The Role of Economic Analysis in EU Competition Law

International Competition Law Series

VOLUME 39

Editor

In its series editor, Alastair Sutton, Kluwer is fortunate to engage and benefit from the experience and expertise of one of the world's outstanding authorities on European Union and international economic law.

Introduction

In their efforts to regulate competition in an increasingly complex business environment, competition authorities face a daunting task. The European Commission and Courts, as well as national courts and legislatures, policymakers, and regulators, are constantly proposing, enacting, reviewing, and enforcing new legal measures, often addressing novel situations. Every industry and service is affected.

Contents/Subjects

With many titles currently available and new ones appearing regularly, the series' coverage includes detailed analyses of relevant legislation and case law in major global trading jurisdictions, defences used in cases involving the digital network economy, state aid cases, enforcement methodologies and a great deal more.

Objective & Readership

The purpose of Kluwer's International Competition Law Series is to follow the ever-changing contours of this dynamic area of the law, keeping the practice in sharp focus so that practising lawyers (including in-house counsel) and academics can be assured of the most up-to-date guidance and sources, in the widest possible range of applications.

The titles published in this series are listed at the end of this volume.

The Role of Economic Analysis in EU Competition Law

The European School

Fourth Edition

Doris Hildebrand

Published by:
Kluwer Law International B.V.
PO Box 316
2400 AH Alphen aan den Rijn
The Netherlands
Website: www.wklawbusiness.com

Sold and distributed in North, Central and South America by:
Wolters Kluwer Legal & Regulatory U.S.
7201 McKinney Circle
Frederick, MD 21704
United States of America
Email: customer.service@wolterskluwer.com

Sold and distributed in all other countries by:
Turpin Distribution Services Ltd
Stratton Business Park
Pegasus Drive, Biggleswade
Bedfordshire SG18 8TQ
United Kingdom
Email: kluwerlaw@turpin-distribution.com

MIX
FSC® C103993

Printed on acid-free paper.

ISBN 978-90-411-6245-8

© 2016 Kluwer Law International BV, The Netherlands

All rights reserved. No part of this publication may be reproduced, stored in a retrieval system, or transmitted in any form or by any means, electronic, mechanical, photocopying, recording, or otherwise, without written permission from the publisher.

Permission to use this content must be obtained from the copyright owner. Please apply to: Permissions Department, Wolters Kluwer Legal & Regulatory U.S., 76 Ninth Avenue, 7th Floor, New York, NY 10011-5201, USA. Website: www.wklawbusiness.com

Printed in the United Kingdom.

Table of Contents

Foreword	xv
List of Figures	xvii
List of Tables	xix

CHAPTER 1
The Frame 1
1.1 Introduction to the Frame 1
    1.1.1 The Equality Principle in EU Competition Law 3
    1.1.2 More Economics Based Approach/European School 5
    1.1.3 Other Schools of Thought in Competition Law 5
    1.1.4 Tensions between Different Schools of Thought? 6
    1.1.5 The Confusion 6
    1.1.6 Differences between the European Approach and Chicago Scholars 7
    1.1.7 Aim of This Book 9
    1.1.8 Guidance 9
1.2 Development of the European School Frame 10
    1.2.1 Drafting the EU Competition Provisions 10
        1.2.1.1 World War II Period 10
        1.2.1.2 Treaty of Paris 1951 11
        1.2.1.3 Spaak Report 1956 13
        1.2.1.4 From the Spaak Report to the Treaty of Rome 1957 14
    1.2.2 Modernisation Process 15
1.3 The Legal Framework 17
1.4 The Economic Framework 22
    1.4.1 Orientation 22
        1.4.1.1 Strategic Level 23

Table of Contents

		1.4.1.2	Operational Level	23
		1.4.1.3	Tactical Level	24
	1.4.2	Chicago School		24
		1.4.2.1	The 'Consumer Welfare' Story	26
		1.4.2.2	Marshallian Concept of Total Surplus	26
		1.4.2.3	*Williamson's* Trade-Off Model	27
		1.4.2.4	The 'Chicago Trap'	30
		1.4.2.5	Wealth Distribution in the Chicago School	30
		1.4.2.6	Chicago School in US Case Law	31
		1.4.2.7	Conclusion	32
	1.4.3	European School		32
		1.4.3.1	Emergence of the European School	32
		1.4.3.2	Core Concepts	33
		1.4.3.3	Ordoliberal Thinking	34
		1.4.3.4	Social Market Economies	37
		1.4.3.5	The Frame of the European School	38
		1.4.3.6	Implementation of the European School into EU Competition Law	39
			1.4.3.6.1 Article 101 TFEU	39
			1.4.3.6.2 Article 102 TFEU	39
1.5	Contrasting the Schools			41
	1.5.1	Merger Case		42
		1.5.1.1	The Case	42
		1.5.1.2	The Transaction	42
		1.5.1.3	Chicago School	43
		1.5.1.4	European School	44
	1.5.2	Horizontal Agreement with a Price Element		45
		1.5.2.1	The Case	45
		1.5.2.2	Chicago School	46
		1.5.2.3	European School	46
	1.5.3	Vertical Restraints		47
		1.5.3.1	The Case	47
		1.5.3.2	Chicago School	48
		1.5.3.3	European School	49
	1.5.4	Abusive Behaviour		50
		1.5.4.1	The Case	50
		1.5.4.2	Chicago School	51
		1.5.4.3	European School	51
	1.5.5	Lessons Learned		52

CHAPTER 2
EU Competition Policy and EU Institutions 55
2.1 Introduction 55
2.2 Competition Concept in the Lisbon Treaty 56

	2.2.1	Concept of a Social Market Economy	57
	2.2.2	Diffusion of Economic Power and Protection of Freedom	58
	2.2.3	Internal Market Objective	59
	2.2.4	Social Market Economy Objective	60
2.3	EU Institutions		61
	2.3.1	European Commission	61
	2.3.2	Court of Justice of the EU	63
2.4	Article 101 TFEU		64
	2.4.1	Article 101(1) TFEU	64
		2.4.1.1 Agreement, Decision and Concerted Practice	65
		2.4.1.2 Appreciability	67
		2.4.1.3 Object and Effect	68
	2.4.2	Article 101(3) TFEU	71
2.5	Article 102 TFEU		72
	2.5.1	General Principles	72
	2.5.2	Dominance	73
	2.5.3	Abuse	77
		2.5.3.1 Imposition of Unfair Purchase or Selling Prices or Conditions (Article 102(a))	77
		2.5.3.2 Limiting Production, Markets or Technical Development to the Prejudice of Consumers (Article 102(b))	78
		2.5.3.3 Applying Dissimilar Conditions to Equivalent Transactions (Article 102(c))	79
		2.5.3.4 Tying Practices (Article 102(d))	80
		2.5.3.5 Exclusionary Abuses Not Directly Covered by the Examples in Article 102(a)-(d)	80
		2.5.3.6 Refusal to Supply	80
		2.5.3.7 Predatory Pricing	82
		2.5.3.8 Exclusionary Rebate Schemes	83
2.6	EU Merger Control		85
	2.6.1	The Evolution of Concentration Control in Europe	85
	2.6.2	Merger Regulation 139/2004	86

CHAPTER 3
Competition Theory   87

3.1	School of Thoughts in Competition Theory		87
	3.1.1	Objectives Assigned to Competition Policy	87
		3.1.1.1 United States (US)	89
		3.1.1.2 European Union	89
	3.1.2	School of Thoughts in Competition Theory	90
		3.1.2.1 Role of Economics	90
		3.1.2.2 Mainstream Economics	91
		3.1.2.3 Appropriate School of Thought?	91
3.2	Origins of Modern Competition Theories		93

Table of Contents

	3.2.1	Classical Theory	94
	3.2.2	Neoclassical Theory	96
		3.2.2.1 Perfect Competition	97
		3.2.2.2 Monopoly	98
		3.2.2.3 Imperfect Competition	100
3.3	Developments in Modern Competition Theories		102
	3.3.1	Workable Competition	102
		3.3.1.1 John Maurice Clark (1940)	102
		3.3.1.2 Erhard Kantzenbach	104
	3.3.2	Effective Competition	106
		3.3.2.1 John Maurice Clark (1961)	106
		3.3.2.2 Joseph A. Schumpeter	107
	3.3.3	Harvard School of Thought	109
		3.3.3.1 Edward S. Mason	109
		3.3.3.2 Industrial Organisation Theory	113
		3.3.3.3 Contestable Markets Theory	118
		3.3.3.4 Game Theory	121
	3.3.4	Chicago School of Thought	128
		3.3.4.1 Attack on the Harvard's School Concentration Doctrine	128
		3.3.4.2 The Efficiency Doctrine	132
		3.3.4.3 Policy Implications of the Chicago School	133
		3.3.4.4 The Post-Chicago School	135
	3.3.5	Concept of Freedom of Competition	138
		3.3.5.1 The Austrian School	139
		3.3.5.2 The Neo-Austrians	141
	3.3.6	Development towards the European School of Thought	144
		3.3.6.1 Role of the State	145
		3.3.6.2 Need for a Constitutional Framework	146
		3.3.6.3 Free Competition	147
		3.3.6.4 Role of Competition Law	147
		3.3.6.5 Influence of Ordoliberalism in the Early Years of the European Commission's Work	148
		3.3.6.6 Critics on the Ordoliberal Concept	148
3.4	Appendix: Basic Economics		149

CHAPTER 4
Competition Practice 161

4.1	Changes in the Enforcement System	161
	4.1.1 The 2000 Proposal	161
	4.1.2 Legislative Process	163
	4.1.3 Regulation 1/2003	168
	4.1.4 German Clause in Regulation 1/2003	170
	4.1.5 Revision Regulation 1/2003	175

4.2	Market Definitions			175
	4.2.1	Necessity for Market Definitions		175
	4.2.2	Market Definition Principles		180
	4.2.3	Market Definition Tools		183
		4.2.3.1	Price Tests	183
		4.2.3.2	Hypothetical Monopolist Test	189
			4.2.3.2.1 US Approach	189
			4.2.3.2.2 European Approach	190
			4.2.3.2.3 Initial Price Analysis	192
			4.2.3.2.4 Modelling Customer Choice with Conjoint Analysis	195
			4.2.3.2.5 Estimation of the Utility Functions	199
			4.2.3.2.6 Preference Function	199
		4.2.3.3	Other Empirical Tests	202
	4.2.4	Relevant Product Market		207
		4.2.4.1	Basic Assumptions	207
		4.2.4.2	Market Definition Practice	212
			4.2.4.2.1 Type of Evidence	212
			4.2.4.2.2 Practice of the Commission	214
	4.2.5	Relevant Geographic Market		227
		4.2.5.1	Basic Assumptions	227
		4.2.5.2	Market Definition Practice	229
			4.2.5.2.1 Type of Evidence	229
			4.2.5.2.2 Practice of the Commission	232
4.3	Market Analysis			248
	4.3.1	Analysis of Market Shares		248
	4.3.2	Evaluation of the Market Position		250
	4.3.3	Analysing Buyer Power		251
	4.3.4	Analysis of Resources		251
	4.3.5	Analysis of Access to Supply and Sales Markets		252
	4.3.6	Competition from (Imperfect) Substitutes		252
	4.3.7	Assessment Barriers to Market Entry/Potential Competition		252
	4.3.8	Market Phase, Level of Trade and Nature of the Product		256
	4.3.9	Bidding Analysis		258
		4.3.9.1	Economics in Bidding Markets	259
		4.3.9.2	Independent Customer Surveys	259
		4.3.9.3	Analysis of Customer Surveys	260
		4.3.9.4	Encounter Ratio between the Merging Parties	260
		4.3.9.5	Encounter Ratio between Two Other Bidders	260
		4.3.9.6	Size of Other Bidders	261
		4.3.9.7	Runner-Up	261
		4.3.9.8	Price Difference	261
		4.3.9.9	Further Analyses	262
4.4	European Economic Approach in Article 101			262

Table of Contents

4.4.1	Object and Effect		262
4.4.2	Ancillary Restrictions		265
4.4.3	Effect on Trade between Member States		269
	4.4.3.1 Developments in the Effect on Trade Concept		269
	4.4.3.2 Guidelines on the Effect on Trade Concept		272
		4.4.3.2.1 Trade between Member States	272
		4.4.3.2.2 Appreciability of Affecting Trade between Member States	273
4.4.4	Appreciability Test of the Agreement/'*De Minimis*'		274
	4.4.4.1 Developments in the Appreciability Test		275
	4.4.4.2 *De Minimis* Notice		276
4.4.5	Economic Analysis in Article 101(1)		277
	4.4.5.1 Vertical Agreements		281
		4.4.5.1.1 Vertical Exclusive Dealings	281
		4.4.5.1.2 Vertical Absolute Territorial Protection	283
		4.4.5.1.3 Vertical Selective Distribution	287
		4.4.5.1.4 Vertical Licensing	291
		4.4.5.1.5 Vertical Franchising	292
		4.4.5.1.6 Vertical Exclusive Purchasing	294
		4.4.5.1.7 Conclusion	299
	4.4.5.2 Horizontal Agreements		300
		4.4.5.2.1 Horizontal Cooperation Agreements	300
		4.4.5.2.2 Horizontal Price-Fixing Agreements	305
		4.4.5.2.3 Horizontal Concerted Practices	307
		4.4.5.2.4 Conclusion	309
4.4.6	Economic Analysis in Article 101(3)		311
	4.4.6.1 First Condition of Article 101(3)		312
		4.4.6.1.1 Cost Efficiencies	314
		4.4.6.1.2 Qualitative Efficiencies	315
	4.4.6.2 Second Condition of Article 101(3)		315
	4.4.6.3 Third Condition of Article 101(3)		317
	4.4.6.4 Fourth Condition of Article 101(3)		318
4.4.7	EU Competition Rules for Distribution		320
	4.4.7.1 Types of Vertical Restraints		322
		4.4.7.1.1 Exclusive Distribution Group	322
		4.4.7.1.2 Single Branding Group	324
		4.4.7.1.3 Resale Price Maintenance Group	324
		4.4.7.1.4 Market Partitioning Group	325
		4.4.7.1.5 Combinations of Vertical Restraints	325
	4.4.7.2 Economics of Vertical Restraints		326
		4.4.7.2.1 Beneficial Effects of Vertical Restraints	326
		4.4.7.2.2 Anti-competitive Effects of Vertical Restraints	328
		4.4.7.2.3 Different Schools of Thought	332

		4.4.7.2.4	EU Policy Conclusions on Vertical Restraints	334
		4.4.7.2.5	Block Exemption Regulation 330/2010	338
		4.4.7.2.6	EU Guidelines on Vertical Restraints	341
	4.4.8	EU Competition Rules for Cooperation		343
		4.4.8.1	Block Exemption Regulations	343
		4.4.8.2	EU Guidelines on Horizontal Cooperation Agreements	345
4.5	European Economic Approach in Article 102			347
	4.5.1	Market Definitions in Article 102		348
		4.5.1.1	Product Market Definitions	349
		4.5.1.2	Geographic Market Definitions	355
		4.5.1.3	The Time Factor	358
		4.5.1.4	Substantial Part of the Common Market	359
	4.5.2	Economic Analysis in Article 102		360
		4.5.2.1	Market shares	362
		4.5.2.2	Barriers of Entry	367
		4.5.2.3	Assessing Single Dominance	371
		4.5.2.4	Assessing Collective Dominance	373
		4.5.2.5	Commission's Rules on Article 102	378
		4.5.2.6	More Economics Based Approach	379
		4.5.2.6.1	Economics of Exclusionary Conduct	381
		4.5.2.6.2	As-Efficient-Competitor Test	382
		4.5.2.6.3	Possible Defences	385
		4.5.2.6.4	Predatory Pricing	386
		4.5.2.6.5	Rebate Systems	388
		4.5.2.6.6	Tying and Bundling	391
		4.5.2.7	Economic Analysis in Cases on Rebates	392
		4.5.2.7.1	Michelin II	392
		4.5.2.7.2	British Airways	394
		4.5.2.7.3	Tomra	396
		4.5.2.7.4	Intel	398
		4.5.2.7.5	Post Denmark II	403
		4.5.2.8	Economic Analysis in Other Article 102 Cases	405
		4.5.2.8.1	Tetra Pak II	405
		4.5.2.8.2	AstraZeneca	408
		4.5.2.8.3	Microsoft	410
4.6	European Economic Approach in Mergers			414
	4.6.1	Role of Economic Analysis in EU Merger Control		417
	4.6.2	Guidance by the Court of Justice of the EU		422
		4.6.2.1	GE/Honeywell	424
		4.6.2.1.1	Theory of Harm/Competition Concerns	425
		4.6.2.1.2	The Judgment	425
		4.6.2.2	Schneider/Legrand	426
		4.6.2.2.1	Theory of Harm/Competition Concerns	426

		4.6.2.2.2	The Judgment	427
	4.6.2.3	Tetra Laval/Sidel		427
		4.6.2.3.1	Theory of Harm/Competition Concerns	427
		4.6.2.3.2	The Judgment	428
	4.6.2.4	Impala		429
	4.6.2.5	Ryanair		430
		4.6.2.5.1	Theory of Harm/Competition Concerns	430
		4.6.2.5.2	The Judgment	431
4.6.3	EU Merger Guidelines			432
	4.6.3.1	Horizontal Merger Guidelines		432
		4.6.3.1.1	Purpose of the Guidelines	432
		4.6.3.1.2	Market Entry	433
		4.6.3.1.3	Efficiency	436
	4.6.3.2	Non-Horizontal Merger Guidelines		438
		4.6.3.2.1	Purpose of the Guidelines	438
		4.6.3.2.2	Analysis of Tying and Bundling	440
		4.6.3.2.3	Analysis of Input and Customer Foreclosure	443
		4.6.3.2.4	Actual and Potential Competition	447
4.6.4	Collective Dominance			451
	4.6.4.1	Developments in the Case Law		451
		4.6.4.1.1	The 'Checklist'	452
		4.6.4.1.2	Development of the Collective Dominance Doctrine	454
	4.6.4.2	Assessment of Coordinated Effects in the Merger Guidelines		460
		4.6.4.2.1	Reaching Terms of Coordination	461
		4.6.4.2.2	Monitoring Deviations	461
		4.6.4.2.3	Deterrent Mechanisms	462
4.6.5	Merger Simulation Models			462
	4.6.5.1	The Specification Stage		463
		4.6.5.1.1	Model Selection	463
		4.6.5.1.2	Auction Models	465
	4.6.5.2	The Estimation Stage		467
		4.6.5.2.1	Linear and Log-Linear Demand System	468
		4.6.5.2.2	Logit and Nested Logit Demand Systems	469
		4.6.5.2.3	Almost Ideal Demand System	471
		4.6.5.2.4	Proportionally Calibrated AIDS	473
	4.6.5.3	The Simulation Stage		475
4.6.6	Commission's Use of Merger Simulation Models			477
	4.6.6.1	Linear Demand Model		477
		4.6.6.1.1	The Case	477
		4.6.6.1.2	Merger Simulation Model	477
	4.6.6.2	Nested Logit Models		477

			4.6.6.2.1	*Scania/Volvo*	478
			4.6.6.2.2	*Lagardère/Natexis/VUP*	479
			4.6.6.2.3	*Unilever/Sara Lee*	480
			4.6.6.2.4	*Kraft Foods/Cadbury*	481
			4.6.6.2.5	*Tomtom/Tele Atlas*	482
		4.6.6.3	Use of Auction Models		482
			4.6.6.3.1	*Sydkraft/Graninge*	482
			4.6.6.3.2	*Oracle/Peoplesoft*	483
			4.6.6.3.3	*Vattenfall/Elsam and E2 Assets*	485
			4.6.6.3.4	*Thales/Finmeccanica/Alcatel Alenia Space/Telespazio*	485
4.7	State Aid Provisions				486
	4.7.1	Economics in the EU State Aid Rules			488
	4.7.2	Balancing Test in Article 107(3)			490
	4.7.3	State Aid Modernisation			494
		4.7.3.1	EU Guidelines		494
			4.7.3.1.1	Rescue and Restructuring Aid	495
			4.7.3.1.2	Regional Aid	495
			4.7.3.1.3	State Aid for Research and Development and Innovation (R&D&I)	496
			4.7.3.1.4	State Aid in Agriculture, Forestry and Rural Areas	497
			4.7.3.1.5	Environmental and Energy Aid	497
			4.7.3.1.6	State Aid to Promote Important Projects of Common European Interest	498
			4.7.3.1.7	Risk Finance	498
			4.7.3.1.8	Broadband	499
			4.7.3.1.9	Aviation Guidelines	499
		4.7.3.2	EU Regulations		499
			4.7.3.2.1	General Block Exemption Regulation	500
			4.7.3.2.2	*De Minimis* Regulation	500
			4.7.3.2.3	Procedural Regulation	501
		4.7.3.3	Notion of State Aid		501
		4.7.3.4	*Ex Post* Evaluations		502
			4.7.3.4.1	Linear Regression	502
			4.7.3.4.2	Matching Techniques	502
			4.7.3.4.3	Difference-in-Difference	503
			4.7.3.4.4	Instrumental Variables	503
			4.7.3.4.5	Regression Discontinuity Design	503

Bibliography	505
Index	543

Foreword

This book is in its fourth edition and written by an economist for people interested in the role of economic analysis in EU competition law.

As European competition economics is evolving over time, the content of this book is progressing too. The inspiration for this book goes back to 1992, when I wrote, under the supervision of Jonathan Faull, a master paper on vertical restraints in EU competition law. The first edition of this book was my Ph.D. thesis at the University of Brussels (VUB) in 1998 documenting my research work on European competition economics in the period 1992–1998. The chair of my Ph.D.-Commission was then EU Commissioner for Competition Karel van Miert who initiated at the same time the so-called 'more economics based approach' in EU competition law. Karel acknowledged that economic analysis is of crucial importance in any EU competition law enforcement. Tom Ottervanger was my Ph.D.-thesis supervisor at that time and remained to be a sponsor of my work since then. Other distinguished members of my Ph.D.-Commission who continuously show their interest in my work over the last twenty years are current President of the European Court of Justice Koen Lenaerts as well as Barry Hawk, Fordham University. My special thanks go to all my fellows who contributed to this project from the very beginning and continue to believe in the importance of this subject.

Whereas in 1998 the first edition of this book was advocating a 'more economics based approach' rooted in EU competition law, the novelty in this fourth edition is that finally the economic school of thought applied in EU competition law, the European School, is properly defined. This genuine European economic approach is much more fundamental than just introducing a few new economic concepts. It actually implements the European cornerstones of freedom of contract, social fairness and equality. At the heart of the European School is the concept of a social market economy. Since 2009, the Lisbon Treaty has made an explicit reference to this concept thereby distinguishing the European economic approach applied in EU competition law from schools of thought applied in other jurisdictions. It is misleading to assume that an economic approach needs to be the same in all antitrust laws around the world. As values, common objectives and the law itself vary throughout societies, the appropriate economic approach in antitrust law differs as well. Thus, one aim of this book is to

Foreword

define why the European approach is unique compared with competition economics in the US, for example. Another aim is to substantiate that EU competition policy represents an essential foundation of the EU. Without the EU competition law provisions, the concept of social market economies would not work at all. The new first chapter on 'The Frame' elaborates on this aspect.

When the 'more economics based approach' was implemented in 1998, I left academia and founded the economic consultancy company EE&MC – European Economic & Marketing Consultants (www.ee-mc.com). EE&MC is a group of competition economists with offices in Bonn, Brussels and Vienna. For almost twenty years, EE&MC has been active in a broad range of industries and has been consultants in a significant number of competition cases. EE&MC clients include mostly enterprises in the Fortune Global 500, as well as competition authorities and courts. EE&MC provides consultancy services on how to apply in real world cases the European school of thought, as defined in this book. That makes this book particularly attractive to people interested in the practical application of the European approach.

I would like to thank the inspiring people working with EE&MC who contributed to this fourth edition, in particular my assistant Katrin Siebertz who managed all the references and footnotes as well as Mark Twemlow who has been involved with finding the appropriate English wording for the past couple of editions. The appropriate English wording is of particular importance in this current fourth edition since the main language used to discuss in the past the explicit link between EU competition policy and the concept of social market economies is German.

My special thanks go to my family too. My four children – Philip, Pascal, Bastian and Nicole – have been involved throughout the years in various roles in all the four editions so far. Although they are starting their own careers now, they have continued to motivate me to finalize my work on the European school of thought. They view this project as an important contribution for the next generation of Europeans. I am vastly grateful to them – not only for their encouragements but also for their understanding that their mother was not always on hand for them. The same is true for my husband, Nico, who is probably one of my strongest supporters in this project. I am sure that they are as happy as I am that this fourth edition is published now.

Doris Hildebrand,
February 2016

List of Figures

Figure 1.1	Overview of Differences in Schools of Thought	8
Figure 1.2	Marshallian Total Surplus Model	26
Figure 1.3	Williamson's Trade-Off Model	28
Figure 3.1	Structure-Conduct-Performance Paradigm (SCP-Paradigm)	111
Figure 3.2	Demand Curve	150
Figure 3.3	Different Demand Curves and Market Demand Curve	151
Figure 3.4	Costs and Supply Curve	151
Figure 3.5	Perfect Competition	153
Figure 3.6	Model of Competition	155
Figure 3.7	Model of Monopoly	155
Figure 3.8	Cournot Model of Oligopoly	158
Figure 4.1	Effect of the Price Increase	191
Figure 4.2	Hypothetical Monopolist Profit	193
Figure 4.3	Hypothetical Monopolist Profit after Price Increase	194
Figure 4.4	Hypothetical Monopolist Test Step 1	196
Figure 4.5	Hypothetical Monopolist Test Step 2	197
Figure 4.6	Example of a Conjoint Question	197
Figure 4.7	Relative Importance of the Attributes in the Fibre Example	199
Figure 4.8	Price Response after a 5% Price Increase in the Fibre Example	200
Figure 4.9	Example of Competitive Pressure between Three Firms	260
Figure 4.10	Type of Efficiencies	312
Figure 4.11	Economic Effect of Health Services	493

List of Tables

Table 1.1	A Comparison of the Competition Provisions: Treaty of Rome 1957 and Lisbon Treaty 2007	19
Table 1.2	European School and Chicago School: A Comparison	41
Table 3.1	Prisoners' Dilemma	124
Table 3.2	Overview Concepts of Competition	159

CHAPTER 1
The Frame

What makes a social market economy social?
The answer is the equality principle in EU competition law.

1.1 INTRODUCTION TO THE FRAME

In plain language, European politicians used to refer to 'consumer welfare' when they spoke about the goal of European Union (EU) competition law.[1] Recently this language has become more nuanced mentioning the 'well-being of people' instead[2] suggesting that consumer interests need to be more broadly defined.

In this sense, EU competition law is not only concerned with the direct harm to consumer interests but also about actions that indirectly might harm their interests, for example by attacking a competitive market structure as such. This broader definition of consumer interests entails that people are privileged beneficiaries of an internal market where competition is not altered.[3]

The 'well-being of people' is defined as an objective in Article 3[4] of the Lisbon Treaty.[5] Other Article 3 objectives in the Lisbon Treaty are the establishment of an internal market and its work for the sustainable development of Europe based on a

---

1. *'Consumer welfare is not just a catchy phrase. It is the cornerstone, the guiding principle of EU competition policy.'* (Almunia J., Competition – what's in it for consumers?, 2011).
2. *'The strongest incentives remain consumers' demand and competitive markets. These are the main factors that push companies to bring new products and services to the market, create wealth, and improve our well-being.'* (Vestager 2015).
3. (Tizzano 2014, 20).
4. *'The Union's aim is to promote peace, its values and the well-being of its peoples.'* Art. 3(1) TEU.
5. The Lisbon Treaty (used in the following) or Treaty of Lisbon entered into force 1 Dec. 2009 and amends the two treaties which form the constitutional basis of the European Union (EU): Treaty on European Union (TEU) and the Treaty establishing the European Community (TEEC) which is also known as Treaty of Rome (1958) and renamed at Lisbon to the Treaty on the Functioning of the European Union (TFEU).

highly competitive social market economy. The combination of the internal market objective with the concept of a social market economy confirms the broader view on consumer interests post-Lisbon.[6]

A market system is an effective instrument to meet the demand from consumers for goods and services. It motivates profit-maximizing companies to increase productivity, to expand, to innovate and to create jobs. These exposed market forces are the generator of prosperity thereby creating wealth. The idea behind the social market economy is that market freedom is combined with social balance. A 'social market economy' is a market system that unifies the principle of freedom with the social equality and fairness objectives.[7] A social market economy recognises that a functioning economy is indispensable in producing the material basis without which human society with all its other non-economic – human and cultural – dimensions cannot exist. *'Where no wealth is created in the first place, none can be re-distributed.'*[8]

A social market economy does not work with the idea of *laissez-faire* capitalism. Instead, it requires government involvement. For this very reason, the European idea is not to leave a market economy alone to any development it might take, but to create a strong framework that ensures:

- First, that social standards and other objectives of the society are respected.
- Second, that the beneficial workings of the market forces are not blocked, restrained or distorted by short-sighted actions of the market actors themselves. This is the crucial importance of a strong EU competition law framework.[9]

The most important objective related to social equality and social fairness in a social market economy is that wealth gains – as a result of a competitive market process – are distributed equally and thereby fairly between all market actors, producers and consumers alike. This principle makes sure that a market economy operates in a social way thereby broadly addressing the well-being of people defined as direct and indirect consumer interests.

A fair distribution of created wealth means that no market participant receives a bundle that is worse for his preferences than an equal split of the available gains. What actually matters from the citizens' perspective is not the amount of gains they obtain. What matters is how they value these benefits compared to alternative bundles.

In contrast to companies that are clearly profit (and thereby price) driven, consumers and citizens are not particularly rational behaving entities. Consumer benefits or utilities derive from multiple sources. This means that the satisfaction

---

6. Article 3(3) TEU. The first reference to a social market economy is found in the draft of the 2004 Rome Treaty and was retained in Lisbon in 2007.
7. (Müller-Armack 1956, 390).
8. (Monti, Competition in a Social Market economy, 2000).
9. It seems to be that then Commissioner Mario Monti is the first one who explicitly pronounced the link between the European model of a social market economy and EU competition law in 2000, quite some time before the European model of a social market economy was declared as a European Union objective in Art. 3 Treaty on the European Union. See (Monti, Competition in a Social Market economy, 2000).

Chapter 1: The Frame

consumers receive from consuming a good or service depends on various attributes. One of them is price. A focus on price only in the assessment of consumer interests does not value the whole set of consumer preferences appropriately. It is the combination of price and other dimensions that defines consumer interests in a broad manner.

In a social market economy, these broadly defined consumer/citizen interests are balanced with the profit-oriented efficiency-enhancing interests of companies.

A social market economy, therefore, represents a humanistic societal order that implements producer and consumer preferences by a holistic conception, namely EU competition law, based on the values of the EU.[10]

Thus, the European model of a social market economy comprises of (1) a legal framework with a (2) pre-defined economic order based on (3) social constituents.[11]

All these three features are embodied in EU competition law thereby enabling European citizens to achieve economic progress as well as societal advancement by satisfying their interests in an optimal way. A market economy – that is structured and maintained according to the EU competition law principles – generates market as well as social effects automatically and directly. The gains of such an embedded competitive market process are distributed in fact equally and thereby fairly between all market actors, producers and consumers.

1.1.1 The Equality Principle in EU Competition Law

There are different meanings attached to equality in EU competition law.

Equality can be understood as equal and fair distribution of income or wealth between the market actors. It also means equal and fair competition conditions for all market actors. Here are some concrete examples:

(1) The equality principle inherent in a social market economy as outlined above is implemented in *Article 101(3) TFEU*. Where an agreement restricts competition but on the other hand improves the production or distribution of goods or promotes technical or economic progress, the resulting benefits / wealth gains should be redistributed fairly and on an equal footing between the market participants – producers and consumers alike. The economic order in the EU legal framework states that such an agreement escapes the nullity provision of Article 101(2) TFEU. The requirement is that consumers get their fair share of the wealth gains achieved.[12] In US anti-trust law, a similar pre-defined provision does not exist. Within a rule of reason approach as applied in US anti-trust law, the economic assessment of an agreement is open-ended with no clear pre-stated preference in the law which economic

---

10. The values of the European Union, as stated in Art. 2 Lisbon Treaty, are respect for human dignity, freedom, democracy, equality, the rule of law and respect for human rights.
11. *Müller-Armack* used the term 'ordo-liberalism'. As we will show further below, the EU competition rules are based partly on ordo-liberalism (Müller-Armack, Soziale Marktwirtschaft, 1956, 245).
12. Technically a balancing between the anti-competitive effects takes place against the pro-competitive effects for both groups, producers and consumers.

3

actor should benefit from the wealth gains achieved. In particular, in US anti-trust law there are no rules on how to redistribute wealth gains resulting from competition restraints between producers and consumers.

(2) When it comes to abuse cases (*Article 102 TFEU*), the economic order in EU competition law applies the equality principle as well. Monopolies or dominant positions themselves are not a problem in Europe. Instead, EU competition law maintains that the behaviour of companies should be on an equal footing: A dominant company is supposed to behave in the same manner as a non-dominant company (*'as-if'* competition).[13] The true challenge is to identify normal acts of competition for both, dominant and non-dominant companies.

On top of that, a dominant company has special responsibilities. It should refrain from any abusive conduct. Some cases are not clear-cut. A dominant company might apply a conduct that when performed by a non-dominant company is legitimate. However, the same conduct might produce negative competitive effects when applied by a dominant company. Again, in such a situation the dominant company should refrain from such a conduct.

In this context, the implementation of the equality principle requires the assessment of the conduct in order to identify whether the behaviour of a dominant company is abusive or not.

Thus, competitive actions which are the result of normal competition are acceptable for both, dominant and non-dominant companies. In fact, the economic order in EU competition law requires equality between the market actors in this regard. Abusive behaviour is a conduct that infringes this equality principle since abusive behaviour is an action a non-dominant company has no (economic) incentive to engage in.[14]

(3) Other applications of the equality principle relate to the EU state aid rules. Governments and companies are treated alike in EU competition law:
- The market investor principle requires the same treatment of subsidies no matter whether financial means are given by a government or a private investor.
- Competition needs to take place on an equal footing despite the fact that a recipient has received a government subsidy.

The equality principle has been inherent in EU competition law since 1958. Competition rules in the Treaty of Rome accommodated the objectives of economic performance (growth, innovation, efficiency) as well as of equality (greater income equality, dispersion of concentrated economic and political power, fostering business

---

13. This position neither is an ordoliberal one nor can be found in German competition law. see (Schweitzer 2007, 15).
14. This does not rule out the efficiency argument. A dominant company can produce efficiencies as non-dominant companies do. These efficiencies can be taken into account in the assessment.

opportunities).[15] The Lisbon Treaty reiterates these goals by making explicit reference in Article 3 TEU to the concept of a social market economy.

Whereas in the past the establishment of an internal market was the focus of EU competition law, post-Lisbon the attention is changing in favour of and accommodating social features like social fairness and equality. Nevertheless, social properties have always been part of EU competition law.

1.1.2 More Economics Based Approach/European School

The approach implementing those principles, 'more economics based approach',[16] was introduced about two decades ago because of the rigidity of the previously applied formalistic methodology. The new approach contributes to a better understanding and enforcement of the rules. Instead of focusing on legal provisions only, agreements are assessed in their economic context. This enables a better understanding of the functioning of markets, the competition in these markets and thereby the social components. Thinking within this approach is becoming known as the European School. This advanced approach facilitates the identification and the application of the equality principle and other social constituents in the EU competition rules thereby improving the application of the economic order underlying the law.

The economic order requires that within Europe social market economies prevail that address in particular the social fairness aspect within the economy (Article 3 TEU). As already stated, the fair distribution of wealth gains throughout society is a pillar in such a social market economy concept. The other pillar is the measurement of consumer utilities goods or services offer. This measurement differs depending on which economic school of thought is applied.

1.1.3 Other Schools of Thought in Competition Law

One of the decisive differences between societies is that the values of the citizens differ. There is no fundamental problem related to this. Different societies can reach diverse conclusions about the appropriate goals of competition law.[17]

Even within the US, discussions about the goals of anti-trust law are variegated.[18] According to *Posner*, the only goal of US anti-trust law should be to promote economic welfare.[19] *Bork* stated in one of his most cited quotes that the goal of US anti-trust law is consumer welfare by which he meant total welfare.[20] Based on a neoliberal, *laissez-faire* approach, a prevailing assumption in the US today is that markets will

---

15. Chicagoans on the other hand ignore the transfer of wealth within anti-trust law since in their opinion there are other arms of public policy that are better suited. See (Ahdar 2002, 345).
16. www.ee-mc.com.
17. (Kerber 2007, 17).
18. US anti-trust enforcement varies too depending on which enforcer applies the law.
19. (Posner R. A., Antitrust Law, 2001, ix).
20. (Bork, The Antitrust Paradox: A Policy at War with Itself, 1978, 90). When writing about consumer welfare, *Bork* argued that those who continue to buy after a monopoly is formed pay more for the same output thereby shifting income from them to the monopoly and its owners,

manage any possible anti-trust problems by themselves. Intervention in market forces is almost not required. In the case of anti-trust enforcement, the focus should be on economic efficiencies only.[21] This efficiency-based-thinking is in accordance with the Chicago School discussed further below.

1.1.4 Tensions between Different Schools of Thought?

In Europe, an important tool that makes markets function in a social way is EU competition law: (1) First, this legal framework protects the competition process as such to create wealth and (2) secondly, it regulates that the results of the competition process are distributed fairly within the society in accordance with consumer utilities. Thus, EU competition law enables the proper functioning of a social market economy for the well-being of people in Europe. In this sense, Europe is rooted in a pro-regulatory philosophy: The economic order was defined upfront in the Treaty of Rome and is implemented by independent authorities and courts accordingly.

There are differences between US anti-trust law and EU competition law. This is perfectly fine in a world with different viewpoints.

The tension starts when a school of thought developed for the application in US anti-trust law is imported to another one, namely EU competition law, by the back door. This is the case when Chicago scholars advocate their specific type of economic analysis in EU competition law. The application of the Chicago *laissez-faire* ideology to competition problems simply does not fit with the aims of EU competition law, which is embedded in a clearly pre-defined economic order thereby integrating the values and objectives of the European society.

Chicago anti-trust concepts do not match with the European School.

1.1.5 The Confusion

The period since the modernisation of EU competition law in the late nineties towards the European School is marked by several attempts to transfer Chicago views into EU competition law. This has created confusion and tensions within the European competition community:[22]

- EU competition lawyers find it difficult to position Chicago School thinking in EU case law. Although Chicago School thinking might offer neat explanations

---

who are also consumers. *Bork* did not consider this as deadweight loss due to restriction in output but merely as a shift in income between two classes of consumers. This will be elaborated on further below.
21. More recently, maybe inspired by the European approach, discussions in the US have emerged as to whether in the US an efficiency-based approach is really the appropriate one to deal with current challenges.
22. Such a transfer for example takes place when US trained Chicago competition economists consult in EU cases. The line of argumentation they present might change in the long run the European approach (drip-drip-effect). This is particularly ridiculous since the US courts themselves do neither favour nor apply Chicago School thinking.

Chapter 1: The Frame

for why dominant companies behave like they do or a merger should go through because of economic efficiencies, the arguments themselves are 'toothless'. Authorities and in particular courts do not usually receive those Chicago arguments favourably. They simply do not fit.
- Longer established authorities like the European Commission or the German *Bundeskartellamt* are criticised when they do not follow the views of US trained Chicago experts. The burden is particularly high for the European Commission since considerable resources are needed to maintain the European approach and 'to keep the whole unit on track' despite all the attempts and criticism.
- On the other hand, newer authorities are much more open to Chicago views. This is mostly due to the fact that their economists were trained in the US, in particular in industrial organisation. A significant part of the academic literature on competition theories relates to US based thinking too. Thus, for younger authorities with less experience it is difficult to distinguish what is Chicagoan and what is the European approach.
- Sometimes even within authorities opinions are mixed about how to deal with Chicago School insights in EU competition law. Whereas some wings might want to introduce Chicago School thinking to EU competition law (for the sake of conformity with US enforcement and the huge pressure they receive), other wings oppose this. They believe that Europe should continue to apply its own genuine European approach as defined in the Lisbon Treaty entailing an economic order within a given legal-institutional framework based on the objectives of freedom as well as equality and social fairness.
- The Court of Justice of the EU increasingly tries to provide orientation to both the competition community in the Member States as well as to the European Commission on how to apply the European approach in EU competition law.

1.1.6 Differences between the European Approach and Chicago Scholars

In Europe, any economic analysis in EU competition law mirrors the pre-defined economic order as well as the other social objectives as determined by the law. The interests of 'average consumers' are measured by their utilities. This measurement lies at the heart of any economic analysis.

Consumer interests are so broadly defined that focusing on prices (and efficiencies) only is not the appropriate tool for an economic assessment. Thus, Europe applies a holistic concept which integrates the values and objectives of the European society, namely prosperity as well as the social responsibility to redistribute wealth fairly and in accordance with consumer preferences.

Chicago scholars do not integrate any policy objective other than the economic one with a special focus on efficiencies. This narrow view is equated with 'consumer welfare'.

With respect to economic analysis, another important difference is that the outcome of economic analysis in EU competition law cases cannot alter the pre-defined economic order including the social policy objective. Economic analysis in the European tradition improves the understanding of how markets work and what type of economic effects are produced by agreements or mergers. Economic analysis in the EU style is particularly valuable and indispensable in assessing facts such as market definition or prognosis of merger effects. However, economic analysis in the European School is rather more a supplement underpinning the law.

The burden on a Chicago style economic analysis is much heavier since this type of analysis needs to determine the order and the related policy objectives case-by-case.

On top of that, the Chicago School needs to compete in the US in every assessment with other Schools of thought, for example the Harvard School. Interestingly neither is considered the leading one. While Chicagoans strongly promote their insights within the economic community, US jurisprudence rarely applies Chicago insights.

The following illustration shows the differences between the two schools of thought.

Figure 1.1   Overview of Differences in Schools of Thought

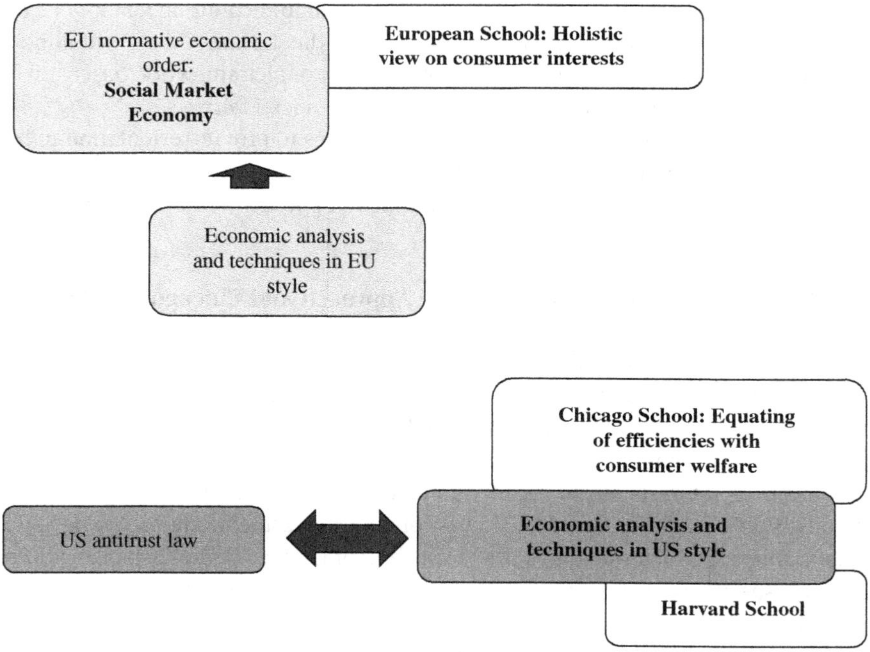

1.1.7 Aim of This Book

The European School is founded on a solid core of research into how markets should ideally function and on layers of practical experiences of how to successfully implement a social market economy thereby offering a practicable solution to many problems Europe is currently facing. The challenge is to get the message across that the competition community in Europe can have confidence in the European economic approach that values social objectives in its competition law assessments, in contrast to the Chicago School in the US which does not.

Within social market economies EU competition law is the vehicle guaranteeing that markets work and produce prosperity that is fairly distributed and in balance with social objectives. The focus in the economic assessment is on consumer interests expressed by consumer preferences and utilities. Thus, the economic approach or 'European School' as discussed in this book offers practitioners in EU competition law the tools available to economists to fulfil the pledges of the Lisbon Treaty.[23]

The tools have been developing for over sixty years with a dynamic expansion in the last two decades.

Economic analysis techniques of the European School can be compared with a colour palette or a set of instruments. By mixing colours artists produce various shades depending on their imagination. The same is true for practitioners in EU competition law. However, the mixing of techniques or instruments needs to be done with caution. Otherwise, the result is discordant with the law.

Some of the burden of getting things right rests on the shoulders of the European Commission. Thus, it is crucial how the European Commission continues to perceive and advocate the genuine European competition approach in accordance with the concept of a social market economy.

This book offers inspiration and fodder for such a task.

However, it might not be that appealing for the European Commission to tell the business community that Europe is pursuing an economic as well as a social agenda. In particular, US businesses might consider social elements within an economic order as precarious. Nevertheless, the 2014 European Commission made economic growth and social fairness their top priorities. Both priorities are already perfectly implemented in EU competition law by the European School.

1.1.8 Guidance

The genuine European approach represents a useful guidance for Member States and national courts that increasingly apply EU competition law. The insights of the European School of thought are even more crucial for those new Member States that have no long-standing experiences with market economies or competition issues in general but are much more acquainted with established traditions in social cohesion.

---

23. Namely to work for the sustainable development of Europe based on balanced economic growth and a highly competitive social market economy (Art. 3 TEU).

The European competition approach also provides guidance for jurisdictions outside the EU that apply similar constitutional competition frameworks. This is what makes Europe special: social market economies that can become role models for other countries worldwide. In this context, the European School competes with the insights of the Chicago School even worldwide.

In the following sections[24], the development of the economic approach in EU competition law is described followed by an overview of the two different schools, the Chicago School and the European School. Then a list of examples is given indicating the differences between these two diverse schools of thought. The section concludes with a comparison of hypothetical cases treated under a Chicago School approach and the European School approach.

1.2 DEVELOPMENT OF THE EUROPEAN SCHOOL FRAME

The economic school of thought in EU competition law is well-developed.

To better understand the EU style of economic analysis, a historical perspective is presented first.

With respect to economic thinking, two periods mark this development: (1) the actual drafting and implementation of the competition rules in the Treaty of Rome which have remained unchanged since, and (2) the modernisation process which started in the mid-1990s.

1.2.1 Drafting the EU Competition Provisions

Despite the fact that different nations are part of the EU, the values shared by the people are the same. The EU is a peace project strongly related to values people within Europe share as well as to economic integration. These basic values are implemented in the competition law provisions.[25] The following is a historical description of the events during the drafting of these provisions.

1.2.1.1 World War II Period

The development of the European concept to competition dates back to the time during World War II, when *Jean Monnet* and other scholars, for example at the University of Freiburg, developed their visions about a peaceful Europe post-World War II. The Freiburg School of thought,[26] active during 1930–1950, was a decisive influence with

---

24. The structure of the following sections in this chapter is the result of a conversation with then Director-General Alexander Italianer of DG Competition on 22 May 2015.
25. The provisions themselves are discussed further below.
26. The *Freiburg Ordoliberal School* was founded in the 1930s in Germany by the economist *Walter Eucken* (1891–1950) and the two lawyers, *Franz Böhm* (1895–1977) and *Hans Großmann-Doerth* (1894–1944). As *Böhm* later said in retrospect, the founders of the school were united in their common concern for the question of the constitutional foundations of a free economy and society. (Vanberg 2002, 38).

respect to the drafting of the competition law provisions and the economic order post-World War II. Scholars in the tradition of Freiburg ordoliberal thinking developed the 'social market economy' concept (now embodied in Article 3 TEU).

1.2.1.2 Treaty of Paris 1951

The 1951 Treaty of Paris which served as the basis for the European Coal and Steel Community (ECSC) included competition related provisions and addressed the equality principle.[27] The ECSC was the result of a May 1950 proposal by *Robert Schuman* to create a West European common market in coal and steel. The Schuman Plan[28] applied the strategy of pursuing European integration by way of market integration.

Jean Monnet contributed with his team to the Schuman Plan that led to the April 1951 Treaty of Paris.[29]

In *Monnet's* opinion, economic cooperation with Germany was essential, particularly given Germany's central position in Europe and its industrial potential.[30] *Monnet* viewed the coal and steel pool as an indispensable but transitional stage on the way to creating a European federation. The first step was the establishment of a common market based on the coal and steel sectors.[31]

Monnet's considerations were coherent with the objectives of the US occupation forces in Germany at that time. One of their aims was to deconcentrate Germany's heavy industry and, more concretely, to break up large firms in general as well as the vertically integrated coal and steel firms in the *Rhein-Ruhr*-region in particular. The US viewed Germany's pre-World War II highly concentrated heavy industry as one of the main causes for the evil that happened during the Nazi regime.

During the negotiations prior to the ECSC, the US exercised pressure on the German government to agree with *Monnet's* proposal for de-concentration and in particular the competition provisions.[32] Finally, Germany accepted an agreement calling for some vertical disintegration, a limitation on self-supply by the remaining vertically integrated Ruhr firms, and the abolition of the *Deutscher Kohlen-Verkauf*

---

27. Article 3 Treaty of Paris already focused on the 'equality' principle by mentioning that the institutions of the Community shall:

    (b) assure to all consumers in comparable positions within the common market equal access to the sources of production; (e) promote the improvement of the living and working conditions of the labor force in each of the industries under its jurisdiction so as to make possible the equalization of such conditions in an upward direction; (f) ...see that equitable limits are observed in prices charged on external markets.

28. The Schuman Plan was based on the assumption that the integration of Germany into a permanent European structure was the best way to prevent Germany from being a threat to its neighbours and, at the same time, guarantee peace in Europe.
29. (Martin S. 2007, 48).
30. The vision of *Monnet* was the creation of a European industrial pool. He foresaw a Europe built on a functional basis by integrating key sectors of the economy in order to create genuine solidarity between the partners and thereby peace in the long-term.
31. (CVCE 2015).
32. (Bowie 1988).

(DKV), the major Ruhr coal joint sales agency. In exchange, Germany got an international agreement that German firms would operate according to the same competition rules as all other firms in the ECSC.[33]

The actual drafting of the competition provisions for the Treaty of Paris was done by *Robert Bowie*, a Harvard anti-trust expert and professor.[34] *Bowie*'s drafts were rewritten in French by *Maurice Lagrange*[35] who put these provisions 'into French treaty language'. In retrospect, more than mere translation was involved.[36]

Thus, the Treaty of Paris 1951 already included some competition related provisions. In Chapter VI on agreements and concentrations, Article 60(1) prohibited unfair competitive practices, in particular purely temporary or purely local price reductions whose purpose is to acquire a monopoly position within the common market, as well as discriminatory practices involving the application by a seller within the single market of unequal conditions to comparable transactions, especially related to the nationality of the buyer.[37] This provision was intended to limit German sales at lower prices to other countries, in particular France. Transparency of prices was another requirement in Article 60.

Article 65(1) prohibited all agreements among enterprises that would distort competition within the common market.[38] Article 65(2) gave the High Authority the right to permit certain types of agreements that were prohibited by paragraph 1, if specified conditions were met.[39] However, Article 65 did not include a provision similar to Article 101(3) TFEU namely that consumers need to get a fair share of the

---

33. (Martin S. 2007, 51). Gerber's guess is that already at this point ordoliberal scholars influenced German's decision-making. (Gerber, Law and Competition in Twentieth Century Europe Protecting Prometheus, 2001).
34. *Bowie* was general counsel to *Jack McCloy*, the Allied High Commissioner for Germany, in 1950–1951 and responsible for the enforcement and the application of the laws dealing with the de-concentration of German industry, coal and steel industry in particular. By chance, *Bowie* became involved in the Monnet-Schuman-Plan. (Bowie 1988).
35. Maurice Lagrange was subsequently the first Advocate General at the Court of Justice.
36. (Bowie, Réflexions sur Jean Monnet in Témoignages à la mémoire de Jean Monnet, 1981, 6); (Lagrange 1980).
37. Today this provision would relate to predatory pricing, price and sales condition discrimination, particularly discrimination based on nationality.
38. Article 65(1):

    All agreements between undertakings, decisions by associations of undertakings and concerted practices tending directly or indirectly to prevent, restrict or distort normal competition within the common market shall be prohibited, and in particular those tending: (a) to fix or determine prices; (b) to restrict or control production, technical development or investment; (c) to share markets, products, customers or sources of supply.

39. Article 65(2):

    However, the High Authority shall authorize specialization agreements or joint buying or joint selling agreements in respect of particular products, if it finds that: (a) such specialization or such joint buying or selling will make for a substantial improvement in the production or distribution of those products; (b) the agreement in question is essential in order to achieve these results and is not more restrictive than is necessary for that purpose; and (c) the agreement is not liable to give the undertakings concerned the power to determine the prices, or to control or restrict the production or marketing,

resulting benefits in order to apply the exemption provision. Article 66 contained detailed merger provisions and a rudimentary clause on abuse of economic power in Article 66(7).[40]

1.2.1.3 Spaak Report 1956

The next initiative unifying Europe related to a common market.

After having encountered failure in the military and political spheres in the mid 1950s, European revival became crucial in the economic sphere.[41] *Paul-Henri Spaak* was asked to draw up ideas for economic integration in the so-called Spaak Report.[42]

The German vision of a common integrated market including competition provisions was drafted as early as April 1955 and outlined in a ministerial note on European economic integration by a team around *Hans von der Groeben*. The concern of *von der Groeben* was that existing monopolies or abusive practices would frustrate a common market goal. Therefore, he considered rules for the protection of free competition within a common market as essential.

The reasoning was that the common market would not itself result in a more rational distribution of activities if suppliers remained able to provide users with goods or services on different terms and conditions, especially if such differences pertained to nationality or country of residence. The advantages of a wider geographic market were – according to *von der Groeben* – making large-scale production possible without the necessity for monopolies. By combining different national markets, large enough outlets that permitted the use of the most advanced production techniques could be created. Moreover, in a wider market it would no longer be possible to maintain outmoded methods of production with their two-fold effects of high prices and low wages. Instead of remaining static, commercial forces would have to pursue a go-ahead investment policy in order to increase production, improve quality and modernise the methods in a larger market: companies must make progress or fail.

---

of a substantial part of the products in question within the common market, or to shield them against effective competition from other undertakings within the common market.

40. Article 66(7):

If the High Authority finds that public or private undertakings which, in law or in fact, hold or acquire in the market for one of the products within its jurisdiction a dominant position shielding them against effective competition in a substantial part of the common market are using that position for purposes contrary to the objectives of this Treaty, it shall make to them such recommendations as may be appropriate to prevent the position from being so used.

41. Address given by Paul-Henri Spaak to the ECSC Common Assembly, Strasbourg, 13 Mar. 1956.
42. The Spaak Report was drafted by the Spaak Committee and approved in May 1956 thereby leading to the Treaties of Rome being signed in 1957 which established the European Economic Community (EEC) and the European Atomic Energy Community (Euratom) among the members of the ECSC.

Another perception was that a common market needed tools to fight both private and public restraints on competition, including state-granted financial assistance favouring certain enterprises that distorted competition.

It needs to be recalled that these ideas date back to 1955. They were transferred directly into the Spaak Report.[43] The Spaak Report contained in Title II on Rules and Common Action the rules concerning competition (Chapter 1). Section 2 discussed the rules concerning financial assistance granted by the states. *Spaak* himself unified the six founding members of the European Economic Community (EEC) around these ideas.

1.2.1.4 *From the Spaak Report to the Treaty of Rome 1957*

The next step was the drafting of the Treaty of Rome. Two German experts, *Alfred Müller-Armack* and *Hans von der Groeben*,[44] were part of the Common Market Group. *Müller-Armack* was the founder of the social market economy concept as applied in Germany (now in Article 3 TEU). The group was headed by *von der Groeben*.

The drafting process of the competition rules was subject to fierce negotiation with numerous different versions of the competition related provisions.

It is understood from the minutes of a meeting of the Common Market Group that during the negotiations the German delegation suggested a *differential* treatment of agreements and monopolies whereas the French delegation proposed that they should be subject to the same test. The French opinion was that all cartels, monopolies and abusive practices, which have the object of hindering competition, should be treated in the *same way*. The suggestion of the German delegation was that an outright prohibition should not be adopted for monopolies and oligopolies. Rather, they should only be subject to the *control of abuse*.

Müller-Armack stated, after declaring that it was necessary to distinguish between monopolies and oligopolies on the one hand and cartels on the other, that monopolies and oligopolies were not necessarily incompatible per se with a system of competition. In *Müller-Armack's* view it was only necessary to address abuses to which certain monopolistic situations could lead. By advocating two separate rules – one for anti-competitive agreements and the other one for the abuse of dominance – the German proposal differed significantly from the other ones. Moreover, the German position was that these two rules should be applicable for both private and public entities.

The German proposal was opposed by the Italian delegation as well. The French and the Belgium-Dutch drafts continued to treat agreements and monopolies on the same footing.

---

43. *Von der Groeben* wrote these ideas for the Spaak Report together with *Pierre Uri* in a period of just four weeks at Grand Hotel Cap Ferrat. See (von der Groeben, Europäische Integration aus historischer Erfahrung, 2002).
44. The author interviewed *von der Groeben* on the drafting of the competition provisions, which finally led to Arts 85 and 86 TEEC and on *von der Groeben's* experiences as first Commissioner for Competition.

Chapter 1: The Frame

The French delegation also argued for a no-direct effect of the competition rules in the common market. Instead *von der Groeben* urged that the Commission should be the only authority making decisions on competition issues subject to review by a second instance. Because of the importance attached to competition policy in a common market, the German position was that an independent authority, the Commission, and not the political Council should be the appropriate decision-making body with respect to competition law.

While preparing the texts for the Treaty of Rome, the German delegation counselled that competition itself was not the consequence of a very complicated legal discipline nor could it only be assured by law. On the contrary, the German position was that the most immediate and direct source of competition lay in a vast market. Thus, German experts supported from the very beginning the notion that a common market needs to be based on the *principles of a market economy*. The French delegation on the other hand supported a more *dirigiste* approach, with further potential for market interventions and economic planning by the Member States.[45]

Until the signing of the Treaty of Rome on 25 March 1957, several more drafts of the competition rules were negotiated between the delegations.

The final provisions were a compromise between the delegations, with the Germans influencing the drafting much more than any other delegation.

Von der Groeben expressed in a personal conversation with the author his view that at this stage he experienced *no influence from the US* at all.[46] The whole discussion with respect to the drafting of the EU competition rules took place between the six founding members of the EEC and was substantially influenced by the German social market economy concept and the French position. The negotiation process itself is well-documented and made public. Indeed the only US intervention was at the time the Treaty of Paris was drafted as observed in the previous section.

Von der Groeben became the first Commissioner for Competition (1958–1970). In retrospect, *von der Groeben* was convinced that the approach selected with respect to EU competition law was 'the' success factor of the European common market in its early years.

1.2.2 Modernisation Process

In the mid 1990s two issues occurred that required a re-thinking of the economic approach in EU competition law:

- The EU Merger Regulation came into force in 1990. For the first time, the European Commission was forced to assess markets and economic effects in mergers and acquisitions within tight review periods.[47] It quickly emerged that

---

45. See also e.g., (von der Groeben 1995, 269, 276–279) (Schweitzer 2007, 11).
46. In spring 1998 in Rheinbach, Germany.
47. In the very beginning, some of the reviews even failed to reach these timelines.

proper guidance over which kind of economic analysis should be applied was required. The main aims were to speed up procedures and increase legal certainty.
- Another avenue to modernisation started in 1995 when participants at the First European Competition Forum judged that the European Commission's practices for handling vertical restraints were too formalistic. The experts advocated that market analysis should be made as an initial step in analysing vertical restraints thereby refraining from the previously applied formalistic approach. Their view was that economic analysis on a case-by-case basis might improve the enforcement of the competition rules. They were motivated among other things by the case law of the Court of Justice at that time (*Delimitis* and *Danish Furs*). The Court proscribed in these cases that the economic context should be considered in determining whether an agreement constituted a restriction of competition or not.[48]

Karel van Miert, Commissioner for Competition 1993-1999, initiated this modernisation process. Both in his political function as well as in his academic environment, *Van Miert* became engaged. He supported academic research activities on EU competition economics as professor at the Free University of Brussels (VUB) where he was teaching.[49] In his political role as Commissioner for Competition, *Van Miert* requested DG Competition, the Directorate General for competition, to pursue a modernisation process towards an increasing use of modern economic tools: in particular he asked for a review of the vertical restraints policy and called for guidelines with respect to market definition.

The adoption of the 'Green Paper on Vertical Restraints' on 22 January 1997 by the European Commission was the first working product in this modernisation process. The publication of the Notice on market definition published later that year on 9 December 1997[50] was another milestone. This Notice has remained unchanged since then.

Van Miert spoke about these first two achievements of the 'more economics based approach' on 10 November 1997 at a conference in Copenhagen:[51]

---

48. The first European Competition Forum was held on 'vertical restraints' on 3, 4 Apr. 1995. Tom Ottervanger, Leiden University, was one of the experts advocating for a need to change the application.
49. In memory of *Karel van Miert* the VUB named in 2010 one of the buildings after him that is currently home to the Institute of European Studies (IES). Research activities with respect to EU competition economics are still ongoing in the *European Competition Economics and Policy* (ECEP) research cluster at the VUB.
50. Actually, the first edition of this book was originally a Ph.D.-doctorate under the supervision of *Karel Van Miert* at the Free University of Brussels (VUB). The final version of the Ph.D.-thesis was approved in an internal defence at the VUB on 9 Dec. 1997 the same day the Commission's market definition notice discussed in s. 4.2. came into force.
51. (van Miert 1997).

There is no answer to these concerns but several changes and reforms are needed. Within the Commission minds are turning to these issues. In some areas: our recent paper on vertical restraints, or the notice on market definition, the process of reform and modernisation is underway.

In his well-known direct and open-minded manner, *Van Miert* insisted:

We need to be clear in our approach. We need to ensure that the outside world understand how we think. We need to be consistent.

The events in 1997 marked the time when the European School as a genuine economic school of thought in EU competition law got attention and raised its profile. As *Van Miert* stated, the understanding of this specific economic thinking in a European way is essential particularly for Member States and courts that engage increasingly in the application of the EU competition rules. On top of that, foreign countries consider how the EU treats competition policy and its application as helpful.[52] It is likely that the current Commissioner for Competition *Margrethe Vestager* (appointed in 2014) will continue promoting the European competition culture in this respect.

Without a proper definition of the European approach, the risk is that the European model is (or will be) mixed with and undermined by other economic schools of thought. The most contrary school of thought, the US Chicago School, dispose of the highest influence at the moment as well.

These two economic schools of thought distinguish themselves by the ideology they apply and adhere to.

Whereas lawyers have difficulties understanding that economists' opinions do differ, economists are used to a manifold world of different schools of thought.[53] Economists are able to position different norms and postulations whereas competition lawyers and enforcers face more difficulties in distinguishing the theories. Thus, a clear explanation of the framework of the European approach or European School of thought as documented in this book provides an orientation to enforcers, academics and practitioners.

In the following, the EU legal framework is discussed first before returning to the economic frame of both schools of thought, the Chicago School and the European School.

1.3 THE LEGAL FRAMEWORK

The Treaty establishing the European Economic Community (TEEC or Treaty of Rome signed in 1957) was replaced by the Treaty of Lisbon (or Lisbon Treaty signed in 2007). The Lisbon Treaty came into force in 2009 and consists of the two core functional

---

52. This in particular relates to the work DG Competition pursues in the ICN (International Competition Network).
53. Chapter two provides a comprehensive overview on some of these different concepts.

Treaties of the EU: the Treaty on European Union (TEU) and the Treaty on the Functioning of the European Union (TFEU).

The following table illustrates the transition from the Treaty of Rome to the Lisbon Treaty with respect to the competition provisions. While Articles 85 and 86 TEEC have remained content wise unchanged, the numbering has been adjusted. They are now Articles 101 and 102 TFEU. Some competition related values previously expressed in the preamble to the TEEC were 'upgraded' to Articles. On top of that, new elements with respect to the social agenda have been added.

The *2007 Lisbon Treaty* declares that the EU is founded on the values of freedom, equality and the rule of law (Article 2 TEU). These values – freedom, equality and the rule of law – are important values related to the economic concept as applied in EU competition law. Considering the history of European society, these values are of significant importance and therefore carefully treasured and adhered to.

The Lisbon Treaty also states in Article 3 TEU that the EU's aim is to promote peace, its values and the well-being of its peoples. The well-being of people does not focus on economic aspects only. It includes social issues as well. Working for sustainable development in Europe based on a *highly competitive social market economy* is one of the principal aims in this regard.

A social market economy is a form of market capitalism combined with social objectives. A social market contains central elements of a free market economy such as private property, free trade, exchange of goods, freedom of contract and free formation of prices. However, in contrast to a free market economy the state is not passive. It actively implements regulatory measures, in particular, with respect to *protecting free market forces*. Integrated within these regulatory measures are social policy objectives that include a balancing of the distribution of gain and gain growth between the different economic actors. These elements are supposed to diminish many of the recurring problems of a free market economy. Thus, within a social market economy, the state's responsibility is to actively improve the market conditions and simultaneously to pursue a social balance.[54]

The people in the EU believe that prosperity and social progress strengthen the economic ties further between the Member States. Strong economic ties in turn lead to a peaceful Europe. In this respect, the EU competition rules are of significant importance in maintaining peace in Europe by supporting the establishment of the internal market and integrating the objectives of prosperity and social progress.

---

54. This responsibility lies according to the Lisbon Treaty with the European Commission as an independent authority.

Chapter 1: The Frame

Table 1.1   A Comparison of the Competition Provisions: Treaty of Rome 1957 and Lisbon Treaty 2007

Treaty Establishing the European Economic Community (TEEC)		Treaty on European Union (TEU) & Treaty on the Functioning of the European Union (TFEU)	
Preamble	'...RESOLVED to ensure the economic and social progress of their countries by common action to **eliminate the barriers which divide Europe**, AFFIRMING as the essential objective of their efforts the constant **improvement of the living** and working conditions **of their peoples**, RECOGNISING that the removal of existing obstacles calls for concerted action in order to guarantee steady expansion, balanced trade and **fair competition**,...RESOLVED by thus pooling their resources **to preserve and strengthen peace and liberty**, and ...'	Article 2 TEU	'The Union is founded on the values of respect for human dignity, **freedom**, democracy, **equality**, the **rule of law** and ...'[55]
Article 2 TEEC	'The Community shall have as its task, by establishing a **common market** and an economic and monetary union and by implementing common policies or activities referred to in Articles 3 and 4, to promote throughout the Community a harmonious, balanced and sustainable development of economic activities, ..., a high degree of competitiveness and convergence of economic performance, ..., the raising of the standard of living and quality of life, ...'	Article 3 TEU	1. The **Union's aim is to promote peace, its values and the well-being of its peoples**. 3. The Union shall establish an **internal market**. It shall work for the sustainable development of

---

55. In French: '*L'Union est fondée sur les valeurs de respect de la dignité humaine, de liberté, de démocratie, d'égalité, de l'État de droit*' and in German: '*Die Werte, auf die sich die Union gründet, sind die Achtung der Menschenwürde, Freiheit, Demokratie, Gleichheit, Rechtsstaatlichkeit*'.

Treaty Establishing the European Economic Community (TEEC)		Treaty on European Union (TEU) & Treaty on the Functioning of the European Union (TFEU)	
			Europe based on balanced economic growth and price stability, a highly competitive **social market economy**, aiming at full employment and social progress, and …
Article 3 TEEC	1. For the purposes set out in Article 2, the activities of the Community shall include, as provided in this Treaty and in accordance with the timetable set out therein: (g) a system ensuring that **competition in the internal market is not distorted**;	**Article 3 TFEU**	1. The **Union shall have exclusive competence** in the following areas: (b) the **establishing of the competition rules** necessary for the functioning of the internal market;
Article 4 TEEC	1. For the purposes set out in Article 2, the activities of the Member States and the Community shall include, …, the adoption of an economic policy which is based on the close coordination of Member States' economic policies, on the internal market and on the definition of common objectives, and conducted in accordance with the **principle of an open market economy with free competition**.	**Article 119 TFEU**	1. For the purposes set out in Article 3 of the TEU, the activities of the Member States and the Union shall include, …, the adoption of an economic policy which is

Treaty Establishing the European Economic Community (TEEC)		Treaty on European Union (TEU) & Treaty on the Functioning of the European Union (TFEU)	
			based on the close coordination of Member States' economic policies, on the internal market and on the definition of common objectives, and conducted in accordance with the **principle of an open market economy with free competition**.
		Protocol No. 27 on the internal market and competition	CONSIDERING that the **internal market as set out in Article 3 of the TEU includes a system ensuring that competition is not distorted,** have agreed that: To this end, the Union shall, if necessary, take action under the provisions of the Treaties, including under Article 352 of the TFEU.

EU competition rules implement the concept of a social market economy in practice. Both, the EU competition rules as well as the concept of a social market economy are interchangeable notions. This is due to the fact that both notions have been developed by the same people based on the same ideology.

One of their beliefs was that competition rules should not be subject to political decision-making and influences from outside. Instead an independent authority needs to implement the competition rules that are mandatory for a social market economy to work. That is why until today, the EU has had the ongoing exclusive competence in establishing and being the guardian of the competition rules (Article 3 TFEU).

The principle of an open market economy with free competition is reiterated in Article 119 TFEU and the link between the internal market and a system with distortion-free competition is repeated in Protocol No. 27.[56]

What is new is that the concept of a social market economy found its way via the Rome Treaty in 2004[57] to the Lisbon Treaty 2007.

In the following, the economic frame based on these legal provisions is elaborated.

1.4 THE ECONOMIC FRAMEWORK

1.4.1 Orientation

Definitions and treatments of economic power may vary. However most concepts recognise the need to control economic power. While differences are fine in general, tensions occur when societies address the same problem from different angles.

There are currently two leading anti-trust jurisdictions: the US and the EU. The distinctions between the two relate to (1) the law itself and (2) the eminent schools of economic thinking they apply. Schools of economic thought are used to structure thoughts and to shape the conditions for decisions necessary in the application of the law. With respect to economic thinking in the US, the Chicago School is a popular approach (however rarely applied in court) whereas in the EU the European School has an increasingly significant profile. These two schools of thought include economic concepts and values people share in their respective societies.

Economic concepts perform different functions in competition law systems. The identification of these different roles helps to clarify the functioning of economic analysis in competition law regimes. By using business economics terms the following roles of economics can be distinguished.

Economics comes into play on the *strategic* level, namely when the economic order is developed and defined as a normative principle. The practical application of economic analysis and theories of harm comes into play at the lower (2) *operational* and (3) *tactical* levels.

The main differences between the Chicago School and the European School relate to the economic analysis on the strategic and on the operational level.

---

56. The actual meaning of the Protocol is less known.
57. This Rome Treaty was signed on 29 Oct. 2004 by representatives of the then twenty-five Member States and was later ratified by eighteen Member States, which included referendums endorsing it in Spain and Luxembourg. However, the rejection of the document by French and Dutch voters in May and June 2005 brought the ratification process to an end.

1.4.1.1 Strategic Level

The market concept applied in both schools of thought is similar: Competition among firms to obtain the backing of consumers spurs firms to produce those goods and services that are most highly valued by consumers at the lowest possible cost. Firms drive prices down towards the marginal cost of production thereby resulting in output up to the point at which additional value to consumers no longer exceeds the additional cost to society.[58]

In principle, both schools of thought follow the paradigm that in a particular market the sum of producer and consumer surplus should be maximised (total surplus standard).[59] The main distinction between the two systems is that within Europe the redistribution of wealth gains within society is predetermined by the legal order to assure that the benefits of the market are social, equitable and fairly shared. This is a normative approach which lacks an equivalent in the Chicago School. In Chicago School thinking, social aspects are simply less popular. Consumer welfare in the Chicago style is enhanced by the creation of efficiencies as such, no matter which market participant receives the actual wealth created.

Thus, the important point here is that in the two schools of thought some values are similar and some are dissimilar. Similar, in that market economies are the preferred system whereas the social equality interest diverges in these two schools of thought.

US Chicago scholars would not accept a pre-determination by law about how wealth gains created by the market process should be distributed between the members of the society, namely equitable and thereby fairly. Social policy considerations are not part of US anti-trust law either.

US Chicago scholars would also not accept that a market system needs government intervention by the creation of a legal framework in order to protect the competition process as such.

Such divergences on the normative level are logical considering the differences in historical development, political orientation and ideology of the people within these two societies. The call for convergence at the strategic level does not make any sense at all. It is perfectly agreeable that societies and schools of thought apply different ideologies that then lead to different results on the operational level too. It is important to know therefore in which system the economic analysis is applied.

1.4.1.2 Operational Level

The economic order on the strategic level represents the guiding principle for the actual application of economic analysis on the operational level.

As stated, the normative economic order in EU competition law is based on the values and objectives of the Lisbon Treaty. Economic analysis in EU competition law

---

58. (Heyer 2006).
59. Total welfare and total surplus are used in the following as synonyms.

can neither change the values nor the objectives of the Treaty. In a hierarchical system, *economic analysis* at the lower operational level *needs to respect the pre-determination at the higher strategic level.*

On the operational level, economic analysis in accordance with the Chicago School provides much more room for elucidation. This is particular true in a case-by-case rule of reason approach as applied in the US. Within a rule of reason approach, the case specific economic analysis is decisive for the outcome without any further guidance from an economic order predetermined in the law on the strategic level. Whereas EU competition law includes for example in Article 101(3) TFEU policy objectives like social fairness and equality (consumers' fair share) there is no similar equivalent in US anti-trust law. US law focuses on anti-trust issues only, neglecting further (social) policy objectives.

In the EU on the other hand, on the operational level economic analysis enriches the understanding of markets or the behaviour in question. The results of the economic analysis cannot alter the pre-defined legal framework on the strategic level. EU style economics is applied according to the rules. This does not mean that economic analysis is of less importance in the EU frame. The difference from the Chicago School relates to the location and meaning which is assigned to economic analysis.

1.4.1.3 Tactical Level

On the *tactical* level, the role of economics is to describe data and identify the relationships among variables. This type of economics is universal and used to describe market facts. It increases the amount and information available to evaluate competition issues.[60]

To conclude: Differences in economic analysis between the Chicago and the European School relate to the strategic and the operational levels.

The differences on the strategic level are almost self-explanatory.

The explanation of why economic analysis on the operational level might produce different results needs further elaboration. The examples at the end of this chapter in section 1.5 provide some insights in this respect.

In order to make a clear distinction between the two schools of thought, the concept of the Chicago School is discussed first. The scope and framework of the European School, namely social market economies, are presented subsequently. Examples of hypothetical cases evaluated under the Chicago School approach and the European School one will be given in the following.

1.4.2 Chicago School

Current economic thinking in US anti-trust economics is based on the Chicago School and what is known as the 'consumer welfare standard' in particular. Synonyms for this approach are 'big is beautiful', 'the market will manage' and 'efficiencies'.

---

60. (Gerber David J. 2013–2014).

Chicago scholars begin with the premise that the sole goal of anti-trust is the achievement of economic efficiency.[61] Then, they apply price theory as the vehicle for determining efficiency effects. Entry is generally thought to be easy and monopoly is therefore most likely self-correcting. Hence, Chicagoans have a strong belief in the functioning of markets, not competition, advocating a *laissez-faire* approach. The Chicago School is confident that markets will manage and correct themselves without government interventions. On the other hand Chicagoans fear the likely harmful efficiency effects from the application of anti-trust laws.[62]

A fundamental premise in Chicago School thinking is that most real-world prices and quantities, most of the time, can be treated as if they were long run perfectly competitive equilibrium prices. This is called the 'good approximation assumption'.[63] By accepting the good approximation assumption, practices like price discrimination, tying and bundling, exclusive dealing contracts, loyalty discounts, and Resale Price Maintenance (RPM) improve market performance or, at least, not worsen it. Nor can mergers worsen market performance. Moreover, any anti-trust activity that goes beyond the prohibition of collusion is considered to be anti-consumer.[64]

The basic features of the Chicago School rely heavily on industrial organisation economics and include the following beliefs:

- Efficiencies associated with economics of scale and scope are of primary importance.
- Most markets are competitive, including many in which relatively few firms are competing.
- Monopoly power is not likely to be durable, since supra-competitive profits will induce entry.
- Barriers to entry (excepting those that are government created) are likely to be less significant than previously thought.
- Monopoly leveraging (e.g., conditioning the purchase of one 'tying product' on the purchase of another 'tied product') is not a sensible strategy since there is a 'single monopoly rent' i.e., the monopoly profits generated through the sale of the tying product will be such that there are no additional profits to be enjoyed through a tying strategy.
- Anti-trust enforcement is only appropriate if there is a substantial likelihood that it will increase consumer welfare.
- Vertical restraints are deemed to be per se legal (subject occasionally to a rule of reason approach) and horizontal price-fixing cartels are per se illegal.

---

61. This thinking may even lead to the 'Efficiency Paradox' which in the name of efficiency protects inefficient conduct by dominant firms thereby protecting inefficiency.(Fox E. 2009, 88).
62. (Bork, The Antitrust Paradox: A Policy at War with Itself, 1978) (Posner R., The Chicago School of Antitrust Analysis, 1979).
63. Mainstream industrial economists have never accepted this theorem. See (Martin S. 2007, 32).
64. (Martin S. 2007, 32).

1.4.2.1 The 'Consumer Welfare' Story

Anti-trust analysis in the Chicago School focuses on the 'consumer welfare' paradigm which is actually the *most abused term* in competition economics.[65]

In practice, applied welfare economics uses the notion of consumer surplus to measure consumer welfare. When measured over all consumers, consumer surplus is a measure of aggregate consumer welfare.

In the following some basic economic concepts are described first before explaining the so-called 'Chicago trap'.

1.4.2.2 Marshallian Concept of Total Surplus

Marshall used price theory for describing the relationship of demand and supply. The following simple graph in the *Marshallian* tradition (1898) illustrates total surplus comprising of consumer surplus and producer surplus. By focusing on costs *Marshall* noted that, in the short run, supply cannot be changed and market value depends mainly on demand.

The excess of a price a consumer would be willing to pay rather than go without the product, over what he actually does pay, is defined as consumer surplus. Producer surplus is the difference between the amount a seller is paid for a good and the seller's cost of providing it (profit). Total surplus or aggregate welfare in the graph below is the joint area of consumer surplus and producer surplus.

Figure 1.2 Marshallian Total Surplus Model

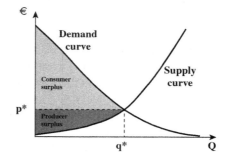

The logic in Chicago School thinking is that markets should maximise total surplus. Nothing is said about the distribution of total surplus between producers and consumers.

The graph illustrates that the focus of this type of analysis is on the relationship between price and quantity. Other non-price and non-quantity related aspects are not

---

65. (Brodley 1987, 1032).

considered thereby neglecting, for example, quality aspects or service level preferences that also might improve consumer utilities.

In the *Marshallian* tradition, price equals marginal costs. Short-term production can be expanded by existing facilities. These fixed costs have little influence on the price. *Marshall* preferred partial equilibrium models over general equilibrium models since the dynamic element in economics made the former more practically useful.

This basic total surplus model is used to discuss the *Williamson's* trade-off model in the following.[66] It becomes clear at that point why Chicago insights cannot be used in any meaningful economic analysis in EU competition law.

1.4.2.3 Williamson's *Trade-Off Model*

In 1968, *Oliver Williamson* discussed the need to weigh the benefits of improved efficiency against the costs of allocative *in*efficiency ('deadweight loss'). His trade-off model[67] shows that society is in most cases better off despite monopoly enhancement because of a merger.

As illustrated in the graph below, following a merger, market power increases: output is reduced from Q1 to Q2 and price increases from P1 to P2. The loss in allocative efficiencies is represented by the triangle A1 ('deadweight loss'). The merger generates cost savings from AC1 to AC2. However, the industry is now less competitive. Since the firm is no longer a price taker, the price P2 it charges is above the (now lower) unit cost AC2.[68]

The striped rectangle, W, represents a loss of consumer surplus (gain in monopoly profits) that the merger produces. Thus, income or *wealth is transferred from consumers to producers*. This means that the amount of consumer surplus, the area below the demand curve and above the price P2, Z, is lower post-merger. Previously consumer surplus was Z plus W plus A1 (area above P1).

---

66. (Williamson, 1968) Deadweight welfare loss is a measure of allocative *in*efficiency.
67. The model is based on strict assumptions: perfect competition, merging firms are duopolists, homogenous products, constant unit cost of production etc.
68. For a monopoly the price will be set where the unit/marginal cost intersects marginal revenue.

Figure 1.3 Williamson's Trade-Off Model

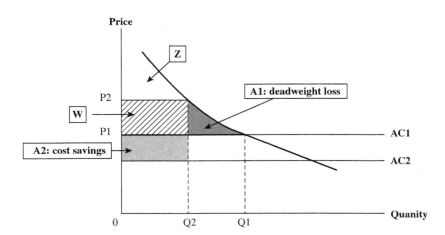

The *total welfare standard* asks whether additional producer surplus (which might accrue through an increase in productive efficiency[69] created by the merger) is larger than any additional allocative inefficiency ('deadweight loss') that results from an increase in market power.

Williamson concluded that cost savings need not be very high to compensate for deadweight losses induced by price increases. The net allocative effect of the merger is assessed by comparing the triangle A1 (deadweight loss) with the rectangle A2 (cost savings) confirming that a merger quite often yields a net-efficiency gain. However, income (or wealth) is transferred from consumers to producers.

When a *consumer welfare standard* is used the merger assessment needs to focus on consumer surplus only. The consumer surplus standard allows, in contrast to the total welfare standard, *no* disadvantages to the consumer. According to this approach, a merger that leads to increased consolidation, higher prices and negative effects for competition can only be approved if the *consumer benefit increases post-merger*. The achievable efficiency gains of a merger must be at least partly passed on to the consumer. This 'consumer pass on' of efficiency gains is mainly measured in prices. Accordingly, a merger that entails projected price increases would not be approved, independent of whatever advantages it may have for the total welfare.[70]

This means that depending on the welfare standard applied, results in the economic analysis differ. An anti-trust standard which puts consumer interests on the forefront could never approve a merger without an increase in consumer surplus.

---

69. *Productive efficiency* (or technical efficiency) describes the level of utilisation of resources in the economy and is maximised with various combinations on the production possibility frontier (PPF) of the economy. It is a situation in which the economy could not produce any more of one good without sacrificing production of another good. Put simply, optimal productive efficiency exists where the economy utilises resources in the least expensive way possible. See (OECD, Glossary of Industrial Organisation Economics and Competition Law, 1993).
70. See also (Ahdar 2002).

Where price decreasing effects through efficiencies are smaller than price increasing effects through additional market power of producers but gains in productive efficiencies are larger than the additional allocative inefficiencies ('deadweight loss'), a consumer welfare standard leads to a negative assessment whereas total welfare would be increased.[71]

To conclude, the Chicago position is that consumer welfare is another name for allocative efficiency or total welfare. This means that the *Chicago School applies a total welfare standard* and not a consumer welfare or consumer surplus standard as articulated by many Chicagoan contributors.

Deciding which welfare standard shall be applied cannot be reached through welfare theory itself, but must be decided normatively. Practically, this means that the decision over which approach to apply is a political one.

In EU competition law both goals – efficiencies as synonym for economic progress and a fair distribution of wealth gains between producers and consumers – are equally important. EU competition law has a built-in preference as to how prosperity should be distributed. The European position is that welfare gains because of a merger should not be attributed mainly to one group (such as the producer in the *Williamson's* trade-off model) but distributed fairly and equitably between both groups, consumers and producers. Whereas the Chicago School believes that in the long run consumers will benefit anyway, the European School prefers a fair distribution at the time the worsening of the competition process takes place.

Returning to the *Williamson* graph above consumer surplus before the merger is the entire area above AC1 (the triangle A1, the rectangle W, and Z the white area above W). Following the merger, consumer welfare/consumer surplus is reduced to Z alone. A1 is gone, a deadweight social loss, and W belongs to the producer.

In the Chicago view, the redistribution of income in *Williamson's* trade-off model is 'neutral'. This is a strange definition considering the fact that producers get richer at the expense of consumers. In the US, there is empirical evidence indeed supporting this observation and indicating that monopoly power, past and present, has contributed significantly to the above average wealth of the already wealthiest families.[72]

---

71. *Allocative efficiency*: Every good or service is produced up to the point where the last unit provides a marginal benefit to consumers equal to the marginal cost of producing it. In the usual interpretation at the point of allocative efficiency, price is equal to marginal cost. In principle, at this point production equals consumer preferences by focusing on the consumer's willingness to pay. At this point surplus is maximised with no deadweight loss. Allocative efficiency can be referred to as *Pareto efficiency* that occurs when resources are so allocated that it is not possible to make anyone better off without making someone else worse off. When referring to a situation as Pareto efficient, it is usually assumed that products are being produced in the most efficient (least cost) way. In anti-trust economics, allocative or economic efficiency arises when inputs are utilised in a manner such that a given scale of output is produced at the lowest possible cost. An increase in efficiency occurs when an existing or higher scale of output is produced at lower cost. See (OECD, Glossary of Industrial Organisation Economics and Competition Law, 1993).
72. See also (Ahdar 2002, 346).

1.4.2.4 The 'Chicago Trap'

Probably the confusion over whether the 'consumer welfare standard' relates to consumer surplus or total welfare was never intended by the Chicago School.

The confusion was introduced to US anti-trust law by *Bork* one of the founders of the Chicago School.[73] He mixed up the term 'consumer welfare' with 'total welfare'.[74] To reach a maximum of confusion, *Bork* also called consumer welfare 'the wealth of the nation'[75], a term economists refer to as 'social welfare'.

In *Bork's* view, consumer welfare is the greatest when society's economic resources are allocated so that consumers are able to satisfy their wants as fully as technological restraints permit. In his view, allocative efficiency and productive efficiency together make up the overall efficiency that determines the level of society's wealth.[76] *Bork* further explained that consumer welfare is net social welfare, the sum of producer surplus and consumer surplus. *'Those who continue to buy after a monopoly is formed pay more for the same output, and that shifts income from them to the monopoly and its owners, who are also consumers'.*[77] Thus, *Bork* qualified both monopolists and normal people as consumers. In *Bork's* view consumer welfare is in fact total welfare.

Bork's main contribution to the Chicago trap[78] is the call for maximising consumer welfare as a dominant goal of anti-trust.[79] *'The whole task of antitrust can be summed up as an effort to improve allocative efficiency without impairing productive efficiency so greatly as to produce either no gain or a net loss in consumer welfare.'*[80]

1.4.2.5 Wealth Distribution in the Chicago School

Bork maintained that anti-trust law has nothing to say about the ways prosperity is distributed or used. In the Chicago view, there is no need to consider a distributional effect of income (or wealth transfer) since it does not affect total welfare as the sum of consumer and producer surplus.[81] In this sense, according to Chicago School thinking US anti-trust legislation is not a process for deciding who should be rich or poor. Chicagoans simply ignore the transfer of wealth. In the Chicago view, anti-trust policy

---

73. In 1966, Bork analysed the legislative intent of the Sherman Act. He argued that economic efficiency should be the guiding principle which means total welfare but he called this 'consumer welfare'. (Bork R., Legislative Intent and the Policy of the Sherman Act, 1966).
74. (Bork, The Antitrust Paradox: A Policy at War with Itself, 1978, 90).
75. *'Consumer welfare, in this sense, is merely another term for the wealth of the nation'.* (Bork, The Antitrust Paradox: A Policy at War with Itself, 1978, 90).
76. *'These two types of efficiencies make up the overall efficiency that determines the level of our society's wealth, or consumer welfare.'* (Bork, The Antitrust Paradox: A Policy at War with Itself, 1978, 91).
77. (Bork, The Antitrust Paradox: A Policy at War with Itself, 1978, 110).
78. (Cseres, Competition Law and Consumer Protection, 2005, 332).
79. (Bork, The Antitrust Paradox: A Policy at War with Itself, 1978, 50).
80. (Bork, The Antitrust Paradox: A Policy at War with Itself, 1978, 91).
81. (Kerber 2007, 6).

is more rigorously economic and less concerned with protecting non-economic values that are impossible to identify and weigh.[82] Thus, in the Chicago School *no distributional issues of income* are included.

Chicago scholars argue that other public policies are better suited to deal with equity goals: '*Antitrust thus has a built in preference for material prosperity, but it has nothing to say about the way prosperity is distributed or used.*'[83] The Chicago school considers efficiency gains as politically neutral but regards wealth transfers as politicised: '*Wealth should go where it is the most appreciated.*'[84]

It has to be noted that a total welfare standard is not compatible with the Pareto-criterion because it allows for redistribution between consumers and producers and therefore a balancing between the positive and negative wealth effects between different persons.[85] This means that the concept of a total welfare standard is indeed not that useful to address distributional issue.

As a matter of fact the contributions of welfare economics to anti-trust analysis in US case law are limited too.

1.4.2.6 Chicago School in US Case Law

Until now in the US, clear guidance from the Supreme Court over which standard, the consumer welfare or the total welfare standard should be applied, is missing. '*The goal of antitrust has not been articulated by the Supreme Court.*'[86] Thus, neither has the US Supreme Court decided about the appropriate economic standard to be applied nor about which school of thought should be applied. Nor is there acceptance by industrial economists that Chicago School thinking on anti-trust is well founded in economics.[87]

In its *Trinko* case (2004), the Supreme Court completely ignored Chicago School literature. In *State Oil* (1997) the Supreme Court adopted the rule of reason rather than the per se legality call of the Chicago School for maximum RPM. In *Leegin Creative Products* (2007), the Supreme Court adopted the rule of reason for minimum RPM too. No one called for the Chicago School's per se legal position. Recent case law in tying and exclusive dealing has been driven mainly by the Harvard School and not the Chicago School approach. One place where the Supreme Court applied Chicago School thinking is the indirect purchaser rule which awards the full trebled overcharge to direct purchasers and no damages at all to indirect purchasers.[88]

Several critical voices argue that the normative foundation of the Chicago School is flawed. They mention that the fundamental goal of anti-trust policy is not increasing economic efficiency. '*It is protecting consumers in the relevant market from practices that deprive them of the benefits of competition and transfer their wealth to firms with*

---

82. (Hovenkamp H. 2010, 1).
83. (Bork, The Antitrust Paradox: A Policy at War with Itself, 1978, 90).
84. (Posner R., The Economics of Justice, 1981, 92).
85. (Kerber 2007, 7).
86. (Blair & Sokol 2012, 473).
87. (Martin S. 2007).
88. (Hovenkamp H. 2010, 4–7).

market power.'[89] According to these voices, the end result of the economic goal of anti-trust should be the enhancement of aggregate social wealth (economic efficiency) subject to the constraint that consumers shall receive an appropriate share of such wealth (consumer welfare). In their view, the appropriate share is the share that would be provided by a competitive market.[90] Actually, these critical US voices sound very much like the European ones.

1.4.2.7 Conclusion

Despite the 'Chicago trap' and the lack of acceptance by the US Supreme Court and other US courts, the Chicago School continues to put strong emphasis on efficiency gains and producer surplus. In the Chicago view, an economy is operating at maximum efficiency when society is squeezing the greatest value out of its scarce resources. The independent actions of profit and utility-maximising economic agents work towards producing this desirable outcome. The Chicago School considers a policy, which produces greater gains to businesses than losses to consumers to be efficient. Chicagoans even consider a monopoly, which produces cost savings but at the same time higher prices for consumers as legitimate.[91]

It has to be noted that the Nobel Prize-winning track record of the Chicago School is very impressive. Between 1969 and 2004, fifty-seven economists related to the University of Chicago had received this honour.[92] Nevertheless, the importance of Chicago School insights for the European approach is very limited.

1.4.3 European School

New challenges such as the increasing decentralised application of EU competition law, the enlargement of the EU, critics on Chicago School learning and the economic and social challenges Europe is currently facing are encouraging a re-focusing of economic analysis in EU competition law.

The following section touches on these more recent developments but also discusses where the European School is coming from. This school of thought needs to be viewed in its historical context.

1.4.3.1 Emergence of the European School

In the last twenty years (1995–2015), all policy areas in EU competition law have been modernised towards a rock-solid coherent European approach.

The modernisation areas include all aspects of competition law namely mergers, agreements, abuses and state aid as discussed in this book.

---

89. (Kirkwood & Lande 2009, 97).
90. (Brodley 1987, 1023).
91. (Cseres, The Controversies of the Consumer Welfare Standard, 2007, 125).
92. (Overtveldt Johan Van 2007, 1).

During these twenty years, diverse Commissioners for Competition have contributed in different ways: while one of the most important changes took place during the time of Commissioner *Mario Monti*'s tenure (1999–2004), namely the decentralisation of the application of the competition rules by Regulation 1/2003, Commissioners *Nellie Kroes* (2004–2010) and *Joaquin Almunia* (2010–2014) focused much more on the modernisation of the state aid provisions. What is clear from these past twenty years is that within Europe the deliberation with respect to economics in EU competition law has raised the European School's profile. The European School as an economic frame and the application of this economic thinking to EU competition law is well-accepted today throughout the competition community.

The economic logic and thinking applied in EU competition law is deeply rooted in the foundations of the Lisbon Treaty and has been further developed by different sources: the academic society[93] as well as the decisional practice and the policy guidance of the Commission. However, the most decisive and influencing elements in this school of thought originate from the case law of the Court of Justice of the EU. In fact, the European concept has been thoroughly researched, subsequently developed further and has been applied in practice for almost six decades.

The remainder of the book discusses this thinking. To begin with some main facets are presented.

1.4.3.2 Core Concepts

The core concept of the European School is that economics plays an important role in the application of the EU competition law principles.

The European School itself is rooted in the economic order and the social policy objectives attached to that order. Thus, the anchor of the European approach is the current legal system.[94] Economic analysis in the European tradition supplements the law thereby enabling the proper application of the legal rules.[95]

The protection of individual (economic) freedom of action as a value in itself against any impairment of excessive economic power lies at the heart of the European School. Economic actors are free to make their own choices. However, society demands that these choices are based on the principle of equality and social balance within a properly pre-defined framework grounded on the rule of law.

Economic analysis in the EU tradition improves the legal order.

In contrast, in the US economic analysis under a rule of reason approach replaces such an economic order. This is due to the flexibility within the US anti-trust provisions. Either a conduct is qualified as per se illegal or the conduct needs to be

---

93. Just a few examples are the inaugural speeches of Tom Ottervanger at the University of Leiden (Ottervanger 2010) or of Wouter Devroe at the University of Maastricht (Devroe 2013).
94. The 'more economics based approach' was never supposed to change the rule of law.
95. The theory of industrial organisation does not focus its research on normative questions. Usually the normative question in this theory is narrowed down to the question of total welfare versus consumer welfare standard. (Kerber 2007, 1).

assessed on a case-by-case basis under the rule of reason.[96] The outcome of such an assessment is open depending on the guidance received by the economic analysis. The outcome in turn depends on the school of thought applied being either Chicago School or Harvard School thinking, thereby producing different and sometimes conflicting outcomes.[97] With respect to economic analysis, coherence in the application of US anti-trust law is missing. Moreover, neither an economic order nor other policy objectives are attached to US anti-trust law compared to EU competition law. Economic analysis in EU competition law is instead rooted in a pre-regulatory and interventionist approach.

This approach reflects ordoliberal thinking and its further development towards the concept of a social market economy.

1.4.3.3 Ordoliberal Thinking

Post-World War II Europe feared communism on the one hand and a revival of fascism and nationalism on the other hand. Ideologically in terms of organising an economy both options – centrally planned economies of socialism or a *laissez-faire* liberalism – were 'no options'.

Europeans were traumatised by the concentrations of power in both public and private spheres which distorted the functioning of their economies. Pre-World War II well-run German cartels like *IG Farben* resulted in a high concentration of economic power. During World War II, scholars had identified that a major 'success factor' of the totalitarian Nazi regime was its ability to turn private economic power quite easily into political power by misusing the German industries and in particular the iron and steel industry.[98] The Nazi regime transformed these powerful private economic entities quite quickly into a war-machine controlled by political power.

In sharp contrast to these experiences ordoliberal scholars identified that peace and the economic and social well-being of people are strongly correlated. It is less likely that a society with a high level of employment and social protection as well as a rising standard of living and quality of life is vulnerable to an ideology as experienced prior to World War II.

---

96. Since the *Leegin* case for example in the US, minimum vertical price-fixing is no longer prohibited per se but will be analysed under the rule of reason. The problem with a full rule of reason standard is that it often operates as a de facto legality rule. Another test (often used in horizontal restraints cases) is the 'quick-look' rule of reason test. A quick-look evaluation considers whether a full rule of reason test is done or not. A full rule of reason test requires significant resources complainants might not dispose of thereby making the application of a full rule of reason test less likely. See (Lao, 216).
97. Within Chicago a view conduct can be found to be not abusive due to its pro-competitive effects. Thus, efficiencies brought about by the conduct may outweigh likely negative effects on competition and possible consumer harm in the long run. The Harvard School instead applies the Structure-Conduct-Performance paradigm (SCP) thereby focusing on the market structure. The emphasis on conduct is minimised and market power is considered to be harmful.
98. (Gormsen Liza Lovdahl 2007, 332); (Röpke 1934, 24–27).

The values of the ordoliberal concept – a neoliberal approach putting emphasis on a framework – has found its way into the Lisbon Treaty. Prominent values of ordoliberalism are 'freedom' and 'equality' as implemented in the EU competition rules.[99]

The actual goal of ordoliberalism lies in the protection of individual economic freedom of action as a value in itself through the restraint of undue power.

The realisation of individual freedom of action is paramount in a market system. Economic efficiency as a generic term for growth, for the encouragement and the development of the technical process, and for allocative efficiency is a consequence of freedom of action and thereby an indirect and derived goal of ordoliberalism as well.[100]

Thus, in the ordo-view a legal system is essential in order to protect the liberty of action by individuals as well as by the government from distortions.[101] Ordoliberal scholars assumed that the accumulation of economic power during the Nazi regime was the consequence of not having such an independent legal system.

'The freedom of the sheep to coexist with the wolf is meaningless in the absence of a shepherd.'[102]

In the ordoliberal opinion, the weakness of the state to establish such a legal system resulted in unrestrained economic and political freedom thereby enabling a dictatorship that finally led to World War II.

By assuming that the working properties of market processes depend on the nature of the legal-institutional framework within which they take place, a market order should be a constitutional one. In ordoliberal thinking, the long-term viability of free markets requires a rule-bound and limited, yet powerful form of government intervention. To quote *Röpke*, one of the ordoliberal scholars:

> *A market economy and our economic program presuppose the following type of state: a state which knows exactly where to draw the line between what does and what does not concern it, which prevails in the sphere assigned to it with the whole force of its authority, but refrains from all interference outside its sphere – an energetic umpire whose task it is neither to take part in the game nor to prescribe their movements to players, who is rather, completely impartial and incorruptible and sees to it that the rules of the game and of sportsmanship are strictly enforced. That is the state without which a genuine and real market economy cannot exist.*

Thus, according to the ordoliberals a market should be embedded in a constitutional framework, which protects the process of competition from distortion by private and public power and minimises state intervention in the economy. This requires that the state must create a proper legal environment for the economy and maintain a

---

99. This German concept is in many ways different from the ideas that are nowadays connected with the term 'neo-liberalism'. *Alexander Rüstow* defined the term 'neo-liberalism' in 1938 at the Colloque Walter Lippmann. The colloquium defined the concept of neoliberalism as involving 'the priority of the price mechanism, the free enterprise, the system of competition and a strong and impartial state'. (Mirowski & Plehwe 2009).
100. (Möschel, The Proper Scope of Government Viewed from an Ordoliberal Perspective: The Example of Competition Policy 2001, 4).
101. *Ibid.*, 8.
102. (Gerber D. J., Constitutionalizing the Economy: German Neo-Liberalism, Competition Law and the 'New' Europe, 1994, 29) (Adams 1976, 13).

healthy level of competition through measures that adhere to market principles. If the state does not take active measures to foster competition, firms with monopoly (or oligopoly) power will emerge, which will not only subvert the advantages offered by the market economy, but also possibly undermine good government.

This claim is very well researched and documented.[103] According to one of the founders of ordoliberalism, *Walter Eucken*, history has demonstrated that competition tends to collapse, because enterprises prefer private (i.e., contractual) regulation of business activities rather than competition and because enterprises are frequently able to acquire such high levels of economic power that they can eliminate competition. In this thinking, competition law is viewed as a means of preventing degeneration of the competitive process. Competition law *enforces* competition by creating and maintaining the conditions under which it can flourish.[104]

The logic is that economic freedom entails the potential for its own destruction. The inherent and unavoidable tendency of private business to restrict competition for the sake of monopoly profits induces companies to agree on cartels, on tying arrangements, on exclusive dealership clauses and other restrictive practices. They use their liberty to narrow their own and their competitor's freedom of contract. Such a decomposition of the market economies has to be prevented by legislation designed to protect competition.[105]

As *Eucken* stated:

> *A liberal market economy cannot survive for long in a totalitarian state, nor can a democratic state under the rule of law survive if economic power is highly concentrated.*[106]

Thus, a system ensuring that the market is protected from destructive influences of political and economic power is required:[107]

> *The market could not be allowed to function as an independent entity without any control.*[108]

Ordoliberal thinking found its way to the European School by defining the 'rules of the game' that are essential for a competitive market economy. In contrast to the belief in self-healing forces of markets – as known for example in the Chicago School – Europeans apply a 'framework' approach instead to protect competition in the long run. In accordance with ordoliberal thinking, the competition process itself is protected by EU competition law.

---

103. Unfortunately, most of the documentation is in German thereby reducing a broader distribution of these insights in the international competition community.
104. (Gerber D. J., Constitutionalizing the Economy: German Neo-Liberalism, Competition Law and the 'New' Europe, 1994, 50).
105. (Eucken, Grundsätze der Wirtschaftspolitik, 1990), (E. Mestmäcker 1980).
106. (Eucken 1939).
107. When competition cannot generate the expected results due to market failures like natural monopolies, external effects, or asymmetric information of the parties, legislation regulating specific economic sectors can be used.
108. (Gerber D. J., Constitutionalizing the Economy: German Neo-Liberalism, Competition Law and the 'New' Europe, 1994, 25).

It is important to note that this ordoliberal concept was further developed towards a concept, which became known as the 'social market economy'.

The European approach today is not about ordoliberalism. It is the further development in academic thinking and practical application towards the concept of social market economies.

1.4.3.4 Social Market Economies

Another important European dogma is that competition is the appropriate tool to manage markets and so create wealth. *Alfred Müller-Armack* is one of the founders of this social market economy concept. He was also part of the Common Market Group when the EU competition rules were drafted for the Treaty of Rome (see section 1.2.1).

As Germany was faced with the results of its military catastrophe, the need for social responsibility was strongly felt. *Müller-Armack* blamed capitalism for betraying the basic principles of the market economy, namely competition and price freedom. In his view, consumer choice has the power to establish real prices and encourage production.

By using the term 'social market economy' *Müller-Armack* developed a third system replacing both collectivist controls and *laissez-faire* mentioned before. In this third way a 'social market economy' is not just a liberal market economy left to function by itself. It is steered in a *socially acceptable direction*.

The main point is that '*it is impossible to choose an economic solution which contradicts the fundamental spiritual values to which one is committed*'.[109]

Social security should be achieved, for example, by the following measures: the creation of a system of work which treats employees as human beings and gives them what is described as the 'social right to participate' in the organisation of their work without reducing managerial initiative and the responsibility of the employer.

Another critical issue in a 'social market economy' – that is of particular relevance in EU competition law – is that access to freedom needs to be equal for all actors. Under the order of free competition within a social market economy, all economic players meet as legal equals. A private law society consists of equally free people with equal rights, a society in which '*everyone should have the same rights and status, namely the status of a person under private law*'.[110]

Ludwig Erhard, another important contributor to the concept of a social market economy, confirmed that:

> Today a social and economic policy faces the task of providing all individuals in the economic process with the greatest possible equality of opportunity. It is also the duty of policy makers to eliminate economic privilege and power-concentration.[111]

---

109. (Müller-Armack, The Meaning of the Social Market Economy, 1989, 82–86).
110. (Böhm, Freiheit und Ordnung in der Marktwirtschaft, 1980, 140) (Böhm, Private Law Society and the Market Economy, 1989, 54); (Nicholls 2000, 155).
111. (Erhard 1946).

Thus, the equality principle in EU competition law makes a social market economy social.

This thinking is implemented in the European approach. Based on ordoliberalism and insights on social market economies, it is crucial that markets are not left alone. It is necessary to create a strong framework that ensures (a) that social standards and other objectives of society are respected and (b) that the beneficial workings of market forces are not blocked, restrained or distorted by short-sighted actions of market actors themselves.

In conclusion, a social market economy is a legally protected system of competition designed to ensure that the energies of ambitious individuals are channelled in a beneficial way to the common (public) good.[112]

1.4.3.5 *The Frame of the European School*

It is universally known that markets are framed by different rules. The choice of the 'rules of the game' is decisive with respect to the general working properties of a market process.

The European belief is that a prosperous, free and equitable society can develop only when the market is embedded in a constitutional framework. The framework is necessary to protect the process of competition from distortion, as a means of preventing degeneration of the competitive process itself and in particular assuring that the benefits of the market are equitably distributed throughout society thereby minimising governmental intervention in the economy.[113]

These 'rules of the game' are incorporated into EU competition law that functions as a pillar of the social market economy concept by putting economic policy on a par with social policy. Thus, the law pre-defines the normative economic order based on the values 'liberty', 'social fairness' and 'equality'. The protection of free competition based on equality is the most important *'social'* principle in a social market economy.[114]

Thus, the ultimate aim of the EU competition rules is to maintain and help to establish a social market economy based on competitive market structures for the well-being of people. The competition process should be steered in a socially acceptable direction.

In the European School, the well-being of people includes besides price elements a holistic perception of consumer utilities and preferences. Interests of the 'average consumer' or citizen lie at the heart of the European School. This is not the same objective as for example defined by the consumer surplus/consumer welfare standard of the Chicago School. The European objective is broader and holistic.

---

112. See also (Nicholls 2000, 144).
113. (Gerber D. J. 1998, 232).
114. See also (Müller-Armack, The Meaning of the Social Market Economy, 1989, 82–86).

Consumer interests in the European School embrace beside economic objectives also social ones. The implementation of this approach requires that price and non-price related elements in the purchasing decision of consumers are considered in any competition assessment.

The focus on general consumer interests is evidenced by the wording of the EU competition rules themselves. The basic idea is that consumers should share any efficiency gains and wealth increases with producers and thereby receive a greater offer, better quality, more innovative products and services at lower prices within an internal market.

1.4.3.6 Implementation of the European School into EU Competition Law

The European approach is laid down in the Lisbon Treaty. Two Treaty Articles refer to the objectives as outlined above. These are Articles 101 and 102 TFEU.

1.4.3.6.1 Article 101 TFEU

Agreements can restrict competition under specific circumstances. Again, the logic holds that market actors are treated equally.

If an agreement restricts competition but contributes to improving the production or distribution of goods or to promoting technical or economic progress it may escape the nullity provision. Such an agreement may produce efficiencies which benefit in the first instance the producer.

In order to be exempted from the nullity provision, the pro-competitive benefits need to outweigh anti-competitive effects. Equality is introduced because it is not the producer alone who benefits; consumers must get a 'fair share' as well.

This does not necessarily mean that consumers must get the same amount of wealth gains as producers because producers need to be compensated, for example, for their innovation efforts and risks. However, the distribution needs to be 'fair'. The analysis considers other non-price related benefits a consumer might receive in compensation for an increase in market power.

In this higher hierarchy canon of freedom, social fairness, equality and rule of law, economic efficiency is of lower importance. Benefits are shared between the two market sides equally. If consumers would not get a fair share, then only producers would benefit. This would be single-sided thereby contradicting the equality and social fairness criteria of the concept of social market economies.

1.4.3.6.2 Article 102 TFEU

Firms are supposed to engage in performance competition or 'competition on the merits'. That is normal competition which improves the performance of a firm and is in the long-term interest of the consumer: better goods, lower prices, better services and an increase in innovation. This type of competition translates into benefits to the consumer.[115] In this sense, the entrepreneur's pursuit of profit is directly related to the consumer.[116] *'The only road to business success is through the narrow gate of better performance in service of the consumer'.*[117]

Performance competition needs to be distinguished from non-performance competition. This latter competition is not in the long-term consumer interest but takes place for other reasons such as the hindrance of competitors or undue enrichment. Non-performance competition is about lowering the accomplishment of competitors thereby improving one's own relative performance (but without an absolute improvement).[118] And it is also about unduly increasing one's own profits at the expense of others.

The logic of equality implies that since non-performance competition is not a type of competition a firm would engage in as normal business conduct, a firm holding economic power should refrain from such a type of competition as well. This is consistent with the 'rules of the game' namely that firms with and without economic market power need to behave equally.

If an individual firm has economic power that power must be controlled. This means that by applying an *'as-if'*-standard, firms need to refrain from conduct that they would not engage in at all if they had no economic power. The rule of law organises an equal treatment of these firms despite whether they have economic power or not. Thus, firms with economic power should behave equally, *'as if'* these firms do not hold economic power.

In order words, firms with economic power should not abuse this power. Their actions must not deviate from the actions of companies that operate in competitive markets. Otherwise their actions could be regarded as unfair and abusive even if they could prove to be welfare-enhancing. In this respect, firms with economic power have a special responsibility.

To conclude, a competition policy in the view of the European School focuses on the legitimisation of economic freedom based on social fairness and equality, which thereby prevents that freedom from not being destroyed by its own preconditions. The framework assures the free and fair play of the actors but also guarantees at the same time equal conditions for each actor and player.

Next, the main aspects of the European School are compared with the Chicago School in a summary.

---

115. (Eucken 1999, 43).
116. (Böhm, The Non-State ('Natural') Laws Inherent in a Competitive Economy, 1982, 109).
117. (Röpke, A Humane Economy: The Social Framework of the Free Market, 1960, 31).
118. (Eucken, Die Überwindung des Historismus, 1938, 81) (Eucken, Grundsätze der Wirtschaftspolitik, 1990, 267, 329, 358f).

1.5 CONTRASTING THE SCHOOLS

Table 1.2 European School and Chicago School: A Comparison

	European School	Chicago School
1.	Social policy objectives are included	Social policy objectives are not included
2.	School of thought is pre-defined in the law as a constitutional economic order	School of thought is flexible and not pre-defined in the law
3.	Companies with economic power need to behave in the same way as companies without economic power: focus on competition on the merits with special responsibilities	'Big is beautiful': dominant companies that innovate should be rewarded for their efforts; new market entry is likely downplaying any economic power in the long run; no need to intervene
4.	Vertical agreements may create economic power to the detriment of consumers	Vertical restraints are lawful since they do not harm competition; in contrast: they are needed to increase innovation and service efforts
5.	Merger control: economic power post-merger is a concern; consumers' interest is decisive	Merger control: economic power post-merger is of less concern; efficiencies usually outweigh any increase in market power
6.	Price-fixing agreements are permitted when consumers get a fair share of the generated benefits	Price-fixing agreements are per se illegal
7.	Focus on consumer utilities with respect to price, choice, quality, innovation, et al.	Focus on price theory
8.	Welfare economics in the Marshallian tradition is not helpful; focus on the creation of wealth gains and the equal and fair redistribution of these gains in society	Total welfare standard = consumer surplus + producer surplus; increase in producer surplus is enough to clear a merger even if consumer prices increase
9.	Anti-trust authorities should be independent	Political variations possible
10.	State Aid control: economic power can derive from private and public entities	No State Aid control

In the following, we discuss hypothetical cases related to mergers, agreements and abuse. As we will see, depending on the school of thought applied, the outcome of the cases differs.

1.5.1 Merger Case

1.5.1.1 *The Case*

Let's assume a village with three Italian restaurants. Within a market of out-of-home consumption for Italian food, every restaurant has a market share of about 33% each. All three businesses are family managed.

One Italian restaurant specialises in pastas, the other one in pizzas whereas the third one offers the full range of Italian food including pastas and pizzas. The two specialist restaurants are well-known for the quality of their respective products whereas the third full range restaurant offers a medium quality. Prices in all the three restaurants are comparable at a medium price level. They are competing with other restaurants in the village (Greek food, local food, etc.). All three restaurants have a simple style including red white checkered paper tablecloths, one type of house-wine etc. To attract more customers, the Italian restaurants offer special packages like 'all you can eat' on Tuesdays and Wednesdays for a fixed price or 'kids up to 7 eat free' on weekends. The village itself is mainly home to normal families (two adults, two kids) with medium incomes. The relevant geographic market is the village.

Pre-merger a family with different tastes needs to decide either to go to the pizzeria (for the benefit of the family members who prefer pizzas and to the detriment to the others who prefer pastas) or to the pasticceria (again for the benefit of the other family members and to the detriment of those who prefer pizza). The third option is to go to the medium quality full range Italian restaurant. There, all family members can enjoy, depending on their individual preferences, either pastas or pizzas but the quality is lower than in the specialised restaurants.

The village has a considerable number of other restaurants. Just a few additional permits to open a new restaurant or appropriate facilities are available.

1.5.1.2 *The Transaction*

The merger is a three to two transaction.

The two Italian restaurants, the one specialising on pizzas and the other one on pastas, merge. The new entity offers a full range of Italian meals post-merger.

Post-merger it is likely that families prefer the new entity since it combines both pizzas and pastas at a higher quality than the third restaurant.

The prognosis is that the original full range restaurant is put under pressure post-merger since it has to compete with another full range restaurant with high quality products. It is likely that the quality of the food and the service in this third restaurant is going to improve as well. Probably this restaurant will hire a new chef and use better quality ingredients, which in turn increases its costs and prices.

It is also likely post-merger that the new merged entity increases prices. The popularity of this restaurant attracts visitors from outside the small village. Thus, the relevant geographic market is enlarged as well. Post-merger more people want to order food in the new merged restaurant.

The restaurant has already moved to the larger unit of the two and has closed down the other smaller one. They might increase the number of seats in the current restaurant or the times of opening hours but it is likely that the seating capacity will soon be reached. Probably the restaurant will stop offering special deals like 'all you can eat' etc. to manage seating capacities better. However, as competition *for* places in this restaurant increases, it is most likely that the new restaurant responds with higher prices. To increase profits even further, the new entity will start offering better and enhanced services such as linen tablecloths and cloth napkins, amuse from the kitchen, a broader assortment of Italian starters and desserts, an extended wine list, candles on the tables and live music in the background.

1.5.1.3   Chicago School

The transaction is cleared with no remedies.

Post-merger families have an additional 'one stop facility' for Italian out-of-home consumption at an excellent quality. All family members are served by one location with their favourite meals. There are no discussions anymore within families as to which Italian restaurant to go to.

The new entity is able to produce significant efficiencies by combining the two restaurants into one outlet. Post-merger just one kitchen is required thereby downsizing fixed costs considerably (however probably with two chefs). Costs for service personal are reduced as well because of the overall reduction in seating numbers at the new entity. Where the restaurant needs to modernise its furniture, costs are also considerably lower. All other variable costs for electricity, heating/cooling, etc. will go down as well. The buyer power of the restaurant is going to increase enabling the owners to get a better bargain. Transaction costs for shopping supplies are lower too.

Despite these cost reductions, post-merger prices are increased which in turn leads to an increase in profits, and thus a producer surplus.

Post-merger the duopoly of the two Italian restaurants in the village will lead to market entry in the long run (despite the limited number of permits available). New restaurants are attracted by the high profits that can be earned in this small village. Although the loyalty of people to their favourite Italian restaurant is high, this does not cause a problem.

The village even starts becoming known regionally as the 'place to be' for excellent Italian food attracting visitors from far away. There is even the chance that the post-merger restaurant will be awarded with a Michelin star. This excellence criterion in turn will be paid for by the additional visitors attracted by this award. The expectation is that the quality of the Italian food will increase even further post-Michelin star.

Based on Chicago School thinking, we see a clear increase in producer welfare thereby increasing total welfare. The issue that families pay more post-merger does not matter since clients are awarded with an excellent top-ranked Italian restaurant in their small home village.

1.5.1.4 European School

Post-merger two outlets remain with the same product portfolio at different service levels.

The question is whether the transaction creates consumer benefits and whether the benefits are redistributed between market participants in an equal and fair manner.

Efficiency gains that accrue directly in a profit increase for the owners is one element in the European School but definitely not the decisive one. The European School cares about the average consumer/customer, in our case the middle-class families (two adults, two kids) in the village. In this case, it depends on how the existing customers balance the economic effects of the transaction. The question to address is whether the wealth gains (increase in owners' profits) are fairly distributed between the customers and the owners.

In this assessment consumer perceptions, consumer benefits and consumer utilities are of importance. Modern economic tools like conjoint analysis offer techniques to measure these consumer utilities and preferences.

Utility is measured in terms of economic choices. In its simplest form, utility is revealed in people's willingness to pay different amounts for different goods. Thus, utility is defined as the satisfaction experienced by the consumer of a good in satisfying human needs.

In our hypothetical case, prices for out-of-home consumption in an Italian restaurant is one element in consumers' interest. Other elements are the satisfaction, fun and ease families experience in having Italian food at a simple place nearby. Probably for average families even Italian restaurants are the first choice when going out for dinner.

Post-merger the most likely result is that within the newly created duopoly prices go up. We will also see an upgrade of the product range and services offered as well as a fancier restaurant. But is this exactly what the average family is looking for?

From the outset the new combined offer (pizzas and pastas in one outlet) and the upgrade in services and products sounds good. However, a more detailed economic analysis reveals that customers' utilities might decrease post-merger.

Despite the price increases for Italian food which will be in the area of 30–40% (pizza price pre-merger EUR 7; post-merger EUR 9.80) families may face less utility post-merger in going to such a place. Since costs for dining out become more expensive, families will go less often. Spontaneous decision-making (like 'let's go!') are not possible anymore, because advance reservations and planning are required. The house-wine is gone and replaced by a list of exclusive wines making choices even more difficult. Maybe these families even perceive the red white checkered paper tablecloths as well as the simple furniture as utility increasing since nobody really cares when the children mess around. The situation is different in a fancy restaurant causing more stress for parents with children. All these elements influence customer satisfaction that can be measured.

There will be a few new customers going to the fancy restaurant who did not visit the simple Italian pizzeria or trattoria before. The utility of these new customers is increased but cannot compensate for the reduced utilities of the average families.

In any assessment, the efficiency gains created by the merger need to be compared with customer utilities pre- and post-merger.

In a European School approach, remedies are likely.

One remedy could be for example that the new restaurant offers a take away facility at the lower prices they used to charge before. This can even be combined with an online-order business.

Another remedy could be that the newly created fancy restaurant adds an additional outlet in the previous house-style next to the up-market restaurant for the local average families. Then it is up to the customer to decide which outlet he prefers: the chic new one or the traditional pizzeria.

In this sense, the European School represents from the customer/consumer perspective a holistic view by integrating the different utility elements price, choice, quality and innovation. Decisive is the fair redistribution of the wealth gains between the market actors created by the merger.

1.5.2 Horizontal Agreement with a Price Element

Horizontal agreements between competitors have the potential to restrict competition. On the other hand, such agreements may also generate substantial economic benefits – both for the participating companies as well as for consumers. The following hypothetical case relates to a horizontal price-fixing agreement in the heating oil industry.

1.5.2.1 The Case

Sales of heating oil are under heavy competitive pressure because other types of energy like natural gas or renewable energies, are increasingly available to households. Currently about 50% of households use natural gas whereas heating oil has a share of about 30%. This share is decreasing rapidly.

Since the number of households using heating oil is going down, heating oil producers and importers are worried. They decide to establish a subsidy programme that contributes a specific amount to new heating oil boiler installations. Households receive a non-repayable lump sum for modernisation.

The grant per renewed heating oil boiler is EUR 1,500. The goal is that each year approximately 200,000 modernisations of installations are financially supported. The programme is planned to go on for five years. This means that the total budget for this funding programme is EUR 1.5 billion. To finance such a funding an agreement between all market participants is necessary. The fund is financed by contributions from the heating oil producers and importers. Technically this is a *horizontal agreement* between producers and importers of heating oil. It is estimated that per litre of heating oil sold 1 cent will be added to the supply price by the producers for this promotion to finance the fund. Thus, the fund has a price increasing effect for heating oil.

The fund is managed by a trustee, who obtains from each participating company based on its sales volume the calculated fund contribution. The trustee pays the grant of EUR 1,500 to the households as a contribution to the renewal of the heating oil boiler. The financial contribution as a direct financial subsidy represents an incentive for households to modernise their heating oil installations. The aim is to subsidise by a fixed amount the replacement of old and inefficient heating oil systems.

The modernisation of heating oil systems means there will be a decrease in the consumption of heating oil since because of improved boiler technology less oil is used. Consumption of heating oil depends on the type of the boiler. Old equipment uses a larger volume of oil. Systems installed before 1978 consume an average of 4,300 litres per year, those that were installed 1979–1986 have a heating oil demand amounting to an average of 4,000 litres per year. Even low-temperature systems that consume less (between 3,200–3,400 litres per year) need modernisation. The most modern boilers require an annual average of only 3,000 litres or almost one third less than those that were built before 1987. Although modern heating oil installations use less oil, in the long run these households will remain heating oil customers by not switching away to other types of heating systems. This is the aim of the heating oil fund programme.

The initiative improves the efficiency of the heating oil systems in the market. Because of the advanced age of a large part of the existing heating oil boilers, most of the heating oil systems used are outdated. The modernisation backlog is amazing. A heating oil system needs modernisation after fifteen years. More than 60% of all heating oil installations are above this fifteen-year-limit. The most frequently cited reason by non-modernisers is that in 96% of the cases the boiler still works. Modernisation is thus deemed to be unnecessary.

The decision about which heating system to purchase depends on costs. Apart from the one-off investment costs in the installation itself, costs of heating oil consumption after installation and the expected rate of energy savings are important.

1.5.2.2 Chicago School

Since the agreement includes a price-fixing element, it is likely that the agreement is considered to be illegal per se.

1.5.2.3 European School

The methodology applied is the 'counterfactual analysis' that compares the market conditions with and without the agreement.

In this case, the market for heating oil is investigated with and without the heating oil fund programme. By comparing the two market situations, the net effect is calculated.

In essence, two modes of action are examined:

Firstly, the collection of the contribution to finance the heating oil installation fund leads to an increase in costs. However, an investigation into whether and to what

Chapter 1: The Frame

extent this increase in costs leads to an increase in the prices for heating oil, that can be passed on to the end customer, depends on the elasticity of demand.

Second, the accelerated implementation of heating oil boiler modernisation leads to a change in demand for heating oil. Modern systems have a much lower average fuel consumption than old equipment. A decrease in demand leads ceteris paribus to a price reduction.

Within the counterfactual analysis, both effects are modelled. The supply-side induced changes in the cost structure are compared with the demand side reduction in consumption. The forecast net change in the price is gauged by an equilibrium model. This equilibrium model defines the market price at the intersection between supply and demand. The model is based on historical market data and uses prognosis techniques.

The market simulation shows that households are better off with the heating oil funds model. The price increase based on the agreement is compensated for by observed price decreases which are a result of a reduction in the heating oil demand because of the modernised boilers. This modernisation-based decline in demand leads to a decrease in heating oil prices to all end users.

According to the European School the net effect for all consumers is positive: The heating oil prices for all consumers' decrease. This means that the fund system will not lead to price increases and that the horizontal agreements can be exempted from the cartel prohibition under Article 101(3). Consumers get a fair share of the resulting benefits. Consumers benefit not only through the modernisation-related lower heating oil consumption and the thereby associated lower costs. They also benefit from general lower heating oil prices and the subsidy itself. On top of that, a reduction in environmental emissions for the benefit of all consumers is achieved.[119]

1.5.3 Vertical Restraints

This case is about vertical agreements/restraints related to online-distribution.

1.5.3.1 *The Case*

The product is a well-known established brand of golf clubs. The market share of this brand is 45%. The shares of the other brands are between 10–20%. The manufacturer used to sell its products through multiple channels of retailers – specialised golf shops but also discounters.

Customers increasingly show a tendency to visit brick-and-mortar retailers that offer different brands of golf clubs. Pre-sale services at these retailers are high, including a club customising service, being assisted by a well-known golf expert and even access to a practice area attached to the golf shop. The retailer also offers a relaxed atmosphere at special club customising days.

---

119. The German Bundeskartellamt (BKartA) exempted the heating oil fund model from the cartel prohibition. The numbers in the case given are not the exact numbers used for modelling the counterfactual scenario.

Customers learn about the golf clubs at these retailers. They select their favourite golf clubs there. Then they visit an online-retailer to do the actual purchasing of the golf clubs over the internet. Home-delivery of the golf clubs increases convenience. The online-retailer itself does not offer any additional services. However, the purchase price of the golf clubs is 15% lower online.

In this situation, the selling efforts of one retailer affect the sales of another. The ability of low-price online-retailers to free ride on the efforts of the high-service golf shop may lower the high-service golf shop's incentives in the long run to offer such services at all.

The brick-and-mortar retailer could even consider charging for these services. If the customer actually purchases the golf clubs from this retailer, he would receive a refund of the money for the service he received.

RPM is another option to address the inefficiencies associated with the risk of underprovision of services and the free riding by online-retailers. By internalising service externalities and by making decisions as an integrated unit, the manufacturer and retailers maintain the service level they want and thereby sales.

Another option is to build a selective distribution system that was not applied previously. Through the new selective distribution systems, the brand owner of the golf clubs is able to limit sales to certain channels or authorised dealers. This discriminates against some actors in the distribution systems. In particular, the brand owner does not want to see his products sold at online market places, such as Amazon, eBay and/or at price comparison websites. The brand manufacturer's argument is that these third party platforms cannot guarantee an appropriate brand-friendly product presentation. Online sales should only be possible via websites, which are authorised by the brand manufacturer. As brick-and-mortar retailers' complaints increase, the manufacturer decides to limit the amount of online sales to members of the newly established selective distribution system. In the manufacturers' view, such a restraint is necessary to preserve and maintain the high value attached to the brand.

Thus, the vertical restraint discussed here includes RPM, a selective distribution system, the ban on sales via platforms like Amazon, eBay and a limit on online-sales. Complaints are coming from online-platforms such as Amazon.

1.5.3.2 Chicago School

Based upon a consumer welfare-based anti-trust regime, the per se treatment of vertical restraints is abandoned. Instead, a rule of reason analysis needs to be applied to assess the competitive effects of such agreements on a case-by-case basis. *The heavy burden to prove the antitrust problem is on the online-platform sellers.*

Under a rule of reason, the practitioner weighs up all of the circumstances of a case in deciding whether a restrictive practice should be prohibited for imposing an unreasonable restraint of competition or not. The criterion applied is its impact on competition. Thus, both the anti-competitive effects as well as the pro-competitive benefits of the conduct are considered. Factors relevant to the rule of reason analysis include the market power of the entities involved, the scope of the restraint, the number of entities within the market adopting the restraint and the restraint's source.[120]

Based on the economic thinking in the Chicago School, it is less likely that a vertical restraint causes a competition problem at all. Vertical restraints are even often regarded as positive. Every party in a vertical agreement is considered to be a natural ally of the consumer.[121]

This means that with respect to vertical restraints almost everything is possible according to the Chicago School, established on the assumption that such business behaviour benefits consumers.

1.5.3.3 European School

Based on the equality principle both brick-and-mortar retailers as well as online-retailers compete on an equal footing. This means that the volume of sales should not be limited because the retailer is selling online. Both retailers, brick-and-mortar as well as online, are allowed to sell the products.

However, since freedom of action is another guiding principle as well, a manufacturer can limit online-sales. This limitation becomes a competition concern when the manufacturer is above a specific market share threshold (30%). Below this market share threshold, the assumption is that the manufacturer has not the strength to alter competition conditions substantially. Thus, the other golf brands below the 30% market share threshold can limit online sales. The leading brand cannot.

With market shares of 45%, negative competition effects of vertical restraints are likely. With such high market shares, the free rider problem is of less concern in the European School. The free rider is seen now as a vital element being active on the competitive fringe disciplining the strong market player.

Consumers value services on the one hand but also lower prices on the other hand. Consumer sovereignty means that consumers decide how they structure their shopping behaviour. A strong market player should not be able to pre-define whether a consumer is asking for advice in a brick-and-mortar shop and then complete the actual purchasing at a lower price online. A consumer can decide himself what to do.

It is estimated that asking for advice offline and then purchasing online does not apply to the majority of golf players. Just below a specific golf-handicap, the choice of the golf clubs might be so important that golf players even have a higher willingness to pay for proper services. They would even probably consider that the golf clubs need to be specially customised to their swings and body profile. However, the consumer is free to choose which purchasing strategy to pursue.

If the brick-and-mortar shop continues to suffer from online-competition it needs to become more creative either by lowering the price or by adding other purchase incentives – thereby increasing consumer utilities. This behaviour increases

---

120. (ICN 2015, 29).
121. (Verouden 2008, 1838).

competition in turn. When the strongest market player is offering golf clubs at lower prices or with more services attached, it is likely that the rest of the market will follow thereby creating even more consumer benefits.

The offer of the golf clubs at Amazon, eBay and/or at price comparison websites does not hurt the golf club brand either. In principle, it depends on the product itself whether services and positioning of the product in the market is important. Most golf clubs are associated with a strong brand. This is because golf in some countries is considered to be an exclusive sport. Within such an exclusive environment, brands are essential: most golf clubs are branded products. Since most of the golf clubs are branded, the brand of the market leader with 45% does not need any special protection.

With respect to RPM, the rule in the European School is that every market participant is free to decide on prices. This means that retailers are free to set their own prices thereby increasing intrabrand-competition. Freedom of action is an important element in the European School.

Thus, it is likely that most of the vertical restraints discussed in this case will be valued as a competition concern under the European School.

1.5.4 Abusive Behaviour

1.5.4.1 *The Case*

Within Europe, large fixed line incumbents in the telecom sector exist. Based on previous investments made by governments they own 100% of the fixed line network. Next to the traditional fixed line networks, other types of data and voice connections are increasingly available like fibre-optic networks in local areas, cable networks, mobile/wireless networks etc. offering similar (sometimes even better) bandwidth and quality of services. These networks are owned by various commercial operators.

The fixed line incumbent is active in the upstream market for wholesale access to the fixed line to downstream competitors and in the downstream market for retail access services to end-customers. Both markets are closely linked to each other.

We assume that prices are not regulated on the wholesale level.

The issue is what a fixed line incumbent is charging for access to new entrants. Entrants without their own networks need wholesale access to the incumbent's network in order to offer products on the downstream retail level. The business model of the entrant is such that his margin depends on the retail price he can charge to the end customer, minus the wholesale price he is paying to the incumbent, and minus his own distribution costs at the retail level such as marketing, billing, debt collection etc.

A margin squeeze exists if a vertically integrated incumbent charges prices for wholesale access, which are so high that competitors are forced to charge their end users prices that are higher for similar services than the ones claimed by the vertically integrated operator from its own end users. If the wholesale charges are higher than retail charges, the competitors, even if they are at least as efficient as the dominant operator, can never make a profit, because on top of the wholesale charges they also have other costs to bear before being able to make a comparable retail service offering.

Thus, a margin squeeze exists by charging new entrants higher fees for wholesale access than the fees that their own customers pay for retail fixed lines.

The competition problem is that the incumbent's behaviour discourages new companies from entering the market and reduces for consumers on the retail level the choice of suppliers of telecom services as well as price competition.

1.5.4.2 *Chicago School*

'Big is beautiful'. The market will manage any competition problem in the long run by itself. Market entry is most likely when the fixed line network market offers high profits. Entrance to services at the retail level will probably come from other cable networks or mobile networks.

The Chicago School does not recognise any anti-trust duty to act at the wholesale level when there is no predatory pricing at the retail level. An incumbent is not required to price both of the services, upstream and downstream, in a manner that preserves its rival's profit margin. Margin squeeze is therefore not an anti-trust law violation.

According to the Chicago argument, an upstream monopolist has no incentive to evict its downstream rivals ('single profit theorem'). The Chicago School contends that an upstream monopolist protected by durable barriers to entry can claim a monopoly profit, but only once. If an upstream monopolist can use contracts to extract fully a monopoly profit from a downstream market, then there is no role for vertical integration to play in leveraging monopoly power to obtain *any additional profit*. The single monopoly theory presumes that vertical integration has some purpose other than leveraging monopoly power.

This means that it is likely that an assessment based on Chicago School thinking will not confirm a competition problem.

1.5.4.3 *European School*

The thinking of the European School is that an incumbent needs to behave in the same manner as a company without economic power. Thus, it needs to be assessed how a non-dominant company would behave in such a situation applying the competition on the merits-principle (*'as if'*-competition).

On the downstream level, a non-dominant company would offer products at a competitive price level. This price level depends on the competitive forces which are generated by the other networks available at the retail level that can serve the customer equally and increasingly even better (mobile, cable, etc.)

The costs for retail services based on fixed line access include costs for the network infrastructure as well as costs at the downstream level. Assuming that a non-dominant company does not need to carry the 'package' of previously hired employees during the times of states' monopolies and that they dispose of a highly flexible and motivated sales force, distribution costs at the retail level are competitive.

With this price/cost level, a non-dominant company is competing with new entrants at the retail level in an equal manner namely wholesale costs plus the distribution costs on the retail level.

The question is whether a non-dominant company would increase prices for a new entrant downstream at the wholesale level. The correct answer is: 'It depends'. Where a non-dominant company can earn higher profits with a lower commercial risk by just providing services on the wholesale level, a non-dominant company will do so. In such a situation market shares of the new entrant downstream increases. Each of the companies is focusing on the business they know the best.

However, the assumption is that the vertically integrated incumbent has already a dominant market share on the downstream retail level since the incumbent was previously the only provider of fixed lines downstream. In our hypothetical situation, we need to assess, what a non-dominant company would do downstream.

A non-dominant company would optimise its revenue streams from both market levels, upstream and downstream. Prices will be set depending on demand elasticities on each level and on the competitive pressure by other networks on the retail level. A vertically integrated non-dominant company would pursue a strategy of optimising profits on both levels. In European School thinking, this is the 'counterfactual situation' which needs to be compared with the actual case.

Where the assessment proves that the incumbent is not applying such a non-dominant strategy a competition problem is likely.

1.5.5 Lessons Learned

Anti-trust issues are of concern in both school of thought.

However, the avenues to achieve results vary. These case examples show that indeed the outcomes of economic analysis differ based on the school of thought applied. These different outcomes in economic analysis in turn affect the evaluation of the related anti-trust problems and thereby sometimes resulting in different conclusions. At this stage, the call for convergence between the two regimes, the US and the EU, does not make any sense at all.

Another lesson learned is that some results of the case analysis are really eye-opening in the sense that they describe concisely in the same hypothetical case the differences between the schools of thought thereby increasing the understanding of the contrasts between the two schools of thought.

The assessment also confirms that practitioners need to be aware in which system they are active. A simple transfer of arguments used in one jurisdiction to another one does not necessarily work. Every jurisdiction deserves its own treatment based on the school of thought applied.

Whereas in both jurisdictions consumer interests lie at the heart of anti-trust enforcers the interpretation of what is in the consumer interest differs. For defining consumer interests Europe applies a broad humanistic social view whereas in the Chicago School the focus is on consumers that are rational *'homo economicus'*. In this

Chapter 1: The Frame

sense, the European approach is much more embedded in real life situations, which display a variety of facets attached to human beings.

The most striking disparity between the two systems is the attachment of the social fairness objective to the market economy principle and the implantation of the equality principle in EU competition law. Whereas the creation of wealth is a top priority in both schools, the *re-distribution of wealth* is a concern just in Europe. Europe achieves this objective by governing and operating a social market economy.

CHAPTER 2
EU Competition Policy and EU Institutions

2.1 INTRODUCTION

On 25 March 1957, the Treaty of Rome establishing the European Economic Community (TEEC) was signed by six countries – France, West Germany, Italy, Belgium, the Netherlands and Luxembourg.[1] Today, the European Union (EU)[2] is a political and economic union of twenty-eight Member States, located primarily in Europe.

The EU has developed a single internal market through a standardised system of laws that apply in all Member States, guaranteeing the freedom of movement of people, goods, services and capital. With almost 508 million citizens (or 7.3% of the world population), the EU Member States combined generates an estimated 24% share of the world's nominal gross domestic product (GDP) making the EU the largest economy in the world.

The need for a common competition policy has been recognised from the very beginning. Both the Treaty establishing the European Coal and Steel Community (ECSC Treaty) signed in Paris on 18 April 1951[3] as well as the TEEC signed in Rome contained a chapter on it. The TEEC was renamed by the Treaty of Maastricht to Treaty establishing the European Community or EC Treaty.[4] The Treaty of Maastricht contained as an Annex an agreement with respect to social policy thereby continuing

---

1. The TEEC came into force on 1 Jan. 1958.
2. The EU was formally established when the Maastricht Treaty came into force on 1 Nov. 1993. In 1995 Austria, Sweden and Finland joined the newly established EU. In 2002, the Euro replaced national currencies in twelve of the Member States. Since then, the Eurozone has increased to encompass nineteen countries. In 2004, the EU saw its biggest enlargement to date when ten new countries, most of which were former parts of the Eastern Bloc, joined the Union. On 1 Jan. 2007, Romania and Bulgaria became members. Since 1 Jul. 2013, Croatia has become the newest Member State of the EU.
3. Under the ECSC Treaty, the Community is responsible for the Community-wide administration of the coal and steel industries, which play a key role in the national economies.
4. The term European Economic Community was replaced by the term European Community throughout the Treaty by Art. G, A, (1) of the Provisions amending the Treaty establishing the

the path laid down in the 1989 Social Charter. The latest treaty in the row is the Treaty of Lisbon (or Lisbon Treaty signed on 13 December 2007).

The Lisbon Treaty came into force on 1 December 2009 and consists of the two core functional Treaties of the European Union: the Treaty on European Union (TEU) and the Treaty on the Functioning of the European Union (TFEU). With respect to competition law, Articles 85 and 86 TEEC have remained content wise unchanged; the numbering was adjusted.

Today the principal competition rules are set out in Articles 101 and 102 TFEU and are positioned in Part Three, Union Policies and Internal Actions, Title VII, Common rules on competition, taxation and approximation of laws, Chapter 1 – Rules on competition. Articles 101–106 TFEU on State Aid are positioned in section 1 – Rules applying to undertakings whereas section 2 – Aids granted by States contains the Articles 107–109 TFEU.

Articles 101 and 102 TFEU relate to anti-competitive behaviour by an enterprise, which has an effect on trade between Member States, and are aimed at preserving and enhancing competition rules by different means. Article 101 TFEU is directed at agreements, decisions or concerted practices between two or more enterprises and includes a possibility for exemption, whereas Article 102 TFEU is aimed at abusive behaviour by monopolies or firms with very considerable market power.

Article 103 TFEU contains the responsibility of the Council to adopt regulations and directives to give effect to the principles set out in Articles 101 and 102 TFEU. Articles 104 and 105 TFEU refer to transition procedures.

Article 106 TFEU (on public undertakings/state aid) takes a special role. This Article is designed to ensure that firms that are publicly owned, regulated or granted privileges do not evade the rules on competition. In EU competition law, the assumption holds that competition can also be distorted when national governments favour certain undertakings, by granting them aid in whatever form, such as outright grants or special tax advantages. This aspect of competition policy is dealt with in section 2 on Aids granted by States by the Articles 107, 108 and 109 TFEU. Article 107 TFEU prohibits government subsidies (state aid) that threaten to distort competition.

Furthermore, provisions placed in other chapters of the Lisbon Treaty for example provisions relating to free movement of goods and services and state monopolies refer to the competition policy as well. In the Lisbon Treaty some competition related values previously expressed in the preamble to the TEEC were 'upgraded' to Articles (see section 1.3).

2.2 COMPETITION CONCEPT IN THE LISBON TREATY

The Lisbon Treaty assumes that the Community is based, except in the sphere of agriculture, on an open market economy. The underlying assumption of a market economy is, that competition, rather than state control, or private monopoly, is the best

---

European Economic Community with a view to establishing the European Community, (Title II) in the Treaty on European Union. The Treaty on European Union was signed in Maastricht on 7 Feb. 1992.

means of bringing about greater efficiency, increased innovation and lower prices, which lead in turn to optimal allocation of resources, rising standard of living and, at least in the long-term, the protection of employment.

To produce these desirable results a market based economy must maintain an effective competitive structure, otherwise it will become costly, inefficient, and unable to supply the needs of consumers at prices they are willing to pay. Thus, the Member States and the Community shall act in accordance with the principle of an open market economy with free competition, favouring an efficient allocation of resources, and in compliance with the principles set out in Articles 2 and 3 TEU as well as Articles 3 and 119 TFEU. The Lisbon Treaty confirms that the EU has the ongoing exclusive competence in establishing and being the guardian of the competition rules (Article 3 TFEU). The principle of an open market economy with free competition is reiterated in Article 119 TFEU and the link between the internal market and a system with distortion-free competition is repeated in Protocol No. 27.

One novelty found in the 2007 Lisbon Treaty relates to social values. The Treaty defines that the EU is founded on the values of freedom, equality and the rule of law (Article 2 TEU). These three values – freedom, equality and the rule of law – are important values related to the economic concept applied in EU competition law. Considering the historical development of European society, these three values are of significant importance and therefore carefully treasured and adhered to. The Lisbon Treaty also states in Article 3 TEU that the EU's aim is to promote peace, its values and the well-being of its peoples. The interpretation of well-being of people does not focus on economic aspects only. It includes a social component as well. Working for sustainable development in Europe based on a *highly competitive social market economy* is one of the principal aims in this regard.

2.2.1 Concept of a Social Market Economy

A social market economy is defined as a form of market capitalism combined with social objectives. The term social market economy has it origin in Germany and is well-known and has been applied for more than six decades as '*Soziale Marktwirtschaft*'.

A social market economy represents a middle path between socialism and capitalism by aiming to maintain a balance between a high rate of economic growth, low inflation, low levels of unemployment, good working conditions, social welfare, and public services based on state intervention. Basically respecting a free market, a social market economy is opposed to both a planned economy and laissez-faire capitalism.

The main train of thought related to social market economies is that a free market economy is social in its origin. A social market contains elements such as private property, free trade, exchange of goods, freedom of contract and free formation of prices. However, in contrast to a free market economy concept based just on capitalism the state is not passive. The state ought to implement regulatory measures, in particular, with respect to protecting free market forces. Integrated within these regulatory measures are social policy objectives that include a balancing of the distribution of gain as well as gain growth between the different economic actors. These elements are supposed to diminish many of the recurring problems of a free market economy. Thus, within a social market economy, the state's responsibility is to improve actively the market conditions and simultaneously to pursue a social balance.[5]

Other aspects, which are basic to EU competition legislation, are the diffusion of economic power, the protection of individual freedom and individual rights. These aspects still occupy an important place. However, two elements in EU competition law play a considerable role namely the diffusion of economic power and the protection of freedom.

2.2.2 Diffusion of Economic Power and Protection of Freedom

Historically, European economies have been inspired by liberal ideas. A free market seems to be a guarantee for wealth and progress. On the other hand, economic freedom bears the potential for its own destruction. The inherent and unavoidable tendency of private business to restrict competition for the sake of monopoly profits induce companies to agree on cartels, on tying agreements, on exclusive dealership clauses and other restrictive practices. They make use of their liberty to narrow their own and their competitors' freedom to contract. Such a decomposition of economy is prevented in Europe by legislation designed to protect competition.[6] In accordance with the European School of thought, a competitive economic system within a well-defined legal framework is valued as a necessary requisite for a prosperous, free and equitable society.

Monopolies and cartels are a radical departure from individualism. In the form of monopolistic dominance of a single firm or of agreements whereby rival firms coordinate their activities, large aggregations of economic power may develop. Such aggregations might threaten political liberty, the democratic process, and the like. The post World War II attitude adopted by German academic scholars with respect to cartels has to be viewed in this light. The Nazis had shown how to transform a highly concentrated and cartelised economy into a central planning system. Boycotts and collective discrimination were applied against outsiders in order to discipline them in the public interest at this time. If the more traditional measures of economic coercion proved insufficient for the purpose, even the formal transformation of private cartels into compulsory cartels was provided for after 1933 by the Nazi regime.

As already discussed at length in the previous chapter, competition carries within it the seeds of its own destruction. An excessive concentration of economic, financial and commercial power can produce such far-reaching structural changes that free competition is no longer able to fulfil its role as an effective regulator of economic activity. This means that private companies must not be allowed to reintroduce the

---

5. This responsibility lies according to the Lisbon Treaty with the European Commission as an independent authority.
6. (Fikentscher 1983, 33–34).

Chapter 2: EU Competition Policy and EU Institutions

barriers that the internal market has abolished and that room must be made for competition in markets that are now subject to extensive regulation.

As identified in Chapter One, a legal framework is regarded to be necessary to protect the process of competition from distortion, to assure that the benefits of the market are *equitably distributed throughout society* and to minimise governmental intervention in the economy. To reach that goal, legal barriers and limits are introduced to the application of the principle of free unrestricted competition and market forces. The EU competition rules lay down such limits and indicate where and how a trade-off has to be made between the different Treaty objectives. On top of that, the establishment of a systematic control over large-scale mergers enables the European Commission to react effectively against structural changes that may jeopardise the continuance of effective competition in the internal market.

Whereas in the past a fundamental objective attached to EU competition law was the promotion of the integration of separate economies into a unified internal market, the Lisbon Treaty added a social objective to EU competition law. These aspects are discussed in the following.

2.2.3 Internal Market Objective

EU competition law ensures that at all stages the completion of the internal market is met and its aims attained. The internal market is an essential condition for the development of an efficient and highly competitive industry. Via the enforcement of the rules ensuring that the regulatory barriers to trade which have been removed are not replaced by private or other public restrictions having the same effect, EU competition law in particular, is an important tool for achieving the goal of, and maintaining, an internal market. Ever since the *Consten & Grundig* case[7] in 1966, the Court of Justice of the EU[8] has made it clear that EU competition law serves European integration. The rules are intended not only to prevent the restriction of production to raise prices, but more importantly to encourage the integration of the market.[9]

In 1957, the fear was that obstacles to freedom of movement and long-standing differences in firms' business environments would tempt Member State governments to take measures to protect certain firms or aggravate the tendency to engage in defensive restrictive practices on the part of the firms themselves. The same protectionist reflexes are still raising their heads particularly at times of economic difficulty, even in an enlarged and unified market, which reproduces 'as far as it can' the characteristics of a domestic market.

---

7. (ECJ, Établissements Consten S.à.R.L. and Grundig-Verkaufs-GmbH v. Commission, Joined cases 56 and 58-64 1966).
8. The Court of Justice of the European Union (Court of Justice of the European Union) is an EU institution seated in Luxembourg. It consists of (1) the Court of Justice, previously known as European Court of Justice (ECJ) (created 1952 as the Court of Justice of the ECSC, later named Court of Justice of the European Communities) and (2) the General Court (created in 1988; formerly the *Court of First Instance*). The Court of Justice of the European Union also has a (3) Civil Service Tribunal, as a specialised court created in 2004.
9. (Horspool and Korah 1992, 385).

In gaining access to markets, the interest of small and medium-sized firms is of significance too. However, integration brings with it the risk that formerly isolated smaller (and even medium-sized) firms may find it difficult to compete successfully with larger firms located both within and without the EU. To mitigate this risk the European Commission has not only tolerated but actually encouraged certain forms of horizontal cooperation among small and medium-sized firms.

Legal conflicts arise in particular when an undertaking[10] seeks market entry and Member States in response restrict entry based on their public policy. Not only Member States but also firms may restrict entry of other firms and thereby limit consumer choice. The avoidance of any 'non-natural' market segregation by private actors, either by contractual arrangements in distribution systems or by abusing industrial or intellectual property rights, is of particular interest for the EU competition rules. If these restrictions are the result of normal competition, the market economy usually will not and cannot object to them. If the restrictions are the consequence of anti-competitive practices like cartels and monopolies, the legal system imposes rules on entry.

Hence EU competition law has been used for decades to open up markets thereby supporting the objective of European market integration. This duty is translated into action by the bulk of the general rules on restrictive practices and State aid and equally by a lengthy series of European Commission decisions in individual cases. There is accordingly a continuing need to forestall and suppress restrictive or abusive practices by firms attempting to divide up the internal market so as to apply artificial price differentials or impose unfair terms on their customers. This assumption holds true in particular with respect to the Digital Single Market (DSM).[11]

The DSM is defined as a market in which the free movement of persons, services and capital is ensured and where the individuals and businesses can seamlessly access and exercise *online* activities under conditions of fair competition, and a high level of consumer and personal data protection, irrespective of their nationality or place of residence. The DSM strategy is built on three pillars: (1) better access for consumers and businesses to digital goods and services across Europe; (2) creating the right conditions and a level playing field for digital networks and innovative services to flourish; and (3) maximising the growth potential of the digital economy.

2.2.4 Social Market Economy Objective

More recently EU competition policy after periods of market integration is about to play a central role *for* a free social market economic policy. This is in clear contradiction to other nation's anti-trust laws, which place competition policy at the forefront of their economic policy and concentrate on the implementation of economic theory considerations only, like, for example in the US.

---

10. The term 'undertaking' is used in EU competition law in place of company, business, firm etc.
11. The Digital Single Market strategy was adopted on the 6 May 2015. (European Commission, Digital Single Market 2015).

Chapter 2: EU Competition Policy and EU Institutions

To understand this point is essential:

Competition law enforcement, which is based on a free market that mainly focuses on economic efficiency considerations, only leads to diverse outcomes, compared to a competition law enforcement that is based on a more holistic free *social market economy* concept. Whereas both concepts focus on consumer (or citizen) welfare, the observed results differ in accordance with the dissimilar underlying market concepts.

The reason for these differences is obvious since the market economy concept applied, places disparate values to various objectives. Welfare perceived by consumers/citizens in a social market economy is not the same as welfare consumers observe in market economies that focus on economic efficiencies only.

Consumers in social market economies, for example, might be prepared to pay higher prices or accept a more limited product range when these market outcomes are more beneficial *for the society as a whole*. Another interpretation might be that even producers are willing to accept lower levels of profits when a *more social equitable distribution of wealth* would mean that consumers receive a fair share of their efficiency gains created by restrictions of competition.

Economic analysis in such circumstances differ, at least from a theoretical point of view.

Since EU competition policy takes into account special EU policy objectives – like the completion of the internal market or social fairness – it is difficult to compare the economic toolbox used in the EU with the toolbox applied in different jurisdictions.

This book is about the economic toolbox used in EU competition law thereby implementing the European School of thought as defined by the law itself and the jurisprudence of the Court of Justice of the EU. This European school of thought is embedded in the concept of social market economies with a focus on social distributed total welfare as well as on the equitable principle.

Chapter Four implements these basic principles in the competition application practice, whereas this chapter outlines the basic legal rules in EU competition law.

2.3   EU INSTITUTIONS

This section introduces the basic EU institutions relevant in EU competition law.

2.3.1   European Commission

In order to ensure the proper functioning and development of the common market, the European Commission (in the following 'Commission') ensures that the provisions of the Lisbon Treaty and the measures taken by the institutions pursuant thereto are applied.

The Commission formulates recommendations or delivers opinions on matters dealt with in the Lisbon Treaty and has its own power of decision. Moreover, the Commission participates in the shaping of measures taken by the Council and by the

European Parliament in the manner provided for in the Lisbon Treaty. The Commission exercises the powers conferred on it by the Council for the implementation of the rules laid down by the latter.[12]

The Commission can be considered to be at the heart of many of the Union's initiatives. It is important to realise when analysing Commission decisions that the Commission has a whole array of powers that are legislative, administrative, executive and judicial in nature. These will be considered in turn.

The Commission also plays a central part in the legislative process of the EU. The Commission possesses the right of legislative initiative.

The common format in the Lisbon Treaty is for the Council to act on a proposal from the Commission when making legislation. In this sense, the Commission's right of initiative places it in the forefront of the development of competition policy. Although the legislative proposals have to be approved by the Council, and depending on the circumstances by European Parliament, the Commission's right of initiative has enabled it to act as a *motor of integration* for the Community as a whole. The capacity of the Commission to act as the motor of integration is also evident in its second role that it plays in the legislation process. The Commission plays a significant role in the development of the Community's overall legislative plan for any single year.

Closely allied to, but distinct from, the above is a third way in which the Commission affects the development of the Union's policy. This is the part that the Commission plays in the evolution of more general policy strategies for the Union as a whole.

A fourth way in which the Commission exercises legislative power is that it has the ability, in certain limited areas, to enact Community norms without the formal involvement of any other institution.

Finally, the Commission exercises delegated legislative power. For example, important regulations relating to competition policy are enacted by the Commission as a result of power delegated to it by the Council.

In addition to its legislative powers, the Commission also has significant *administrative* responsibilities. Policies, once made, have to be administered. Legislation, once enacted, must be implemented. In this capacity, the Commission will normally act as a supervisor and overseer of policy implementation itself. The Commission also possesses responsibilities of an executive nature like those relating to finance and those concerning external relations.

The Commission's judicial powers can be illustrated by the following two aspects. On the one hand, it will be the Commission that will bring actions against recalcitrant Member States when they act in breach of Union law. On the other hand, the Commission will in certain areas act as investigator and initial judge of Treaty violations, whether by private firms or by Member States. In practical terms, two of the most important of these areas are EU competition law and State Aid.

The Commission's decision can be reviewed by the Community's judiciary, and this will normally be by the General Court.

---

12. Article 291 TFEU.

Notwithstanding the existence of this judicial review, the Commission's investigative and adjudicative powers provide it with a significant tool for the development of Community policy. It allows the Commission to devise new strategies in relation to particular aspects of, again, EU competition policy or State Aid; it enables it to employ the power of selective prosecution to take cases which raise significant issues; and it provides a vehicle through which the Commission can give guidance to national courts as to the more precise meaning of broadly framed Treaty Articles.

This means that the Commission is the designer of EU competition policy.

The permanent officials, who work in the Commission, are organised into Directorates General (DG) covering the major policy areas. The department of the Commission responsible for competition policy is DG Competition (formerly DG IV). The Commission's DG Competition is charged with enforcing the competition rules under the instructions of the Member of the Commission responsible for competition, currently Commissioner Margrethe Vestager. As a member of the Commission, she is completely independent in the performance of her duties. She shall neither seek nor take instructions from any government or from any other body.[13]

2.3.2 Court of Justice of the EU

Decisions that have been made by the Commission can be reviewed. This species of review has, since 1989, been undertaken by the Court of First Instance, now known as the General Court.

It follows from Article 256 TFEU and the first paragraph of Article 58 of the Statute of the Court of Justice of the EU that the General Court has exclusive jurisdiction, first, to find the facts, except where the substantive inaccuracy of its findings is apparent from the documents submitted to it, and, secondly, to assess those facts. However, when the General Court has found or assessed the facts, the Court of Justice has jurisdiction under Article 256 TFEU to review the legal characterisation of those facts by the General Court and the legal conclusions it has drawn from them.

In addition, in accordance with the rules relating to the division of powers between the Commission and the Court of Justice of the EU, it is for the Commission, subject to review by the General Court and the Court of Justice, to ensure application of the principles laid down in Articles 101 and 102.

It must also be noted that the principle of effective judicial protection is a general principle of EU law to which expression is now given by Article 47 of the Charter of Fundamental Rights of the EU.[14]

Consequently, the General Court must generally undertake, on the basis of the evidence adduced by the applicant in support of the pleas in law put forward, a full review of whether or not the conditions for applying competition rule provision are met. The General Court must also establish that the Commission has stated reasons for its decision. In carrying out such a review, the General Court cannot use the margin of

---

13. The responsibilities and duties of Commission members are laid down in Art. 17 TEU and Art. 245 TFEU.
14. (ECJ, MasterCard Inc. and Others v. Commission, C-832/12 P 2014).

assessment which the Commission enjoys by virtue of the role assigned to it in relation to competition policy by the Treaties, as a basis for dispensing with an in-depth review of the law and of the facts.

Although the Commission has, in accordance with that role, a margin of assessment with regard to economic matters, in particular in the context of complex economic assessments, that does not mean that the General Court must refrain from reviewing the Commission's legal classification of information of an economic nature. Although the General Court must not substitute its own economic assessment for that of the Commission, which is institutionally responsible for making those assessments, it is apparent from now well-settled case law that not only must the EU judicature establish, among other things, whether the evidence relied on is factually accurate, reliable and consistent but also whether that evidence contains all the relevant information which must be taken into account in order to assess a complex situation and whether it is capable of substantiating the conclusions drawn from it.

Another route to the European Court of Justice (ECJ) on an interpretation of EU competition law principles – increasingly used by national courts – is the request for a preliminary ruling (Article 267 TFEU). Preliminary rulings are final determinations of Union law. The final decision remains with the referring court to be decided after it has received the preliminary ruling.

2.4 ARTICLE 101 TFEU

Article 101 applies at and between all levels in the production and distribution chain, from research and development to retailing.

2.4.1 Article 101(1) TFEU

Article 101(1) provides:

> *The following shall be prohibited as incompatible with the common market: all agreements between undertakings, decisions by associations of undertakings and concerted practices, which may affect trade between the Member States and which have as their object or effect the prevention, restriction or distortion of competition within the common market, and in particular those which:*
>
> *(a) directly or indirectly fix purchase or selling prices or any other trading conditions;*
> *(b) limit or control production, markets, technical development, or investment;*
> *(c) share markets or sources of supply;*
> *(d) dissimilar conditions to equivalent transactions with other trading parties, thereby placing them at a competitive disadvantage;*
> *(e) make the conclusion of contracts subject to acceptance by the other parties of supplementary obligations which, by their nature or according to commercial usage, have no connection with the subject of such contracts.*

Points (a) to (e) are assumed to be a list of examples of conduct which may be considered to be anti-competitive, without any distinction being drawn between arrangements between competitors and those between firms operating at different levels of trade or between restrictions that are necessary to make some legitimate transaction viable and those that are not. In deciding whether any particular transaction falls within Article 101(1), it is necessary to consider:

- whether there exists an agreement, decision or concerted practice made between or observed by undertakings;
- whether competition within the common market may thereby be prevented, restricted or distorted; and
- whether trade between Member States may thereby be affected.

2.4.1.1 Agreement, Decision and Concerted Practice

Article 101(1) requires the existence of an agreement, decision or concerted practice. Agreements create an institutional framework through which the parties sacrifice their autonomous competitive conduct and instead observe discipline.

In Article 101(1), the word agreement is not confined to legally binding contracts only. It clearly includes a contract, but is broader.

Under contract law, legal or quasi-legal duties are preconditions for the enforcement of a contract before a court of law. For an agreement, it is not necessary to be intended as legally binding upon the parties for Article 101 to apply.[15] Informal agreements can be caught under Article 101(1), and the mere fact that parties claim to have terminated them will not be taken to be conclusive. *BP Kemi*[16] is a case about an agreement that had never been signed. The Commission concluded that two separate contracts, one signed and the other one implemented, each dependant on the other, formed part of the same agreement.

However, when a later contract is dependent on the first one but the first contract is made without an assurance that the second one will be made, they form separate agreements.

A morally binding commitment is an agreement within the meaning of Article 101(1) too. Such an agreement may be written or oral. It may be inferred from all the circumstances, or it can exist within the continuing business relationship between the parties.

Accordingly, an agreement exists if the parties reach a consensus on a plan, which limits or is likely to limit their commercial freedom by determining the lines of their mutual action or abstention from action in the market. No contractual sanctions or enforcement procedures are required.[17]

---

15. (ECJ, Heintz van Landewyck SARL and others v. Commission, Joined cases 209-215 and 218/78 1980); (Commission Decision IV/31.149 on Polypropylene 1986).
16. (Commission Decision (79/934/EEC) on BP Kemi – DDSF (IV/29.021) 1979).
17. (Commission Decision IV/31.149 on Polypropylene 1986, para. 101).

Decisions of associations are easily distinguishable from agreements. They typically include articles of incorporation, by-laws, or rules of the association in question, for example, the rules of a trade association.

By its very nature, then, a *concerted practice* does not have all the elements of a contract but may *inter alia* arise out of coordination that becomes apparent from the behaviour of the participants. Any consensus between the parties to regulate their future competitive conduct will suffice to establish a prohibited restraint on their autonomy and independence.[18]

The Court of Justice discussed in the *Dyestuffs*[19] case the term concerted practices:

> *Article 85 (now Article 101) draws a distinction between the concept of 'concerted practices' and that of 'agreements between undertakings' or of 'decisions by associations of undertakings'; the object is to bring within the prohibition of that Article a form of co-ordination between undertakings which, without having reached the stage where an agreement properly so-called has been concluded, knowingly substitutes practical co-operation between them for the risks of competition. By its very nature, then, a concerted practice does not have all the elements of a contract but may inter alia arise out of co-ordination which becomes apparent from the behaviour of the participants. Although parallel behaviour may not by itself be identified with a concerted practice, it may however amount to strong evidence of such practice if it leads to conditions of competition which do not correspond to the normal conditions of the market, having regard to the nature of the products, the size and number of the undertakings and the volume of the said market. This is especially the case if the parallel conduct is such as to enable those concerned to attempt to stabilise prices at a level different from that to which competition would have led, and to consolidate established positions to the detriment of effective freedom of movement of the products in the Common Market and of the freedom of consumers to choose their suppliers. Therefore the question whether there was concerted action in this case can only be correctly determined if the evidence upon which the contested decision is based is considered, not in isolation, but as a whole, account being taken of the specific features of the market in the products in question.*[20]

If the term concerted practice is interpreted too broadly it may label certain behaviour as collusion, even though the identity of pricing policy between the parties is not in fact the result of collusion at all, but rather a rational, natural response of firms in that type of market. In 'normal' competitive markets, firms tend to compete and it is unlikely that they will price at the same level without some sort of collusion, because of cost structure and the like.

In its *Sugar* judgment, the Court of Justice held that a concerted practice was established by evidence. No actual plan was required for a concerted practice to exist.

---

18. (Commission Decision (89/190/EEC) on PVC (IV/31.865) 1988) (Commission Decision (89/191/EEC) on LdPE (IV/31.866) 1988) (Commission Decision IV/31.149 on Polypropylene 1986).
19. (ECJ, Imperial Chemical Industries Ltd. v. Commission, Case 48-69 1972).
20. (ECJ, Imperial Chemical Industries Ltd. v. Commission, Case 48-69 1972, 64–68).

Chapter 2: EU Competition Policy and EU Institutions

The key idea was that each undertaking should operate independently in the market and:

> must be understood in the light of the concept inherent in the provisions of the Treaty relating to competition that each economic operator must determine independently the policy which he intends to adopt on the Common market including the choice of persons and undertakings to which he makes offers or sells. Although it is correct to say that this requirement of independence does not deprive economic operators of the right to adapt themselves intelligently to the existing and anticipated conduct of their competitors, it does however strictly preclude any direct or indirect contact between such operators, the object or effect whereof is either to influence the conduct on the market of an actual or potential competitor or to disclose to such a competitor the course of conduct which they themselves have decided to adopt or contemplate adopting on the market.[21]

Thus, the concepts of 'agreement', 'decision' and 'concerted practice' overlap.

Unilateral measures, such as the mere refusal to supply parallel importers or the decision to reduce output of a product, are not within the scope of Article 101.[22] However, unilateral measures addressed by a seller to his buyer may lead to a concerted practice if it is followed by the buyer and monitored or policed by the seller.[23]

2.4.1.2 *Appreciability*

The prohibition of Article 101(1) against agreements, which prevent, restrict or distort competition, has been limited in the enforcement practice of the Commission and in the judgments of the Court of Justice of the EU by the principle that the restriction must be *appreciable* before Article 101 will apply.

The Court of Justice judges appreciability in the light of the economic and legal setting of the agreement and its object and effects, including the cumulative effects of possible parallel agreements.[24] Any appraisal of an appreciable effect of an agreement includes the assessment of the position and the importance of the parties on the market for the product concerned. This means that it is common to identify the relevant market first i.e., the product and geographical market in which the product competes.

The requirement of appreciable effect relates mainly to (i) the size of the parties concerned and (ii) the parties' market share. That is to say that an agreement needs an economic analysis first in order to determine whether it satisfies the requirement of appreciable effect on competition *or* trade between Member States. Thus, the appreciability doctrine requires a comprehensive economic analysis.[25]

---

21. (ECJ, Coöperatieve Vereniging 'Suiker Unie' UA and others v. Commission, Joined cases 40-48, 50, 54 to 56, 111, 113 and 114-73 1975).
22. (ECJ, Ford of Europe Incorporated and Ford-Werke Aktiengesellschaft v. Commission, Joined cases 228 and 229/82 1984).
23. (Commission Decision (82/367/EEC) on Hasselblad (IV/25.757) 1981) (ECJ, Hasselblad (GB) Limited v. Commission, Case 86/82 1984).
24. (ECJ, L.T.M. v. M.B.U., Case 56-65 1966).
25. (Hawk 1995, 980).

The approach to how to assess appreciability in practice is outlined in section 4.4.4.

2.4.1.3 Object and Effect

Article 101(1) prohibits agreements, decisions and concerted practices which have the *'object or effect'* of preventing, restricting or distorting the competition within the internal market. The restraint of competition may be *either* the object or effect of the enterprise's conduct.

According to established case law, in particular the case *La Societe Technique Miniere (STM) v. Maschinenbau Ulm GmbH*[26] and *Stergios Delimitis v. Henninger Bräu*[27], it is necessary to carry out a two-stage examination: the analysis of whether the restraint of competition may be either (1) the object or (2) the effect of the enterprise's conduct.[28] The three criteria to be examined in such an analysis are (1) first the object of the agreement, then (2) its effects and finally (3) whether it affects intra-Community trade.[29]

Agreements and decisions are often explicit enough for an anti-competitive purpose to be evident which is in clear contradiction to the objectives set out in the Lisbon Treaty without confirmation from other sources. Restrictions by object are restrictions by 'their very nature'.[30]

In other cases, in order to determine whether a given clause has the object of restricting competition within the meaning of Article 101(1), it is necessary to consider the aims pursued by the agreement.[31]

---

26. (ECJ, L.T.M. v. M.B.U., Case 56-65 1966).
27. (ECJ, Stergios Delimitis v. Henninger Bräu AG, Case C-234/89 1991).
28. (ECJ, L.T.M. v. M.B.U., Case 56-65 1966):

    Finally, for the agreement at issue to be caught by the prohibition contained in Article 85(1) it must have as its object or effect the prevention, restriction or distortion of competition within the Common Market. The fact that these are not cumulative but alternative requirements, indicated by the conjunction 'or', leads first to the need to consider the precise purpose of the agreement, in the economic context in which it is to be applied. This interference with competition referred to in Article 85(1) must result from all or some of the clauses of the agreement itself. Where however, an analysis of the said clauses does not reveal the effect on competition to be sufficiently deleterious, the consequences of the agreement should then be considered and for it to be caught by the prohibition it is then necessary to find that those factors are present which show that competition has in fact been prevented or restricted or distorted to an appreciable extent.' p. 249

29. (ECJ, H. G. Oude Luttikhuis and others v. Verenigde Coöperatieve Melkindustrie Coberco BA., Case C-399/93 1995, 11).
30. (ECJ, Miller International Schallplatten GmbH v. Commission, Case 19/77 1978).
31. See, for instance, the judgment in (ECJ, Compagnie Royale Asturienne des Mines SA and Rheinzink GmbH v. Commission, Joined cases 29/83 and 30/83 1984) and in particular (ECJ, L.T.M. v. M.B.U., Case 56-65 1966):

    The competition in question must be understood within the actual context in which it would occur in the absence of the agreement in dispute. In particular, it may be doubted where there is an interference with competition if the said agreement seems really

The determination whether an agreement has as its object a restriction of competition is not dependent on the subjective intent of the parties but on 'its terms, the legal and economic context in which it was concluded and the conduct of the parties.'[32]

In practice, few types of agreements or clauses within an agreement have as their object the restriction of competition. Typically, these are agreements and clauses, which, prima facie, do not appear to have any significant beneficial effects and are entered into solely to restrict competition. Nevertheless, the circumstances and context of the agreement are relevant and in many cases crucial for removing any possible doubt as to the purpose behind it.[33]

According to a fairly well-defined guidance in the case law, it is necessary to consider the aims pursued by the agreement as such in the *light of the economic context* in which the agreement is to be applied in order to determine whether a given clause has the object of restricting competition within the meaning of Article 101(1):[34]

> *In order to establish whether an undertaking can be found to have infringed Article 85 (new Article 101(1)) of the Treaty, the only relevant questions are whether it participated with other undertakings in an agreement having the object or effect of restricting competition and whether that agreement was liable to affect trade between Member States. The question whether the individual participation of the undertaking concerned in that agreement, notwithstanding its limited scale, restrict competition or affect trade between Member States is entirely irrelevant. Moreover, that provision does not require the restrictions of competition ascertained actually to have appreciably affected trade between Member States but merely requires that it be established that the agreement was capable of having that effect.*[35]

This means that if an object to restriction of competition is evident, then the agreement itself, or at least any anti-competitive clause in the agreement, constitutes a restraint of competition 'by its very nature'. For this reason, merely entering into an anti-competitive agreement is prohibited even if, temporarily, it may not be followed by the objectives achieved.[36] Thus, anti-competitive agreements that have not been implemented infringe Article 101(1) and may be exempted from the cartel prohibition only if the conditions set out in Article 101(3) can be applied.[37]

---

necessary for the penetration of a new area by an undertaking. It is appropriate to take into account in particular the nature and quantity, limited or otherwise, of the products covered by the agreement. p. 250

32. (ECJ, NV IAZ International Belgium and others v. Commission, Joined cases 96-102, 104, 105, 108 and 110/82 1983, 23–25).
33. (ECJ, Allgemeine Elektrizitäts-Gesellschaft AEG-Telefunken AG v. Commission, Case 107/82 1983).
34. See, for instance, the judgment in (ECJ, Compagnie Royale Asturienne des Mines SA and Rheinzink GmbH v. Commission, Joined cases 29/83 and 30/83 1984).
35. (CFI, Tréfileurope Sales SARL v. Commission, Case T-141/89 1995, 10).
36. (ECJ, SC Belasco and others v. Commission, Case 246/86 1989, 15); (ECJ, Sandoz prodotti farmaceutici SpA v. Commission, Case C-277/87 1990, 13); (Commission Decision IV/31.149 on Polypropylene 1986); (Commission Decision (89/191/EEC) on LdPE (IV/31.866) 1988).
37. (Commission Decision (72/41/EEC) on Henkel/Colgate (IV/26.917) 1971).

Accordingly, no actual effect on the market is regarded to be necessary for the rule to apply, which corresponds to the preventive nature of the rule. If the agreement seeks to restrict competition within the meaning of Article 101(1), it must be considered to be prohibited automatically. Its effects need not to be considered.[38]

In order to assess whether coordination between undertakings is *by nature* harmful to the proper functioning of normal competition, it is necessary to take into consideration all relevant aspects as well as the real conditions of the functioning and structure of the markets of the economic or legal context in which that coordination takes place, it being immaterial whether or not such an aspect relates to the relevant market. That must be the case, in particular, when that aspect is the taking into account of interactions between the relevant market and a different related market[39] and, all the more so, when, as in the present case, there are interactions between the two facets of a two-sided system.[40]

The Court of Justice clarified this concept in its judgment in *Groupement des cartes bancaires (CB) v. European Commission*.[41] In this case, the Court of Justice reviewed the legal characterisation of facts as performed by the General Court and the legal conclusions the General Court has drawn from them.[42]

The Court of Justice reaffirmed again that certain types of coordination between undertakings reveal a sufficient degree of harm to competition that it may be found that there is no need to examine their effects.[43] Certain types of coordination between undertakings can be regarded, by their *very nature*, as being harmful to the proper functioning of normal competition. Consequently, it is established that certain collusive behaviour, such as that leading to *horizontal price-fixing by cartels*, may be considered so likely to have negative effects, in particular on the price, quantity or quality of the goods and services, that it may be considered redundant, for the purposes of applying Article 101(1) to prove that they have actual effects on the market.[44] The Court confirmed that experience shows that such behaviour leads to falls in production and price increases, resulting in poor allocation of resources to the detriment, in particular, of consumers:

> *Where the analysis of a type of coordination between undertakings does not reveal a sufficient degree of harm to competition, the effects of the coordination should, on the other hand, be considered and, for it to be caught by the prohibition, it is necessary to find that factors are present which show that competition has in fact been prevented, restricted or distorted to an appreciable extent.*[45]

---

38. (ECJ, Verband der Sachversicherer e.V. v. Commission, Case 45/85 1987).
39. (see, by analogy, judgments in (ECJ, Stergios Delimitis v. Henninger Bräu AG, Case C-234/89 1991, paras 17–23); and (ECJ, Allianz Hungária Biztosító Zrt and Others v. Gazdasági Versenyhivatal, Case C-32/11 2013, para. 42).
40. (ECJ, CB v. Commission, Case C-67 / 13 P 2014, para. 79).
41. (ECJ, CB v. Commission, Case C-67 / 13 P 2014).
42. *Ibid.*, para. 41.
43. See (ECJ, Allianz Hungária Biztosító Zrt and Others v. Gazdasági Versenyhivatal, Case C-32/11 2013, para. 34).
44. See (ECJ, BNIC v. Guy Clair, Case C-123/83 1985, para. 22).
45. (ECJ, CB v. Commission, Case C-67 / 13 P 2014, para. 52) and (ECJ, Allianz Hungária Biztosító Zrt and Others v. Gazdasági Versenyhivatal, Case C-32/11 2013, para. 34).

To conclude: In order to determine whether an agreement reveals a sufficient degree of harm to competition that it may be considered a restriction of competition 'by object' within the meaning of Article 101(1), an analysis should include the content of its provisions, its objectives and the economic and legal context of which it forms a part. When determining that context, it is also necessary to take into consideration the nature of the goods or services affected, as well as the real conditions of the functioning and structure of the market or markets in question.

The approach of how to assess 'object and effect' from an economic perspective in practice is outlined in section 4.4.1.

2.4.2 Article 101(3) TFEU

Article 101(2) provides that agreements that infringe the whole of the Article are void.

The Court of Justice has interpreted this to mean that at least those provisions, which restrict competition contrary to Article 101(1) are void.[46]

The prohibition in Article 101(1) is tempered by Article 101(3) and may be declared to be inapplicable to agreements, decisions or concerted practices, or categories thereof, fulfilling the criteria laid down in Article 101(3). Article 101(3) provides that:

> *The provisions of paragraph 1 may, however, be declared inapplicable in the case of:*
> *any agreement or category of agreements between undertakings;*
> *any decision or category of decisions by associations of undertakings;*
> *any concerted practice or category of concerted practices;*
> *which contributes to improving the production or distribution of goods or to promoting technical or economic progress, while allowing consumers a fair share of the resulting benefit, and which does not:*
>
> *(a) impose on the undertakings concerned restrictions which are not indispensable to the attainment of these objectives;*
> *(b) afford such undertakings the possibility of eliminating competition in respect of a substantial part of the products in question.*

In order to qualify for an exemption under Article 101(3) the net effect of the agreement must be beneficial. The benefit must contribute to general welfare, not merely to the parties involved. Benefits accruing to consumers include higher quality of the products offered, the introduction of new and improved products, prices that are more favourable, a broader range of goods, lower costs and hence lower costs for consumers, an efficient operating of customer services, or ensuring regularity of supply. Activities, which jeopardise the single market or put the competitive process at risk are unlikely to meet the requirements of Article 101(3). Price-fixing, quota setting and market sharing are examples of such 'hard core' activities that are unlikely to meet the requirements of Article 101(3).

---

46. (ECJ, L.T.M. v. M.B.U., Case 56-65 1966); (ECJ, Société de Vente de Ciments et Bétons de l'Est SA v. Kerpen & Kerpen GmbH und Co. KG., Case 319/82 1983).

For undertakings seeking an exemption under Article 101(3), it is necessary to produce documentary evidence, that an exemption is justified. This means that the burden of proof to establish the net benefit of an agreement is on the parties.[47]

The evaluation of pro- and anti-competitive effects required by Article 101(3) must be based on both existing and future competitive conditions.[48] Accordingly, the evaluation must take into account, *inter alia*, the nature and quantity of the products and services covered by the agreement, the position and importance of the parties in the market for the products concerned, and the isolated nature of the disputed agreement or, alternatively, its context in a series of agreements.[49] In *SPO v. Commission*[50], the Court of First Instance emphasised once again that the burden of proof in relation to Article 101(3) is upon the undertaking seeking the exemption.

A more detailed guidance in the application of Article 101(3) is provided in section 4.4.6.

2.5 ARTICLE 102 TFEU

2.5.1 General Principles

Article 102 prohibits the abuse of dominant[51] market positions within the internal market or in a substantial part of it, in so far as it may affect trade between Member States.

The avoidance of market dominance is not the aim of Article 102. Article 102 refers to the *abuse* of an already existing dominant position only. This means that:

> (a) finding that an undertaking has a dominant position is not in itself a recrimination but simply means that, irrespective of the reasons for which it has such a dominant position, the undertaking concerned has a special responsibility not to allow its conduct to impair genuine undistorted competition on the common market.[52]

Thus, Article 102 is supposed to limit the way that dominant firms act in order to force them to conduct themselves.

Article 102 provides that:

> Any abuse by one or more undertakings of a dominant position within the common market or in a substantial part of it shall be prohibited as incompatible with the common market insofar as it may affect trade between Member States. Such abuse may, in particular, consist of:

---

47. (ECJ, Vereniging ter Bevordering van het Vlaamse Boekwezen, VBVB, and Vereniging ter Bevordering van de Belangen des Boekhandels, VBBB, v. Commission, Joined cases 43/82 and 63/82 1984, 52).
48. (Ritter, Braun and Rawlinson 1993, 11).
49. (ECJ, Verband der Sachversicherer e.V. v. Commission, Case 45/85 1987, 15).
50. (CFI, Vereniging van Samenwerkende Prijsregelende Organisaties in de Bouwnijverheid and others v. Commission, Case T-29/92 1995).
51. The Sherman Act in the US requires the existence of monopoly power (s. 2).
52. (ECJ, NV Nederlandsche Banden Industrie Michelin v. Commission, Case 322/81 1983).

(a) directly or indirectly imposing unfair purchase or selling prices or other unfair trading conditions;
(b) limiting production, markets or technical development to the prejudice of consumers;
(c) applying dissimilar conditions to equivalent transactions with other trading parties, thereby placing them at a competitive disadvantage;
(d) making the conclusion of contracts subject to acceptance by the other parties of supplementary obligations which, by their nature or according to commercial usage, have no connection with the subject of such contracts.

Article 102 enumerates certain types of abuses without being exhaustive. The general concept of abuse is broad and difficult to define. The TFEU refers to abuse 'of' a dominant position, but it does not mean that a link of causality must exist between the dominant position and the abuse.

To conclude, the substance of the prohibition, which is of absolute character and does not provide any exemption, is the abuse of a dominant position. In deciding whether any particular action falls within Article 102, certain conditions must be present at the same time:

(1) There must exist a dominant position held by one or more undertakings within the common market or a substantial part of it.
(2) The dominant position must be abused.
(3) The abuse must have an effect on trade between Member States.

The first two criteria are briefly discussed in the following.

2.5.2 Dominance

The first step in applying Article 102 is to define the relevant degree of economic power, *dominance*.[53]

The TFEU in fact gives no definition of dominance. It is thus left to the Commission subject to the control of the Court to determine whether or not a dominant position exists by reference to the relevant market factors. Article 102 applies not only to abuse of a dominant position by a single firm, but also to abuses by 'one or more' firms acting together.

The Court of Justice examined the concept of market dominance in *Sirena v. Eda*[54], where the Court defined it as the ability or power to prevent effective competition in an important part of the market, considering the position of producers or distributors of similar products. In *Michelin v. Commission*[55], the Court of Justice clarified the definition of dominant position:

---

53. The attempt to define dominance can be traced back to the year 1621, when Leonardo Lessius defined in his work 'Gerechtigkeit, Recht und andere Kardinaltugenden' dominance as the ability of one or a few offerers to sell a specific kind of good for a certain price, which is freely chosen and independent from competitors as well as buyers.
54. (ECJ, Sirena S.r.l. v. Eda S.r.l. and others, Case 40-70 1971).
55. (ECJ, NV Nederlandsche Banden Industrie Michelin v. Commission, Case 322/81 1983).

> It exists when an undertaking enjoys a position of economic strength which enables it to hinder the maintenance of effective competition on the relevant market by allowing it to behave to an appreciable extent independently of its competitors and customers and ultimately of consumers.

Dominance, therefore, is the power to hinder effective competition, which means the power to behave independently in the market.

In *United Brands*[56], the Court held that dominance did not require the elimination of all competition. The fact that there had been '*a lively competitive struggle*' did not, therefore, negate dominance, especially in circumstances where the competition did not succeed in increasing their market share and the competition was limited in time and space.

Since *United Brands*, the Court of Justice has used a standard definition for dominance. The Court of Justice stated that:

> *Undertakings are in a dominant position when they have the power to behave independently without taking into account to any substantial extent, their competitors, purchasers and suppliers... . It is not necessary for the undertaking to have total dominance such as would deprive all other market participants of their commercial freedom, as long as it is strong enough in general terms to devise its own strategy as it wishes.*[57]

In order to determine whether a position is dominant, it must be viewed in relation to the relevant product market and the relevant geographical market.[58] Depending on the case, the time factor may be considered as well.

That means that in determining whether a firm has a dominant position on a market, the first – often most difficult – step is to define the market concerned, the relevant market, in term of products and geography and time.[59] These concepts will be discussed in section 4.5.1.

Once the relevant product, geographical, and temporal elements of the market are defined, it has to be decided whether the undertaking is dominant within that sphere. Some measurement of the *market power* possessed by the undertaking is therefore necessary, which the Court employed in *United Brands:*[60]

> *a position of economic strength enjoyed by an undertaking which enables it to prevent effective competition being maintained on the relevant market by affording it the power to behave to an appreciable extent independently of its competitors, its customers and ultimately of the consumers.*

---

56. (ECJ, United Brands Company and United Brands Continentaal BV v. Commission, Case 27/76 1978).
57. (ECJ, United Brands Company and United Brands Continentaal BV v. Commission, Case 27/76 1978).
58. See United Brands v. Commission.
59. (ECJ, Coöperatieve Vereniging 'Suiker Unie' UA and others v. Commission, Joined cases 40-48, 50, 54 to 56, 111, 113 and 114-73 1975).
60. (ECJ, United Brands Company and United Brands Continentaal BV v. Commission, Case 27/76 1978).

Chapter 2: EU Competition Policy and EU Institutions

This test was quoted with approval in *Hoffmann-La Roche*[61] and the Court added that:

> Such a position does not preclude some competition which it does where there is a monopoly or quasi-monopoly but enables the undertaking which profits by it, if not to determine, at least to have an appreciable influence on the conditions under which that competition will develop, and in any case to act largely in disregard of it so long as such conduct does not operate to its detriment.
>
> A dominant position must also be distinguished from parallel courses of conduct which are peculiar to oligopolies in that in an oligopoly the courses of conduct interact, while in the case of an undertaking occupying the dominant position the conduct of the undertaking which derives profits from that position is to a great extent determined unilaterally. The existence of a dominant position may derive from several factors which, taken separately, are not necessarily determinative but among these factors a highly important one is the existence of very large market shares.[62]

The test whether the dominant firm is an 'unavoidable trading partner' *(partenaire obligatoire)*, i.e., other firms have no real alternative to dealing with the dominant firm, is an often used tool in assessing dominance.[63]

The structure of the relevant market must be such as to give the firm the ability to act in a largely unconstrained manner because of the absence of effective competition. The main variables are the firm's market share, its lead in terms of market share over its rivals, the degree of dependence of its customers or suppliers, and its ability to set its prices and terms and conditions of sale without serious regard to the competitive response of smaller competitors.

Market share is only one of the decisive factors.

The actual size of the market share possessed by the undertaking is of interest to the determination of whether it has market power in the sense set out above. In *Hoffmann-La Roche*, the Court stressed the importance of market shares:

> Furthermore although the importance of the market shares may vary from one market to another the view may legitimately be taken that very large shares are in themselves, and save in exceptional circumstances, evidence of a dominant position. An undertaking which has a very large market share and holds it for some time, by means of the volume of production and the scale of the supply which it stands for - without those having much smaller market shares being able to meet rapidly the demand from those who would like to break away from the undertaking which has the largest market share - is by virtue of that share in a position of strength which makes it an unavoidable trading partner and which, already because of this secures for it, at the very least during relatively long periods, that freedom of action which is the special feature of a dominant position.
>
> ... The existence of a dominant position may derive from several factors which taken separately are not necessarily determinative but among these factors a highly important one is the existence of very large market shares.[64]

---

61. (ECJ, Hoffmann-La Roche & Co. AG v. Commission, Case 85/76 1979, 39).
62. See also (ECJ, NV Nederlandsche Banden Industrie Michelin v Commission, Case 322/81 1983, 30).
63. (CFI, Radio Telefis Eireann v. Commission, Case T-69/89 1991).
64. (ECJ, Hoffmann-La Roche & Co. AG v. Commission, Case 85/76 1979, 41).

Whilst the Commission had placed weight in *Hoffmann-La Roche* on the pure size of the company and the volume of turnover, which it provided, the Court did not accept that size and turnover alone could indicate dominance. The Court also placed far less reliance than the Commission on the range of products produced by Roche as well as the fact that it had retained market share over a continuous period of time, pointing out that this could be explained by a large number of other factors, including simply its ability to compete effectively in a normal manner. Save in exceptional circumstances, the existence of a very large market share, which was held for some time, would in itself be indicative of dominance: it would secure for the undertaking concerned the freedom of action which was the hallmark of a dominant position.[65]

Thus a large market share is necessary, though rarely sufficient alone, to prove the existence of a dominant position. *'A trader can only be in a dominant position on the market for a product if he has succeeded in winning a large part of this market'.*[66]

Market shares above 80% are noticeably high and are usually enough to conclude a dominant position.[67]

In *Continental Can*[68], the Court laid down the test of market dominance as the ability of competitors to constitute an adequate counterweight.

In *United Brands*[69], where it was held that a market share of 45% of the banana market constituted market dominance, the fact that the largest competitor had a market share of only 9% was an important consideration. Other factors in this case were the high barriers against new entrants to the market, such as penetration costs, access to sources of supply, and the need for large investment.

In the *AKZO*[70] case, the Court held that a market share of 50% could be said to be very large, and hence indicative of a dominant position.

Except in the most obvious of cases, such as *Suiker Unie*[71], where one of the suppliers had a massive share of a commodity product, the proof of significant market share is seldom a substitute for a full economic analysis of the issue of dominance.[72] *'Market shares are limited in their power of indication'.*[73]

An analysis in section 4.5.2 shows that market share is not the only or even decisive factor. An essential aspect of the analysis relates to barriers to entry and potential competition.

---

65. (ECJ, Hoffmann-La Roche & Co. AG v. Commission, Case 85/76 1979, 41); (CFI, Hilti AG v. Commission, Case T-30/89 1991), a market share of 70% was, in itself, indicative of market dominance.
66. (ECJ, United Brands Company and United Brands Continentaal BV v. Commission, Case 27/76 1978).
67. (ECJ, Coöperatieve Vereniging 'Suiker Unie' UA and others v. Commission, Joined cases 40-48, 50, 54 to 56, 111, 113 and 114-73 1975).
68. (ECJ, Europemballage Corporation and Continental Can Company Inc. v. Commission, Case 6/72 1973).
69. (ECJ, United Brands Company and United Brands Continentaal BV v. Commission, Case 27/76 1978).
70. (ECJ, AKZO Chemie BV v. Commission, Case C-62/86 1991).
71. (ECJ, Coöperatieve Vereniging 'Suiker Unie' UA and others v. Commission, Joined cases 40-48, 50, 54 to 56, 111, 113 and 114-73 1975).
72. (Child and Bellamy 1993, 605).
73. (Langen and Bunte 1994, para. 22 no. 62).

2.5.3 Abuse

Since the dominant position itself is not prohibited, there should plainly be no restraint on the reasonable and normal conduct of that undertaking like expanding output, innovation, cost reduction, efficient organisation and so forth. However, the distinction between what is permissible conduct by a dominant firm and conduct, which is prohibited as abusive, is often a difficult one.

Article 102 gives examples of abuse. The list of abuses is illustrative and not exhaustive, and it is for the Commission and Court to determine, in each individual case, whether the practice or activity complained of is an abuse of a dominant market position.

Article 102 nominates four examples of abuse:

Such abuse may, in particular, consist in:

(a) directly or indirectly imposing unfair purchase or selling prices or other unfair trading conditions;
(b) limiting production, markets or technical development to the prejudice of consumers;
(c) applying dissimilar conditions to equivalent transactions with other trading parties, thereby placing them at a competitive disadvantage;
(d) making the conclusion of contracts subject to acceptance by the other parties of supplementary obligations which, by their nature or according to commercial usage, have no connection with the subject of such contracts.

2.5.3.1 Imposition of Unfair Purchase or Selling Prices or Conditions (Article 102(a))

A dominant firm abuses its dominant position according to Article 102(a), if it charges its customers unfairly high prices or extorts unfairly low prices from its suppliers, or if it imposes 'other unfair trading conditions' or terms on its customers or suppliers.

This is a typically exploitative abuse. It is to be distinguished from the exclusionary abuse of predatory pricing, i.e., price-cutting to injure or remove a competitor which is discussed together with other exclusionary practices in the section below.

However, the Court of Justice seems to consider predatory pricing, too, as a form of unfair pricing falling within Article 102(a).[74]

A firm that holds a dominant position may have sufficient market power to charge its customers unfairly high prices. Often the overpricing may be selective, i.e., it may involve price discrimination between different customers or geographic markets. Discrimination exists when cases are not treated alike. In other words, different prices are not discriminatory unless there is no objective justification for the difference. For the dominant firm, however, an allegation of price discrimination is likely to raise difficulties under Article 102 if third parties are placed at a real economic disadvantage

---

74. (ECJ, Ahmed Saeed Flugreisen and Silver Line Reisebüro GmbH v. Zentrale zur Bekämpfung unlauteren Wettbewerbs e.V., Case 66/86 1989).

as a result of the policy followed. Multinational companies that practise discriminatory pricing to different national markets are particularly susceptible to the charge of excessive pricing.

In *Sirena*, for example, the Court stated that excessive prices might constitute an abuse of a dominant position. *'As regards the abuse of a dominant position, although the price level of the product may not of itself necessarily suffice to disclose such an abuse, it may, however, if unjustified by any objective criteria and if it is particularly high, be a determining factor.'*[75]

In *General Motors Continental* the Commission found that charging excessive fees for certification of automobile imports constituted an abuse of a dominant position. The Court stated that an abuse could include:

> the imposition of a price which is excessive in relation to the economic value of the service provided, and which has the effect of curbing parallel imports by neutralising the possibly more favourable level of prices applying in other sales areas in the Community, or by leading to unfair trade in the sense or Article 102(2)(a).[76]

The Court in *United Brands* specified further the status of excessive pricing as an abuse of dominant position. The Court posited the following test for excessive pricing:

> The question therefore to be determined is whether the difference between the costs actually incurred and the price actually charged is excessive, and, if the answer is in the affirmative, whether a price has been imposed which is either unfair in itself or when compared to competing products.[77]

The Court also said in that case that the burden of proof of overpricing rests on the Commission or other persons alleging it. Since *United Brands*, the Commission has been reticent about taking decisions on 'unfair prices' except where the price differentials in question perpetuate market division.[78]

2.5.3.2 Limiting Production, Markets or Technical Development to the Prejudice of Consumers (Article 102(b))

A dominant firm that limits 'production, markets or technical development to the prejudice of consumers' may infringe Article 102(b). These forms of abuse require that consumers be directly or indirectly prejudiced.[79]

As regards *limitation of production*, an example is the discontinuance of the production of spare parts for a car model that is no longer in production.[80] Restrictions

---

75. (ECJ, Sirena S.r.l. v. Eda S.r.l. and others, Case 40-70 1971, 17).
76. (ECJ, General Motors Continental NV v. Commission, Case 26-75 1975, 12).
77. *Ibid.*
78. For example, (ECJ, British Leyland Public Limited Company v. Commission, Case 226/84 1986).
79. (Ritter, Braun and Rawlinson 1993, 299).
80. (ECJ, Consorzio italiano della componentistica di ricambio per autoveicoli and Maxicar v. Régie nationale des usines Renault, Case 53/87 1988).

Chapter 2: EU Competition Policy and EU Institutions

imposed on third parties such as licensees or suppliers, through contract terms that limit them to producing for an overly narrow field of use or territory or in unduly small quantities may constitute an abuse.

Limitation of markets may be caused through contractual terms or by unilateral action like refusal to supply. Contractual restrictions on the markets or customers to which a firm may sell or the suppliers from which it may buy ordinarily infringe Article 101(1) unless exempted under Article 101(3). If such restrictive agreements infringe Article 101 when made by non-dominant firms, it constitutes a serious infringement of Article 102, when dominant firms impose them. On the other hand, unilateral actions by a dominant firm to restrict the markets or customers supplied by distributors or to cut off supplies to certain purchasers may also infringe Article 102. Generally, even a firm in a dominant position is free to determine its marketing policy and to select its customers, but the firm has to take into account the particular degree of dependence of its customers owing to the fact that the customers have few alternative suppliers. A dominant firm is entitled to review its entire distribution system and to phase out certain customers over time. However, it may infringe Article 102 if it withdraws supplies suddenly or without notice.[81]

A dominant firm may infringe Article 102(b) by restricting access to or the use or the development of a new technology to the detriment of consumers i.e., *limitation of technical development*. A dominant firm may fall foul of Article 102 by restricting access to or the use or development of a new technology to the detriment of consumers.

2.5.3.3 *Applying Dissimilar Conditions to Equivalent Transactions (Article 102(c))*

The third example of abuse of dominance given in Article 102 is 'applying dissimilar conditions to equivalent transactions with other trading parties, thereby placing them at a competitive disadvantage' (Article 102(c)).

In other words, a dominant firm can abuse its dominant position by discriminating between different trading partners (customers or suppliers) in its terms and conditions of trading with them, with the result that some are disadvantaged. Failing to treat cases alike and treating unlike cases are both discriminatory. To show discrimination it is necessary to determine whether or not transactions are alike, or rather equivalent in the words of Article 102(c). Given that transactions are rarely exactly alike, Article 102(c) does not require a dominant firm to offer identical prices and conditions throughout the Community.

Price differences are only regarded as abusive once a certain tolerance level is exceeded and they become significant and unjustifiable. The tolerance level is less in cases where the discrimination is part of a clear policy of dividing markets or excluding competitors. Article 102(c) has been found applicable most often in cases of price discrimination. Price discrimination may constitute selective unfair pricing, falling under Article 102(a), if some of the prices are unfair.

---

81. (Commission Decision (87/500/EEC) on BBI/Boosey & Hawkes (IV/32.279) 1987).

2.5.3.4 Tying Practices (Article 102(d))

The final example of abuse of dominance given in Article 102 is *tying*, i.e., making the conclusion of contracts subject to acceptance by the other parties of supplementary obligations which, by their nature or according to their commercial usage, have no connection with the subject of such contracts.

The dominant firm may not be dominant in the supply of the tied product. The mischief of the conduct might be that it attempts to extend the market strength of the dominant firm from the market of the tying product to that of the tied product.

The concept of the tying clause presupposes the supply of two distinct products rather than a combination of different components in a single-product so that, for example, the supply of shoe laces in shoes, or buttons on clothing is not regarded as tie-in.[82]

Illegal tying can occur only where the two products by their nature or according to commercial usage need not be sourced from the same supplier, although they may be closely related. Aggregated rebate schemes[83] may have the same effect as direct tying clauses and can be caught by Article 102(d).

2.5.3.5 Exclusionary Abuses Not Directly Covered by the Examples in Article 102(a)–(d)

Article 102 prohibits practices which may be permissible in a normal competitive situation but are not permissible for dominant firms which should have a 'special responsibility'[84], since their behaviour may cause a prejudice to competition in general and to the interests of competitors, suppliers, customers and consumers in particular. In the following, some examples are analysed in more detail, namely:

- refusal to supply;
- predatory pricing;
- fidelity rebates and similar practices;
- other kinds of price discrimination will be discussed in the following section.

2.5.3.6 Refusal to Supply

The most characteristic types of exclusionary conduct that have been found to be prohibited by Article 102, but which are not in all cases directly covered by the examples given in the Article, is conduct that may be aimed directly at the actual or potential competitor, as in the cases of refusal to supply and refusal of access to a

---

82. (CFI, Hilti AG v. Commission, Case T-30/89 1991) and (Commission Decisions (92/163/EEC) on Tetra Pak II (IV/31043) 1991).
83. That is, arrangements under which the supplier grants a rebate based on the customer's total purchases from it of different products.
84. (ECJ, NV Nederlandsche Banden Industrie Michelin v. Commission, Case 322/81 1983, 57).

Chapter 2: EU Competition Policy and EU Institutions

market, or aimed at the competitor via its actual or potential customers or suppliers, as in the cases of exclusionary (or predatory) pricing and exclusionary dealing arrangements.

As already stated, a firm in a dominant position is free to determine its marketing policy and to select its customers, but the firm has to take into account the particular degree of dependence of its customers owing to the fact that they have few alternative suppliers. However, it may infringe Article 102 if it withdraws supplies suddenly or without notice.

A dominant undertaking will generally need to show an 'objective justification' for a refusal to supply an existing customer. The same applies to a refusal to supply on unreasonable terms. That is so even if the refusal to supply affects competition in a market, which is separate from, or ancillary to, the market in which the supplier is dominant.

Precisely what constitutes an 'objective justification' is not clear, but a desire to enter a new market oneself, thereby substituting for the customer, or to retaliate disproportionately against the customer's trading policies, is not sufficient. Leading cases are *Commercial Solvents, United Brands, Hugin* and *Telemarketing*.

The Court of Justice cleared this concept in *Commercial Solvents*. The Court held that:

> *However, an undertaking being in a dominant position as regards the production of raw material and therefore able to control the supply to manufacturers of derivatives, cannot, just because it decides to start manufacturing these derivatives (in competition with its former customers) act in such a way as to eliminate their competition which, in the case in question, would amount to eliminating one of the principal manufacturers of ethambutol in the Common Market. Since such conduct is contrary to the objectives expressed in Article 3(g) of the Treaty and set out in greater detail in Article 85 and 86 (now Articles 101 and 102), it follows that an undertaking which has a dominant position in the market in raw materials and which, with the object of reserving such raw material for manufacturing its own derivatives, refuses to supply a customer, which is itself a manufacturer of these derivatives, and therefore risks eliminating all competition on the part of this customer, is abusing its dominant position within the meaning of Article 86(new Article 102).*[85]

In the context of intellectual property rights, the judgment of the Court of Justice in the *Magill* Case[86] on 6 April 1995 is of importance. This case can be viewed as a true landmark decision, as it establishes a number of important principles concerning the borderline between competition law and intellectual property law.

In this case, a number of television stations in the UK and Ireland published their own weekly television guide covering exclusively their own programmes. No comprehensive weekly television guide was available. Each of the TV stations claimed, under Irish and UK legislation, copyright protection for its own weekly programme listings in

---

85. (ECJ, Istituto Chemioterapico Italiano S.p.A. and Commercial Solvents Corporation v. Commission, Joined cases 6 and 7-73 1974, 25).
86. (ECJ, Radio Telefis Eireann (RTE) and Independent Television Publications Ltd (ITP) v. Commission, Joined cases C-241/91 P and C-242/91 P 1995).

order to prevent their reproduction by third parties. The TV stations only provided their programme schedules free of charge, on request, to daily and periodical newspapers, accompanied by a licence for which no charge was made, setting out the conditions under which that information could be reproduced. Magill TV Guide Ltd attempted to publish a comprehensive weekly television guide but was prevented from doing so by TV stations, which obtained injunctions prohibiting publication of weekly television listings.

The Court found that the TV stations' refusal to provide basic information as to the channel, day, time and title of programmes based on its reliance on national copyright provisions prevented the appearance of a new product, a comprehensive weekly guide to TV programmes, which the TV stations themselves did not offer and for which there was a potential consumer demand. The Court added that there was no justification for such refusal either in the activity of television broadcasting or in that of publishing TV magazines. Finally, the Court held that the TV stations, by their conduct, reserved for themselves the secondary market of weekly TV guides, by excluding all competition on that market. This judgment is interesting in particular from the point of view that the Court of Justice has taken the opportunity to confirm its earlier jurisprudence that Article 102 can apply to protect competing suppliers of spare parts or services regardless of existing intellectual property protection. It has also confirmed the view of the Commission that the balance between intellectual property protection and competition is not to be left entirely to the legislature.

2.5.3.7 *Predatory Pricing*

The expression *predatory pricing* is associated with pricing by a dominant undertaking, which has, as a principal objective, the elimination or serious weakening of a competitor.

Predatory pricing normally but not necessarily involves: (i) selective price-cutting; (ii) unprofitable or barely profitable price levels; and (iii) pricing 'aimed at' a specific competitor. However, predatory pricing must not be confused with normal price competition, the latter being a natural and expected feature of the competitive process. Price reductions, whether initiated by the dominant firm or by others, and whether across the board or on specific contracts, may be evidence of the competitive process at work, even in a dominated market, and should not be prohibited merely upon proof that a competitor has suffered some disadvantage. It is therefore a matter of some difficulty to distinguish between a legitimate competitive response and 'predatory' or 'abusive' action.

AKZO is the leading case.

The Court of Justice adopted in *AKZO*[87] a cost-based test, applying the principle that abuse is an objective concept.

The Court held that prices below variable costs through which an undertaking tries to eliminate the competitor, must be considered abusive. This is because each sale

---

87. (ECJ, AKZO Chemie BV v. Commission, Case C-62/86 1991, 69).

at such prices causes a loss, the only possible rationale for such prices being that in the long run elimination of the competitor must be considered as abusive. Where the price is higher than average variable cost but lower than average total cost, abuse may be found when prices are fixed in the context of a plan to eliminate a competitor. Nevertheless, this constitutes a subjective element in an objective concept.

In *Tetra Pak II*[88], for example, the Commission found that Tetra Pak had engaged in predatory pricing of its non-aseptic cartons in Italy. These cartons were sold considerably below cost price (i.e., total average cost) over a period of seven years. The company had a dominant position on the market for aseptic cartons and the Commission found that it had used profits from this market to subsidise sales on the market for non-aseptic cartons, selling the latter at a loss below average variable cost in seven of the Member States. The Commission looked in detail at the Italian market, finding that the pricing policy was deliberately aimed at eliminating competition.

In an Article 102 investigation by the Commission against Deutsche Post AG[89] the Commission set forth a standard for measuring 'cross-subsidies' between the reserved area and competitive activities that result in predatory prices in the latter: any service provided by the beneficiary of a monopoly in open competition has to cover at least the additional or incremental cost incurred in branching out into the competitive sector. This so-called 'increment cost test' was proposed by the economic expert to Deutsche Post AG in this case and became later on the standard.

The Commission considers that any cost coverage below this level is predatory pricing which falls foul of Article 102. In order to ensure the requisite level of transparency of financial relations between its monopoly and business parcel services, Deutsche Post AG had undertaken with reference to the Commission to create a separate company ('Newco') to supply business parcel services. Newco would be free to procure the 'inputs' necessary for its services (such inputs include, for example, sorting, transport and delivery services) either from Deutsche Post AG or from third parties or produce these 'inputs' itself. Should Newco choose to purchase the 'inputs' from Deutsche Post AG, the latter would have to provide to Newco all goods and services at market prices. In addition, Deutsche Post AG had undertaken that all 'inputs' it supplied to Newco would be supplied to Newco's competitors at the same price and under the same conditions. This formal decision under Article 102 of the Treaty clarified the Commission's position on the costs to be covered by a multi-product monopoly operator that offers an additional line of products in markets open to competition.

2.5.3.8 *Exclusionary Rebate Schemes*

A dominant firm may also infringe Article 102 by certain types of dealing arrangements with its customers that tend to exclude competitors. Such arrangements include long-term requirements (exclusive dealing) or part-requirements contracts and equivalent

---

88. (Commission Decisions (92/163/EEC) on Tetra Pak II (IV/31043) 1991).
89. (Commission Decision (2001/354/EC) on Deutsche Post AG (Case COMP/35.141) 2001).

informal relationships secured by pressure or threats, clauses requiring customers to disclose more favourable offers received from competitors, supply contracts associated with the leasing of equipment, and *exclusionary rebate schemes*.

Certain kinds of price discounts can tie customers to a supplier just as effectively as requirements contracts or can reinforce the effect of such contracts. This is especially the case with rebates, i.e., discounts paid retrospectively in respect of past purchases. Rebate schemes, whether in conjunction with requirements contracts or by themselves, granted by dominant firms in return for securing all or an increased proportion of the business of customers may well infringe Article 102 in the absence of some objective justification.

As the Court of Justice stated in *Hoffmann-La Roche*:

> *An undertaking which is in a dominant position on a market and ties purchasers - even if it does so at their request - by an obligation or promise on their part to obtain all or most of their requirements exclusively from the said undertaking abuses its dominant position within the meaning of Article 102 of the Treaty, whether the obligation in question is stipulated without further qualification or whether it is undertaken in consideration of the grant of a rebate.*
> *The same applies if the said undertaking, without tying the purchasers by a formal obligation, applies, either under the terms of agreements concluded with these purchasers or unilaterally, a system of fidelity rebates, that is to say discounts conditional on the customer's obtaining all or most of its requirements - whether the quantity of its purchases be large or small - from the undertaking in a dominant position.*

Special financial rebates or discounts granted by dominant firms in return for securing all or an increased proportion of the business of customers are exclusionary in effect and may well infringe Article 102 in the absence of some objective justification, such as a cost-based quantity discount. That principle was first established in *Sugar*[90], where the Court held that Article 102 was infringed by the system of pricing of SZV which:

> *is not to be treated as a quantity rebate exclusively linked with the volume of purchases from the producer conceded but has rightly been classified by the Commission as a 'loyalty' rebate designed, through the grant of a financial advantage, to prevent customers obtaining their supplies from competing producers.*

Similarly, in *Hoffmann-La Roche*[91], Roche had entered into a number of fidelity rebate arrangements with various customers. In finding an abuse under Article 102, the Commission held that abuse was established by:

> *The fact that customers are bound by an exclusive or preferential purchasing commitment in favour of Roche for all or for a very large proportion of their requirements either as a result of an express obligation of exclusivity, or fidelity rebates, or other means.*

---

90. (ECJ, Coöperatieve Vereniging 'Suiker Unie' UA and others v. Commission, Joined cases 40-48, 50, 54 to 56, 111, 113 and 114-73 1975).
91. (Commission Decision (76/642/EEC) on Vitamins (IV/29.020) 1976, 60).

Chapter 2: EU Competition Policy and EU Institutions

> *The fact that the price advantages granted are based not on the differences in costs borne by Roche in relation to the quantities supplied, but on the supply of all or a very large proportion of a customer's requirements.*
>
> *The fact that in certain cases the rebate is based on all purchases, so that purchases of vitamins of one group are aggregated with purchases of vitamins of other groups ('across the-board rebates').*
>
> *The fact that the agreements generally contain a provision known as the 'English clause,' the significance of which is as follows; purchasers are obliged to inform Roche of offers from other manufacturers more favourable than those of Roche; should Roche not match such offers, purchasers are free to purchase from such manufacturers without losing the rebate in respect of purchases made from Roche. In some agreements Roche stipulate that the offers should emanate from 'reputable' manufacturers (thereby excluding dealers and brokers).*

The Court[92], affirming the Commission's decision, expressed its conclusions forcefully:

> *An undertaking which is in a dominant position on a market and ties purchasers - even if it does so at their request - by an obligation or promise on their part to obtain all or most of their requirements exclusively from the said undertaking abuses its dominant position within the meaning of Article 86 (now Article 102) of the Treaty whether the obligation in question is stipulated for without further qualifications or whether it is undertaken in consideration of the grant of a rebate.*
>
> *The same applies if the said undertaking, without tying the purchasers by a formal obligation, applies either under the terms of agreements concluded with these purchasers or unilaterally, a system of fidelity rebates, that is to say discounts conditional on the customer's obtaining all or most of its requirements - whether the quantity of its purchases be large or small - from the undertaking in a dominant position.*

A more detailed overview on the economic analysis related to rebates under Article 102 is provided in section 4.5.2.7.

2.6 EU MERGER CONTROL

2.6.1 The Evolution of Concentration Control in Europe

The TFEU does not contain explicit concentration control provisions.

Nevertheless, public discussion on a possible European control of concentrations started early and resulted in the 1966 EC Commission's Memorandum[93] on Concentration.

In that memorandum, the Commission identified two broad categories of transactions: concentrations and cooperations (i.e., cartel-type arrangements). 'The term "concentration of enterprises" is used where several enterprises are brought together under a single economic management at the expense of their independence in a manner indicating permanence.'[94] The Commission clarified that the most important

---

92. (ECJ, Hoffmann-La Roche & Co. AG v. Commission, Case 85/76 1979, 120).
93. (Commission Memorandum on the Problem of Concentration in the Common Market 1966).
94. *Ibid.*, para. 51.

types of concentrations are: a company's acquisition of holdings in other companies, the total or partial acquisition of the capital assets of other companies, and the merger of two or more legally independent companies into a new company. Cooperations, on the other hand, resulted in behavioural change and involved coordination of the market behaviour of enterprises that remain economically independent.

The conclusion at that time was that the best instrument for the Commission to engage in the control of concentrations would be a separate Regulation.

The first proposal for such a Regulation was submitted to the Council as early as 1973. In the period 1973–1987, only a few modifications to and discussions regarding the 1973 proposal took place. The efforts to adopt a Merger Regulation were renewed when fresh proposals in 1988 and 1989 were presented.[95] The attempts gained further momentum, with the Court's Judgment in *Philip Morris*.[96]

Claiming that Philip Morris opened the door to the application of Article 101 to concentrations, the Commission used the judgment as argument to force the adoption of its proposal by the Council.

Finally, Council Regulation (EEC) No. 4064/89 of 21 December 1989[97] – also called the Merger Regulation – was adopted.

The Regulation applied to concentrations. It divides responsibility for the 'control of concentrations' between the Commission and the Member States on the basis of turnover thresholds. Once a concentration meets the Community-dimension criteria, it must be notified to the Commission for analysis.

2.6.2 Merger Regulation 139/2004

The Merger Regulation was amended by the Council Regulation (EC) 139/2004 of 20 January 2004 on the control of concentrations between undertakings (the ECMR). The ECMR came into force on 1 May 2004 and introduced some flexibility into the investigation timeframes while retaining the much praised predictability. It reinforced the 'one-stop shop' concept, and clarified that the Commission has the power to investigate all types of harmful scenarios in a merger, from dominance by a single firm to the effects stemming from a situation of oligopoly that might harm the interests of European consumers.

A novelty in the ECMR is the notion of 'significant impediment to effective competition' – SIEC in Article 2(2) and (3) – requiring an extension beyond the concept of dominance.

The role of economic analysis in the 2004 ECMR is discussed in section 4.6.

---

95. Amended proposal for a Council Regulation (EEC) on the control of concentrations between undertakings, 25 Apr. 1988, (1988) O.J. C 130/4: Amended proposal for a Council Regulation (EEC) on the control of concentrations between undertakings, 30 Nov.1988, (1989) O.J. C 22/14.
96. (ECJ, British-American Tobacco Company Ltd and R. J. Reynolds Industries Inc. v. Commission, Joined cases 142 and 156/84 1987).
97. (Regulation 4064/89 on the control of concentrations between undertakings 1989).

CHAPTER 3
Competition Theory

3.1 SCHOOL OF THOUGHTS IN COMPETITION THEORY

3.1.1 Objectives Assigned to Competition Policy

For centuries the core problem for every economic society has been to determine what commodities shall be produced and in what quantities, how they will be produced and for whom.

Different economic systems tried to solve these questions. First, 'custom' might be a solution: society uses a set of pre-ordained rules with reference to previous practices. Secondly, 'dictate' is another option. Those holding power simply decree their preferred answers to each question.[1] Alternatively, thirdly, a 'market mechanism' can be applied. The latter dominates in a free democratic society and is determined primarily by *competitive markets*.

The general assumption shared today by most industrialised countries is that a competitive market system is the least bad for promoting economic and political freedoms. It also represents the best chance of achieving a high standard of living.[2] For the citizens of the European Union (EU), the Lisbon Treaty confirms that a highly competitive social market economy is the most proficient tool to increase the well-being of its people. The market mechanism and the functioning of a market economy are central themes in a market system.

Objectives assigned to a market system – and implemented by competition policy and law – are the protection of individual freedom and individual rights as well as the diffusion of economic power. The interaction between these objectives need to be balanced:

---

1. Central planned economies proved us that this system is not successful.
2. (Jacquemin 1990, 1).

- The protection of the economic freedom of the market participants is one of the most important assets in any democratic economic order. This protection of freedom is sometimes in conflict with other objectives assigned to competition policy. Examples for this conflict are abusive practices by powerful firms endangering the existence and thereby the freedom of weaker participants. This type of behaviour could cause a weakening of the competition process. They are mainly addressed by national laws under 'unfair competition'. These laws intend to ensure that competitors compete in a fair way, and carry out their social functions according to an ethical code of honest trade practices. The code is determined by common sense.[3] On the other hand, these types of law restrict the freedom of the powerful firms to act. Thus, their economic freedom is constrained by law in favour of a competitive market process.
- The diffusion of both private and public economic power is another essential feature assigned to competition policy and law. Interestingly, the diffusion of economic power and the correlated desire to limit the size of firms has never played an appreciable role in long established constitutional democracies such as Britain, the Netherlands or Switzerland. It was Germany that voiced its concerns post-World War II in favour of a diffusion of economic power.[4] Addressing economic power by law also contradicts the concept of economic freedom. Thus, convincing arguments are necessary to support why limitations of economic freedom induced by law are for the benefit of the people. These arguments are elaborated on in each of the different competition theories.

Economics assumes that markets that are more competitive improve economic performance and generate benefits for the well-being of people. This thinking has been dear to the hearts of economists since *Adam Smith* and the Classical School of economics. In an economist's view, the ultimate aim within society is to establish and maintain competitive market structures. An unrestrained interaction of competitive forces yields the best allocation of scarce economic resources, the lowest prices, the highest quality and the greatest material wealth, while at the same time providing an environment conducive to the preservation of democratic, political and social institutions.[5] In their view, competition is regarded as the only means that ensures entrepreneurial forces are mobilised and the full potential of a firm's efficiencies is exploited. A competitive process leads not only to greater overall economic efficiency and to competitiveness, but in particular to increased consumer welfare.[6] Thus, economic efficiencies and consumer welfare are the 'hot topics' discussed in competition theories.

---

3. (Jacquemin 1990, 3).
4. (de Jong 1990a, 120).
5. (Northern Pacific Railway Company and Northwestern improvement company v. United States of America 1958). Full case explanations and details on (Cornell University Law School 1992).
6. (Schmidt and Rittaler 1989, XIV).

3.1.1.1   United States (US)

In the US, the focus of anti-trust policy is on efficiencies. Competition policy is supposed to '... *promote and maintain a process of effective competition so as to achieve a more efficient allocation of resources.*'[7] Judge Posner pronounced in *Olympia Equip. Leasing Co v. Western Union Tel. Co*[8] that '*the emphasis of anti-trust policy has shifted from the protection of competition as a process of rivalry to the protection of competition as a means of promoting economic efficiency...*'. Bork[9], a leading representative of the US Chicago School, has made the neatest affirmation of a purely efficiency-directed US anti-trust policy.

Bork defined efficiency by both allocative and productive efficiency. Bork stated that '*... business efficiency necessarily benefits consumers by lowering the costs of goods and services or by increasing the value of the product or service offered.*'[10] In his view, anti-trust law needs to challenge inefficient conduct and in his opinion, this objective should be *the* goal of competition. A necessary (but not sufficient) attribute of inefficiency is a restriction of output beyond levels that would prevail under competitive conditions. In his *laissez-faire* view, conduct not so identified must be presumed to enhance efficiency, and should not be the subject of any legal sanction.[11] Despite the fact that the efficiency goal of competition is the most prominently pronounced one in all jurisdictions, some societies attach other policy objectives to competition as well.

3.1.1.2   European Union

Within the EU, for decades now, the integration of the internal market was seen as an important objective attached to EU competition law. More recently, introduced by the Lisbon Treaty, other objectives are becoming more relevant thereby putting European citizens in particular at the centre of competition policy. Today, the main concern is the achievement of an effective and socially balanced competition process for the benefit and well-being of the people. The classical consumer welfare objective as pronounced by US commentators coexists with these aims too. But it is not in the centre of EU competition law enforcement.

New to Europe is the general acceptance that the preferred market system is that of a highly competitive social market economy. This newly added feature in the Lisbon Treaty mandates a more holistic approach in EU competition policy and law than applied so far. It means that all relevant aspects related to a social market economy need to be taken into account in a legal assessment.

One example of such a holistic approach is the assessment of the Commission in an Article 102 case on the duty to deliver 'services of general interest' by a powerful

---

7. See discussion in (Vickers and Hay 1987, 2).
8. (Olympia Equipment Leasing Company, ALFCO v. Western Union Telegraph Company 1986). see also (Leagle 2013).
9. (R. Bork 1978, 54).
10. (R. Bork 1978, 7).
11. (R. Bork, The Goals of Antitrust Policy 1967).

postal service provider. The allegation was that the postal operator, mainly active in the reserved letter monopoly area, abused his dominant position by granting fidelity rebates to selected clients and by engaging in predatory pricing in the competitive market for business parcel services. By defining a new standard for measuring 'cross-subsidies' between the reserved letter monopoly area and the competitive business parcel activities, the European Commission acknowledged that the majority of the postal network costs are necessary to perform the public services. According to the European Commission's standard established in this case, postal services provided by a monopoly player has to cover at least the incremental cost incurred in branching out products or services into a competitive sector (*incremental cost test*). Any cost coverage below this level is considered predatory pricing which falls foul of Article 102. This incremental cost test in the *Deutsche Post* case[12] is a classic example of the genuine European approach that considers both competition related goals and other policy objectives related to social aims. *GE/Honeywell*[13] and *Microsoft*[14] are other cases where by integrating other policy objectives the European Commission's and the Court's economic assessments deviated considerably from the US approach.

For competition economists rooted in the European approach, these outcomes are not surprising at all. It makes sense that any competition assessment in EU competition law considers the specificities of the EU. When the Treaty of Rome was drafted, broader competition policy objectives were already being applied. The philosophy has now been revitalised in the Lisbon Treaty. The European competition concept is flexible. It applies standardised criteria and is built on established economic traditions thereby representing a solid balance between theory and practice.

3.1.2 School of Thoughts in Competition Theory

3.1.2.1 *Role of Economics*

Compared with the clearly determined natural sciences, economics offers a broad range of possible – sometimes even conflicting – elucidations about market interactions. In fact, economics tries to simplify complex market relations. Moreover, economic models tend to focus only on specific research subjects thereby neglecting other aspects considered not so relevant for the research topic under scrutiny. Thus, common within all economic theories is the attempt to transfer complex market interactions into lines that are easy to understand. Simplicity is the skill that characterises economics.

Another feature inherent in economics is its strong relationship with political and social choices. In this sense, economics is a sparkling science. Unlike hypotheses in mathematics or physics, economics is subjective, value-laden and, ultimately,

---

12. Case COMP/35.141 *Deutsche Post AG*, D., Commission, 20.3.2001, (2001) OJ L 125/27. The author proposed the incremental cost test in these proceedings to the European Commission that decided to use this test as its future standard.
13. For the anatomy of the GE-Honeywell Disaster see (Elliot 2001).
14. (Microsoft Corp. v. Commission of the European Communities 2007).

imprecise, offering most of the time no unique answers. In particular, competition theories are considered to be manifold undergoing constant change, review and advancement, both in the US and in Europe.

3.1.2.2 Mainstream Economics

Positions on economics shared and accepted by a significant number of economists are called 'mainstream economics'.[15] Within mainstream economics opposing views on competition theories are categorised into schools of thought. They are defined as a set of ideas or opinions that a group of people share about a particular matter. Systematic economic schools of thought have been developing mainly since the beginning of what is termed the modern era. While some individuals often do not fit into particular schools of thought, especially in modern times, classifying economic insights into 'schools' is useful. The point is that different economists have diverse perspectives on various topics depending on the school of thought preferred and applied. This means that the same empirical facts can be interpreted in different ways. As we will see later, most economic schools of thought are easy to work with despite the schools of thought having evolved over time in a variety of directions. The main distinction between these economic schools of thought is the belief, which underpins the various schools. In this respect, ideology and historical evolutions are important features. Another distinction lies in the purpose a school of thought is used for.

3.1.2.3 Appropriate School of Thought?

This book deals with the European School of thought applied in EU competition law. The thinking is characterised by a clear reference to EU competition policy and the ideology shared by the people living in the EU. While US schools of thought as applied in US anti-trust policy are less suitable for Europe, a genuine European School is essential.

One of the most controversial issues between the European approach and US thinking relates to welfare economics. What is the appropriate surplus standard[16] that should be applied in the economic assessment within competition law: the consumer surplus standard or the total welfare standard? Whereas both jurisdictions claim that consumer welfare is their ultimate goal in any anti-trust enforcement, the underlying assumptions differ significantly. This irritates the legal community.

---

15. Mainstream economics today is often associated with neoclassical theories. Several economists in different places at about the same time (end of the nineteenth century) began to base value on the relationship between costs of production and 'subjective' elements.
16. Total welfare is the sum of consumer surplus and producer surplus. The consumer surplus is the amount that consumers benefit by; the difference between what consumers would be prepared to pay for goods and what they do pay. The producer surplus is the amount that producers benefit by selling goods above the cost of production (Jones und Sufrin 2010, 13). Some anti-trust authorities pursue a consumer surplus standard, while others pursue a total welfare standard.

Europe employs a much broader understanding of consumer welfare by combining the assessment of efficiency gains with other economic objectives like market integration and social fairness aspects. This is due to the ideology Europeans share. On the other hand, in the US, the consumer welfare approach is embedded in the general valuation of market interactions favouring a vastly competitive and producer focused market economy. These different interpretations on consumer welfare are embodied in competition law itself, as Chapter One revealed.

A few economists argue that the *socio-political goals as assigned to EU competition law* and policy could be achieved more economically through other means. For example, they convincingly debate that transferring wealth directly to a particular category of economic agents is less costly to society than interfering with competitive market forces. However, it depends on the applied market model. When the underlying market model is a social one then competition law is just a tool that makes markets work in a socially desirable manner. If the underlying market model favours a *laissez-faire* approach, then a direct transfer of wealth would be more appropriate. This might be the case in the US.

Another argument used against the broader policy objectives in EU competition law and policy is that the use of the law for political goals rests on assumptions that have no empirical support.[17]

This statement is not entirely accurate with respect to the economic concept of social market economies. The concept of a social market economy has existed for more than six decades now in Germany including competition law provisions that mirror EU competition law. The balancing of social and economic objectives within a social market system and particularly a fair distribution of wealth gains between producers and consumers made post-World War II Germany become one of the most important European and international economies. Thus, the integration of broader policy objectives in competition law is already a success story not lacking empirical evidence.

Lawyers mainly voice a further argument against a more holistic European approach. They argue that current competition theories do not provide a stable setting as required by law.

It is true that the nature of European competition economics has been undergoing significant changes in recent years. This does not mean that economic insights should be skipped. While lawyers might consider none of the competing theoretical frameworks as adequate, they still provide useful guidance.

Lawyers also argue that the level of detail required to guide them through the practical application in individual cases is missing. As shown in Chapter Four on competition practice, the available economic frame and tools are and can be applied properly in practice. On the other side, European competition economists have to admit that in the past they were not very successful in producing guidelines for lawyers enabling them to successfully apply competition theory in a European School tradition to real life cases. To that extent, economists have failed and the criticism raised by lawyers is justified.

---

17. Discussed in (Jenny 1994, 218).

One response to this is that the answers received from economists depend inevitably upon the questions posed by lawyers. If such questions beg generalised discussions, then these imprecise answers are the responsibility of the questioner. The ability to ask the 'right' questions to competition economists necessitates having a basic knowledge of competition theories.

This issue is stressed in this book too: lawyers can become better acquainted with economic thinking in the European tradition. Today's competition theory does provide a *frame* for economic analysis and in particular, a way of organising economic thinking on the sometimes very complex issues involved in EU competition law. Recent developments in the field offer the prospect of clearer and more concise operational analysis; moreover, advanced analytical methods are broadly available.[18]

Still, economists' answers have to focus on the facts presented as well as on the legal assessment as required by the law. Understanding how EU competition law works in practice or, in other words, knowing what the European Commission and courts applying EU competition law need, in order to assess the application of the competition rules, is obligatory for competition economists, while also bridging the gap between economics and law. Such an interdisciplinary approach is compulsory in any professional activity related to competition law. This books aims to respond to this need by addressing both groups of lawyers and economists.

3.2 ORIGINS OF MODERN COMPETITION THEORIES

The German word *Wettbewerb* is an equivalent term for *Konkurrenz* which has its source in the Latin word *concurrere*. The corresponding French word is *concurrence*. *Concurrere (lat.)* means to start with a fight, struggle or rivalry for supremacy (lat. *competitio*). The English word competition originates from this Latin word *competitio*.

'Competition' is usually used in the sense of rivalry in a race – a race to get limited supplies or a race to be rid of excess supplies. Each competitor pursues the same goal. Each competitor wants to pass the other one or as a minimum requirement to keep pace with the other competition. In a dynamic, ongoing environment, being a competitor at a relative standstill means being left behind by the other competitors. The sociological interpretation of 'competition' is the rivalry between two or more persons or groups for an object desired in common, usually resulting in a victor and a loser or losers but not necessarily involving the destruction of the latter. The natural phenomenon of 'competition' is integrated into our society: in sports, in culture, in politics and in the economy.

For our means competition can be understood to be a process of responding to a new force and a method of reaching a new equilibrium.[19]

In the US, competition policy is referred to as anti-trust policy.

---

18. Some examples of these analytical methods are the counterfactual method in cartel cases, merger simulation models in merger cases or the net additional cost test in state aid cases. These methods are elaborated upon in s. 4.6.5.
19. (G. J. Stigler 1986, 266).

3.2.1 Classical Theory

This competition concept was described for the first time in the classical school of thought. Classical theory developed in the late eighteenth century and reached its maturity in the middle of the nineteenth century. Important contributors[20] are *Adam Smith, David Ricardo, Thomas Robert Malthus* and *John Stuart Mill*. These economists shared a perspective on value theory and distribution theory. The value of a product depends on the costs involved in producing that product. The distribution of the output produced among the different social groups is in accordance with the costs borne by those groups in producing the output. Classical theory also states that the economy will be most successful when people are allowed to work at jobs that interest them, and businesses are allowed to compete without being controlled by the government.[21] During the reign of the classical economists, competition was recognised as crucial for a healthy economy.

The classical concept of competition is based on the *concept of freedom* and needs to be seen as part of what the society believes at that time. Freedom of competition and freedom of consumers to choose one of the alternatives offered by the market are considered to be natural freedoms of human beings. Competition in this classical interpretation is a *dynamic* process of action and reaction. Using the freedom of competition and thereby favouring individual interests enables every economic entity to get what it deserves.

Adam Smith[22], as one of the leading representatives, suggested that the forces of competition (the *'Invisible Hand'*) lead to a reconciliation of private, self-interested behaviour with general social aims. The 'Invisible Hand' generates harmony of all interests. State intervention could only disturb this harmony.[23] In this classical view, a competitive economy will automatically achieve efficiency without any need for government intervention. This *'Laissez-faire'* approach does not mean that the state has no function at all. The classical concept requires the state to provide an appropriate framework in order to facilitate the functioning of the markets. Law and order, the reduction of inflationary tendencies and the establishment of infrastructures are the essentials.

Stigler (1957) defines the five conditions for *Smith*'s concept of competition:[24]

- Rivals must act independently, not collusively.
- The number of rivals, potential as well as present, must be sufficient to eliminate extraordinary gains.
- The economic units must possess tolerable knowledge of market opportunities.
- There must be freedom (from social restraints) to act on this knowledge.

---

20. Adam Smith (1723–1790) and David Ricardo (1772–1823) developed and described for the first time the price mechanism.
21. (Cambridge University Press 2013).
22. (Smith 1776).
23. (I. Schmidt 2012, 3).
24. (G. Stigler 1957, 2).

– Sufficient time must elapse for resources to flow in the directions and quantities desired by their owners.

Many of the fundamental concepts and principles were set forth in Smith's *An Inquiry into the Nature and Causes of the Wealth of Nations* (1776). *Smith* strongly opposed the mercantilist[25] theory and policy that had prevailed in Britain since the sixteenth century. *Smith* argued that the entire community benefits most when each of its members follows his or her own self-interest. In a free enterprise system, individuals make a profit by producing goods that other people are willing to buy. By the same token, individuals spend money for goods that they want or need most. *Smith* demonstrated how the apparent chaos of competitive buying and selling is transmuted into an orderly system of economic cooperation that can meet individuals' needs and increase their wealth. He also observed that this cooperative system occurs through the process of individual choice as opposed to central direction. *Stigler* (1957) concluded that:

> Modern economists have a strong tendency to read more into such statements than *Smith* and his contemporaries meant. *Smith* did not state how he was led to these elements of a concept of competition. We may reasonably infer that the conditions of numerous rivals and of independence of action of these rivals were matters of direct observation.[26]

The reduction of monopolistic behaviour is another issue addressed by classical economists.

According to *Smith*, the narrowing of competition is always against the interest of the public, and only serves the dealers[27] because it enables them to raise their profits above what they naturally would be, and to levy for their own benefit, an absurd tax upon the rest of their fellow citizens.[28] In that context, one of *Smith's* famous quotes stated that:

> People of the same trade seldom meet together, even for merriment and diversion, but the conversation ends in a conspiracy against the public, or in some contrivance to raise *prices*. It is impossible indeed to prevent such meetings, by any law which either could be executed or would be consistent with liberty and justice.[29]

Smith, as the leading representative of the classical theory, argued powerfully in his works against monopolies. A monopolist or cartel has the power to affect the price by output decisions. Generally, price decreases with each successive unit of output. That means that the monopolist's marginal revenue[30] will always be less than the price paid by consumers. Consequently, the monopolist is not interested in selling more

---

25. Mercantilism is the idea that a country's government should try to influence trade and business, especially by encouraging exports and putting limits on imports (Cambridge University Press 2013).
26. (G. Stigler 1957, 2).
27. Smith used 'dealers' in his work, but it can be assumed that he referred to sellers in general.
28. (de Jong 1985, 38).
29. (Smith 1776, 54).
30. The marginal revenue is the amount of money a company can make by selling one more unit of something (Cambridge University Press 2013).

units at a cheaper price. The profit-maximising output will be below that which would predominate under competition, and at a higher price.[31] In *Smith's* view, *'the price of monopoly is upon every occasion the highest which can be got. The natural price, or the price of free competition, on the contrary, is the lowest, which can be taken, not upon every occasion indeed, but for any considerable time together.'*[32]

Smith contested permanent monopolies, because monopolies limit the 'natural' freedom of individuals and result in a considerable decrease in welfare. In contrast, he supported the idea of a temporarily limited monopoly, caused by the building up of trade relations with foreign countries. In his book he stated the following:

> When a company of merchants undertake, at their own risk and expense, to establish a new trade with some remote and barbarous nation, it may not be unreasonable to incorporate them into a joint stock company, and to grant them, in case of their success, a monopoly of the trade for a certain number of years. It is the easiest and most natural way in which the state can recompense them for hazarding a dangerous and expensive experiment, of which the public is afterwards to reap the benefit. A temporary monopoly of this kind may be vindicated upon the same principles upon which a like monopoly of a new machine is granted to its inventor, and that of a new book to its author.[33]

Smith's work was almost forgotten when neoclassical economics became the new mainstream.

3.2.2 Neoclassical Theory

Under the influence of the French economist *Antoine Augustin Cournot*, competition theory focused on a static price theory. In his book on *'Researches on the Mathematical Principles of the Theory of Wealth'* (1838) *Cournot* used for the first time mathematical formulas and introduced the ideas of functions and probabilities into economic analysis. He was the first one to describe supply and demand as a function of price. *Cournot* extensively used equilibrium models that described the end-version of markets. External factors were neglected, in particular the time factor. Since *Cournot* it became common to classify markets according to the number of sellers (or buyers) into the market forms polypoly, oligopoly, duopoly, and monopoly (polypsony, oligopsony, and monopsony).

Under the increasing influence of mathematics, *Alfred Marshall* established the crucial relationship between costs and income in his work *'Principles of Economics'* (1890).[34] As a result, the concept of competition has been progressively narrowed down until economists generally associate the term with a very particular type of industrial structure known as *'perfect competition'*. A perfectly competitive industry has several distinguishing characteristics, including: many firms, homogenous products, low-entry barriers and high information. The term perfect competition is also

---

31. (R. A. Posner 1976, 237).
32. (Smith 1776) in (Scherer 1993, 12).
33. (Smith 1776) in (Scherer 1993, 18).
34. (Marshall 1890).

Chapter 3: Competition Theory

used in neoclassical economics to describe a market in which no buyer or seller has market power. Thus, the markets are competitive. They are by nature allocative and productively efficient.[35]

Perfect competition forms the basis of a very important and widely used model of economic behaviour. Under the ideal model of perfect competition, where a large number of independent manufacturers of equal strength are supplying identical goods to customers all in possession of complete, or perfect market information, no one manufacturer has a sufficient market share to influence price by altering output. The assumption is that all firms are aiming to make maximum profit and that entry to the industry is unrestricted. In such an environment economic efficiency is automatically achieved.[36]

To support the understanding of these economic fundamentals, *Appendix A to this chapter* provides further elaborations. Figures 3.1–3.3 describe demand and supply curves.

3.2.2.1 Perfect Competition

The importance of this neoclassical competition concept derives from the fact that only if prices are treated by consumers and firms as parameters, is the standard maximum utility condition achieved. This means that the *marginal utility* of the last unit of money spent on each good must be the same. The standard maximum profit condition also requires that the firm must produce the quantity that renders the marginal cost equal to the product's price, and must employ the quantity of a factor that renders the factor's 'price' (i.e., rental) equal to the factor's marginal revenue product. These conditions allow the derivation of the demand and supply functions on which the neoclassical approach bases its determination of equilibrium prices as equating supply and demand without anybody consciously acting to such an end.

To sum up the illustrations in Appendix A: Economic efficiency is achieved if an economy produces the amount of each commodity indicated by the intersection of the demand curve and the marginal cost curve for that commodity. In a market economy, of course, where commodities are sold, rather than distributed freely, the sale of the optimal level of output requires that the price be set equal to the marginal cost of producing the optimal quantity (P for Price in Figure 3.5). This requirement for *price to equal marginal cost*[37] is an important one in the economic analysis of competition and monopoly and is still used today to simplify complex market interactions. It has to be recalled that this model of perfect competition uses unrealistic assumptions like perfect information. However, this simple model allows us to structure and orientate our thinking on the issues that matter.

A direct comparison of the Figures 3.6(a) and 3.3(b) in the Appendix reveals that under perfect competition, the result, which a market mechanism automatically produces, is the same as an 'efficient' result. This is a modern version of *Smith's*

---
35. (Knight 2002, 78–86).
36. (G. Stigler 1957, 1–17).
37. Marginal cost is defined as the costs required to produce one more unit of a good.

original 'Invisible Hand' proposition discussed above namely that self-interested behaviour on the part of individuals, when moderated by competition, provides a socially desirable result. Price equals automatically marginal cost of output for every firm in the industry, and the economically efficient level of output will be produced.[38]

Perfect competition will also guarantee another result, although only in the long-term. This is the elimination of any excess profits through the mechanism of perfectly free entry. If the established firms in the industry are making a return on capital, which is larger than in other industries, then new firms will be attracted in, and they face no hindrance. However, their entry will tend to push down the price and render the industry less profitable until the return on capital is just equal to that which can be earned elsewhere. The mechanism of entry, or even more simply the threat of entry, is an important aspect of the competitive process, not only in perfect competition, but also in more complex structures. The conditions under which entry can take place are frequently of interest to those concerned with framing and implementing competition law.

The economic theory outlined in the Appendix, is also called 'price-theory' because of the relations identified above. The theory explains the formal analytical reasons for regarding perfect competition as an optimal form of market structure producing ideal results. However, this 'static' price theory concept of nineteenth century competition with the basic assumptions of a hypothetical equilibrium, perfect competition and perfect information, a description of an end-state model represents – according to later findings – an unrealistic situation.[39] Nevertheless, these findings are still positively recognised by society, namely that a polypolistic market structure should be preferred over monopolies.[40] The neoclassical theory of perfect competition is not designed to describe specific real-world cases. It is just a theoretical model organising our thinking. The model itself is frequently used by competition authorities to explain real-world behaviour and to predict economic consequences of changes in the different variables contained in the model. Similarly, this also applies to the analytical model of monopoly.

3.2.2.2 *Monopoly*

'Pure' monopoly is defined as a situation where one company has complete control of the supply of a product or service.[41] So a monopoly situation occurs in an industry in which there is only one producer in a market, and there is no possibility of future entry. In that case, it can be shown quite simply that that industry's performance will be sub-optimal. While monopolists have no *direct* competitors that sell the same product, they do have *indirect* competition i.e., that a good substitute product is available to consumers.

---

38. (Agnew 1985, 26).
39. (Möschel 1983, 43).
40. (Emmerich 1991, 8).
41. (Cambridge University Press 2013).

Chapter 3: Competition Theory

Figure 3.7 in the Appendix features the demand curve and the marginal cost curve as well as competitive prices and monopoly prices. If the industry is in the hands of a single firm – a monopolist – then the supply curve for that firm represents the industry supply as a whole. *Posner* described this situation as follows:

> A monopolist is a seller (or a group of sellers acting like a single seller) who can change the price at which his product will sell in the market by changing the quantity that he sells. This 'power over price', the essence of the economic concept of monopoly, derives from the fact that the price that people are willing to pay for a product tends to rise as quantity of the product offered for sale falls. Some people will value the product more than other people do and will *therefore* bid more for it as the quantity available shrinks in order to make sure that they get it. The seller who controls the supply of a product can therefore raise its price by restricting the amount supplied.[42]

The monopolist will always charge a higher price than the competitive price (Pc in Figure 3.7) if demand at the competitive price is inelastic, that is, if the proportional reduction in the quantity demanded as a result of the higher price is less than the proportional increase in price.[43] In this situation, where price equals marginal cost (output Q_c at price P_c in Figure 3.7), the firm will make maximum profit by producing less, limiting output to the level where marginal cost equals the increase in revenue earned by producing one more unit (*marginal revenue*). The profit-maximising point is achieved at an output Q_m of price P_m as illustrated in Figure 3.7. The optimum monopoly price may be much higher than the competitive price, depending on the intensity of consumer preference for the monopolised product in relation to its costs.

The first charge levelled at monopoly, then, is that it leads to economic *inefficiency*. Price will be higher than marginal cost, and output is smaller under monopoly than under competition. The second charge is slightly different, but corresponds more closely to common sense complaints about monopoly behaviour. This is the charge that a firm in a monopoly position will have the freedom to allow its costs to rise above the minimum level necessary, without suffering any penalty. Economists were obliged to give this aspect of inefficiency a new name, having confusingly requisitioned the word 'efficiency' to mean 'economic efficiency' or 'price equal to marginal cost'. Thus such behaviour is most frequently described as 'managerial inefficiency' or '*X-inefficiency*'.[44]

Four social consequences, which may arise from a monopolist's conduct, are important:

(1) Monopoly pricing will yield a greater profit to the producer than he will gain under competition, thus transferring wealth in the economy. Transfer payments are of no importance in classical theory, total wealth being unaffected, but are of clear concern to governments operating consumer protection policies. Moreover, the ability to make monopoly profits may cause a firm

---
42. (R. A. Posner 1976, 8).
43. (R. A. Posner 1976, 9).
44. See (Agnew 1985, 28) and (Leibenstein 1966, 392–415).

under competition to seek dominance over production, wasteful advertising and excess product differentiation, all of which increase the costs of production.[45]

(2) In the absence of competition, poor quality service may be provided to customers, contract terms may be unduly oppressive and arrogant attitudes may be adopted towards compliance with contracts.

(3) The monopolist is under less pressure to control his costs and may thus slide into productive *in*efficiency. 'X-inefficiency' may penetrate a dominant firm.

(4) Inadequate research and development programmes may result: the aggregate costs of duplication under competition may be far outweighed by the lack of incentive to innovate under monopoly.

The *allocative inefficiency* arising from monopoly may, however, be offset in one or more of three ways. First, a monopolist will normally be able to take advantage of the economies of large-scale production. Thus, for example, bulk-buying of raw materials, specialised plant, the absence of duplication in research and development, the elimination of surplus capacity and cheaper distribution of goods may all serve to bring the costs below those which would prevail under competition, so that the *dead-weight loss* of monopoly may be eliminated. Secondly, misallocation theory can only predict the effect of monopoly in one industry. Indirect competition amongst the producers of substitutes may negate any misallocation effect. Thirdly, the monopolist has the crucial ability to adopt a policy of price discrimination, subsidising one class of customers by profits earned from others, thereby facilitating supply to persons who under competition would have been neglected.[46] Another main effect of reduced output under monopoly is that consumers who would have bought the monopolised product are forced to switch to substitutes (if available), scarce resources thus being diverted to a second best and costlier use. The same effect will result from a cartel.

The two market structures we have analysed so far – perfect competition and monopoly – are extremely useful tools for economic analysis, even though neither accurately depicts real-world situations. For instance, both models ignore the real-world conditions of a large number of firms selling slightly different products known as *monopolistic competition*; or a few firms that sell either identical or differentiated products referred to as *oligopoly*. A sharp distinction between these market structures cannot be made and is determined by the sellers' positions.

3.2.2.3 Imperfect Competition

A kind of revolution in neoclassical price theory took place at the beginning of the 1920s, which was initiated by *Piero Sraffa*[47] and later developed – at the same time but

---

45. (R. A. Posner 1976, 8–22).
46. (Merkin and Williams 1984, 2).
47. (Sraffa 1926, 535–550).

Chapter 3: Competition Theory

independent from each other – by *Edward Chamberlin*[48] and *Joan Robinson*[49]. One of their basic assumptions is that real competition is imperfect.

Perfect competition and perfect contestability are but ideals that real markets can rarely if ever attain. Actual markets deviate from these two benchmarks both in their structure and in the conduct of the firms that populate them.[50] Thus in economic theory, imperfect competition is the competitive situation in any market where the conditions necessary for perfect competition are not satisfied. *Monopolistic competition* and *oligopoly* are considered as imperfectly competitive market structures that result from a change in the assumptions underlying the theory of perfect competition as discussed above.

At first sight, the term monopolistic competition is a contradiction. However, it can be interpreted that although a tendency towards a monopoly exists, competition does take place. Monopolistic competition is characterised by a large number of buyers and sellers, easy entry and exit by producers, and market participants that have perfect information. It is seen as a result of product differentiation. When products are differentiated, non-price market strategies become an important competitive tool. Advertising and changes in product qualities are the two most central means by which a firm can increase market shares and profits. Gains from such strategies are short run under monopolistic competition. In the long run, a successful competitive move is generally matched by other competitors and profits return to normal.[51]

By differentiating between larger and smaller groups, *Chamberlin* introduced the problem of oligopoly to price theory. Because of interdependence, there is no complete theory of oligopoly.[52] Oligopolies are characterised by a few firms in a market. In contrast to perfect competition, barriers to entry exist. In addition, oligopoly sellers may offer differentiated products. Behaviour in oligopoly is determined by how well rivals recognise their interdependence with other oligopolists. Broadly speaking, an oligopolist can be cooperative or non-cooperative with rivals. The degree to which oligopolists do cooperate determines, to a large extent, market prices and output. Oligopoly can closely resemble conditions of perfect competition or monopolistic competition, if products are differentiated. An oligopoly can also approach a monopoly situation if cooperation is close among sellers. The most extreme form of cooperation is a *cartel*. In a cartel oligopolists explicitly agree or conspire on output, price, or both. In some cases, firms can be so well organised that behaviour is closely akin to a monopoly. However, cartels are fragile, because incentives to cheat are inherent within any cartel agreement. A 'cheater' can gain at the expense of other members if the cheating firm is not caught. Oligopoly requires more units of resources per unit of output than are absolutely necessary. Price is frequently higher than both average and marginal costs.[53]

---

48. (Chamberlin 1933).
49. (Robinson 1933).
50. (J. A. Ordover 1990, 7).
51. (Maurice, Phillips and Ferguson 1982, 484).
52. Perfect competition, monopoly and monopolistic or imperfect competition are the only three which can be clearly distinguished.
53. (Maurice, Phillips and Ferguson 1982, 485).

The analysis of *Sraffa, Chamberlin* and *Robinson* showed that an oligopoly market structure can lead to the same deficient economic performance as a monopoly situation. Their work on the so-called price theory revolution was significantly influential on the development of economic theory, since it describes a more realistic world. However, the influence of this work on competition law was rather limited, because it still used a static equilibrium model. The analysis referred to the start, transformation and end situations of markets and did not reflect the change and/or adaptation process, which does represent an essential part of dynamic and uncertain competition. It is interesting to note that some of the arguments on imperfect competition were transposed to the Ordoliberal School of thought[54] (*Eucken, Böhm*) at least verbally.[55]

3.3 DEVELOPMENTS IN MODERN COMPETITION THEORIES

3.3.1 Workable Competition

3.3.1.1 John Maurice Clark (1940)

In contrast to other economists, *John Maurice Clark* focused mainly on the effects of competition thereby initiating discussions, which are still ongoing. In his work '*Towards a Concept of Workable Competition*' (1940) *Clark* criticised and questioned the model of perfect competition.[56] The concept he developed is seen as an attempt to go 'beyond' perfect competition. The assumptions in the perfect competition concept were thought to be overly rigorous. The formal criteria were too exacting in the real life circumstances (e.g., perfect knowledge) and there were many instances known to practical investigators where, when all relevant factors were considered, no action of public policy was likely to improve performance even in a highly concentrated industry.[57]

Clark's article, in which he coined the term *workable competition*, was a pioneering effort to identify the factors that led to 'the closest available working approximation to (the standard of pure and perfect competition) under actual conditions.'[58] *Clark* was most concerned with short run problems stemming from a high ratio of fixed to variable costs coupled with instability and unpredictable fluctuations in demand. Under such conditions, unregulated price competition can be destructive throughout an industry. If perfect competition is not achievable in many sectors of industry, the one possible response is to attempt to identify 'workable competition'.

---

54. The Ordoliberal School of thought which is the academic cradle of EU competition law is analysed in a later section.
55. (Möschel 1983, 44).
56. (J. M. Clark 1940, 241).
57. (Markham 1950, 349–361).
58. (J. M. Clark 1940, 241).

Workable competition, *Clark* contended, would have to be something intermediate between pure oligopoly and the ruinously low prices likely to result from unlimited market chaos.[59]

This concept of workable competition is seen as the attempt to develop conditions for forms of competition, which are economically desirable. The approach is a *normative* one i.e., that norms are used to judge whether certain economic circumstances are positive or negative. Depending on the result, instruments of competition policy are used to adapt the competition process. According to *Clark*, workable competition is defined as 'the most desirable form of competition, selected from those that are practically possible, within the limits set by conditions which we cannot escape.'[60]

In *Clark's* view, many of the departures from purely competitive structure and conduct that make short run competition workable are consistent with long run performance approximating the efficient resource allocation of the competitive model. Potential competition and the competition of substitutes play important roles in monopolistic competition. Both of these factors tend to increase the elasticity of the demand curve facing the firm, particularly in the long run. Many large firms take a long run viewpoint, recognising the threats of potential competition and substitute products and, hence, refrain from restrictive practices that would increase short run profits.[61]

Another of *Clark's* insights is that competition can be viewed as workable when both buyers and sellers have access to a substantial number of alternatives and are able to reject those found to be relatively unsatisfactory.[62]

'Workable competition' though rarely discussed in the context of formal theory, has had a pervasive influence on the literature of industrial economics.[63] Most attempts by successive writers to define workable competition further are tautological – defining workable competition as that which gives the best available result. Those attempts to identify workability usually consist of long lists of structural and behavioural 'norms' that an industry should achieve before being deemed workably competitive. As many of the norms amount to approximations to perfect competition, it is difficult to see for some commentators what has been gained through the search for workability.[64]

In his earlier work, *Clark* also discussed possible solutions with respect to the concept of perfect competition. *Clark* wrote:

> If there are, for example, five conditions, all of which are essential to perfect competition, and the first is lacking in a given case, then it no longer follows that we are necessarily better off for the presence of any one of the other four. In the absence of the first, it is *a priori* quite possible that the second and third may become positive detriments; and a workable satisfactory result may depend on achieving some degree of 'imperfection' in these other two factors.

---

59. (J. M. Clark 1940, 253).
60. (J. M. Clark 1940, 242).
61. (J. M. Clark 1940).
62. (Edwards 1949, 9).
63. (Auerbach 1988, 20).
64. (Agnew 1985, 34).

> Suppose the first requisite is perfect two-way mobility of the factors of production, with no specialised and irrecoverable fixed capital. Granted this, an industry can stand the most rigorous competition in all other respects.... Take away the saving grace of perfect two-way mobility and leave the other conditions; let demand decline, and competition becomes too strong: you have a 'sick industry' on your hands. Reduce the number of producers and let them sell on quoted prices and anticipate one another's reactions and you have a form of 'oligopoly.'[65]

It is neither intuitively obvious nor demonstrable from the perfect competitive model whether the 'sick industry' or the 'oligopoly' *Clark* mentioned is preferable from a welfare standpoint.

With his theory of *'second best'* *Clark* addressed this issue within a general equilibrium framework. If anywhere in the economy one of the optimality conditions of the perfect competitive model is missing, the next- or second best situation probably is not one in which the rest of these conditions hold. The general theorem for the second best optimum states that:

> if there is introduced into a general equilibrium system a constraint which prevents the attainment of one of the Paretian conditions[66], the other Paretian conditions, although still attainable, are, in general, no longer desirable. In other words, given that one of the Paretian optimum conditions cannot be fulfilled, then an optimum situation can only be achieved by departing from all the other Paretian conditions.[67]

Clark contributed to this discussion with the proposal that if a market contains a few imperfections it is possible by implementing additional imperfect conditioning factors to reactivate competitive activities by, for example, the reduction of market transparency. Given that imperfect forms of competition are the most effective in the absence of the ideal perfect competition scenario, the addition of imperfect conditions represents the least undesirable form of uncertainty. This approach is called 'remedial imperfections' (*German*: Gegengiftthese).[68]

To conclude: In Clark's concept, welfare may increase by the addition of imperfect conditions to an imperfect market situation.[69] According to Clark, this could mean that concentrations are less critical than perfect competition.[70]

3.3.1.2 Erhard Kantzenbach

Clark's dynamic theory of workable competition found adherence among some European economists, of whom the most prominent one is *Erhard Kantzenbach* with

---

65. (J. M. Clark 1940, 242).
66. 'Pareto efficiency', or 'Pareto optimality', is defined as a situation of allocation of resources in which it is impossible to make any one individual better off without making at least one individual worse off.
67. (Lipsey and Lancaster 1956, 11).
68. (J. M. Clark 1940, 249).
69. (I. Schmidt 2012, 10).
70. (Krimphove 1992, 24).

his work on *'Konzept des Funktionsfähigen Wettbewerbs'*.[71] His view on competition provoked an extensive and influential debate within Germany.

Rejecting static equilibrium theory, *Kantzenbach* described competition as an evolutionary and disequilibrium process, in which rivalry wins. In his view, competition rivalry is only an instrument to achieve social welfare goals, of which three are outstanding: the growth of the social product, the optimal product differentiation and market transparency. Competition, as an instrumental concept, is therefore seen as a means to an end, in accordance to *Clark's* concept, and intends to achieve five economic goals. These functions of competition consist of:[72]

(1) A functional distribution of income on the basis of market results.
(2) An adjustment of supply and demand.
(3) An efficient allocation of the factors of production.
(4) A flexible adjustment of production capacity to extra-economic factors.
(5) A continuing technological progress in products and production methods.

In *Kantzenbach's* view, competition policy's task is to counter situations and tendencies in which the intensity of competition potentially is either sub-optimal (e.g., promotion of concentration, the raising of scale of operations and an increase in product differentiation or particular cartel types) or over optimal (some splitting up of trusts, the prevention of some mergers, or the prevention of oligopolistic price wars in order to avoid the formation of uncontrolled monopolies). Essentially, in *Kantzenbach's* view, polypolistic competition lacks dynamic progress, while tight oligopoly ensures an optimal intensity of competition.[73]

An oligopoly represents the dependency of a particular seller on the behaviour of an individual competitor, who may threaten his existence. This situation creates a high degree of insecurity, which is at a maximum in a homogeneous duopoly situation and very low in polypolistic markets. This insecurity depends on the divergence of cost functions, relative liquidity reserves of the companies concerned and short-term demand shifts in the market, which are all difficult to identify. The assumption is that both owner controlled and management controlled firms strive for long-term security. Potential and effective intensity of competition diverges as the number of competing oligopolists decreases and the more homogeneous the products sold become. For *Kantzenbach*, the distinction between potential and effective intensity of competition is the decisive issue.[74]

Kantzenbach stated that 'potential competition intensity rises when less and less sellers of homogeneous goods threaten to wipe out one of them by means of unforeseen actions. The same facts induce restraints on competition though, because nobody wants to be wiped out.'[75] In *Kantzenbach's* view, oligopolistic interdependency is not

---

71. See also (Kantzenbach and Kalfass 1981, 103).
72. (Vedder 2003, 33).
73. (Möschel 1983, 45).
74. (de Jong and Shepherd 2007, 43).
75. (de Jong and Shepherd 2007, 44).

restricted to horizontal relations between firms, but also relate to vertical liaisons. This includes engaging in long-term delivery agreements, vertical mergers and takeovers, and, as in horizontal coordination, common capital participations and interlocking directorates defined as board members of one company serving board positions in multiple corporations.[76]

The strongest arguments against the concept of workable competition came from *Hayek* and *Hoppmann*.[77] In addition, in the US, legal scientists in particular, questioned the concept of workable competition. A study by *Dirlam* and *Kahn* in 1954 concluded that a radically imperfect market structure would sooner or later produce a defective performance and that economic sciences did not deliver useful criteria concerning the elements of market structure, results, and performance. They concluded that the use of the concept of workable competition in competition law would lead to a softening and a replacement of earlier unambiguous norms.[78]

As a result of these debates further concepts of competition have been developed. Moreover the level of uncertainty has increased over whether state interventions in a competition process are necessary at all.[79]

3.3.2 Effective Competition

3.3.2.1 John Maurice Clark (1961)

Clark, who based his assumptions in earlier works on a static model, recognised in later works that the use of static models was inadequate. He criticised himself and rejected in his more recent work on '*Competition as a Dynamic Process*' (1961) the static concept of perfect competition, which concentrates on the creation and conservation of a desirable idealistic market structure.

Clark in his more recent work, views competition as a dynamic process. He started to focus on the steering of the continuously changing and developing conduct of all market participants.[80] A dynamic process is, according to *Clark*, the result of moves and responses. He states that 'these moves and responses may influence production, products or prices, and their various combinations.'[81] The activities of pioneering companies and the quick response of so-called imitating followers or other innovating companies are the essentials. The time factor is crucial for providing incentives for firms to initiate competitive moves, giving them an advantage, albeit a temporary one, over the competitors. Under the condition that the process stays free, the circle will never end. In *Clark's* view, stronger market positions are allowed for a limited period of time as long as market entry is always possible.[82]

---

76. (de Jong and Shepherd 2007, 44).
77. (Emmerich 1991, 12).
78. (Uitermark 1990, 161).
79. (Emmerich 1991, 12).
80. (Cox, Jens and Markert 1981, 14).
81. (J. M. Clark 1955, 457).
82. (J. M. Clark 1962).

Effective competition makes the market system perform well and prevents firms from raising their prices much above their costs. Monopoly power does the reverse; it usually impairs that performance. When the monopolist raises its price above costs the buyers have no alternative to turn to, and so the monopolists' sales go down only moderately. A competitive firm, by contrast, has little choice or control, because its customers do have a wide range of choice and can turn to other suppliers. To be 'effective' the continuing competition process has to be open and free.[83]

In his more recent work, *Clark* also steered away from his theory of 'second best', which represented in 1940 workable competition for him. His new reasoning was that market imperfections are necessary requirements for technical progress. *Clark* tried to concentrate on the dynamic process oriented element thereby integrating the *Schumpeterian* theory of innovation in his 'concept of effective competition'.[84]

3.3.2.2 Joseph A. Schumpeter

Joseph A. Schumpeter described in his famous work *'Capitalism, Socialism and Democracy'*[85] competition as a dynamic process of creative destruction. He argued that technical progress and the economic growth it caused are far more important than static efficiency in resource use. *Schumpeter* wrote:

> system - *any* system, economic or other - that at every given point of time fully utilises its possibilities to the best advantage may yet in the long run be inferior to a system that does so at no given point of time, because the latter's failure to do so may be a condition for the level or speed of long-run performance.[86]

Schumpeter views competition as an ongoing process, rather than a sequence that reaches a terminus. Interactions occur in a variety of structures and reward patterns, which can change. Because technology and demand are not rigid, they too can change as events progress.[87] *Schumpeter* is quite contemptuous of what he calls the glorified ideal of a perfectly competitive economy, which in reality never exists.[88]

Schumpeter's thoughts concerning competition focussed on competition caused by innovations. Innovation means for the entrepreneur a limited time lead against the competition. This monopoly situation allows him to make profit for a limited time. Followers and imitators arise and the profit level turns down. The accumulated profit till this point is enough to pay back the risk and the invested capital. Competition is only 'temporarily suspended'. In *Schumpeter's*[89] scheme of things, this is part of the process of 'creative destruction', which marks the downswing of the business cycle.[90]

---

83. (J. M. Clark 1962).
84. (I. Schmidt 2012, 10) and (Kantzenbach and Kalfass 1981, 120).
85. (Schumpeter 1942).
86. (Schumpeter 1942, 83).
87. (Shepherd 1986, 26).
88. (Schumpeter 1942, 81).
89. (Schumpeter 1942, 81–86).
90. (Haberler 1986, 83).

However, what is more important in *Schumpeter's* view is that profit stimulates other entrepreneurs in the future to take risks and invest capital. Although in the beginning there is a reduction in welfare, ultimately the advantage for society is more welfare since society got better and (or) cheaper products. Discrepancies like product differentiation and non-transparency of the market in the model of perfect competition are necessary for the functioning of the competition process.[91]

Based on *Schumpeter's* theory that prices set by innovation monopolies are higher for a limited period of time and therefore cause a negative impact on the welfare, stimulates innovation monopolies to introduce new and better products. In later works, *Schumpeter* recognises that large entities are in a better position to organise expensive and complex innovation processes. Because of their market power, they are in a better position to protect their innovations against imitation competition. *Schumpeter* stated that technological progress will be faster under monopoly than under competition because, among other things, of the difficulty for competitive firms to secure outside financing for risky R&D investments. In *Schumpeter's* words, 'what we have to accept is that [the large-scale establishment or unit of control] has come to be the most powerful engine of (economic) progress'.[92]

Shepherd concludes that 'the Schumpeterian version of competition is almost the exact reverse, point by point, of the neo-classical equilibrium analysis.'[93]

Competition theory defined at that time certain conditions where effective competition occurs in economic markets:

- Buyers have access to alternative sellers for the products they desire (or for reasonable substitutes) at prices they are willing to pay.
- Sellers have access to buyers for their products without undue hindrance or restraint from other firms, interest groups, government agencies, or existing laws or regulations.
- The market price of a product is determined by the interaction of consumers and firms. No single consumer or firm (or group of consumers or firms) can determine, or unduly influence, the level of the price.
- Differences in prices charged by different firms (and paid by different consumers) reflect only differences in cost or product quality/attributes.

In *effective* competitive markets, consumers are protected to some degree from exploitative prices that firms, acting unilaterally or as a collusive bloc, could charge. Likewise, firms are protected from manipulation by large individual consumers (or groups of consumers) and from disruption or interference from other firms.

Competition occurs on the basis of both price and the quality or features of the product. Products are often differentiated, that is they are not identical across firms. One form of a product is usually a reasonable substitute for another form of that product. This is often referred to as 'functional equivalence'. Sellers may also offer

---

91. (Schumpeter 1942).
92. (Jenny 1994, 205).
93. (Shepherd 1985, 57).

product combinations or bundles that appeal to specific consumers or consumer segments. Effective competition can occur even in markets with relatively few firms that differ substantially in size, market share, and *tenure*. However, for such markets to be competitive, it is important that there are *no barriers* to entry and exit. Various models show how these barriers affect the behaviour of firms and the overall performance of the industry and any artificial barrier to competition may reduce the efficient allocation of resources.[94]

3.3.3 Harvard School of Thought

Since the 'workability' concept as discussed in the previous section is a normative one, the structural elements of the different industries become important. The discussion initiated by *Clark* led to a wave of publications that are condensed under the name the *'Harvard School'*.

The emphasis of the Harvard School of thought is on markets. Attributes prominent in the Harvard School are market structure, market conduct or behaviour, and market result or performance. The circular combination of these three elements is called the structure-conduct-performance paradigm (SCP paradigm).

3.3.3.1 Edward S. Mason

Edward S. Mason was the first author who discussed the merits of the structure-conduct-performance approach. This approach aims to turn away from price theory and attempts to examine the facts of industries' operation in order to identify those factors which lead companies to behave in acceptable ways, and those which lead to satisfactory performance.[95] The structure-conduct-performance paradigm or SCP-paradigm is widely accepted and a leading research topic of *Industrial Organisation (IO)*.[96] It stems from various concepts of interactions between industry or market structure, business conduct and the social and economic performance of an industry. The thesis is that the structure of a market structure influences to some degree the behaviour and performance of firms. Conversely, each firm's performance can influence to some degree its future market position.[97]

Mason, based in Harvard, assumed that market structure exerts a major influence on business conduct.[98] 'The structure of a seller's market, then,' he wrote, 'includes all those considerations which he takes into account in determining his business policies and practices. His market includes all buyers and sellers, of whatever product, whose

---

94. (Lutz, Kemp and Dijkstra 2010, 21).
95. (Agnew 1985, 35).
96. For example, in (Bain 1968).
97. (Shepherd 1986, 23).
98. (Baldwin 1987, 108).

action he considers to influence his volume of sales.'[99] *Mason* went on to describe the structural conditions that would be likely to have the greatest impact on conduct. These included:

- The product's economic characteristics, such as whether it is a consumer or producer good, durable or non-durable, and differentiated or standardised.
- The firm's cost and production conditions, including ratios of fixed to variable costs at various levels of output.
- The numbers and relative sizes of buyers and sellers whose actions the firm has to take into account and the ease of entry for new firms.
- Demand conditions including sales trends, seasonal or cyclical fluctuations around these trends, and buyers' knowledge of the product's characteristics.
- The nature of the distribution channels.

The fundamental causal relationship between structure and conduct is inherent in the framework of microeconomic theory, as illustrated by the following propositions:

(1) Firms will be able to set price (a form of conduct) only if their products are sold in the structural setting of a less than purely competitive market. Otherwise, all they can do is decide how much they wish to sell at the price determined by the impersonal market forces of supply and demand.
(2) Successful collusion depends on structural characteristics; the two most important are the number of possible conspirators and the ease with which newcomers can enter the market.
(3) Price discrimination requires at least two sets of customers with different demand elasticities, so that the profit-maximising prices charged to each set will differ. In addition, there must be some barrier to prevent those paying the lower price from reselling to customers charged the higher price.
(4) The nature of the product and its users will determine whether false or misleading advertising is likely to be a profitable form of conduct.
(5) The higher the target firm's fixed costs relative to its variable costs, the more effective a tactic of predatory pricing is.
(6) The degree of competition in and the ease of entry into the market for a potential new product are important considerations in a firm's R&D planning.

To sum up, the relationships among structure, conduct, and performance that appear in the real-world markets are complex and interactive, as presented by the figure below.

---

99. (Mason 1939, 69).

Chapter 3: Competition Theory

Figure 3.1   Structure-Conduct-Performance Paradigm (SCP-Paradigm)

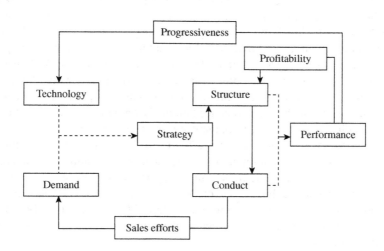

Structure and conduct are partly influenced by underlying demand conditions and technology. In Figure 3.1, structure affects conduct on the one hand but on the other hand conduct as strategic behaviour also affects structure. Structure and conduct interact to determine performance. Sales efforts, being a part of conduct, also feedback and affect demand. Performance, in turn, has its feedback on technology and structure. Progressiveness (referring to the rate of technological progress) influences the available technology. Profitability, which determines the attractiveness of entering the market, has a dynamic (intertemporal) effect on market structure.[100]

The evaluation of performance is able to ascertain whether governmental interference in private markets is justified and, if so, what the probable effects of various policy actions might be. Performance is a multidimensional concept. In his initial discussion, *Mason* identified two aspects: the allocation of resources among different users and the stability of production at full employment levels. Today, many economists would add equitable distribution of income to this list of performance criteria. In the traditional Harvard view, a precise and value-free standard of equity (or equality) in income distribution cannot be formulated. *Mason* suggested in an article '*Monopoly in Law and Economics*'[101], that:

> it is not ... sufficient to conduct purely analytical and descriptive studies of various types of control situation ... A further study of different types of industrial markets and business practices and of the effects on prices, outputs, investment and employment designed to indicate means *of* distinguishing between socially desirable and undesirable ... is the only way in which economics can contribute directly to the shaping of public policy.

---

100. (Martin 1994, 7–8).
101. (Mason 1937, 25–471).

He stated further that 'with respect to the monopoly problem it is not altogether clear whether the work of economists should be oriented toward the formulation of public policy or toward analysis of market situations; the trend however is towards the latter.' In *Mason's* opinion, if this trend continued, the gap between legal and economic reasoning would widen. In his mind the subject that matters in economic analysis and competition law are 'restrictions of trade' and 'control of the market'. However, restraints of trade may occur separately from anything the courts would be willing to call control of markets. On the other hand, from the economic point of view control of the market may occur without any practice that the law would call restraint of trade.[102]

At this point, it becomes clear that lawyers and economist use economic terms in distinctly different ways. For lawyers the term monopoly is used as a standard of evaluation, designating a situation not in the public interest. Competition, in comparison, designates situations in the public interest. For the lawyer, monopoly means a restriction of the freedom of business to engage in legitimate economic activities. From the legal point of view, monopoly is the counterpart of free competition, but the latter is often quite compatible with the presence of monopoly elements in the economic sense of the word monopoly.

To an economist trained in the Harvard School tradition the correct comparison is between monopoly and pure competition and differs in the ways in which market transactions occur and resources are allocated under the two. A monopolist (or oligopolist) is able to influence the market price. Consequently, a firm's output decisions are made keeping in mind the potential effect on price. A (pure) competitor, on the other hand, cannot influence the market price, and as a result seeks to maximise profits by producing until marginal costs equal price. A firm with monopoly power will produce at a lower output level and charge a higher price than an identical firm in a competitive market. Clearly, forcing a monopolist to act like a competitive firm could increase total surplus. Moreover, issues like social justice and equity (or equality) may also be relevant. Yet, whether such coercion could or should be adopted was the difficult question at that time.[103]

Mason stated that monopolistic elements are practically omnipresent and concluded that the economic analysis of monopolistic situations lost their value in anti-trust policy and law. In the legal context, this may lead to a conflict situation, because of the impossibility of distinguishing injury to a competitor and the nature of the injury to the public. *Mason* stated further that anti-trust law was not sufficiently developed and required renewal. For *Mason* it was clear that the preservation of all competitive elements and the suppression of monopolistic power would be in the public interest.[104]

---

102. (Mason 1937, 34).
103. (Hirsch 1988, 9).
104. (Mason 1937, 49).

3.3.3.2 Industrial Organisation Theory

Since *Mason's* pioneering work, the concept of business conduct has been expanded to include areas other than determination of price and output. Industry structure has been studied to explain the forces either stimulating or retarding research and development (R&D) efforts, advertising, merger and acquisition activities, and product diversification. Whereas *Mason's* basic insight is fundamental to the SCP-paradigm, *'Industrial Organisation'* is the overall name given to discussions and research on this topic.[105]

Industrial Organisation is a field of economics that studies the strategic behaviour of firms, the structure of markets and their interactions. The study of Industrial Organisation adds to the perfectly competitive model *real-world frictions* such as limited-information, transaction costs and cost of adjusting prices, government actions, and barriers to entry by new firms into a market. Industrial Organisation then considers how firms are organised and how they compete.

Research results in Industrial Organisation influenced economic policy, especially competition or anti-trust policy. The theory of Industrial Organisation became a specific economic playing field. In the past, traditional Industrial Organisation was attacked as being too empirical or case study oriented. However during the late 1970s, potential shortcomings of this approach were made explicit and model based time series analyses were promoted as the solution to the problem of empirical research. In more recent years Industrial Organisation was supplemented by sophisticated game theoretical models. During the 1980s Industrial Organisation accepted that the decision-makers in firms began with optimisation problems. The theory then took the lead in promoting the concept that in a world of just a few firms, strategic behaviour and actions are very important. Firms optimise their behaviour within an environment in which other firms are, at the same time, practising the same way. Decisions within the Industrial Organisation concept were modelled as non-cooperative games. At the same time economists have tried to drive forward the attempts to integrate the phenomenon of market power into their market models. Although to a degree Industrial Organisation can claim respectable theoretical origins, the subject matter does not rest firmly on a broad theory. Empirical work was frequently undertaken to pursue in measurable terms relationships thought to be important.

In Industrial Organisation, market structures are seen as complex and evolving, and the influences exerted by structure are seen as tendencies, not laws. Market imperfections are recognised to be significant in many cases, and strategic techniques of exploiting market power are explored. Technological progress is regarded as important, as *Schumpeter* has stressed, and is probably more important than static efficiency. Free entry could be powerful, and some dominant firms had justly earned their positions by displaying superior performance in the past. According to Industrial Organisation insights, a competitive market structure has the performance outcome of lower costs and lower prices. Pure competition is seen merely as a set of theoretical conditions, not as a practical goal for policy in any real industries.[106] Dominance is an

---
105. (Shepherd 1985, 1).
106. (Shepherd 1991, 11).

important problem, usually causing social costs, and *market share* is seen as the unifying basis for evaluating market power, pricing behaviour and restrictive actions.[107] Shepherd, as one of the leading representatives in the industrial organisation field, described a basic concept of competition in the following brief form:[108]

(1) In every market, firms try to attain and exploit large market shares, as they attempt to maximise their profits.
(2) When these firms' strivings hold each other in check, no firm is able to capture a large market share. The result is a healthy process of competition, which holds down prices, forces firms to be efficient, and stimulates innovation.
(3) But if one or several firms do attain high market shares, they can usually get extra profits by setting prices above costs and restricting output. Their monopoly power can impose social losses by causing inefficiency, a retarding of innovation, and unfair shifts in income and wealth.
(4) These costs of monopoly may possibly be offset, in part or whole, by benefits from scale economics or an increase in innovation.

There is, however, one feature of structure, the numbers and relative sizes of buyers and sellers, that is amenable to numerical measurement and for which substantial data is available. The use of concentration indices as explanatory variables in studies comparing the performance of various industries was encouraged and given greatly enhanced statistical legitimacy by a 1955 study in which *Widen Rosenbluth* reported that the most widely used concentration indices and bases were highly consistent with one another.[109]

Concentration, however measured, is one aspect of structure. However, in the theory of oligopoly, concentration is crucial, since control of a large share of an industry's market by a small number of firms is necessary though not sufficient to sustain prices above costs and restrict output. Other important attributes of structure, such as barriers to entry, degree of product differentiation, and economies of scale are commonly associated with concentration as well, so that a concentration index can often serve as a proxy for a set of structural conditions conducive to or limiting exercise of market power.

A number of economists have emphasised industrial concentration as the primary determinant of economic performance. Their broadly shared conclusions, especially those pertaining to the relationship between concentration and profits, have been called the *'concentration doctrine'*. The concentration doctrine is a variant of the structuralist position. *Concentration is regarded as clear and convincing evidence of the existence of market power* and adherents contend that economic performance will be improved (those espousing various versions of the doctrine emphasise different aspects of performance) by reducing concentration in most industries in which it

---
107. (Shepherd 1985, 53).
108. (Shepherd 1985, 2).
109. (Rosenbluth 1955, 69).

exceeds some predetermined standard. The doctrine, as stated here in its simplest and most general form, is predicated on the assumption that in a majority of industries, or at least in enough to justify sweeping public action, existing levels of concentration are not the result of real economies of scale or the technological pre-eminence of large firms achieved through their own innovative efforts.[110] One criticism of the concentration doctrine is that its adherents link concentration too directly to market power, sometimes even indiscriminately equating the two.

Joe S. Bain advocated a pragmatic justification for the structuralist approach in his book *'Industrial Organisation'*[111]. Business conduct can take numerous, very different forms, within which various tactics are possible. Particular levels of industry price and output might, for example, be established by any one of several forms of overt collusion. Such collusion might involve either the price level or the rate of production. It could also include various tactics such as conspiratorial meetings, agreed-upon signals, regular exchange of statistical data, or communication through an intermediary such as a trade association or interlocking memberships on boards of directors. If one type of collusion was suppressed, firms might find it easy to adopt another. Further, in many if not most structural situations, different forms of conduct might lead to almost exactly the same results for price and output. Even if all possible collusive tactics could be eliminated, perhaps much the same outcome would be obtained through price leadership, actual or threatened predatory pricing, or merger of troublesome independent small firms with larger ones. Only the collective ingenuity of the nation's business people limits the nature and types of business conduct. The conclusion is that many different types of conduct will yield virtually identical levels of price and output and, therefore, economic performance as long as the structural setting remains unchanged.

Thus, an investigator may find it impossible to identify the conduct actually practised in an industry. Firms engaged in illegal or unethical conduct will try to hide it. In addition, honest and ethical firms may have legitimate competitive reasons for not wanting rivals to know their tactics. Both diversity and obscurity of conduct, *Bain* argued, lead to a situation in which we find that actual patterns of market conduct cannot be fully enough measured to permit us to establish empirically a meaningful association either between market conduct and performance, or between structure and market conduct.[112]

Bain also identified and quantified 'barriers to entry' into non-competitive industries by measuring factors such as initial capital requirements, the threat of price-cutting by established firms, and product differentiation. He found that industry profitability (a measure of performance) was positively and significantly correlated with two indices of industry structure: (1) the seller concentration ratio and (2) a subjectively estimated categorisation of the height of barriers to new entry.[113]

---

110. (Baldwin 1987, 306).
111. (Bain 1968).
112. (Bain 1968, 344–345).
113. (Scherer 1986, 6).

Bains' findings are interpreted by Chicago School representatives (discussed in the following section) in a way that shows there are no indications that concentration is the reason for oligopolistic restraints on competition. They see it the other way around namely, that competition led to the success of the most cost efficient firms on the market and afterwards to concentration.

Harvard School representatives have to admit that this theory represents an argument against their favoured oligopoly thesis. Nevertheless, Harvard scholars counter that besides large-scale cost efficiency, individual market power also influences the profits of large firms. The reasoning lies in the fact that extensive financial resources enable large firms to improve their products continuously and to increase the attractiveness of their products by massive promotional efforts.[114]

Nevertheless *Bains'* results were enthusiastically received, in part because they reached an economic profession eager to utilise 'new' econometric tools and because the ideological climate of the time (1960s) favoured public intervention to nullify the price-raising effects of monopoly and oligopoly. The ultimate goal for the advocates of the Harvard School was to identify in their mainly empirical work restraints to competition and develop intervention criteria for US anti-trust policy.[115] 'The "Harvard School" requires - in order to make their whole concept work - state intervention'.[116] The anti-trust policy implications of this approach are broad prohibitions or strict scrutiny of all arrangements and practices, including vertical practices and conglomerate mergers. Partially because of this temporary convergence between economic thinking and political philosophy, US anti-trust activity reached new heights of expansion in the late 1950s, 1960s and early 1970s. One of the commentators on EU competition law even compares the economic analysis as applied by the European Commission with the Harvard School of anti-trust in the mid-twentieth century, which had its heyday in the Warren Court of the 1960s.[117]

Many studies in the basic *Bain* tradition have been carried out, most – but not all – indicating that industry profits, variously measured, rise with industry concentration, variously defined. The focus of this work on *concentration ratios* was partly artificial, reflecting the sheer abundant availability of those ratios. On the positive side, it could be noted that many (though by no means all) of the studies have confirmed the existence of a positive relationship between the level of concentration and the level of profits, thereby suggesting to some writers, that concentration confers monopoly power which in turn allows higher profits to be earned and which therefore justifies government regulation of highly concentrated industries. However, there are a number of reasons why such a conclusion cannot be held with any great confidence:[118]

(1) In the first place, there are problems with the statistical method, which makes it difficult to measure the various different concepts used showing the extent

---

114. Daimler-Benz cars represent a good example of both effects.
115. (E. J. Mestmäcker 1994, 289–302).
116. (I. Schmidt 2012, 24).
117. (Hawk 1990, 7).
118. (Agnew 1985, 35).

Chapter 3: Competition Theory

of the links between them. Most of the central concepts – concentration, entry barriers, and product differentiation – are difficult to measure and have to be approximated rather unsatisfactorily by the use of 'proxies'. As a result, the findings are sensitive to the samples chosen and the sources of data, so that very similar studies might produce contrasting, even diametrically opposite, results.

(2) Secondly, there are problems with the misspecification of relationships between the variables. In the simple standard approach to structure-performance investigations, it is usually taken for granted that the direction of causation runs from industry structure to industry performance. However, even within a simple model such as perfect competition it is clear that performance can have an impact on structure. If the relationships between structure and performance work in both directions then the results of simple statistical techniques tell us very little about the industry's workings. More complex models are required.[119]

(3) The third problem is even more fundamental because it concerns the interpretation of the results and the use to which they are put. If we accept, for the sake of argument, that the evidence shows a factual link between profitability and high levels of concentration, the most common interpretation placed on that fact is that a high level of concentration gives monopoly power to firms. This in turn allows them to make monopoly profits that reflect a misallocation of resources. The conclusion to be drawn for policy, then, is that concentration is a 'bad thing' and that there are gains to be had from an active policy against concentration and mergers. However, as *Demsetz*[120], a leading Chicago School representative, and others have noted, the same factual relationship between concentration and profitability could arise from a wholly different mechanism. It is perfectly possible that higher profits are simply the result of greater efficiency and that high levels of concentration are simply the incidental result of output becoming concentrated in the hands of those companies who have 'got it right'.[121]

There are, therefore, two completely different lines of thought about the implications of the concentration-profitability-relationship. The 'market power' interpretation sees it as evidence of powerful companies' ability to acquire and use costly monopoly power. The 'competitive' view argues that concentration may be the result of a desirable competitive process. Attempts have been made to devise tests that would allow us to decide between these conflicting hypotheses, but they are inconclusive, and it is very unlikely that any definitive conclusion will ever be reached to everyone's satisfaction.

The 'competitive' interpretation of the concentration profitability-relationship clearly implies a very different conception of competition from that derived from the

---
119. see (Phillips 1976).
120. (H. Demsetz 1973).
121. (Agnew 1985, 37).

perfectly competitive model. It is important to appreciate the alternative notions of competition that coexist in economic analysis. *Shepherd* and *Gale* (both 1972)[122] made telling contributions. They used company, rather than industry data and attempted to measure not only the conventional industry concentration ratio, but also the market shares possessed by individual firms. What they found was that individual market shares were more strongly associated with profitability than concentration.[123] As a result of a better source of business data in the US, it was possible to substantiate these findings.[124] Research on this subject is still ongoing. Recent insights, for example, indicate that the influence of the concentration ratio on profit disappears when individual market shares are seen as independent variables in the regression analysis.

3.3.3.3 Contestable Markets Theory

High firm concentrations in a given market may not translate to market power. Even in markets where only one or a few firms can efficiently operate (e.g., due to *economies of scale*), it is possible for competition to work. This is known as one of the basic principles in microeconomic theory. Monopolistic profits cannot remain in the long run unless there is some barrier to entry. In the *theory of contestable markets,* which lies very much in the mainstream of industrial economics, the crucial structural precondition for socially optimal pricing is frictionless entry to and costless exit from markets, rather than the inability of any firm to influence price by changing its output.

A market is said to be contestable when barriers to entry and exit are so low that the threat of potential entry prevents the incumbent from exercising market power. Contestability requires that there are no sunk costs for market entry. That is, should an entrant fail, it can recover its fixed costs, for example by selling assets or reusing them elsewhere. In their 1982 book on *Contestable Markets*[125] *William J. Baumol, John C. Panzar, and Robert D. Willig* showed that in purely monopolistic and oligopolistic markets with certain cost and demand configurations, not only will economic profit be eliminated but price will equal marginal cost, provided entry and exit are unimpeded in the sense of being, respectively, frictionless and costless. A market that fully meets their conditions qualifies as 'perfectly contestable.'[126]

A perfectly contestable market is defined as one in which entry is free, exit is costless, existing firms and entrants compete on equal terms and potential entrants are not deterred from entering by the threat of retaliatory price-cutting by incumbents. Should an incumbent firm increase prices above the normal level of profits, then new firms will enter the market and force prices down again. In such a market, it can be

---

122. (Shepherd 1972, 25).
123. (Scherer 1986, 7).
124. The PIMS (Profit Impact of Market Strategies) and the Federal Trade Commission's LB – Line of Business Data.
125. (Shepherd 1986) The 'contestability' and 'sustainability' ideas of William Baumol and his team were developed on the Bell payroll. This is only one of a few examples that indicate that in the last two decades in the US the anti-trust field has experienced a rising tide of money from the industry for research into economic studies and expert testimonies.
126. (Baumol 1988, 256).

shown that the benefits previously associated with perfect competition alone will accrue, even if there are very few firms in the industry. As the contestability theorists themselves put it:

> *Monopolists and oligopolists who populate such markets are sheep in wolves' clothing, for under this arrangement potential rivals can be as effective as actual competitors in forcing pro-social behaviour upon incumbents, whether or not such behaviour is attractive to them. As we have seen ... this may be true where observed market phenomena are far from the competitive norm, and even where they superficially assume some pattern of behaviour previously thought to be pernicious per se.*[127]

Obviously, the idea of a contestable market is related to the idea of entry barriers and such a market might be thought of as one where barriers to entry are relatively limited. However, the theory also suggests that in many instances entry barriers are less dreadful than has often been assumed. The essential idea is straightforward. If entrants to an industry can exit quickly and with little or no loss of *sunk costs*[128] incumbent firms, however monopolistic their structural position may be, are constrained from raising prices above the least-cost level by fear of 'hit and run' entry that captures the incumbent's market share and profits. Thus, sunk costs as the major real deterrent to entry is essential. If sunk costs are small, then new entrants may have little difficulty in competing with existing firms on equal terms and the threat of this competition will force incumbents to behave like perfect competitors.[129] All that is important is the ability to enter and exit (in the extreme case) at no cost. The greater the costs associated with exit the less contestable, and by inference the less competitive, the market will be and *vice versa*.

The 'run' part of 'hit and run' entry comes from the exit of new entrants whenever the incumbents respond by reducing their prices to entry-inhibiting levels, only to be 'hit' again if they attempt after exit to raise prices. The theory offers the not entirely new insight that the ability of potential competition to constrain incumbents' pricing depends not only upon the 'height' of entry barriers, but also upon how readily entrants can liquidate their investments if the incumbents react in a hostile manner. Its main limitation is the difficulty of finding real-world cases in which liquidation of entry investments are quick and not subject to 'fire sale' losses.

Thus, in a perfectly contestable market with a sustainable equilibrium price, entry to the market must be free and exit costless; incumbents and potential entrants must face identical cost functions; incumbents must be able to earn revenues equal to total costs of production at a market-clearing price; and there must be some lag between the response of demand to an entrant's lower price and the incumbent's response, so that potential entrants can use the incumbent's existing price to calculate the prospective profit from hit-and-run entry. Given these assumptions, a perfectly

---

127. (Baumol, Panzar and Willig 1982, 350).
128. Sunk costs, as the name implies, are those costs that cannot be eliminated, even by cessation of production.
129. (Agnew 1985, 44).

contestable market will yield the socially optimal price and output under a wide range of cost and demand configurations, even though occupied by only one firm.

Perhaps the classic application of the theory of contestability lies in the aviation industry. A good example, provided by *Baumol* et al. (1982), is a small airline market. If we consider the market for air travel between two small towns, where the number of people travelling is only sufficient to fill one aircraft per day, we have an example of a 'natural monopoly'. These markets, notes *Elizabeth E. Bailey* in a foreword to *Contestable Markets,* are 'characterised both by easy entry and exit and significant economies of scale. Even if a route is flown by a single carrier, other carriers who have stations at both endpoint cities can readily enter if monopoly profits become evident.'[130]

It will always be cheaper for the route to be serviced by a single airline than for two planes to fly in competition, and we would expect that market to be monopolised, in the sense of there being only one supplier. However, that one supplier will not be free to behave like a 'textbook' monopolist. If aircraft can be rented, or if there is an active second-hand market for planes, then sunk costs are relatively low. In that case, it is possible, at little cost, for a carrier to move in and out of serving different routes, according to demand, suffering little or no irrevocable loss. All an entrant has to do, if the incumbent 'monopolist' is creating a profitable opportunity by charging high fares, is to fly his aircraft on to the tarmac, undercut the incumbent and make a profit. If the incumbent then cuts his price, the entrant can literally fly away and either use the plane on another route or sell it (or cease renting it). The absence of substantial sunk costs makes entry cheaply reversible and the threat or the reality of easy entry will discipline the incumbent 'monopolist'. Air travel, then, provides a useful example of a contestable market and its outcome.[131] The theory of contestability has proved very influential in the US experience of deregulation and liberalisation of air routes and may yet prove so in Europe.

The contestable markets approach has a number of implications for policy towards competition. The approach shows quite clearly that it is not appropriate to decide on whether to intervene in an industry by making reference to the degree of departure from the conditions of perfect competition. It is also of interest that the theory provides an alternative benchmark to the unattainable criterion of perfect competition, that of contestability, and suggests that policies designed to improve contestability are the most appropriate form of competition policy.

This statement needs further elaboration. When considering the structure and behaviour of an individual industry, the first step is to decide whether or not it constitutes a contestable market. If it does, then government interference is not needed, even if the industry exhibits symptoms that in the past have been accepted as indicators of poor market performance, such as high concentration, price discrimination, mergers and horizontal or vertical integration. If, on the other hand, the industry is not contestable then intervention in order to make it so needs to be considered. It should be noted in this context that the European Commission can only act against

---

130. (Baumol, Panzar and Willig 1982, XXI).
131. (Agnew 1985, 44).

Chapter 3: Competition Theory

(1) restraints of competition, (2) abuse of a dominant position, and (3) certain mergers. The European Commission cannot interfere simply because an industry is not contestable.

At least in theory governments are required to consider methods by which entry and exit to an industry can be made easier. In particular, policies are needed which reduce sunk costs, the main impediment to contestability. Such measures could include having sunk costs borne by government, which would then lease facilities to firms, or by mandating that sunk costs be shared by a consortium. Alternatively, sunk costs might be reduced by tax advantages for rapid depreciation, for retooling, or for the reuse of old plant in new activities.[132]

The theory leads to the same result as perfect competition, given that any industry organisation, which does not maximise profits, attracts (costless) entry and exit. Criticism of the contestability idea is that it disregards externalities, strategic considerations and irreversibilities, as well as the internal consistency of its assumptions.[133] The contestable market theory was also attacked on the grounds that the necessary assumptions are so stringent as to rob the model of most of its empirical and theoretical relevance.[134] *Baumol* et al. have two responses. First, the principal value of the model is normative rather than descriptive:

> *Perfect contestability is not likely to be satisfied exactly by any real market. Yet it does provide a standard against which actual markets can be compared, no matter if the relevant production techniques and market demands dictate production by a single giant firm or by a multitude of independent enterprises....There are objective structural market conditions that can be examined to determine the relevance of contestability in practice. And where these conditions do not hold even approximately, actual industry configurations can, nevertheless, be usefully compared to those that would result if the markets were structurally contestable.*[135]

Further, *Baumol* et al. argue, contestability as described in the model approximates actual conditions in some markets, such as airline service between city pairs. *Baumol* characterised this theory of contestability as 'no less than a unifying theory as a foundation for the analysis of industrial organisation.'[136] In *Scherer's*[137] view the contestability theory is circles within circles – an aesthetically pleasing creation whose conformity to reality is at best questionable.

3.3.3.4 Game Theory

Game theory is a branch of applied mathematics that is used in the social sciences, most notably economics. It is a clear and interdisciplinary approach to the study of human behaviour. There are many scientific spheres that are involved in game theory

---

132. (Agnew 1985, 45).
133. (Pitelis 1991, 65).
134. (Baldwin 1987, 259).
135. (Baumol, Panzar and Willig 1982, 35-45).
136. (Baumol 1988, 15).
137. (Scherer 1986, 13).

like mathematics, economics and the other social and behavioural sciences. The mathematician *John von Neumann* initiated game theory. The first important work was *'The Theory of Games and Economic Behaviour'* in 1944, which *von Neumann* wrote together with the mathematical economist *Oskar Morgenstern*. Both brought ideas from neoclassical economics into their collaboration.

Game theory is considered to be the mathematical theory of bargaining and represents a distinct, interdisciplinary approach to the study of human behaviour. With the work of *Neumann* and *Morgenstern* 'games' became a scientific metaphor for a wide range of human interactions in which the outcomes depend on the interactive strategies of two or more persons or parties. The intention of game theory was to provide a theory of economics and strategic behaviour when people interact directly, rather than 'through the market.' Games became a scientific metaphor for a much wider range of human behaviour and serious interactions in which the results depend on the interactive strategies of a number of persons, who have contrasting motives or at best mixed ones. It is about such serious interactions as market competition, arms races and environmental pollution.

Serious interactions are typical within game theory. That means the individual's choice or behaviour is essentially a choice of a strategy, and the result of the interaction depends on the strategies chosen by each individual. Game theory attempts to mathematically capture behaviour in strategic situations, in which an individual's success in making choices depends on the choices of others. Traditional applications of game theory attempt to find equilibria in these games.

The aim of neoclassical economic theory is to choose rationally in order to maximise an individual's outcomes. This is a mathematics problem because it is necessary to choose the activity that maximises rewards under given circumstances. In game theory, the case is more complex because the result depends on the one hand on the individual's own strategies and on the market conditions, but on the other hand directly on the strategies chosen by others. We may still think of rational behaviour as a mathematical problem: That it is possible to maximise the rewards of a group of interacting decision-makers and so gain a rational outcome as the 'solution' of the game.

Rationality is the most discussed issue between neoclassical economics and game theory.

The neoclassical theory is based on the assumption that human beings are absolutely rational in their economic choices and behaviour. The key assumption is that each human being maximises the rewards – profits, incomes or subjective benefits – within a certain situation. Thereby the range of possibilities is narrower because absolute rational behaviour is more foreseeable than irrational behaviour. In addition, it provides a criterion for the evaluation of the efficiency of an economic system. If the results lead to a reduction in the rewards for the actors, without producing more than compensating rewards to others (costs greater than benefits, broadly) then something is wrong. The rational neoclassical individual is confronted with a specific system of institutions, including property rights, money and highly competitive markets. All these effects must be considered in order to maximise the results. This means that it is not *necessary* for the human being to take into account interactions with other individuals. Each individual has to consider only their own situation and their interactions on the market. The recurring issue is that it limits the range of the theory. When competition is restricted and there is no monopoly, or property rights are not fully defined, consensus neoclassical economic theory is inapplicable. Neoclassical theory has never produced a generally accepted extension of the theory to cover these cases. Those decisions that were taken outside the money economy are another problem for the neoclassicists.

In the 1980s, game theory became the instrument of prime importance for the development of models that were specific to problems of industrial economics, also called *'New Industrial Economics.'*[138] New Industrial Economics follows a behaviour oriented analytical approach that tries to find out more about types of actions the firms currently operating in a marketplace can be expected to take under different types of economic circumstances. The most important difference between the game theoretical approaches from the traditional microeconomic approach of oligopolistic interdependence is that it assumes each supplier will try to realise his best strategy, which is based on the analysis of the 'best' strategies of their competitors.[139]

Contemporary game theorists search for so-called *Nash equilibria* that occur when each player's strategy is optimal given the strategies of the other players. A player's best response (or best strategy) is the strategy that maximises that player's payoff, given the strategies of the other players. In this situation, the strategies of each player and the given strategies of the other players lead to the result that the first player has no incentive to change the strategy. An analysis of a game permits players to locate the equilibria, and thus to predict those states of play that will be stable, barring exogenous interference. Such equilibria are stable, but not necessarily desirable; for example, in what is undoubtedly the best-known and most discussed instance of a game, the Prisoner's Dilemma, the unique *Nash equilibrium* is a state in which both of the two players are as badly off, given their utility function.[140]

The classic example of the Prisoners' Dilemma is illustrated by the following little story: Bonnie and Clyde are captured near the scene of a burglary. The police put them in jail separately and each of the two has to choose whether or not to confess and implicate the other. If neither of them confesses, then both will serve three years in prison. If each confesses and implicates the other, both will go to prison for four years. However, if one of them confesses and implicates the other the person who does not confess will go to prison for eight years. The strategic choice for both is to 'confess' or 'not confess.' This can be expressed in a 'payoff table' of a kind that has become standard in game theory. The payoff table for the Prisoners' Dilemma game is as follows:

---

138. See (Tirole 1988) and (Fudenberg and Tirole 1991, 259–327).
139. See (Kantzenbach, Kottmann and Krüger 1996, 20).
140. (Dixit und Skeath 2004), (Luce und Raiffa 1957).

Doris Hildebrand

Table 3.1   Prisoners' Dilemma

		Clyde	
		Confess	Not Confess
Bonnie	Confess	Four years each	One year for Bonnie and eight years for Clyde
	Not Confess	Eight year for Bonnie and one years for Clyde	Three years each

The table above has to be read like this: Each prisoner chooses one of the two strategies. For example, Bonnie has to decide between the strategies to confess or not confess. For her there are two possible courses that Clyde can take. The first one is that he will confess. In that case, if Bonnie chooses not to confess, she will go to prison for eight years, while if she does confess, she will go to prison for four years. Therefore, in the situation where Clyde does confess the best strategy for Bonnie is to confess, too.

If Clyde does not confess then Bonnie again has the choice of whether to confess or not. If she does, she will go to prison for one year. If not, she will go to prison for three years. In this case, Bonnie's best strategy is to confess.

What strategies are 'rational' if Bonnie and Clyde want to minimise the time they spend in jail? Bonnie's best strategy is to confess. If Clyde reasons in the same way, and they both confess, then they each go to prison for four years each. This is a less beneficial situation than if they had acted irrationally and kept quiet and not confessed in which case they each would have gotten off with three years each.[141] It should be noted that in reality strategies must be undertaken without the full knowledge of what other players will do.

The *Nash equilibrium* is applicable to a wider variety of games than the criterion proposed by *von Neumann* and *Morgenstern*. This equilibrium is sufficiently general, allowing for the analysis of non-cooperative games in addition to cooperative ones.

Game theory experienced a flurry of activity in the 1950s, during which time the concepts of the core, the extensive form game, fictitious play, repeated games, and the Shapley value were developed.

The concept of the Nash equilibrium in pure strategies was first developed by the French economist Antoine Augustin Cournot in his theory of oligopoly in 1838. *Cournot competition* is an economic model used to describe an industry structure in which companies compete over the amount of output they will produce, which they decide on independently of each other and at the same time. Firms choose a quantity of output to maximise their own profit. However, the best output for one firm depends on the outputs of others. Cournot equilibrium occurs when each firm's output maximises its profits given the output of the other firms, which is pure-strategy Nash equilibrium.

---

141. (Rapoport und Chemmah 1965).

Chapter 3: Competition Theory

With the Cournot competition model, the following criteria apply:

- There is more than one firm and all firms produce a homogeneous product, i.e., there is no product differentiation.
- Firms do not cooperate, i.e., there is no collusion.
- Firms have market power, i.e., each firm's output decision affects the good's price.
- The number of firms is fixed.
- Firms compete in quantities, and choose quantities simultaneously.
- The firms are economically rational and act strategically, usually seeking to maximise profit given their competitors' decisions.

The essential assumption of this model is that each firm aims to maximise profits, based on the expectation that its own output decision will not have an effect on the decisions of its rivals. The cost functions may be the same or different among firms. The market price is set at a level such that demand equals the total quantity produced by all firms. Each firm takes the quantity set by its competitors as a given, evaluates its residual demand, and then behaves as a monopoly.

However, the modern game theory concept of the Nash equilibrium is defined in terms of mixed-strategies, where players choose a probability distribution over possible actions.

Bertrand competition is another model of competition used in economics, named after the French economist *Joseph Louis François Bertrand* (1822–1900). Specifically, it is a model of price competition between duopoly firms, which results in each charging the price that would be charged under perfect competition, known as marginal cost pricing. The Bertrand competition model has the following assumptions:

- There are at least two firms producing homogeneous products.
- Firms do not cooperate.
- Firms have the same marginal cost (MC).
- Marginal cost is constant.
- Demand is linear.
- Firms compete in price, and choose their respective prices simultaneously.
- There is strategic behaviour by both firms.
- Both firms compete solely on price and then supply the quantity demanded.
- Consumers buy everything from the cheaper firm or half at each, if the price is equal.

Competing on price means that firms can easily change the quantity they supply, but once they have chosen a certain price, it is very hard, if not impossible, to change it. Some examples of firms that might operate in this way are bars, shops or other companies that publish non-negotiable prices. There are two plausible outcomes: colluding to charge the monopoly price and supplying one half of the market each, or not colluding and charging marginal cost, which is the non-cooperative Nash equilibrium outcome. If one firm has lower average cost (a superior production technology), it will charge the highest price that is lower than the average cost of the other one (i.e., a price *just* below the lowest price the other firm can manage) and take all the business. This is known as 'limit pricing'.

The *Bertrand* and the *Cournot* competition models have similar assumptions. However, their implications are different. *Bertrand* predicts that a duopoly is enough to push prices down to marginal cost level and that a duopoly will result in perfect competition. Neither model is necessarily 'better'. The accuracy of the predictions of each model varies from industry to industry depending on the closeness of each model to the industry situation. If capacity and output can be easily changed *Bertrand* is generally a better model of duopoly competition. Or, if output and capacity are difficult to adjust, then *Cournot* is generally preferred.

Under some conditions the *Cournot* model can be recast as a two-stage model, where in the first stage firms choose capacities, and in the second they compete in *Bertrand* fashion. The most critical flaw in the *Bertrand* model is the assumption that firms compete in one period, the price being chosen and set forever. However, as it is unreasonable to expect the other firm to indefinitely keep higher prices and sell nothing, each firm must expect that lowering the price will almost immediately be met with the same move by the other firm, thus no firm can expect to get bigger market share by cutting price, and the preferred strategy is keeping prices at monopoly price level. The situation is analogous to the prisoner's dilemma, as the single-period version has completely the opposite implications than the iterated version.

Another criticism with respect to the two models is the focus purely on price, ignoring non-price competition. Firms can differentiate their products and charge a higher price. If a firm does undercut a rival and get full market share, it now has to supply the whole market. Many firms however would not have the capacity to do this. In general, the greater the overall capacity constraints, the higher the prices are over marginal cost. These elaborations already indicate that those models can only be used to structure our thinking but not to deliver exact mathematical results with respect to competition.

The *Stackelberg leadership model* is another model of a strategic game in economics in which the leader firm moves first and then the follower firms move sequentially. It is named after the German economist *Stackelberg* who published his contribution on *Market Structure and Equilibrium (Marktform und Gleichgewicht)* in 1934.

In game theory terms, the players of this game are a *leader* and a *follower* and they compete on quantity. The *Stackelberg* leader is sometimes referred to as the market leader. There are some further constraints upon the sustainability of the *Stackelberg* equilibrium. The leader must know *ex ante* that the follower observes his action. The follower must have no means of committing to a future non-*Stackelberg* follower action and the leader must know this. Indeed, if the 'follower' could commit to a *Stackelberg* leader action and the 'leader' knew this; the leader's best response would be to play a *Stackelberg* follower action. Firms may engage in *Stackelberg* competition if one has some sort of advantage enabling it to move first. More generally, the leader must have commitment power. Moving clearly first is the most obvious means of commitment: once the leader has made its move, it cannot undo it – it is committed to that action.

Chapter 3: Competition Theory

Moving first may be possible if the leader was the incumbent monopoly of the industry and the follower is a new entrant. Holding excess capacity is another means of commitment.

In 1965, *Reinhard Selten* introduced his solution concept of *subgame perfect equilibria*, which further refined the *Nash* equilibrium.

In 1967, *John Harsanyi* developed the concepts of complete information and Bayesian games.

Nash, *Selten* and *Harsanyi* became Economics Nobel Laureates in 1994 for their contributions to economic game theory.

In recent years, there has been an explosion of work, mostly mathematical, on theories of strategic behaviour and especially entry deterrence. In building an adequate, integrated theory, it became a major issue to incorporate not only the mandates of long run profit maximisation, but also the strategies through which firms move toward their goals in an environment characterised by small numbers of meaningful competitors.

The most interesting work on *strategic deterrent behaviour* has emphasised three notions: (1) 'prepositioning', for example. investing in reserve capacity so as to keep one's marginal costs on reactive output low and hence enhance one's price war fighting credibility; (2) 'pre-emption', or being first on the market with a new product, plant, or advertising campaign; and (3) 'inculcating' in rivals' minds the expectation that one might react to an incursion irrationally. All three have received rich theoretical development. On the empirical side, by far the most important advance is the illumination of the role 'first mover' advantage plays in building product differentiation. It was once argued seriously that firms could, by spending enough, advertise their way to monopoly power in consumer goods markets. This hypothesis is no longer empirically tenable, its demise explaining *inter alia* why all firms do not choose to advertise their way to monopoly power.[142] However, advertising does tend to fortify dominant firms against small rivals and new entrants.[143]

The critical insight is that advertising per se is not sufficient. To be effective in building a long run strategic position, it must be accompanied by something more: usually some element of innovation, either in physical product characteristics or in the characteristics advertising imparts to the product. 'Innovation' here means being the first mover, although there is also a 'fast second' theory explaining why being literally first is not always essential. In any event, it has become clear from several empirical studies that firms who have led some field of product development build up substantial reputational capital that can be exploited in at least three important ways: (1) in the ability to charge premium prices without suffering severe customer defection; (2) in the ability to expand one's customer base at lower advertising costs per unit than firms lacking a first mover reputation; and (3) in the opportunity to race down learning curves before rivals, building market share and securing production cost advantages both through learning-by-doing and conventional scale economies. Once a firm has gained such first mover advantages, it becomes difficult to displace even though it

---

142. (Scherer 1986, 15).
143. (Shepherd 1985, 49).

commands supranormal profits. This set of relationships is almost surely why market share and profitability are strongly correlated.[144]

3.3.4 Chicago School of Thought

The major attack on the concentration doctrine in the Harvard School tradition came from a cluster of economists and lawyers (also called the *Chicago School*) who hailed their own collective approach as the 'new learning' of Industrial Organisation. These economists and lawyers shared a tradition associated with the University of Chicago's Department of Economics and its Law School, stressing a commitment to the economic, political, and social values of a free market system and a corresponding antipathy toward most government interference with its workings. Prominent among this group, and concerned with concentration and anti-trust policy, include *Robert H. Bork, Ward S. Bowman, Jr., Harold Demsetz, John S. McGee, Stanley I. Ornstein, Sam Peltzman, Richard A. Posner, George J. Stigler, Lester G. Telser* and *Milton Friedman*.

The Chicago School of thought emphasises non-intervention from government and rejects regulation in *laissez-faire* free markets as inefficient. The Chicago School is also associated with neoclassical price theory.

3.3.4.1 *Attack on the Harvard's School Concentration Doctrine*

The liberal Chicago School de-emphasised market structure, 'concentration' and 'barriers to entry' and denied the extensive possibility that Harvard scholars could prove empirical relationships. They questioned in particular the structure-conduct-performance framework and criticised the empirical studies concerning the SCP-paradigm. They demonstrated that the relationship between concentration, entry barriers and monopoly profits is not stable or sometimes does not exist at all. One of the major results of their work was that there is no causal link between high concentration and high profit. In their view, history and data demonstrate that concentration and collusion, either tacit or explicit, are not synonymous. Mutually recognised interdependence, the hallmark of oligopoly by one definition, does not characterise concentrated industries any more than unconcentrated. Neither is it a sufficient condition to produce tacit or express collusion in either concentrated or unconcentrated industries.[145]

The US Supreme Court has discussed the Chicago School approach in several cases[146] without confirming that this School of thought is the most preferred one in the US.

---

144. (Scherer 1986, 15).
145. (Brozen 1977, 854).
146. *Continental T.V., Inc. v. GTE Sylvania Inc.*, 433 US 36 (1977); *Broadcast Music, Inc. v. Columbia Broadcasting System, Inc.*, 441 US 1 (1979); *National Collegiate Athletic Assn. v. Board of Regents of Univ. of Okla.*, 468 US 85 (1984); *Spectrum Sports, Inc. v. McQuillan*, 506 US 447 (1993); *State Oil Co. v. Khan*, 522 US 3 (1997); *Verizon v. Trinko*, 540 US 398 (2004); *Leegin Creative Leather Products Inc. v. PSKS Inc.*, 551 US (2007).

Chapter 3: Competition Theory

The assumption in the Chicago School tradition is that competition in industrial markets even with a high concentration ratio functions reasonably well because of the self-regulation powers of uninfluenced industrial markets under the precondition that no *legal* barriers to entry exist. Different concentration ratios are only the result of different cost structures, in particular of economies of scale. An increasing concentration ratio in one industry is explained through the economic advantages accruing to large-scale firms.[147]

The Chicago School views competition as a dynamic process. This implies that a certain distance from the static model of the neoclassicists is maintained, whereas, their idea of equilibrium fictions clearly resembles the concept developed by the neoclassicists.[148]

Contrary to the classical approach, which is dynamic and emphasises the tendency for rates of return to equalise between different economic activities through the behaviour of profit-seeking individuals, the neoclassical, static notion analyses interactions in the context of a specified environment, so that a situation is defined as competitive if a predetermined set of structural characteristics (large number of participants etc.) are found to be present. Since the neoclassical model identifies the level of competition with some measure of concentration in a particular market, an exact and consistent measure of its boundaries is a necessity.[149]

In analysing industrial markets, *George J. Stigler*, a leading Chicago school representative, refers to pure economic theory i.e., neoclassical price respectively resource allocation theory, rejecting the field of research that is called Industrial Organisation.

Stigler deduces a model of perfect competition, which is characterised by certain conditions, such as the largest firm in an industry makes a trifling fraction of the industry's sales or purchases. It follows that there are many firms in the industry; or that these many firms are assumed to act independently (polypoly); or that there exists a complete knowledge of offers to buy and sell by the participants of the market.[150]

It is clear that these assumptions of perfect competition have to be criticised because they are unrealistic and, as already stated, remedial imperfections are necessary for competition, as a dynamic process, to evolve. Market imperfections like product heterogeneity, lack of market information, lack of foresight, adjustments lags, etc. are the prerequisites and effects of a dynamic competitive process, which is characterised by never ending phases of moves and responses. The analysis of economic behaviour in the neoclassical theory is in essence reduced to optimal behaviour under familiar conditions. These familiar limiting conditions apply to (1) preferences, (2) technological data and (3) the availability of the means of production. Identification of the limiting conditions is followed by the query for optimisation. Alert participants of the market process generate market signals through which a tendency is created towards a general economic equilibrium. However, owing

---

147. (Kantzenbach and Kalfass 1981, 119).
148. (Hoff & Stiglitz 2010).
149. (Auerbach 1988, 13).
150. (G. Stigler 1968, 5).

to continuous change in the limiting conditions identified above, this equilibrium is never achieved. Due to the disequilibrium and its inherent uncertainty the model of perfect competition is simply inadequate.[151]

Robert Bork in his book *The Antitrust Paradox* evaluates an optimal resource allocation attained in market equilibrium:

> Changing wants and technologies are in themselves sufficient to prevent the attainment of such equilibrium. But the forces of competition in open markets cause the actual allocation of resources to be ever *shifting* in pursuit of the constantly moving equilibrium point.[152]

This statement clearly affirms that Chicago scholars do not see the market equilibrium in the neoclassical tradition as a final state that will actually be reached. For them, it is more or less a guiding star, which has to be followed in all of its movements. This pursuit is not achieved by conscious public policy; only competition without any public interference forces the economy to adapt constantly to this ever-changing equilibrium. The view of the Chicago School that the *movement* towards equilibrium should be examined rather than the conditions required for maintaining such an equilibrium, means that the Chicago School emphasises a classical view close to that of *Adam Smith*. However, the analysis of competition perceived in such a specific way is done in a comparatively static manner, which again leads to the omission of the dynamic aspects of competition.[153]

Nevertheless anti-trust is analysed in the Chicago School tradition by means of neoclassical microeconomics, which means that the models of perfect competition and monopoly serve as standards of reference.[154]

Neither perfect competition nor monopolies in the structural sense are seen as states that should be reached. They simply serve as a model for the purpose of economic analysis for the sake of analytical clarity and for legal certainty.

Basically the understanding of the Chicago School using neoclassical price theory is:

- the understanding of market behaviour as a free game of forces without any state intervention. The market process is seen as the free play of economic moves and responses and according to *Stigler* as the 'survival of the fittest' – so-called 'Economic Darwinism';
- the push-back of state intervention; the state should only provide a minimum legal framework;
- transfer of economic thinking to all aspects of living ('economics of marriage'); and
- a liberal-conservative attitude of the representatives of the Chicago School, which is interpreted as an entrepreneur friendly (pro big-business) and union hostile attitude.

---

151. (Groeneveld, Maks und Muysken 1990, 3).
152. (R. Bork 1978, 98).
153. (Schmidt and Rittaler 1989, 2).
154. (H. Demsetz 1976, 371).

Chapter 3: Competition Theory

Representatives of the Chicago School are concerned about economic efficiency and consumer welfare as well as the protection of competition rather than competitors. Furthermore, in their view only a few acts should be prohibited, namely cartels that fix prices and divide markets, mergers that create monopolies, and dominant firms pricing predatorily, while allowing such practices as vertical agreements and price discrimination on the grounds that it did not harm consumers. In general, the Chicago School rejects structural remedies based on the argument that the organisation of an industry that has developed over time without any legal restrictions is the result of the underlying cost situation ('survival of the fittest').[155] Chicagoans value a high degree of concentration as the result of the superior abilities of entrepreneurs.[156] Consequently, the industry's structure is the result of the differing efficiencies of firms over time.

The Chicago School's attack on the concentration doctrine centres on the contention that economic efficiency is the primary cause of concentration. The concentration doctrine, which states that industrial concentration leads to excessively high or rigid prices or to persistent excess profits, is asserting in general, that concentration is a cause of economic *in*efficiency. The Chicago School denies that this assumption has ever been demonstrated; to the contrary, they consider economic efficiency as the principal cause of concentration. The position of the Harvard School that market concentration is an indication of collusion is therefore heavily criticised on the grounds that it might discourage competitive conduct that promotes efficiency.[157] In the Chicagoan view concentration in markets could increase the danger of collusion, but this could be easily recognised and prosecuted. To conclude, concentration is viewed in the Chicago School as necessary in order to achieve economic efficiency.

State interventions such as market structure interference, except in the case of some horizontal mergers, are judged as too extensive. Chicago School adherents generally view barriers to entry as low and it is assumed that potential competitors and buyers have perfect information about their profit-making and cost saving opportunities. Their concept of competition is long-term oriented and has a strong thrust in market power. Since the wisdom of the Chicago School is that the ultimate goal of competition policy is consumer welfare, expressed by efficiency, other goals are not considered explicitly.[158]

Robert Bork, who undertook a comprehensive analysis of the legislative history of the Sherman Act to attempt to ascertain Congress' true motives, revealed that the US Congress' principle concern was that firms through cartels, mergers, and other means, might achieve the power to raise prices to consumers. In exploiting his result, *Bork* believed that the only *evil* resulting from market power is that it leads to a form of economic efficiency. He stated in a dissenting comment in the *Neal* Report[159]:

---

155. (H. Demsetz 1976, 375).
156. (E. J. Mestmäcker 1994, 286).
157. (H. Demsetz 1976, 383).
158. (Emmerich 1991, 16).
159. In 1968, a special task force set up by President Lyndon B. Johnson submitted the Neal Report (named after task force chairman Phil C. Neal, dean of the University of Chicago Law School, but far from being a Chicagoan).

> When firms grow to sizes that create concentration or when such a structure is created by merger and persists for many years, there is a very strong prima facie case that the firms' sizes are related to efficiency. By efficiency I mean 'competitive effectiveness' within the bounds of the law, and competitive effectiveness means service to consumers. If the leading firms in a concentrated industry are restricting their output in order to obtain prices above the competitive level, their efficiencies must be sufficiently superior to that of all actual and potential rivals to offset that behaviour. Were this not so, rivals would be enabled to expand their market shares because of the abnormally high prices and would thus deconcentrate the industry. Market rivalry thus automatically weighs the respective influences of efficiency and output restriction and arrives at the firm sizes and industry structures that serve consumers best.[160]

In *The Antitrust Paradox* in 1978 *Bork* added:

> Today, I would add only two thoughts. First, I doubt that there is any significant output restriction problem arising from the concentration of any industry. Second, there is no coherent theory based on consumer welfare that supports a policy of industrial deconcentration when concentration has been created either by the internal growth of the firms or by merger more than ten or fifteen years old.[161]

This attack on the concentration doctrine of the Harvard School has led to a public policy position labelled the *'efficiency doctrine'*.

3.3.4.2 The Efficiency Doctrine

Bork's attack on the Harvard School has led to a public policy position labelled the *'efficiency doctrine'*. *Bork* in particular contends that the founding fathers of US anti-trust law pursued only the goal of maximisation of consumer welfare. For *Bork* and most of the members of the Chicago School, maximisation of economic benefits to consumers is clearly equated with economic efficiency. *Bork* asserts that the responsibility of the courts 'requires that they take consumer welfare as the sole value that guides anti-trust decisions.'[162] He therefore concludes, that the sole goal of the anti-trust laws is to increase overall economic efficiency.[163] Two types of economic efficiency, in turn, determine consumer welfare:

- allocative efficiency (macroeconomic optimalisation of the allocation of resources); and
- productive efficiency (efficient usage of resources in the individual firm gained by economies of scale or transaction-cost efficiency).[164]

Bork concludes that 'the whole task of anti-trust can be summed up as the effort to improve allocative efficiency without impairing productive efficiency so greatly as to

---

160. (R. Bork 1968, 54).
161. (R. Bork 1978, 178).
162. (R. Bork 1978, 51).
163. (R. Bork 1978, 90–91).
164. see also (I. Schmidt 2012, 20).

Chapter 3: Competition Theory

produce either no gain or a net loss in consumer welfare.'[165] *Posner* in adding to this discussion says that efficiency means exploiting economic resources in such a way that 'value' – human satisfaction as measured by aggregate consumer willingness to pay for goods and services – is maximised.[166]

While the efficiency doctrine sets very different criteria for appropriate anti-trust activities from those of the concentration doctrine, an emphasis on economic efficiency in and of itself in no way weakens the underlying case against tolerating monopolistic restraints on output and enhancement of price. But when coupled with the Chicago School's assumptions that competition among a few firms may be just as effective as competition among many and that efficiency is the primary cause of concentration, the efficiency doctrine does suggest that structural remedies are usually inappropriate in instances short of pure monopoly and that the major job of the anti-trust authorities should be to control or eliminate overtly collusive conduct.[167]

In 1973, *Harold Demsetz* described the market concentration doctrine simply as the widespread belief '... *that a reliable index of monopoly power can be obtained by measuring the degree to which the output of an industry is produced by a few firms.*'[168] Demsetz and others of the Chicago School deny that there is acceptable theoretical support for the contention that higher levels of concentration are associated with lower degrees of competition. In addition, they believe that concentration is more often a consequence of economic efficiency than a cause of allocative inefficiency.

Overall, empirical work gives limited support to the Chicago view. The traditional view that market power matters seem unshaken. Whether this power can be exercised by only one pure monopolist or can be effectively shared among two, three, or some other number of the larger firms in an industry is uncertain. Probably, the critical number of firms or market shares vary from industry to industry, depending on elasticity of demand for the product, ease of entry and intra-industry mobility, economies of scale, homogeneity of product, and other structural features. Thus, the Chicagoans' contention that differences in profitability among US firms is almost inevitably the result of differences in efficiency and not in market power has not been sustained. However, the view has held that, in some markets at least, large shares have been won by superior efficiency. The statistical difficulties in ascertaining how frequently this occurs are challenging. Finally, the relationship between concentration and economic performance is more complex than presumed in the simpler versions of the concentration doctrine.[169]

3.3.4.3 *Policy Implications of the Chicago School*

In the late 1970s and early 1980s, the *Chicago School* achieved broad ascendancy in US anti-trust policy, ushering in a new era of analysis dominated by a strong reliance on

---

165. (R. Bork 1978, 91).
166. (R. Posner, Economic Analysis of Law 2nd edition 1977, 10).
167. (Baldwin 1987, 320).
168. (H. Demsetz 1973, 2).
169. (Baldwin 1987, 315).

economic theory. Anti-trust policy changed from rather rigorous law enforcement to a very passive, almost *laissez-faire* policy, which is justified by its supporters through purely economic reasoning. Although the US Supreme Court has never said that only efficiency counts, it has stated on many occasions that efficiency is extremely important.[170]

A permissive view toward many arrangements (such as vertical practices and exercise of intellectual property rights) is taken because of their perceived efficiencies, particularly transaction-cost reductions and avoidance of free rider effects. The general purpose of US anti-trust law at that time was to inhibit any kind of restraints of competition. This is done by per se prohibitions of certain market behaviour. With respect to other kinds of behaviour the rule of reason is applied, i.e., agreements, which upon further analysis prove to be acceptable or even beneficial to the interests of consumers or suppliers, are removed from the ambit of the general rule.[171] However, even in the latter cases there is no room in US anti-trust law for balancing the goal of free competition with possibly conflicting policy goals such as the promotion of exports or employment for example. The rule of reason is only applied to the question, whether or not certain market behaviour has under the given circumstances restrictive effects or not.[172]

Deregulation of industries, which are controlled by the state, is considered desirable. With regard to deregulation, the Harvard and the Chicago schools take a similar view although the motives for deregulation are somewhat different. Whereas the Harvard School stresses the necessity of restoring competition as far as possible in all markets, the Chicagoans first look at abolishing government interference, thereby creating a free enterprise system in unregulated markets. This policy aims at abolishing the regulation of prices and market access in industries in which a competitive structure is possible. However, the representatives of the Harvard School contend that the Chicago School wants to extend deregulation to industries that need government protection. In markets in which economies of scale prevent a competitive market structure, especially concerning a natural monopoly, monopoly profits should be avoided by regulation; in such a case, a policy of deregulation would allow monopolists to skim off monopoly profits.[173]

With regard to other schools of thought within the field of anti-trust theory, similarities between the Chicago School and the Neo-Austrian School can be recognised as far as the transaction-cost approach is concerned. Although concepts are quite different in terms of their theoretical approach, they show a considerable degree of similarity with respect to policy implications.

---

170. (Lande, Chicago's False Foundation: Wealth Transfers (Not Just Efficiency) Should Guide Antitrust 1989, 633).
171. (Peeters 1989, 521).
172. (I. Schmidt 2012, 24).
173. (Schmidt and Rittaler 1989, 90).

3.3.4.4 The Post-Chicago School

The link between anti-trust law and economics in the US has remained intact since the beginning of the 1990s, but the Chicago school has fallen under increasingly forceful attacks from so-called *Post-Chicago* theorists:

> Post-Chicago antitrust economics is a world of the imagination, an intellectual neighbourhood where a number of economists, lawyers, judges, and enforcement officials are to be found these days. It is a neighbourhood in transition, not a well-planned, fully wrought new town.[174]

It defines itself largely by the ways it differs from the anti-trust thinking associated with *Posner* and *Bork,* labelled the Chicago theory and in vogue during the 1980s. Unlike Chicago theory, post-Chicago is not ideologically driven.

According to *Lande,* the primary purpose of the anti-trust laws is to prevent consumers from paying prices that exceed competitive levels. In effect, Congress in the US gave consumers the property right to purchase competitively priced goods and therefore declared that higher-than-competitive prices constitute unfair takings or extractions of consumer's property. The US anti-trust laws mandate that these fruits of American capitalism – competitively priced goods – belong to consumers, not cartels.[175] Based on the assumption that the US Congress was concerned with more than economic efficiency in 1890, when the Sherman Act was passed, some scholars contemplate what difference it would make if anti-trust analysis incorporates wealth transfer effects. If the efficiency paradigm would be replaced by a policy that blocked any merger that is likely to lead to consumers paying higher prices, a tighter merger enforcement would be the result. The switch can be caused either by the use of relatively stricter Herfindahl-Hirschman Index[176] standards in merger enforcement or through a higher burden for those who justify a merger by demonstrating enhanced efficiency.[177]

Another influence on the post-Chicago anti-trust discussion has been the US Supreme Court's 1992 decision in *Eastman Kodak Company v. Image Technical Services, Inc.*[178], which has been heralded by many as a breakthrough for Post-Chicago economics. In the view of post-Chicago scholars, what many consider to be the crowning achievement of the Chicago School – namely that anti-trust issues can be analysed through the simple lens of neoclassical price theory – may cause the downfall of the Chicago School. The difference between Chicago and post-Chicago thinking about competition and monopoly is related to the difference often noted between neoclassical price theory and Industrial Organisation economics. Both recognise the

---

174. (Sullivan 1995, 669).
175. (Lande, Chicago's False Foundation: Wealth Transfers (Not Just Efficiency) Should Guide Antitrust 1989, 632).
176. The Herfindahl-Hirschman Index is defined in the section on US anti-trust law.
177. (Lande, Chicago's False Foundation: Wealth Transfers (Not Just Efficiency) Should Guide Antitrust 1989, 642).
178. (Eastman Kodak Company v. Image Technical Services, Inc. 1992).

efficiency of competition and the allocative costs of monopoly.[179] However, post-Chicago thinkers showed that the Chicago School's simplified economic models are of limited usefulness in understanding complex economic forces that operate in the real-world.[180]

Post-Chicago anti-trust study starts from essentially the same position as the Chicago analysts but, in the Industrial Organisation tradition, digs into empirical material in an effort to illustrate the significance of observed distinctions between neoclassic models and the configuration of the particular market under examination. This encourages efforts to refine and particularise the models. It is important to note that the post-Chicago approach invites detailed factual analysis.[181]

Post-Chicago economic analysis was born out of, and in essence is defined by, criticism of the Chicago School. The standard post-Chicago criticisms include:[182]

(1) *Chicago models are too abstract and simplistic to address market realities.*
Post-Chicago theorists believe that just a few, if any, real world markets operate as efficiently as these 'static' models suggest. Post-Chicagoans prefer more 'dynamic' models that are individually tailored to the market under examination and take account of market imperfections, external forces that may alter market outcomes, and the potential for strategic behaviour among market participants.[183]

(2) *The Chicago School relies too heavily on economic theory, as opposed to facts, to decide cases.*
The Chicago School is well known for its use of economic filters and efficiency-based defences. Unlike their Chicago School counterparts, post-Chicagoans tend to use economic theory to highlight uncertainties and thus to justify keeping the doors open to further factual investigation.[184]

(3) *The Chicago School places too much confidence in the discipline of the market.*
The Chicago School adheres to the view that market forces tend to discipline anti-competitive or inefficient practices and correct for periodic imbalances[185] Thus government intervention is unnecessary in most cases. Many Post-Chicagoans regard such views as naive. Post-Chicagoans see far more potential for market imperfections (such as information failure) and barriers to entry to inhibit the competitive process and thus greater need for government action.[186]

(4) *The Chicago School adheres to an overly narrow view of market power.*
According to the Chicago School, in the absence of market power[187] firms acting alone cannot harm competition.[188] Post-Chicago theorists tend to believe that even firms lacking market power can in some situations

---

179. (Sullivan 1995, 670).
180. (Royall 1995, 445).
181. (Sullivan 1995, 673).
182. (Royall 1995, 445).
183. (Hovenkamp, Antitrust Policy after Chicago 1985, 256).
184. see (Hovenkamp 1994).
185. (R. Bork 1978, 195–196).
186. (Lande 1994, 631–644) or (Baker, Recent Developments in Economics that Challenge Chicago School Views 1989, 651–652).
187. Market power is defined as the ability to raise market prices and restrict market output.
188. (R. Posner 1979, 928).

Chapter 3: Competition Theory

unilaterally restrict competition by, for instance, taking actions that have the effect of raising rival's costs[189] or by exploiting captive consumers who lack perfect information.[190]

(5) *The Chicago School's concept of efficiency is too limited.*[191]
The Chicago School stands strongly in favour of the proposition that economic efficiency is the exclusive goal of the antitrust laws.[192] Post-Chicago scholars argue among other things that Congress never intended to enshrine the concept of efficiency as the sole concern of antitrust laws.[193] Post-Chicagoans have stressed the importance of considering not only the 'allocative' and 'productive' efficiency implications of antitrust policy, but also the prospects for 'dynamic' efficiency gains - i.e. future improvements in existing market conditions precipitated by present investments in innovation.[194]

Norm-oriented Chicago anti-trust analysts focus on improvements in science. Fact-oriented post-Chicagoans deny such a claim because their analyses typically – and usually quite frankly – end in judgments. This means that roles are changing for anti-trust actors as post-Chicago analysis became more common. Post-Chicagoans persuade a Court or jury to accept their way of organising and evaluating myriad factual details to reach a judgment that is factual and in particular, not normative and universal. Post-Chicagoans are supposed to determine purpose and effect by empirical inquiry and analysis.[195]

Concerning the anti-trust treatment of vertical mergers, Chicago School commentators view vertical mergers as generally competitively neutral or even pro-competition.[196] This more benign view formed the foundations of the 1985 Vertical Restraints Guidelines.[197] However, a renewed concern among economists is that vertical mergers can lead to anti-competitive effects under certain circumstances. On this point, post-Chicago theories neither ignore nor reject the economic analysis of the Chicago School. Instead, they apply a newer methodology of modern industrial organisation theory to more realistic market structures in which vertical mergers can have anti-competitive effects.[198]

The extension of economic models with more realistic assumptions enables Post-Chicago economists to reach a refined understanding of foreclosure. Modern industrial organisation literature has formulated models of vertical integration in which vertical mergers lead to real foreclosure and the net supply of inputs available to rivals is decreased. Also models have been formulated in which monopoly power may be created or enhanced – and monopoly profits thereby increased – by vertical mergers

---

189. (Krattenmaker and Salop 1986, 209).
190. (Kattan 1993).
191. (I. Schmidt 2012, 23).
192. (R. Bork 1978, 91).
193. (Hovenkamp 1985, 249–255).
194. (Ordover and Willig 1985, 311).
195. (Sullivan 1995, 678).
196. see (R. Bork 1978).
197. These Guidelines were rescinded by the Clinton Administration in 1993.
198. See (Krattenmaker and Salop 1986).

that have little or no efficiency benefits. In these post-Chicago models, some vertical mergers can be anti-competitive, although others are still pro-competitive.

Post-Chicago analysis also relaxes the restrictive assumptions upon which the single monopoly profit theory is based.[199] As a starting point, post-Chicago industrial economics accepts the criticisms of pre-Chicago foreclosure theory. The mere fact that a vertical merger blocks rival firms' access to the supply of inputs produced by one input supplier does not mean that the net supply of inputs available to those rival firms has been reduced. Instead, it merely realigns purchase patterns among competing firms.

Post-Chicago thinking provides some useful insights. Although the Post-Chicago School has developed over the past decade,[200] the federal agencies' anti-trust enforcement is still largely shaped by the Chicago School's rational choice theories. These theories are still applied to various conducts, such as vertical restraints, conduct by a monopolist, and tying.[201]

3.3.5 Concept of Freedom of Competition

The attack on the concept of workable competition did not only come from the Chicago School. In academic discussions and professional journals other critiques also gained ground. Based on classical liberal thoughts and rooted in *Adam Smith*, neoliberal authors started to introduce the so-called neoclassical concept of freedom of competition.

In particular, some German authors, especially *Erich Hoppmann*[202] and *Dieter Schmidtchen*[203] have the view, that competition policy, because of its very nature, can only pursue one goal, namely freedom of competition.[204] *Hoppmann* defines competition as a complex, open system of market processes that is based on the freedom to

---

199. (Riordan and Salop 1995, 517).
200. See, e.g., (Hovenkamp 2001) One area where post-Chicago School thinking has made some slight inroads is predatory pricing. For the Chicago School, given that profits are sacrificed by predatory pricing in order to drive out a competitor, and the risks of recouping the profits, 'there is no sufficient reason for anti-trust law or the courts to take predation seriously.' Frank H. Easterbrook (1981) REV. 263, 264. The Supreme Court, relying upon the Chicago School's writings, concluded that 'there is a consensus among commentators that predatory pricing schemes are rarely tried, and even more rarely successful.' Matsushita Elec. Indus. Co. v. Zenith Radio Corp., 475 US 574, 589 (1986); Brooke Group Ltd. v. Brown & Williamson Tobacco Corp., 509 US 209, 226 (1993). As the Tenth Circuit noted in the government's most recent predatory pricing case, '... recent scholarship has challenged the notion that predatory pricing schemes are implausible and irrational.' United States v. AMR Corp., 335 F.3d 1109, 1114–15 (10th Cir. 2003) (citing Patrick Bolton et al., *Predatory Pricing: Strategic Theory and Legal Policy*, 88 GEO. L.J. 2239, 2241 (2000) '... modern economic analysis has developed coherent theories of predation that contravene earlier economic writing claiming that predatory pricing conduct is irrational.'). Thus, the Tenth Circuit stated, 'Although this court approaches [the government's predatory pricing claims] with caution, we do not do so with the incredulity that once prevailed.' *AMR Corp.*, 335 F.3d at 1115.
201. (Stucke, Behavioral Economists at the Gate: Antitrust in the 21st Century, 2007).
202. For example, in (Hoppmann 1966, 286–323).
203. For example, in (Schmidtchen 1978).
204. (Möschel 1983, 46).

take part in the market processes and to act freely within the system.²⁰⁵ Freedom of competition in *Hoppmann's* view furthers the freedom of competitors to act and imitate (parallel process) as well as in partner selection on the market side (exchange process).

Freedom is interpreted as:

- freedom in the sense of absence of dictates by third parties (freedom of decision); and
- freedom as absence of restraints on exchange transactions (freedom of action).²⁰⁶

Freedom of competition is not the only requirement; 'spirit of competition' is obligatory with the aim of leading to an efficient coordination of the plans and actions of market players, supported by economic incentives and sanctions. Under these circumstances, freedom of competition is an economic advantage for all market participants.²⁰⁷

The only criterion in evaluating a competitive process, according to *Hoppmann* and *Schmidtchen*, is the individual market behaviour, whether it impairs the competitive freedom of other firms in the market or not. The authors in particular reject the use of market structure and market performance criteria to evaluate competitive processes. Market structures in their view are rather results than causes of market processes. Neither the resulting market structure nor the common performance criteria justify any conclusion, whether the underlying market process had been competitive or not. From this point of view, many anti-trust actions are criticised as interventionist and directed against the free economic order.²⁰⁸

These authors are deeply influenced by the work and thinking of the Austrian School.

3.3.5.1 The Austrian School

The birth of the *Austrian School of economics* is usually recognised as having occurred with the 1871 publication of *Carl Menger's Grundsätze der Volkswirtschaftslehre*. Two younger economists, *Eugen von Böhm-Bawerk* and *Friedrich von Wieser* became enthusiastic supporters of the new ideas put forward in *Menger's* book. During 1880s a vigorous outpouring of literature from these two followers, from several other *Menger* students, and in particular a methodological work by *Menger* himself, brought the ideas of *Menger* and his followers to the attention of the international community of economists. The Austrian School consequently became a recognised entity.²⁰⁹

The scene in Austrian economics changed during and after the World War II and was rather different from what it had been before. A new group of younger students came to the fore, many of whom were to become internationally famous economists in

---

205. (E. Mestmäcker 1984, 31).
206. (I. Schmidt 2012, 14).
207. (I. Schmidt 2012, 14).
208. According to (Hoppmann 1966) and (Schmidtchen 1978).
209. (Kirzner 1992, 57).

later decades. These economists include in particular *Friedrich A. von Hayek, Gottfried Haberler, Oskar Morgenstern* and *Fritz Machlup.*[210] *Ludwig von Mises* is another outstanding scholar.[211]

Austrian economists reject statistical methods and artificially constructed experiments as tools applicable to economics, saying that while it is appropriate in natural sciences where factors can be isolated in laboratory conditions, the actions of human beings are too complex for this kind of treatment. Austrian scholars view entrepreneurship as the driving force in economic development and see private property as essential to the efficient use of resources. Usually (if not always) government interference in market processes are regarded as counterproductive. In this, their views do not differ greatly from those of the Chicago School.

Austrian economics can be broken into two general trends. One, exemplified by *Friedrich A. Hayek*, while distrusting most neoclassical concepts (like the entire corpus of macroeconomics), generally accepts a large part of the neoclassical methodology. The other, exemplified by *Ludwig von Mises*, seeks a different formalism for economics. The main area of contention between the mainstream and the Austrian School is on their view of the market system as a process, not only to be studied using equilibrium models, but to be viewed as an incessant process that only tends toward a constantly changing equilibrium. This difference is the root of the Austrian business cycle theory, the economic calculation debate, and their different views of monopoly and competition. The second primary area of contention between neoclassical theory and the Austrian school is over the possibility of consumer indifference. Neoclassical theory says it is possible, whereas *Mises* rejected it as being '*impossible to observe in practice.*' The third major dispute arose when Mises and his students argued that utility functions are ordinal, and not cardinal; that is, the Austrians contend that one can only rank preferences and cannot measure their intensity, in direct opposition to the neoclassical view at the time. Finally, there are a host of questions about uncertainty raised by *Mises* and other Austrians, who argue for a different means of risk assessment. These questions are directly linked to the market process approach to economic theory, since the world of probabilistic uncertainty is the equilibrium world. The market process theory is relevant only when immersed in a world of genuine uncertainty.

Friedrich A. von Hayek stands for a dynamic vision on competition. He sees market economy as a complex evolutionary market system, which is based on spontaneous, closely associated, independent, and not predictable actions of the market players. Competition is seen as a discovery journey, which leads to open and unique results and which is based on the spontaneity of the independent decisions of the competitors. Competition is viewed as an overall market process.[212] In *Hayek's* 1946 lecture, '*The Meaning of Competition*' he distinguished the state of perfect competition from the dynamic competitive process. One of the conditions required for the former is perfect knowledge; the central achievement of the latter that 'it is only

---

210. (Kirzner 1992, 62).
211. (von Mises 1949).
212. (Möschel 1983, 47).

Chapter 3: Competition Theory

through the process of competition that the facts will be discovered'.[213] He is referring to the process of the formation of opinion. This process of opinion formation is one built out of a series of entrepreneurial steps, made possible by the competitive freedom of entrepreneurial entry, and exemplified by the entry of one 'who possesses the exclusive knowledge ... to reduce the cost of production of a commodity by 50% and thus reduces its price by 25%.'[214]

In a free unrestricted competition environment, without any arbitrary restraints, production is directed towards consumer wishes, economic performance of producers' increase, costs are reduced and technical-economic progress is realised by the efforts of dynamic entrepreneurs.[215] These insights were deepened and made even more explicit in *Hayek's* later work on *'Competition as a Discovery Procedure'*. In this paper it is emphasised that it is not that prices act as signals transmitting existing information but rather that it is the competitive process which *digs out* what is in fact discovered. In effect, 'competition is valuable only because, and so far as, its results are unpredictable and on the whole different from those which anyone has, or could have, deliberately aimed at'.[216]

Hayek stated in his work *'Der Wettbewerb als Entdeckungsverfahren'* (Kiel 1968) that interventions in the field of competition are wrong and lack content. The most important task of competition policy and competition law is to ensure free markets.[217] *Hayek* denied that this could be reached with the help of state interventions. In his opinion state interventions are used to raise barriers to market entry.[218] The neoliberal law philosophy of *Hayek* is marked by the recommendation that the state should only enact common rules like contract law, incorporation law and patent law with the aim that competition is favoured under all circumstances and restraints on competition are prohibited without exception. Particularly, *Hayek* was against special laws like the German competition law and against a monopoly commission, if they have room for discretionary interpretation. The state should limit its role to providing an appropriate, clear, and always guilty framework, without the necessity of continuous state interference.[219]

Critics of *Hayek's* concept question whether free competition in a social market economy as the only coordination instrument, is sufficient.[220]

3.3.5.2 The Neo-Austrians

Since about 1970 the term 'Austrian economics' has experienced a revival with respect to the ideas of *Carl Menger* and the earlier Austrian School, as developed through the work of *Mises* and *Hayek*. This revival has occurred particularly in the US where a

---

213. (von Hayek 1949, 106).
214. (von Hayek 1949, 101).
215. (Cox und Hübner 1981, 28).
216. (von Hayek 1978, 180).
217. (von Hayek 1969).
218. (von Hayek 1960, 256).
219. (Cox und Hübner 1981, 30).
220. (Baumbach and Hefermehl 1993, 34).

sizeable literature emerged from a number of economists. This literature includes works by *Murray N. Rothbard, Israel Kirzner, Gerald P. O'Driscoll, Mario J. Rizzo* and *Roger W. Garrison.*

The thrust of this literature has been to emphasise the differences between the Austrian understanding of markets as processes and that of the equilibrium theorists whose work has dominated much of modern economic theory.[221] Contemporary neo-Austrian economists claim to adopt economic subjectivism more consistently than any other school of economics and reject much neoclassical formalism. For example, while neoclassical economics formalises the economy as an equilibrium system with supply and demand in balance, Austrian economists' emphasise its dynamic, perpetually disequilibrium nature. As a result of this emphasis the term 'Austrian economics' has often come to be understood as a refusal to adopt modern mathematical and econometric techniques that standard economics adopted largely as a result of its equilibrium orientation. In other words, the difference between the Austrians and mainstream economics can be seen as the difference between a creative art and a dull, predictable science.

The economists in this group of modern Austrians, sometimes called *neo-Austrians*, do see themselves as continuers of an earlier tradition, sharing with mainstream neoclassical economics an appreciation for the systematic outcomes of markets, but differing from it in the understanding of how these outcomes are in fact achieved. Largely as a result of the activity of this group, many classic works have recently attracted a considerable readership.[222]

For mainstream microeconomics, the term 'competition' has for many decades meant the state of affairs associated with the conditions of the perfectly competitive equilibrium market. That state of affairs is the one in which, for each market participant, market price is given, not subject to modification by any one agent's bids or offers. Such conditions imply that the market price is already assumed to be the equilibrium price. Neo-Austrians believe that although there is a tendency towards equilibrium, the economic process should not be analysed on the basis of a model of equilibrium based on perfect competition. For the reason that with such an analysis the nature of the adaptation processes, which are characteristic of the dynamics of disequilibrium in a market economy, disappears. The neo-Austrians, joined by certain neoclassical economists and the monetarists, are of the opinion that competition refers not to a state of affairs but to a dynamic process. Neo-Austrians also contend that government intervention, which goes beyond the supposed intervention in the minimal state, actually increases disequilibrium. Government intervention changes the price structure in such a way that reactionary conduct from the private sector does not lead to a tendency of equilibrium. Thus, adaptation processes are delayed and disturbed.[223] In their view, according to competition law, the principle task of government should be to eliminate obstacles that prevent markets operating smoothly.

---

221. (Kirzner 1992).
222. (Kirzner 1992, 68).
223. (Groeneveld, Maks und Muysken 1990, 2).

Chapter 3: Competition Theory

In the neo-Austrian view the entrepreneurial market process is a competitive process in the sense that it relies on the freedom of potential entrepreneurs to enter markets in order to compete for perceived available profits. Were incumbent firms arbitrarily protected against competitive entry by government measures, the market process would be hampered or halted. 'A market', in *Kirzner's* words:

> is competitive only insofar as it expresses the discoveries of entrepreneurial market participants each of whom is aware that, unless he stays on his toes, others may steal a march on him, and that he is himself free to take advantage of any market opportunity that he believes himself to have detected. In order to be completely competitive, in this sense, we do not require that there be many firms in any one industry; all we require is *that* there is complete freedom for entrepreneurial entry. No market participant enjoys the privilege of being protected against competitive entry.[224]

Although competition policy authors of the neo-Austrian school reach quite similar final conclusions, they may not be confused with the Chicago School, with *Richard Posner, Harold Demsetz, Yale Brozen* and others. The starting points of those two schools are quite different. For Chicagoans economic efficiency is seen as the only goal of anti-trust legislation. For Neo-Austrians, efficiency is a collectivistic (holistic) fiction with no expressive power at all. What should be taken into account are only individual goals. Individual freedom is seen as the only possible criterion for a free economic order.[225] The issue of freedom was analysed in a two dimensional way: the relationship between state and private actor and the relationship between private actors themselves.[226]

But what both have in common is the conclusion that, using *Yale Brozen's* words:

> we make the mistake of thinking that the antitrust laws were designed and applied to keep markets competitive or to make them competitive where they are not. On rare occasions they do that. Most of the applications of the antitrust laws however serve as a restraint on entrepreneurial discovery and on competition. They serve largely to preserve competitors, not competition.[227]

The neoclassical concept of freedom of competition is today one of the most important concepts in competition. Critically, the very often discussed contradiction between economic freedom and economic advantage (*dilemma-problem*) has to be mentioned. The basic statement of the dilemma-problem is that extensive promoting of competition can lead to a conflict with other important economic and meta economic goals.[228] Other critics are against this theoretical approach and the requirement for per se prohibitions for practical competition law.[229]

---

224. (Kirzner I. M. 1990, 32).
225. (Kantzenbach 1990, 203).
226. (I. Schmidt 2012, 18).
227. (Y. Brozen 1990).
228. (Emmerich 1991, 19).
229. (Clapham 1981, 145).

3.3.6 Development towards the European School of Thought

Post-World War II, the ordoliberalism concept of Freiburg scholars contributed significantly to the creation of the Social Market Economy concept the German economy is based on. The protection of free competition is one of the most important 'social' principles in a Social Market Economy. The other one is the equitable distribution of the wealth gains achieved by free competition within society.[230]

Free competition and economic liberty have to sustain many restrictions. Economic freedom bears the potential for its own destruction. The inherent and unavoidable tendency of private business to restrict competition for the sake of monopoly profits induces companies to agree on cartels, on tying arrangements, on exclusive dealership clauses and other restrictive practices. They make use of their liberty in order to narrow their own and their competitor's freedom of contract. This spontaneous decomposition of the market economy has to be prevented by legislation designed to protect competition.[231]

Where competition could not generate the expected results due to market failures like natural monopolies, external effects, or unequal information of the parties, legislation regulating specific economic sectors can be used. As *Eleanor Fox* pointed out, 'Europeans tend to be less hostile to government as regulator and more sceptical of private corporations as servants of the public interest.'[232]

The ordoliberal thought added new legal and social dimensions to the liberal tradition. The legal dimension requires law to protect the market from destructive influences of political and economic power. 'The market could not be allowed to function as an independent entity without any control.'[233]

In the ordoliberal view, competition and competition law is not viewed as automatism, but as a task of active governmental economic policy. Monetary and other policies designed to foster competition would have little effect, ordoliberal scholars argued, if firms could act in concert in setting prices or determining output or if firms with economic power could use that power to foreclose opportunities for competition.

The *Freiburg Ordoliberal School* was founded in the 1930s in Germany by the economist *Walter Eucken* (1891–1950) and the two lawyers, *Franz Böhm* (1895–1977) and *Hans Großmann-Doerth* (1894–1944). As *Böhm* later said in retrospect, the founders of the school were united in their common concern for the question of the constitutional foundations of a free economy and society.[234] The Freiburg School also includes such authors as *Constantine von Dietze, Leonhard Miksch, Wilhelm Röpke* and *Alexander Rüstow,* notwithstanding more politically notable personalities such as *Alfred Müller-Armack* and *Ludwig Erhard.*

As outlined in detail in Chapter one, the drafters of the Treaty of Rome were inspired by the ideas on ordoliberalism of the Freiburg School. During World War II,

---

230. (Müller-Armack, The Meaning of the Social Market Economy 1989, 82–86, 84).
231. see also (W. Eucken 1990) and (E. Mestmäcker 1980).
232. (Fox 1986, 983).
233. (D. J. Gerber 1994, 25).
234. (Vanberg 2002, 38).

Chapter 3: Competition Theory

scholars at the University of Freiburg in Germany developed their thoughts and ideology with respect to a Europe post-world war. Today it is known and widely accepted[235] that the ideas of the Freiburg School, not US ideology, determined the legal language in Articles 101 and 102 and were the guiding principles in the drafting of EU competition law.

3.3.6.1 Role of the State

Ordoliberalism passionately encourages competitive free markets. This is motivated by the historical observation that concentrations of power in both public and private spheres distort the functioning of economies. Thus, in the Freiburg School view the long-term viability of free markets requires a rule-bound and limited yet powerful form of government intervention. To quote the prominent liberal academic *Wilhelm Röpke*:

> A market economy and our economic program presuppose the following type of state: a state which knows exactly where to draw the line between what does and what does not concern it, which prevails in the sphere assigned to it with the whole force of its authority, but refrains from all interference outside its sphere - an energetic umpire whose task it is neither to take part in the game nor to prescribe their movements to players, who is rather, completely impartial and incorruptible and sees to it that the rules of the game and of sportsmanship are strictly enforced. That is the state without which a genuine and real market economy cannot exist.[236]

Thus ordoliberalism is a school of neoliberalism emphasising the need for the state to ensure that the free market produces results close to its theoretical potential. Ordoliberal theory suggests that the state must create a proper legal environment for the economy in order to maintain a healthy level of competition through measures that adhere to market principles. The concern is that, if the state does not take active measures to foster competition, firms with monopoly (or oligopoly) power will emerge, which will not only subvert the advantages offered by the market economy, but also possibly undermine good government. Based on its own historical experiences, the fear in Germany is that strong economic power can be transformed into political power quite smoothly. Therefore, defining the 'rules of the game' of a competitive market society is an Ordoliberal scholar's underlying mission.

An otherwise competitive marketplace often failed from lax legal structures. Examples include: (a) the sub-optimal allocation of resources based on monopoly-skewed pricing, (b) de facto closing of previously accessible markets to other producers, (c) overly-generous patent protections, (d) limited liability law, and (e) an arbitrary application of liability law.[237] These restrictions threaten the efficiency and equity of unencumbered market distribution. Thus, anti-monopoly policy in particular needs to be embedded into a state's legal system.[238]

---

235. See for example (Gerber 2001, 264); (Gormsen 2006); (Cseres 2005, 82); (Marenco 2002, 303).
236. (Röpke 1950, 192).
237. (Eucken 1959).
238. (Möschel 1989, 142–159).

3.3.6.2 Need for a Constitutional Framework

Freiburg School thinkers agreed with earlier conceptions of liberalism in considering a competitive economic system to be necessary for a prosperous, free and equitable society. They were convinced that such a society could develop only where the market was embedded in a constitutional framework. This framework was necessary to protect the process of competition from distortion, as a means of preventing degeneration of the competitive process, to assure that the benefits of the market were equitably distributed throughout society and to minimise governmental intervention in the economy.[239]

Thus, the ordoliberalism of the Freiburg school starts from the very premise that the market order is a constitutional order, that it is defined by its institutional framework and, as such, subject to explicit or implicit constitutional choice. It assumes that the working properties of market processes depend on the nature of the legal-institutional frameworks within which they take place.[240]

Eucken showed that the specific way in which an economic process develops is dependent upon the specific kind of economic system that prevails. However, every specific kind of economic system is but a combination of a quite limited number or elementary constituting elements, e.g., property rights, competition and money. *Eucken* discovered what could be called the interdependence of the economic and political systems of a national state. A liberal market economy, he argued, cannot survive for long in a totalitarian state, nor can a democratic state under the rule of law survive if economic power is highly concentrated. Economic systems differ in their implications for individual freedom.[241] *Eucken* continued his work during the time of the totalitarian Hitler regime. After World War II, a carefully thought-out programme was ready which gained influence in the emerging institutions of the new democracy.

Eucken's view was that the only way to achieve sustained economic performance and stability was through an economic order based on competition. Competition, however, cannot fulfil its integrative function if it is not of the appropriate form. Competition creates an integrated whole from the aggregate of economic processes only if it itself is provided with the necessary structure. This means in turn that the market form of perfect competition[242] must be restored and maintained.[243] *Eucken* understood this to imply that market power should be diffused as far as possible. Moreover, depending on the configuration of the other factors conditioning competition, market power may be diffused even if the market tends toward oligopoly or even monopoly.

Another Freiburg scholar was *Leonhard Miksch*. For structural reasons, *Miksch* developed a scheme of market forms to classify economic phenomena. His classification of supply and demand into competition, oligopoly, and monopoly is a refinement

---

239. (D. Gerber 1998, 232).
240. (Vanberg, April 2011).
241. see (Eucken 1939).
242. Perfect competition as used here does not refer to the stationary state, but rather to the behaviour that takes prices as given and equates them with marginal costs.
243. (Eucken 1959, 160).

of *Heinrich von Stackelberg's* work. *Miksch*, in his scheme, included partial monopolies and partial oligopolies. In addition, *Miksch* related the number of market participants to the market size, that is, to the conditions of uniform markets, uniform goods, and sufficient market transparency. Using this scheme of market forms, *Miksch* assigned market orders to the respective markets:

> It is the task of competition policy to endow each market with the appropriate market order. Doing that, attention must be paid to the existing market form; market forms *cannot* be changed by legislative means at all, but only by economic policy, and even so only in restricted scope and in a long-term time frame.[244]

3.3.6.3 Free Competition

Competition, then, is the primary regulative principle, because only in an environment of competition can economic actors optimally unfold their creativity and coordinate it in voluntary decisions. Accordingly, all markets that are characterised by the market form of 'perfect competition', or in which this market form can be established, must be safeguarded by the market order of 'free competition'. Here, the state should only intervene by way of a proper execution of general competition law. Nonetheless, on markets that are characterised by 'imperfect competition,' the state must actively intervene to establish a market order of 'ordered regulated competition' ('geordnete gebundene Konkurrenz'), for only state interventions in the market can remove market disruptions and 'maintain the general societal interest.' This moreover applies for monopolies.

3.3.6.4 Role of Competition Law

According to *Eucken* and his colleagues, history has demonstrated that competition tended to collapse, because enterprises preferred private, contractual regulation of business activities rather than competition and because enterprises were frequently able to acquire such high levels of economic power that they could eliminate competition. Competition law was viewed as a means of preventing this degeneration of the competitive process. Competition law would *enforce* competition by creating and maintaining the conditions under which it would flourish.[245]

The model of complete (perfect) competition provided the substantive standards for competition law, requiring that law be used to prevent the creation of monopolistic power, to abolish existing monopoly positions where possible and, where this was not possible, to control the conduct of monopolies. The monopoly prohibition was directed primarily at cartels and other anti-competitive agreements between competitors. An independent monopoly office would enforce those principles.[246] This conception of competition law focused attention on one core problem – private economic power.

---

244. (Miksch 1947).
245. (D. J. Gerber 1994, 50).
246. (Lipps 1975, 20).

This fundamentally new concept was a particular application of the German *Ordnungspolitik* and rested on its theoretical underpinnings. The ordoliberal conception of competition law is viewed as having played a key role in the success of the social market economy in Germany and in the evolution of German thought and attitudes about economy and society in general. German competition law was and still is heavily influenced by ordoliberal thoughts.[247] German ordoliberal influence has been particularly direct and obvious in relation to EU competition law. As already stated in Chapter One, EU competition law provisions were included in the Treaty of Rome with German support.[248]

3.3.6.5 Influence of Ordoliberalism in the Early Years of the European Commission's Work

The Ordoliberal thoughts of the Freiburg School extended beyond Germany and have penetrated the thought, institutions and practices of the European Community, as well as various Member States throughout the Community. Most of the leading German representatives in the founding of the European Communities were closely associated with ordoliberalism or at least shared an appreciation for it.[249] As a matter of fact, ordoliberal influence has been particularly direct and obvious in relation to EU competition law. In the 1950s, Germany had comprehensively debated the role of competition, and had passed Europe's first modern national competition statute. As a result, the German competition community emerged as leaders in this area – as illustrated, by the appointment of *Hans von der Groeben* as the first Commissioner for Competition Policy of the European Commission. Especially in the early years of the application of EU competition law, ordoliberal thought set the tone for thinking about competition law within the European Commission.

3.3.6.6 Critics on the Ordoliberal Concept

Critics however emerged. The ordoliberal programme appeared to become outdated in many respects. The economic theory at the time of the development of the ordoliberal

---

247. Most leading scholars in the area of competition law have been closely associated with Ordoliberalism. The strength of this tradition was even on a personal level. One of *Böhm's* scholars, who is a major contributor to the Ordoliberal concept, was *Mestmäcker*, who became the first president of the German Monopoly Commission. Scholars of Mestmäcker like *Immenga* or *Möschel* followed this tradition.
248. (Bayliss and El-Agraa 1990, 137).
249. *Walter Hallstein*, for example, was one of the founders of the European Communities and the first president of the European Commission. He had been a law professor in Germany and a friend of *Heinrich Kronstein*. He became associated with the Ordoliberals during the 1940s, acquiring a high regard for the ideas of *Walter Eucken*. Many of his views on the role of law in shaping the future of European institutions clearly reflect Ordoliberal ideas. Another key figure was *Hans von der Groeben*, one of the two principal drafters of the so-called '*Spaak*-Report', the document on which the Rome Treaty was based. Although they supported the process, Ordoliberals did not provide the primary political impetus for establishing a European common market.

concept (the static neoclassical price theory, as outlined in the previous section) was according to Freiburg scholars not suitable for an analytical model. The principle weakness of the Freiburg school's notion of restriction on economic freedom was, according to *Hawk:*

(1) its failure to generate precise operable legal rules (i.e., failure to provide an analytical framework);
(2) its distance from and tension with (micro) economics that does provide an analytical framework;
(3) its tendency to favour traders/competitors over consumers and consumer welfare (efficiency) and;
(4) its capture of totally innocuous contract provisions having no anti-competitive effects in an economic sense.[250]

These assumptions, which are grounded on failures of the neoclassical model and explained in previous sections, are justified and supported by the findings of the Post-Chicago School.

Nevertheless, economic theory has developed over the years and today provides an analytical model that is possibly suited for the specific situation of EU competition law. The European School of thought is explored and defined in Chapter One.

3.4 APPENDIX: BASIC ECONOMICS

An economy consists of many firms and many more households. Households are concerned with distributing their available time, wealth and skills across a range of different activities in ways, which suit them best. Firms are mainly concerned with making profits. These two groups of economic factors are linked together through two sets of markets. (1) First, there are the markets for goods and services. In these markets, firms supply those goods, which are demanded by households who are willing to sacrifice part of their income and time in order to acquire them. (2) Second, there are the markets for factors of production, including all the different types of resource, which can be used to produce goods and services. In these markets, households are the suppliers, seeking to earn income, and firms are the demanders, seeking to buy or hire the resources, they need in order to produce products.

Demand is defined as a list of prices and of corresponding quantities that consumers are willing and able to buy at each price. The market demand curve shows the quantity that consumers are willing to purchase at different prices. The curve is obtained by asking at each price how much each person demands. Adding up the quantities demanded by all of the consumers at that price we obtain the total quantity that is demanded at each price (market demand curve). As the price is reduced, each person will increase the quantity demanded. That means the total quantity demanded must also increase as the price for the commodity falls. The market demand curve is the

---

250. (Hawk 1995, 978).

horizontal addition of the individual demand curves. The quantity demanded varies inversely with price. Demand elasticity measures the responsiveness of the quantity demanded to price changes. The more (or less) responsive quantity demanded is to price, the more elastic (or inelastic) is the demand.

The following Figure 3.2 represents a 'demand curve', showing the amounts which consumers are willing and able to buy at each price. If consumers are deemed to be rational and self-interested, then the price that a consumer is willing to pay for a unit of the commodity can conveniently be taken as a monetary measure of the satisfaction he expects to get from having that unit of the commodity.

Figure 3.2   Demand Curve

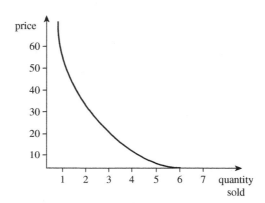

The market demand curve is the horizontal sum of individual demand curves.

Figure 3.3 below illustrates this relationship. If the price is 25, for example, the quantity demanded by consumer A is 2 units and the quantity demanded by consumer B is 1 unit. The total quantity demanded in the market at a price of 25 is 3 units, as shown on the market total demand curve. Position A shows the point where the demand curve is kinked; this is the price at which consumer B first comes into the market. At the point where the demand curve reaches the x-axis so many units have been produced that no one is willing to pay for a further unit (saturation quantity). If the demand curve reaches the y-axis, the price is so high that no one wants any further unit of the commodity (prohibition price).

Chapter 3: Competition Theory

Figure 3.3 Different Demand Curves and Market Demand Curve

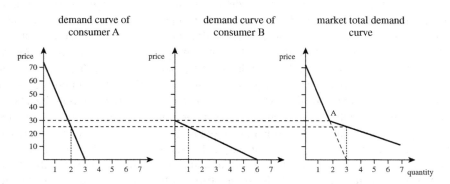

In the very simple example given (Figure 3.2) consumer saturation is achieved by producing six units of the commodity shown.

However, most goods and services cannot be produced without cost, and it has to be remembered that each unit produced requires resources that could have been used to produce other things. Clearly, this needs to be taken into account when deciding on the most efficient level of output to produce. Therefore, it is necessary to discuss cost curves and supply.

Figure 3.4 illustrates the elements of the basic competitive model. Figure 3.4(a) below refers to a typical firm. Figure 3.4(b) describes the entire market.

Figure 3.4 Costs and Supply Curve

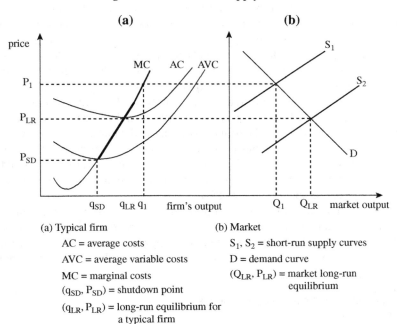

(a) Typical firm
AC = average costs
AVC = average variable costs
MC = marginal costs
(q_{SD}, P_{SD}) = shutdown point
(q_{LR}, P_{LR}) = long-run equilibrium for a typical firm

(b) Market
S_1, S_2 = short-run supply curves
D = demand curve
(Q_{LR}, P_{LR}) = market long-run equilibrium

151

Figure 3.4(a) illustrates the firm's cost curves – the average cost curve, the average variable cost curve and the marginal cost curve. The average cost (AC) or unit cost is equal to total cost divided by the number of goods produced and the average variable cost (AVC) is variable cost per each unit of output. Short run average cost and average variable cost curves are usually drawn with the parabolic shape of Figure 3.4(a). This shows the law of the diminishing marginal productivity. That means that an increasing number of variable inputs are combined with a given amount of fixed inputs. A point is reached after which output per unit of variable inputs begins to decline. The marginal cost is the change in cost per unit change in output. If there are low output levels, additional production factors (e.g., workforce) are very productive and the cost of an additional unit of output is relatively small. The marginal cost declines as output rises from low levels and the workforce approaches the most efficient size for the capital stock. It can be observed that the marginal cost begins to rise as the point of diminishing marginal productivity is reached.[251]

Supply is the list of prices and the corresponding quantity that will be supplied at each price on the list. It is illustrated by the market supply curve. Supply elasticity measures the responsiveness of quantity supplied to changes in price.

Market equilibrium exists when the price in a market is such that the quantity demanded equals the quantity supplied.[252] It is illustrated by the intersection of the market demand and the supply curves.

A firm in a competitive market tries to earn as large a profit as possible by choosing the output that makes marginal cost equal to the market price. As long as marginal cost is less than the market price, the firm will gain by increasing its output. At the point when the firm reaches the output that makes its marginal cost equal to the market price, it will not profit by further increases in output. The output level q1 in Figure 3.4(a) makes marginal cost equal to the market price P1. This output is the profit-maximising level for the firm. The point (q1, P1) is one point on the firm's supply curve that shows the output that the firm will bring to the market at different prices. For prices like P1, the firm supply curve coincides with the firm's marginal cost curve.

If the firm shuts down, the losses equal the rental cost of the fixed factors of production. This cost must be covered no matter how much output is produced. In the case where the price falls below its average variable cost, the loss to the firm would be even more than the fixed cost if the firm puts output on the market. The firm would not only lose its fixed cost, but would have an additional loss on every unit sold. This means a shortfall of price from the firm's average variable cost. Firms can avoid such a loss. The profit-maximising firm will shut down if the market price falls below the minimum average variable cost (price PSD).

These arguments show that the supply curve of a single firm in a competitive industry is the marginal cost curve above the shutdown point.[253] The market supply curve is obtained by adding up the individual supply curves of the firms within the market. Figure 3.4(b) shows the initial short run market supply curve S1. The short run

---

251. see (Martin 1994, 17 ff).
252. see also (Maurice, Phillips and Ferguson 1982, 62).
253. (Martin 1994, 17 ff).

Chapter 3: Competition Theory

market equilibrium exists at the point of intersection of the market demand, which shows the quantity that consumers will purchase at different prices and the supply curves. The initial short run equilibrium price is P1 and the corresponding output is Q1. A typical firm will produce output q1 in short run equilibrium. In this case, new firms will enter the market in the long run or firms that are in the market will set up new plants. When additional plants are built the output, which is produced at different prices, are added to the short run market supply curve. That means the short run supply curve shifts to the right and market equilibrium slides down the demand curve. The short run equilibrium price falls and the quantity supplied increases. As long as there is a profit to be made by market entrance, which means as long as the price exceeds the firm's average cost, the process will continue. The price could fall until it reaches the minimum average cost. This is the price PLR. For the single plant firm the long run equilibrium is q LR and the industry output in long run equilibrium is QLR.

Within long run equilibrium, each firm's marginal cost equals the market price. Therefore, each firm is maximising its profit. Market price equals average cost and firms earn only a normal rate of return on investment. Individual profit is maximised and it can be expected that no firm would change its behaviour. When the economic profit is zero, neither new firm have an incentive to enter the industry nor firms in the industry have a reason to exit. This equilibrium will exist unless an external force shifts firm cost curves or the market demand curve.[254] In Figure 3.4(b), the demand curve and the cost curve are brought together, identifying the optimal output of this commodity at the point of intersection of the demand and supply curves. Thus markets characterised by the assumptions of perfect competition have the following properties:

- price is equal to marginal cost;
- price is equal to average cost (thus implying that marginal cost is equal to average cost);
- no firm makes profits above the normal level of profit.

These above-mentioned properties are shown in Figure 3.5.

Figure 3.5 Perfect Competition

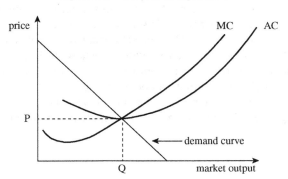

---

254. (Martin 1994, 20 f).

To conclude, a firm chooses the output at which marginal revenue MR equals marginal cost MC. The firm then checks that it is covering average costs. A competitive firm aims for MR to equal price. That means that selling an extra unit of output does not bid down the price and reduce the revenue earned on previous units. The price at which the extra unit is sold gives a change in total revenue.

Under the conditions specified, no firm has any market power. As far as each individual firm is concerned the price of the industry's product is determined by market forces, and each firm has to accept that price and shall sell as much as to yield maximum profit. As the firm gets the same price for each unit of output it sells, regardless of the amount produced, the firm aiming for maximum profit will increase its output up to the level where the price it gets for a further unit sold is just equal to the extra cost incurred in producing that unit. In other words, price will be equal to marginal cost, giving the socially optimal result described above. This point is set out in more detail in Figure 3.6 below.

Figure 3.6(a) shows the situation facing an individual firm in a perfectly competitive industry. The horizontal line PD shows the demand curve facing the firm, indicating that the firm can sell any amount at price P, but nothing at a higher price. The line MC shows the firm's marginal costs for each level of output. If the firm wishes to make maximum profit, it will choose to produce at a level of output Q. This situation facing each individual firm under 'atomistic competition' (another term sometimes used to describe perfect competition) is directly related to the overall industry position shown in Figure 3.6(b).

Figure 3.6(b) shows the demand curve for the product as a whole (as opposed to the demand for an individual firm's output shown in Figure 3.6(a)) and the 'supply curve', which shows the amount of the product which firms in the industry will choose to produce at each price. The market price is determined by the intersection of these two curves, with price P and quantity Q. However, the supply curve is simply the marginal cost curve for the industry as a whole, showing as it does the amount which all firms taken together will choose to supply at each price (which is, of course, directly related to the marginal cost of each firm in the industry).

A direct comparison of Figures 3.6(a) and 3.6(b) reveals that under perfect competition, the result which the market mechanism automatically produces is the same as the industry efficient result. This is a modern version of *Smith's* original 'Invisible Hand' proposition – that self-interested behaviour on the part of individuals, when moderated by competition, can provide a socially desirable result. Price will automatically equal the marginal cost of output for every firm in the industry, and the economically efficient level of output will be produced.[255]

Figure 3.6(a) shows the horizontal demand curve D crossing the marginal cost curve MC and Figure 3.6(b) shows the industry supply and demand curves.

---

255. see (Agnew 1985, 26).

Chapter 3: Competition Theory

Figure 3.6   Model of Competition

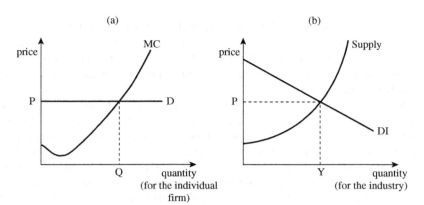

In contrast, the demand curve of the *monopolist* is the industry demand curve, which slopes down. There is only one supplier and entry is blocked. That means that the monopolist faces no actual and no potential competition. The marginal revenue is less than the price at which the extra output unit is sold. The monopolist recognises that extra output reduces revenue from previous units because price falls as we move down the demand curve. Figure 3.7 is a reminder of the previous discussion about the relationship between price, marginal revenue and total revenue when the demand curve slopes down.

Figure 3.7   Model of Monopoly

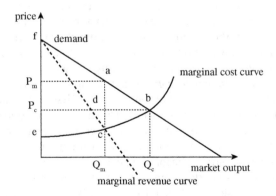

The monopolist is a price maker unlike the competitive firm, which is a price taker. That means a competitive firm takes the market price as given and varies the output until its marginal cost equals price.

A high inelasticity of the demand curve demonstrates that an extra unit of output will bid down the price and will reduce the revenues from existing units. The monopolist must move down the market demand curve if he produces and sells an extra unit of output, which causes a price reduction and leads to the marginal revenue concept.

Marginal revenue means the change in total revenue for each unit change in the demanded quantity. These revenues are lower than the price because selling an additional unit of the commodity requires a downwards movement on the demand curve. That means a reduction in price and a loss in revenue on units that could have been sold at a higher price.

The monopolist chooses the output that makes its marginal cost equal to its marginal revenue in order to earn as large a profit as possible (Figure 3.7). At an output less than Q_m, the marginal revenues would exceed marginal cost. By increasing the output, revenues would increase more than its cost. This means that the profit would increase. Therefore, the monopolist will increase output as long as marginal revenue exceeds marginal cost. At the point where marginal revenue is equal to marginal cost, the monopolist maximises his profit (output Qm). This is the same logic that is used to show that a competitive firm will maximise its profit by picking the output that makes its marginal cost equal to the market price. The difference is that a competitive firm can sell all it wishes at the market price and a monopolist must lower the price when he wants to increase sales. When the profit-maximising output is found then the monopoly price can be reached by going up the demand curve. This is shown in Figure 3.7 where the price Pm is the price at which Qm units of output will be the quantity demanded.[256] The point on the total demand curve which represents the profit maximising point for the monopolist, defined by Pm and Qm is called the *Cournot Point*.

The traditional measure of social welfare is made up of two parts. The first is the consumer surplus and the second is the producer surplus. Consumer surplus is the area under the demand curve but above the price (the area aP_mf in Figure 3.7). This area shows the sum of how much each unit sold is valued by consumers above its price. The area abP_cP_m in Figure 3.7 is the loss of the consumer surplus due to the monopoly. The area $aceP_m$, the area above the marginal cost curve but below the price is the producer's surplus. The area *abcd* shows the deadweight social welfare loss from monopoly. That means the cost to society of a market not operating efficiently.

An industry with *monopolistic competition* has many sellers that are producing commodities that are close substitutes for one another. That means that every firm has just a limited ability to affect its output price.[257] The theory of monopolistic competition is characterised by a large number of small firms so that each firm can neglect the possibility that its own decisions cause any adjustment in the other firms. Free entry and exit from the industry in the long run can be assumed. This framework seems to resemble the discussion of perfect competition but the difference is the fact that each firm faces a downwards-sloping demand curve. This theory shows an industry in which each firm can influence its market share by changing its price relative to its competitors. The demand curve is not horizontal because products are limited

---

256. see (Martin 1994, 23 ff).
257. see (Begg, Fischer und Dornbusch 1997, 146).

substitutes. Reducing prices attracts only some customers from other shops but each shop will always have some local customers for whom the importance of a nearby shop is more important than a few pence on the price of a product. That means that monopolistic competition shows product differentiation, for example by location or brand loyalty, which may allow firms to charge slightly different prices from other firms in the industry without losing all its customers. Monopolistic competition requires on the one hand product differentiation and on the other hand limited opportunities for economies of scale so that there are numerous producers who can largely neglect their interdependence with any particular rival.

The market shares of each firm depend on the number of firms within the market and the prices charged. If there are a given number of suppliers, the shift in the industry demand curve will affect the demand curve of every single supplier. That means that an increase in the number of suppliers in the industry will shift the demand curve for the individual firms to the left thereby decreasing market shares. To some extent, a firm can increase its market share by reducing prices. There will be new entrants as long as there is the possibility of realising short run profits. Just at the point where each firm's demand curve has shifted so far to the left that the price is equal to the average cost, market entry stops. At this point, firms are breaking even.[258]

An *oligopoly* is an industry with only a few producers who may recognise that its own-price depends not merely on its own output but also on the actions of its important competitors in the industry.[259] Oligopolistic industries are faced sometimes with the need for each firm to examine how its own actions will affect the decisions of its relatively few competitors. That means firms may take the commercial decisions of their competitors into account when they are formulating their own strategy. Advances in game theory have resulted in significantly more sophisticated economic models of competition by taking explicit account of the interactions between competing firms. A 'new' branch of economics (non-cooperative game theory) initiated by Neumann and Morgenstern (1944), arose which addressed the strategic interactions between the different firms. The examination of oligopoly received little attention until the 1970s because of the lack of tools which were required in this area.

The assumptions of the *Cournot model of oligopoly* are that each firm competes by setting their output so as to maximise profits given the output of their competitors. It is also assumed that the firms set their quantities only once and the competitive outcome is a non-cooperative Nash equilibrium (see also the Prisoners' Dilemma). Figure 3.8 illustrates the Cournot Model of Oligopoly. The decision-making process of firm 1 is that for each amount of output which is produced by firm 2 there is a unique output that maximises firm 1's profit which is shown by the reaction curve R_1. Each given level of output of firm 2 corresponds with the reaction curve of firm 1 which indicates the level of output that will maximise the profit of firm 1 by a given output of firm 2. It can be said that for each amount of output that is produced by firm 1, there is a unique output that maximises the profit of firm 2 (shown by the reaction curve R_2). To sum up, along the reaction curve R_1 firm 1 is choosing its output level in order to maximise its

---

258. (Begg, Fischer und Dornbusch 1997, 149).
259. (Begg, Fischer und Dornbusch 1997, 146).

profits given the output of firm 2 and along reaction curve R_2, firm 2 behaves in the same way given the output of firm 1. The point of intersection (E) of both reaction curves is the non-cooperative Nash equilibrium which means that both firms are maximising their profits given the output of the other firm (the Cournot equilibrium). The Cournot model is characterised by the fact that price is higher than marginal cost. With an increasing number of firms price moves closer to marginal costs but still remains above marginal costs.

Figure 3.8   Cournot Model of Oligopoly

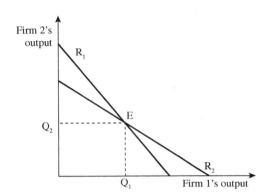

The assumption that different firms compete by setting their prices and not their quantities is a feature of the *Bertrand model* differentiating it from the Cournot model which takes into consideration quantities supplied by firms. The Bertrand model assumes that there are two firms, each of them aiming to maximise its profits and being able to compete with each other by setting its price, based on information of the price set by the other firm. The other assumptions are that the products supplied by the firms are homogeneous; the firms set their prices only once, the marginal costs of the firms are identical and constant, and that the outcome of competition is a non-cooperative Nash equilibrium. Any price firm 2 sets, firm 1 can maximise its profits by setting a price just slightly lower than firm 2 and by supplying the whole market. That means leaving firm 2 with a demand of zero. Firm 2 has an incentive to just undercut the price that is set by firm 1. This will not happen if one of the firms sets the price at marginal cost, since at this point it does not pay to undercut this price. The consequence is that firms set the price at marginal cost, there is allocative efficiency and the outcome of competition under Bertrand competition is similar to that under perfect competition. The outcome is not dependent on the number of firms. Critics of this model say no firm will lose all of its demand because of capacity or preferences. Also the model does not consider the implications of capacity constraints and on the other hand it assumes that products are homogeneous.

This section concludes with an overview of the different concepts of competition as discussed in this chapter.

Table 3.2   Overview Concepts of Competition

	Chicago School	Harvard School	Austrian School
Aims	Consumer welfare, meaning a favourable relationship between price and quantity (economic aim) No consideration of meta economic aims	Economic aims (functions of competition) e.g.: – Distribution equity – Consumer sovereignty – Optimal factor allocation – Adaptation flexibility – Technological progress – Meta economic aims – Decentralisation of economic power	Freedom of competition as the final aim resulting in individual economic advantage (Non-dilemma thesis)
Research method	Neoclassical analysis in the interests of 'analytical clarity' and the legal certainty of firms	Empirical examination and legal case studies in order to develop further empirical price and competition theories rich in content	Model-predictions about characteristics and economic advantages of competition systems; no single statement about the concrete shaping of the system
Horizon	Long-term	Short and middle-term	Long-term
Competition approach	Approach of behaviour (the problem is not concentration but collusion)	Market structure, market conduct, market performance paradigm	Competition as nomocratic order which means that the competition aims regarding contents are left open (refusal of the teleocratic approach)

	Chicago School	Harvard School	Austrian School
Concept of measurement	Allocative efficiency that means an optimal allocation of resources Productive efficiency, meaning an efficient use of resources within the different firms (e.g., realisation of economies of scale or transaction-cost economies)	Market structure, market conduct, market performance which correspond to normative aims (categorical approach)	Refusal of welfare economic efficiency concepts and econometric models for the analysis of competition processes; but restriction of freedom of competition (test of market power)
Competition policy	Survival of the fittest, just exceptional structural interventions because the market regulates itself; breaking up just in exceptional areas. Per se ban in case of horizontal agreements; vertical agreements are subject of per se-legality, unless essential negative horizontal effects appear (rule of reason).	Governmental competition policy opposite concentration (merger control and break up) and pursuit of negotiation and hindrance strategies; partly per se-rule, partly rule of reason	Drawing up general rules of conduct (per se-rules), which secure the competition system.
Exceptions	Deregulation of state controlled branches of industry and far elimination of exception areas.	Criticism of the too extensive exemptions concerning the exceptions of competition	Original acceptance of natural competition hindrance (e.g., because of economies of scale); elimination of political exceptions as artificial competition hindrances.

Source: (Schmidt & Haucap, 2012, p. 14 ff).

CHAPTER 4
Competition Practice

4.1 CHANGES IN THE ENFORCEMENT SYSTEM

At the beginning of this century, the Commission reviewed its anti-trust enforcement rules and procedures with respect to Articles 101 and 102 TFEU.[1]

The Community legislature, within the limits of the general principles of the TEU, is empowered to lay down rules on the application of Articles 101 and 102 by bodies other than the Community institutions as well as rules on the interaction between the different decision-makers. This power was applied with respect to Regulation 1/2003. In the following discussion the legislative process itself is discussed first before the basic principles enshrined in Regulation 1/2003 are elaborated. Special attention is given to the so-called 'German clause' in Regulation 1/2003.

4.1.1 The 2000 Proposal

The proposal of the Commission for a new regulation replacing Regulation 17/62 dates back to 2000.[2] The aim of the reform was to give the Commission new anti-trust powers and procedures for an enlarged and more mature European Union (EU). Another intention of the reform was that national competition authorities (NCAs) should take part more extensively in implementing EU anti-trust rules.[3] The reform also requested that Member States' courts and competition authorities should make a greater contribution to the enforcement of the EU anti-trust rules. At the same time, the goal was the creation of a level playing field for business, as all enforcers should have an obligation to apply the EU anti-trust rules to cases that affect trade between Member States.

---

1. In the following Arts 101 and 102 TFEU are just mentioned as Arts 101 and 102. The same applies for Arts 2 and 3 TEU.
2. (Commission Proposal for a Council Regulation on the implementation of the rules on competition 2000).
3. (Commission proposes regulation that amends system for implementing Arts 81 and 82 2000).

In 2000, national courts and NCAs had been applying Article 101(1) and Article 102 for almost forty years. However, in contrast to Regulation 1/2003, Regulation 17/62 gave the Commission the sole power to declare Article 101(1) inapplicable pursuant to Article 101(3). The 2000 reform stopped the Commission from having an exemption monopoly on Article 101(3) by enabling the direct applicability of the exception rule in the Member States. Article 102 had been applied consistently by the Commission, national authorities as well as national courts since 1958. Accordingly, the 2000 proposal provided for certain rules to be respected by NCAs and/or courts when applying Articles 101 and 102 as well as rules on cooperation between them and with the Commission.

Another objective of the 2000 proposal was to exclude the application of national competition law to agreements and practices that affect trade between Member States. Such agreements and practices should only be subject to a single set of rules. This was considered essential in order to ensure that competition in the internal market is not distorted because of differences in the legal framework.

The objective of a coherent application of EU anti-trust law was manifested in the 2000 proposal in Article 3.[4] The proposed Article 3 stipulated that when an agreement or practice is capable of affecting trade between Member States only EU anti-trust law should be applied. In the system in place before Regulation 1/2003, the same agreement or conduct was subject to Community competition law and several national competition laws. In accordance with the principle of primacy of Community competition law, established by the Court of Justice in the *Walt Wilhelm*[5] case, national law can be applied only as far as it does not prejudice the uniform application of the Community competition rules throughout the single market. Thus, the primacy principle resolves clear conflicts in favour of Community law thereby removing the costs attached to the parallel application of Community law and national laws for both competition authorities and business.

The uniform application of EU anti-trust law in the Community was considered to be of fundamental importance. Not only the fundamental objective of equal conditions of competition for companies on the single market but also the concern for uniform protection of consumer interests in the entire Community would be undermined if in the actual enforcement of the anti-trust rules of Articles 101 and 102 significant disparities occur. For that reason, the objective of a uniform application of Articles 101 and 102 was a central theme running throughout Regulation 1/2003.[6]

In this context, Article 3 of Regulation 1/2003 addresses the relationship between national competition laws and EU anti-trust law. This rule is the so-called '*convergence*

---

4. Article 3 2000 Proposal:

   Where an agreement, a decision by an association of undertakings or a concerted practice within the meaning of Article 81 of the Treaty or the abuse of a dominant position within the meaning of Article 82 may affect trade between Member States, Community competition law shall apply to the exclusion of national competition laws.

5. (ECJ, Walt Wilhelm and other v. Bundeskartellamt, Case 14/68 1969).
6. (Opinion of Advocate General Kokott, Case C-8/08, T-Mobile Netherlands BV and Others 2009, para. 85).

Chapter 4: Competition Practice

clause'. The convergence clause is evident where NCAs or courts apply both European and national competition law in parallel, the application of the latter is subject to an obligation of convergence as defined in Article 3(2) Regulation 1/2003.

Regulation 1/2003 does not preclude Member States from implementing on their territory national legislation, which protects legitimate interests other than anti-trust law.[7] However, when it comes to the application of Article 101 the rule is clear: NCAs and courts need to apply Article 101 as well. The same is true for Article 102: Where the competition authorities of a Member States or national courts apply national competition law to any abuse prohibited by Article 102, they shall also apply Article 102 of the Treaty (Article 3(1) Regulation 1/2003).

In relation to Article 102, the convergence clause is weakened by Recital 8 in the preamble of Regulation 1/2003:

> *Member States should not under this Regulation be precluded from adopting and applying on their territory stricter national competition laws which prohibit or impose sanctions on unilateral conduct engaged in by undertakings. These stricter national laws may include provisions which prohibit or impose sanctions on abusive behaviour toward economically dependent undertakings.*

The application of the exemption to the convergence clause enshrined in Recital 8 depends thus on (i) whether trade between Member States is affected, (ii) whether the national legislation can be classified as competition law and (iii) whether the behaviour in question is a unilateral conduct and not an agreement under Article 101. In such a case, stricter national laws may include provisions, which prohibit or impose sanctions on abusive behaviour toward economically dependent undertakings.

To conclude, the Commission's 2000 Proposal focused on a consistent application of competition rules in an enforcement system in which parallel powers to apply Articles 101 and 102 are exercised by the Commission, national authorities and national courts. The conclusion at that time was that it is crucial to adopt measures addressing the danger of inconsistent application effectively.

4.1.2 Legislative Process

The legislative process started in September 2000 with the consultation of the European Parliament and the Economic and Social Committee.

The European Parliament voiced concerns that a greater decentralisation of the EU anti-trust rules must under no circumstances lead to any re-nationalisation of the

---

7. In so far as such national legislation pursues predominantly an objective different from that of protecting competition on the market, the competition authorities and courts of the Member States may apply such legislation on their territory. Accordingly, Member States may under Regulation 1/2003 implement on their territory national legislation that prohibits or imposes sanctions on acts of unfair trade practice, be they unilateral or contractual. Such legislation pursues a specific objective, irrespective of the actual or presumed effects of such acts on competition on the market. This is particularly the case of legislation which prohibits undertakings from imposing on their trading partners, obtaining or attempting to obtain from them terms and conditions that are unjustified, disproportionate or without consideration. See also Recital 9, Regulation 1/2003.

competition policy as such.[8] All economic agents should be treated on a non-discriminatory basis throughout the Community. The Parliament recognised that as the prohibitions of Articles 101 and 102 tend by their very nature to produce direct effects in relations between individuals, the Articles create rights directly in respect of the individuals concerned, which national courts must safeguard. The Parliament supported an autonomous decision-making power for the Commission as retained in the 2000 proposal. The setup of an information and cooperation mechanism in the 2000 proposal received approval by the Parliament too since it was supposed to guarantee a consistent application of the rules within the Community.

The Economic and Social Committee commented in a similar way:[9] Article 3 in the Commission's 2000 proposal was qualified as solid. The Committee confirmed that the relationship between Articles 101 and 102 and national competition laws is clear and remarkably bold in its conciseness and brevity in the 2000 proposal, thereby removing one of its main causes for concern. The Committee agreed in particular with the mandatory application of Community law as provided under the proposed Article 3, when the facts or practices may affect trade between Member States. The Committee regarded this as the most appropriate response to concerns about the re-nationalisation of competition rules. Consequently, EU anti-trust law was supposed to be superior to national legislation in all instances.

During the first working debates in the legislative process at the Council, the German and French delegation expressed opposition to Article 3 of the Commission's 2000 proposal. Both argued that it went beyond codifying the principle of primacy of EU law over national law and that it would supersede national competition law in important areas where national rules currently are applied. Germany entered a general reservation to Article 3, while all other delegations (including France) stated that Article 3 was central to the entire reform package and that they could take a view on it once other elements had been clarified.[10]

Germany has a national Act against Restraints of Competition (ARC).[11] Germany applies this Act in all cases when there is *no* effect on trade between Member States.

---

8. (Draft Legislative Resolution A5-0229/2001, 2001).
9. (European Commission, Opinion of the Economic and Social Committee on the Proposal for a Council Regulation on the implementation of the rules, 2001, 73–80).
10. (Council of European Union, Note from General Secretariat of the Council to the Delegations 5158/01 2001, 10).
11. The national German Act provides for a prohibition of unfair hindrance, which applies to firms holding a superior bargaining position as well as dominant undertakings. Regarding the superior bargaining position, s. 20(2) of ARC stipulates that a firm holds a superior bargaining position if small or medium-sized enterprises as suppliers or purchasers of certain kinds of goods or commercial services depend on this firm in such a way that sufficient and reasonable possibilities of resorting to other undertakings do not exist. Such dependence exists only if besides the undertaking allegedly holding a superior bargaining position in the relevant market no other undertakings exist which would be able and willing to supply the respective small or medium-sized undertaking on reasonable terms. The presumption of a superior bargaining position applies only to buyers although a supplier as well as buyer may hold a superior bargaining position in relation to another undertaking. According to the law, a supplier of certain kind of goods or commercial services shall be presumed to depend on a purchaser within the meaning of s. 20(2) of ARC if this purchaser regularly obtains from this supplier, in addition to discounts customary in the trade or other remuneration, special benefits which are

Chapter 4: Competition Practice

Probably, Germany's concern was that because of ongoing European integration national cases might be qualified as supra-national cases and thereby give precedence to EU anti-trust law. Since the request to deviate from the general convergence clause in Article 3 can be traced back to Germany, the exemption to Article 3 is called the 'German' clause.[12]

During the legislative process, Germany consistently (e.g., in January[13] and June 2001[14]) continued to express a general reservation against Article 3 and claimed that the application of stricter national anti-trust law should be possible.[15] France and Austria, who pronounced general reservations as well, followed Germany. In May 2002, France proposed that Article 3 must not put into question the application of specific national law provisions permitting a reaction in a suitable manner to specific problems arising on one Member States' territory that Community law cannot deal with appropriately.[16] Germany maintained its general reservation by again requesting new language on unilateral behaviour and stricter national rules to be included in the text.[17] France did not concur in that regard anymore. In September 2002, Finland held that Article 3 must not put into question the application of specific national law provisions permitting States to react in a suitable manner to specific problems arising on one Member States' territory and that Community law cannot deal with appropriately. Germany continued with its general reservations (9 September[18] and 1 October 2002[19]). On 15 November 2002, Germany was the only country left with a general

---

      not granted to similar purchasers. Section 20(4) of ARC sets forth that firms with superior bargaining power shall not hinder small or medium-sized competitors, in particular by offering goods or services below cost price without objective justification and by implementing a cost price squeeze.

12. See new Art. 3(1) and (2) in (Council of European Union, Progress Report from the presidency to the COREPER/Council (Industry/Energy) 13563/01 2001, 20) The new Art. 3(2) has been integrated in Art. 3(1) in the Report from the Competition Working party to the Permanent Representatives Committee (Council of European Union, Report from the Competition Working party to the Permanent Representatives Committee 11791/02 2000, 17).
13. (Council of European Union, Note from General Secretariat of the Council to the Delegations 5158/01 2001).
14. (Council of European Union, Note from the General Secretariat of the Council to the Delegations 9999/01 2001).
15. (Council of European Union, Note from General Secretariat of the Council to the Competition Working Party 13451/02 2002, 18), (Eibl and Schultze 2005, 526) (Klees 2006, 406).
16. France suggests inserting an additional paragraph with the following wording:

    *This provision is without prejudice to the implementation by national competition authorities or national courts of national law provisions that **mainly pursues a different or complementary objective** from that assigned to articles 81 and 82 of the Treaty. This is the case of national provisions that prohibit or punish on national territory unilateral acts of companies that, without holding a dominant position, can affect competition or acts of companies that affect fair trade.*

17. (Council of European Union, Progress Report from the presidency to the permanent representatives Committee/Council 8383/02 2002).
18. (Council of European Union, Report from the Competition Working party to the Permanent Representatives Committee 11791/02 2000).
19. (Council of European Union, Report from Competition Working Party to the Permanent Representatives Committee 12998/02 2002).

reservation stating that the application of stricter national law should be possible.[20] The same holds for the version published on 21 November 2002.[21]

The Commission participated in this discussion with the Council working group with a Staff Working Paper on 'Article 3 – the relationship between EC law and national law'. The Commission confirmed again that Article 3 was intended to ensure that agreements and practices capable of affecting cross-border trade should be scrutinised under a single set of rules only, to the exclusion of both more lenient and stricter national competition laws applicable to such agreements and practices.[22] Article 3 was supposed to promote a level playing field throughout the Community and remove the costs attached to the parallel application of EU competition law and national laws for NCAs, national courts and undertakings.

The Commission identified in its paper that differences in national competition law standards create an inherent risk of compartmentalisation and distortion of competition in the internal market. Stricter national standards in some Member States make it more difficult for firms, engaging in intra-Community trade, to pursue a coherent strategy in several Member States or the Community as a whole, for example, by employing a common distribution strategy. The prohibition of agreements or obligations to modify them significantly may force the undertakings concerned to change their commercial strategy on the market, which in turn can lead to a loss of economic welfare. This contradicts the very aim of EU anti-trust law, which is to promote economic welfare in the Community.[23]

With respect to the interpretation of Article 3, the Commission stated that Article 3 in the 2000 Proposal form does not eliminate the application of national competition law. It remains applicable to all agreements and practices that do not affect trade between Member States.[24]

As regards unilateral conduct, the Commission interpreted Article 3 – interestingly now – as applying only to practices that constitute an abuse of a dominant position within the meaning of Article 102. It does not exclude the application of stricter national laws that regulate the unilateral behaviour of undertakings whether dominant or not. In the context of Article 3, the prohibition rule of Article 102, as far as it applies to unilateral conduct, thus constitutes only a minimum standard that must be applied throughout the Community.[25]

Thus, the Commission deviated from the previous standpoint in paragraph 60 by stating that the need to exclude the application of stricter national laws to the behaviour of dominant undertakings is less compelling as long as such national laws do

---

20. (Council of European Union, Report from General Secretariat of the Council to the Permanent Representatives Committee 14327/02 2002).
21. (Council of European Union, Report from Permanent Representatives Committee to the Council 14471/02 2002).
22. (European Commission, Commission Staff Working Paper on Art. 3, SEC (2001) 871 2001, 6).
23. *Ibid.*, para. 11.
24. *Ibid.*, para. 40.
25. *Ibid.*, para. 73.

Chapter 4: Competition Practice

not impinge on pro-competitive or non-restrictive agreements.[26] The Commission finally stated that Article 3 does not exclude the application of stricter national competition laws to the unilateral behaviour of companies. On the other hand, to the extent that the abusive behaviour is based on an agreement within the meaning of Article 101, only Articles 101 and 102 can apply if the case affects trade between Member States. In other words – according to the Commission – as regards unilateral conduct Article 3 only excludes the application of national rules that are equivalent to those contained in Article 102. If it is alleged that a dominant firm has committed an abuse of the type covered by Article 102, for example discriminatory pricing, Article 3 must be applied. National law, on the other hand, remains applicable to the extent that it applies to the unilateral conduct of non-dominant firms or regulates the unilateral conduct of dominant firms in a stricter way than Article 102. In the field of unilateral conduct, the main effect of Article 3 is thus to ensure that practices covered by Article 102 become subject to a common standard and to the cooperation mechanisms of the network of competition authorities.[27]

On 13 December 2002, the Council published the political agreement, which includes the revised 'German clause' whereby the original text has been amended and Article 3(2) reads as follows: *'Member States shall not under this Regulation be precluded from adopting and applying on their territory stricter national laws which prohibit or sanction unilateral conduct engaged in by undertakings.'*

Neither the White Paper nor the Commission's 2000 Proposal nor the European Parliament nor the Economic and Social Committee discussed the possibility that a NCA can apply a stricter national anti-trust law provision under Article 102. Within the legislative procedure, as shown above, it was clear to everybody involved that since the time the Treaty went into force in 1958, Article 102 was applied consistently throughout the EU: by the Commission, by national authorities as well as by national courts. The very objective of the Commission's 2000 proposal was to enhance the protection of competition and to create a level playing field for business throughout the Community. In particular, the aim was to ensure that Articles 101 and 102 together are applied in a consistent manner by the various decision-makers involved in their application. As we will see in the following, this aim was not achieved.

The 2000 proposal led to the adoption of Regulation 1/2003 on 16 December 2002. On 1 May 2004 the new anti-trust enforcement regulation as well as documents, which cover such things as treatment of complaints, the issuance of guidance letters and the functioning of the European Competition Network (ECN) linking the European family of competition authorities, came into effect. Recital 8 in the preamble of Regulation 1/2003 states that stricter national laws may include provisions which prohibit or impose sanctions on abusive behaviour toward economically dependent undertakings.

---

26. *Ibid.*, para. 60.
27. *Ibid.*, para. 60.

4.1.3 Regulation 1/2003

Regulation 1/2003[28], the 'Modernisation' Regulation, introduced changes in the enforcement system of EU anti-trust law. Regulation 1/2003 abolishes the notification to the Commission of business agreements, a system that had been created in 1962 but had become unnecessarily bureaucratic as companies operating in Europe were now familiar with competition rules. By removing the centralised notification and authorisation system for the application of Article 101(3), an agreement that has anti-competitive effects can nonetheless be found legal, if it produces sufficient countervailing benefits that are passed on to consumers. Under the new Regulation, Article 101(3) can be directly invoked by undertakings before a national court or NCA. The agreement, decision or conduct in question is found legal if the party can show that it fulfils the conditions set out in Article 101(3). Thus, the major changes in Regulation 1/2003 are the abandonment of the notification system, the introduction of a duty for NCAs to apply Articles 101 and 102, and the transformation of Article 101(3) into a 'legal exception' directly applicable by all enforcers and judges. Regulation 1/2003 also set out mechanisms for cooperation between the Commission and national authorities and courts, provided for a new category of decisions, and expanded the Commission's remedial and investigative powers in competition cases. Finally, Regulation 1/2003 consolidates into a single piece of legislation the many procedural rules that were scattered in separate instruments or derived from the case law of the Court of Justice.

Article 5 of Regulation 1/2003 states that despite the fact that NCAs have the power to apply Articles 101 and 102 in individual cases, the Commission may – where the Community public interest to the application of Articles 101 and 102 so requests – find by decision that Article 101 is not applicable either because the conditions of Article 101(1) are not fulfilled, or because the conditions of Article 101(3) are satisfied.[29] In exceptional cases, where the public interest of the Community so requires, it may also be expedient for the Commission to adopt a decision of a declaratory nature finding that the prohibition in Articles 101 or 102 does not apply, with a view to clarifying the law and ensuring its consistent application throughout the Community, in particular with regard to new types of agreements or practices that have not been settled in the existing case law and administrative practice.

Thus, Regulation 1/2003 necessitates undertakings to make their own assessment of the compatibility of any restrictive practices with Article 101(3), in the light of the legislation in force and the case law. Six Notices are included in the 'modernisation package' beside the Regulation. The six Notices provide further clarification on aspects such as on the effect on trade, on the application of Article 101(3), on informal

---

28. (Council of European Union, Report from Competition Working Party to the Permanent Representatives Committee 12998/02 2002).
29. According to Art. 11(6) of Regulation 1/2003, the initiation by the Commission of proceedings for the adoption of a decision shall relieve the national competition authorities of their competence to apply Arts 101 and 102.

guidance relating to novel questions concerning Articles 101 and 102, on the handling of complaints as well as on the cooperation with national courts and with NCAs within the ECN.

One of the central elements of the package was the *Notice on Cooperation within the Network of competition authorities* (ECN). The coming into force of the legal framework activates a range of new cooperation mechanisms between the Commission and the Member States' competition authorities. The Notice provides guidance, among other things, on the work sharing between the public enforcers, mutual information about pending cases at different stages of the procedure and the exchange of information for the use in evidence. In order to promote a coherent application and provide guidance to businesses, another Notice sets out the *methodology for the application of Article 101(3)*. The Notice does not replace but complements the extensive guidance already available in Commission Guidelines on particular types of agreements, in particular the Guidelines on horizontal cooperation agreements and the Guidelines on vertical restraints. The 'modernisation package' further comprises:

Guidelines on the effect on trade: The effect on trade is the jurisdictional criterion that determines the reach of the EU anti-trust rules. It is of particular importance in the system which obliges Member States' courts and competition authorities to apply the EU anti-trust rules to all agreements and practices that may affect trade between Member States.

The *Notice on the cooperation between the Commission and the national courts*: The Notice is intended to serve as a practical tool for national judges when they apply EU anti-trust law. It explains in particular the tools for cooperation foreseen in Regulation 1/2003, which include, *inter alia*, the possibility for the national courts to ask for information and opinions from the Commission on cases pending before them that concern the application of the Community competition rules.

The *Notice on informal guidance to business* (guidance letters): While the abolition of the notification system for the application of Article 101 was a central element of the reform, the Commission remained open to discuss specific cases with undertakings when appropriate. The Commission is in particular prepared to provide guidance to businesses where novel questions make it difficult for them to assess their agreements or conduct under EU anti-trust law. For this type of situation, the Notice sets out the possibility of issuing *guidance letters* to business. Guidance letters are reserved for cases where a genuinely novel question concerning Articles 101 or 102 arises and are subject to the Commission's enforcement priorities. They will be reasoned and published.

The *Notice on the handling of complaints by the Commission*: The Notice explains both the possibility of providing market information to the Commission in an unbureaucratic way and the procedures applicable to formal complaints. It is intended to encourage citizens and businesses to come forward with information on suspected infringements of the competition rules.

4.1.4 German Clause in Regulation 1/2003

The 'German clause' in Article 3(2) Regulation 1/2003 reads as follows: 'Member States shall not under this Regulation be precluded from adopting and applying on their territory stricter national laws which prohibit or sanction unilateral conduct engaged in by undertakings.' This exemption started significant discussions after Regulation 1/2003 entered into force. All major competition institutions worldwide started a review of the concept of unilateral conduct and its possible abusive behaviour. Germany as well as the Commission played an active role in all these discussions. In case of buyer power which benefits consumers there is no need for stricter national dominance laws. In the case of EU anti-trust law, this law even contradicts the basic objectives as set out in the TFEU. In the following, these discussions are organised in a chronological order.

In 2008, the International Competition Network (ICN) conducted a survey with thirty-two jurisdictions about the concept of abuse of a superior bargaining position (ASBP).[30] The reason for this survey was that in several jurisdictions concerns had arisen particularly in business-to-business relations. These concerns were not limited to the retail sector. ASBP here typically includes a situation in which a party makes use of its superior bargaining position in light of normal business practices, relative to another party to unjustly cause the other party to provide money, service or other economic benefits. The theoretical relationship between specific provisions on ASBP and competition rules regulating unilateral conduct was not clear from the responses to the ICN survey.[31]

The Commission responded to this survey that powerful buyers could be characterised as dominant vis-à-vis their suppliers whether or not they are with respect to their customers. In addition, their suppliers could possibly be abused either through 'exploitation' (i.e., prices below competitive levels) or through 'exclusion' (i.e., efforts to discourage others from offering them access to consumers). Besides imposing lower prices on input suppliers, a dominant buyer may employ a number of practices other than pricing behaviour, with potentially anti-competitive effects. Examples of strategic buyer behaviour include (a) exclusive selling obligations, (b) predatory overbuying of inputs or (c) raising rivals costs through overbuying or (d) refusal to purchase. These practices may serve a number of different purposes. Some can enhance efficiencies, some can distort competition, while others allow buyers to obtain a greater share of profits, so-called rent shifting.[32] The Commission replied thus by making reference to Article 102 as understood by EU anti-trust law.

Later in 2008, the OECD conducted a policy roundtable on monopsony[33] and buyer power.[34] According to the OECD, buyer power is concerned with how downstream firms can affect the terms of trade with upstream suppliers. There are two types

---

30. (ICN Report on Abuse of Superior Bargaining Position 2008).
31. *Ibid.*, 27.
32. *Ibid.*, 22.
33. Monopsony is a market form in which only one buyer interfaces with would-be sellers of a particular product.
34. (OECD Policy Roundtables on Monopsony and Buyer Power 2009).

of buyer power: monophony power and bargaining power. The welfare implications, and therefore the appropriate enforcement policies, of the two types of buyer power are very different. Both result in lower input prices, but the exercise of monophony power usually results in higher prices downstream. Reductions in input prices in the case of bargaining power are typically beneficial.

The Commission confirmed it its submission[35] that buying power is an increasingly hot topic within the competition community by referring to the declaration of the European Parliament on investigating and remedying the abuse of power by large supermarkets operating in the EU from 19 February 2008. In its submission, the Commission also made clear that much of the current interest in buyer power highlights the plight and problems faced by small suppliers. It is clear that some of these concerns relate to issues that are not a matter of anti-trust law but rather highlight social or political concerns. Thus, according to the Commission, these concerns are not covered by EU anti-trust law. The basis of EU competition policy is that the ultimate end user of any product – the consumer – should be at the centre of anti-trust law. This means that the ultimate focus should be on the demand side. It is competition that brings about low prices and better choice for consumers and guarantees that companies' offers adapt to the preferences of the demand side. It is also this process that drives efficiency, innovation and productivity benefits. Nevertheless, there are certain potential situations where buyer power can lead to a competition problem if it has an effect on competition on the sales market – either in terms of higher prices or loss of choice or quality (for instance if there is significant supplier exit). These would lead to direct disadvantages for the consumer, which should be addressed by competition law.

At the same time, the Commission published in 2009 a Communication on the food supply chain.[36] The Commission stated that a key lesson stemming from analyses carried out involving stakeholders and NCAs is the necessity to draw a clear distinction between concerns about potentially unfair trading practices – related to the imbalances in bargaining power of contracting parties – and concerns about anti-competitive practices. The ability of suppliers and/or buyers to exercise their market power in a manner that distorts competition to the detriment of consumers depends primarily on the type of supply chain and on local market conditions. In addition to classic cartels and Resale Price Maintenance (RPM), other practices were deemed to deserve special attention by NCAs, such as joint commercialisation agreements, tying and bundling, joint purchasing agreements (buying alliances) and the increasing use of private labels. For such practices, a careful balancing of efficiency-enhancing and potentially anti-competitive effects is needed. No sweeping generalisation can be made and a case-by-case analysis based on the specifics of local market conditions is necessary in order to establish the existence of a possible competitive harm.[37]

---

35. *Ibid.*, page 255 onwards.
36. (Communication from the Commission on a better functioning food supply chain in Europe 2009).
37. *Ibid.*, 6.

The Staff Working Document[38] found that when negotiations occur between retailers and large multinational suppliers, who are often producers of a portfolio of goods that are in some cases must-carry brands, suppliers may have significant market power. In such cases, the buyer power of even the largest retailers may be offset by the market power of the suppliers. The profit margins of such 'unavoidable' suppliers are generally higher than those of retailers.[39] These differences in profitability can be explained by the fact that retailers compete mostly on price-related criteria whereas branded good producers compete on other factors in addition to price including brand image, product characteristics, consumer preferences for special flavours, etc. This change in the balance in bargaining power has – so the Commission believes – contributed to an increased concentration of retailers and the development of buying platforms destined to pool purchase volumes together so as to negotiate better terms from such suppliers.[40]

The Commission noted that NCAs have been very active over recent years in terms of their enforcement actions on food markets. However, by 2009, *no* abuse of dominance against retailers had been found, even though investigations had been carried out at national level.[41] The Commission concluded that an important caveat needs to be made from the outset in terms of the application of competition rules to buyer power related issues. The primary objective of EU competition policy is to ensure well-functioning markets to the benefit of citizens and businesses in the EU. NCAs consequently tackle buyer power to the extent that it harms, or could potentially harm, the competitive process and thereby consumer welfare. In this regard, the Commission said that unequal bargaining power does not always present a '*buyer power*' problem, in terms of anti-trust law. Therefore, the two concepts should – according to the Commission – be carefully distinguished. Abuses of buyer power are contrary to EU anti-trust law where there is a proven detriment to downstream consumers. However, much of the political interest is in fact focused on issues of 'unequal bargaining power' which needs to be distinguished from issues of 'buyer power', and actually highlights problems faced by small suppliers in the context of contractual negotiations with stronger buyers. EU anti-trust law is not concerned with particular outcomes of contractual negotiations between parties unless such terms would have negative effects on the competitive process and ultimately reduce consumer welfare. It is not the aim of the EU anti-trust rules to interfere in the bargain struck between contractual parties, in the absence of proven competitive harm.[42]

---

38. (Commission Staff Working Document on Competition in the food supply chain 2009, 17–18).
39. As an illustration, on average in 2006, the average net profit margins of European retailers were around 4%, whereas these same margins in the case of The Coca-Cola Company and the Group Danone were around 20% and 11%, respectively.
40. *Ibid.*, 7.
41. *Ibid.*, 16.
42. *Ibid.*, 18.

Chapter 4: Competition Practice

In 2009, the Commission informed the European Parliament about the functioning of Regulation 1/2003. At that time, Regulation 1/2003 had been in place for five years.[43]

The Commission[44] discussed the last sentence of Article 3(2) Regulation 1/2003 where Member States are not precluded from adopting and applying stricter national laws, which prohibit or sanction unilateral conduct: Unilateral behaviour capable of affecting trade between Member States can thus be prohibited by national law, even if it occurs below the level of dominance or is not considered abusive within the meaning of Article 102. The Commission confirmed in its submission to the Parliament, that the last sentence in Article 3(2) contains an exception from the level playing field and implies that undertakings doing cross-border business in the internal market may be subjected to a variety of standards as to their unilateral behaviour. Besides the rules applicable to unilateral behaviour by firms that expressly extend to undertakings that do not have a dominant position in the market within the meaning of Article 102, national laws may also foresee different standards for assessing dominance as well as stricter national provisions governing the conduct of dominant undertakings.[45]

The Commission noted that the business and legal communities had called for an extension of the convergence rule to national laws covering unilateral conduct. Feedback from stakeholders suggested that diverging standards fragment business strategies that are typically formulated on a pan-European or global basis. This is not *a priori* contradicted by the fact that some of the national provisions on unilateral conduct appear to be rarely applied in the practice of NCAs.[46] Against this background, the exclusion of unilateral conduct from the scope of the convergence rule was considered to be a matter of high importance, which should be further examined, both in terms of evaluating the extent of any potential problems and assessing the need for action at European level.[47] The Commission commissioned a study on the impact of national rules on unilateral conduct that diverge from Article 102. The study results were delivered to the Commission in summer 2011. The study itself was made available to the public in 2015.[48] The main task of the study was to evaluate the exception of the convergence rule.[49] In January 2012, DG Comp set up a Task Force on food retailing.

In May 2012, the ECN published a study on competition law enforcement and market monitoring activities by ECAs in the food sector. The study took a closer look at the cases in which the ECAs applied only national competition law and came across

---

43. (Communication from The Commission to the European Parliament and the Council on the functioning of Regulation 1/2003 2009).
44. (European Commission, Communication from The Commission to the European Parliament and the Council on the functioning of Regulation 1/2003 2009, paras 21, 22).
45. *Ibid.*, para. 21.
46. *Ibid.*, para. 177.
47. *Ibid.*, para. 179.
48. (European Commission 2012).
49. (European Commission, Call for Tender for Study on the impact of national rules on unilateral conduct that diverge from Art. 102 of the Treaty on the Functioning of the European Union 2010).

a group of cases in which the ECAs applied stricter national rules that target abusive conduct by undertakings, which goes beyond Article 102. This has been the case in sixteen investigations.

In its study, the ECN defined unequal bargaining power as existing whenever one party to a proposed contract, be it either the supplier or the buyer, can 'drive a hard bargain'. That means that the party can impose upon the other contracting party terms and conditions that are deemed unfavourable by that other party. Unequal bargaining power and resulting contractual imbalances do not necessarily imply a competition infringement in most cases. Buyer power, by contrast, exists if a market is concentrated to such an extent that a particular buyer has not only power over a particular supplier but over suppliers in general. From the perspective of EU anti-trust law, the power of a buyer over its suppliers can constitute a problem, for instance, if this position is used to *foreclose* (potential) rivals to the detriment of consumers. However, buyer power can also be to the benefit of consumers, for instance, by acting as a countervailing power that exerts competitive constraints on a powerful supplier or by creating purchase efficiencies that are passed on to consumers.

In October 2013, another OECD policy roundtable on 'Competition Issues in the Food Chain Industry' took place.[50] The Commission reported in its submission, that NCAs have investigated cases, which involved abusive conduct by dominant operators. These abuses mainly involved strategies to *foreclose* competitors, such as exclusivity obligations, minimum purchasing obligations, tying and refusals to supply, but also some *exploitative* abuses, such as unjustified contractual obligations. The large majority of these cases related to abusive conduct subject to Article 102 or equivalent national rules. However, some NCAs applied stricter national rules, beyond the scope of Article 102 such as the abuse of economic dependency. This was especially the case in the area of retail where cases concerned abusive terms in contracts between retailers and their suppliers (such as unfair risk-sharing terms, retroactive changing of contract terms, the abusive charging of certain fees, etc.).[51]

In September 2014, the Task Force of DG Comp finally published its study on 'The economic impact of choice and innovation on modern retail in the EU food sector'. In his press release, then Commissioner Almunia stated that the retailers' bargaining power does not seem to have a negative impact on choice and innovation. In moderately concentrated retail markets, retailers' stronger bargaining power vis-à-vis suppliers does not seem to lead to less choice and innovation in food products either.[52]

In July 2014, the Commission published its most recent report to the Parliament on 'Ten Years of Antitrust Enforcement under Regulation 1/2003'.[53] This publication does not address Article 3. Neither the convergence clause nor the 'German clause' with respect to Article 102 is mentioned. The report gives the impression that with respect to substance there is no issue at all. However, as we will see in the following, some Member States apply the exemption to the convergence clause exhaustively

---

50. (OECD, Competition Issues in the Food Chain Industry 2013).
51. *Ibid.*, 112.
52. (European Commission, Commission publishes results of retail food study 2014).
53. (Commission Notice on the notion of State aid pursuant to Art. 107(1) TFEU 2014).

Chapter 4: Competition Practice

thereby contradicting the basic principles of EU anti-trust law. However, it is also fair to note, that it is neither France nor Germany that applies the clause. We see the application of the German clause in particular in the new EU Member States.

4.1.5 Revision Regulation 1/2003

The entry into force of Regulation 1/2003 in 2004 transformed the competition enforcement landscape, giving NCAs and national courts a key role in applying the EU rules on restrictive business practices and abuses of dominant market positions (Articles 101 and 102).

In 2015, the Commission started a consultation procedure[54] on potential EU legislative actions to empower NCAs to be truly effective enforcers of the EU competition rules. This initiative covers four areas of action as identified in the 2014 Commission's Communication on Ten Years of Council Regulation 1/2003, namely to guarantee that they (1) have an effective enforcement toolbox; (2) can impose effective fines; (3) have effective leniency programmes in place which facilitate applying for leniency in multiple jurisdictions and (4) have adequate resources and are sufficiently independent when enforcing the EU competition rules.

Where the same substantive rules are being applied, it needs to be ensured that divergence in procedural rules do not undermine the level playing field. It appears that NCAs may face difficulties relating to their powers of investigation (e.g., some national competitions authorities cannot gather evidence stored on digital devices when inspecting the premises of a suspected cartelist – laptops, tablets, etc.) or to their ability to impose effective fines for anti-competitive behaviour (e.g., some national competitions authorities cannot fine cartelists for the full period of their participation in the cartel).[55]

4.2 MARKET DEFINITIONS

The definition of the relevant market is an essential part in any competitive assessment. Economic analysis is crucial is such market definitions.

4.2.1 Necessity for Market Definitions

The first step in any competition analysis is the definition of the relevant market. A market definition is required in order to check firstly whether an agreement can escape EU competition provisions and if not, what the economic effects of the agreement in the previously defined relevant market are. In determining whether an appreciable restriction of competition exists under Article 101(1) or in establishing if the conditions under

---

54. (European Commission, ECN Plus: Empowering the national competition authorities to be more effective enforcers – Consultation Strategy 2015).
55. (Commission Press release on boosting enforcement powers of national competition authorities 2015).

Article 101(3) for an exemption from prohibition are met, markets need to be defined first. The same is true for the application of Article 102 and merger assessments. Thus in applying the EU competition rules, it is necessary to determine the position of the concerned parties on the relevant geographic market, the relevant product market as well as the time period in question. It is further necessary to find out to what degree market conditions change by an agreement or a merger.[56] In order to calculate market shares and to assess the overall degree of the concentration market definitions are essential. The relevant product and geographic markets determine the scope within which market power is assessed.

The objective of defining a market in both its product and geographic dimension is also crucial in identifying actual and potential competitors that are capable of constraining the behaviour of undertakings and of preventing them from behaving independently of an effective competitive pressure. Clearly, an incorrect market definition leads to different results. Market definitions that are too narrow, either in product or geographic terms, might result in the paradox that operations with an essentially pro-competitive effect in the broader, actual market are obstructed or hindered on competition grounds. Market definitions that are too broad do not allow the identification of the dangers of a merger that might result in positions of market power.

The need for market definitions became clear in cases like *Kali and Salz v. Commission*[57], where the Court annulled the Commission's decision for failure to demonstrate that two types of fertiliser constituted separate markets. The Court mandated that the Commission needs to delineate the relevant market first and to establish then how the share of the market affected by the agreement relates to the unaffected portion.[58]

The Court of First Instance confirmed in *SPO v. Others*,[59] that it was necessary, at the outset, to determine the scope of the Commission's obligation to define the relevant market before finding an infringement of Articles 101 and 102. According to the Court, the approach to defining the relevant market differs as to whether Article 101 or Article 102 has to be applied. For the purposes of Article 102, the proper definition of the relevant market is a necessary precondition for any judgment as to allegedly anti-competitive behaviour[60] since, before an abuse of a dominant position is ascertained, it is necessary to establish the existence of a dominant position in a given market, which presupposes that such a market has already been defined. On the other hand:

---

56. For ECJ decisions on relevant market under Art. 101 see e.g., (ECJ, Hasselblad (GB) Limited v. Commission, Case 86/82 1984); (ECJ, Miller International Schallplatten GmbH v. Commission, Case 19/77 1978) and (ECJ, SA Musique Diffusion française and others v. Commission, Joined cases 100-103/80 1983) the precise definition of the relevant market was left open, since from any viewpoint the effect of the parties' conduct was appreciable.
57. (ECJ, Kali und Salz AG and Kali-Chemie AG v. Commission, Joined cases 19 and 20/74 1975).
58. (Decision IV/30.129 on Carlsberg 1984).
59. (CFI, Vereniging van Samenwerkende Prijsregelende Organisaties in de Bouwnijverheid and others v. Commission, Case T-29/92 1995, paras 73 and 74).
60. (CFI, Società Italiana Vetro SpA, Fabbrica Pisana SpA and PPG Vernante Pennitalia SpA v. Commission, Joined cases T-68/89, T-77/89 and T-78/89 1992, 315).

Chapter 4: Competition Practice

For the purposes of applying Article 81 (new Article 101), the reason for defining the relevant market is to determine whether the agreement, the decision by an association of undertakings or the concerted practice at issue is liable to affect trade between Member States and has as its object or effect the prevention, restriction or distortion of competition within the Common market.[61]

In *Schöller*,[62] a case on exclusive purchasing agreements for ice cream, the Commission was criticised by the Court of First Instance for adopting a too narrow definition of the relevant market.[63] In order to establish whether the definition of the relevant market adopted by the Commission in point 87 of its decision is correct, the Court observed at the outset, that a delineation of the relevant market is essential. The requirement in this case was to analyse the effects of the exclusive agreements on competition and, in particular, to analyse the possibilities available to new domestic and foreign competitors to establish themselves in the ice cream market or to increase their market shares thereof.[64]

In this context, it is established law in Articles 101 and 102 cases that account must be taken of the *consumer's point of view*.

The Court of Justice already held in *Continental Can*[65], a case concerning the application of Article 102, that the possibilities of competition can only be judged in relation to those characteristics of the products in question by virtue of which of those products are particularly apt to satisfy an inelastic need and are only to a limited extent interchangeable with each other. As regards the product market, the Court of Justice has held, more specifically, that the concept implies that there can be effective competition between the products, which form part of it, and this presupposes that there is a sufficient degree of interchangeability between all the products forming part of the same market.[66]

Moreover, as regards the possibility of taking account of other factors, the Court observed that an examination limited to the objective characteristics of the relevant products cannot be sufficient: the competitive conditions and the structure of supply and demand on the market must also be taken into consideration:[67]

> The Court must therefore examine the definition of the product market adopted by the Commission in the light of those considerations. It must be borne in mind that, in point 80 of its decision, the Commission stated that scooping ice-cream and craft-trade ice cream served for immediate consumption in the street, that is to say

---

61. (CFI, Vereniging van Samenwerkende Prijsregelende Organisaties in de Bouwnijverheid and others v. Commission, Case T-29/92 1995, para. 74).
62. (CFI, Schöller Lebensmittel GmbH & Co. KG v. Commission, Case T-9/93 1995).
63. Schöller then claimed that the Commission disregarded the effect of the supply agreements on competition. The third claim of Schöller was that the Commission is not empowered by Art. 2 of Regulation No. 17 to prohibit all the existing exclusive agreements, including those not covered by the prohibition contained in Art. 81(1) of the Treaty.
64. According to (ECJ, Stergios Delimitis v. Henninger Bräu AG, Case C-234/89 1991, paras 15 and 16).
65. (ECJ, Europemballage Corporation and Continental Can Company Inc. v. Commission, Case 6/72 1973).
66. (ECJ, Hoffmann-La Roche & Co. AG v. Commission, Case 85/76 1979).
67. (ECJ, NV Nederlandsche Banden Industrie Michelin v. Commission, Case 322/81 1983, para. 37).

> *without the provision of any catering services, and impulse ice cream sold at the same place are, from the consumer's point of view, equivalent products.*
>
> *The Court considers, first, that the Commission was therefore right to exclude icecream offered as part of a catering service, that is to say some industrial ice cream for bulk-buying customers and craft-trade ice cream, since that market, according to the case law of the Court of Justice (Delimitis, cited above, paragraph 16), constitutes a separate market, the consumption of ice creams in restaurants generally involving the provision of a service and being less often affected by considerations of an economic nature than purchases, for example, in a grocery store.*
>
> *The Court also considers that it is also necessary to exclude, as contended by the Commission, ice-creams stored in private freezers at consumers' homes, since they are not available to satisfy a need arising away from home, in particular an impulse need, and are only to a limited extent interchangeable with products sold in the street. They are take-home ice cream, which in general is purchased with a view to home storage, and single-item ice creams delivered to the doorstep. The Court considers that the place of consumption was correctly considered by the Commission to be a decisive factor in determining the market in this case, since the products in question can be stored for only a very limited time without refrigeration and must therefore necessarily be consumed in the immediate neighbourhood of the last place where cold storage was possible.*[68]

As regards craft-trade ice creams, the documents before the Court showed that ice cream of that kind is generally offered for sale at or close to the place of production. It was not therefore covered by the contested supply agreements. In those circumstances, the Court considered that the assessment of the effects on competition, in particular regarding access to retailers, of the supply agreements at issue, was not likely to change if those ice creams are included in the product market. Accordingly, the Court confirmed that the Commission was right to exclude them from the product market.

On one point, the Court criticised the Commission. The Court stated that the Commission had not put forward any evidence to show that there are different patterns of demand for the two categories of product, within the meaning of the *Michelin*[69] judgment, which could justify a delineation of the market that excludes scooping ice cream sold in the street. The Court considered that although there are various channels of distribution that fact is not sufficient in itself to exclude ice cream for bulk-buying customers sold in individual portions for consumption outside catering establishments. The Court considered that Schöller was right to claim that the mere division into individual portions carried out by a trader in the traditional trade does not constitute a 'catering service' within the meaning of *Delimitis*.

The question arose whether the Commission should have included the proportion of catering ice cream sold in individual portions and in competition with impulse ice cream in the street in several types of outlet, those two categories of product being interchangeable from the consumer's point of view. The Court considered however that the decision not to include scooping ice cream in the relevant market did not substantially affect the assessment made of the effects on competition of the supply

---

68. (CFI, Schöller Lebensmittel GmbH & Co. KG v. Commission, Case T-9/93 1995) paras 41–43.
69. (ECJ, NV Nederlandsche Banden Industrie Michelin v. Commission, Case 322/81 1983).

Chapter 4: Competition Practice

agreements at issue, in particular, as to whether access to the market was closed or considerably hindered by the existence of the agreements.

By analysing step by step the Commission's definition of the relevant product market, the Court confirmed in the most relevant parts the view of the Commission.

Concerning the relevant geographical market, it was apparent in this case that the distribution of industrially produced ice cream is always undertaken at national level and that national characteristics are reflected in differences in market structure, product ranges and prices. The Court confirmed that the Commission acted correctly and in accordance with the case law in treating the German market as constituting the relevant geographical market.[70]

Trefileurope Sales v. Commission[71] is another case about a cartel where the Court of First Instance confirmed the Commission's approach of defining the relevant market. The case concerns Commission Decision 89/515/EEC[72] of 2 August 1989 relating to a proceeding under Article 101, in which the Commission imposed a fine on fourteen producers of welded steel mesh for having infringed Article 101(1). The product with which the contested decision is concerned is welded steel mesh. It is a prefabricated reinforcement product made from smooth or ribbed cold-drawn reinforcing steel wires joined together by right-angle spot welding to form a network. It is used in almost all areas of reinforced concrete construction.

In the findings of the Court as to an infringement of Article 101(1), the Court followed the Commission's approach in defining the relevant product market and considered *'that the Commission's analysis of the product market is not incorrect.'*[73] The market for the different kinds of welded steel mesh (including standard mesh, catalogue mesh, Listenmatten and tailored mesh) constitutes for the purpose of Article 101(1), a single market in welded steel mesh. The Court considered the influence of the prices of standard mesh on the prices of *Listenmatten* and tailor-made mesh. In other words, the substitutability for *Listenmatten* and tailor-made mesh was analysed.

These examples show that market definition is so essential in the application of the EU competition rules. Depending on the markets defined, the outcome of an anti-trust investigation might change. That is the reason market definitions are discussed upfront in the following sections at length.

The point is that a thorough market definition requires know-how about the methodology as well as substantial application experience. In 1997, the Commission published its Notice on the Definition of the Relevant Market for the Purposes of Community Competition Law[74] in order to clarify the market definition principles. The Notice is described and analysed in more detail in the following section. The 1997 Notice was actually the first initiative in EU competition law by then Commissioner Karel van Miert to introduce the more economics based approach (see section 1.2.2).

---

70. See (ECJ, Stergios Delimitis v. Henninger Bräu AG, Case C-234/89 1991, 18) and (ECJ, NV Nederlandsche Banden Industrie Michelin v. Commission, Case 322/81 1983, 25–28).
71. (CFI, Tréfileurope Sales SARL v. Commission, Case T-141/89 1995).
72. (Decision 89/515/EEC on proceeding under Art. 85 (Welded steel mesh) 1989, 1).
73. (CFI, Tréfileurope Sales SARL v. Commission, Case T-141/89 1995, 29).
74. (Commission Notice on the definition of relevant market 1997, 5).

The challenge for an economist working with anti-trust authorities is also to understand that the definition of the relevant market makes or dismisses a case for an authority. Since authorities show a tendency to keep control over business transactions, discussions on market definitions with authorities are demanding. The situation is much better in court cases, since a court does not have a hidden and sometimes even political agenda thereby addressing market definition in a transparent and objective manner.

The general drawback is that only in rare cases are market definitions, for example that the Commission applies, challenged at the Court of Justice at the EU. Therefore the competition community trusts the Commission that the methodology discussed in the following chapter is applied thoroughly. In principle, the Commission discusses with the parties in an open and transparent manner how they intend to deal with critical issues in market definitions. In particular, the Chief Economist Team of the Commission (CET) is very helpful in cooperating with the parties on critical market definition issues. Discussions on data gathering and data analysis are quite frequently held with the CET. While a few of the national authorities' competition economists still show a hostile attitude towards discussing market data and market analysis with parties, the CET handles those discussions in a professional way. Modern competition economics, as illustrated in the following sections, provides highly sophisticated quantitative and econometric tools to define relevant markets in accordance with legal requirements. This approach on market definition with the support of modern econometric tools is generally applicable and yields testable hypotheses. In this analysis, both qualitative and quantitative methods are applied. Qualitative methods, for example, include an examination of product characteristics and the intended use of a product by consumers, whereas quantitative methods involve the examination of price trends or the estimation of cross-price-elasticities.

However, in the majority of the cases, the Commission does not define a relevant product and geographic market leaving market definitions open. In this respect, the Commission's approach is a pragmatic one. Often the Commission concludes that even with the narrowest possible market definition, no competition problem arises. The Commission is satisfied by looking at different possible markets or categories of businesses and reaches a decision on compatibility without having to decide on all the various issues involved in defining a market.

4.2.2 Market Definition Principles

Companies often use the term 'market' to refer to the area where they sell their products or to refer broadly to the industry or sector which they belong to. However in anti-trust analysis, market definition is a tool to identify and define the boundaries of competition between firms.

In general, the more narrowly the market is defined the more likely a firm or firms will be found to have market power. Thus, the main purpose of market definition is to identify in a systematic way the competitive constraints that companies face. The objective of defining a market in both its product and geographic dimension is to

Chapter 4: Competition Practice

identify actual and potential competitors that are capable of constraining companies' behaviour and of preventing them from behaving independently of effective competitive pressure.

The main train of thought in defining relevant markets is to apply the concept of 'substitutability' as developed by the Court of Justice. Firms are subject to three main sources of competitive constraints: demand substitutability, supply substitutability and potential competition.

From an economic point of view, demand substitution constitutes the most immediate and effective disciplinary force on the suppliers of a given product, in particular in relation to their pricing decisions. The basic insight is that interchangeability, referred to as 'substitutability', is considered from the viewpoint of the consumer and customer. That is to say, that the relevant market must include all those products and regions that are substitutable with the products sold by the parties. Basically, the exercise of market definition consists of identifying the effective alternatives for the consumers. The Commission's 1997 Notice on the definition of the relevant market for the purposes of EU competition law[75] describes this methodology in a very detailed way.

According to the 1997 Commission's Market Definition Notice, when considering the degree of *demand-side substitutability* it has to be clarified which products or services are considered substitutes against each other from the customers' perspective. Thus, the aim of the definition of the relevant market is to identify the relevant choice set of customers according to the competitive forces in the market. The basic question to answer is whether the consumer would switch from one product to another in the case of a price increase. Therefore, demand-side substitutability is used to measure the extent to which consumers are prepared to substitute other services or products for the service or product in question. A firm or a group of firms cannot have a significant impact on the prevailing conditions of sale, such as prices, if its customers are in a position to switch easily to other products.

The main train of thought with respect to demand-side substitutability holds for both dimensions of the relevant market: for the product as well as for the geographic scope of a market. The relevant *product* market consists of all those products and services that are seen as substitutable with regard to their characteristics, price, and intended use by its customers. As to the definition of the relevant *geographic* market, the degree of substitutability from the view of the customers is fundamental too. The relevant geographic market, hence, comprises all areas in which the conditions of competition are homogeneous for the firms supplying the products or services under consideration and which are considerably different to other areas. The question to be answered is whether customers would switch to readily available substitutes or suppliers located elsewhere in response to a price increase in the products and areas being considered.

A heavy focus on demand-side substitutability may result in narrow market definitions. Whereas demand-side substitutability measures the extent to which

---

75. (European Commission, Notice on the definition of relevant market 1997, 5–13).

consumers or customers are prepared to substitute other products or services for the product or service in question, *supply-side substitutability* indicates whether suppliers other than those offering the product or services in question would switch their line of production to other regions or offer the relevant products or services without incurring significant additional costs. Substitutability on the supply-side occurs when producers that are currently supplying different products possess those skills and assets that make it possible to switch production in a short period of time if a price rise occurs. In this case, the competitive constraint would not come from the fact that a considerable part of demand would be addressed to competing products when the price rises, but rather that the price rise attracts producers that are currently selling some other products. However, there are several conditions that should be fulfilled for supply substitutability to widen the relevant market. In particular, switching production must be easy, rapid and feasible. Considerable sunk costs should not occur and barriers to entry must be surmountable in a rapid and relatively cheap way.

A full integration of demand- and supply-side substitution into the relevant market concept is found in the 1992 US Department of Justice's Merger Guidelines, which indicates that:

> *The Agency's identification of firms that participate in the relevant market begins with all the firms that currently produce and sell in the relevant market. This includes vertically integrated firms to the extent that such inclusion accurately reflects their competitive significance in the relevant market prior to the merger.*[76] *In addition, the Agency will identify other firms not currently producing or selling the relevant product in the relevant area as participating in the relevant market if their inclusion would more accurately reflect probable supply responses. These firms are termed 'uncommitted entrants'. These supply responses must be likely to occur within one year and without the expenditure of significant sunk costs of entry and exit, in response to a 'small but significant and not transitory' price increase.*[77]

The reasons why supply-side substitution has to be included in the market definition is straightforward: the additional production which would be put in the market at once, would have a similar disciplinary effect on the competitive behaviour of the merging parties as the possible loss of customers arising from demand substitution. '*Supply side substitutability should therefore enlarge the product market definition when its effects on competition might be assimilated to those of demand substitution.*'[78]

Supply substitutability plays in practice a minor role. In its decisions, the Commission traditionally focuses on the demand side of the market, i.e., the customer side, and normally limits its analysis to demand side factors. Supply-side factors are rarely considered by the Commission and even where they are considered, their contribution to market definition analysis remains limited. In second-phase investigations, however the Commission demonstrates an increasing willingness to analyse the supply-side of the market.

---

76. (US Merger Guidelines 1992, point 1.31).
77. *Ibid.*, point 1.32.
78. (Alonso 1994, 205).

Chapter 4: Competition Practice

Potential competition is not measured at all when defining markets: the bulk of the analysis is related to demand substitutability.

The following section addresses the economic tools applied in market definitions.

4.2.3 Market Definition Tools

The following section discusses the tool box available to economists for market definition purposes. In some elaborations formulas and graphs are used to explain the role of economic analysis in a more detailed way. For the convenience of the reader the use of formulas and graphs is rather limited and in case their presentations are necessary, a step by step approach is applied to guide non-economists through.

4.2.3.1 Price Tests

As a general rule, the comparison of absolute prices of two (or more) products is not a valid means of determining whether those products are in the same product market. *Price discrimination* is part of normal business conduct and occurs when the same good or service is sold to different groups of buyers at different prices. Price differences can be based on transport costs especially with regard to rural as compared to urban prices. It is common for variations in price to be explained by differences in cost.

However *patterns in price changes* can be informative. For example, two products showing the same pattern of price changes, for reasons not connected to costs or general price inflation, could be – although not proven – close substitutes.

Another useful tool is to look at the *correlation of prices* over time (i.e., to analyse the relative price changes over time rather than to look at absolute prices). If prices are highly correlated, the products may fall within the same market. However, correlation does not tell us much (if anything) about causation. A high correlation coefficient might be explained by the similar underlying factors pushing the changes of both prices while there could be little real competition between the two products. Correlation between prices may diverge or get closer over time, due to such things as changes in underlying costs, or changes in service quality, or a different level of common influence imposed by some other factor. In the absence of being able to explain the price movement, it can be dangerous to draw inferences about market definition from price correlation data.

The *speed of adjustment* of a product price or geographic area to a price change of another product or geographic area, can also be used as a test for market definition. The test suffers from much the same problems as the price correlation analysis.

Customer reactions to price changes in the past may also be relevant. Evidence that a relatively large proportion of customers had switched to a rival product in response to a relatively small price rise would provide evidence that these two goods are close substitutes. Equally price divergence over time, without significant levels of substitution, would be consistent with the two products being in separate markets.

Evidence of *own or cross-price elasticities* of demand is helpful too. The own-price elasticity of demand measures the rate at which demand for a product changes when its price goes up or down. A high price elasticity of demand indicates that a small change in price will result in a proportionately much larger change in quantity demanded; i.e., it is price elastic. Where this is the case, firms will not be able to increase profits by raising price, since consumers would respond to such an increase by switching away. This would be the case even for a hypothetical monopolist. However, the simple statistical observation that over a certain period of time, say, a 10% increase in price is associated with, say, a 2% decrease in demand does not automatically imply a price elasticity of –0.2. A number of other variables may probably explain the change in demand. These aspects need to be considered when estimating the own-price elasticity for a certain product from such historical data.

In addition to own-price elasticities, *cross-price elasticities* might help to understand the competitive constraints exercised by other products or regions. The cross-price elasticity of demand measures the rate at which demand for a product (e.g., a rival product) changes when the price of another product goes up or down. When the own-price elasticity for the product considered, say product A, is high enough to lead one to believe that a hypothetical monopolist would not profitably raise prices of A in a small but significant way, it becomes important to clarify which products exercise a constraint on A. Cross-price elasticities might help to identify the close substitutes.[79] A high cross-price elasticity of demand suggests that the two goods or services are good substitutes for each other, suggesting that the goods or services are in the same product market.[80] Again, as in the case of own-price elasticities, when it comes to estimating cross-price elasticities from historical data one has to carefully consider which other variables are likely to have an impact on the demand of the product under consideration – apart from its price and the prices of substitutes.

A direct way of estimating own- and cross-price elasticities in a certain market is to *estimate the elasticities from time series data* of prices and sales. However, when dealing with differentiated product industries building econometric models of those markets will rapidly lead to models of very high dimensionality which might render the task of estimating elasticities from historical data cumbersome. Suppose for instance attempting to estimate market power in a market characterised by n differentiated products. This would lead to a specification of an econometric model of n demand equations where the demand for each product is expressed as a function of the n prices of all products in the market and, say, k exogenous variables. Thus, even with linear or log-linear demands, estimating such a system would imply the estimation of $n*(n + k)$ parameters since each of the n demand equations will contain all the n prices plus the k additional explanatory variables. Such systems will rapidly become intractable due to lack of sufficient data.[81]

---

79. (Werden, Demand Elasticities in Antitrust Analysis, 1998), for example, proposes using the cross-price elasticities to rank the substitutes which might be included in the relevant market according to the HMT.
80. *Ibid.*, (Froeb and Werden 1992, 241–247), for a discussion of some of the problems that can arise.
81. Suppose, for example, one wants to analyse a market with six products and there are four additional exogenous explanatory variables considered relevant in explaining quantities sold. Then one would have to estimate a system of six equations each containing the six prices of the

Evidence on the price-concentration relationship might be informative as well. *Price-concentration studies* examine how the price of a product in a distinct area varies according to the number (or share of supply) of other products sold in the same area. These studies are useful where data is available for several distinct areas with varying degrees of concentration. There is usually a high correlation between firms having a high market share and firms having market power. High market shares are, nevertheless, not sufficient of themselves to confer market power. However, where market power appears to be absent but an entity has very high market share, it places an additional burden on the parties to define correctly the relevant product market. Where concentration is very high and prices are not statistically different from those in other areas where concentration is low, this can suggest that: (1) the market has been defined too narrowly. For example, if a firm had 100% of a market in location X, and 20% of the market in location Y, and prices were not statistically different between X and Y, it may be that either the product or the geographic market definition is too narrow. (2) The market is subject to 'hit and run' entry or firms in nearby markets are able to switch capacity fairly easily, so that the apparently dominant firm has no market power as a result of the ease of supply-side substitution. This issue can be solved by a price-concentration analysis.

Other, more sophisticated econometric techniques for aiding in the delineation of anti-trust markets are for example '*Granger causality tests*' and '*tests for co integration*'. The Granger causality test is a test for feedback effects between two price series, and can be used to determine whether determinants of prices for x include previous prices for y. It can be used as a test for erogeneity (whether disturbances in y are also influential in causing changes in x). On the other hand, the co integration test is a test used to determine whether two series with no apparent short run relationship share a common trend in the long run. Specifically, two non-stationary series are co integrated if there exists a linear combination of them which renders the relationship stationary.[82] Both, the Granger causality and the co integration tests suffer from problems similar to those affecting tests for correlation.

If firms provide goods or services on the basis of longer-term contracts or large-volume contracts, the closer the firms will compete with each other. In these circumstances, it would be expected that they work with the same clients. Such *client studies* do not typically involve econometric tests, and thus provide rather more general evidence than much of what is discussed above.

If available, *natural experiments* can be another suitable empirical methodology to define relevant markets. Laboratory experiment is a common methodology used in many scientific studies. In principle, scientists design two groups, a group in which the experiment will take place, and a control group. The effect of the experiment will be measured by comparing the outcome between the experimental group and the control

---

products and the four additional exogenous variables. That is, there are 60 parameters to be estimated. If there were additional seasonal and cyclical patterns and a trend in the series, as probably often will be the case, data requirements will become even more inflated.

82. (Werden & Froeb, Correlation, Causality, and All that Jazz: The Inherent Shortcomings of Price Tests for Antitrust Market Delineation, 1993, 344).

group. Natural experiments are somewhat similar, but the experiment does not take place in a laboratory but outside in the real-world. Negative supply shocks for example can yield an unexpected output decline. They can provide useful information about the strength of the competitive reactions of producers located in other regions of the world.

Event studies[83] are other tools not directly related to product prices and are used to illustrate implications for the expected future profitability or valuation of firms typically resulting in share price movements. Where information is released which indicates a change in a company's competitive position, the information will result in a more or less immediate change in the company's share price. For market definition purposes, relative share price movements of firms competing within or offering potential substitutes for products in the candidate market can provide information about the market's view of the degree of competition between firms or products. Thus, event studies might provide a valuable source of information relevant to market definition too.

For financial markets, such events appear as information is released onto the market. Where information is released which indicates a change in a company's competitive position, the information will result in a more or less immediate change in the company's share price. Equity markets have been shown to be extremely good at interpreting information with implications about a firm's future profitability. Indeed, the response of equity markets to specific pieces of information can provide valuable empirical evidence regarding the real effect on a firm of a specific event. The theoretical basis for this conclusion is found in a moderate version of the *Efficient Markets Hypothesis*. The hypothesis states that all publicly available information is incorporated into the stock price, such that no one can systematically bet against the market and win on the basis of information about which the market knows. There is much empirical evidence supporting this hypothesis. Events that move stock prices can provide information that assist in defining markets. These events may include: earlier merger and acquisition (M&A) activity, announcements about new products or services, technological developments, announcements about changes in regulation, sharp exchange rate changes when they occur within or near the candidate market and change in the potential profitability of a good or service in comparison to other (substitute or complementary) goods or services. For market definition purposes, relative share price movements of firms competing within, or offering potential substitutes for services in the candidate market can provide information about the market's view of the degree of competition between firms or products.

The causes of share price movements can be complex, and the link between events and share price changes need to be understood to avoid conclusions being drawn about causation that are not consistent with the underlying facts. Indeed, empirical attempts to translate the effects of events (external to the firm or strategic corporate decisions) face methodological difficulties that cannot be overcome easily.

---

83. These events may include: earlier M&A activity, announcements about new products or services, technological developments, announcements about changes in regulation, sharp exchange rate changes, etc.

However, event studies can provide a valuable source of information relevant to market definition when undertaken objectively, rather than to support an *a priori* position.

In some cases, *critical loss analysis (CLA)*[84] may be relevant. One definition of critical loss is the minimum percentage loss in volume of sales required to make a 5% or 10% price increase on a product unprofitable. The critical percentage tends to be lower when an undertaking has a high mark-up over unit costs (since each sale lost entails a relatively large loss in profit). However, the fact that an undertaking can set a high mark-up might also demonstrate that its current customer base is not particularly price sensitive. These potentially opposing effects might need to be balanced and assessed in conjunction with other evidence (e.g., estimates of elasticities of demand). CLA has been applied in the US in recent years whereas Europe prefers the Hypothetical Monopolist Test (HMT) discussed further below.

The calculation of the critical loss is purely an arithmetical exercise. The benefit to the hypothetical monopolist from a price increase is the amount of the price increase, Δp, times the quantity that will be sold at the new price, $(q + \Delta q)$, i.e., $\Delta p(q+\Delta q)$. The cost to the monopolist of the price increase is equal to lost sales, i.e., to the pre-merger margin, $(p-c)$, where c denotes average variable cost (AVC), times the quantity reduction, Δq, caused by the price increase, i.e., $-(p-c)\Delta q$. The critical loss is the percentage reduction in quantity that just balances the benefit and cost of the price increase, that is, for which

$$\Delta p(q+\Delta q) = -(p-c)\Delta q, \quad (1)$$

holds.

Solving for the critical loss, $-\Delta q/q$, yields[85]

$$-\frac{\Delta q}{q} = \text{Critical Loss} = \frac{\Delta p/p}{\Delta p/p + m}, \quad (2)$$

where $m = (p-c)/p$ is the contribution margin measured as a percentage of the price.

The actual loss in the single-product case can be easily calculated as

$$\text{Actual Loss} = \varepsilon \frac{\Delta p}{p}, \quad (3)$$

where ε denotes the own-price elasticity (commonly just referred to as the 'price elasticity') of demand, which is defined as the percentage change in the quantity demanded that follows a 1% increase in the price of the product.[86]

---

84. Its basic idea is simple. One asks, given a certain price increase, what the percentage loss in unit sales would have to be to render the price increase unprofitable. If the actual loss is less than the critical loss, the price increase would be profitable, otherwise it would not and the definition of the relevant market has to be broadened by further substitutes or geographical areas.
85. See (O'Brien & Wickelgren 2003, 9).
86. Mathematically, the (own) price elasticity ε is defined as $\varepsilon = \frac{\Delta q}{\Delta p}\frac{p}{q}$, where p denotes price and q the quantity of the product under consideration.

Thus, if

$$\text{Actual Loss} = \varepsilon \frac{\Delta p}{p} > \frac{\Delta p/p}{\Delta p/p + m} = \text{Critical Loss}, \quad (4)$$

a price increase by $\Delta p/p$ would be profitable and the relevant market has to be augmented. Equation (4) also indicates that the price elasticity, ε, plays a decisive role in the determination of whether a price increase would be profitable or not.[87]

In the multi-product case, the analysis is more complex. However, the same basic reasoning applies. If a hypothetical monopolist increases the prices of more than one product, the actual loss is reduced compared to the single-product case because some fraction of the reduction in the demand for the individual products is recaptured by the other products of the monopolist. The extent to which this occurs is measured by the cross-price elasticity or the diversion ratio.

For notational convenience, let us consider the symmetric case of two products, A and B, as an example.[88] The cross-price elasticity between products A and B is defined as the percentage change in the demand for product B when there is a 1% increase in the price of product A.[89] A $\Delta p/p$ percent increase in the price of product A causes the unit sales of product A to fall by the amount of the price increase times the own-price elasticity of demand, i.e., by $\varepsilon \Delta p/p$. Similarly, the price increase causes the unit sales of product B to rise by the amount of the price increase times the cross-price elasticity of demand, i.e., by $\varepsilon_{AB} \Delta p/p$. Since products A and B are symmetric in this example, a $\Delta p/p$ percent increase in the price of product B causes the unit sales of product B to fall by $\varepsilon \Delta p/p$ and the unit sales of product A to rise by $\varepsilon_{AB} \Delta p/p$.

Combining both effects, a price increase of $\Delta p/p$ percent for both products causes a reduction in unit sales of $(\varepsilon - \varepsilon_{AB})\Delta p/p$ percent for both products. Thus, the actual loss for the hypothetical monopolist from a $\Delta p/p$ percent price increase is[90]

$$\text{Actual Loss} = \frac{\Delta p}{p}(\varepsilon - \varepsilon_{AB}). \quad (5)$$

Equation (5) shows that because some of the loss in sales is recaptured by the other product of the hypothetical monopolist, the actual loss due to a price increase is reduced compared to the single-product case.

---

87. Indeed, the analysis of the profitability of a hypothetical price increase sometimes is cast in terms of the 'critical elasticity', $\varepsilon = \dfrac{1}{\Delta p/p + m}$. See (Massey 2000, 320). This formula for the critical elasticity can easily be derived from equation (4).
88. Symmetry refers to the assumption that prices, quantities and elasticities are equal for both products. The basic argument given above can be extended to the n-product case and to asymmetric cases. See (O'Brien & Wickelgren 2003).
89. The cross-price elasticity ε_{AB} between products A and B is defined as $\varepsilon_{AB} = \dfrac{\Delta q_B}{\Delta p_A} \dfrac{p_A}{q_B}$, where p_A denotes the price of product A and p_B the quantity of product B.
90. See (O'Brien & Wickelgren 2003, 12).

Chapter 4: Competition Practice

4.2.3.2 Hypothetical Monopolist Test

The most advanced methodology to measure demand-side substitutability in market definition is the so-called Hypothetical Monopolist Test (HMT).[91]

4.2.3.2.1 US Approach

In the US, a similar test, the Small but Significant Non-transitory Increase in Prices Test (SSNIP) is used.[92] The US Department of Justice Merger Guidelines describe the procedure:

> The Department will begin with each product (narrowly defined) produced or sold by each merging firm and ask what would happen if a hypothetical monopolist of that product imposed a 'small but significant and non-transitory' increase in price.[93] If the price increase would cause so many buyers to shift to other products that a hypothetical monopolist would not find it profitable to impose such an increase in price, then the Department will add to the product group the product that is the next-substitute for the merging firm's product and ask the same question again. This process will continue until a group of products is identified for which a hypothetical monopolist could profitably impose a 'small but significant and non-transitory' increase in price. The Department will consider the relevant product market to be the smallest group of products that satisfies this test.[94]

Accordingly, in the US a 'market' is defined as a product or group of products and a geographic area in which it is produced or sold such that a hypothetical profit-maximising firm, not subject to price regulation, and as the only present and future producer or seller of those products in that area, would likely impose at least a 'small but significant and nontransitory' increase in price, assuming the terms of sale of all other products are held constant. A relevant market is a group of products and a geographical area that is no bigger than necessary to satisfy this test. In the US, a 5% price increase over a period of one year is given as a fair benchmark for most purposes, although higher or lower levels may be used depending on the industry. In considering the likely reaction of buyers to a price increase, the US authorities consider all relevant evidence, including, but not limited to, the following: evidence that buyers have shifted or have considered shifting purchases between products in response to relative changes in price or other competitive variables; evidence that sellers base business decisions on the prospect of buyer substitution between products in response to

---

91. The concept of the HMT was introduced in the US Merger Guidelines in 1984 as the SNIPP-test. The test is used by many European anti-trust authorities.
92. (U.S. Department of Justice and Federal Trade Commission 1992), (US Non-Horizontal Merger Guidelines 1984, Ch. 4).
93. What constitutes a 'small but significant and nontransitory' increase in price will depend on the nature of industry, and the Department at times may use a price increase that is larger or smaller than 5%.
94. (US Merger Guidelines 1992).

relative changes in price or other competitive variables; the influence of downstream competition faced by buyers in their output markets; and the timing and cost of switching products.

It is always possible to improve those price tests and it is even possible to construct more sophisticated tests based on the econometric estimation of demand elasticities. However, in its present form, the SSNIP test and HMT provide useful evidence on market definition and hence have greater economic relevance than an approach based on casual observations of product characteristics and prices. The logic of the economic approach to product market definition is that two products neither have to look the same nor have to have the same price in order to be included in the same market. Nor do they necessarily have to be completely interchangeable. What is required is that enough consumers or producers are willing to switch from one product to the other in order to act as an effective market discipline on either group of suppliers.[95]

4.2.3.2.2 European Approach

In its analysis the Commission makes use of both qualitative and quantitative methods. Competition economists on behalf of the parties support the Commission in this exercise by providing price analyses to ensure that the Commission possesses all the relevant information to assess a merger properly. Qualitative methods, for example, may include an examination of product characteristics and the intended use of a product by consumers, whereas quantitative methods may involve the examination of price trends and the estimation of cross-price elasticities by the use of econometric methods. The analyses of more recent Commission's decisions illustrate that a more consistent approach to the definition of the relevant product market has emerged. In particular, the Commission's Notice on the definition of the relevant market has improved this situation. In the following, the appropriate methodology for market definition, the HMT, is discussed at length.

The methodology the Commission applies to measure demand and supply substitutability as well as to define the relevant product and geographic market is the so-called *HMT*.[96] The HMT is an experiment, postulating a hypothetical small, non-transitory change in relative prices and evaluating the likely reactions of customers to that increase.

The Commission's 1997 Notice refers in paragraphs 16 and 17 to this speculative experiment. The Notice states that:

> Conceptually, this approach means that, starting from the type of products that the undertakings involved sell and the area in which they sell them, additional products and areas will be included in, or excluded from, the market definition depending on

---

95. (Bos, Stuyck, & Wytinck 1992, 337).
96. The HMT has received a considerable amount of discussion in recent years. (Harris & Simons 1989); (Baumann & Godek 1995); (Johnson 1989); (Werden, Four Suggestions on Market Delineation, 1992); (Gasmi, Laffont, & Sharkey 2002); (Dobbs 2007).

Chapter 4: Competition Practice

whether competition from these other products and areas affect or restrain sufficiently the pricing of the parties' products in the short term.'

'The question to be answered is whether the parties' customers would switch to readily available substitutes or to suppliers located elsewhere in response to a hypothetical small (in the range 5% to 10%) but permanent relative price increase in the products and areas being considered. If substitution were enough to make the price increase unprofitable because of the resulting loss of sales, additional substitutes and areas are included in the relevant market. This would be done until the set of products and geographical areas is such that small, permanent increases in relative prices would be profitable.

Thus, the methodology of the HMT focuses on demand as well as on supply substitutability. In practice, the HMT is a two-step procedure:

- The shift in the number of consumers who do not buy the product due to an increase in price has to be calculated. This analysis depends on the own-price elasticity of the product or service as well as on the cross-price elasticities of the products or services under consideration.
- A calculation has to show whether the price increase was profitable. This calculation depends on the margin of the product or service in question.

Figure 4.1 illustrates this relationship.

Figure 4.1   Effect of the Price Increase

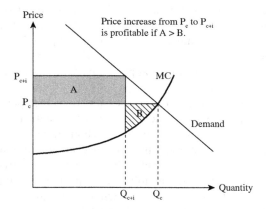

The Notice gives as a practical example for the HMT a merger between soft drink bottlers. An issue to examine in such a case would be to decide whether different flavours of soft drinks belong to the same market. In practice, the question to address would be whether consumers of flavour A would switch to other flavours when confronted with a permanent price increase of 5% to 10% in flavour A. If a sufficient number of consumers would switch to, say flavour B to such an extent that the price increase in flavour A would not be profitable due to the resulting loss of sales, then the market would comprise at least flavours A and B. The process would have to be repeated for flavours C and D, and so on until a set of products is identified for which a price increase would not induce a sufficient substitution in demand.[97]

The price to take into account will be generally and in particular for the analysis of merger cases, the *prevailing market price*. Since the analysis of mergers is prospective, the focus is on how the merger itself might lead to the creation or reinforcement of dominance. It is conceivable therefore, that if prices have been increased substantially in the past, additional price increases in the future are in fact constrained by other products. In such situations, the relevant market might be different for the purpose of analysing a merger.

Before describing the HMT in detail, it should be emphasised that defining a market in strict accordance with the test's assumptions is a demanding task. If customers or consumers are asked directly how they would react to a hypothetical price rise, their answers should be treated with caution. In this respect, survey evidence might provide additional information, for example, evidence on how customers rank particular products, whether and to what extent brand loyalty exists, and which characteristics of products are the most important ones to their decision to purchase. The main conclusion is that defining a market requires the balancing of various types of evidence and the exercise of judgment.[98]

4.2.3.2.3   Initial Price Analysis

The HMT provides a well-defined and coherent approach to market definition, but it has to be made operational. Indeed, by its very nature of describing a hypothetical (monopolist) situation it implies that no actual data is available that would allow for a literal application of the test. One should bear in mind the hypothetical nature of the test when assessing any implementation. The following section elaborates on the economics of the HMT.

One of the first components in the application of the HMT is the examination of pricing and pricing related issues.

Another aspect, which needs a cautious treatment, is the appropriate price level. Where an undertaking already has market power it may operate in a market where the current price is substantially different from the competitive price. In such a case, cross-price elasticity for demand might provide misleading information, as prices are likely to have been raised to a level already where demand is relatively price sensitive (i.e., at or near monopoly levels at the limit of what people are willing to pay). Other products appear to be adequate substitutes when this may not be the case. This phenomenon is known as the 'Cellophane Fallacy'.[99] In a case involving cellophane, the US Supreme Court considered that a significant price rise would bring cellophane into competition with other products. This led the Supreme Court to conclude that other products served as sufficiently good substitutes to cellophane, so that cellophane could not be considered as being in a separate market. However, the then current prices

---

97. *Ibid.*, para. 18.
98. (Office of Fair Trading 2004, point. 2.14).
99. (U.S. Supreme Court, United States v. E. I. du Pont de Nemours & Co., 351 U.S. 1956).

were already far above the price that would prevail if the market was competitive.[100] To solve the Cellophane fallacy the analyst must use a price that would prevail if the market was competitive. In practice, a benchmarking of prices solves this problem.

In the following figure, MC represents the marginal cost curve and D the demand curve of the hypothetical monopolist that is formed from the consolidation of a number of firms, which were in competitive equilibrium. The hypothetical monopolist is assumed to inherit a situation where price is initially equal to marginal cost. The marginal cost at Q_0 is MC_0, and the profit in this situation is $Profit_0$, which equals the firms' revenues (P_0Q_0) minus the total costs incurred in producing Q_0. The total cost covers variable and fixed costs. The variable cost term is equal to Q_0 times average variable cost ($Q_0 * AVC_0$) or the sum of all points along the marginal cost curve from one to Q_0, this means $\sum_{i=1}^{Q_0} MC_i$. So the profit is defined as: $Profit_0 = P_0Q_0 - Q_0 * AVC_0$ − Fixed Costs. Figure 4.2 shows the situation after the hypothetical price increase.

Figure 4.2 Hypothetical Monopolist Profit

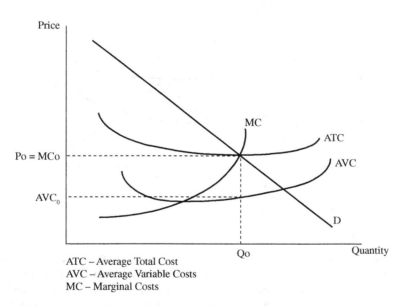

ATC − Average Total Cost
AVC − Average Variable Costs
MC − Marginal Costs

P_0 = initial price, Q_0 = initial quantity
Source: (Frank 1997).

---

100. Essentially, even where a product has no close substitutes, if the price is already high and a hypothetical price rise occurs, consumers would tend to switch to poorer substitutes more readily than they would if the price rise had occurred from a significantly lower level (such as would prevail if the market was already relatively competitive).

The increased price is P1; the new quantity is Q1; and the marginal cost is MC1. Profit1 is equal to P1Q1 - Q1 * AVC1 - Fixed Costs. The conclusion is that the critical loss in sales that would make a given price increase unprofitable is the level of output that makes firms indifferent between the market prices P0 and P1. So the critical loss is the level that implies that Profit0 equals Profit1. As illustrated, the effects on a firm's profits are determined by the difference between the additional revenue gained from the price increase and the decreased costs caused by a reduction in sales or production and the loss in revenue resulting from a sales reduction. Thus, it is necessary to calculate the profits before and after the price increase in order to determine whether the price increase will be profitable or not, as well as the reactions of consumers to a (hypothetical) price increase.

Figure 4.3   Hypothetical Monopolist Profit after Price Increase

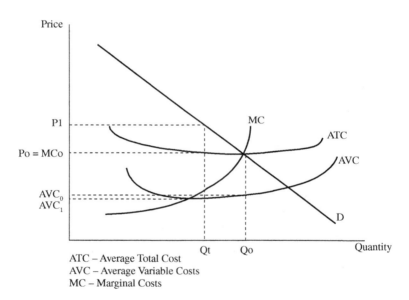

ATC – Average Total Cost
AVC – Average Variable Costs
MC – Marginal Costs

Source: (Frank 1997).

Thus, one can conclude from the discussion above that both the own-price as well as the cross-price elasticities are decisive in evaluating whether a price increase by a hypothetical monopolist would be profitable or not and hence how to define the relevant market. In other words, the eventual change in the profit of a hypothetical monopolist after a price increase can only be answered empirically.

In order to implement the HMT the purchasing decisions of customers need to be evaluated. Probably the most widely used method of price analysis in market research is the so-called '*Conjoint Analysis*'. Conjoint Analysis is an empirical tool, which allows a proper performance of the HMT. Customers buy products not only based on price, but also consider in their buying decisions other factors, such as quality, service, past experiences etc. In general, few consumers are willing to fill in simple paper & pencil questionnaires asking whether he or she would accept a price increase in the range of 5% to 10%. As a consequence, markets would be defined very narrowly. Conjoint Analysis instead examines the benefit a product represents for the customer and values it. Pricing and market segmentation are typical areas where Conjoint Analysis is frequently used. Competition analysis is another one.[101]

4.2.3.2.4 Modelling Customer Choice with Conjoint Analysis

The course of Conjoint Analysis follows a well-established methodology.[102] Preferably a computer-based Conjoint Analysis is applied to examine the benefit a product represents for the customer and how he or she values it. Different software packages are available to conduct Conjoint Analyses. The software permits the analysis of the relationship between the prices of a product and the choice behaviour of consumers. Recently there has been a continuous development within Conjoint Analysis.[103] One focus of these extensions has been on the modelling of individual differences in choice-based models based on hierarchical Bayesian methods.[104]

Conjoint Analysis deals with preference intensity and can be used to estimate the best possible predictive validity of marketplace behaviour and consumer reaction.[105] At its heart lies the estimation of a formal model of choice, usually a so-called *logit model*. The components of this method are:

- a technique of data collection requiring a respondent to consider 'trade-offs' among desirable alternatives;
- a computational method which derives 'utilities' accounting as nearly as possible for each respondent's choice behaviour.

There are many product attributes for which ideal levels in fact differ from customer to customer such as promotional support or brand awareness. For attributes such as convenience, economy, or level of performance, however, it can be assumed that every customer would prefer a product having as high a level of each attribute as possible. What is needed in such cases is information about customers 'trade-offs'. It is relevant to determine how customers value various levels of each attribute and the extent to which they would forego a high level of one attribute to achieve a high level

---

101. The choice-based approach of Conjoint Analysis employing a logit model is based on McFadden, in: (Zarembka 1974). It has been adapted to marketing research by (Punj & Staelin 1978) and (Gensch & Recker 1979).
102. Most studies of conjoint analysis have involved a verbal description of product profiles. Due to increased computing capabilities, ongoing research has developed approaches to integrate virtual reality and conjoint analysis. See, e.g., (Dijkstra & Timmermans 1997).
103. For an overview see, e.g., (Green & Srinivasan, Conjoint Analysis in Marketing: New Developments with Implications for Research and Practice 1990); (Werden, Froeb and Scheffman 2004); (Rao 2008).
104. See, e.g., (Allenby, Arora, & Ginter 1995); (Lenk, DeSarbo, Green, & Young 1996).
105. For a discussion of Conjoint Analysis see, e.g., (Aaker, Kumar, & Day 2003); (Gustafsson, Herrmann, & Huber 2000).

of another. Customers make a selection of different product concepts, which are marked by different sets of characteristics. The price determines the decision to buy a product as well as the possibilities to use it. By carrying out the HMT with support of Conjoint Analysis, the attractiveness of products or the utilities of each product attribute are determined. The utilities of individual customers are added up and transferred into a demand curve. The result of a Conjoint Analysis is a demand curve function, which is used to examine hypothetical price changes and their effect on demand.

With the implementation of the HMT, the so-called 'Choice-Based Conjoint' Analysis (CBC) is applied in most studies. CBC software provides all the tools needed to conduct a choice-based conjoint study: a questionnaire module for designing and conducting PC-based interviews, three analysis modules, and a market simulation module for testing 'what if' scenarios. The output is used by the market simulation module, which estimates the share of choice for products that are made up of combinations of the study's attributes. The main characteristic distinguishing choice-based from other types of Conjoint Analysis is that the respondent expresses preferences by choosing concepts from sets of concepts, rather than by rating or ranking them.[106] Below are two schemes of the key processes.

Figure 4.4   Hypothetical Monopolist Test Step 1

Step 1: Conjoint Analysis

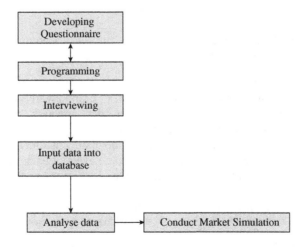

---

106. (DeSarbo, Ramaswamy, & Cohen 1995).

Figure 4.5 Hypothetical Monopolist Test Step 2

Step 2: Calculation of Profitability

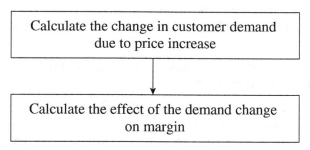

Step 1: Conjoint Analysis

Within Conjoint Analysis different product options characterised by a variety of different attributes, only one of them being its price, are presented. Consumers are asked to evaluate these different product concepts. This evaluation is often done by binary choice, i.e., by presenting two different product concepts to the respondent and asking him to make a decision for one out of the two.[107]

Figure 4.6 shows an example of such a choice question.[108]

Figure 4.6 Example of a Conjoint Question

Which fibre purchase would you prefer?	
Viscose The fibre is biodegradable € 1,20 /kg (US $ 1,47 /kg) The level of quality is high and steady	Lyocell Wet tenacity is essential. € 2,25 /kg (US $ 2,76 /kg) The quality of fibers is low (e.g. causing standstill period)

Thus, Conjoint Analysis is based on a formal, structural model of consumers' choice, which implies that:

107. The choice-based approach of Conjoint Analysis employing a logit model is based on McFadden in: (Zarembka 1974). It has been applied to marketing research by (Punj & Staelin 1978) and (Gensch & Recker 1979).
108. Due to increased computer capacities, approaches have been developed to integrate virtual reality systems into Conjoint Analysis. See, e.g., (Dijkstra and Timmermans, Exploring the possibilities of conjoint measurement as a deision-making tool for virtual wayfinding environments 1997).

- consumers aim to satisfy a need. This need is satisfied by the utility derived from the consumption of the product and its perceived attributes;
- the comparison of the benefits and costs of the different product concepts lead to a preference towards the product;
- the buying intention becomes an actual buying decision by devoting real resources to it.

The reasons why Conjoint Analysis is especially well-suited to estimate price sensitivity of demand within the HMT are:

- the possibility of jointly considering the elements relevant to a consumer's buying decision;
- the high similarity of the choice decision with real buying decisions. It is because of this realistic choice situation that respondents are expected to give very valid responses of their true preferences and buying motives.

Conducting a Conjoint Analysis reveals the attractiveness, called the 'part-worths', of each attribute of the product to the respondent. The sum of the part-worths of the combined product features gives the utility of that certain product concept to the consumer. The wording 'conjoint' relates to the fact that relative utilities of certain product features might not be measurable if considered separately but that a joint consideration of the different product features will reveal the relative utilities of the distinctive features.

In accordance with legal requirements each product concept is characterised by the product, its price, quality, and its intended use. The application of various 'what if' scenarios allows the estimation of the importance of these product features when the price is changed (*relative price increase*). In these simulations, the part-worth of each attribute of the products is evaluated. The sum of all part-worths of the attributes of a certain product determines its utility from the point of view of the consumer. Finally, these utilities of different product concepts derived from the choices of the respondents can be aggregated to conduct market simulations of different, hypothetical price scenarios. Based on the choices of the respondents, the hypothetical changes in demand for a certain product after a hypothetical price change are estimated. The market simulation module allows the analyst to determine the products considered in different scenarios of competition, to evaluate the part-worths based on these scenarios, to aggregate the utilities of the products and to model the behaviour of the respondents within this market.

Figure 4.7 illustrates the relative importance of the attributes of the products under consideration in the fibre example. It shows that the product itself is the most important aspect in the choice of customers with a weight of 41% in his decision process. Quality contributes to 22% and price to 32% to the decision. Intended use is of only minor importance in shaping the choice of the customers with a weight of 5%.

Chapter 4: Competition Practice

Figure 4.7 Relative Importance of the Attributes in the Fibre Example

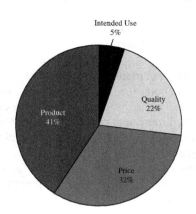

The two fundamental concepts to this methodology are the concept of a utility function for individual product concepts and a preference function summarising the utilities derived from the different product concepts. These two concepts will be discussed briefly.

4.2.3.2.5 Estimation of the Utility Functions

The first step in applying the above outline of the decision model is to derive the utility functions. The utility function maps the specifications of the different product attributes onto a value called the *utility* of this particular product concept. This mapping reveals how the different attributes are valued by consumers.

Consumers choose between different product concepts. Conjoint Analysis estimates the part-worth of each product attribute based on the choice decisions of the respondents. Utilities are a linear combination of the part-worths of the product's attributes:

$$U_j = \alpha_j - \beta p_i + \gamma x + e_{ij},$$

where U_j denotes the consumer j's utility derived from product i, α_j is a constant basis level of utility, β is a parameter of the consumer's price sensitivity, p_i the price of product i, x a vector of other product attributes, y a vector of the part-worth of these attributes, and e_{ij}, a random component. The estimates of the utility function are deduced indirectly from the choice decisions of the respondents.

4.2.3.2.6 Preference Function

Based on the utilities derived from certain product concepts, the share of preferences a certain product concept receives within a given set of products can be calculated. The share of preferences for a certain product is given by the logistic distribution function with product utilities as the input variables. The utilities are rescaled such that the sum of the (antilog of the) utilities of all products equals 100. That is,

$$P_i = \frac{u_i}{\Sigma_{t \in C} u_t},$$

where P_i denotes the share of preferences of product i, $u_i = expU_i$ and C is the set of possible choices. Thus, P_i denotes the probability that product i will be chosen. From the part-worth of the attribute 'price', price and cross-price elasticities are computed. These, in turn, can be applied to evaluate the competitive constraints of the products in the market on the product under consideration and to implement the HMT to define relevant product and geographic markets.

Figure 4.8 shows the effect of a 5% price increase on demand in the fibre example. The price response function is not very steep implying that a price increase leads only to a minor response.

Figure 4.8 Price Response after a 5% Price Increase in the Fibre Example

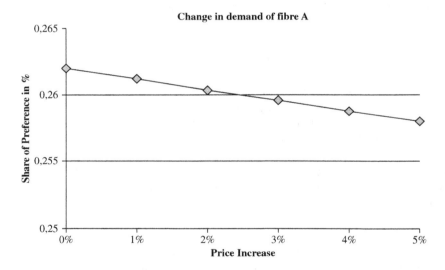

Step 2: Calculation of Profitability

The calculation of the profit of a hypothetical price increase is the second step in the application of the HMT after the estimation and calculation of the price elasticity on the demand side. Both, the likely decrease in demand as well as the change of the contribution margin in the case of a hypothetical price increase, influence the profit or loss situation. To calculate the profits, turnover data (NOS – Net Outside Sales) as well as variable cost data (TDC – total direct costs) are required. These data are provided by the company under investigation. TDC or the equivalent of Cost of Goods is the sum of the cost for raw materials, packaging materials (e.g., bottles, labels), conversion costs

Chapter 4: Competition Practice

to finished products (e.g., labour cost, machine depreciation), and delivery cost (e.g., transportation and warehousing cost from the manufacturing plant to the customers warehouse). Costs for marketing are also included in the TDC.

The volume of the product is defined in statistical units (SU) upon which the accounting system of the company is based. This converts the amount of the product sold into a common measure, i.e., statistical units.

The contribution margin is defined as NOS minus TDC. The profit or loss of the hypothetical price increase is calculated by comparing the contributions margins before and after the price increase.

After the provision of the accountancy data by the company, the profit or loss of the hypothetical price increase is calculated on the basis of the following steps:

- First, the reduction in volume in SU (Statistical Units) is calculated by means of the price elasticity using the market simulator with the conjoint analysis.
- Secondly, change in turnover (NOS) is calculated. In most cases, a price increase for the product under investigation results in a reduction in the purchase likelihood. This figure is used to calculate the reduction in volume terms. The hypothetical volume is multiplied by the price resulting in the new, hypothetical turnover.
- In the next step, changes in TDC are calculated. This is done by reducing the TDC of the base scenario by the percentage in changes of demand, which results in hypothetical TDC.
- Finally the hypothetical profit has to be identified. The hypothetical profit is calculated as hypothetical NOS minus hypothetical TDC.

If this profit is lower than the profit before the price increase, a price increase is obviously not profitable for the company, which proves that the relevant market is wider. Other products in the consumers' choice set exercise a competitive constraint on the product under consideration.

If the profit is higher than the profit before the price increase, the price increase is profitable. This means that substitutability is not enough to constrain a hypothetical monopolist. Thus, the relevant market has to be defined narrowly.

To conclude, the process of market definition is ultimately an empirical matter, although in many cases the relevant market can be determined sufficiently accurately without the need for complex econometric studies. Obtaining accurate consumer information through surveys about future (hypothetical) economic behaviour is a critical task in the implementation of the HMT. Econometric techniques that are based on historical data are backward-looking, and thus define markets as they were in the past. In the case of market definition for merger cases these definitions may not hold. Where markets need to be defined by reference to empirical methods, however, experts should apply modern tools.

4.2.3.3 Other Empirical Tests

Excess capacity, transportation costs, and costs of local distribution are relevant factors in defining a geographic market. These factors provide evidence of likely supply responses to hypothetical price increases. If there is excess capacity existing in plants serving a defined geographic market, it is more likely that there would be a significant supply response if the price was increased in the defined area. In addition, the lower the transportation costs, the greater the outside area from which it would be economic to ship into the defined area, or the smaller the hypothetical price increase that would induce shipments into the defined area. And finally, the lower the costs of local distribution, the easier it will be for firms located outside the defined hypothetical monopoly area to ship into and sell in the area.[109]

Landes and *Posner*[110] use the so-called *diversion approach*, for their definition of the geographical market in anti-trust cases. If a distant seller has some sales in a local market, all its sales, wherever made, should be considered a part of that local market for purposes of computing the market share of a local seller. This is because the distant seller has proved its ability to sell in the market and could increase its sales there, should the local price rise, simply by diverting sales from other markets. The analysis involves showing that the supply response of the competitive fringe is an increasing function of the ratio of the distant seller's sale in their other markets to their sales in the local market. The higher that ratio, the higher their supply response will be because it is easier for distant sellers to divert a small fraction of their output to the local market should the price rise there than it would be to divert a large fraction of their output to the local market.[111] The idea is not a new one, but *Landes* and *Posner* make the novel claim that a local seller's market power often can be estimated without examining the costs of transportation or other distance related costs that sellers located in another country bear.

Shipment tests are perhaps the most widely used empirical test method for delineating relevant geographic markets. Shipment patterns are difficult to interpret and have to be used with care. The rule of thumb, subject to many exceptions, is that an exporting area may be a market, while an area with substantial imports probably is not.[112] Some assumptions are necessary for the interpretation of trade flows, for example, as to whether buyers and sellers respond to exchange rate fluctuations in the same way that they would respond to hypothetical cartel price increases.

The most common way to measure the relevant geographic market is by the use of the *Elzinga-Hogarty*[113] test. This test uses shipments data to define two ratios: LOFI, 'little out from inside,' and LIFO, 'little in from outside'. LOFI and LIFO are defined as:

---

109. (Klein 1987, 268).
110. (Landes & Posner 1981, 937–982).
111. *Ibid.*, 693.
112. (Owen 1987, 212).
113. in: (Elzinga & Hogarty 1973, 45).

$$\text{LOFI} = \frac{\text{Sales by firms in the market to customers in the market}}{\text{Total sales by firms in the market to customers both inside and outside the market}}$$

and

$$\text{LIFO} = \frac{\text{Sales by firms in the market to customers in the market}}{\text{Total purchases by in the market}}$$

These ratios are designed to determine the smallest geographic region where nearly all production in that region is purchased by consumers in the region (LOFI) and where nearly all purchases by consumers in the region come from firms located in the region (LIFO). It may be extremely difficult to obtain shipment data on an origin and destination basis for the merged firms and all other firms in the market. However, assuming this data or some approximation is available; *Elzinga* and *Hogarty* use the following steps to construct these ratios:

- They start with the largest of the merging firms (or its largest plant) and try to find the minimum area required to account for at least 75% of the appropriate shipments of that firm. This is the first hypothetical geographic market. (If plants are geographically separate, the calculation is done for each plant.)
- Next they determine if 75% of the total sales of this product within the hypothetical area are shipped from plants located within this area. If not, the hypothetical market area must be expanded until this point is reached (LIFO).
- Finally, it has to be determined if at least 75% of the shipments by the firms within the hypothetical market area are to customers within the area. If not, the hypothetical market area must be expanded until this point is reached (LOFI).

Economic problems may arise in interpreting export flows out of an area when using the LOFI ratio. There are two major reasons why large export flows out of a local area are an indication that the relevant geographic market is larger than the local area. First, if shipments are being made from one production area to another, it is an indication that transportation costs are such that trade flows could be reversed if price were increased in the local area. Secondly, and perhaps more importantly, large exports are an indication that local market shares do not accurately reflect market power. Any local producer outside the merger presumably can divert its exports to the local market. Therefore, even if the merged firm has a large post-merger local market share, it would not necessarily have the ability to increase local price. An economically relevant market share of the merged firm in the local market, that is, a share that accurately reflected market power, should be calculated by using the merged firm's sales in the local market, but total sales in all markets (or total capacity) for the other local firms. In this case, the share of local sales by the merged firm does not accurately reflect the merged firm's ability to control supply of the product in the local market.

However, even though large exports out of an area suggests a larger geographical market, a merger of firms within the narrow area may create some market power; for example, a situation where there are only two firms in an isolated area, both exporting to a world market with many other firms. The merger of these two firms would permit the merged firm to increase price in the local market by the transportation costs from that market to the outside world. For example, although the crude oil market is a worldwide market, if there were only two crude oil producers in Alaska, a merger would give them the ability to collect local rents by increasing the price they charge local refiners.

In addition to large import flows not being a necessary condition for the expansion of the geographic market, it is not always a sufficient condition. This is because, although imports may be large, the hypothetical supply response to a price increase may be small. Trade barriers like duties or quotas can be the reason for that. Tariffs act like transport costs in constraining the extent to which importers can discipline price increases. However, if tariffs are trivial compared to the differences between foreign costs and domestic prices, they are no barriers. Quotas, voluntary or otherwise, clearly do constrain the ability of foreign suppliers to discipline a domestic market. An example is the Japanese automobile imports into Europe. Although they are large, the supply response may be limited because of the existence of import quotas.

The major difficulty with the Elzinga-Hogarty test is that it draws inferences about relevant geographic markets by examining current shipment data, rather than, as required by the Guidelines and sound economic analysis, by examining the changes that would occur in shipments if relative prices changed. For example, consider the problems of interpreting import flows into an area when using the LIFO ratio. The lack of import flows into an area (meeting the LIFO test) does not imply that the market should not be expanded beyond the geographic area under investigation. The important economic point is that small or non-existing imports into an area do not indicate that significant imports would not be forthcoming in response to a small but significant non-transitory price increase. The important economic point is that in defining a geographic market what one would like to measure ideally is the elasticity of supply.[114] Critics state that since the Elzinga-Hogarty test is independent of the supply elasticity of the exporting region, the test cannot identify anti-trust markets.[115]

In the case of homogeneous goods, transport costs might be a crucial factor. Prices of commodities like oil or sugar significantly differ from one area to the other, and after taking due account of transport costs, such areas may represent separate markets. Otherwise trade flows or arbitrage would take place tending to equalise prices. In the absence of current trade flows, a *transport costs test* sheds light on whether imports could constrain a hypothetical domestic cartel. Transportation costs can actually provide measures of supply responses to hypothetical price increases. If transport costs significantly exceed price differences, the two areas are separate markets at competitive prices.

Another factor used to analyse the relevant geographic market is the similarity or differences in *price movements* between two areas. The basis of this approach is to examine movements over time in the price levels of two products believed to compete in the same market. If they really represent effective substitutes, provided that product

---

114. (Klein 1987, 266).
115. (Scheffmann & Spiller 1987, 129).

quality variations over time do not prevent the data from giving a like comparison, then their prices would be expected to move broadly in parallel fashion. To the extent that their prices diverge, it is possible to verify whether this divergence is accompanied by a significant proportion of consumers switching to the consumption of the product with the lower price.

A number of economists, including *Stigler* and *Sherwin*,[116] use *similarity of price movements*, rather than price uniformity, as a more appropriate measure of defining the relevant market. Because of common time trends, reflecting technological change or inflation, serial correlation may be expected in models comparing price levels. *Stigler* and *Sherwin* therefore proposed that the test for grouping either geographical areas or product ranges into the same markets should be the correlation between percentage changes in their prices. The authors asserted this approach is more powerful than attempts to measure cross-elasticity of demand and supply to determine substitution.

Economic theory gives according to *Stigler* and *Sherwin* strong support for the use of evidence on price similarity for the purposes of market definition. The prices of the same product at the same horizontal stage will be equal in two places A and B if at least *one* of the following conditions is fulfilled:

- There are no barriers to (or costs involved in) the transfer of demand between A and B, so that for any one product the cross-price-elasticity of demand between them would be infinite. This condition will be sufficient to bring about price equality even if there are major differences in the level and elasticity of demand for the product between the two areas.
- Each of a large number of competing suppliers has equal access to A and B, with no cost differences. If the price in A exceeded that in B, then supply to A would rise relatively to supply to B, causing price equality.
- Given monopoly or collusive oligopoly across both A and B, the price elasticity of demand at any single price is the same in each area. A company with a Community-wide monopoly may vary prices geographically, according to local price elasticities.

Economic theory implies that these different price zones, national or otherwise, constitute separate markets.

The economic rationale behind examining price movements between two areas is that an increase in price in one area, say, due to a rise in costs or demand in that area will, if there is substitution, lead to an increase in price in the other area as firms in the other area expand their shipments of the product into the original area. Therefore, an examination of changing production and shipments in response to relative price changes would represent a direct test of substitutability between the areas. There is no necessity for any price correlation between the areas. For example, if there were constant costs of producing the product, the increase in price in the first area would merely increase shipments and extend shipping distances from the second area into the first with no change in prices in the second area.

---

116. (Stigler & Sherwin 1985).

Another factor that must be examined when using price correlations as an indication of relevant geographic market is whether the cause of the change in price in one area also is the same in the other area. Without correcting for these common influences on the two prices, the correlation does not give any evidence of competitive substitutability. For example, if a price increase in one area is due to a rise in costs of factors that similarly affect firms in other areas, then the high correlation of prices between the two areas is a spurious measure of substitutability. This is why one can often obtain nonsensically high correlations between two unrelated products such as two distinct elements of the Consumer Price Index, or two clearly non-competitive products such as the price of pizza in one city and the price of pizza in another city.

While this close *correlation of prices* in the two areas might be due to the fact that the two areas are in the same market, it may also be caused by the fact that both sets of producers purchase inputs from common labour and capital markets. For instance, pizza prices are likely to be very highly correlated because they are both responding to common price changes in the underlying inputs, such as tomatoes, cheese, etc. and not because they are in the same geographic market. If the costs of labour or capital used by both sets of producers move in unison, then so will the output prices regardless of the geographic market for the output. Similarly, common factors such as the business cycle or the inflation rate may affect demand in two distinct markets in very similar ways.

Some common changes may affect demand facing competitive firms in opposite directions, leading to a negative price correlation. For example, population shifts between two areas may lead to an increase in demand in one area and a decrease in demand in the other, with corresponding price changes in the respective areas. The products in both areas may be highly substitutable with one another on the margin yet they exhibit a negative price correlation. This suggests that subtracting out common influences to obtain an economically meaningful test may be an extremely difficult exercise to perform. One, ideally, needs to find an event that affects one area while having no direct effect on the other area.[117]

Buyers may have preferences for domestic products even when the products are physically identical. Such preferences may turn on the risks associated with the supply disruptions intrinsic to foreign trade, risks of trade barriers being imposed, risks of exchange fluctuations, or simply because information about distant suppliers may be costly to obtain and to evaluate. The issue however is whether these preferences would persist in the face of a small but significant and non-transitory domestic price increase.

It is the possibility that imports will increase in response to higher domestic prices that disciplines the domestic market, preventing or discouraging cartelisation. If foreign producers have capacity and if that capacity could not profitably be redirected to respond to the domestic price increase, then this foreign capacity is excluded from the market. It is generally capacity, not sales, that constitutes the most important competitive constraint. However, capacity data is often not available, and sales may be the best proxy.

---

117. (Klein 1987, 274).

Chapter 4: Competition Practice

In the case of heterogeneous goods, the problem is more difficult if the product market includes imperfect substitutes, as is most often the case. Price differences may simply reflect qualitative differences among the products. Prices should, taking due account of information lags, at least move in a coordinated fashion. Otherwise, the two areas are probably in different markets. In short, high-price correlations over a sustained period tend to suggest that the two areas are in the same market. However, this evidence is not conclusive because it is also consistent with other hypotheses, for example similar cost phenomena in both markets.

4.2.4 Relevant Product Market

4.2.4.1 Basic Assumptions

The process of defining relevant markets is a structured exercise. On the basis of preliminary information available possible candidate markets are identified within which, for instance a concentration or a restriction of competition has to be assessed. In principle, the Commission follows an open approach to empirical evidence and does not follow a rigid hierarchy of different sources of information or types of evidence. Existing case law on market definitions provides further guidance with respect to the first working assumptions to start with. This case law is discussed further below.

In general, and for all practical purposes when handling individual cases, the question will usually be to decide on a few alternative possible relevant markets. For instance, with respect to the product market, the issue is often to establish whether product A and product B belong to the same product market or not. It is often the case that the inclusion of product B would be enough to remove any competition concerns. Under such circumstances, it is not necessary to consider whether the market also includes additional products and reach a definitive conclusion on the precise scope of the product market. If under the conceivable alternative market definitions the operation in question does not raise competition concerns, the question of market definition will be left open, reducing thereby the burden on companies to supply information.

According to the Notice on the Definition of the relevant market,[118] the relevant product market:

> *comprises all those products and/or services which are regarded as interchangeable or substitutable by the consumer, by reason of the products' characteristics, their prices and their intended use.*

Thus, product characteristics, intended use and prices are the issues that need to be investigated.

In fact, market definition depends to a large extent on how customers value the different characteristics. The drawing of a relevant product market is mainly focussed on an analysis of consumer/customer criteria. Consumer preferences are considered to

---

118. (European Commission, Notice on the definition of relevant market 1997, para. 7).

be important in determining the substitutability of different products on the demand side. Qualitative and quantitative information with respect to the view of competitors, customers and consumers is the type of evidence that is considered in assessing whether two products are demand substitutes.[119]

In the Commission's view, supply-side substitutability does not merit the same competitive effects as demand-side substitutability. In its Notice on the Definition of the Relevant Market, the Commission explains that supply-side substitutability is supposed to be taken into account only in those situations in which its effects are equivalent to those of demand substitution in terms of effectiveness and immediacy:

> This means that suppliers are able to switch production to the relevant products and market them in the short term without incurring significant additional costs or risks in response to small and permanent changes in relative prices. When these conditions are met, the additional production that is put on the market will have a disciplinary effect on the competitive behaviour of the companies involved. Such an impact in terms of effectiveness and immediacy is equivalent to the demand substitution effect.[120]

In the footnote to this point, an indication is given of how long 'a short period' of time is: *'i.e. the period which does not imply a significant adjustment of existing tangible and intangible assets.'* The meaning of supply substitutability is limited in the Notice by paragraph 23. *'When supply substitutability would entail the need to adjust significantly existing tangible and intangible assets, additional investments, strategic decisions or time delays, it will not be considered at the stage of market definition.'* The Notice nominates the area of consumer products, in particular for branded beverages, as an example where supply-side substitution should not be used to enlarge the market. This example relates to the *Nestlé/Perrier*[121] case. In this case, Nestlé's submission that the relevant product market comprised all non-alcoholic refreshment beverages (including bottled source water and soft drinks) was rejected.

In *Nestlé/Perrier*[122], the Commission established the notion of substitution, namely that:

> a limited substitutability in terms of functionality alone is not sufficient to establish substitutability in competition terms. In the present case, if the only criteria to establish substitutability were to be quenching thirst, many products of very different nature, which fulfil that function, would have to be considered as belonging to the same market (tea, milk, beer, certain fruits, etc...). Several factors however indicate the existence of a distinct market for bottled source waters, where operators are able to act with a significant independence of the actions of companies selling soft drinks, in particular in the area of pricing.[123]

From the demand side, the Commission studied the motivation of final consumers to purchase bottled water originating from a natural source, differences in the

---

119. Ibid., paras 38–43.
120. (European Commission, Notice on the definition of relevant market 1997, para. 20).
121. (Commission Decision 92/553/EEC on Nestlé/Perrier 1992).
122. Ibid.
123. Ibid., para. 9.

composition of the products, their taste and intended use, the low cross-price elasticity of demand, the evolution of prices over time and the views of retailers. The Commission concluded that pointing to a narrower market, the market for bottled source water was distinct from that for soft drinks, in view of substantial differences in consumption patterns and present and historic price levels, despite a limited substitutability in terms of functionality. However, certain supply-side factors, such as the fact that most companies market both still source and sparkling and flavoured source waters, and that a bottler of still source water could easily switch production to a sparkling or flavoured source water, militated against a narrower market. On the supply-side, the Commission further examined the regulatory requirements for the production of spring and mineral water, the differences in the types of sellers in the market, the pricing of manufacturers and supply-side substitutability. It is a clear case of where the technical possibility of manufacturing the relevant product is not enough to enlarge the market on the basis of supply-side substitutability. In principle, all soft drink producers have the assets and technical possibilities to bottle purified tap water. In fact, they just need to bypass in their manufacturing process the addition of flavours in order to produce bottles of drinkable water. The Commission did not contest that soft drink producers could easily produce bottled tap water. However, it contested that this bottled water could be marketed in competition with spring waters in France. Careful and long-standing marketing of spring waters in France, their high brand awareness combined with high advertising budgets was an indication that selling bottled tap water in France was commercially not attractive for competitors.[124] Therefore, the Commission determined that the relevant product market was the market for bottled source water.

Alongside demand-side substitutability and supply-side substitutability potential competition might influence market definition, however the Notice on the Definition of the Relevant Market does not take into account potential competition when defining markets. The argument is that conditions under which potential competition will actually represent an effective competitive constraint depend on the analysis of specific factors and circumstances related to the conditions of entry. The Notice states that *'if required, this analysis is only carried out at a subsequent stage, in general once the position of the companies involved in the relevant market has already been ascertained, and when such position gives rise to concerns from a competition point of view'*.[125]

The view that market shares should reflect potential competition arose in particular from US researchers like *Landes* and *Posner*. According to them, competition has to be defined among different products and among alternative actual and potential sources of supply. The market has to include producer's substitution of one product for another. This is mathematically obvious from the *Lerner* index[126], which shows that elasticity of supply of competitors influences the price elasticity of demand faced by the

---

124. *Ibid.*, para. 18.
125. (European Commission, Notice on the definition of relevant market 1997, para. 24).
126. The concept of market power as the setting of price in excess of marginal cost is formalised in the Lerner index, which measures the proportional deviation of price at the firm's profit-maximising output from the firm's marginal cost at the output.

individual firm.[127] Therefore, it is necessary from the US point of view to evaluate both the probable demand responses and the probable supply responses.

Analyses of the product characteristics and the intended use of the product are supposed, as a first step, to limit the field of investigation of possible substitutes. However, product characteristics and intended use are insufficient evidence to conclude whether two products are demand substitutes. Generally, functional interchangeability or similarity in characteristics does not provide in themselves sufficient criteria because the responsiveness of customers to relative price changes may also be determined by other considerations. Conversely, differences in product characteristics are not in themselves sufficient to exclude demand substitutability, since this will depend to a large extent on how customers value different characteristics.

One of the most common misconceptions in the approach to product market definition is that all products in the relevant market must be substitutable for all the others – in other words that they should be *perfect substitutes* for one another. The fallacy in this conception is readily apparent where real life examples of highly competitive consumer product markets are considered. It is almost impossible to conceive a market in which two brand products are perfect substitutes for one another, since there is invariably an element of consumer loyalty towards one product. However, because of similar products' characteristics, intended use and price those different products may be part of the same relevant product market. Where suppliers generally sell a portfolio of products, the entire portfolio determines the product market when the buyers regard the portfolio and not the individual products as substitutes.[128]

The Commission's Notice does not clarify whether captive production or used, recycled or reconditioned goods are included in the market size.

Furthermore, the discussion about supply-side substitution in defining relevant product markets confuses more than clarifies. The relevant product market is supposed to encompass all products that are substitutable in demand and supply. The current sales of those products need to be combined to calculate the total value or volume of the market.

A practical example related to supply-side substitutability is the case of paper. Paper is usually supplied in a range of different qualities, from standard writing paper to high quality papers to be used for instance to publish art books. From a demand point of view, different qualities of paper cannot be used for a particular purpose, i.e., an art book or a high quality publication cannot be made of lower quality papers. However, paper plants are prepared to manufacture the different qualities, and production can be adjusted in a short time frame by incurring minor additional costs. In the absence of particular difficulties in distribution, paper manufacturers are able therefore to compete for orders of various qualities, in particular if orders are passed with a sufficient lead time to allow modification of production plans. The Commission sometimes stick to the opinion, that various qualities should not be included in the

---

127. The Lerner index measures the difference between price and marginal cost as a fraction of the price of a product in order to determine the extent of the industry mark-up thus $L = (P-MC)/P$ see also in: (Landes & Posner 1981, 945).
128. (Commission Guidelines on Vertical Restraints 2000, 91).

Chapter 4: Competition Practice

relevant market. There, sales are not added up to estimate total market value and volume. The market definition therefore might be adjudged too narrow.

Another issue is that the Commission refuses to take into account potential competition when defining markets, but does not provide solid arguments why it includes supply substitution.

Chains of substitution are another aspect. In paragraph 57 of the Notice, the Commission states that chains of substitution might lead to the definition of a relevant market where products or areas at the extreme of the market are not directly substitutable. For example, product B can be a demand substitute for products A and C. Even if products A and C are not direct demand substitutes, they might be found to be in the same relevant product market since their respective pricing might be constrained by substitution to B. One potential error which often occurs when relying on chains of substitution to delineate markets is that, while A may be a good substitute for C, it cannot be assumed that C will be as good a substitute for A. In extreme cases, this would amount to one-way substitutability.

Chains of substitution do not only apply to products but also to the geographic scope of markets. An ice cream seller at one end of a long beach at a holiday resort is not competing with the ice cream seller at the other end of the beach. However, if there is an ice cream seller every hundred metres, then the chain of substitution will put the seller at either end of the beach in the same product market. The pricing and service provided by these two ice cream sellers will constrain each other through the constraint each one in the chain imposes on other nearby ice cream sellers. It tends to be more difficult to determine whether chains of substitutes in products put them in the same product market, or whether the chain has a sufficient gap somewhere to delineate one of the market boundaries.

The factors that link or potentially break the chain of substitution between products can be abstract, and it may be very difficult to get the quality of information needed in order to arrive at a well-informed judgment about whether a 'chain' is broken or otherwise. In some cases, both substitutes and complements will need to be studied.

In assessing a relevant product market, product characteristics, price and intended use play an important role. In that context, the Commission checks marketing studies, clients surveys and advertising in order to describe the relevant characteristics, product differentiation and brands. In individual cases, certain types of evidence will be determining the product market, depending on the characteristics and specificity of the industry and products or services that are being examined. According to the Notice on the Definition of the Relevant Market a decision will be based, in most cases, on the consideration of a number of criteria and different items of evidence. The following section discusses a few merger cases, since in those cases the Commission usually discusses market definitions at length.

The kind of information required to assess the relevant product market depends heavily on the products and/or services in question. Several sources of information on consumer preferences such as past market research, scanner data on prices and quantities sold by retailers, studies based on usage diaries or attitudinal studies might be used. *'For practical reasons the Commission does not order this kind of research for a specific case.*'[129] The Commission uses other sources namely the information provided by the notifying parties of a merger in the Form CO and the replies to the Commission's questionnaires that are sent to the customers, competitors and/or suppliers.

In certain cases, the nature of the activities undertaken by the parties requires a unique assessment, especially if the activities involved are the distribution of products, the provision of services or where the products have special chemical properties.

4.2.4.2 Market Definition Practice

4.2.4.2.1 Type of Evidence

The type of evidence considered to reach a conclusion on the definition of the relevant product market might be classified as follows:

- Evidence of substitution in the recent past.
- Quantitative Tests.
- Views of customer and competitors.
- Consumer Preferences.
- Barriers and Costs associated with switching demand to potential substitutes.
- Different categories of customers.
- Price Discrimination.

4.2.4.2.1.1 Evidence of Substitution in the Recent Past

Evidence relating to recent past events or shocks in the market that offer actual examples of substitution between two products is useful. If there have been changes in relative prices in the past (all else being equal), the reactions in terms of quantities demanded may determine substitutability. Launches of new products in the past are also considered to offer useful information, when it is possible to precisely analyse which products lost sales to the new product. Past evidence has two critical aspects: the European single market was maybe not fully integrated at the time of previous evidence and a merger has a strong prospective element.

4.2.4.2.1.2 Quantitative Tests

There are a few quantitative tests useful for the purpose of delineating markets. These tests consist of various econometric and statistical approaches: estimates of elasticities and cross-price elasticities for the demand of a product, tests based on similarity of price movements over time, the analysis of causality between price series and similarity of price levels and/or their convergence.

---

129. (Alonso 1994, 200).

Chapter 4: Competition Practice

4.2.4.2.1.3 Views of Customers and Competitors

The main customers and competitors can provide additional views on the boundaries of the product market as well as most of the factual information required in reaching a conclusion on the scope of the market. The Commission takes reasoned answers from customers and competitors into account as to what would happen if relative prices for the candidate products would increase in the candidate geographic area by a small amount (for instance of 5%-10%).

4.2.4.2.1.4 Consumer Preferences

In cases of consumer goods, it might be difficult for the Commission to gather personally the views of end consumers about substitute products. Marketing studies that companies have commissioned in the past and that are used by companies in their own decision-making as to pricing of their products and/or marketing actions may provide useful information for the Commission's delineation of the relevant market. Consumer surveys on usage patterns and attitudes, data from consumer's purchasing patterns, the views expressed by retailers and more generally, market research studies submitted by the parties and their competitors may be taken into account to establish whether an economically significant proportion of consumers consider two products as substitutable, also taking into account the importance of brands for the products in question. It is interesting to note that the Commission will give less weight to ad hoc studies:

> The methodology followed in consumer surveys carried out ad-hoc by the undertakings involved or their competitors for the purposes of a merger procedure or a procedure under Regulation 17 will usually be scrutinised with utmost care. Unlike pre-existing studies, they have not been prepared in the normal course of business for the adoption of business decisions.

4.2.4.2.1.5 Barriers and Costs Associated with Switching Demand to Potential Substitutes

There are a number of barriers and costs that might prevent the Commission from considering two prima facie demand substitutes as belonging to one single-product market. The Notice does not include an exhaustive list of all the possible barriers to substitution and of switching costs. These barriers or obstacles might have a wide range of origins. In the past, the Commission has been confronted with regulatory barriers or other forms of State intervention, constraints arising in downstream markets, the need to incur specific capital investment or loss in current output in order to switch to alternative inputs, the location of customers, specific investment in the production process, learning and human capital investment, retooling costs or other investments, uncertainty about quality and the reputation of unknown suppliers and others.

4.2.4.2.1.6   Different Categories of Customers and Price Discrimination

The extent of the product market might be narrowed in the presence of distinct groups of customers. A distinct group of customers for the relevant product may constitute a narrower, distinct market when such a group could be subject to price discrimination. Price discrimination occurs when the same good or service is sold to different groups of buyers at different prices. This will usually be the case when two conditions are met: a) it is possible to identify clearly which group an individual customer belongs to at the moment of selling the relevant products to him, and b) trade among customers or arbitrage by third parties should not be feasible. It is interesting to note that price discrimination is a topic in the product market definition but not in the geographic market definition. An entity is able to discriminate profitably because it is able to identify a group of buyers who are significantly less able (e.g., because of price intensity) or willing (e.g., because of relatively high switching costs) to switch to other suppliers. Differential pricing, however, will not always turn out to be actual price discrimination. Transport costs can result in price differences. It is common for variations in price to be explained by differences in cost. For price discrimination to be sustainable, buyers must be prevented from reselling the product to the group being asked to pay more.

4.2.4.2.2   Practice of the Commission

In the example of *KNP/Bührmann Tetterode/VRG*[130], the Commission found that the concentration affected the distribution and servicing of printing presses, with manufacturers and distributors supplying a complete range of printing press equipment. The Commission also found that from the perspective of the customers of printing presses (i.e., the printers), effective service and maintenance are very important for their business. The Commission concluded that, since the parties were engaged in the supply of a service 'rather than in the manufacture of goods', it was not necessary to define different product markets for each type of machine according to their technical characteristics. The distribution and servicing of printing presses was, therefore, the relevant product market. Another example is *MBB/Arospatiale*[131] where the Commission included product support activities in the assessment of the primary development and production market of a particular product.[132]

In *Renault/Volvo*[133], the Commission did not accept Renault's and Volvo's view that trucks above 5 tonnes are considered a single market. Technical configurations – regarded as the key components such as the type of engine, the number of axles, and the trailer – were cited in order to subdivide the market above 5 tonnes. The technical aspects of the upper range, above 16 tonnes, were considered to be more sophisticated because the requirements of durability and operating costs were greater than for the

---

130. (Commission Decision on KNP/Bührmann-Tetterode and VRG 1993).
131. (Commission Decision on Aérospatiale / MBB 1991).
132. at point 5.
133. (Commission Decision on RENAULT / VOLVO 1990).

intermediate range, a segment between 5 and 16 tonnes. The Commission saw that the marketing of trucks was influenced by these technical product characteristics and stated that the intermediate range trucks and the upper range trucks are not normally considered by customers as interchangeable or substitutable products and constitute therefore two different relevant product markets.[134]

In contrast, in *MBB/Aerospatiale*[135] the Commission treated the entire range of military helicopters as a single-product market. If the Commission had performed a more detailed analysis, it would probably have found differences in specification, use and capability between different types of helicopters, which at least matched the differences between intermediate and upper range trucks found in *Renault/Volvo*. However, it seems that the Commission explicitly recognised supply-side substitution as decisive to group together unlike products in the same market. Products, which are technically substitutable, may nevertheless, be classified as belonging to separate markets.

In *Aerospatiale - Alenia/de Havilland*[136], the notifying parties contended that their customers, the airlines, consider other factors such as technical characteristics and direct operating costs in their decisions about which aircraft to acquire as relevant. It was said that on this basis aircraft in different size segments are competing directly. The Commission considered that the parties drew an incorrect conclusion and that in fact customers take into account several factors in making their decisions as to which aircraft to acquire.

The *Du Pont/ ICI case*[137] serves as an example to show how the Commission's mode of operation defines the relevant product market from the demand side. This case analysed the proposed acquisition of the worldwide nylon operations of Imperial Chemical Industries plc (ICI) by E.I. Du Pont de Nemours and Company (Du Pont). In these proceedings, the Commission analysed the market from the perspective of the carpet manufacturers, who were the customers for the nylon fibres for carpets sold by ICI and Du Pont.

In analysing the relevant product markets the Commission first found that nylon fibres for textile applications and for industrial applications were not substitutable for nylon fibres for carpets. Since the Commission found no horizontal overlap in the market of nylon fibres for textile applications and no cause for competitive concern in the market of nylon fibres for industrial applications, these markets were discussed briefly in the decision.

The Commission did, however, examine the relevant product market for nylon fibres for carpets because the transaction gave rise to serious doubts as to its compatibility with the common market in that specific market. In examining substitutability from the demand side, that is, from the perspective of the carpet manufacturers, the Commission stated that:

---

134. *Ibid.*, paras 8–10.
135. (Commission Decision on Aérospatiale / MBB 1991).
136. (Commission Decision 91/619/EEC on Aerospatiale- Alenia/de Havilland 1991, 17).
137. (Commission Decision 93/9/EEC on Du Pont/ICI 1992).

> There is a relevant product market comprising all nylon fibres used for carpets. The different types of nylon fibre compete within this overall market. Other fibres used for carpet manufacturing, such as polypropylene, wool, polyester and acrylic are not regarded by the carpet manufacturers as interchangeable or substitutable to a significant extent with nylon carpet fibres, by reason of their characteristics, their prices and their intended use in the manufacturing process.[138]

Based on its examination of demand-side substitutability, the Commission concluded that nylon and polypropylene fibres were not substitutable and therefore did not belong to the same product market. The Commission held that there was a distinct market for nylon fibres, as against other fibres, for the purpose of carpet manufacture, given the superior performance characteristics of nylon and its substantially higher price. The decision of the Commission in the *Du Pont/ICI* provides a clear and concise formulation of the notion of substitution in demand:

> For two products to be regarded as substitutable, the direct customer must consider it a realistic and rational possibility to react to, for example, a significant increase in the price of one product by switching to the other product in a relatively short period of time. Each product must be a reasonable alternative for the other in economic and technical terms. In this context, industrial customers will usually make an objective evaluation of alternative inputs.[139]

This formulation is in principle consistent with basic economic principles, that is that two products are substitutes if purchasers are able and willing to modify the quantities demanded of each in reaction to a change in their relative prices. This also points to the practical difficulties in establishing whether two products are substitutes, since it includes two aspects involving a certain scope for subjective judgment: the need for the changes in relative prices to be sufficient ('a significant increase') and the need to establish a certain time scope within which substitution might take place ('a relatively short period of time').[140]

Consumer preferences and the actual motivation for end consumers to demand a product are not easily established. The main problem in this area is not conceptual, but rather a matter of what evidence to gather and assess. As in *Allied Lyons/HWE-Pedro Domecq*[141], it was found that, because of its particular flavour, consumers usually regard whisky as distinct from other spirits. Whisky may be further segmented, but a more precise definition of the market was not necessary in this case. While products may seem fungible in terms of purpose, switching costs may indicate a limited substitutability, as *Tractabel/Distrigaz*[142] II illustrates. In this case, gas and electricity were viewed as separate markets. Based largely on what is perceived as the different needs of business and leisure travellers, the Commission in *Havas Voyage/American Express*[143] regarded travel agencies serving business travellers in a market different

---

138. *Ibid.*
139. *Ibid.*, point 23.
140. (Alonso 1994, 196).
141. (Decision IV/M.400 on Allied Lyons/HWE-Pedro Domecq 1994).
142. (Decision IV/M.493 on Tractebel/Distrigaz II 1994).
143. (Decision IV/M.564 on Havas Voyage/American Express 1995).

Chapter 4: Competition Practice

from those serving those travellers travelling for leisure. In *Medeol/Elosua*,[144] bottled olive oil was distinguished from bottled sunflower oil partly because the two products appealed to different groups of consumers. Olive oil was generally purchased by those who like its taste and its health benefits, while sunflower oil appealed to those with different tastes and attracted to its sharply lower prices.

The Commission has also demonstrated a willingness to divide markets into segments and to define the relevant product market according to different distribution channels. In *Henkel/Nobel*,[145] the Commission found the relevant product market in the cosmetics sector comprising the following five main market segments based upon demand substitutability: body care products, skin care products, oral hygiene products, hair care products and scents. The Commission also noted that several of these market segments had links with each other both on the demand and supply-side. On the demand side, the supermarket chains bought the entire product range, and not merely a single-product. On the supply-side, the producers adopted uniform marketing strategies covering different but complementary products.

Varta/Bosch[146] is a case that demonstrates that the Commission takes into account situations where the need exists for manufacturers to adapt different business policies for the same product in view of the divergent demand structures found in the original equipment manufacturers (OEM's) and replacement markets like in *Magnet Marelli/CEAC*[147] and *Mannesmann/Boge*.[148] An important element establishing different conditions of competition in the *Varta/Bosch* case was the structure of the demand side. Substantial differences were found in the spread and importance of the different distribution channels. The Commission divided the starter battery market into two distinct product markets and based its assumptions not on a difference in the product itself or on the function of the product, but on the fact that the conditions of competition differ significantly on the two markets. The producers are forced to adapt their commercial and entrepreneurial policies to the different requirements of the two sales markets:

- the original equipment market, which comprises the supply of starter batteries for vehicle producers for the initial equipment of new vehicles; and
- the replacement market, which comprises the supply of replacement batteries to the retail market for the equipment of used cars.[149]

In general terms, the original equipment market is characterised by its specific demand side, the automobile industry, which gives the market specific features. The quality and the standards are prescribed and controlled by the car manufacturers and linked to R&D cooperation for new products with the car manufacturers. Distribution on the original equipment market means just-in-time delivery to a small number of

---

144. (Decision IV/M.431 on Medeol SA/Elosua SA 1994).
145. (Decision IV/M.186 on Henkel/Nobel 1992).
146. (Decision IV/M.12 on Varta/Bosch 1991).
147. (Decision IV/M.43 on Magneti/Marelli/CEAc 1991).
148. (Decision IV/M.134 on Mannesmann/Boge 1991).
149. *Ibid.*, point 12.

217

clients. Supply to the replacement market, on the other hand, implies strong seasonal fluctuations in demand for a large number of battery types, with a variety of different distributors ranging from purchase organisations, wholesalers, car producers and department stores to ultimate dealers. Despite the fact that one type of replacement battery can be used for a number of different types of cars, more than 400 different types of replacement batteries are currently produced in the Community. Each type varies in relation to size and power, etc. Distribution on the sales markets requires therefore the existence of a distribution and service network system because a number of clients require delivery to the local outlets and service.[150] The arguments of the parties that the original equipment sector and the replacement sector for starter batteries belong to the same product market were waived for the reasons given by the Commission.

The Commission's methodology for defining the relevant product market can also be illustrated with cases from the medical and consumer products sectors. In the medical sector, medicines are broken down into therapeutic classes according to the Anatomical Therapeutic Classification (ATC) recognised and used by the World Health Organisation. In particular, the third level of this classification provides a classification according to the therapeutic properties of products, i.e., their intended use. This level may therefore be accepted as a first operational market definition. In *Ciba-Geigy/Sandoz*[151], the Commission addressed for the first time in more depth the issue that, while market definition on this basis should be appropriate in many cases, the analysis should not necessarily be limited to delineation according to the third level of the ATC classification. Such delimitation may be too narrow on the indication for which they are approved or prescribed or on their demand-side substitutability from the point of view of the consumer for OTC products. In the case of prescription drugs, it would depend therefore on the point of view of the prescribing doctors who regularly base their prescription decision on objective findings about efficiencies and similarities between drugs. For this reason, in this case, the Commission took into account whether the pharmaceuticals grouped in a particular ATC class, third level, really have the same intended use, or whether pharmaceuticals in other ATC classes have similar intended use and efficiencies.

Narrowing the relevant market is an important issue. In *Unilever France/Ortiz-Miko*[152], Unilever France acquired a majority stake in Safral, whose main holding in France was Ortiz Miko, a company chiefly operating in the ice cream, sorbet and frozen food market. In that case, the Commission first distinguished between three different relevant ice cream markets: the take-home, restaurant, and impulse ice cream markets. It was possible to divide the relevant markets further into sub-markets, because there appeared to be a possibility that in one segment – defined as 'industrial, wrapped non-artisanal ice cream', which involved only 12% of the notified operation's value – dominance would be created. The analysis was complicated by the fact that there was a trend toward concentration in this market. In view of the fact that it could not be

---

150. *Ibid.*, point 15.
151. (Decision IV/M.737 on Ciba-Geigy/Sandoz 1996).
152. (Decision IV/M.422 on Unilever France/Ortiz Miko (II) 1994).

Chapter 4: Competition Practice

shown that the transaction itself would be the catalyst for creating dominance in the market and that defining such a specific market would likely have led to an excessively narrow definition, the case was cleared.[153]

In *Shell/Montecatini*[154], the Commission defined a separate relevant product market for the granting of licences for technology. Shell Petroleum NV (the holding company of Royal Dutch Shell group) and Montedison Nederland (a subsidiary of the Ferruzi group, whose interests are held by Montecatini through Himont Inc.) decided to set up a joint venture, Sophia. Initially, the plan was to transfer all Montedison's and almost all Shell's polyolefin interests to the new entity. The Commission decided that there were two markets: the market for the granting of licences for the technology involved in the manufacture of polypropylene, a world market, and the market for the production and sale of polypropylene, which is still a West European market. What is interesting is that the market for the licensing of the technology required for polypropylene is deemed to be distinct from that for the production and sale of polypropylene. Any polypropylene producer must use a catalyst and a technological process that enables it to carry out the polymerisation of the propylene. However, not all polypropylene producers have their own technology, and they must consequently make use, under licence, of the technology of a third party, which generally provides the associated services and the catalysts. This feature of the sector has led to the development of a specific licensing activity, which constitutes a separate market. It emerged during the investigation that the licensing market was a world market with very few operators and that demand derived from producers who had not developed a technology, notably because of the cost of research and development in this sector.

This decision was followed in *Union Carbide/Enichem*[155], which dealt with the licensing of polyethylene technology. The Commission examined the effects of the proposed operation of the three separate markets: the market for the production and sale of Polyethylene ('PE') resins, the upstream market for the supply of ethylene (which is the raw material used in the production of PE), and the market for PE technology licensing. The Commission concluded that the operation would not create or strengthen a dominant position in any of these markets.

In respect of product markets, price analysis in the decisions of the Commission is generally geared to a study of price levels and price differences among substitutes. In the *Medeol/Elosua*[156] case for example, different product characteristics as well as different price levels were used to consider the markets for bottled sunflower oil and bottled olive oil as two different product markets.

In the decision concerning the *Tetra Pak/Alfa-Laval*[157] concentration, the Commission seems to have adopted an explicit and formal economic framework in assessing the relevant market. There, in assessing whether septic and non-septic packaging machinery compete in the same market, the Commission relied on an

---

153. (Lowe 1995, 140).
154. (Decision IV/M.269 on Shell/Monecatini 1994).
155. (Decision IV/M.550 on Union Carbide/Enichem 1995).
156. (Decision IV/M.431 on Medeol SA/Elosua SA 1994).
157. (Decision IV/M.68 on Tetra Pak/Alfa-Laval 1991).

evaluation of how customers of both products would react in response to a small but significant price increase. Besides focusing on the precise kind of switching at the margin, which economists would advocate as the acid test of effective substitutability, those familiar with the US Department of Justice Merger Guidelines will recognise this phrase as being taken almost word-for-word from those guidelines. The formal economics based approach used by the Commission in this case is underlined further by the assessment of substitutability in terms of evidence on elasticity of demand. This decision clearly stands for a flirtation with the US approach to market definition.

An attempt to investigate price elasticities was made in the *Costa Crociere/ Chargeurs/Accor*[158] case, where a widespread enquiry among customers, tour operators and travel agencies revealed that a 10% increase in the price of cruises would depress demand from about half of consumers, but would not affect the other half. In *Thomson/Shorts*[159], very short-range missiles and short-range missiles were each held to constitute separate product markets because, *inter alia*, for each range of rocket prices were significantly higher than those of the range below. For the inquiry into whether goods are interchangeable, data concerning the cross-elasticity of demand is useful. In the case of a high cross-elasticity of demand between certain products, a slight increase in the price of one product causes a considerable number of customers to switch to other products, thereby indicating that the products compete in the same relevant product market. Cross-elasticity of demand therefore directly measures the degree of interchangeability of certain products.

In *Du Pont/ICI*[160], a large price difference existed between nylon fibres and polypropylene fibres in general. The Commission checked the general price development in the Community of nylon fibre and polypropylene fibre for use in carpets over the last five years. No indication was found that the polypropylene fibre price has a significant influence on the nylon fibre price. Polypropylene fibre prices for carpets had fallen by between 10% and 11% in nominal terms over the previous five years, whereas nylon fibre prices for carpets had increased in nominal terms by between 3 and 4% over the same period. During this period the share of nylon fibres in total carpet fibre usage remained largely constant, so these figures do not indicate significant positive cross-price elasticity between nylon and polypropylene fibres for carpets.[161]

The *Procter & Gamble/VP Schickedanz*[162] case may serve as an example too, because the definition of the relevant product market was of crucial importance in that particular case. Procter & Gamble acquired the German manufacturer of paper products, Vereinigte Papierwerke Schickedanz AG. Through the deal, Procter & Gamble was to acquire the popular 'Camelia' brand of sanitary napkins. Given the strong position of its own 'Always' brand, the Commission took the view that the proposed transaction would place Procter & Gamble in a dominant position on the German and Spanish markets for sanitary towels. Procter & Gamble would have accounted for about

---

158. (Decision IV/M.334 on Costa Crociere/Chargeurs/Accor 1993).
159. (Decision IV/M.318 on Thomson/Shorts 1993).
160. (Decision IV/M214 on Du Pont/ICI 1992).
161. *Ibid.*, point 28.
162. (Decision IV/M.430 on Procter & Gamble/VP Schickedanz (II) 1994).

two-thirds of the German market (by value), while slightly increasing its already dominant share in Spain. The question was specifically, whether the substitutability on the demand side was strong enough to consider tampons and sanitary napkins as one market.

The Commission had to examine a wealth of qualitative and quantitative evidence in order to decide on this question. As an example of the use of quantitative techniques, the Commission in this case partly relied on econometric estimation, based on supermarket scanner data of cross-price elasticities as well as cross-promotional elasticities, i.e., the elasticities of different types of promotions. The cross-price elasticities, as well as the cross-promotional elasticities, were all either insignificant or very low. The Commission eventually concluded, based on the examination of qualitative as well as quantitative evidence, that tampons and towels were two separate product markets.

This case serves as an example to show that different parties can interpret economic data in different ways in order to reach different goals. The notifying parties and third party competitors presented in that case conflicting econometric calculations concerning the question of whether the demand substitutability was sufficiently strong to consider tampons and pads as a single market. In that particular case the Commission asked for independent analysis of the comprehensive data and held several hearings in which it received testimonies from outside experts. The Commission also relied on indices to establish that consumer behaviour was significantly influenced by factors other than price, namely performance and brand familiarity, and that consumer preferences were based on complex cultural, psychological and physical influences and motivations.

The existence of separate customer categories or market segments is mentioned in some decisions. Different categories of customers are examined with a view to the existence of possible captive groups. Captive customers can be defined as a group of consumers who are not able or willing to switch to a substitute, although such substitution is possible for the rest of consumers. Price discrimination thus becomes important in order to define separate product markets. In two cases, *Otto/Grattan*[163] and *Redoute/Empire Stores*[164], the Commission analysed price discrimination marginally.

When defining the relevant product market in these two cases, the Commission took into account the fact that retail shops and catalogue mail-order are not substitutes for a segment of consumers by reason of objective factors. More specifically, the elderly, disabled and people living in remote areas are considered 'captive' for mail-order services. Nevertheless, the existence of a captive group in those cases did not suffice in itself to define a separate product market. The Commission rejected in *Otto/Grattan* the parties' claims that their mail-order businesses competed directly in the same market as conventional non-food retailers. In doing so, the Commission cited, besides the fact that consumers may be captive to the mail-order catalogues, a number

---

163. (Decision IV/M.070 on Otto/Grattan 1991).
164. (Decision IV/M.80 on La Redoute/Empire 1991).

of differences between mail-order and retail sales including free delivery and inspection, credit terms at no extra cost and reduced price flexibility.

While all these features are present, none of the factors noted in the decision reflect whether mail-order catalogues are allowed to price their products independently of the prices that are charged in retail outlets. This is an empirical question, which can only be answered by comparing trends in mail-order catalogue prices relative to retail prices over a period of time. The existence of captive mail-order customers is largely irrelevant under the circumstances. Provided such customers are in the minority, and there is no way for the mail-order supplier to price-discriminate against this group of customers, they are equally protected by the general requirement that mail-order prices remain competitive with retailers.

In *Costa Crociere/Chargeurs/Accor*,[165] the Commission focused on the cruise market as a distinct segment within the package holiday market because it found that a significant proportion of customers (around half) were 'captive' to cruises and insensitive to significant price increases. The Commission did not go as far as investigating the possibility of price discrimination by cruise operators against these captive customers.

In the *Mannesmann/Boge*,[166] case, conditions for defining separate product markets were met. In that case it was found that clients in the aftermarket pay much higher prices than car manufacturers for the same shock absorbers. Factors such as 'just in time' deliveries to motor vehicle manufacturer, market access conditions to the OEM/OES, or the need for a dense distribution network and a wide product range to supply the aftermarket explain the possibility of price discrimination between both markets and constitute identified barriers to possible arbitrage. The different categories of customers are explicitly put in relation to the differences in the prices charged to each.[167]

In the following, the economic work carried out by the Commission in the merger decision *Omya/JM Huber*[168] is described.[169] The merging companies produce and sell calcium carbonate, an industrial mineral largely used in paper manufacturing. One of the major issues the Commission faced during this merger investigation was to determine whether ground calcium carbonate (GCC) and precipitated calcium carbonates (PCC) belong to the same relevant market. The notifying party claimed that sales of PCC form a distinct market, a market definition that produces a minimal overlap, while third parties argued that GCC and PCC are considered interchangeable by customers. In this case the Commission used customer level data to estimate the substitution pattern between the different suppliers of calcium carbonate filler for the paper industry. The dataset consisted of detailed information on annual shipments from the major suppliers to paper mills in the EEA. The Commission applied an

---

165. (Decision IV/M.334 on Costa Crociere/Chargeurs/Accor 1993).
166. (Decision IV/M.134 on Mannesmann/Boge 1991).
167. *Ibid.*, at para. 11.
168. (Commission decision COMP/M.3796 on OMYA/J.M. HUBER PCC 2006).
169. (Durand und Pesaresi 2007, 92).

Chapter 4: Competition Practice

econometric model that was used in conjunction with other pieces of evidence to allow the Commission to take a considered view of the market.

PCC and GCC are both used for various applications in the paper industry, in particular for 'filling' applications. This industrial procedure consists of adding the mineral to the cellulose slurry before it is formed into the sheet. The filling application improves the quality of paper in terms of whiteness, opacity, brightness and colour; furthermore, it increases its dimensional stability and bulkiness. The economic study applied a *discrete choice approach* to estimate the substitution patterns between the various producers of carbonates filler. The model adopted in this study assumes that each paper mill will select a supplier of calcium carbonates filler that is located within a certain geographic distance. A nested logit model can be estimated in one of two ways: by first estimating the conditional probability and then the marginal probability, or by estimating the entire probability model using standard maximum-likelihood. The nested logit specification adopted by the Commission in this study models the choice probabilities as a function of observed variables. Once such a model is estimated it is useful to know the extent to which these probabilities vary in response to a change in price. The data analysed by the Commission sheds light on the substitution pattern between GCC and PCC. The purpose of this work was to check and possibly complement other evidence about the market definition collected by the Commission during its investigation. Contrary to the notifying party's claim, interviews with customers and switching evidence pointed toward a broad market including both filling PCC and GCC. The elasticities results of the choice model support the existence of a broad market.

One of the key issues in the Lufthansa/SN Airholding airline merger[170] was the product market definition on the Brussels-Frankfurt route, and in particular whether air travel competes with train travel. While it was relatively straightforward to estimate the actual loss with a survey that was conducted at the airport gates in Brussels by asking respondents whether they would have decided to travel by train if airfare was 5–10% more expensive, the calculation of the critical loss brought up a number of issues.

First, while CLA assumes that a single price is charged to all customers, the airline industry is characterised by significant price discrimination (as for example business passengers tend to pay significantly higher prices than leisure passengers). Thus it does not seem to be reasonable to expect (as the CLA assumes) a hypothetical monopolist to increase the average price by 5–10%. Second, notwithstanding the fact that the gross margins will differ significantly across the different customers according to what they paid for their tickets (and thus the average gross margin on which the critical loss is based is likely not appropriate for the CLA calculations), the application of CLA to an airline industry that is characterised by high fixed costs also brings up an important question of what the appropriate measures of variable costs and hence gross margins are. In particular, while it is true that in the short run, variable costs per seat are likely best approximated by catering and fuel costs along with departure taxes, the 5–10%

---

170. (Regulation 139/2004 on Merger Procedure, COMP/M.3796 – OMYA/HUBER PCC 2006).

price increase may actually (over the two-year time horizon that is relevant for merger control) have an effect on the number of frequencies/airplanes that the airline may use on a given route. It is thus important to properly measure the effect of the price increase on the behaviour of the airline, otherwise the estimate of the variable costs may be too low (and the margins too high), which may incorrectly imply that the market is wide, and air travel competes with train travel (as the critical loss may be lower than it would be in reality). For example, sensitivity analysis can be used for that purpose to test what effect different assumptions on costs have on the magnitude of the critical loss.[171]

The Arjowiggins/Reflex case demonstrates the use of different tools in pricing analysis. The key market reviewed in this transaction was the carbonless paper market.[172] Carbonless paper comprises of three layers of paper (CB top sheet, CFB middle sheet, and CF bottom sheet) and is used to make duplicate copies without a carbon layer. It is sold either in reels or sheets (sheets are created by cutting reels into smaller pieces). In an all carbonless EEA-wide market, the combined entity would have around half of the market (with the top five producers accounting for about 90% of the market). The position of the merged entity would however be significantly more pronounced if national markets for reels and sheets were considered separately, as the market share data showed significant variations among the different national markets.

Thus, the Commission undertook pricing analysis to examine whether (i) the carbonless market should be split into separate reels and sheets markets, and (ii) whether national boundaries defined geographic markets, or whether there was a single EEA-wide market. To determine whether reels and sheets are in the same product market, correlation coefficients were calculated for six Member States to see how closely the market prices of reels and sheets move. The resulting correlations ranged from – 0.32 to 0.50 and on their own suggested that prices of reels and sheets do not move closely together. This conclusion was further strengthened with the use of benchmarking, as it was accepted that the three layers of carbonless paper (CB, CF and CFB) are all part of the same market based on the qualitative results of the market investigation and the finding that almost all correlation coefficients between the three layers of carbonless paper (CB, CF and CFB) ranged from 0.8 to 0.98. It thus followed that reels and sheets were unlikely to be in the same market, as the correlation coefficients between reels and sheets were significantly lower than the correlations between the three layers of carbonless paper.[173]

In *Campina/Friesland*, two independent dairy cooperatives merged.[174] Their activities overlapped in several markets along the dairy food product chain, from the procurement and processing of fresh milk to the production of a variety of dairy and non-dairy products. The case also raised difficult questions regarding the significance of supply-side substitutability in product market delineation. By definition, raw milk is the primary ingredient in all dairy products, and dairy companies can switch

---

171. (Amelio and Donath 2009).
172. (Decision M.4513 on Arjowiggins/M-real Zanders Reflex 2008).
173. (Amelio and Donath 2009).
174. (Decision M.5046 on Friesland Foods/Campina 2008).

Chapter 4: Competition Practice

production (or 'valorise the milk' in the industry jargon) from one dairy product to another with relative ease. For example, it is hard to think of significant barriers to switching from producing a 'young' cheese to producing a relatively more mature cheese. Supply-side substitution first requires (i) entry at short notice, (ii) at low cost, and (iii) without incurring irreversible investments – circumstances that hardly apply in most cases, particularly when it is recognised that these conditions apply not only to production but also to distribution and marketing. Moreover, market aggregation – a broadening of market boundaries to include a larger group of products or geographical area – only makes sense when supply-side substitution is found to be technologically feasible and economically viable for most, if not all, firms that sell one or more of the products in question (the so-called 'near universality' criterion). Whereas one competitor may be able to shift swiftly from producing and distributing (say) 'young cheese' to 'mature cheese', only if all (or nearly all) competitors can do the same would it be possible to include both types of cheese in the same market. However, nothing of substance is lost since the competitive pressure potentially exerted by such rivals was taken into account in the assessment of merger-induced entry.[175]

The *OneWorld Airline Alliance* case concerned a set of agreements that were concluded between British Airways (BA), American Airlines (AA), and Iberia (IB) to establish a revenue-sharing joint venture that would cover all three parties' passenger air transport services on routes between Europe and North America.[176] The agreements foresee cooperation on pricing, capacity, and scheduling coordination, as well as sharing of revenues.

In airline cases, the Commission has traditionally defined markets based on the origin-and-destination (O&D) city-pair approach: a demand side perspective whereby customers consider all possible alternatives of travelling from a city of origin to a city of destination. However, in this case the issue was whether on short-haul routes one-stop services would be part of the market for non-stop services. Furthermore, particularly in long-haul, it may be necessary to differentiate between services for premium and non-premium passengers. Demands from each of these groups differ in terms of travel comfort, service frequency, travel time, etc.

Supported by extensive qualitative evidence, the Commission first showed that for the affected routes, premium and non-premium services are parts of separate markets. The Commission conducted a price correlation analysis that was based on data submitted by the parties (BA, IB, and AA) and a competitor Virgin Atlantic (VA) as well as a customer survey at Heathrow Airport that complemented and ultimately reinforced this conclusion.

Parties had argued that all tickets irrespective of cabin class and flexibility (in terms of changes and refunds) could be considered as part of the same market, since tickets are differentiated by characteristics along a continuum. Hence, changes in the price of a given set of tickets would influence the demand for a second set of tickets that are similar in some dimension, in turn this leading to second-order effects on the demand for a third set of tickets, similar to the second set, and so on, until the whole

---

175. (Neven and De la Mano 2009).
176. (Decision COMP/39.596 on BA/AA/IB 2010).

market is covered. According to this argument, it is thus not possible to delineate clear boundaries between different sets of tickets such that a hypothetical monopolist would find it profitable to increase significantly and permanently the price of the tickets included in one well-defined set. The purpose of the fare correlation analysis was to test this hypothesis and was limited only to assess whether different sets of non-stop fares within a route could indeed constitute different markets.

The Commission used monthly average net return fares, across cabin class, ticket flexibility and type of customer (tickets sold under a corporate contract were separate from tickets sold to individual passengers). The analysis was done using alternative standard correlation techniques to address in varying ways the potential problem of spurious correlation: the risk that correlation coefficients are biased due to factors such as common costs, seasonality, or other common patterns in demand. The results of this analysis indicated that the prices of non-fully flexible (i.e., restricted) corporate and non-corporate economy tickets are statistically independent from the prices of (1) business and first class tickets or (2) the fully flexible premium economy booking class. This provides an additional indication that non-fully flexible (restricted) corporate and non-corporate economy tickets do not belong to the same product market as business or first class tickets.

By contrast, the results also showed that the prices in the three low-fare booking classes tend to show a relatively strong co-movement, indirectly validating the methodology. At the same time, the price correlations in the higher fare classes (first and business classes and the fully flexible premium economy class) tend to be weaker than those in the lower classes. This might indicate that non-price, yet relevant, dimensions of competition such as quality of service and schedule convenience are more important in the high-fare classes than in the lower fares. One explanation is that among higher-priced tickets there is more product differentiation and thus greater scope for segmentation.

The Commission conducted a customer survey at Heathrow Airport. The Commission designed the questionnaire and processed and analysed the responses. The purpose of the survey was to obtain a representative sample of responses from non-stop passengers who were departing from London and flying to a number of destinations in the US. The questionnaire was intentionally short, and all questions were 'multiple choice' and were aimed at collecting information on passengers' characteristics, passengers' past behaviour ('revealed preference' questions), and passengers' likely reaction to hypothetical situations, such as a price increase in their flight ticket (stated preference questions). The results of the survey provided further evidence as regards the definition of the boundaries of the product market in terms of the substitutability between premium and non-premium tickets and between non-stop and one-stop flights. In particular, the results showed that first class and business class passengers share common travel preferences, which differ from the travel preferences of passengers travelling in restricted economy class – particularly as regards the purpose of travel, the time at which the ticket was booked and the length of stay at destination. Furthermore, upper class passengers appear to be much more likely to

Chapter 4: Competition Practice

switch airline in the event of a price increase instead of reducing the comfort or the flexibility of their travel by switching to a lower fare class.[177]

4.2.5 Relevant Geographic Market

4.2.5.1 *Basic Assumptions*

Market definition consists of two components: product market definition and geographic market definition. Product market definition was discussed in the previous sections and seeks to include all products that are meaningful substitutes.

Geographic market definition is a key step in a competition analysis, requiring informed judgment, common sense and accuracy. Optimally, the procedure involves the following three steps: measuring the extent of inter-market penetration, identifying the leading substitutes, and evaluating the effects of external influences. Whereas the analysis of the relevant product market seems to be more complex at first sight, the analysis of the relevant geographic market is more important for the outcome of the assessment. Markets that are defined too narrowly will typically result in market shares that overstate the actual degree of market power. Markets that are defined too broadly will typically understate the degree of market power by including in the market share calculations sources of competition that are distinctly inferior as a threat to the exercise of market power.

The relevant geographic market is defined in the Commission's market definition Notice as follows:

> *The relevant geographic market comprises the area in which the undertakings concerned are involved in the supply and demand of products or services, in which the conditions of competition are sufficiently homogeneous and which can be distinguished from neighboring areas because the conditions of competition are appreciably different in those areas.*[178]

The Court of Justice in United Brands gives the almost 'classical' geographic market definition test in EU competition law.[179] In that case, the Court of Justice held that there has to be '*a clearly defined geographic area in which (the relevant product) is marketed and where the conditions of competition are sufficiently homogeneous for the effect of the economic power of the undertaking concerned to be evaluated.*'[180] In order to calculate the merged firm's market share, a geographic boundary that separates firms that are competing with the merged firm from those firms that are not competing with the merged firm, is essential.

---

177. (Neven and De la Mano 2010).
178. (European Commission, Commission Notice on the definition of relevant market 1997, para. 8).
179. (ECJ, United Brands Company and United Brands Continentaal BV v. Commission, Case 27/76 1978).
180. *Ibid.*, at para. 11.

The Commission itself considers in its Market Definition Notice that the process of defining the geographic dimension of the relevant market is not significantly different from that of defining product dimension. The approach can be summarised as follows: the Commission will take a preliminary view of the scope of the geographic market on the basis of broad indications regarding the distribution of market shares of the parties and their competitors, as well as a preliminary analysis or pricing and price differences at national and EU or EEA level. This initial view is basically a working hypothesis.

In paragraph 29 of its Notice, the Commission explains the need to explore the reasons behind any particular configuration of prices and market shares:

> *Companies might enjoy high market shares in their domestic markets just because of the weight in the past, and conversely, a homogeneous presence of companies throughout the EEA might be consistent with national or regional geographic markets. The initial working hypothesis will therefore be checked against an analysis of demand characteristics (importance of national or local preferences, current patterns of purchases of customers, product differentiation/brands, other) in order to establish whether companies in different areas do really constitute an actual alternative source of supply for consumers. The theoretical experiment is again based on substitution arising from changes in relative prices, and the question to answer is again whether the customers of the parties would switch their orders to companies located elsewhere in the short term and at negligible cost.*

If necessary, a further check on supply-side factors will be carried out. This analysis will include an examination of requirements for a local presence in order to sell in that area, the conditions of access to distribution channels, costs associated with setting up a distribution network, and the existence or absence of regulatory barriers arising from public procurement, price regulations, quotas and tariffs limiting trade or production, technical standards, monopolies, freedom of establishment, requirements for administrative authorisations, packaging regulations etc. In short, the Commission will focus on the identification of possible obstacles and barriers isolating companies located in a given area from the competitive pressure of companies located outside that area.

The *actual pattern and evolution of trade flows* offer useful supplementary evidence as to the economic importance of each demand or supply factor mentioned above, and the extent to which they may or may not constitute actual barriers creating different geographic markets. The analysis of trade flows will generally address the question of transport costs and the extent to which these may hinder trade between different areas having regard to plant location, costs of production and relative price levels. The Notice does not mention the parties own shipment patterns. In fact, the Commission itself appears to consider the parties' shipment patterns more frequently than those of the customers.[181]

---

181. (Decision IV/M.430 on Procter & Gamble/VP Schickedanz (II) 1994); (Decision IV/M.603 on Crown Cork & Seal/CarnaudMetalbox 1995); (Decision IV/M.582 on Orkla/Volvo 1995).

4.2.5.2 Market Definition Practice

4.2.5.2.1 Type of Evidence

The evidence the Commission intended to use according to the Notice is categorised as follows:

- Past evidence of diversion of orders to other areas.
- Basic demand characteristics.
- Views of customers and competitors.
- Current geographic pattern of purchases.
- Trade flows and pattern of shipments.
- Barriers and switching costs associated with diverting orders to companies located in other areas.

4.2.5.2.1.1 Past Evidence of Diversion of Orders to Other Areas

The Commission believes that in certain cases, evidence on changes in prices between different areas and consequent reactions by customers might be available. Generally, the same quantitative tests used for product market definition might also be used in geographic market definition, bearing in mind that international comparisons of prices might be more complex due to a number of factors such as exchange rate movements, taxation and product differentiation.

4.2.5.2.1.2 Basic Demand Characteristics

The nature of demand for the relevant product may in itself determine the scope of the geographical market. Factors such as national preferences or preferences for national brands, language, culture and life style, and the need for a local presence have a strong potential to limit the geographic scope of competition. The same view on consumer preferences as expressed in the discussion on the definition of the relevant product market can be taken here.

4.2.5.2.1.3 Views of Customers and Competitors

As in the discussion on the definition of the relevant product market, the Commission might contact the main customers and competitors of the parties in its enquiries, to gather their views on the boundaries of the geographic market as well as most of the factual information it requires reaching a conclusion on the scope of the market.

4.2.5.2.1.4   Current Geographic Pattern of Purchases

A strong factor is the examination of the customers' current geographic pattern of purchases which provides useful evidence as to the possible scope of the geographic market. When customers purchase from companies located anywhere in the EU or the EEA on similar terms, or they procure their supplies through effective tendering procedures in which companies from anywhere in the EU or the EEA do submit bids, the geographic market will usually be considered Community-wide.

4.2.5.2.1.5   Trade Flows and Pattern of Shipments

When the number of customers is so large that it is not possible to obtain a clear picture of geographic purchasing patterns, information on trade flows might be used as an alternative, provided that the trade statistics are available with a sufficient degree of detail for the relevant products. Trade flows provide useful insights and information for the purpose of establishing the scope of the geographic market but are not in themselves conclusive.

4.2.5.2.1.6   Barriers and Switching Costs Associated with Diverting Orders to Companies Located in Other Areas

The absence of trans-border purchases or trade flows, for instance, does not necessarily mean that the market is at most national in scope. Still, barriers isolating the national market have to be identified before concluding that the relevant geographic market in such a case is national. European Integration as a dynamic process plays a decisive role in this discussion.

Perhaps the clearest obstacle for a customer to divert its orders to other areas is the impact of transport costs and transport restrictions arising from legislation or from the nature of the relevant products. The impact of transport costs will usually limit the scope of the geographic market for bulky, low-value products, bearing in mind that a transport disadvantage might also be compensated for by a comparative advantage in other costs (labour costs or raw materials). Access to distribution in a given area, regulatory barriers still existing in certain sectors, quotas and custom tariffs might also constitute barriers isolating a geographic area from the competitive pressure of companies located outside that area. Significant switching costs in procuring supplies from companies located in other countries constitute additional sources of such barriers.

The Notice also mentions that the factors described above will not be used in each individual case. Often in practice the evidence provided by a subset of these factors will be sufficient to reach a conclusion. This assumption is supported by the findings of past decisions by the Commission.

Chapter 4: Competition Practice

The Commission uses the HMT for the definition of the relevant geographic market too.[182] The HMT is discussed in section 4.2. To apply the HMT for the purpose of geographic market definition, evidence about elasticities is used to indicate whether a price increase would be profitable. For example, consider two groups of producers manufacturing the same commodity that are located in two different regions that we call A and B. Historically prices in the two regions have been moving in parallel, with the price gap reflecting differences in transportation costs. When one producer attempts to raise prices, such an attempt is doomed to fail in this market. The presence of suppliers that could easily expand output provides sufficient discipline to prevent any profitable deviation from the actual equilibrium price. As a result, A and B belong to the same economic market. Now consider that the group of producers located in region A forms a cartel, and attempts to restrict output in order to raise prices. Assume that the producers located in B are unable to exercise arbitrage because they all produce at full capacity, and further their existing capacity is not sufficient to satisfy consumer demand in B. That is, producers located in A export to region B, where prices tend to be higher. In this case, a hypothetical monopolist controlling the production facilities located in A could successfully raise prices. Producers located in B would have neither the ability to increase production nor the incentive to sell their existing production to A as prices in B remain at higher levels. As a result, region A could constitute a separate anti-trust market. The example shows that the anti-trust market and the economic market are two different concepts that need not coincide. As a result, it is important to bear in mind such a distinction when using empirical techniques to support a particular market definition.

To conclude, factors exerting a possible determining influence in the Commission's analysis of conditions of competition in geographic markets include the almost classical geographical distribution of market shares[183] and relative prices.[184] Examples of specific demand side factors cover determinants of consumer preferences[185] such as language and cultural differences, as well as brand loyalty[186], and consumers' final purchasing patterns. Shipment patterns[187] and cross-border imports and exports[188] are others. Factors considered cover both supply and demand characteristics.

The factors deliberated upon in the analysis of geographic markets can be summarised as follows:

(A) in support of a *wider geographic* market:
- absence of entry barriers enabling quick and easy transfer of supply;
- absence of price differences;
- presence of the major suppliers in all the Member States;
- substantial cross-border trade and imports;

---

182. (European Commission, Commission Notice on the definition of relevant market 1997).
183. For example, (Decision IV/M.197 on Solvay-Laporte/Interox 1992).
184. For example, (Decision IV/M.190 on Nestlé/Perrier 1992).
185. For example, (Decision IV/M.27 on Promodes/Dirsa 1990).
186. For example, (Decision IV/M.190 on Nestlé/Perrier 1992).
187. For example, (Decision M.180 on Steetley/Tarmac 1992).
188. For example, (Decision IV/M214 on Du Pont/ICI 1992).

- low transport costs;
- international / European buying policy and lack of strong national preferences; and
- similar distribution systems throughout the EU.

(B) in support of a narrower (national) geographic market:
- existence of price differences;
- national suppliers holding high market shares and appreciable differences in market shares in the various territories considered;
- low cross-border trade and imports;
- high transport costs or difficult transport links;
- just-in-time deliveries and security of supplies;
- import tariffs;
- legal or technical entry barriers, national specification requirements and approval systems;
- limited freedom to establish or provide cross-border services, for example in the life insurance sector;
- existence of language and cultural barriers;
- public purchasers with strong national buying preferences;
- importance of national brands;
- different distribution channels and marketing methods in the Member States.

In the following section, the above-mentioned factors are considered.

4.2.5.2.2 Practice of the Commission

Factors considered include both general indicators, as well as factors exerting a possible determining influence on market delineation. The use of general indicators like the geographical distribution of market shares, relative prices as well as the location of major suppliers is illustrated by several decisions. In *BSN/EURALIM*[189], the fact that major food producers, despite being present in most Member States, had very different market shares in each Member State, was considered as indicating national markets for ready-prepared meals. In *Rhone-Poulenc/SNIA II*[190], the absence of price differences for an intermediate product (nylon textile fibres) was held to indicate a market as wide as Western Europe. Conversely, in *Nestlé/Italgel*[191], price differences between countries indicated a predominantly national market for a consumer product (ice cream). Regarding price tests, European Merger control follows to a great extent the US approach discussed earlier. The same critical remarks have to be reiterated, namely the relevance of price discrimination and the difficulties of obtaining reliable

---

189. (Decision IV/M.445 on BSN/Euralim 1994).
190. (Decision IV/M.355 on Rhône-Poulene/SNIA (II) 1993).
191. (Decision IV/M.362 on Nestlé/Italgel 1993).

Chapter 4: Competition Practice

data. Nevertheless, the Commission usually defines markets as national[192] when companies charge different prices in different Member States.[193]

Price analyses are based upon the Marshallian definition of an economic market as the area where prices tend to uniformity, taking account of transportation costs. Marshall's criterion for market definition assumed perfect competition. Although this definition may be useful for some purposes, it is not generally useful for analysing a geographic market in the context of a competition law action.

Horowitz[194] urged the use of *price equality* as the basis for market definition, pointing out the near-impossibility of direct assessment of substitutability, either to customers or suppliers. Horowitz suggested that geographical areas could be grouped into the same market if any differences in price between the same products were tending to zero over time.[195]

One may be able to use *price uniformity* in defining geographic markets for homogeneous products, but it makes no sense for most real-world products and markets. For example, it is certainly difficult to claim a national or worldwide market for gasoline on the basis of price uniformity, accounting for transportation costs, when gasoline stations across the street from one another are selling gasoline at markedly different prices. Although the prices may be different, the stations are likely to be competing with one another. Similarly, if foreign firms are selling products in Europe net of transportation costs at a lower price than in their home country, it makes no sense to claim that the markets are separate and distinct.

On the other hand, detailed calculations of numerous *price correlations* among different products may contribute to the definition of product as well as geographical markets.[196] Price correlations measure the extent to which price movements are similar from one geographical region to the other. The correlations are measured in coefficients ranging from zero, which indicates absence of correlation, to one, which indicates perfectly correlated price movements. If prices in different markets move independently of each other, one can reasonably conclude that the markets are separate and that the suppliers are able to discriminate with regard to prices. Consequently, a weak price correlation coefficient would tend to indicate separate geographic markets. However, the opposite is not necessarily true. A certain degree of price correlation cannot indicate the existence of a homogeneous geographic market in the absence of other factors such as mutual interpenetration or similar structures of supply and demand in the different regions.

The correlation coefficients of the prices of steel tubes in separate geographical areas were examined in *Mannesmann/Vallourec/Ilva*[197], with a view to determining

---

192. For example, (Decision IV/M.070 on Otto/Grattan 1991, 11); (Nestlé/Perrier 1992, 21); (Decision IV/M.43 on Magneti/Marelli/CEAc 1991, 16); (Decision IV/M.12 on Varta/Bosch 1991, 18).
193. (Canenbley, Die Abgrenzung des Geographisch Relevanten Marktes in der EWG-Fusionskontrolle 1993, 243).
194. see (Horowitz 1981).
195. (Fishwick & Denison 1992, 137).
196. (Carlton & Bishop 1994, 422).
197. (Decision IV/M.315 on Mannesmann/Vallourec/Ilva 1994).

whether each area constituted a separate geographic market. In this case, price movements correlated in a similar fashion in Europe and the US. Nevertheless, this argument was dismissed upon closer examination since the differences between absolute price levels remained substantial and fluctuated considerably from one year to another.

Another example, the high correlation of prices of solid benzoic acid in the EEA, Asia and North America was used as supporting evidence in the *Arsenal/DSP* decision[198] to define the relevant geographic market for solid benzoic acid as wider than the EEA. In that case the Commission's findings were robust to adjustments for toluene prices that were, according to the notifying party, driving the results of the Commission's price correlation analysis.

When assessing price correlations, careful attention should be paid to the selection of reliable and representative data. The investigation in the *Mannesmann/Vallourec/Ilva* case showed that similarities in the pricing behaviour of different suppliers could be explained by common characteristics shared by the suppliers. In that case, a western European market for such tubes was found, and it was argued in the decision that whereas non-correlated prices tend to indicate separate markets, the existence of positive price correlations does not in itself indicate an integrated market if other indicators of such integration (such as mutual market interpenetration) are absent.

To conclude, geographic reference markets are defined on the basis of a *variety of factors* such as tariff barriers, price levels, transport costs, the degree of mutual interpenetration and the structure of supply and demand. Special attention is given to shipment data tests and, as already discussed, to price correlations.

Examples of specific demand side factors cover determinants of consumer preferences[199] such as language and cultural differences, as well as brand loyalty[200], and consumers' final purchasing patterns.

As far as specific demand factors are concerned, the relevance of inherent *consumer preferences and characteristics* and the effect of advertising were noted in cases involving final consumer products. In *Newspaper Publishing*[201], markets for newspapers were found to be national because of linguistic and cultural specificities. In *Kirch/Richemont/Telepiù*[202], it was decided that television broadcasting markets remain essentially national because of linguistic and cultural barriers, despite an increase in cross-border satellite television broadcasting. In *Allied Lyons/HWE-Pedro Domecq*[203] and *BSN/EURALIM*[204], the markets for alcoholic spirits and ready-prepared meals, respectively were found to remain essentially national because of the existence of national brands corresponding to national consumer preferences. In *Nestlé/Italgel*[205],

---

198. (Decision M.5153 on Arsenal/DSP 2009).
199. For example, (Decision IV/M.27 on Promodes/Dirsa 1990).
200. For example, (Decision IV/M.190 on Nestlé/Perrier 1992).
201. (Decision IV/M.423 on Newspaper Publishing 1994).
202. (Decision IV/M.410 on Kirch/Richemont/Telepiù 1994).
203. (Decision IV/M.400 on Allied Lyons/HWE-Pedro Domecq 1994).
204. (Decision IV/M.445 on BSN/Euralim 1994).
205. (Decision IV/M.362 on Nestlé/Italgel 1993).

ice cream markets were held to be predominantly national in view of national consumer profiles and consumption habits, and national brand loyalty. In *Costa Crociere/Chargeurs/Accor*[206], markets for cruises and package holidays were held to be national because of, *inter alia*, national differences in consumption patterns, the need for brochures to be published in several languages, and the existence of advertising campaigns targeting national audiences.

Again, *consumers' final purchasing patterns* were found to be an important factor for the determination of geographical markets. In *SNECMA/TI*[207], the market for civil aircraft landing gear was deemed to be worldwide because aircraft manufacturers commission and purchase civil aircraft components worldwide and in a single currency. In that case, the continuing emergence of potential competition arising from licensees and subcontractor-manufacturers was taken into account. At the same time that buyers extend the area within which they search for the relevant product, comparing quality and price, sellers will extend the areas within which they seek business, comparing long-term profitability. *KNP/BT/VRG*[208] illustrates a similar effect for intermediate goods. The market for the distribution and servicing of printing presses was found to be national, principally because customers (printers) insist that distributors have a well-developed local service network for maintenance and repairs. In the *Pilkington-Techint/SIC* case[209], rapid response times and the quality of local service for the supply of certain kinds of glass used in the building trade seemed to suggest national or even regional markets.

Supply substitution, both by firms already present in the market and by new entrants, is the next stage of analysis. The elasticity of supply by firms already selling to the relevant geographical market and entry by other firms with no current significant sales in that area has to be considered.[210] Supply- and demand substitution are, of course, complementary and reciprocal. It may be difficult to distinguish the two from their net effects. It is, however, useful to analyse supply substitution separately, because it arises from a different motivation.

With regard to entry by firms not currently selling the relevant product within the relevant market, attention will focus mainly on those already selling the relevant product elsewhere. The other form of cross-entry, by firms already selling other products within the relevant geographical area, may also be of interest and entry conditions may be most favourable for companies combining these two conditions – the relevant product elsewhere plus other products within the geographical area. In assessing the probability of new entry, analysts must identify any sunk costs, which might be involved and also consider the potential for defensive measures by incumbent firms. Competition from new entrants is more probable in expanding market.[211]

Usually, the Commission examines entry barriers like governmental regulations (price regulations, quotas, tariffs, technical standards) and supplier constraints such as

---

206. (Decision IV/M.334 on Costa Crociere/Chargeurs/Accor 1993).
207. (Decision IV/M.368 on SNECMA/TI 1994).
208. (Decision IV/M.291 on KNP/Bührmann-Tettorde/VRG-Group 1993).
209. (Decision IV/M.358 on Pilkington-Techint/SIV 1993).
210. (Fishwick & Denison 1992, 52).
211. *Ibid.*, 139.

transport costs and distribution systems as well as the geographical location of major suppliers. Entry barriers may take a number of different forms, though competition economists differ as to the weight, which should be attached to different kinds of obstacles. A consensus is that regulatory and legal barriers are capable of giving significant protection to firms already established in a market.[212]

Legal prohibitions, formal barriers to trade and transport costs are considered by the Commission as barriers with regard to supply to a new geographical market by an existing producer of the relevant product. As far as specific supply factors are concerned, the effect of governmental regulations such as technical standards and tariffs can be found to be important for the delimitation of geographical markets. In *Electrolux/AEG*,[213] the existence of European standards for electrical equipment was taken to indicate European markets for domestic appliances. In *Philips/Hoechst*[214], it was suggested that the market for magnetic optical discs could be worldwide given product standards established by the International Standardisation Organisation. *Philips/Grundig*[215] is another example where harmonisation of technical standards was taken to indicate EC-wide markets for electronics products. In *British Telecom/MCI*,[216] the Commission concluded that the relevant market was one which was opening up to world competition, because of liberalisation and technological advances, and that it was therefore necessary for firms to adjust to this new environment. This case demonstrates the importance that the Commission attaches to the need to place agreements, referred to in their context, and its concern to adopt decisions, which take account of the particularities of each sector.

In other cases, however, the Commission used Member States' territories as the relevant geographical market for reasons such as quantitative and regulatory restrictions.[217] National regulations were considered to contribute to national markets in pharmaceuticals as demonstrated in *Roche/Syntex*[218] and other decisions in this sector. In *Accor/Wagons-Lits*[219], the relevant market for motorway restaurants was held to be France in view of the regulatory barriers, which made it more difficult for non-French enterprises to operate in this sector. In *Talanx International/Meiji Yasuda Life Insurance Company/HDI Poland*[220] and *Vienna Insurance Group/EBV*[221] the Commission considered that the geographic market for life insurance is the national market due to differing regulatory frameworks (among other aspects).

---

212. (Cook & Kerse 1996, 50).
213. (Decision IV/M.458 on Electrolux/AEG 1994).
214. (Decision IV/M.406 on Philips/Hoechst 1994).
215. (Decision IV/M.382 on Philips/Grundig 1993).
216. (Decision IV/M.353 on British Telecom/MCI 1993).
217. (Decision IV/M.98 on ELF/BC/Cepsa 1991) and (Decision IV/M.72 on Sanofi/Sterling Drug 1991, 17).
218. (Decision IV/M.457 on La Roche/Syntex 1994).
219. (Decision IV/M.126 on Accor/Wagons-Lits 1992).
220. (Decision M.6743 on Talanx International/Meiji Yasuda Life Insurance Company/HDI Poland 2012).
221. (Decision M.5075 on Vienna Insurance Group/EBV 2008).

The problem of estimating the time frame over which regulatory barriers may be eroded by single market legislation was alluded to in *American Cyanamid/Shell*.[222] The existence of an EC external tariff was taken to indicate Community-wide markets for industrial goods in *Harrisons&Grosfield/AKZO*.[223] In *Mannesmann/Vallourec/Ilva*[224], the existence of significant tariff barriers was an element indicating separate markets (the US, Japan, and Western Europe) for steel tubes, whereas the absence of barriers was taken to indicate worldwide aircraft markets in *Dasa/Fokker*.[225]

Excess capacity, transportation costs, and costs of local distribution are other relevant considerations in the definition of the geographic market. These factors provide evidence of likely supply responses to hypothetical price increases. If excess capacity exists in plants serving a defined geographic market, it is more likely that there would be a significant supply response if the price were increased in the defined area. In addition, the lower transportation costs, the greater the outside area from which it would be economic to ship into the defined area, or, similarly, the smaller the hypothetical price increase that would induce shipments into the defined area. And finally, the lower the costs of local distribution, the easier it will be for firms located outside the defined hypothetical monopoly area to ship into and sell in the area.[226] This argument follows *Landes* and *Posner*[227] who argued that if a distant seller has some sales in a local market, all its sales, wherever made, should be considered a part of that local market for purposes of computing the market share of a local seller. This *Landes* and *Posner* approach is based on the assumption that the 'foreign' and 'domestic' products are identical and that the elasticity of total supply faced by undertakings which increase their sales to the domestic market is infinite, i.e., they face constant marginal cost.

The economics of entry into the relevant product and geographical market for a firm not currently supplying depends on whether the firm:

(1) currently sells other products within the geographical market and/or;
(2) currently sells the relevant product in other geographical markets.

Examples include *Tarmac/Steetle*[228], where local markets for bricks were established since bricks are both very heavy and bulky and transport represents a significant percentage of the total selling price. Conversely, in the *Pilkington-Techint/SIV*[229] case, markets for some kinds of flat glass were held to be EU-wide since transport costs were found to be relatively low in relation to the high-value-added products transported. In *CGP/GEC ALSTHOM/KPR/Kone Corporation*,[230] high transport costs were indicative of

---

222. (Decision IV/M.354 on Cyanamid/Shell 1993).
223. (Decision IV/M.323 on Procordia/Erbamont 1993).
224. (Decision IV/M.315 on Mannesmann/Vallourec/Ilva 1994).
225. (Decision IV/M.237 on DASA/Fokker 1993).
226. (Klein 1987, 268).
227. (Landes & Posner 1981, 937–982).
228. (Decision M.180 on Steetley/Tarmac 1992).
229. (Decision IV/M.358 on Pilkington-Techint/SIV 1993).
230. (Decision IV/M.420 on CGP/GEC Alsthom/KPR/Kone 1994).

a national market for cranes; in *Electrolux/AEG*,[231] on the other hand, a western European market for domestic appliances was found to exist in view of the fact that major manufacturers adopt a strategy of establishing centralised, large-volume assembly-line plants, with corresponding economies of scale, from which products are shipped throughout Europe.

In the case of concentrations in the retail sector the Commission has taken account of the choice of retail outlets available to shoppers in the areas covered by the concentration. As in *Promodes/BRMC*,[232] the geographic market for retail distribution of consumer food and related products was held to be local, since consumers are unwilling to travel more than a certain distance to make such purchases.

The *ratio of transport costs to the value of the transported product* is critically important. Its importance will increase where:

- low-value consignments cannot be combined to allow sharing of transport costs;
- value is low in relation to volume or bulk;
- value is low in relation to the cost of maintaining the quality of the product during transport; this may still apply (for example) to some perishable foods and fragile goods and volatile chemicals, though transport facilities for such products have been developing and becoming more economic.

The situation described in (a) applies particularly to the geographical area likely to be considered by the individual consumer of a product. In the *Promodes/Dirsa* case,[233] concerning concentration in the food and non-food retailing sector in Spain, the Commission defined local markets for consumer grocery purchasing. In its decision, the Commission, in acknowledging the homogeneity of conditions of competition, referred exclusively to conditions as perceived by or pertaining to consumers and took no notice of the fact that large retailers compete with each other at a nation-wide level (strangely the Commission did, however, acknowledge that Promodes had achieved its rank as the largest retailer in the Spanish market through its concentration with Dirsa). The Commission went further than suggested by the parties themselves and held that the relevant geographical market was not regional, as suggested by Promodes, but local as a result of the homogeneity of competition conditions.[234] In the similar *Spar/Dansk*[235] case, the Commission defined a zone 'within 20 minutes' driving distance. In *Rewa/Billa*[236] and *Kesko/Tuko*,[237] the relevant geographical markets were from the point of view of the consumer local markets in which companies concerned had their retail outlets. Although those markets can be defined in the Commission's

---

231. (Decision IV/M.458 on Electrolux/AEG 1994).
232. (Decision IV/M.242 on Promodes/BRMC 1992).
233. (Decision IV/M.27 on Promodes/Dirsa 1990).
234. *Ibid.*, para. 8.
235. (Decision IV/M.179 on SPAR/Dansk Supermarked 1992).
236. (Decision IV/M.803 on Rewe/Billa 1996).
237. (Decision IV/M.784 on Kesko/Tuko 1996); the Commission prohibited the proposed merger of two Finnish companies after an investigation initiated at the request of the Finish Office of Free Competition pursuant to Art. 22 of the Merger Regulation.

Chapter 4: Competition Practice

view as markets covering a circle with a radius of approximately 20 car-minutes, an assessment limited to these local markets is considered inappropriate if a large number of local markets affected by the concentration are so closely interlinked that they overlap and thus cover a larger or even the entire territory of a Member State. In this context, it is necessary to take into account that the competitive relations between the large retail chains are not limited to local competition, but take place on a much wider geographical dimension. This can be seen for example through the largely centralised decision taken by the large retail chains about the product ranges to offer.

In the *Rewe/Meinl*[238] case, the Commission discussed at length the geographic market definition. The acquisition concerned the Austrian food retail market and several Austrian procurement markets for daily consumer goods. In particular the issue was whether the food retail market had a national scope and whether the procurement markets for daily consumer goods are larger than Austria. Although there are considerable aspects that would support such a view, the Commission defined the relevant procurement markets still as nation-wide. The Commission's investigation resulted in the conclusion that the market shares on the food retail market in Austria would increase from 30% to at least 37% with the closest competitor (Spar) having 26%. In particular the fear was that the position of Rewe/Billa would have been strengthened considerably by the acquisition of Meinl through, for example, the chain of highly productive large outlets, the strong position in urban centres and the advantage of centralised organisation. In addition, the proposed concentration would, in the eyes of the Commission, further increase the already existing high entry barriers to the Austrian food retail market. A strong issue in this case was also the buyer power in respect of several procurement markets, particularly for dairy products, bread and pet food. The Commission stated that suppliers to the food sector would on average depend for 29% of their turnover on sales to *Rewe/Billa/Meinl*, some product groups showing a significantly higher degree of dependency. In evaluating the degree of dependency, the Commission took notice of structural elements existing for *Rewe/Billa* such as the centralised buying structure and its strong position in Eastern Austria. In order to remove the Commission's concerns the parties offered modifications on the original proposed operation.

In *Mannesmann/Vallourec/Ilva*,[239] shipment data was considered in defining the extent of the geographic reference market. The Commission examined in particular the usefulness of the *Elzinga-Hogarty test*. The Elzinga-Hogarty test relies on the assumption that a given area belongs to a wider geographic market if either 10% or more of production is exported or a similar proportion of consumption is imported. However, the Commission questioned the reliability of this method since it could lead to a wider market definition even if market interpenetration was not mutual. In this case, exports from Western Europe exceeded 10%, but imports were found to be below this threshold. The Commission concluded that the fact that exports exceeded 10% would

---

238. (Decision IV/M.1221 on Rewe/Meinl 1999).
239. (Decision IV/M.315 on Mannesmann/Vallourec/Ilva 1994).

not be sufficient in itself to find that the relevant geographic market was wider than Western Europe, given that imports were small.[240]

In *BMW/Rover*,[241] national differences in distribution systems for cars were taken as an indication that national markets may still exist. Further the need for local facilities and separate catalogues[242] as well as strong national buying preferences[243] indicate national geographical markets. *Nestlé-Perrier*[244] may serve as an example too. The Commission defined the relevant market as France, including among its reasons a number of factors, which are related specifically to potential supply. Imports of mineral water to the French market are insignificant (less than 2% of the market) with similar situations in Italy (imports less than 1%) and Germany (about 3%). In contrast, Belgium exports 42% of production and imports 51% of consumption, so is not considered to be a national market.

In *Harrisons & Crosfields/AKZO*,[245] the geographical market for three industrial product groups was held to be Community-wide in view of, *inter alia*, the presence of major suppliers in several Member States, with significant market shares. In *Thomson/Shorts*,[246] the presence of a national supplier for defence equipment was held to be sufficient for the establishment of a national market.

With respect to geographic market definitions, the Commission frequently stresses the point that the assessment to be made is a dynamic one, taking into account in particular the effect of market integration. A merger resulting in a national champion in a Member State may factually impede the development of the Single European market and point towards the relevant geographic market being the national market. On the other hand, a merger between undertakings from different Member States may be viewed as part of a trend towards increased cross-border trade in the affected product market.

As a general rule for jurisdictional reasons, the Commission is supposed to focus on market shares at the Community or European level while taking account of the worldwide context. Where there is significant actual or realistic potential competition from imports outside Europe, the Commission may recognise the existence of a worldwide market.

An example is the *Aerospatiale-Alenia/de Havilland* case.[247] In this case, regional turboprop aircraft (commuters) were said to be a world market from an economic point of view. The market concerned was characterised by a significant mutual interpenetration, there were no tangible barriers to import these aircrafts into the EC and costs of transportation were negligible.

Although the Commission itself emphasises a dynamic assessment, it typically adopts a static 'short term' market analysis (as opposed to a 'long term' dynamic one)

---

240. (Lowe 1995, 148).
241. (Decision IV/M.416 on BMW/Rover 1994).
242. (Decision IV/M.070 on Otto/Grattan 1991, 11).
243. (Decision IV/M.4 on Renault/Volvo 1990, 17 and 18).
244. (Decision IV/M.190 on Nestlé/Perrier 1992).
245. (Decision IV/M.310 on Harrisons & Crosfield/AKZO 1993).
246. (Decision IV/M.318 on Thomson/Shorts 1993).
247. (Decision IV/M.53 on Aerospatiale-Alenia/de Havilland 1991).

Chapter 4: Competition Practice

in its cases, leaving the dynamic elements to be taken into account at a later stage when the merits of the transaction have to be assessed.

Examples of the Commission's static approach to determine the geographic market can be found in the Commission's decisions in *American Cyanamid/Shell*[248] and *Mannesmann/Hoesch*.[249] In both cases, the Commission discounted the market effects of the Community regulatory regime. The expectation was that changes brought by Community legislation would not occur in the short-term. In *Hafnia/Codan*, a case in the insurance market[250] the gradual opening up of the Community insurance markets as a result of Community legislation and other factors were discounted by the Commission in its relevant geographic market definition. Based on a static analysis of the competitive conditions, the Commission defined the relevant geographic market in the insurance sector as a national one.

In its assessment the Commission also considers whether a firm operates in a number of different geographic markets. Commercial banks may serve as an example. They supply multiple services to multiple types of customers. Large corporations, for example, obtain credit from many sources and the geographic market is very broad, probably worldwide, for this type of banking services. On the other hand, the geographic market is likely to be much narrower for small customers demanding retail banking services in their neighbourhood. This geographic division adds a dimension, which is treated carefully.

However, the Commission has a very strong record in defining geographic markets as being national, regional or local in scope.
In *Nestlé/Italgel*[251], the Commission noted that the geographic markets for ice cream are predominantly national since ice cream markets are subject to national legislation on labelling, air expansion coefficient and product contents. In addition, consumer profiles, seasonal factors, habits of consumption, channels of distribution, the importance of the artisanal section, internal segmentation (in terms of impulse ice cream, take-home ice cream and catering), prices and margins, sizes and brand names varied between Member States.

In *Costa Crociere/Chargeurs/Accor*[252], markets for cruises and package holidays were held to be national because of, *inter alia*, national differences in consumption patterns, the need for brochures to be published in several languages, and the existence of advertising campaigns targeting national audiences.

In *Kali and Salz/MdK/Treuhand*,[253] the Commission concluded that, for agricultural potash products, Germany was separable from the rest of the Community and constituted one relevant geographic market while the remainder of the Community constituted another relevant geographic market. The Commission based its conclusion upon the absence of appreciable imports into the German market (which was characterised by excess supply), the demand of German customers for magnesium containing

---

248. (Decision IV/M.354 on Cyanamid/Shell 1993, 20–22).
249. (Decision IV/M.222 on Mannesmann/Hoesch 1992, 71).
250. (Decision IV/M.344 on CODAN/HAFNIA 1993).
251. (Decision IV/M.362 on Nestlé/Italgel 1993).
252. (Decision IV/M.334 on Costa Crociere/Chargeurs/Accor 1993, 17–19).
253. (Decision IV/M.308 on Kali und Salz v. MdK v. Treuhand 1993).

potash products and their long established supply relationships with German suppliers who are the only producers of magnesium containing potash products in the Community. The Community apart from Germany constituted a separate geographic market (rest of Europe) because of significant trade flows between the Member States and generally homogeneous competitive conditions.[254]

In *Mercedes-Benz/Kässbohrer*,[255] although the bus market throughout the EU would be affected, the Commission considered the German market required particular attention. This market was characterised by low imports, strong brand loyalty and close customer-supplier relationship. The Commission therefore considered that the German bus market was a national market.

In *ABB/Daimler Benz*[256], the Commission believed that the market for local trains had remained national in Germany although, in other Member States, the lack of major national rail transportation industries had already resulted in wider geographic markets. The proposed operation would have led to the creation of a dominant duopoly in the German market for local trains. In order to alleviate the Commission's concern, the parties agreed on the sale of Kiepe Elektrik GmbH, a Daimler Benz subsidiary, specialising in electrical supplies for local trains. As a result of this divestiture, a competent producer of electrical components that was independent of the parties would remain on the German market.

Some determinations of the geographic market have provoked controversy, particularly in cases where markets are still divided along national lines despite moves towards a single European market. For example, in *Magneti Marelli/CEAc*[257] and *Varta/Bosch*[258], the Commission considered that the market for replacement starter batteries was national, so that the concentrations resulted in high market shares in individual Member States. The shares would have been significantly lower at a Community or wider European level.

One of the most prominent cases with respect to geographic market definition was *Volvo/Scania*.[259] For a number of reasons, including different technical requirements and purchasing habits, the Commission established that the markets for heavy trucks and buses were still national in scope. This conclusion was particularly based on observed differences in technical requirements, purchasing habits and market shares in various Member States. Therefore, the Commission reached the conclusion, that a merger between Volvo and Scania would have led to a market share of 90% in Sweden and of between 50% and 70% in Ireland, Norway and Finland. In this case of classical horizontal overlaps and large market shares, the unilateral effects of the concentration were investigated. The Commission stated that the dominance test had to be applied to any relevant geographic market independently of its size. The spirit of the ECMR has to guarantee consumers protection from the effects of dominance in small and large markets alike. Furthermore, the investigation led the Commission to the conclusion

---

254. (Heistermann 1995, 61).
255. (Decision IV/M.477 on Mercedes-Benz/Kässbohrer 1995).
256. (Decision IV/M.580 on ABB/Daimler-Benz 1995).
257. (Decision IV/M.43 on Magneti/Marelli/CEAc 1991).
258. (Decision IV/M.12 on Varta/Bosch 1991).
259. (Decision COMP/M.1641 on Linde/AGA 2000).

Chapter 4: Competition Practice

that the barriers to entry or for expansion in these markets were high. For these reasons the Commission came to the conclusion that, if approved, the concentration would have significantly changed the structure of the market for heavy trucks in Sweden, Norway, Finland and Ireland and created a dominant position on each of those markets. Since the commitments proposed by the parties did not resolve the competition concerns the Commission finally prohibited the operation and thereby stressed the need for firms that have overlapping market positions to carefully assess all elements that are relevant for the assessment of the scope particularly of the geographic markets concerned.

The Commission used to define *regional markets* as relevant geographic markets too. In *KNP/Bührmann Tetterode/VRG*[260], the Commission concluded that the relevant geographic market for the distribution and service of printing presses was national. The analysis was based on an appraisal of distribution arrangements, purchasing patterns of customers and differences in price levels between the various Member States. Furthermore, the Commission found that the relevant geographic markets for board products for transport packaging were regional markets crossing national borders. One region consisted of the Benelux countries, northern France and central Germany. Another regional market covered southern Germany, eastern France, Austria and Switzerland. The Commission's finding of regional markets was based upon significant trade flows between these countries, time constraints on delivery imposed by customers and an analysis of transport costs. In *VIAG/Continental*,[261] the Commission considered as the relevant geographic market a cross-border regional market within the Community namely Germany, the Benelux countries and North of France. The reason was that transport and administrative costs increase in importance as the ratio of value to weight or volume falls. The cost of transporting empty cans is so high in relation to their volume that it becomes uneconomic to transport them much more than the average shipping distance of 200 km[262]; with glass bottles the economic range of supply is even less. The approach is correct from the economic point of view, since economic realities do not follow political borders.

Sanitec/Sphinx[263] was a case featuring high market shares in the Nordic countries. The Commission found that the operation in the form it had been notified would have led to adverse competition effects in ceramic sanitary-ware and other bathroom products in the Nordic countries. Since there are particular national standards for sanitary products the markets were specified to be national in scope. The high market shares (up to 90%) and absence of countervailing buying power led the Commission to the conclusion that the operation would have had negative effects on the Nordic customers. Subsequently *Sanitec* offered remedies in the Nordic countries.

Promodes/Dirsa[264] is a case concerning concentration in the food and non-food retailing sector in Spain. The Commission went further than suggested by the parties

---
260. (Decision IV/M.291 on KNP/Bührmann-Tettorde/VRG-Group 1993).
261. (Decision IV/M.81 on VIAG/Continental Can 1991, 16–17).
262. The 200 km limit was first defined in the Continental Can case under Art. 82 (1972).
263. (Decision IV/M.1578 on Sanitec/Sphinx 1999).
264. (Decision IV/M.27 on Promodes/Dirsa 1990).

themselves and held that the relevant geographical market was not regional, as suggested by Promodes, but a *local market* as a result of the homogeneity of competition condition.[265] In its decision, the Commission, in acknowledging the homogeneity of conditions of competition, referred exclusively to conditions as perceived by or pertaining to consumers and took no notice of the fact that large retailers compete with each other at a nation-wide level (strangely the Commission did, however, acknowledge that Promodes had achieved its rank as the largest retailer in the Spanish market through its concentration with Dirsa).

There were other cases where the geographic reference market was local as in *BP/Petromed*.[266] In this case, the Canary Islands constituted a distinct geographic market. By contrast, in *Cargill/Unilever*[267] the Commission held that in spite of the existence of different local markets, so much inter-linkage existed that segmentation into different relevant geographical markets could not to be shown and that further, no indication existed that appreciably different conditions of competition were present in the various agricultural areas of Great Britain. Similar to the situation in *Promodes/Dirsa*[268], in this instance various competitors were active in a significant number of localities and competed with each other and with the other parties to the concentration in practically every area.

In its investigation of the proposed acquisition of Acetex, an active producer in the acetyls and plastic business, by Blackstone, a US private merchant-banking company, in the so-called *Blackstone/Acetex case*[269] the Commission used econometric analysis for its geographic market definition. One of the companies controlled by Blackstone, Celanese, is active on the same product markets as Acetex. One of key issues in this transaction was the delineation of the relevant geographic market for each product affected by the transaction. In this merger, the markets concerned were in particular the markets for acetic acid, vinyl acetate monomer (VAM), acetic anhydride, and polyvinyl alcohol (PVOH).

The merging parties argued that the relevant geographic markets are worldwide and substantiated their view with several econometric studies. A price correlation analysis was submitted that demonstrated a high correlation of the prices worldwide that supports the thesis of a worldwide market. These results were completed with a co integration and a Granger causality analysis using prices of acetic acid in different regions of the world. The study showed that there is a long-term relationship between the prices in different world regions. Furthermore, a study illustrated that unexpected plant outages caused price increases in other regions leading to the conclusion of a globally integrated market. Additionally, the geographical market definition as world market was supported from the analysis of the impact of unexpected plant outages on trade flows.

---

265. *Ibid.*, para. 8.
266. (Decision IV/M.111 on BP/Petromed 1991).
267. (Decision IV/M.26 on Cargill/Unilever 1990).
268. (Decision IV/M.27 on Promodes/Dirsa 1990).
269. (Decision M.3625 on Blackstone/Acetex 2005).

Chapter 4: Competition Practice

Based on a fairly detailed *correlation and co-integration analysis*, the studies showed that historical prices from various regions of the world move mutually. The studies concluded that the relevant markets are worldwide. Showing that prices from two regions are correlated over time may indicate that these regions belong to the same economic market. However, how strong the correlation needs to be to validate such a claim is anyone's guess. In addition, the correlation of two price series may be the result of common factors, such as input prices or seasonality. Hence it is important to remove these common factors that would explain a strong association between price movements before claiming that prices are actually correlated as a result of market forces.

The Commission replicated and confirmed the results of the submitted studies and performed in some cases additional tests and examinations. Although the Commission criticised certain model specifications and pointed out that the results were inconclusive, the Commission concluded:

> *On the basis of all of the above considerations, including a more thorough examination, in the light of the latest evidence, of the factors taken into account in the decision to initiate proceedings, and in spite of the inconclusiveness of some of the studies mentioned, the balance of evidence now available clearly points to the conclusion that the geographic market for acetic acid should be defined as global for the purposes of this decision.*[270]

The other three product markets were also defined as world markets. This definition led to the approval of the merger without remedies. This case illustrates that the Commission increasingly applies – by implementing the standard of proof as defined by the European Courts – econometric studies. These studies can contribute considerably to a correct market definition and, hence, to the approval of a merger.

In 2007, the British company Ineos Group Limited (hereinafter 'Ineos') notified the Commission of its proposed acquisition of the Norwegian company Kerling ASA (hereinafter 'Kerling'). Both companies were active, amongst others, in the market of Standard PVC (hereinafter 'S-PVC').

The main issue in this *Ineos/Kerling case*[271] was the assessment of the relevant geographic market. This case exemplifies the complementary nature of *quantitative and qualitative evidence* in making an overall assessment of a merger. It is apparent from this case that quantitative data, to the extent it helps to form a better understanding of the functioning of the affected markets allows the Commission to minimise the risk of error, including the wrongful prohibition of neutral or pro-competitive mergers. Therefore, the Commission advocates that parties of an efficiency-enhancing merger feel encouraged to provide relevant and accurate quantitative data to substantiate their case.

In the assessment of market definition, the Commission had conflicting information. On the one hand, the parties claimed that the UK S-PVC market was part of a broader European S-PVC market on the basis of a substantial level of imports from

---

270. (Decision M.3625 on Blackstone/Acetex 2005, 49).
271. (Decision M.4734 on INEOS/Kerling 2008).

Western Europe (over 30% of UK demand). On the other hand, a number of UK customers argued in favour of a national S-PVC market, on the grounds that it would be difficult to rely on importers for substantial and reliable supplies. The existence of imports into the UK is a necessary condition for a broader relevant geographic market, but not a sufficient one. The presence of flows between countries does not necessarily imply the existence of a sufficiently competitive constraint on the domestic production, and certainly not the ability to defeat a SSNIP by a potential monopolist. In order to test the existence of a UK national market in this specific context, the Commission applied two alternative and complementary techniques to implement the SSNIP test.

First, it can be estimated whether a SSNIP by the hypothetical monopoly in the UK S-PVC market created by the merger would be profitable by means of a (1) *Critical Loss Analysis* (CLA). The second way to test the existence of a UK national market is to look at (2) the *elasticity of supply* of imports with respect to the prices charged by UK producers. The higher the elasticity of supply, the more a given price increase will lead to increased imports into UK, and the more likely that such a price increase will be defeated. This was done through a 'natural experiments analyses'.

The dataset passed through a detailed consistency check, which allowed the Commission to identify a number of mistakes in the dataset and to secure explanations from the parties on outlier observations. It was also ascertained that the transaction data received did not reflect the real economic trade-offs being made by the buyers, and might bias the analysis. Indeed, this accounting based data, which are often the type of (price and quantity) transaction data delivered to the Commission, may not reflect the real economic trade-offs being made by the buyers due to asynchronous recording of quantity returns, discounts or rebates in accountancy systems. The discrepancies between the accountancy-based dataset and a *dataset reflecting economic trade-offs* were also addressed by the parties, so that the analysis could be done on data reflecting the actual economic transactions.

The CLA builds directly on the definition of an anti-trust market contained in the Notice on Market Definition, that is: a market is the smallest group of producers that, if they behaved as a single hypothetical profit-maximising firm, would impose at least a small but significant and non-transitory increase in price. In the context of this decision, the logic of the test is to identify the group of producers in the UK (the hypothetical geographic market) that would be able to exercise market power if they could coordinate their pricing and output behaviour. If the hypothetical monopoly could profitably exercise market power by raising prices by 5%–10% (or reducing output accordingly), then the anti-trust relevant geographic market would be the UK. If not, the market is broader. The profitability test is constructed by comparing the critical loss and the actual loss estimated on the basis of the elasticity. The price rise is profitable for the hypothetical monopoly if the actual loss is lower than the critical one.

The second assessment, the natural experiment in this case also illustrates the importance of having an extensive and complete dataset concerning the key parameters of competition such as sales volumes, transaction prices, margins, costs, etc. A significant increase in imports following Ineos' outage would suggest that the geographical market is broader than the UK, while no response would suggest the contrary. This conclusion can only be reached once the dataset has been built and validated, and the plant outages may offer competitors opportunities to increase their sales and or obtain higher margins (by extracting a premium paid by customers) on their additional sales, assuming they have the ability to expand output or otherwise reallocate sales to the affected customers. An *analysis of the evolution of volumes, prices and margins over the outage period* can therefore provide additional evidence on the scope of the geographic market.

Situations of this type offer the conditions for 'natural experiments analysis' which permits the calculation of the rivals' elasticity of supply. Specifically in this case, Ineos' plant in Barry (UK) had an unexpected partial shutdown in June 2004. Given the strong production linkages between the two plants, this also affected the level of production at Ineos' other UK plant, in Runcorn. As a result, this outage substantially affected the volume of S-PVC produced by Ineos in the UK (a loss of 10% of the 2002–2006 average yearly sales) for a period of five months during which this plant was producing at approximately 50% of its maximum technical capacity, as opposed to 90% under normal conditions. This outage is reflected in the transaction data and constitutes a very interesting experimental base for analysing competitors' reactions to a sudden drop in the parties' supply of S-PVC in and into the UK. The analysis showed that the volumes lost by Ineos were not completely captured by Kerling, as customers looking for alternative sources of supply turned to imports. In fact, more of these sales were captured by the importers than by Kerling. Moreover, Kerling's margins did not rise over this period, which is a clear indication that Kerling was constrained in its price reaction to Ineos' supply reduction by the importers. The combination of these two elements suggested that not only Kerling but also importers were in a position to swiftly react to any attempts by Ineos to constrain output so as to increase prices. This provided further evidence that both Ineos and Kerling are constrained by importers, even in the event of an output shortage, which suggests that the market is indeed wider than the UK.

The Commission reached the conclusion, that the process of market definition is ultimately an empirical matter, although in many cases it can be determined sufficiently accurately without the need to adopt empirically-based techniques. Where markets need to be defined by reference to empirical methods, however, it should be done by experts. Even apparently simple econometrics can turn out to be very complex. The complexity of many econometric techniques means that the courts may be left to balance the evidence presented by both (interested) sides, but are unlikely to be able to assess the merits of the econometrics employed without seeking expert assistance.

A final and important lesson from this case is that a close cooperation between the Commission services and the merging parties in generating the most accurate and extensive data set will generally allow the Commission to make a more informed decision to the advantage of parties involved in a neutral or pro-competitive merger. Indeed, in this case, an in-depth investigation, solidly grounded on factual evidence allowed the Commission to avoid making the likely mistake of accepting unnecessary remedies in phase I. Remedies, which would have been costly for the merging parties to implement and might have disrupted the functioning of the market.[272]

In *Omya/Huber PCC*[273] the Commission had evidence that discrimination was feasible at the level of individual customers. It avoided giving a geographic market definition in the traditional sense of describing the precise physical borders of each geographic market. Instead it focused directly on what the merger would mean to the various customers of the merging parties.

In *Campina/Friesland*[274], it was initially far from clear whether the presence of large retailer chains implied that the wholesale market might extend beyond the Netherlands, even if the retail (or end-consumer) market were regarded national in scope. Campina and Friesland Foods were two independent dairy cooperatives at the time of notification. Their activities overlapped in several markets along the dairy food product chain, from the procurement and processing of fresh milk to the production of a variety of dairy and non-dairy products. Both companies were predominantly based in the Netherlands. Parties argued that the procurement market would be narrower than national, given the location of the dairy plants, the dispersion of farmers, and other factors that affect transaction costs. In the end, markets at all three levels of the supply chain were considered to be national in scope. In large part, this was because of strong evidence indicating that Dutch consumers (and consequently derived demand by retailers) have a very strong preference for Dutch dairy products. Respondents to the market investigation pointed out that the merging parties, both independently and under the umbrella of the Dutch Dairy Organisation, have incurred substantial expenditures over the last decades to promote Dutch dairy products. The success of this strategy is evident from the fact that the merging parties explicitly labelled a large majority of their dairy products as coming from Dutch cows.[275]

4.3 MARKET ANALYSIS

4.3.1 Analysis of Market Shares

In the assessment of the market position of the supplier, market shares on the relevant product and geographic market provide first indications. Market shares are a vital indicator to estimate the economic impact of agreements. They signify the market performance and future scope for action.

A substantial market share generally suggests that the ability of the opposite side of the market to switch to other undertakings is limited. As a result, the undertaking in question has an increased scope for action. The larger the absolute market share of an undertaking, the greater the likelihood that it has a scope for action that is not sufficiently controlled and the greater its ability is to restrict other market participant' use of competition parameters.

---

272. (Amelio, De La Mano and Godinho de Matos 2008, 63).
273. (Regulation 139/2004 on Merger Procedure, COMP/M.3796 – OMYA/HUBER PCC 2006).
274. (Decision M.5046 on Friesland Foods/Campina 2008).
275. (Neven and De la Mano 2009).

Chapter 4: Competition Practice

Overall, market shares are calculated on the basis of the relevant product and geographic market. Market shares can be measured either in sales value or in sales volume. Market shares, in particular the market shares for markets with heterogeneous products, are preferably defined in value terms, i.e., expressed by turnover, and not in terms of quantity. Market shares in sales value reflect more accurately the market conditions. If uncertainties still exist regarding the market definition and as a result about the size of market shares, a tolerance threshold may be used when calculating market shares.[276]

If direct and indirect sales have become increasingly substitutable due to, for example, the increased sensitivity of retailers with regard to prices, the pure reliance on market shares and their aggregates as such are not really appropriate to determine market power.

The market share difference in relation to the closest competitor, the market share structure in general as well as the market share development over several time periods have to be evaluated. Market share differences and the distribution of market shares show a competitor's ability to offer the other side of the market alternative choices should the market leader use its scope for action to restrict competition via an agreement. The greater the difference (gap) between an undertaking's market share and that of its largest competitor and/or the more fragmented market shares are, the greater the likelihood that the market (share) leader has scope for restrictive action. In addition, the competitors' production capacities and their degrees of utilisation may be considered.

Yet, even in markets with a large market share gap, market entry might be possible. Therefore, the existence of a gap in market shares has to be assessed. Additional indicators like the nature of the market and its stage in the life cycle point to the fact that many individual small firms may enter and exit the market depending on the competitive setting. These undertakings do not have large disadvantages compared to large undertakings.

The development of market shares over time is another useful indication of the economic effects of an agreement. Competition is a dynamic process of initial moves by one competitor and the responses by others to catch up with it. In a competitive market, market shares therefore generally fluctuate over time. Just as a sustained high market share is an indicator of uncontrolled scope for action, market share fluctuations combined with changing market leadership, or sustained heavy market share losses suggest such an uncontrolled scope for action does not exist. In situations of intense price competition, for example market share losses indicate that the negative economic effects of an agreement are less likely.

The time frame to consider depends on the duration of the agreements and related contract terms. In cases where products are purchased infrequently on the basis of long-term contracts, an analysis of market shares over a longer time period provides

---

276. (Bundeskartellamt, Principles of Interpretation 2010).

indications about the competitive process in this market. In analysing market shares over time, other possible causes for market share developments have to be considered as well. The longer the time frame, the less significant market share fluctuations become.

The Commission itself is not coherent when it comes to the size of market shares. From a competition economist perspective, the assumption holds that a high market share is usually a good indicator of market power. However, in the case of low entry barriers it may not indicate market power.[277] Therefore, a more thorough approach is necessary in order to deduce conclusions from the height of market shares.

4.3.2 Evaluation of the Market Position

Negative effects on competition within the relevant market are likely to occur when the parties individually or jointly have or obtain some degree of market power and the agreement contributes to the creation, maintenance or strengthening of that market power or allows the parties to exploit such market power.[278] In markets with high fixed costs, undertakings must price significantly above their marginal costs of production in order to ensure a competitive return on their investment. The fact that undertakings price above their marginal costs is therefore not in itself a sign that competition in the market is not functioning well and that undertakings have market power that allows them to price above the competitive level. It is when competitive constraints are insufficient to maintain prices and output at competitive levels that undertakings have market power within the meaning of Article 101(1).[279] The market position of the supplier could be further strengthened – depending on the facts of the case – if he has certain cost advantages over his competitors. These competitive advantages may result from a first mover advantage (having the best site, etc.), holding essential patents, having superior technology, being the brand leader or having a superior portfolio.

A similar approach is applied when the market position of competitors is assessed. The stronger the established competitors are and the greater their number, the less likely is the risk of the supplier or buyer in question being able to foreclose the market individually and of a reduction in inter-brand competition. However, a market structure where the number of competitors becomes rather small and their market position (size, costs, R&D potential, etc.) is rather similar, may increase the risk of collusion. Fluctuating or rapidly changing market shares or market positions are in general an indication of intense competition.[280]

---

277. (Commission Guidelines on Vertical Restraints 2000).
278. Market power is defined as the ability to maintain prices above competitive levels for a significant period of time or to maintain output in terms of product quantities, product quality and variety or innovation below competitive levels for a significant period of time.
279. (Guidelines on the Art. 81(3) of the Treaty 2004, 25).
280. (Commission Guidelines on Vertical Restraints 2000, 124).

4.3.3 Analysing Buyer Power

A high level of concentration of firms on the buyer side of the market is not in itself sufficient evidence to disprove market power of a supplier, since any buying power initially affects all suppliers to an equal extent. This is particularly the case when the level of concentration on the supply-side is equal or even superior to the level of concentration on the demand side.

Instead of this, a prerequisite for buyer power is that a powerful buyer awards its contracts according to market-strategic considerations, so as not to become dependent on suppliers with market power. Buyer conduct is likely to be based on market-strategic considerations when the purchasing market for the purchasing firm is especially important, e.g., because the cost of the primary product has a major effect on the sales price of the finished product. If purchases by one customer make up a major part of the production on the supply-side of the market, this, too, is an indication of buyer power. If there are competitors with adequate capacities to meet demand, a buyer's threat to switch to another supplier may have a considerable disciplinary effect on a supplier with market power that sells a major part of its production to a single buyer.[281]

Buyer power can only preclude market power on the supply-side of the market when all significant buyers pose a comparable potential threat. Thus, buyer power derives from the market position of the buyer.

A first indicator of buying power is the market share of the buyer on the purchase market. This market share reflects the importance of his demand for his possible suppliers. Other indicators focus on the market position of the buyer on his resale market including characteristics such as own brands of the buyer/distributor, wide geographic spread of his outlets and his image amongst final consumers. The effect of buying power on the likelihood of anti-competitive effects is not the same for the different vertical restraints. Buying power may in particular increase the negative effects in cases of restraints from the limited distribution and market partitioning groups such as exclusive supply, exclusive distribution and quantitative selective distribution.[282]

4.3.4 Analysis of Resources

Superior financial strength may provide a firm with a scope for action, in particular as regards the use of parameters of competition such as price, investment, research and advertising. The same applies, for example, to a comprehensive production programme or range of products, or resources that are specific to a particular sector or market, in particular technological resources. Superior resources result in a paramount market position if they limit the alternatives available to buyers and have discouraging and deterrent effects on competitors. In some cases, profits can be transferred and

---

281. (Bundeskartellamt, Principles of Interpretation 2010, 31).
282. (Commission Guidelines on Vertical Restraints 2000, 125).

losses can be balanced out from one market to another. Such effects manifest themselves in existing competitors refraining from engaging in active competition and potential competitors refraining from entering the market. The assumption that superior resources are actually used has to be well substantiated.

In order to determine the financial strength of an enterprise, numerous criteria such as turnover, cash flow, profits, liquid funds, annual surplus or access to national and international capital markets have to be assessed. Turnovers on their own are only of limited significance with regard to the capital available for shifting resources within an enterprise, and are thus not always a suitable indication of the financial strength of an enterprise. Opportunities for innovative enterprises to make profits, for example in view of the development of high-tech share prices, must be increasingly taken into account in assessing a firm's resources.

The manner in which advantages arising from other resources affect the markets concerned also has to be examined. In markets where customer relations and the users' trust in an established and comprehensive range of products are important factors, a wide range of products, production volumes and established sales structures may replace financial strength as a core parameter of competition. In markets where research and development plays an important role, qualified human resources or a considerable innovation potential may gain importance.[283] Therefore an assessment of the resources also has to take place.

4.3.5 Analysis of Access to Supply and Sales Markets

A firm's easier access to the supply or sales markets in relation to its competitors may give it a paramount market position. This is the case if a powerful firm (in terms of its market share) can make access to such markets difficult or even impossible for its rivals on account of its own very good access to the supply or sales markets (raising the barriers to entry or risk of foreclosure).

4.3.6 Competition from (Imperfect) Substitutes

The scope for action of powerful firms may be limited to a certain extent by firms supplying imperfect substitute goods or services to those in the market concerned, which may replace them to a limited extent or under certain circumstances. Since indications exist that such substitutes are available, the competitive constraints from these substitutes will be illustrated.

4.3.7 Assessment Barriers to Market Entry/Potential Competition

Barriers to entry and potential competition are important indications of a market position. Whereas market shares provide only limited insights, an analysis of barriers

---

283. (Bundeskartellamt, Principles of Interpretation 2010, 17).

Chapter 4: Competition Practice

to entry embodies the relevant information on the significance of competitive constraints available in a market. This means that even a firm with a high market share cannot apply excessive prices since in the case of low barriers to entry, it is very likely that potential competitors would be able to enter the market quickly and limit the scope of anti-competitive action of a company with high market shares.[284] On the other hand, if barriers to entry are high, this might be an important indication that a firm has a paramount market position as it is able to secure its market position against new entrants.

Consequently, entry barriers are important in establishing whether there is real foreclosure.[285] Entry barriers arising from vertical agreements are therefore measured by the extent to which undertakings can increase their price above the competitive level, usually above minimum average total costs (ATCs), and make supra-national profits without attracting entry. Without entry barriers, easy and quick entry would eliminate such profits and hence make the negative effects of vertical agreements very unlikely. As far as effective entry is likely to occur within one or two years, entry barriers can be said to be low.[286]

Entry barriers can originate from many sources and factors. In the following, a short description of these will be given to explain how entry barriers are assessed in practice. Without barriers to entry, no increases in market power or negative effects are expected in the case of vertical agreements.[287] In such a case, a very dynamic and unpredictable 'competitive fringe' is able to put appreciable pressure on any large firm, ensuring that competitive forces remain even after the proposed merger.

Entry barriers may result from a wide variety of factors such as economies of scale and scope, government regulations (especially where they establish exclusive rights), state aid, import tariffs, intellectual property rights (IPR), ownership of resources (where the supply is limited due to for instance natural limitations), essential facilities, a first mover advantage and brand loyalty of consumers created by strong advertising. Vertical restraints and vertical integration may also work as entry barriers by making access more difficult and foreclosing (potential) competitors. Entry barriers may be present at only the supplier or buyer level or at both levels.

Market entry is thus not a firm-related, but a market-related structural criterion. Disproportionately high costs of market entry or a high risk of failure indicate that the barriers to entry are high.[288] The height of entry barriers depends on related sunk costs that have to be incurred to enter the market but that are lost when the market has to be exited.[289] The more sunk costs there are, the higher the risk is that potential market entrants face when they consider entering the market and the more credibly already

---

284. (BKartA Grundsatzabteilung E/G 4, Auslegungsgrundsätze zur Fusionskontrolle, 2000, 25).
285. In assessing the possible anti-competitive effects of exclusive distribution, entry barriers that may hinder suppliers from creating new distributors or finding alternative distributors are less important. Foreclosure of other suppliers does not arise as long as exclusive distribution is not combined with single branding.
286. (European Commission, Commission Guidelines on horizontal mergers 2004, para. 74).
287. (The Law and Economics of Mergers 2002).
288. See in: (Waterson & Dobson, Vertical Restraints and Competition Policy 1996, 27).
289. (Commission Guidelines on Vertical Restraints 2000, 128).

established suppliers (incumbents) can threaten that they will match new competition. It is useful to consider the extent to which sunk costs give these incumbents a significant advantage over potential new market entrants and to what extent sunk costs might influence their decision to enter the market. Yet, the mere existence of sunk costs in a market does not necessarily mean that entry barriers are so high that competition within the market cannot be effective. New market entrants must often incur various market specific start-up costs like investments in elementary equipment like buildings, machines, infrastructure, advertising etc. Even if new suppliers have some disadvantages to suppliers already active in the market, what counts is the proportionality between sunk costs and the likelihood of the return of these costs by making profit out of the investments made. If the return on investment is unlikely to reach the breakeven point (all incurred costs are covered) entry barriers are significantly high and deter potential new suppliers to enter the market.

In knowledge based production, it cannot be assumed that incumbent companies and potential entrants have the same knowledge. A potential entrant who wants to start a new production line needs to firstly find retailers on the downstream market willing to distribute the products invented. This innovator may need even more given the substantial transaction costs of finding somebody willing to experiment with something new. If a substantial number of retailers are already tied to other producers' entry can become really difficult.[290]

In evaluating potential competition, examination should be made of whether effective entry and relevant competition is possible and feasible. In addition, entry must take place within a time period that is short enough to discourage the firms concerned from exploiting their market power. Market entry costs should not be disproportionately high either. Potential entry must also be expressed in sufficiently concrete terms. According to established practice, barriers to entry can be roughly divided into three categories:

- *structural barriers to entry* usually arise from certain technological or demand-related industry characteristics, but may also lie in the resources that are required to be successful on the market. They are not generally created intentionally to prevent entry;
- *strategic barriers to entry* are intentionally set up by market leaders in a market in order to deter potential suppliers from entry;
- *statutory barriers to entry* are those set up in the context of the state's monopoly on power in the form of laws, regulations and administrative practices.

These barriers will be addressed forthwith.

Structural barriers are not created on purpose by either the government or the established suppliers to prevent entry. These barriers to entry usually arise from certain technological or demand-related market characteristics, but may also lie in the undertaking's resources that are required to enter the market successfully. Generally,

---

290. (Kerber & Vezzoso 2004, 17).

the higher the future profit prospects are considered to be, the more likely it is that new market players will enter the market. New and growing markets or markets with excess demand have – compared to stagnant markets characterised by excess capacities – lower barriers to entry. Additionally, market entry is unlikely if limited time is available to gain a return on new investments due to a decline in the market. In principle potential foreign competitors have to be evaluated in the same way as potential domestic competitors. Yet, they may face extra barriers to market entry if the markets have national features which make market entry from abroad more difficult for legal or practical reasons. That may be the case when there are tariff or non-tariff barriers to trade, or language barriers, or if buyers prefer domestic suppliers. Other typical structural barriers to entry arise from economies of scale[291] and scope.[292]

In markets where economies of scale are significant, entry on a small-scale is extremely difficult unless the new market entrant can successfully find a market niche, invent a new product and make profit out of supplying consumers' demand as part of this target group. Economies of scope may have similar implications, as a potential entrant would prefer to enter the market with many products as opposed to comparably few products. In the presence of large economies of scale, a potential supplier needs the capacity to enter the market on a large-scale (in relation to the size of the market) in order to compete successfully within the market of active suppliers. Large-scale entry might require relatively large sunk costs. Again, significant sunk costs raise obstacles to market entry of new competitors or suppliers and may constitute barriers to entry. If, for example, long contract durations lock-in customers to primarily deal with the established suppliers, new market entrants might not be able to achieve an efficient scale of production over a short or medium time period. This could hinder the market entry of new suppliers. Even when entry is not completely deterred, potential market entrants need time to achieve efficient levels of production, obtain the relevant information, raise capital and build the necessary plant and machinery. In this case, even if entry occurs, the established suppliers could nevertheless retain market power for a substantial period of time or in the worst case even drive upcoming competitors out of the market by, for example, pursuing aggressive pricing strategies. In particular, diversified firms often have advantages through economies of scope. These arise when a firm is engaged in a number of commercial activities at lower costs than would be incurred if different firms carried on each activity separately. Economies of scope are also involved when vertically integrated firms have advantages that may require a new entrant to enter the market at more than one level at the same time.

Strategic barriers to entry are intentionally set up by established suppliers in a market in order to deter potential suppliers from entry. The most common practice of an established supplier to prevent market entry is to conclude long-term supply contracts or exclusive contracts with customers. Demarcation and concession agreements, industry-wide or individual firms' standards for complementary goods or the development of propriety technical access systems have similar effects. If they have

---

291. Economies of scale exist where average costs fall as output rises.
292. Economies of scope mean that it costs less to produce two types of products together than to produce them separately.

been created by advertising and inter-brand competition, buyer preferences may suggest that there are strategic barriers to entry. This may entail cost disadvantages for new market entrants (e.g., sunk costs) in relation to established suppliers until the former have attracted attention and won a reputation of their own. Conversely, strategic market conduct by customers and the threat that they may switch to another supplier can lead to potential competitors effectively limiting the scope of powerful undertakings. Finally, strategic barriers could be barriers designed by suppliers already active in the market like aggressive price strategies, advertising campaigns or specific long-term contracts etc.

In theory, strategic barriers to entry exist if they are voluntarily set by the current market players to hinder entry in the market. The most frequent strategic barrier to entry is brand loyalty. Companies create brand loyalty that prevents potential competitors from entering the market because customers have such high brand loyalty that they would not switch to the newcomer anyway.

Statutory barriers to entry are those set up by either the government in the form of laws, regulations and administrative hurdles that hinder effective market entry or by established suppliers. An example of the latter case is the targeted and comprehensive use of commercial legal protection, particularly the method of protecting the whole environment around an innovation and possible technological alternatives by protective rights (so-called 'ring fencing').

Effectiveness of market entry: Another important part of the analysis is the effectiveness of market entry:

- *Timeliness of Entry*: In order to deter or counteract the competitive effects of concern, entrants must quickly achieve a significant impact on price in the relevant market. Generally, a market entry is considered timely only when it can be achieved *within two years* from initial planning to significant market impact.
- *Likelihood of Entry*: An entry alternative is likely if it would be profitable.
- *Sufficiency of Entry*: In as much as multiple entry generally is possible and individual entrants may flexibly choose their scale, committed entry generally is sufficient to deter or counteract the competitive effects of concern whenever entry is likely.

4.3.8 Market Phase, Level of Trade and Nature of the Product

The market phase refers to the development stage of a market and hence to the stability of its competitive conditions. It is thus not an independent factor, but provides important information for evaluating market shares and their developments. In particular, there may be differences between the two early market phases, the experimental and the growth phases, and the two later stages, the maturity and stagnation phases.

In markets which are just beginning to develop and where the speed of innovation is high, a large market share or even a sole position is not necessarily to be seen as

Chapter 4: Competition Practice

market power. Markets and market power may still be unstable or incalculable. The competitive conditions are subject to rapid change and are therefore unable to indicate a permanent scope for action. While the relevant good or service may have found a market, it can still be developed or improved, and other applications have not yet been discovered. Many competitive parameters can be used and their use may create a new demand rather than channelling demand away from existing competitors.

In the maturity and stagnation phase the competitive conditions in the market concerned generally change at a considerably slower pace than in the experimental and expansion phase. In relation to the general trend, market growth is below average. Products or production processes can hardly be improved any further and all possible uses and applications of the goods concerned have been discovered and tested. In markets in which the technology has been developed to such an extent and turnover volumes are declining or stagnating, competition through innovation and market entry tends to be rare. Any remaining competition parameters can only be used to respond to competitors' moves. Since current competitors in the market orient themselves in relation to existing competitive conditions, large market shares are less likely to decrease in later than in earlier market phases. The competitive advantages which individual firms may enjoy, for example because of their superior financial strength or excellent access to supply or sales markets, impede the progress of competitors and tend to squeeze out less integrated firms or companies with weaker resources. New entry is rather unlikely, especially if the market is stagnating.[293]

The level of trade and nature of the product are examined too. Level of trade is linked to the distinction between intermediate and final goods and services. Negative effects are in general less likely at the level of intermediate goods and services. The nature of the product plays a role in particular for final products in assessing both the likely negative and the likely positive effects. When assessing the likely negative effects, it is important whether the products on the market are more homogeneous or heterogeneous, whether the product is expensive, taking up a large part of the consumer's budget, or is inexpensive and whether the product is a one-off purchase or repeatedly purchased. In general, when the product is more heterogeneous, less expensive and resembles more a one-off purchase, vertical restraints are more likely to have negative effects.[294]

In the assessment of particular restraints *other factors* may have to be taken into account. Among these factors can be the cumulative effect, i.e., the coverage of the market by similar agreements, the duration of the agreements, whether the agreement is 'imposed' (mainly one party is subject to the restrictions or obligations) or 'agreed' (both parties accept restrictions or obligations), the regulatory environment and behaviour that may indicate or facilitate collusion like price leadership, pre-announced price changes and discussions on the 'right' price, price rigidity in response to excess capacity, price discrimination and past collusive behaviour.

---

293. (Bundeskartellamt, BkartA Grundsatzabteilung E/G 4, Auslegungsgrundsätze zur Fusionskontrolle, 2000, 33-34).
294. Paragraph 132.

4.3.9 Bidding Analysis

Competition in bidding markets is characterised by a few, typical elements: tenders take place infrequently; the value of each individual contract is usually very significant and contracts are typically awarded to a single successful bidder (the so-called 'winner-takes-all' principle). Thus, bidding markets can be described as:

- Competition is 'winners take all', so each supplier either wins all or none of the order.
- Competition is 'lumpy'. That is, each contest is large relative to a supplier's total sales in a period, so that there is an element of 'bet your company' in any contest.
- Competition begins afresh for each contract and for each customer. That is, if there is any repetition of a contest, there is no 'lock-in' by which the outcome of one contest importantly determines another.
- Sometimes, a fourth characteristic is assumed either implicitly or explicitly: Entry of new suppliers into the market is easy.[295]

For these reasons, market shares in bidding markets are of limited importance. Market shares as at a given date are less significant for the analysis of a bidding market. In such a market the fact that a particular company has had a number of recent 'wins' does not necessarily mean that one of its competitors will not be successful in the next round. Provided that it has a competitive product and that other factors are not heavily weighted in the first company's favour, a competitor can always win a valuable contract and increase its market share considerably at one go. However, as the Court stated in *GE/Commission* such a finding does not mean that market shares are of virtually no value in assessing the strength of the various manufacturers on a market of that kind, especially where those shares remain relatively stable or reveal that one undertaking is tending to strengthen its position. In this instance, an analysis over a five-year period provided additional insights. Thus, the Court reached the conclusion that:

> *even on a bidding market, the fact of a manufacturer maintaining, or even increasing, its market share over a number of years in succession is an indication of market strength. A time must come when the difference between one manufacturer's market share and that of its competitors can no longer be dismissed as a function of the limited number of competitions that constitute demand on the market.*[296]

These new requirements of the Court of First Instance comprise further economic analyses. Where market shares remain stable over time or even increase further economic assessment in bidding markets is required. In the following, the methodology of how to assess bidding markets is described.

---

295. (Klemperer 2005, 6).
296. (CFI, General Electric Company v. Commission, Case T-210/01 2005, 149-151).

Chapter 4: Competition Practice

4.3.9.1 *Economics in Bidding Markets*

The intensity of competition in bidding markets can be evaluated by means of bidding market analyses. This approach is based on the analysis of whether the two merging parties are close competitors and whether the merger leads to a reduction of the competition intensity. The 'closeness of the firms' indicates the competitive pressure of one company on the other. First, an analysis takes place of whether tenders are really important in the market concerned. The number of public tenders (e.g., in the building industry) can provide information on the importance of tenders in an industry. If such information is not publicly available, merging parties provide the required data. However, for detailed economic analyses the data provided by the parties lacks completeness. This is quite self-evident since the parties should not possess crucial information on pricing and offers of their competitors. Therefore, customer surveys are appropriate tools to obtain all the necessary information about the bidding behaviour for further analyses. The issues which should be covered by customer surveys in the course of bidding market analyses are the following:

- Are the merging parties close competitors and are the merging parties able to exercise competitive pressure on each other?
- Is the bidding price in a tender influenced by the participation of one or both merging parties?

Since such data is rarely available, the instrument of an independent customer survey is preferred.

4.3.9.2 *Independent Customer Surveys*

To perform the customer surveys, electronic questionnaires are developed and programmed. Since in most cases the customers are business customers, an interview over the internet is efficient and non time-consuming. Specific survey software is used which avoids any form of abuse and guarantees confidentiality. This is a very important issue since highly confidential data about an industry are exchanged. The questionnaires are designed based on working assumptions about the relevant product and geographic markets. In the design of the questionnaires particular attention is given to the market conditions. Before the actual performance of the interviews takes place, the comprehensibility of the questionnaire is checked in a pre-test-phase.

The issues to be covered as well as the number of customers to be interviewed influence the representativeness of the customer survey. Usually about 50% of the customers – either in absolute numbers or by revenues generated – should be questioned. Where few customers generate a significant part of the revenues, an analysis of these customers provides more insights than an analysis of a considerable number of customers which account for only a small part of turnover.

The time period to be covered should be over several years; however, this depends on the issues as well as on the number of customers. Customer data such as contacts, e-mail addresses etc. are usually available from the merging parties.

4.3.9.3 Analysis of Customer Surveys

After the appropriate data are generated by means of a customer survey, data is analysed according to established standards.[297] Whereas the data of each single tender may include useful information, further statistical analyses focus on the following key figures:

- Encounter ratio between the merging parties.
- Encounter ratio to other bidders.
- Size of the other bidders.
- Runner-Up.
- Price difference.

In the following, those key figures are discussed.

4.3.9.4 Encounter Ratio between the Merging Parties

Firstly, the analyses are focused on how often the merging parties take part at the same time in a tender procedure. The number of encounters is an indicator of the so-called 'closeness of the companies'. Since suppliers of goods cannot take part in all tenders, they concentrate on those tenders, where they assume they have the best chance of winning the tender due to technical specifications.

4.3.9.5 Encounter Ratio between Two Other Bidders

The number of encounters between the merging parties is compared to the number of encounters with other bidders. That firm which bears the most competitive pressure on the merging parties is identified. This kind of encounter ratio with other firms shows how often two firms compete in tenders and therefore illustrates the existing closeness of these firms.

Figure 4.9 Example of Competitive Pressure between Three Firms

Tender	Firm A in 000's	Firm B in 000's	Firm C in 000's	First Best Bid	Second Best Bid
1*	187	192	78	C	A
2	125	158	131	A	C
3	104	89	93	B	C
4	65	85	69	A	C
5	189	147	156	B	C

---

297. A framework for statistical analyses of bidding markets can be found in (Loriot, Rouxel, & Durand 2004).

Chapter 4: Competition Practice

Tender	Firm A in 000's	Firm B in 000's	Firm C in 000's	First Best Bid	Second Best Bid
6	65	116	78	A	C
Total Sales	255	236	78		
Market Shares	45%	41%	14%		

*Example: Firm A has in tender 1 a bid of 187.000. The other bids from firm B are 192.000 and from firm C 78.000. Firm C won the tender. Firm A had the second best offer.

Although the market share of firm C is only 14%, the competitive pressure of firm C on firm A with a market share of 45% is the highest one. In all the six tender procedures, firm C exercised the most competitive pressure on firm A.

4.3.9.6 Size of Other Bidders

In addition to the occurrence of encounters between firms, an analysis of the size of these firms is important. Did only small firms on the fringe bid or did the merging parties compete with huge international players? In the latter case, the competitive pressure on the merging parties is more significant.

4.3.9.7 Runner-Up

The second best bid is in the view of a customer nearly as good as the first bid. The second best bid therefore exercises the most competitive pressure on the first bid. For this reason, the Runner-Up in all tenders is analysed in detail. In doing so it is important to check whether one of the merging parties was often the Runner-Up to the other merging party. The aim is to discover which of those firms, bears the most competitive pressure on the merging parties.

4.3.9.8 Price Difference

A statistical analysis of the effects of the bidding behaviour of the merging parties on absolute prices can be determined by considering the unit prices of the announced products. For this reason – only for homogenous products – information about the total value of the tender as well as the number of products in the tender is required. With this data it can be tested whether merging parties have an effect on the price difference between the first and the second best bid. More specifically the relative price differences between the first and the second best bid are compared. If the differences are smaller between the merging parties than the differences between other competitors, then the competitive pressure between the merging parties is higher and has more influence on prices than other competitors.

4.3.9.9 Further Analyses

The statistical analyses described previously answer the question of whether the merging parties impose competitive pressure on each other or not. Further analyses include the assessment of the degree of competitive pressure. The degree of competitive pressure can be estimated by means of an econometric model. The model analyses the influence of the participation of a merging firm on the price. Besides the information about the first and the second best bid, information about the project size, the number and identity of the other bidders, the products in question as well as the price per unit is necessary for these analyses. With this data the influence on the price difference can be obtained using the following model:[298]

$$\left(1 - \frac{P_{2,i}}{P_{1,i}}\right) = \beta_0 + \beta_1 DUM_i + \beta_2 NUM_i + \beta_3 VOL_i + \beta_4 FOR_i + \mu_i$$

Respectively

$$P_{ppu,i} = \beta_0 + \beta_1 DUM_i + \beta_2 NUM_i + \beta_3 VOL_i + \beta_4 FOR_i + \mu_i$$

This model tests whether the participation of the second merging firm does influence the price difference in tenders where the first merging firm gave the best bid. The endogenous variable is the price per unit or the price difference and can be quantified here. If one merging firm does impose competitive pressure on the other merging firm β_1, the coefficient of the dummy variable for the participation of the first firm, has to be negative and significant.

4.4 EUROPEAN ECONOMIC APPROACH IN ARTICLE 101

Competition practitioners acknowledge that any assessment in Article 101 involves economics. As we will see in this chapter, the scope of economic analysis depends on the agreement and the related economic circumstances.

The Court of Justice of the EU has developed over the years' solid jurisprudence about the type of economic analysis requested. This section covers the main case law whereas the following sections provide practical guidance about how to perform such an economic analysis despite the fact that the applicant of the legal rules is not a trained competition economist.

4.4.1 Object and Effect

Article 101(1) prohibits agreements, decisions and concerted practices whose *'object or effect'* is the prevention, restriction or distortion of competition within the Common Market. Thus, Article 101(1) distinguishes between those agreements that have a

---

298. This model is based on Bajari and Ye. (Bajari & Ye 2003).

restriction of competition as their object and those agreements that have a restriction of competition as their effect. The analysis of the object and the analysis of the effect of an agreement need to be clearly separated. The first is intended to assess the objective function of a particular set of conditions in its contractual context. The second one is designed to establish whether, an agreement whose object is not anti-competitive is nevertheless liable, in the specific market context in which it is to operate, to affect appreciably competition in the common market.

The restraint of competition may be *either* the object or effect of the enterprise's conduct. Once it has been established that an agreement has as its object the restriction of competition, there is no need to take account of its concrete effects. In other words, for the purpose of applying Article 101(1) no actual anti-competitive effects need to be demonstrated where the agreement has a restriction of competition as its object.

Restrictions of competition *by object* are those that by their very nature have the potential of restricting competition. These are restrictions, which, in light of the objectives pursued by the Community anti-trust rules, have such a high potential for negative effects on competition that it is unnecessary for the purposes of applying Article 101(1) to demonstrate any actual effects on the market.

The distinction between 'restrictions by object' and 'restrictions by effect' arises from the fact that certain forms of collusion between undertakings reveal such a sufficient degree of harm to competition that there is no need to examine their actual or potential effects.[299] Such types of coordination between undertakings can be regarded, by their very nature, as being harmful to the proper functioning of normal competition.[300] These are restrictions which in the light of the objectives pursued by the competition rules are so likely to have negative effects on competition, in particular on the price, quantity or quality of goods or services, that it is unnecessary to demonstrate any actual or likely anti-competitive effects on the market.[301] The types of restrictions that are considered to constitute restrictions 'by object' differ depending on whether the agreements are entered into between actual or potential competitors or between non-competitors (e.g., between a supplier and a distributor). In the case of agreements between competitors (horizontal agreements), restrictions of competition by object include, in particular, price-fixing, output limitation and sharing of markets and customers. As regards agreements between non-competitors (vertical agreements), the category of restrictions by object includes, in particular, fixing (minimum) resale prices and restrictions which limit sales into particular territories or to particular customer groups.[302]

---

299. Judgments in (ECJ, CB v. Commission, Case C-67 / 13 P 2014, para. 49); (ECJ, Dole Food and Dole Fresh Fruit Europe v. Commission, C-286/13 P 2015, para. 113).
300. See for example the judgments of the Court of Justice in (ECJ, CB v. Commission, Case C-67 / 13 P 2014, para. 50); (ECJ, Dole Food and Dole Fresh Fruit Europe v. Commission, C-286/13 P 2015, para. 114); (ECJ, Expedia, C-226/11 2012, para. 36 and case law cited).
301. Judgments in (ECJ, CB v. Commission, Case C-67 / 13 P 2014, para. 51); (ECJ, Dole Food and Dole Fresh Fruit Europe v. Commission, C-286/13 P 2015, para. 115).
302. (Commission Staff Working Document on restrictions of competition 'by object' for the purpose of defining which agreements may benefit from the De Minimis Notice 2015).

This presumption is based on the serious nature of the restriction and on the experience that restrictions of competition by object are likely to produce negative effects on the market as such thereby jeopardising the objectives pursued by the EU competition rules. Restrictions by object directly harm consumers because they have to pay higher prices for the goods and services in question.[303]

Agreements and decisions are often explicit enough for an anti-competitive purpose to be evident that might be in contradiction with the objectives set out in the Treaty of Lisbon without confirmation from other sources. Nevertheless, the circumstances and context of the agreement or decision are relevant and in many cases crucial for removing any possible doubt as to the purpose behind it.[304] According to a fairly well-defined guidance in the case law, in order to determine whether a given clause has the object of restricting competition within the meaning of Article 101(1), it is necessary to consider the aims pursued by the agreement as such in the *light of the economic context* in which the agreement is to be applied:[305]

> In order to establish whether an undertaking can be found to have infringed Article 85(1) (new Article 101(1)) of the Treaty, the only relevant questions are whether it participated with other undertakings in an agreement having the object or effect of restricting competition and whether that agreement was liable to affect trade between Member States. The question whether the individual participation of the undertaking concerned in that agreement, notwithstanding its limited scale, restricts competition or affects trade between Member States is entirely irrelevant.
> Moreover, that provision does not require the restrictions of competition ascertained actually to have appreciably affected trade between Member States but merely requires that it be established that the agreement was capable of having that effect.[306]

Accordingly, no actual effect on the market is regarded to be necessary for the rule to apply, which corresponds to the preventive nature of the rule. If the agreement seeks to restrict competition within the meaning of Article 101(1), an automatic prohibition must be considered.[307] For this reason merely entering into an anti-competitive agreement is prohibited even if, temporarily, it may not be followed by the objectives achieved.[308] Thus, anti-competitive agreements that have not been implemented infringe Article 101(1) and may be validated only if an exemption under Article 101(3) is granted.[309]

The assessment of whether or not an agreement has as its object the restriction of competition is based on a number of factors. These factors include, in particular, the

---

303. (European Commission, Communication from the Commission Notice Guidelines on the application of Art. 81(3) of the Treaty 2004).
304. (ECJ, Allgemeine Elektrizitäts-Gesellschaft AEG-Telefunken AG v. Commission, Case 107/82 1983).
305. (ECJ, Compagnie Royale Asturienne des Mines SA and Rheinzink GmbH v. Commission, Joined cases 29/83 and 30/83 1984).
306. (CFI, Tréfileurope Sales SARL v. Commission, Case T-141/89 1995, 10).
307. (ECJ, Verband der Sachversicherer e.V. v. Commission, Case 45/85 1987).
308. (ECJ, SC Belasco and others v. Commission, Case 246/86 1989, 15); (ECJ, Sandoz prodotti farmaceutici SpA v. Commission, Case C-277/87 1990, 13); (Decision IV/31.149 on Polypropylene 1986, 29–30); (Decision 89/191/ on LdPE IV/31.866 1988, 33–34).
309. (Decision 72/41 on Henkel/Colgate IV/26.917 1971).

Chapter 4: Competition Practice

content of the agreement and the objective aims pursued by it. It may also be necessary to consider the context in which it is (to be) applied and the actual conduct and behaviour of the parties on the market. In other words, an examination of the facts underlying the agreement and the specific circumstances in which it operates may be required before it can be concluded whether a particular restriction constitutes a restriction of competition by object. The way in which an agreement is actually implemented may reveal a restriction by object even where the formal agreement does not contain an express provision to that effect. Evidence of subjective intent on the part of the parties to restrict competition is a relevant factor but not a necessary condition.[310]

Where the object is not anti-competitive, the analysis proceeds to the second-phase, regarding the *impact*, which the agreement is specifically likely to have on competition. Account must be taken of both actual and potential effects. For an agreement to be restrictive by effect it must affect actual or potential competition to such an extent that on the relevant market negative effects on prices, output, innovation or the variety or quality of goods and services can be expected with a reasonable degree of probability. Such negative effects must be appreciable. The prohibition rule of Article 101(1) does not apply when the identified anti-competitive effects are insignificant. Again, this test reflects the economic approach needed to assess Article 101(1). The prohibition of Article 101(1) only applies where on the basis of proper market analysis it can be concluded that the agreement has likely anti-competitive effects on the market.[311] It should also be borne in mind that the general criterion for deciding whether an agreement has the object or effect of restricting competition is how competition would have operated in the market in question in the absence of that agreement, the counterfactual analysis.

To summarise, the analysis of the object and the analysis of the effect are to be clearly distinguished. Whereas the Commission used to state quite frequently in the past that a particular agreement infringes Article 101(1) in the case law of the Court of Justice of the EU, now, this distinction is observed more clearly. However, it is less clear which principle is applied.[312] A clear, perhaps the clearest, example of the application of the analytical approach based on the distinction between object and effect can be found in *Delimitis v. Henninger Bräu* discussed further below.[313]

4.4.2 Ancillary Restrictions

The economic approach in the assessment of Article 101(1) is controlled by the insistence of both the Commission and the Court of Justice of the EU to analyse whether restrictive clauses in agreements, which fall outside Article 101(1), are really

---

310. (Guidelines on the Art. 81(3) of the Treaty 2004, 22).
311. See in this respect (CFI, ENS, Eurostar (UK), EPS, UIC, NS and SNCF v. Commission, Joined cases T-374/94, T-375/94, T-384/94 and T-388/94 1998).
312. Opinion of the Advocate General Tesauro in (ECJ, Gøttrup-Klim e.a. Grovvareforeninger v. Dansk Landbrugs Grovvareselskab AmbA, Case C-250/92 1994, 16).
313. (ECJ, Stergios Delimitis v. Henninger Bräu AG, Case C-234/89 1991).

necessary to secure the implementation of a lawful agreement. The Court of Justice of the EU confirmed in a number of judgments, that certain provisions and obligations fall outside Article 101(1) even though the freedom of the parties to the agreement or of third parties is clearly restrained. The ancillary restraints doctrine emerged.

It is apparent from the case law of the Court of Justice that if a given operation or activity is not covered by the prohibition rule laid down in Article 101 EC, owing to its neutrality or positive effect in terms of competition, a restriction of the commercial autonomy of one or more of the participants in that operation or activity is not covered by that prohibition rule either, if that restriction is objectively necessary to the implementation of that operation or that activity and proportionate to the objectives of one or the other (see judgments in (*ECJ, Remia BV and others v. Commission*, Case 42/84 1985, paragraphs 19 and 20); (ECJ, *Pronuptia de Paris GmbH v. Pronuptia de Paris Irmgard Schillgallis*, Case 161/84 1986, paragraphs 15–17); (ECJ, *Gøttrup-Klim e.a. Grovvareforeninger v. Dansk Landbrugs Grovvareselskab AmbA*, Case C-250/92 1994, paragraph 35), and (ECJ, *H.G. Oude Luttikhuis and others v. Verenigde Coöperatieve Melkindustrie Coberco BA.*, Case C-399/93 1995, paragraphs 12–15).[314]

The Court of Justice clarified this doctrine in its *Mastercard* judgment. Where it is not possible to dissociate such a restriction from the main operation or activity without jeopardising its existence and aims, it is necessary to examine the compatibility of that restriction with Article 101 in conjunction with the compatibility of the main operation or activity to which it is ancillary, even though, taken in isolation, such a restriction may appear on the face of it to be covered by the prohibition rule in Article 101(1). Where it is a matter of determining whether an anti-competitive restriction can escape the prohibition laid down in Article 101(1) because it is ancillary to a main operation that is not anti-competitive in nature, it is necessary to inquire whether that operation would be impossible to carry out in the absence of the restriction in question. Thus, the objective necessity test concerns the question whether, in the absence of a given restriction of commercial autonomy, a main operation or activity which is not caught by the prohibition laid down in Article 101(1) and to which that restriction is secondary, is likely not to be implemented or not to proceed.[315] Only those restrictions which are necessary in order for the main operation to be able to function in any event may be regarded as falling within the scope of the theory of ancillary restrictions'.

In *Gottrup-Klim v. Dansk Landbrugs*,[316] the Court of Justice found that in order to escape the prohibition laid down in Article 101(1) the restrictions imposed on members must be limited to what is necessary to ensure that the cooperative functions properly and maintains its contractual power in relation to producers. Thus, even when an agreement is not a restriction of competition it is still required to ensure that the restrictive clauses are objectively necessary.[317]

---

314. (ECJ, MasterCard Inc. and Others v. Commission, C-832/12 P 2014, 89).
315. (ECJ, MasterCard Inc. and Others v. Commission, C-832/12 P 2014, 90–93).
316. (ECJ, Gøttrup-Klim e.a. Grovvareforeninger v. Dansk Landbrugs Grovvareselskab AmbA, Case C-250/92 1994, 32–34).
317. *Ibid.*, 'The compatibility of the statutes of such an association with the Community rules on competition cannot be assessed in the abstract. It will depend on the particular clauses in the statues and the economic conditions prevailing on the markets concerned.' para. 31

If an agreement in its main parts, for instance a distribution agreement or a joint venture does not have as its object or effect the restriction of competition, then restrictions, which are directly related to and necessary for the implementation of that transaction, also fall outside Article 101(1).[318] A restriction is directly related to the main transaction if it is subordinate to the implementation of that transaction and is inseparably linked to it. The test of necessity implies that the restriction must be objectively necessary for the implementation of the main transaction and be proportionate to it.[319]

Thus, under the ancillary restraints doctrine, the overall agreement is examined in the abstract to determine whether it is restrictive to competition or not. If the agreement is beneficial to competition, restrictions and obligations fall outside Article 101(1) where they are inherent to this agreement. Thus, the concept of ancillary restraints covers any alleged restriction of competition which is directly related and necessary to the implementation of a main non-restrictive transaction and proportionate to it.

The application of the ancillary restraint concept must be distinguished from the application of the defence under Article 101(3) which relates to certain economic benefits produced by overall restrictive agreements and which is balanced against the restrictive effects of the agreements. If, for example, the main object of a franchise agreement does not restrict competition, then restrictions, which are necessary for the proper functioning of the agreement, such as obligations aimed at protecting the uniformity and reputation of the franchise system, fall outside Article 101(1). No exemption according to Article 101(3) is necessary.[320]

The distinction between the ancillary restraint doctrine in Article 101(1) and the indispensability test in Article 101(3) is that under Article 101(3) the test is whether the clause is necessary for the attainment of the benefits identified whereas under Article 101(1), the question is, whether the clause is necessary for the existence and the implementation of the agreement.

The Court of Justice has declared in a growing number of judgments that certain provisions and obligations fall outside Article 101(1) even though freedom of the parties to the agreement or third parties was clearly restrained.

The Court of Justice in *Metro I* applied this line of reasoning[321], for example. In this case, the Court of Justice stated that a particular type of distribution system, which

---

'Prohibition of dual membership does not, therefore, constitute a restriction of competition within the meaning of Article 85(1) of the Treaty and may even have beneficial effects on competition.' para. 34 'So, in order to escape the prohibition laid down in Article 85(1) of the Treaty, the restrictions imposed on members by the statutes of cooperative purchasing associations must be limited to what is necessary to ensure that the cooperative functions properly and maintains its contractual power in relation to producers.' paras 35 and 45.
318. See e.g., (ECJ, H.G. Oude Luttikhuis and others v. Verenigde Coöperatieve Melkindustrie Coberco BA., Case C-399/93 1995, 12–14).
319. (Guidelines on the Art. 81(3) of the Treaty 2004).
320. See (ECJ, Pronuptia de Paris GmbH v. Pronuptia de Paris Irmgard Schillgallis, Case 161/84 1986).
321. (ECJ, Metro SB-Großmärkte GmbH & Co. KG v. Commission, Case 26-76 1977), 'Provided that the obligations undertaken in connexion with such safeguards do not exceed the objective in

limits price competition, could fall outside the prohibition.[322] The judgment of the Court of Justice in *Nungesser*[323] is another example:

> It appears therefore that the contracts at issue, by granting an exclusive license over breeders' rights for INRA maize seeds in respect of Germany, constitute the most appropriate means of attaining the objectives of the common agricultural policy, having regard to the particular requirements inherent in the production and marketing of those seeds.[324]

The Commission applied the doctrine in its decision *P&I Clubs* – Pooling Agreement and found that:

> a claim-sharing agreement such as the Pooling Agreement entails an agreement between the parties on a number of aspects of their insurance activity. Indeed, it is inherent in any claim-sharing agreement that its members decide in common at least the policy conditions and the level of cover offered. ... Such an agreement cannot be considered anti-competitive, at least when the claim sharing is necessary to allow its members to provide a type of insurance that they could not provide alone. Indeed, there cannot be a restriction of competition when the members of the pool are not actual or potential competitors, because they are unable to insure alone the risks covered by the pool. If anything, such claim sharing indeed strengthens competition since it allows several insurers, which are not able to provide such cover to put their resources in common and create a new player. To the extent that the claim sharing does not violate Article 85(1) (new Article 101(1)), the restrictions imposed on the parties to the claim-sharing agreement, which are indispensable to the proper functioning of that claim sharing, are not covered by Article 85(1) (new Article 101(1)). They must be considered ancillary to, or inherent in, the claim sharing.[325]

---

view they do not in themselves constitute a restriction on competition but are the corollary of the principal obligation and contribute to its fulfilment.' para. 27

322. Ibid.:

> For specialist wholesalers and retailers the desire to maintain a certain price level, which corresponds to the desire to preserve, in the interests of the consumers, the possibility of the continued existence of this channel of distribution in conjunction with new methods of distribution based on a different type of competition policy, forms one of the objectives which may be pursued without necessarily falling under the prohibition contained in Article 85(1). para. 21

> This was confirmed in (ECJ, Metro SB-Großmärkte GmbH & Co. KG v. Commission, Case 75/84 1986):

> The Court recognised in that connection in its judgement in Metro I that some limitation in price competition was to be regarded as inherent in any selective distribution system, because the prices applied by specialist dealers necessarily remained within a much narrower margin than would be expected if there were competition between specialist dealers and non-specialist dealers. para. 45

323. (ECJ, L.C. Nungesser KG and Kurt Eisele v. Commission, Case 258/78 1982) 'Having regard to the specific nature of the products in question, the Court concludes that, ... the grant of an open exclusive license ... is not in itself incompatible with Article 85(1) of the Treaty.' para. 58
324. Ibid., para. 21.
325. (Decision IV/D-1/30.373 and No. IV/D-1/37.143 on P & I Clubs, IGA and P & I Clubs, Pooling Agreement 1999, 65–68) and (ECJ, Gøttrup-Klim e.a. Grovvareforeninger v. Dansk Landbrugs

Chapter 4: Competition Practice

In its most recent Notice on the applicability of Article 101 to horizontal cooperation agreements,[326] the Commission clarified its position on the doctrine further. The Commission stated that it is inherent to the functioning of a production joint venture, which also markets the jointly manufactured goods that decisions on prices need to be taken jointly by the parties to such an agreement. In this case, the inclusion of provisions on prices or output does not automatically cause the agreement to fall under Article 101(1). The provisions on prices or output will have to be assessed *together* with other effects of the joint venture on the market to determine the applicability of Article 101(1).[327]

In general, ancillary restraints are those which are directly related to the agreement and objectively necessary for its existence. However, they also must remain *subordinate* in importance to the main object of the agreement.[328] Thus for an R&D joint venture the 'main object' of the agreement would be the complete or partial integration of the R&D operations of the parties in a particular field of research. An obligation on the parties not to carry out research independently in this area for the lifetime of the joint venture could, if it were objectively necessary for the implementation of the agreement, be described as a subordinate clause. On the other hand it would be difficult to argue persuasively that a clause which prevented these parties from competing with each other in another, unrelated field is directly related to the agreement or objectively necessary for its existence.[329]

4.4.3 Effect on Trade between Member States

In order for Article 101(1) to apply the agreement must have an effect on trade between Member States. This hurdle is of significance since if it is not satisfied, the matter in question remains within the jurisdiction of the relevant Member State.

4.4.3.1 Developments in the Effect on Trade Concept

The Court has frequently ruled that the condition concerning the effect on trade between Member States, contained in Articles 101 and 102, is intended to determine the scope of Community law in relation to that of the laws of the Member States.[330]

As early as in *Wilhelm v. Bundeskartellamt*[331], the Court stated in a preliminary ruling that some agreements may be subject to both national and Community law. The

---

Grovvareselskab AmbA, Case C-250/92 1994), where the restrictions necessary for the proper functioning of a cooperative were considered not to be covered by Art. 101(1).
326. (European Commission, Commission Notice – Guidelines on the applicability of Art. 81 of the EC Treaty to horizontal cooperation agreements 2001).
327. *Ibid.*, para. 90 and footnote 18.
328. (European Commission, Commission Notice concerning the assessment of cooperative joint ventures pursuant to Art. 85 of the EEC Treaty 1993).
329. (Faull & Nikpay 1999, 92).
330. (ECJ, Établissements Consten S.à.R.L. and Grundig-Verkaufs-GmbH v. Commission, Joined cases 56 and 58-64 1966).
331. (ECJ, Walt Wilhelm and other v. Bundeskartellamt, Case 14/68 1969).

condition about trade between Member States limits the scope of Community law. It limits that of national law only to that extent that Community law takes precedence.[332]

The concept of 'effect on trade between Member States' is thus best understood as a rule of jurisdiction, enabling Community law to regulate all restrictive agreements having appreciable repercussions at Community level. Whether an agreement affects trade between Member States is closely connected with the question of whether the agreement prevents, restricts or distorts competition and whether, if it does, the effect of the agreement is appreciable.

The hurdle has not, however, proven too difficult for the Court to surmount. The concept of trade has been described by the Court as having a wide scope. It covers all economic activity, including not only the supply of goods but also the supply of services[333] and even the right of a trader in one Member State to set up business in another, like in *Pronuptia*[334], where the Court included in the concept of effect on trade between Member States the possibility of a firm becoming established in another Member State.

The Court adopted a broad test in *Consten and Grundig*. The Court held that in order for an agreement to affect trade between Member States:

> *it must be possible to foresee with a sufficient degree of probability on the basis of a set of objective factors of law or of fact that it may have an influence, direct or indirect, actual or potential, on the pattern of trade between Member States such as might prejudice the aim of a single market in all the Member States.*[335]

The condition that trade between Member States be affected is easily satisfied. In practice, this requirement is met if the agreement alters the normal flow or pattern of trade, or causes trade to develop differently from the way it would have developed in the absence of the agreement. Restrictions that affect intra-state trade stand in contradiction to the principle of a unified common market with no internal borders or other obstacles to free trade.

The Court of Justice also held that, for restrictive arrangements to be prohibited by Article 101(1) it is not necessary for them to appreciably affect trade between Member States but merely to be capable of having that effect.[336]

Building and Constructions Industry[337] is another case where the Commission considered that trade between Member States is affected appreciably by the agreement. The very nature of the rules and regulations in question had the effect of influencing trade flows between Member States.

---

332. (Korah 1994, 50).
333. such as banking and money transmission, insurance loss adjustment, foreign exchange brooking, the management of artistic copyrights, the organisation of trade fairs, agency services, message forwarding services, television broadcasts, including broadcasts by satellite, and the services of public utilities, such as gas and electricity, the performance of individual artists and the provision of consulting services by an individual have been held to be trade.
334. (ECJ, Pronuptia de Paris GmbH v. Pronuptia de Paris Irmgard Schillgallis, Case 161/84 1986).
335. (ECJ, Établissements Consten S.à.R.L. and Grundig-Verkaufs-GmbH v. Commission, Joined cases 56 and 58-64 1966).
336. (ECJ, Miller International Schallplatten GmbH v. Commission, Case 19/77 1978, 15).
337. (Decision IV/31.572 and 32.571 on Building and construction industry in the Netherlands 1992).

Chapter 4: Competition Practice

Even an agreement confined to activities in a single Member State may infringe Article 101(1). In *Vereeniging van Cementhandelaaren v. Commission*[338], a Dutch trade association, of which most Dutch cement dealers were members, recommended prices at which its members should sell in the Netherlands. It was argued that, as this did not apply to exports, it did not 'affect trade between Member States '. But the Court stated that:

> *An agreement extending over the whole of the territory of a member state by its very nature has the effect of reinforcing the compartmentalisation of markets on a national basis, thereby holding up the economic interpenetration which the Treaty is designed to bring about and protecting domestic production.*

> *In particular, the provisions of the agreement which are mutually binding on the members of the applicant association and the prohibition by the association on all sales to resellers who are not authorised by it make it more difficult for producers or sellers from other Member States to be active in or to penetrate the Netherlands market.*[339]

The finding that an agreement which extends over the whole territory of one Member State has the effect of reinforcing compartmentalisation of national markets has been confirmed in several other judgments,[340] because such agreements result in the subdivision of the Common market into several national markets characterised by artificially differentiated conditions.[341]

The Court of Justice of the EU does not apply a quantitative test for appreciability, but as the Court established in a preliminary ruling on *Völk v. Vervaecke*,[342] an agreement falls outside Article 101(1) if it is unlikely to have an appreciable effect on competition or trade between Member States, even if its object is plainly a restriction of competition:[343]

> *If an agreement is to be capable of affecting trade between Member States it must be possible to foresee with a sufficient degree of probability on the basis of a set of objectives, factors of law or of fact that the agreement in question may have an influence direct or indirect, actual or potential, on the pattern of trade between Member States in such a way that it might hinder the attainment of the objectives of a single market between States. Moreover the prohibition in Article 81(1) (new Article 101(1)) is applicable only if the agreement in question also has as its object or effects the prevention, restriction or distortion of competition within the Common market. Those conditions must be understood by reference to the actual circumstances of the agreement. Consequently an agreement falls outside the prohibition in Article 81 (new Article 101(1)) when it has only an insignificant*

---

338. (Decision 8/72 on Vereeniging van Cementhandelaren 1972, 29).
339. *Ibid.*, paras 29–30.
340. (ECJ, Remia BV and others v. Commission, Case 42/84 1985, 22).
    (ECJ, Bundeskartellamt v. Volkswagen AG and VAG Leasing GmbH., Case C.266/93 1995, 26).
341. (ECJ, SC Belasco and other v. Commission, Case 246/86 1989).
342. (ECJ, Franz Völk v. S.P.R.L. Ets J. Vervaecke, Case 5/69 1969).
343. Völk made less than 1% of the washing machines produced in Germany, and the Court ruled that even absolute territorial protection granted to its exclusive distributor for Belgium and Luxembourg would not infringe Art. 81(1), if it did not restrict competition and noticeably affect inter-state trade.

effect on the markets, taking into account the weak position which the persons concerned have on the market of the product.[344]

The Court of First Instance confirmed in *SPO v. Commission*[345] the finding of the Commission and added that since potential effect is sufficient, future development of trade may be taken into account in assessing the effect of the restrictive arrangements on trade between Member States, whether or not it was foreseeable. The applicants could not invoke the limited extent between the Member States on the building sector since a mere potential effect on trade is sufficient for infringement of Article 101(1).

4.4.3.2 Guidelines on the Effect on Trade Concept

In their interpretation of Articles 101 and 102, the then Court of Justice of the EU has already substantially clarified the content and scope of the *concept of effect on trade* between Member States. To clarify some issues, however, the Commission published guidelines on the effect on trade concept in 2004.[346] They spell out a rule indicating when agreements are in general unlikely to be capable of appreciably affecting trade between Member States.

The effect on trade criterion is an autonomous Community law criterion, which must be assessed separately in each case. It is a jurisdictional criterion, which defines the scope of application of Community competition law with respect to Articles 101 and 102.

In the case of Article 101, it is the agreement that must be capable of affecting trade between Member States. It is not necessary, for the purposes of establishing Community law jurisdiction, to establish a link between the alleged restriction of competition and the capacity of the agreement to affect trade between Member States. Non-restrictive agreements may also affect trade between Member States.

In the case of Article 102, it is the abuse that must affect trade between Member States. This does not imply, however, that each element of the behaviour must be assessed in isolation. Conduct that forms part of an overall strategy pursued by the dominant undertaking must be assessed in terms of its overall impact. Where a dominant undertaking adopts various practices in pursuit of the same aim, for instance practices that aim at eliminating or foreclosing competitors, in order for Article 102 to be applicable to all the practices forming part of this overall strategy, it is sufficient that at least one of these practices is capable of affecting trade between Member States.

4.4.3.2.1 Trade between Member States

The Commission states in its guidelines that an effect on trade 'between Member States' implies that there needs to be an impact on cross-border economic activity

---

344. (ECJ, Franz Völk v. S.P.R.L. Ets J. Vervaecke, Case 5/69 1969, 5–7).
345. (CFI, Vereniging van Samenwerkende Prijsregelende Organisaties in de Bouwnijverheid and others v. Commission, Case T-29/92 1995).
346. (Commission Notice on the effect on trade concept 2004, 81–96).

Chapter 4: Competition Practice

involving at least two Member States. The agreement or practice is not required to affect trade between the whole of one Member State and the whole of another Member State. Articles 101 and 102 may also be applicable in cases involving part of a Member State, provided that the effect on trade is appreciable.

The nature of the agreement and practice provides an indication from a qualitative point of view of the ability of the agreement or practice to affect trade between Member States. Some agreements and practices are by their very nature capable of affecting trade between Member States, whereas others require more detailed analysis in this respect. Cross-border cartels are an example of the former, whereas joint ventures confined to the territory of a single Member State are an example of the latter.[347] The nature of the products covered by the agreements or practices also provides an indication of whether trade between Member States is capable of being affected. The market position of the undertakings concerned and their sales volumes are indicative from a quantitative point of view of the ability of the agreement or practice concerned to affect trade between Member States.[348]

The actual effects on trade between Member States are those that are produced by the agreement or practice once it is implemented. The potential effects are those that may occur in the future with a sufficient degree of probability. In other words, foreseeable market developments must be taken into account. The inclusion of indirect or potential effects in the analysis of effects on trade between Member States does not mean that the analysis can be based on remote or hypothetical effects.[349]

4.4.3.2.2 Appreciability of Affecting Trade between Member States

Agreements and practices fall outside the scope of application of Articles 101 and 102 when they affect the market only insignificantly owing to the weak position of the undertakings concerned on the market for the products in question. Appreciability can be appraised in particular by reference to the position and the importance of the relevant undertakings on the market for the products concerned. The assessment of appreciability depends on the circumstances of each individual case, in particular the nature of the agreement and practice, the nature of the products covered and the market position of the undertakings concerned. When by its very nature the agreement or practice is capable of affecting trade between Member States, the appreciability threshold is lower than in the case of agreements and practices that are not by their very nature capable of affecting trade between Member States. The stronger the market position of the undertakings concerned, the more likely it is that an agreement or practice capable of affecting trade between Member States can be held to do so appreciably.[350] The Commission holds the view that in principle agreements are not capable of appreciably affecting trade between Member States when the following cumulative conditions are met:

---

347. (Commission Notice on the effect on trade concept 2004, 29).
348. (Commission Notice on the effect on trade concept 2004, 30).
349. (Commission Notice on the effect on trade concept 2004, 43).
350. (Commission Notice on the effect on trade concept 2004, 45).

- The aggregate market share of the parties on any relevant market within the Community affected by the agreement does not exceed 5%.
- In the case of horizontal agreements, the aggregate annual Community turnover of the undertakings concerned in the products covered by the agreement does not exceed EUR 40 million. In the case of agreements concerning the joint buying of products the relevant turnover shall be the parties' combined purchases of the products covered by the agreement.

In order to apply the market share threshold, it is necessary to determine the relevant market. This consists of the relevant product market and the relevant geographic market. The market shares are to be calculated on the basis of sales value data or, where appropriate, purchase value data. If value data are not available, estimates based on other reliable market information, including volume data may be used.[351]

In qualitative terms the assessment of agreements covering only part *of a Member State* is approached in the same way as in the case of agreements covering the whole of a Member State.[352] Where an agreement forecloses access to a regional market, then for trade to be appreciably affected, the volume of sales affected must be significant in proportion to the overall volume of sales of the products concerned inside the Member State in question. This assessment cannot be based merely on geographic coverage. The market share of the parties to the agreement must also be given fairly limited weight. Even if the parties have a high market share in a properly defined regional market, the size of that market in terms of volume may still be insignificant when compared to total sales of the products concerned within the Member State in question.[353]

Agreements that are *local* in nature are in themselves not capable of appreciably affecting trade between Member States. This is the case even if the local market is located in a border region. Conversely, if the foreclosed share of the national market is significant, trade is capable of being affected even where the market in question is not located in a border region.[354]

4.4.4 Appreciability Test of the Agreement/'*De Minimis*'

The prohibition of Article 101(1) against agreements that prevent, restrict or distort competition has been limited in the enforcement practice of the Commission and in the judgments of the Court of Justice of the EU by the principle that the restriction must be *appreciable* before Article 101 will apply. Thus, an agreement that obviously restricts competition requires an analysis in order to determine whether the agreement satisfies

---

351. (Commission Notice on the effect on trade concept 2004, 55).
352. (Commission Notice on the effect on trade concept 2004, 89).
353. (Commission Notice on the effect on trade concept 2004, 90).
354. (Commission Notice on the effect on trade concept 2004, 91).

Chapter 4: Competition Practice

(1) the requirement of appreciable effect and (2) in order to establish whether the agreement affects trade between Member States to an appreciable extent, as discussed in the previous section.

4.4.4.1 *Developments in the Appreciability Test*

The Court of Justice of the EU has frequently clarified that the provision is not applicable where the impact of the agreement on trade between Member States *or* on competition is not appreciable.[355] The Court of Justice has also stated that an agreement which may affect trade between Member States and which has as its object the prevention, restriction or distortion of competition within the internal market constitutes, by its nature and independently of any concrete effects that it may have, an appreciable restriction of competition.[356] The Court judges appreciability in the light of the economic and legal setting of the agreement and its object and effects, including the cumulative effects of possible parallel agreements.[357]

Since an appraisal of the appreciable effect of an agreement will include consideration of the position and the importance of the parties on the market for the product concerned, it is necessary to identify first the relevant market i.e., the product and geographical market in which the product competes. The requirement of appreciable effect relates mainly to (i) the size of the parties concerned and (ii) the parties market share. That is to say that an agreement needs economic analysis in order to determine whether it satisfies the requirement of appreciable effect on competition *or* trade between Member States.

In some cases, the Court affirmed an appreciable effect if the parties have more than 5% of the relevant market, even only in one Member State.[358] In *Stergios Delimitis v. Henninger Bräu*,[359] the Court of Justice held that account must be taken of the conditions under which competitive forces operate on the relevant market therefore it is necessary to know the number and the size of producers present in the market and customer fidelity to existing brands. *Schöller v. Commission*[360] may serve as another case, since the Court of First Instance confirmed the Commission's approach of analysing the effect on competition. The Court confirmed that:

> It should be noted at the outset that the Commission was right, in paragraphs 68 to 70 of the decision, to state that the clause contained in the supply agreements whereby the retailer undertakes to sell through its sales outlet only products purchased directly from Schöller contains both an exclusive purchasing obligation and a prohibition of competition, which are capable of giving rise to a restriction of competition within the meaning of Article 85(1) (new Article 101(1)) of the Treaty both between products of the same brand and between products of different brands.

---

355. See (ECJ, Expedia, C-226/11 2012, paras 16 and 17).
356. See (ECJ, Expedia, C-226/11 2012, paras 35, 36 and 37).
357. (ECJ, STM v. MBU, Case 56-65 1966).
358. (ECJ, Miller International Schallplatten GmbH v. Commission, Case 19/77 1978) (ECJ, Allgemeine Elektrizitäts-Gesellschaft AEG-Telefunken AG v. Commission, Case 107/82 1983).
359. (ECJ, Stergios Delimitis v. Henninger Bräu AG, Case C-234/89 1991).
360. (CFI, Schöller Lebensmittel GmbH & Co. KG v. Commission, Case T-9/93 1995).

The Court therefore had to consider whether the Commission has established to the requisite factual and legal standard that the contested supply agreements have, as it contends, an appreciable effect on competition on the market.[361]

In assessing whether the agreement has an appreciable effect on competition on the market, the Court of First Instance found, first, that the applicant holds a strong position in the relevant market. In view of the strong position occupied by the applicant in the relevant market and, in particular, its market share, the Court considered that the agreements contribute significantly to the closing-off of the market. In addition, the Südzucker Group, which directly and indirectly holds 49% of Schöller's capital, declared a turnover of DEM 4.54 billion. According to points 31 and 35 of the Commission's decision, the share held by the applicant of the relevant market amounted to more than 25% of the grocery trade and of the traditional trade in 1991. As far as the quantitative importance of the contested agreements on the relevant market is concerned, the Court found that, in the market as a whole the applicant had tied, by those agreements, more than 10% of the sales outlets. The latter figures confirmed that the agreements appreciably limited the scope for German competitors and competitors from other Member States to establish themselves on the relevant market or to consolidate their market shares.

As regards the impact of networks of exclusive agreements on access to the market, it is also apparent from the case law of the Court of Justice of the EU that first it depends particularly on the number of sales outlets tied to the producers in relation to the number of untied retailers. Secondly, it relies on the quantities to which those commitments relate and on the proportion between those quantities and those, which are sold through retailers that are not tied. Furthermore, the extent of tying-in brought about by a network of exclusive purchasing agreements, although of some importance in assessing the extent to which the market is closed off, is only one factor amongst others pertaining to the economic and legal context in which the agreement or, as in this case, a network of agreements must be assessed.[362]

It is also necessary to analyse the conditions prevailing on the market and, in particular, the actual specific possibilities for new competitors to penetrate the market despite the existence of a network of exclusive purchasing agreements.[363]

4.4.4.2 De Minimis *Notice*

In line with the jurisprudence of the Court of Justice, the Commission sets out in the *De Minimis* Notice[364] how it determines, with the help of market share thresholds, which agreements have no appreciable effect on competition and are thus outside the scope of Article 101. This provides a 'safe harbour' for minor agreements between companies below certain market share thresholds. This does not imply that agreements between undertakings which exceed the thresholds set out in the Notice constitute an

---

361. *Ibid.*, paras 71 and 72.
362. (ECJ, Stergios Delimitis v. Henninger Bräu AG, Case C-234/89 1991, 19 and 20).
363. (CFI, Schöller Lebensmittel GmbH & Co. KG v. Commission, Case T-9/93 1995, 82).
364. (Commission De Minimis Notice 2014).

appreciable restriction of competition. Such agreements may still have only a negligible effect on competition and may therefore not be prohibited by Article 101(1) of the Treaty (3).[365]

The following agreements benefit from the 'safe harbour':

(a) if the aggregate market share held by the parties to the agreement does not exceed 10% on any of the relevant markets affected by the agreement, where the agreement is made between undertakings which are actual or potential competitors on any of those markets (agreements between competitors) (7); or

(b) if the market share held by each of the parties to the agreement does not exceed 15% on any of the relevant markets affected by the agreement, where the agreement is made between undertakings which are not actual or potential competitors on any of those markets (agreements between non-competitors).

In cases where it is difficult to classify the agreement as either an agreement between competitors or an agreement between non-competitors the 10% threshold is applicable.

Agreements which have as their object the prevention, restriction or distortion of competition within the Single Market do not benefit from the Notice's safe harbours. The Commission will not apply the safe harbours to agreements containing any restriction 'by object' or any of the restrictions that are listed as 'hardcore restrictions' in Commission Block Exemption Regulations (BERs) under Article 101(3). 'Hardcore restrictions' are considered by the Commission to generally constitute restrictions by object.

Where, in a relevant market, competition is restricted by the cumulative effect of agreements for the sale of goods or services entered into by different suppliers or distributors (cumulative foreclosure effect of parallel networks of agreements having similar effects on the market), the market share thresholds are reduced to 5%, both for agreements between competitors and for agreements between non-competitors. Individual suppliers or distributors with a market share not exceeding 5%, are in general not considered to contribute significantly to a cumulative foreclosure effect. A cumulative foreclosure effect is unlikely to exist if less than 30% of the relevant market is covered by parallel (networks of) agreements having similar effects.[366]

4.4.5 Economic Analysis in Article 101(1)

The conceptual difficulty of defining a 'restriction of competition' has contributed to differing views on the application of Article 101(1) in the past. The two possible approaches on how to define a 'restriction of competition' relate to the structure of

---

365. See, for instance, (ECJ, Bagnasco and Others, Joined cases C-215/96 and C-216/96 1999, paras 34 and 35).
366. (European Commission, Commission De Minimis Notice 2014, point 10).

Article 101. Whereas Article 101(1) and (2) specify that agreements which restrict competition are void, Article 101(3) identifies the criteria for an exemption from this prohibition.

The first approach is to interpret the prohibition in Article 101 *broadly*, permitting restraints on competition only via a block exemption or an individual assessment under Article 101(3). Based on this broad interpretation almost every restriction is regarded as falling under Article 101(1) and then potentially permitted under Article 101(3).

In the past, the Commission applied such a broad interpretation. Agreements that were pro-competitive in a given market situation were caught by the prohibition of Article 101(1) and (2) and were exempted later on based on the criteria as specified in Article 101(3). In circumstances of vertical restraints, for example, the Commission's policy was to apply Article 101(1) widely because of concerns over threats posed to market integration and the ambiguous nature of their impact on competition.[367] In order to hold an agreement, decision or concerted practice in violation of Article 101(1), the Commission had to establish that (1) a restriction of competition exists, (2) it is appreciable, and (3) it affects trade between Member States. This far-reaching ban was softened by the exemption rule of Article 101(3). The Commission used to have a monopoly in applying Article 101(3) until May 2004 when Regulation 1/2003 entered into force.[368]

The fundamental misconception lying at the heart of such an excessive application of Article 101(1) is the view that any restraint on commercial freedom of action is a restriction of competition. Based on this view any economic analysis in an assessment of Article 101(1) is obsolete thereby unnecessarily widening the scope of Article 101(1). The fact that an agreement contains clauses that limit the commercial freedom of parties is neither a necessary nor a sufficient condition for Article 101(1) to apply.[369] A broad interpretation or definition of 'restriction of competition' shifts any meaningful economic analysis from Article 101(1)–101(3), thus excluding before March 2004 national courts from the more important part of the analysis. The modernisation process and in particular Regulation 1/2003 caused the loss of the Commission's monopoly powers to apply Article 101(3). National courts are now able to apply both limbs of Article 101: Article 101(1) as well as Article 101(3). Thus, national courts increasingly shadow the established case law of the Court of Justice of the EU with respect to the application of Article 101(1) and perform, also in accordance with the 'more economics based approach' developed by the Court of Justice of the EU, a more comprehensive economic assessment under Article 101(1) in order to assess whether an agreement restricts competition or not in the first place.

This second more modern approach to assess a 'restriction of competition' under Article 101(1) entails, from the economic perspective, a competition test which is unique: the European competition test.

---

367. (European Commission, Green Paper on Vertical Restraints in EC Competition Policy 1997, points 20, 37).
368. *Ibid.*, point 37.
369. (Faull & Nikpay 1999, 81–87).

Chapter 4: Competition Practice

The European competition test is a test inherent to EU competition law. The test was developed in practice and applied in several cases by the Court of Justice of the EU.

An important aspect is that this European competition test on what is a restriction of competition needs to be clearly distinguished from the US rule of reason. The quite simple difference lies in the law itself. US anti-trust law does not have similar and, in particular, separate provisions as known in EU competition law: Article 101(1) and 101(3). This means that any economic analysis entailing consumer welfare considerations differs per se between these two jurisdictions since the underlying legal rules vary. A rule of reason analysis, as understood by US authorities, involves the identification of the relevant market, establishing the defendant's market power as well as an analysis of a multitude of other factors used to decide whether the restraint adversely affects competition in the market or not. Both jurisdictions require a case-by-case analysis. However, in the US rule of reason the economic assessment also includes a study of justifications establishing a legitimate objective and the necessity of the restraint to achieve that objective. Such an assessment is not part of an analysis under Article 101(1). Thus, the type of economic analysis applied differs because of the underlying different legal rules in the two jurisdictions. There are significant practical consequences attached to this important difference which will be discussed in the subsequent sections.

The second approach on how to interpretate Article 101(1) is *less broad* than the previous one. The second approach has been developed – as we will also see in the sections below – mainly by the Court of Justice of the EU. This less broadly and in fact more economics modern approach takes the view that not every restriction is necessarily a 'restriction of competition' within the meaning of Article 101(1). Thereby this less broad approach avoids the need for an exemption under Article 101(3) by excluding certain apparently restrictive agreements from the ambit of Article 101(1) in the first place. Since the burden of proof related to Article 101(3) is on the parties seeking an exemption, the less broad approach puts more weight on the authorities and national courts to verify that an agreement really restricts competition.

If for example a vertical agreement is neither *de minimis* nor constitutes one of the two hard core restraints, i.e., RPM or absolute territorial protection for exclusive distributors, according to the case law of the Court of Justice of the EU a case-by-case analysis is required. This analysis should take into account the real economic context of the case to see if competition is appreciably restricted. In the case of healthy inter-brand competition and if distributors as well as consumers have a range of similar products from which to choose, the competitive effects under Article 101(1) have to be analysed by the authorities and the national courts.

This brings us right to the point. The intensity of the debate over the introduction of a European competition test in Article 101(1) between the Commission and the Court of Justice of the EU was not principally about the meaning of the language of Article 101(1). The Commission was fundamentally concerned about who shall interpret and apply the competition rules. Since the Commission gave up its monopoly to apply Article 101(3) in 2004, a shift towards the less broad application of Article 101(1) in accordance with the case law of the Court of Justice of the EU can be seen. The European competition test in Article 101(1) emerged and gained ground.

The Court of Justice of the EU has quite frequently confirmed that the requirement of protection of competition pursued by Article 101(1) cannot be defined in abstract terms but must be seen in the specific economic context in which the conduct of the undertakings came about. Thus, the Court of Justice of the EU has a strong tendency to look on a case-by-case basis beyond the negative elements of agreements in their analysis under Article 101(1) in order to determine the actual economic impacts on the market.[370] An example of this approach is that certain positive aspects of vertical agreements have entered the analysis of the Court of Justice of the EU in Article 101(1), such as their capacities to solve free rider problems among resellers, to reduce commercial risks stemming from intra-brand competition or to protect a producer's brand image.[371] Thus, the Court of Justice of the EU requires under Article 101(1)[372] a full market analysis. It will be outlined in the following sections that in some cases like *Consten-Grundig*, for example, as early as 1966 the Court of Justice did not adopt the Commission's proposed broad definition on restriction of competition[373] but rather formulated a more neutral definition.[374] In the same year in *Technique Miniere*, the Court of Justice stated that an exclusive distributorship agreement does not fall automatically within Article 101(1) thereby advocating a less broad interpretation. Now that it is established case law that Article 101(1) does not apply to certain agreements which apparently limit economic freedom.[375]

However, some scholars still engage in a discussion about the application of Article 101(1) itself. They argue that competition policy should primarily be made in the form of applying general rules ('rule of law') instead of attempting to intervene into the market on a case-by-case basis.[376] An assessment on a case-by-case basis is according to them too costly. US anti-trust policy applies *'per se* rules' implying that

---

370. (Faull & Nikpay 1999, 93).
371. (Verouden 2003, 553).
372. (European Commission, Art. 81 of the EC Treaty (ex Art. 85) n.d.) Some of the following Court judgments and Commission decisions refer to the old Art. 85(1) which is the new Art. 81(1).
373. (ECJ, Établissements Consten S.à.R.L. and Grundig-Verkaufs-GmbH v. Commission, Joined cases 56 and 58-64 1966, 326) According to the Commission:

   the decisive criterion for the coming into force of the prohibition mentioned in Article 85(1) ... consists of the finding that the agreement interferes with the freedom of action of the parties or with the position of third parties on the market not only in a theoretical but also in a perceptible manner.

374. *Ibid.* 'In order to arrive at a true representation of the contractual position the contract must be placed in the economic and legal context in the light of which it was concluded by the parties.' 343.
375. (ECJ, STM v. MBU, Case 56-65 1966, 248):

   In order to be prohibited as being incompatible with the Common Market under Article 85(1) of the Treaty an agreement between undertakings must fulfil certain conditions depending less on the legal nature of the agreement than on its effects on trade between Member States and its effects on competition. Thus Article 85(1) is based on an assessment of the effects of an agreement from two angles of economic evaluation, it cannot be interpreted as introducing any kind of advance judgement with regard to a category of agreements determined by their legal nature.

376. On the application of per se-rules see (Hoppmann 1977).

certain behaviours are generally prohibited as well as the previously discussed 'rule of reason' approach, which means that in a particular case the advantages and disadvantages have to be assessed and balanced in one stage. However, in Europe the European competition test in Article 101(1) is applied in most of the cases thereby avoiding *'per se* rules' and favouring a case-by-case assessment. The European approach is something 'in between'. The majority of the cases do not reach the level of a case-by-case assessment at all because of the extensive use of *de minimis* and market share thresholds that are operated to define the boundaries of the European competition test.

Shortly, examples of this approach are illustrated confirming that the Court of Justice of the EU performs quite comprehensive economic analyses within Article 101(1).

The following section distinguishes economic analysis in either vertical or horizontal agreements. An example of a *horizontal agreement* might be a cartel, which partitions the market and imposes production quotas or selling prices. Agreements between actual or potential competitors that intend to restrict production and/or to raise market prices pose serious competition concerns. Agreements to fix prices or divide markets *'of their nature'* restrict competition within Article 101(1). A clause included in a distribution contract which prohibits the import or export of the product within the internal market or which prescribes the retail prices to be charged for the product in question ('RPM') are typical examples of *vertical agreements* restricting competition. In particular, when it comes to vertical agreements, economic analysis does play a significant role in any appraisal under Article 101(1). Moreover, it is an established trend in the case law that, in order to establish whether a particular clause is anti-competitive in intent, its function in the context of the contractual relationship of which it forms part of has to be assessed.

4.4.5.1 Vertical Agreements

As we will show in the following, EU competition law distinguishes between infringements which qualify as a restriction of competition under Article 101(1) and violations that require economic analysis to assess whether Article 101(1) applies or not. Whereas we see in some areas changes in the jurisprudence over time, the rulings of the Court of Justice of the EU on the role of economic analysis in Article 101(1) are quite consistent.

4.4.5.1.1 Vertical Exclusive Dealings

In 1966, the Court of Justice refused in a preliminary ruling to adopt a per se interpretation of a restriction of competition under Article 101(1) in the *Technique Miniere* case.[377] Instead the Court opted for an individual economic analysis in a European style (also called the 'European competition test').

---

377. (ECJ, STM v. MBU, Case 56-65 1966).

The case concerned a vertical relationship namely an exclusive supply contract, whereby Société Technique Minière (STM) had the exclusive right to sell in France certain grading equipment produced by Maschinenbau Ulm (MBU). The contract did not insulate the French territory. STM could sell the goods outside France too and parallel imports could be obtained from other countries.

The single exclusive dealing agreement between the two companies was found not to be in fundamental conflict with the objectives of the TFEU. The required evidence was a case specific economic analysis in order to qualify whether the agreement was prohibited by reason of its object or of its effect. The Court stated that:

> *Finally, for the agreement at issue to be caught by the prohibition contained in Article 85(1) (new Article 101(1)) it must have as its 'object or effect' the prevention, restriction or distortion of competition within the Common market.*
>
> *The fact that these are not cumulative but alternative requirements, indicated by the conjunction 'or', leads first to the need to consider the precise purpose of the agreement, in the economic context in which it is to be applied. This interference with competition referred to in Article 85(1) must result from all or some of the clauses of the agreement itself. Where, however, an analysis of the said clauses does not reveal the effect on competition to be sufficiently deleterious, the consequences of the agreement should then be considered and for it to be caught by the prohibition it is then necessary to find that those factors are present which show that competition has in fact been prevented or restricted or distorted to an appreciable extent.*
>
> *The competition in question must be understood within the actual context in which it would occur in the absence of the agreement in dispute. In particular, it may be doubted whether there is an interference with competition if the said agreement seems really necessary for the penetration of a new area by an undertaking. Therefore, in order to decide whether an agreement containing a clause 'granting an exclusive right of sale' is to be considered as prohibited by reason of its object or of its effect, it is appropriate to take into account in particular the nature and quantity, limited or otherwise, of the products covered by the agreement, the position and importance of the grantor and the concessionaire on the market for the products concerned, the isolated nature of the disputed agreement or, alternatively, its position in a series of agreements, the severity of the clauses intended to protect the exclusive dealership or, alternatively, the opportunities allowed for other commercial competitors in the same products by way of parallel re-exportation and importation.*

The Court took into account the fact that the exclusive supply contract is a necessary step allowing MBU to penetrate the French market. This was regarded as something to be encouraged. The consequence is that if the agreement does not have as its object the restriction of competition, the effects of the agreement must be analysed to demonstrate that factors are present which prevent, restrict or distort competition to an appreciable extent.[378] The consequences of the agreement are assessed by taking into account a number of economic factors, including whether the agreement is necessary to penetrate the market, the market position of the parties, the nature and quantity covered by the agreement, inter-brand competition and network

---

378. *Ibid.*, 249.

effects. These factors are vital in any economic analysis related to Article 101(1). Actually, the Court requested an evaluation of welfare-reducing and welfare-enhancing effects.

4.4.5.1.2 Vertical Absolute Territorial Protection

Consten and Grundig[379] is a case on export bans. The Court of Justice made clear that irrespective of the effects of an agreement such an agreement is infringing Article 101(1) per se because the clear object of an export ban agreement is to distort competition. Thus Consten and Grundig established in 1966 the basic principle that agreements, which prohibit exports within the internal market of their nature, restrict competition within the meaning of Article 101(1), irrespective of their actual effects. This judgment is seen as 'the' rule against absolute territorial protection conferred by export bans. Export bans preventing parallel imports are considered to infringe Article 101(1) per se.

Grundig concluded with the French company Consten a contract of indefinite duration which granted to the latter exclusive rights in France, the Saar and Corsica for the sale of Grundig radio receivers, recorders, dictaphones and television sets, as well as their accessories and spare parts.

Consten undertook to buy fixed minimum quantities, to order regularly in advance, to maintain a repair workshop with a stock of spare parts, to take over the guarantee and after-sales service, to refrain from selling similar competing products and from delivering directly or indirectly to the markets of other countries. The grant of the exclusive sales right to Consten meant that Grundig was obliged to surrender to Consten retail sales in the contract territory and to refrain from marketing deliveries, either directly or indirectly, to other persons established in the said territory.

Grundig granted the exclusive rights to Consten as recognition for the high investments that Consten had to make to market Grundig products in France. Grundig also agreed to clauses forbidding exportation from distributors in other Member States and upon its German wholesalers, and honouring guarantees only from approved dealers. In 1957, Consten registered under its own name the trademark GINT (Grundig International) for France, in order to prevent parallel imports. However, a parallel importer managed to obtain Grundig products and sold them in France, thereby undercutting Consten.

In its judgment, the Court did not completely reject Grundig's exclusive distribution system, but condemned those contractual elements aimed at or having as effect the absolute territorial protection of participants through clauses on re-exportation, guarantees and trademarks. The argument advanced by the applicants and the German Government was that since the Commission restricted its examination solely to Grundig products, the decision was based upon a false concept of competition

---

379. (ECJ, Établissements Consten S.à.R.L. and Grundig-Verkaufs-GmbH v. Commission, Joined cases 56 and 58-64 1966).

contained in Article 101(1). Maybe the parties were motivated by the *Bosch*[380] case. In that case, the Court stated that it is not possible to form a general opinion on the applicability of Article 101(1) on export prohibitions, but that it is necessary to examine all the facts of the particular case. Thus, the Federal Government of Germany argued that it is necessary to take account of the general situation in the market and also to take into account the competition between similar products from other manufacturers or importers. Both Grundig and Consten, supported by the German government, argued that instead of using a formal analysis, the Commission:

> before declaring Article 85(1) (new Article 101(1)) to be applicable, should, by basing itself upon the rule of reason, have considered the economic effects of the disputed contract upon competition between the different makes. There is the presumption that vertical sole distributorship agreements are not harmful to competition and in the present case there is nothing to invalidate that presumption. On the contrary the contract in question has increased the competition between similar products of different makes.[381]

The Court, however, rejected those arguments, and stated that there was no need for an economic analysis. According to the Court, the agreement had the object of restricting competition since it aimed at isolating the French market for Grundig products and at artificially maintaining a very well-known brand, thereby separating national markets within the Community.[382] The Court stated furthermore that:[383]

> For the purpose of applying Article 85(1) (new Article 101(1)), there is no need to take account of the concrete effects of an agreement once it appears that it has as its object the prevention, restriction or distortion of competition.
> Therefore the absence in the contested decision of any analysis of the effects of the agreement on competition between similar products of different makes does not, of itself, constitute a defect in the decision.

The parties advocated for economic analysis just to legitimise a scheme, which gave absolute territorial protection to the French distributor. Indeed, an economic analysis can involve trade-offs between pro- and anti-competitive effects of an agreement, which could even warrant in theory an absolute territorial protection. Such protection might indeed be necessary to enable a manufacturer to penetrate a new market. Theory suggests that any reduction in intra-brand competition would be more than offset by an increase in inter-brand competition. Nevertheless, the *Consten and Grundig* case should not be perceived as rejecting economic analysis within Article 101(1), but rather as indicating that such analysis cannot serve to validate absolute territorial protection which is qualified by the Court as a per se prohibition in Article 101(1).

---

380. (ECJ, Kledingverkoopbedrijf de Geus en Uitdenbogerd v. Robert Bosch GmbH and Maatschappij tot voortzetting van de zaken der Firma Willem van Rijn, Case 13/61 1962).
381. (ECJ, Établissements Consten S.à.R.L. and Grundig-Verkaufs-GmbH v. Commission, Joined cases 56 and 58-64 1966).
382. *Ibid.*, 516 and 517.
383. *Ibid.*, 342.

Once it is established that an agreement restricts competition by preventing parallel imports it is irrelevant that such an agreement might increase competition between manufacturers or have other favourable effects. Such effects are for consideration, if at all, in Article 101(3). Export bans are contrary to the fundamental objective of market integration. It is the 'market partitioning' object which justifies such a strict treatment of intra-brand agreements.

In Trefileurope Sales, the Court of First Instance confirmed that:

> *export clauses under which the reseller is required to re-export the goods to a specified country constitute an infringement of Article 85(1) (new Article 101(1)) of the Treaty where they were essentially designed to prevent the re-export of the goods to the country of production so as to maintain a system of dual prices, and thereby restrict competition, within the common market.*[384]

GlaxoSmithKline[385] is another case that is of importance with respect to the economic assessment under Article 101(1). In this case the Court advocated an *analysis of consumer welfare* in Article 101(1) by spotlighting certain assumptions in this respect. The Court confirmed that it follows from previous case law that agreements that clearly intend to treat parallel trade unfavourably must in principle be regarded as having as their object the restriction of competition. In particular, *Consten and Grundig* gave rise to this case law as discussed above. The application of Article 101(1) in *GlaxoSmithKline* however should not depend, according to the Court, solely on the fact that the agreement in question was intended to limit parallel trade in medicines or to partition the common market, which leads to the conclusion that it affects trade between Member States. The Court stated that an analysis designed to determine whether it has as its object or effect the prevention, restriction or distortion of competition on the relevant market, *to the detriment of the final consumer*, is required.

In *Consten and Grundig*, the Court of Justice did not hold that an agreement intended to limit parallel trade must be considered by its nature, that is to say, independently of any competition analysis, to have as its object the restriction of competition. On the contrary, the Court of Justice merely held, first, that an agreement between a producer and a distributor which might tend to restore the national divisions in trade between Member States might be of such a kind as to frustrate the most fundamental objectives of the Community (paragraph 340), a consideration which led it to reject a plea alleging that Article 101(1) was not applicable to vertical agreements (pp. 339 and 340). The Court of Justice then carried out a competitive analysis, abridged but real, during the course of which it held, in particular, that the agreement in question sought to eliminate any possibility of competition at the wholesale level in order to charge prices which were sheltered from all effective competition. These considerations led the Court of Justice to reject a plea alleging that there was no restriction of competition.

In *GlaxoSmithKline*, the Court of First Instance now clarified that, if account is taken of the legal and economic context in which GSK's General Sales Conditions are

---

384. (CFI, Tréfileurope Sales SARL v. Commission, Case T-141/89 1995, 12).
385. (CFI, GlaxoSmithKline Services Unlimited v. Commission, Case T-168/01 2006, 115–118).

applied, it cannot be presumed that those conditions deprive the final consumers of medicines or advantages. In effect, the wholesalers, whose function, as the Court of Justice has held, is to ensure that the retail trade receives supplies with the benefit of competition between producers are economic agents operating at an intermediate stage of the value chain and may keep the advantage in terms of price which parallel trade may entail, in which case that advantage will not be passed on to the final consumers. The Court continued by stating that the objective assigned to Article 101(1), which constitutes a fundamental provision indispensable for the achievement of the missions entrusted to the Community, in particular for the functioning of the internal market, is to prevent undertakings, by restricting competition between themselves or with third parties, from reducing the welfare of the final consumer of the products in question. Consequently, the principal conclusion reached by the Commission in this case, namely that the clause in question must be considered to be prohibited by Article 101(1) in so far as the clause had the object of the restriction of parallel trade, was not upheld by the Court of First Instance. As the prices of the medicines in this case are to a large extent shielded from the free play of supply and demand owing to the applicable regulations and are set or controlled by the public authorities, it cannot be taken for granted at the outset that parallel trade tends to reduce those prices and thus to increase the welfare of final consumers. An analysis of the terms of the clause therefore does not permit the presumption that that provision, which seeks to limit parallel trade, thus tends to diminish the welfare of final consumers. In this largely unprecedented situation, it cannot be inferred merely from a reading of the terms of that agreement, in its context, that the agreement is restrictive of competition, and it is therefore necessary to consider the effects of the agreement, if only to ascertain what the regulatory authority was able to apprehend on the basis of such a reading. The Court concluded that:

> *not every agreement which restricts the freedom of action of the participating undertakings, or of one of them necessarily falls within the prohibition in Article 81(1) EC (now Article 101(1)). In particular, any contract concluded between economic agents operating at different stages of the production and distribution chain has the consequence of binding them and, consequently, of restricting them, according to the stipulated terms, in their freedom of action. In the present case, whatever the price at which the Spanish wholesalers agree to buy a medicine from GW on the Spanish market, they are limited in their freedom of action since, from an economic point of view, they are not capable in the long term of reselling them at a lower price on the other national markets of the Community. However, as the objective of the Community competition rules is to prevent undertakings, by restricting competition between themselves or with third parties, from reducing the welfare of the final consumer of the products in question, it is still necessary to demonstrate that the limitation in question restricts competition, to the detriment of the final consumer.*[386]

Thus, *GlaxoSmithKline* again stressed the importance of a full economic appraisal under Article 101(1) or the European competition test.

---

386. (CFI, GlaxoSmithKline Services Unlimited v. Commission, Case T-168/01 2006, 171).

Chapter 4: Competition Practice

4.4.5.1.3   Vertical Selective Distribution

The approach on how to assess a 'restriction of competition' in selective distribution agreements emerged as early as in 1977 in the *Metro (No. 1)* case[387] later confirmed in 1986 in the *Metro (No. 2)* case.[388]

Both *Metro* cases are preliminary ruling reference cases about a selective distribution system. The Court of Justice decided that certain restrictions do not amount to restrictions on competition within the meaning of Article 101(1) if they are objectively justified by certain policy considerations, such as the need to ensure adequate distribution of high quality or high technology products. The Court ruled in both cases on the compatibility of a selective distribution system for electrical equipment with Article 101(1).

SABA[389], a German subsidiary of the US based GTE company, distributed its products (radios, televisions and tape recorders) through selected wholesalers and retailers in Germany and through sole distributors in the other Member States, with the exception of Ireland, who were in turn in contact with wholesalers and appointed retailers. SABA's distribution system was characterised by four elements:

(1) Distribution was carried out by selected and appointed wholesalers and retailers and by sole distributors.
(2) Any dealer wishing to retail SABA equipment had to keep a specialised shop or department, had to have suitable premises, employ trained staff and be capable of providing after-sales and guarantee services prescribed by SABA. Further they had to be engaged in certain sales promotion activities and to meet certain sales targets (adequate turnover). SABA dealers had to enter into six-month supply contracts for fixed quantities to ensure a stock of the SABA product range as fully as possible in quantities reflecting the turnover level.
(3) Those selling SABA products undertook to supply only other resellers who were appointed distributors and required to submit to checks to ensure that they were. German wholesalers undertook not to supply private consumers in Germany.
(4) Wholesalers, retailers and distributors undertook not to export SABA equipment outside the Community or to import it from third countries. Wholesalers and retailers undertook to achieve an adequate turnover and to keep a stock of SABA equipment.

SABA's criteria were of two kinds. The technical, also called qualitative, requirements were that the dealer specialises in electrical products, maintains adequate premises, employs qualified staff and supplies after-sales services. The commercial or quantitative requirements were for the dealer to be prepared to enter into six-month

---

387. (ECJ, Metro SB-Großmärkte GmbH & Co. KG v. Commission, Case 26-76 1977). (also called the SABA case).
388. (ECJ, Metro SB-Großmärkte GmbH & Co. KG v. Commission, Case 75/84 1986).
389. *Ibid.*

forward supply contracts based on targets set by SABA, to achieve an adequate turnover and to maintain specified stock levels.

SABA refused to supply products to Metro, a German self-service wholesaler trader, because Metro did not satisfy the required conditions. Metro lodged a complaint with the Commission because of an infringement of Articles 101 and 102.

Previously the Court of Justice and the Commission had consistently held that agreements came under the prohibition principle of Article 101(1) if they restricted the business freedom of the parties to such agreements and had a perceptible effect on the supply/demand alternatives offered to third parties. Such agreements had to be analysed pursuant to the conditions laid down in Article 101(3) before the Commission would grant an exemption. The Commission applied this traditional system in the two Metro cases as well. Although holding that the agreement as a whole was incompatible with Article 101(1) and that it had to meet the requirements of Article 101(3), the Commission nevertheless distinguished between the use of qualitative criteria governing the admittance to the SABA distribution system and further obligations.

The Commission[390] held that insofar as the appointment of SABA dealers is based on general qualitative criteria, which are objectively required to ensure an adequate distribution of equipment, and provided that all persons who fulfil these requirements are in fact appointed as SABA dealers, no restriction of competition within Article 101(1) arises. However SABA's additional commercial requirements were not justifiable by the needs of adequate distribution of the products concerned. Such requirements brought the SABA distribution system within Article 101(1), because they led to the exclusion of dealers technically qualified to handle the goods but unable to comply with the additional obligations.

Since the system as a whole led to an improvement in distribution, the Commission granted an exemption under Article 101(3) to the cooperation agreements in regard to the obligation on retailers to stock as full a range of SABA products as possible, to achieve adequate turnover and to keep a corresponding stock, and the requirement that distributors, wholesalers and retailers should check before supplying a reseller that the reseller was an authorised SABA outlet. They were not cleared on the conditions of sale, which prohibited German wholesalers from supplying private consumers within Germany and which prohibited exports from the Community. SABA amended, following intervention by the Commission, the clause prohibiting German wholesalers from supplying trade consumers with the exception of 'institutions, such as barracks, schools, churches and hospitals.' SABA extended the definition of wholesaler to cover the self-service wholesaler trade.

Metro continued to claim the existence of discrimination: (1) the prohibition on supplies by wholesalers to institutional consumers; (2) the requirement that the product purchased from the wholesaler had to be likely to increase the profit-earning capacity of the undertaking concerned; and (3) the obligation to sign a cooperation agreement. Metro appealed to the Court of Justice that, the Commission, by adopting the decision infringed Article 101(3). Metro also claimed infringement of Article 102.

---

390. (Decision IV/847 on SABA 1975).

The Court rejected Metro's application, upholding the Commission in all material respects. In upholding the Commission, the Court found the SABA price structure was 'somewhat rigid'[391], but said that price competition 'does not constitute the only effective form of competition or that to which absolute priority must in all circumstances be accorded.'[392] The Court confirmed the selective distribution mechanism could operate in a restricted area:

> *provided that the resellers are chosen on the basis of objective criteria of a qualitative nature relating to the technical qualifications of the reseller and his staff and the suitability of his trading premises and that such conditions are laid down uniformly for all potential resellers and are not applied in a discriminatory fashion.*[393]

The Court stated further that:

> *The requirement contained in Articles 3 and 85 of the EEC Treaty (new Article 101) that competition shall not be distorted implies the existence on the market of workable competition, that is to say the degree of competition necessary to ensure the observance of the basic requirements and the attainment of the objectives of the Treaty, in particular the creation of a single market achieving conditions similar to those of a domestic market. In accordance with this requirement the nature and intensiveness of competition may vary to an extent dictated by the products or services in question and the economic structure of the relevant market sectors.*[394]

The concept as introduced in *Metro (1)* has been further clarified by the Court of Justice in its *Metro (2)*[395] case. As Advocate General *VerLoren van Themaat* stated in his conclusions in *Metro (2)*, this concept implies that:

> *for the purposes of assessment of an individual selective distribution system such as that concerned here, on the basis of Article 85(1) and (3) (new Article 101(1) and (3)), it is of decisive importance whether, in addition to the distribution system at issue, there are adequate alternative 'channels of distribution' or 'new methods of distribution' in order to provide for the requirements of the various categories of consumers.*

Provided there are a sufficient number of other manufacturers and a variety of distribution systems, competition with other distribution systems will ensure that the 'objective criteria of a qualitative nature' are not fixed at too high a level. That safeguard ceased to operate, however, if the major competitors applied a similar system whereby certain sales methods (such as cash and carry stores which have no trained staff and to which the related obligation to provide pre-sales and after-sales service does not apply) were excluded. The interest of unqualified dealers was not an object of protection under Article 101 from the Commission's point of view. The primary object of protection was the consumer:

---

391. (ECJ, Metro SB-Großmärkte GmbH & Co. KG v. Commission, Case 26-76 1977, 22).
392. (ECJ, Metro SB-Großmärkte GmbH & Co. KG v. Commission, Case 26-76 1977, 21).
393. (ECJ, Metro SB-Großmärkte GmbH & Co. KG v. Commission, Case 26-76 1977, 20–21).
394. (ECJ, Metro SB-Großmärkte GmbH & Co. KG v. Commission, Case 26-76 1977, 20).
395. (ECJ, Metro SB-Großmärkte GmbH & Co. KG v. Commission, Case 75/84 1986).

As long as manufacturers are anxious to maximise profits through selective distribution and as long as workable competition prevails, the interests of consumers seem to be sufficiently safeguarded. If consumers do not wish to take advantage of such selective distribution systems, they are free to move their custom to unqualified dealers and will thereby eventually force manufacturers to abandon selective distribution.[396]

VerLoren van Themaat believed, however, that once specialised dealers comprise a large share of the market, manufacturers cease to have the necessary freedom of choice, since they could not risk being rejected by its category of outlet and that a proliferation of selective distribution systems could effectively deprive the consumer of the freedom to transfer their custom to unqualified dealers.

The Court held in *Metro* that in the case of high quality and technically advanced consumer durables the Commission was justified in recognising that selective distribution systems constituted, together with others, an aspect of competition which did not contravene Article 101(1): provided first, that resellers were chosen on the basis of objective criteria of a qualitative nature and secondly, that such conditions are laid down uniformly for all potential resellers and are not applied in a discriminatory fashion. The Court also said:

For specialist wholesalers and retailers the desire to maintain a certain price level, which corresponds to the desire to preserve, in the interests of consumers, the possibility of the continued existence of this channel of distribution in conjunction with new methods of distribution based on a different type of competition policy, forms one of the objectives which may be pursued without necessarily falling under the prohibition contained in Article 81(1) and, if it does fall there under, either wholly or in part, coming within the framework of Article 81(3). This argument is strengthened if, in addition, such conditions promote improved competition inasmuch as it relates to factors other than prices.[397]

The Metro cases established a further category of agreements, which do not fall within Article 101(1). These are agreements in which the restrictions are 'objectively justified'. Thus, although SABA restricted competition by preventing SABA products being sold by 'cash and carry' houses, the Court of Justice declined to apply Article 101(1) to a system based on qualitative technical criteria adopted by a non-dominant supplier of specialised goods. Moreover, in deciding that the restriction was 'justified' under Article 101(1) the Court balanced the price rigidity that might arise in such systems of selective distribution against the improvement in competition arising in other respects, e.g., the maintenance of standards of service.

That approach, which has been confirmed in subsequent cases, involves a comprehensive economic appraisal under Article 101(1). Taking into account this approach towards the economic function of a selective distribution system, the Court had to recognise that these limitations on the freedom of recognised dealers are necessary if a two tier selective, distribution system is to exist at all. That, in turn, blurs the respective spheres of application of Article 101(1) and Article 101(3). If a particular

---

396. *Ibid.*, 3063.
397. (ECJ, Metro SB-Großmärkte GmbH & Co. KG v. Commission, Case 26-76 1977, 21).

Chapter 4: Competition Practice

restriction is 'justified' under Article 101(1) there is no need to apply Article 101(3) at all. However *Metro* does not yield any clear philosophical basis about where to draw the dividing line between what is justified under Article 101(1) and what is not.

The Court's use of 'balancing' language should not be interpreted as introducing a US rule of reason analysis whereby vertical restraints can only escape the application of Article 101(1) after considering the restrictions on intra-brand and the enhancement of inter-brand competition. One should opt to read the analysis of selective distribution systems as a finding that the restrictions of competition are ancillary if the proper distribution of the products cannot otherwise be ensured.

Bayrische Motorenwerke AG v. ALD Auto-Leasing D GmbH[398] is another case where the Court supported the trend towards a more comprehensive economic analysis in order to assess the object and the effect of the agreement in question. This case concerned the issues of a selective distribution system for motor vehicles, refusal to supply and territorial protection.

4.4.5.1.4 Vertical Licensing

The *Nungesser*[399] case furnishes a further example of the appraisal approach in Article 101(1). This case analysed the necessity of a contractual restriction for the achievement of a legitimate business purpose. It was considered by the Court to be *'necessary to examine whether, in the present case, the exclusive nature of the license, in so far as it is an open license, has the effect of preventing or distorting competition within the meaning of Article 85 (new Article 101) of the Treaty.'*[400]

This case concerned agreements between I.N.R.A., the French national agricultural research institute, and Mr Eisele, trading as Nungesser, whereby I.N.R.A. assigned exclusively to Mr Eisele, in respect of the Federal Republic of Germany, certain plant breeder's rights relating to maize seeds developed by I.N.R.A., and granted Mr Eisele the exclusive right to produce and sell I.N.R.A. seeds in Germany. I.N.R.A. undertook to prevent I.N.R.A. seeds being exported to Germany other than via Mr Eisele. There was also evidence that pressure had been brought to bear on third parties to prevent parallel imports into Germany.

In its legal analysis of the agreement under Article 101(1), the Commission had found restrictions upon the freedom of action of the parties to the agreement and an effect upon third parties. Its decision[401] implied that exclusivity would always be restrictive within the meaning of Article 101(1) and could even not be exempted by means of Article 101(3). The Commission held that Article 101(1) was infringed by (1) the grant by I.N.R.A. to Mr Eisele of exclusive rights to produce and sell the seeds in Germany. I.N.R.A. thereby deprived itself of the ability to license other undertakings

---

398. (ECJ, Bayerische Motorenwerke AG v. ALD Auto-Leasing D GmbH, Case C-70/93 1995).
399. (ECJ, L.C. Nungesser KG and Kurt Eisele v. Commission, Case 258/78 1982).
400. *Ibid.*, para. 54.
401. (Decision IV/28.824 on Breeder's rights – maize seed 1978).

in Germany, or to enter the market itself; (2) by I.N.R.A's undertaking to prevent third parties from exporting to Germany; and (3) by Mr Eisele's use of his plant breeders' rights to prevent parallel imports.

The arguments of the parties were that the exclusive license was necessary to enable I.N.R.A. to enter a new market, and compete with comparable products therein, since no trader would risk launching a new product unless he was given protection from competition from the licensor and other licensees. The Court distinguished between an open exclusive licence, whereby the owner merely undertakes not to compete himself, nor to grant licences to others in the same territory; and an exclusive licence with absolute territorial protection, under which all competition from third parties is eliminated.

The Court of Justice ruled that having regard to the specific nature of the products in question, the grant of an open exclusive license is not in itself incompatible with Article 101(1) of the Treaty.[402] A total prohibition of such licences under Article 101(1) would be prejudicial to the Community interest. *'Such a result would be damaging to the dissemination of a new technology and would prejudice competition in the Community between the new product and similar existing products.'*[403] On the other hand, applying the principles of *Consten and Grundig*, the Court reaffirmed that a protected exclusive licence, which conferred absolute territorial protection and enabled the licensee to prevent parallel imports and, in effect to partition the common market, was contrary to Article 101(1).

It does appear that the Court's reasoning is close to that in *Technique Miniere*. In both cases the Court seems to be saying, in effect, an exclusive right does not 'of its nature' fall within Article 101(1) where the grant of such a right is essential to the penetration of a new market. On the other hand, the Court confirms that an agreement, which grants absolute territorial protection, is 'of its nature' a restriction on competition within the meaning of Article 101(1).

In *Coditel*,[404] the Court held that the grant of an exclusive copyright licence to exhibit a film in a Member State would not in itself infringe Article 101(1) even though the effect of this was to prevent transmission of that film by cable from a neighbouring Member State. It was for the national court to apply an analysis in order to determine whether the restrictions thereby created were artificial and unnecessary in terms of the needs of the cinematographic industry.

4.4.5.1.5 Vertical Franchising

In the *Pronuptia*[405] case, a very important preliminary ruling about a vertical franchising agreement decided in 1986, the Court of Justice had to consider the compatibility of

---

402. (ECJ, L.C. Nungesser KG and Kurt Eisele v. Commission, Case 258/78 1982, 58).
403. *Ibid.*, para. 58.
404. (ECJ, Coditel SA, Compagnie générale pour la diffusion de la télévision, and others v. Ciné-Vog Films SA and others, Case 262/81 1982).
405. (ECJ, Pronuptia de Paris GmbH v. Pronuptia de Paris Irmgard Schillgallis, Case 161/84 1986).

franchising with Article 101(1) and again assessed the pro- and anti-competitive effects under this provision.

In *Pronuptia*, the Court was asked to make a preliminary ruling. *Pronuptia de Paris* and its subsidiaries franchised various retailers to sell wedding gowns, according to its instructions, in shops that looked as if Pronuptia owned them, but in fact belonged to the franchisee. Pronuptia promised to franchise only one person in three cities in Germany – the franchised territories – and the person agreed to sell from the contract premises. Finally when it came to the payment of royalties, the argument that this franchise agreement was anti-competitive occurred.

The Court first took the view that provisions designed to protect the franchisor's know-how and business methods did not constitute restrictions on competition. Thus, the impositions of a non-compete provision or a restriction on transfer of the franchisee's shop without the franchisor's consent are not apparently within Article 101(1).

The Court observed in paragraph 15 that franchising has desirable characteristics. It is a method used by a firm, which has found a good formula to market a product, to exploit this idea without using its own capital for investment. The firm helps new firms to enter the market with directives, assistance and an established reputation. The Court observed that this kind of franchising distribution did not increase competition but neither did it limit competition. To be certain that the marketing strategy works, the franchisor must be able to ensure that the assistance it gives to its franchisees does not benefit its competitors, even indirectly; and it must preserve the identity and reputation of the network.[406] Second, the Court sanctioned measures by the franchisor designed to maintain the identity and reputation of the network. This enabled the franchisor to impose restrictions not only on the method of selling used by its franchisee – for example sales premises, qualifications of sales staff etc. – but also on the selection of goods sold. In the view of the Court, the franchisor is entitled to exercise control over the selection of goods offered by the franchisee so that the public is able to obtain goods of the same quality from each franchisee in the network. In some cases such as the distribution of fashion articles, as in *Pronuptia*, it would be impractical to lay down objective quality specifications:

> In such circumstances a provision requiring the franchisee to sell only products supplied by the franchisor or by suppliers selected by him may be considered necessary for the protection of the network's reputation.

Ancillary restraints, that are needed to support a transaction which is not anti-competitive, do not restrict competition. Nevertheless the Court added that the obligation to sell only from the contract premises restrained the franchisees from opening a second shop without consent and that, coupled with an exclusive territory, gave each franchisee absolute territorial protection, which, in accordance with the Court's judgment in *Consten and Grundig*, would infringe Article 101(1) once the network was widespread.

The Court's statement goes further in *Pronuptia*: The Court suggests that the Commission should exempt even absolute territorial protection. Article 101(1) is not

---

406. (Korah 1990, 150).

infringed if the franchisee is prohibited from opening a shop of the same or similar nature in an area where he might compete with a member of the network during the currency of that agreement and a reasonable period of time after the expiry of the franchise.[407] The Court added again in its summary[408] that the agreement must be judged in the light of the particular provisions in the contract and their economic context.

The Court was not, however, prepared to go so far as to say that a restriction on the franchisee opening a second outlet did not fall within Article 101(1). To have done so would have overturned many of its previous judgments on selective distribution. Indeed the Court seems to have regarded such exclusivity as virtually per se within Article 101(1). The Court did however suggest strongly that such a restriction might be exempted under Article 101(3), since it could be shown that a prospective franchisee would not take up an expensive franchise unless he could expect a degree of protection against competition on the part of the franchisor and other franchisees.

Because of the approach to ancillary restraints and the assessment of pro- and anti-competitive effects in Article 101(1), the judgment was an important one. The underlying approach is to consider first whether a given agreement is likely, in general, to be anti-competitive in nature in the light of the fundamental aims of the TEU. If the answer is no, clauses inherent in the successful operation of the agreement then fall outside Article 101(1). In other words, ancillary restraints necessary to support a legitimate objective, which is not anti-competitive in itself, are not caught by Article 101(1). Effects on inter-brand competition outweigh possible negative effects on competition of restrictions necessary to protect the know-how and assistance provided by the franchisor.

4.4.5.1.6 Vertical Exclusive Purchasing

In *Brasserie De Haecht*,[409] a preliminary ruling case on the issue of exclusive purchasing, the Court held that the effects of such an agreement had to be assessed in the whole economic context in which they occur and where they might combine with others to have a cumulative effect on competition. If no anti-competitive object is established, an agreement, decision or concerted practice will still infringe Article 101(1) if it has anti-competitive effects.

The case concerned the validity of a brewery tie agreement. The Courts' conclusion was that agreements whereby an undertaking agrees to obtain its supplies from one undertaking to the exclusions of all others do not of their nature fall within Article 101(1), but may do so if a market analysis taking account of other similar agreements disclose an appreciable restriction of competition and effect on Inter-State trade. It also follows from that judgment that the cumulative effect of several similar agreements constitutes one factor amongst others in ascertaining whether, by way of

---

407. (ECJ, Pronuptia de Paris GmbH v. Pronuptia de Paris Irmgard Schillgallis, Case 161/84 1986, 16).
408. *Ibid.*, para. 27.
409. (ECJ, SA Brasserie de Haecht v. Consorts Wilkin-Janssen, Case 23-67 1967).

possible alteration of competition, trade between Member States is capable of being affected. However, the outstanding characteristic of this case is that the Court emphasised the importance of the *factors relevant for the economic and legal context*.

The most significant judgment is *Delimitis*, a preliminary ruling on exclusive purchasing decided in 1991. The Court held that vertical agreements that have the effect of tying the distributor to the supplier might be caught by Article 101(1).

In this case the Court broadly stated that beer supply agreements are prohibited by Article 101(1) if two cumulative conditions are met: The first is that, having regard to the economic and legal context of the agreement at issue, it is difficult for competitors who could enter the market or increase their market share to gain access to the national market for the distribution of beer in premises for the sale and consumption of drinks. The second condition is that the agreement at issue must make a significant contribution to the sealing-off effect brought about by the totality of those agreements in their economic and legal context.

In *Delimitis v. Henninger Bräu*[410], the dispute related to an amount claimed from Stergios Delimitis, formerly the licensee of premises for the sale and consumption of drinks in Frankfurt am Main, by the brewery Henninger Bräu, established in Frankfurt. The dispute followed the termination of the contract at Delimitis' request. The contract was a beer supply agreement, entered into between them on the 14 May 1985.

Under the terms of beer supply agreements, the supplier generally affords the reseller certain economic and financial benefits, such as the granting of loans on favourable terms, the letting of premises for the operation of a public house and the provision of technical installations, furniture and other equipment necessary for its operation. In consideration for those benefits, the reseller normally undertakes, for a predetermined period, to obtain supplies of the products covered by the contract only from the supplier. This exclusive purchasing obligation is generally backed by a prohibition on selling competing products in the public house let by the supplier. Such agreements do not have the object of restricting competition. Thus it was in this case necessary to analyse the effects of beer supply agreements. They have to be taken together with other contracts of the same type, to consider the opportunities of internal competitors or those from other Member States, to gain access to the market for beer consumption or to increase their market share and, accordingly, the effects on the range of products offered to consumers.

The Court stated that in making that analysis, the relevant market must be first determined. The relevant market is primarily defined on the basis of the nature of economic activity in question, in this case the sale of beer. Beer is sold through both retail channels and premises for the sale and consumption of drinks. It follows that in *Delimitis*, taking account of the consumer's point of view, the reference market is that for the distribution of beer in premises for the sale and consumption of drinks. Secondly, the relevant market is defined from a geographical point of view. In order to assess whether the existence of several beer supply agreements impedes access to the market as defined, it is further necessary to examine the nature and extent of those

---

410. (ECJ, Stergios Delimitis v. Henninger Bräu AG, Case C-234/89 1991).

agreements in their totality, comprising all similar contracts tying a large number of points of sale to several national producers.[411]

The effect of those networks of contracts on access to the market in *Delimitis* was supposed to depend specifically on the number of outlets, the duration of the commitments entered into, the quantities of beer to which those commitments relate, and on the proportion between those quantities and the quantities sold by free distributors. The existence of a bundle of similar agreements is not, however, sufficient in itself to support a finding that the relevant market is inaccessible, inasmuch as it is only one factor, amongst others, pertaining to the economic and legal context in which an agreement must be appraised.[412]

Other factors the Court considered as important to be taken into account in *Delimitis* are, in the first instance, those relating to opportunities for access. The Court indicated that the key question to be addressed is the existence of other barriers to entry, or to growth, for the participants in the market. If the market analysis discloses that it is difficult to gain access to the relevant market, it is then necessary to assess the extent to which the agreements entered into by the brewery in question contribute to that difficulty. Secondly, account must be taken of the conditions under which competitive forces operate on the relevant market. In that context, it is necessary to know not only the number and the size of producers present in the market, but also the degree of saturation of the market and the customer fidelity to existing brands. It is generally more difficult to penetrate a saturated market in which customers are loyal to a small number of large producers than a market in full expansion in which a large number of small producers are operating without any strong brand names.[413]

The Court decided therefore that if an examination of all similar contracts entered into on the relevant market and the other factors relevant to the economic and legal context in which the contract must be examined shows that those agreements do not have the cumulative effect of denying access to that market to new national and foreign competitors, the individual agreements comprising the bundle of agreements cannot be held to restrict competition within the meaning of Article 101(1). They do not, therefore, fall under the prohibition laid down in that provision.

If such an examination reveals that it is difficult to gain access to the relevant market, it is necessary to assess the extent to which the agreements entered into by the brewery in question contribute to the cumulative effect produced, in that respect, by the totality of similar contracts found in that market[414]. In order to assess the extent of the contribution of beer supply agreements entered into by a brewery to the cumulative sealing-off effect mentioned above, the market position of the contracting parties must be taken into consideration[415]. The most interesting point is, that the Court said that that position is not solely determined by the market share held by the brewery and any other group to which it may belong, but also by the number of outlets tied to it or to its

---

411. (ECJ, Brauerei A. Bilger Söhne GmbH v. Heinrich Jehle and Marta Jehle, Case 43-69 1970).
412. (ECJ, SA Brasserie de Haecht v. Consorts Wilkin-Janssen, Case 23-67 1967).
413. (Jones & Sufrin 2008, s. 240).
414. (ECJ, Stergios Delimitis v. Henninger Bräu AG, Case C-234/89 1991, 24).
415. (ECJ, Stergios Delimitis v. Henninger Bräu AG, Case C-234/89 1991, 25).

Chapter 4: Competition Practice

group, in relation to the total number of premises of sale and consumption of drinks found in the relevant market. The Court indicates by this statement that an analysis of market structure has to be done and follows thereby competition theory, which considers the factor market share only as a starting point. The contribution of the individual contracts to the sealing-off of that market also depends on their duration.

What the Court did in *Delimitis* was in fact an economic assessment of Article 101(1) meaning that the Court did not view Article 101(1) widely. By analysing 'restriction of competition', the Court applied an economic appraisal. This assessment involved the identification of the relevant market (point 16). The Court reflected on the market position (point 25) as well as on a multitude of other factors, which are used to analyse whether the restraint adversely affects competition (number and the size of producers, degree of saturation, customer fidelity and the trend in beer sales; point 22).

Thus *Delimitis* is an important judgment indicating the increasing importance of economic analyses in EC competition law. The judgment supports the need for such an analysis and votes for a two-stage test, which can be referred to as the '*Delimitis* test'.[416] First, it has to be assessed whether the market in which the agreement operates is one that is difficult for new suppliers to enter or in which existing suppliers cannot easily increase their market share. Secondly, if the market poses barriers to entry or growth, whether the agreement in question contributes significantly to those barriers has to be examined. If *Delimitis* is intended to apply to all exclusive purchasing restrictions, it greatly increases the burden for a national court in determining the validity of such clauses.

Mars/Langnese[417] and *Mars/ Schöller*[418] are other cases in this context.

Schöller notified the Commission in a letter on 7 May 1985 that a form of 'supply agreement' governing its relations with its retail distributors existed. The Commission returned a letter stating that if the fixed duration of the agreements to be concluded in the future would not extend to two years, Schöllers Ice Cream Supply-Agreements would be compatible with the competition rules of the EC Treaty. The average duration of Schöllers 'ice cream supply agreements' fall well short of the period of five years laid down in Commission Regulation (EEC) 1984/83 as a precondition for a block exemption to be available in respect of exclusive purchasing agreements.

On 18 September 1991, Mars GmbH lodged a complaint with the Commission against the applicant and against Langnese-Iglo GmbH for infringement of Article 101 and 102 of the Treaty. Mars asked for protective measures to be taken in order to forestall the serious and irreparable damages which, in their opinion, would be caused by the fact that the sale of ice cream would be severely hampered by the implementation of Schöller's and Langnese's agreements. By the decision of 25 March 1992 the Commission by way of an interim measure prohibited Schöller and Langnese from enforcing their contractual rights under the agreements concluded by them or for their benefit, whereby retailers undertook to buy, offer for sale or sell only ice cream from

---

416. (Pheasant and Weston 1997, 328).
417. (Decision IV/34.072 on Mars/Langnese 1992).
418. (Decision IV/31.533 and IV/34.072 on Mars/Schöller 1992).

those producers, to the exclusion of Mars ice cream products. The Commission also withdrew the benefit of the application of Regulation 1983/84. By way of final decisions on the 'supply agreements' at issue, *Mars/Langnese*,[419] and *Mars/ Schöller*,[420] the Commission stated that the agreements requiring retailers established in Germany to purchase single-item ice cream for resale only from Schöller and Langnese infringed Article 101(1).

The Commission made clear whether the agreements concluded by Langnese and Schöller infringed Article 101(1) by applying a three-tier-test:

- Does the agreement itself have an appreciable effect on competition or trade between Member States?
- If not, do all agreements of this kind entered into by the undertaking concerned have this effect?
- If not, do all agreements of this kind, which exist in the relevant market, have this effect?

If one of the questions is answered in the affirmative, the conditions for the application of Article 101(1) are met.

Those decisions were supposed to clarify the Commission's attitude towards exclusive purchasing agreements. In general, the Commission considered these agreements to be beneficial to competition in normal market conditions because they strengthen the position of the undertaking, which has concluded the exclusivity agreement. If, however, access by other suppliers to the relevant market is impeded as a result of the market structure and other significant barriers to entry to this market, the Commission does not accept any further strengthening of that position by exclusivity agreements:

> *Exclusive purchasing obligations also have an indirect effect on competition between suppliers of goods throughout the relevant market (inter-brand competition). They make it more difficult or impossible to set up independent distribution structures such as are necessary if new entrants are to gain access to the relevant market or if an existing market position is to be consolidated.*[421]

The Court of First Instance in 1995 upheld this interpretation in *Schöller v. Commission*[422], an Article 263 case on exclusive purchasing. The Court stated that an examination of all similar agreements concluded on the market and of other aspects of the economic and legal context in which they operate show that the exclusive purchasing agreements by the applicant are liable to appreciably affect competition within the meaning of Article 101(1) of the Treaty.[423]

---

419. (Decision IV/34.072 on Mars/Langnese 1992).
420. (Decision IV/31.533 and IV/34.072 on Mars/Schöller 1992).
421. (Decision IV/34.072 on Mars/Langnese 1992, 72).
422. (CFI, Schöller Lebensmittel GmbH & Co. KG v. Commission, Case T-9/93 1995).
423. (CFI, Langnese Iglo GmbH v. Commission, Case T-7/93 1995, 85).

4.4.5.1.7 Conclusion

The Court of Justice of the EU weighs all the circumstances of the case in deciding whether a restrictive practice should be prohibited as imposing an unreasonable restraint on competition. Such an appraisal of economic effects of an agreement can clearly be evidenced in the case law. This requirement for a comprehensive economic assessment should not be confused with the US term 'rule of reason'. The European appraisal implies a competition test under Article 101(1). Essentially, it means that the ultimate consequences for competition are assessed under that paragraph and not under Article 101(3).

In the past, contrary to such an approach, the Commission adopted a more relaxed interpretation of the applicability of Article 101(1), which resulted in confusion about the exact scope of the competition test. In Commission decisions, the true economic assessment was made when judging whether the agreement should benefit from an exemption under Article 101(3). This approach was based on the monopoly of the Commission to apply Article 101(3). The problem within EU competition law was therefore much more *when* the overall assessment of the competition impact of an agreement should have been made, than *if* this assessment is made at all. The Court of Justice of the EU regularly confirmed that the requirement of protection of competition pursued by Article 101(1) cannot be defined in abstract terms but must be seen in the specific economic context in which the conduct of the undertakings came about. Furthermore, the enforcer of EU competition law is required, in assessing the applicability of Article 101(1), to examine the actual details of the case and cannot rely on hypothetical situations.[424]

It is established case law that an agreement can escape the prohibition laid down in Article 101(1) if it does not significantly contribute to denying access to the market to new national and foreign competitors.[425]

It is also clear by analysing the case law that naked restraints on pricing, market sharing and some kinds of collective boycott are likely to be condemned with a fairly short analysis if they are found capable of restricting trade between Member States. Nevertheless, it should be noted that such a per se approach was criticised and rejected in a few other judgments.

To conclude: The Court of Justice of the EU requests the performance of extensive economic analysis within Article 101(1). In particular, when it comes to vertical agreements, economic analysis does play a significant role. It is an established trend in case law[426] that, in order to determine whether a particular clause is anti-competitive in intent, for the purpose of Article 101(1), that its function in the context of the contractual relationship, of which it forms part of, has to be assessed. Against this background, the Court normally concludes that no anti-competitive object is contained

---

424. (CFI, Schöller Lebensmittel GmbH & Co. KG v. Commission, Case T-9/93 1995, 95).
425. (ECJ, Stergios Delimitis v. Henninger Bräu AG, Case C-234/89 1991, 23–24).
426. Opinion of the Advocate General Tesauro in the (ECJ, Gøttrup-Klim e.a. Grovvareforeninger v. Dansk Landbrugs Grovvareselskab AmbA, Case C-250/92 1994, 16).

in the clauses which are found in the abstract to be *necessary* to ensure that a contract, which is not in itself harmful to competition, can fully discharge of the legal and economic function which it pursues.

4.4.5.2 Horizontal Agreements

The role of economic analysis in Article 101(1) is slightly different in horizontal cases. These are discussed in the following.

4.4.5.2.1 Horizontal Cooperation Agreements

In *Gottrup-Klim v. Dansk Landbrugs Grovvareselskab AmbA*[427], a reference case for a preliminary ruling, the Court confirmed that economic conditions play a decisive role in analysing whether the prohibition laid down in Article 101(1) can be escaped.

A national court was seeking to ascertain whether a provision in the statutes of a cooperative purchasing association, the effect of which is to forbid its members from participating in other forms of organised cooperation, which are in direct competition with it, is caught by the prohibition in Article 101(1). The Court stated that:

> *The compatibility of the status of such an association with the Community rules on competition cannot be assessed in the abstract. It will depend on the particular clauses in the statutes and the economic conditions prevailing on the markets concerned.*[428]

By doing so the Court found that the restrictions imposed by the statutes of cooperative purchasing associations have to be assessed as to what is necessary to ensure that the cooperative functions properly and maintains its contractual power in relation to producers. Certainly it is the task of a court to consider a practice unlawful, but a broader understanding of the relevant economic facts supports courts in doing their job more accurately in particular in cases in which the same facts can be explained differently.

European Night Services v. Commission[429] is the climax of a trend in the case law requiring that the overall anti-competitive effects of agreements need to be assessed in their economic context.

The case concerned the cooperative joint venture European Night Services Ltd. (ENS) which had been set up by railway undertakings established in the United Kingdom (UK), France, Belgium and the Netherlands (the 'parent companies'). The joint venture had as its main business to operate night services on certain routes

---

427. (ECJ, Gøttrup-Klim e.a. Grovvareforeninger v. Dansk Landbrugs Grovvareselskab AmbA, Case C-250/92 1994).
428. *Ibid.*, para. 31.
429. (CFI, ENS, Eurostar (UK), EPS, UIC, NS and SNCF v. Commission, Joined cases T-374/94, T-375/94, T-384/94 and T-388/94 1998).

between the UK and continental destinations. The service was completely new, involved major investments and substantial financial risks. It also required the pooling of know-how by the parent companies.

The Commission found that the joint venture had the effect of restricting competition under Article 101(1). It then exempted the agreements under Article 101(3) but for a period of time shorter than the duration of the joint venture. The exemption was subject to the condition that the parent companies supply the same necessary rail services as they had agreed to supply to ENS to any international grouping of railway undertakings or any transport operator wishing to operate night passenger services through the Channel Tunnel.

ENS and the partner companies brought the case to the Court based on the arguments that the Commission's reasons for holding that the joint venture restricted competition between the parent companies and between the parent companies and ENS were based on a hypothetical assessment of conditions of competition and that the Commission should have weighed the pro-competitive effects.

The Court found that:

> the ENS agreements have effects restricting existing and potential competition (a) among the parent undertakings, (b) between *the* parent undertakings and ENS and (c) vis-à-vis third parties; furthermore (d), those restrictions are aggravated by the presence of a network of joint ventures set up by the parent undertakings.

In paragraph 136 of this judgment, the Court stated that:

> Before any examination of the parties' arguments as to whether the Commission's analysis as regards restrictions of competition was correct, it must be borne in mind that in assessing an agreement under Article 85(1) (now Article 101(1)) of the Treaty, account should be taken of the actual conditions in which it functions, in particular the economic context in which the undertakings operate, the products or services covered by the agreement and the actual structure of the market concerned ... unless it is an agreement containing obvious restrictions of competition such as price-fixing, market-sharing or the control of outlets. In the latter case, such restrictions may be weighed against their claimed pro-competitive effects only in the context of Article 85(3) of the Treaty, with a view to granting an exemption from the prohibition in Article 85(1).

Practitioners have discussed this paragraph at length.[430] One reading is that the Court reaffirmed that an economically realistic approach is necessary in the assessment of any particular case. The Court did not really exclude the balancing of negative and positive effects in Article 101(1) in order to reach a meaningful conclusion on the overall net effects of the agreement on competition. However, the methodology applied by the Court requires, before any such balancing could possibly be carried out, that negative effects be established first. The Court found that the Commission had failed to establish, or to provide adequate reasons for holding, that any of the alleged restrictive

---

430. See for example (Nazzini 2006).

effects occurred or might occur. There was, therefore, no need explicitly to address the question of the balancing of any negative effects against the pro-competitive effects of the agreements.

With respect to a European competition test the reading is that the case emphasises the importance of meaningful economic analysis that takes into account the real conditions of competition on the relevant market. The case also sets out the methodological framework for the analysis of restrictions of competition under Article 101(1). This methodological framework has been further developed in more recent cases.

In *Métropole Télévision (M6) v. Commission*,[431] the Court tried to clarify the exact scope of the economic assessment. The discussion in this case was again about a rule of reason in EU competition law. The Court stated that such a rule has not, as such, been confirmed by the Court of Justice of the EU. On the contrary, in various judgments the Court of Justice and the Court of First Instance indicated that the existence of a rule of reason in Community competition law is doubtful. Instead, in a number of judgments, the Court of Justice of the EU has favoured *a more flexible interpretation* of the prohibition laid down in Article 101(1).[432] Those judgments cannot, however, be interpreted as establishing the existence of a rule of reason in Community competition law. They are, rather, part of a broader trend in the case law according to which it is not necessary to hold, wholly in abstract and without drawing any distinction, that any agreement restricting the freedom of action of one or more of the parties is necessarily caught by the prohibition laid down in Article 101(1).

Jurisprudence requests that in assessing the applicability of Article 101(1) to an agreement, account should be taken of the actual conditions in which it functions, in particular the economic context in which the undertakings operate, the products or services covered by the agreement and the actual structure of the market concerned. Article 101 expressly provides, in its third paragraph, for the possibility of exempting agreements that restrict competition where they satisfy a number of conditions, in particular where they are indispensable to the attainment of certain objectives and do not afford undertakings the possibility of eliminating competition in respect of a substantial part of the products in question. *'It is only in the precise framework of that provision that the pro and anti-competitive aspects of a restriction may be weighed'*. The reasoning the Court provided is that Article 101(3) would lose much of its effectiveness, if such an examination had already been carried out under Article 101(1).

From the economic perspective there seems to be a misunderstanding with respect to the analysis performed in Article 101(1) and Article 101(3). Whereas the

---

431. (CFI, M6, Suez-Lyonnaise des eaux, France Télécom andTF1 v. Commission, Case T-112/99 2001, 74–78).
432. See in particular, (CFI, M6, Suez-Lyonnaise des eaux, France Télécom andTF1 v. Commission, Case T-112/99 2001, para. 75) (ECJ, STM v. MBU, Case 56-65 1966), (ECJ, L.C. Nungesser KG and Kurt Eisele v. Commission, Case 258/78 1982), (ECJ, Coditel SA, Compagnie générale pour la diffusion de la télévision, and others v. Ciné-Vog Films SA and others, Case 262/81 1982), (ECJ, Pronuptia de Paris GmbH v. Pronuptia de Paris Irmgard Schillgallis, Case 161/84 1986) and (CFI, ENS, Eurostar (UK), EPS, UIC, NS and SNCF v. Commission,Joined cases T-374/94, T-375/94, T-384/94 and T-388/94 1998).

economic analysis in Article 101(1) refers to the market situation as such, Article 101(3) deals with the economic situation of an individual undertaking. In Article 101(1), the welfare-reducing effects of an agreement in a given market are assessed taking into consideration possible welfare-enhancing effects of this agreement *in the market* affected. The scope of analysis refers to the overall welfare effects of the agreement under scrutiny representing the *European competition test*. In Article 101(3), the individual productive efficiencies related to a specific undertaking are assessed. This is a different type of economic analysis.

In *O2*,[433] the Court of First Instance clarified this distinction further. The following steps in the analysis were identified. These steps are elementary in the European competition test.

In order to assess whether an agreement is compatible with the common market in the light of the prohibition laid down in Article 101(1), it is necessary to examine the economic and legal context in which the agreement was concluded. That method of analysis is of general application and is not confined to a category of agreements.

Where it is accepted that the agreement does not have as its object a restriction of competition, the effects of the agreement should be considered and for it to be caught by the prohibition it is necessary to find that those factors are present. This shows that competition has in fact been prevented or restricted or distorted to an appreciable extent.

The competition in question must be understood within the actual context in which it would occur in the absence of the agreement in dispute (so-called *counterfactual analysis*). The interference with competition may in particular be doubted if the agreement seems really necessary for the penetration of a new area by an undertaking. Such a method of analysis, as regards, in particular, the taking into account of the competition situation that would exist in the absence of the agreement, does not amount to carrying out an assessment of the pro- and anti-competitive effects of the agreement and thus to applying a rule of reason in a US style. The Community judicature has not deemed to have a place for a US style rule of reason in Article 101(1). Thus, it is necessary to carry out a full analysis *by examining what the competitive situation would have been in the absence of the agreement*. The examination required in the light of Article 101(1) consists essentially of taking account of the impact of the agreement on existing and potential competition (see, to that effect, *Delimitis*, paragraph 21) and the competition situation in the absence of the agreement (see *Société Minière et Technique* at paragraphs 249–250). Those two factors are intrinsically linked.

Such an examination is necessary not only for the purposes of granting an exemption but prior to that, for the purposes of the economic analysis of the effects of the agreement on the competitive situation determining the applicability of Article 101.

In *Österreichische Postsparkasse AG/Bank für Arbeit und Wirtschaft AG v. Commission*,[434] the Court confirmed again that the ultimate purpose of the rules that

---

433. (CFI, O2 (Germany) GmbH & Co. OHG v. Commission, Case T-328/03 2006, 65–73).
434. In (CFI, Österreichische Postsparkasse AG, Bank für Arbeit und Wirtschaft AG v. Commission, Joined Cases T-213/01 and T-214/01 2006).

seek to ensure that competition is not distorted in the internal market is to increase the *well-being of consumers*. That purpose can be seen in particular from the wording of Article 101. Whilst the prohibition laid down in Article 101(1) may be declared inapplicable in the case of cartels which contribute to improving the production or distribution of the goods in question or to promoting technical or economic progress, that possibility, for which provision is made in Article 101(3), is, *inter alia*, subject to the condition that a fair share of the resulting benefit is allowed for users of those products. Competition law and competition policy therefore have an undeniable impact on the specific economic interests of final customers who purchase goods or services.

In 2014, the Court of Justice clarified further in the *Mastercard*[435] case the role of economic analysis in Article 101(1).

The Commission declared in its decision[436] that the multilateral interchange fees (MIFs) applied under the MasterCard card payment system to be contrary to competition law. The MIF corresponds to a proportion of the price of a payment card transaction that is retained by the card-issuing bank. The cost of the MIF is charged to merchants in the more general context of the costs which they are charged for the use of payment cards by the financial institution which handles their transactions. The Commission found that the MIF had the effect of setting a floor under the costs charged to merchants and thus constituted a restriction of price competition that was to their detriment. The Commission also took the view that it had not been demonstrated that the MIF could generate efficiencies capable of justifying its restrictive effect on competition.

In its judgment, the General Court[437] did not accept the arguments of the complainants relating to the objective necessity of the MIF to the operation of the MasterCard payment system. Since the MIF is not objectively necessary for the operation of the MasterCard system, the Commission was entitled to consider its effects on competition independently rather than in conjunction with the effects of the MasterCard system to which the MIF relates. That analysis of the effects of the MIF on competition was also endorsed by the General Court.

In paragraph 89, the Court of Justice reaffirmed that if a given operation or activity is not covered by the prohibition rule laid down in Article 101(1), owing to its neutrality or positive effect in terms of competition, a restriction of the commercial autonomy of one or more of the participants in that operation or activity is not covered by that prohibition rule either if that restriction is objectively necessary to the implementation of that operation or that activity and proportionate to the objectives of one or the other.[438]

---

435. (ECJ, MasterCard Inc. and Others v. Commission, C-832/12 P 2014).
436. (European Commission, Summary of Commission Decision of 19 December 2007 relating to a proceeding under Article 81 of the EC Treaty and Article 53 of the EEA Agreement (Case COMP/34.579 – MasterCard, Case COMP/36.518 – EuroCommerce, Case COMP/38.580 – Commercial Cards) 2009).
437. (ECJ, MasterCard Inc. and Others v. Commission, Case T-111/08 2012).
438. (see to that effect, in particular, judgments in (ECJ, Remia BV and others v. Commission, Case 42/84 1985, paras 19 and 20); (ECJ, Pronuptia de Paris GmbH v. Pronuptia de Paris Irmgard

Chapter 4: Competition Practice

The General Court dismissed the complaints related to a weighing-up of the restrictive effects of the MIF on competition, legitimately established by the Commission, with any economic advantages that may ensue in Article 101(1). By making reference to the judgments in *Van den Bergh Foods v. Commission*, [T-65/98, EU:T:2003:281], paragraph 107 and the case law there cited, the General Court reaffirmed that it is only within the specific framework of Article 101(3) that the pro and anti-competitive aspects of a restriction may be weighed.[439]

The Court of Justice confirmed this interpretation by stating in paragraph 180 of the *Mastercard* judgment that it is evident from the very wording of Article 101 and established that a measure is liable to have an appreciable adverse impact on the parameters of competition, such as the price, the quantity and quality of the goods or services, and is therefore covered by the prohibition rule laid down in Article 101(1), economic advantages can be considered only in the context of Article 101(3):[440]

> In the light of that finding, the General Court therefore correctly concluded, in paragraph 182 of the judgment under appeal, that the criticisms presented to it in relation to the two-sided nature of the system had no relevance in the context of a plea relating to infringement of Article 81(1) EC (now Article 101(1)), in so far as they entailed the taking into account of economic advantages under that paragraph. The General Court also correctly concluded that any economic advantages that may ensue from the MIF are relevant only in the context of the analysis under Article 81(3) EC.[441]

As in some other cartel cases the Court of Justice reconfirmed in the *Mastercard* case that it is apparent that horizontal agreements which include price-fixing elements are infringement of Article 101(1) almost per se. Economic analysis rarely changes such a conclusion.

4.4.5.2.2 Horizontal Price-Fixing Agreements

With respect to Article 101(1) the Court of Justice stated that the MIF stem from a decision by an association of undertakings to set prices and that the resulting anti-competitive effects are obvious:[442]

> In that regard, it is apparent from the case-law of the Court of Justice that certain types of coordination between undertakings reveal a sufficient degree of harm to competition for the examination of their effects to be considered unnecessary (see to that effect, in particular, judgments in LTM, EU:C:1966:38, 249; Beef Industry

---

Schillgallis, Case 161/84 1986, paras 15–17); (ECJ, Gøttrup-Klim e.a. Grovvareforeninger v. Dansk Landbrugs Grovvareselskab AmbA, Case C-250/92 1994, para. 35), and (ECJ, H.G. Oude Luttikhuis and others v. Verenigde Coöperatieve Melkindustrie Coberco BA., Case C-399/93 1995, paras 12–15).
439. (ECJ, MasterCard Inc. and Others v. Commission, Case T-111/08 2012).
440. (ECJ, MasterCard Inc. and Others v. Commission, C-832/12 P 2014).
441. Ibid., para. 181.
442. Ibid., para. 183.

Development Society and Barry Brothers, C-209/07, EU:C:2008:643, paragraph 15; and Allianz Hungária Biztosító and Others, EU:C:2013:160, paragraph 34 and the case-law cited). That case-law arises from the fact that certain forms of coordination between undertakings can be regarded, by their very nature, as being injurious to the proper functioning of normal competition (see to that effect, in particular, judgment in Allianz Hungária Biztosító and Others, EU:C:2013:160, paragraph 35 and the case-law cited).[443]

In *Vereniging van Samenwerkende Prijsregelnde Organisaties in de Bouwnijverheid and Others (SPO v. Others) v. Commission*[444], a reference case about a Dutch cartel, the Court of First Instance dismissed contentions that the Commission decision was void.

SPO is a coordinating organisation set up in 1963 by a number of Dutch associations of building undertakings. Under its statutes, SPO's object is *'to promote and administer orderly competition, to prevent improper conduct in price tendering and to promote the formation of economically justified prices.'* The Commission adopted its decision[445] finding that the statutes and the price regulating rules of the SPO constitute infringements of Article 101(1).[446]

The Court of First Instance confirmed the Commission's decision[447] by stating that the exchange of information constituted a concerted action and thereby restricting competition insofar as it leads to practical cooperation between prospective contractors and to the fixing of certain conditions for the transaction. The Court approved the Commission's view that a joint fixing of price increases constitutes price-fixing within the meaning of Article 101(1)(a). The Court of First Instance rejected the application of a rule of reason within the scope of Article 101(1) for a horizontal agreement, confirming that any advantage created by the concerted behaviour in question, such as the alleged improvement in the transactional structure of the market is irrelevant in the context of Article 101(1) and might only be considered in connection with Article 101(3).[448]

---

443. *Ibid.*, paras 184–185.
444. (CFI, Vereniging van Samenwerkende Prijsregelende Organisaties in de Bouwnijverheid and others v. Commission, Case T-29/92 1995).
445. (Decision IV/31.572 and 32.571 on Building and construction industry in the Netherlands 1992).
446. It also rejected the application for an exemption under Art. 81(3) and imposed on the appellants fines totalling ECU 22,498.000.
447. (CFI, Vereniging van Samenwerkende Prijsregelende Organisaties in de Bouwnijverheid and others v. Commission, Case T-29/92 1995).
448. Their first plea was that the Court of First Instance infringed Art. 81(3) and Art. 190 of the Treaty and Art. 9(1) of Regulation 17/62 or in any event the general principles of Community law requiring reasons to be given for decisions, and failed to observe the rights of the defence. Their second plea concerned the determination of the amount of the fines. Pursuant to Art. 119 of its Rules of Procedure, the Court may, where an appeal is clearly inadmissible or clearly unfounded, by reasoned order dismiss it at any time. Since the Court of Justice found that every plea raised in this Appeal was manifestly unfounded, the Appeal was rejected by means of reasoned order rather than judgment. (ECJ, Vereniging van SAmenwerkende Prijsregelende Organisaties in de Bouwnijverheid and Others v. Commission, Case C-137/95 P 1996).

4.4.5.2.3 Horizontal Concerted Practices

The broad interpretation of the term agreement needs to be borne in mind when *concerted practices* are at stake. By its very nature, then, a concerted practice does not have all the elements of a contract but may *inter alia* arise out of coordination, which becomes apparent from the behaviour of the participants. Any consensus between parties to regulate their future competitive conduct is sufficient to establish a prohibited restraint on their autonomy and independence.[449] The mere existence of parallel conduct in itself is not sufficient to prove the existence of a concerted practice. The formal burden of proving such an infringement of Article 101(1) rests with the Commission or the Courts. Thus, if parties can show that, although there is parallel behaviour, other explanations than the existence of collusion is more likely, Article 101(1) does not apply.[450] Explanations relate to the factual evidence on the nature of the market and the way in which firms behaved therein. If facts do not indicate that the market structure naturally leads to price uniformity, *and* if there are other factors as well, which are indicative of collusion, then the onus shifts to the firms on how the identity of price movements can be explained without some element of collusion. There can be a concerted practice even though there is no actual 'plan' operative between the parties.

Some of the restrictive practices to which Article 101(1) applies only immediately concern relations between the participants, such as agreements to limit production or coordinate technical development or investment. Likewise, the exchange of commercially sensitive information, which may not have an immediately perceptible impact in the marketplace, has been found to violate Article 101(1) insofar as it enables competitors to take their business decisions with knowledge of each other's market strategy and intentions.[451] Only those consequences of the agreement that are inherent or obvious are relevant. This requires a determination of the *'natural and probable consequences'*.[452] It is also possible that parts of the agreement that individually do not infringe Article 101(1) produce anti-competitive effects in combination with one another. The effects of an anti-competitive agreement may be reinforced if there are parallel agreements between the same firms or between third parties.

Authorities are able to act against anti-competitive effects at an early stage. The anti-competitive effects do not need to have an immediate impact in the marketplace or to be perceptible to other market operators. Potential effects are relevant as well as the actual effects.[453]

---

449. (Decision IV/31.865 on PVC 1988, 11) (Decision 89/191/ on LdPE IV/31.866 1988, 32) (Decision IV/31.149 on Polypropylene 1986, 29).
450. (ECJ, Compagnie Royale Asturienne des Mines SA and Rheinzink GmbH v. Commission, Joined cases 29/83 and 30/83 1984).
451. (Decision IV/29.725q on Wood pulp 1984, 20).
452. (Decision IV/27.000 on IFTRA rules for producers of virgin aluminium 1975, 8).
453. (Decision IV/33.814 on Ford/Volkswagen 1992, para. 41).
    (Decision IV/32.688 on Konsortium ECR 900 1990).

In the *Wood Pulp* cartel case, the economic analysis of the market structure played the decisive role in assessing pricing behaviours. The Court's experts illustrated which pricing policies can be expected in an oligopolistic market.

In its *Wood Pulp* decision,[454] the Commission found that forty wood pulp producers and three of their trade associations had infringed Article 101(1) by concerting on prices. According to the Commission, the price parallelism could only be explained by collusion between the producers. In order to analyse this question, the Court[455] decided to obtain an expert's report on parallel pricing. By an order of 25 October 1990, the Court decided to obtain a second expert's report. The experts were requested to describe and analyse the characteristics of the market during the period covered by the decision and to state whether, in the light of those characteristics, the natural operation of the market should lead to a differential price structure or to a uniform price structure.

The experts observed first that the system of announcements at issue must be viewed in the context of the long-term relationships which existed between producers and their customers and which were a result of both the method of manufacturing the pulp and the cyclical nature of the market. The experts found that because of the specific production process, a relationship based on close cooperation was established between the pulp producers and the paper manufacturers. Purchasers demanded the introduction of that system of announcements because they wished to ascertain as soon as possible the prices, which they might be charged in order to estimate their costs and to fix prices of their own products. The announced price was regarded as a ceiling price below which the transaction price could always be renegotiated.[456]

It was apparent from the expert's report that the experts regard the normal operation of the market as a more plausible explanation for the uniformity of prices than collusion. The experts analysed the structure of the market and price trends over the period at issue and maintained that several factors or mechanisms specific to that market were incompatible with an explanation based on concerted action.[457] The experts also directed a number of specific criticisms against the Commission's explanations concerning the impact on prices of transport costs, the size of orders and, in general, differences in costs and the granting of secret rebates.[458]

Following the expert's reasoning, the Court stated that in this case concerted action was not the only plausible explanation for parallel conduct. Parallel conduct cannot be regarded as furnishing proof of concerted action unless concerted action constitutes the only plausible explanation for such conduct. Accordingly, the parallel conduct established by the Commission did not constitute evidence of concerted action. Article 1(1) of the contested decisions was therefore annulled.[459]

---

454. (Decision IV/29.725q on Wood pulp 1984).
455. (ECJ, A. Ahlström Osakeyhtiö and others v. Commission, Joined cases C-89/85, C-104/85, C-114/85, C-116/85, C-117/85 and C-125/85 to C-129/85 1993).
456. *Ibid.*, para. 77.
457. *Ibid.*, para. 115.
458. *Ibid.*, para. 121.
459. *Ibid.*, para. 126.

The Court's decision is of significance in its insistence that rigorous economic analysis may be required in order to determine whether there is another plausible explanation for the parties' conduct on pricing. It was in fact expert evidence, which destroyed the Commission's case before the Court.[460]

In *Philip Morris*[461], a reference case about a minority share acquisition, the Court of Justice analysed whether the acquisition by one company of a minority interest in a competitor had an anti-competitive object or effect. In this case, the Court of Justice reviewed not only whether the agreements included clauses with an anti-competitive object, but also whether the actual effect of the acquisition agreement would be to restrict competition and whether it was *potentially* an instrument for influencing the commercial conduct of a competitor. The Court said that the acquisition of an equity stake could:[462]

> serve as an instrument for influencing the commercial conduct of the companies in question so as to restrict or distort competition on the market on which they carry on business. ... That may also be the case where the agreement gives the investing company the possibility of reinforcing its position at a later stage and taking effective control of the other company. Account must be taken not only of the immediate effects of the agreement but also of its potential effects and of the possibility that the agreement may be part of a long-term plan. Finally, every agreement must be assessed in its economic context and in particular in the light of the situation on the relevant market.

In other words, an analysis to show the economic context was an essential requirement in *Philip Morris*.

4.4.5.2.4 Conclusion

The 'European' approach in the competition assessment in Article 101(1) cannot and should not be compared with the US rule of reason.[463] The straightforward argument is quite simple: *the law is different*. EU competition law entails in Article 101 two economic tests: the first one is the economic assessment of whether competition is restricted in Article 101(1) and the second economic assessment relates to the question of whether such a restriction can be exempted under Article 101(3). Thus, the European approach is a different one and any attempt to streamline the European

---

460. (Van Gerven & Varona 1994).
461. (ECJ, British-American Tobacco Company Ltd and R. J. Reynolds Industries Inc. v. Commission, Joined cases 142 and 156/84 1987, 4577–4583).
462. *Ibid*.
463. The rule of reason is a doctrine developed by the US Supreme Court in its interpretation of the Sherman Antitrust Act. The rule, stated and applied in the case of (U.S. Supreme Court, Standard Oil Co. of New Jersey v. United States, 211 U.S. 1911), is that only combinations and contracts *unreasonably restraining trade* are subject to actions under the anti-trust laws and that size and possession of monopoly power are not illegal. Rule of reason analysis, as understood by US authorities, involves identification of the relevant market, establishing the defendant's market power as well as a multitude of other factors used to analyse whether the restraint adversely affects competition in the inter-brand market, and the justifications establishing a legitimate objective and the necessity of the restraint to achieve that objective.

approach with the US rule of reason needs to fail as it did in the past. The Court of Justice of the EU clarified these differences in a number of cases by stating several times that EU competition law does not entail a US style rule of reason. On the other hand, the Court of Justice of the EU has frequently held that Article 101(1) is not contravened by the following, by virtue of their object:

- An exclusive-supply clause and a non-competition clause included in a franchising contract, in that they were necessary to ensure that that contract could discharge its typical function.[464]
- A non-competitive clause in a contract for the transfer of a business, if not of disproportionate duration, may be necessary to ensure that the transfer has the effect intended.[465]
- A no-challenge clause in a patent-licence agreement (granting a free licence) since it was crucial for the equilibrium of an agreement which has neither as its object nor as its effect the prevention, restriction or distortion of competition.[466]
- An exclusive-supply clause in a brewery agreement, since it was an inherent feature of that form of cooperation between reseller and supplier, based on convergence of interests in promoting sales of the product, which is characteristic of that specific contract.
- As well as in a number of other cases discussed in the previous sections.

As illustrated, the Court of Justice of the EU considers it an essential feature of Article 101(1) that its application in any given case depends upon the economic aims or effects of transactions entered into between undertakings. In this context, the Court has frequently stated that the requirement of protection of competition pursued by Article 101(1) cannot be defined in abstract terms but must be seen in the specific context in which the conduct of the undertakings came about. This requirement means that the nature and intensity of competition may vary according to the products or services concerned and the economic structure of the relevant sectors.[467] The economic test in Article 101(1) refers to competition in a market by taking into account the consumer welfare of EU citizens. The Commission acknowledges this notion in its Notice on horizontal cooperation agreements[468] as well by stating that:

many horizontal agreements, however, do not have as their object a restriction of competition. Therefore, an analysis of the effects of the agreements is necessary. For this analysis, it is not sufficient that the agreement limits competition between the parties. It must also be likely to affect competition in the market to such an extent that negative market effects as to prices, output, innovation or the variety or quality of goods and services can be expected.

---

464. (ECJ, Pronuptia de Paris GmbH v. Pronuptia de Paris Irmgard Schillgallis, Case 161/84 1986).
465. (ECJ, Remia BV and others v. Commission, Case 42/84 1985).
466. (ECJ, Bayer AG and Maschinenfabrik Hennecke GmbH v. Heinz Süllhöfer, Case 65/86 1988).
467. (ECJ, Metro SB-Großmärkte GmbH & Co. KG v. Commission, Case 26-76 1977).
468. (European Commission, Commission Notice – Guidelines on the applicability of Art. 81 of the EC Treaty to horizontal cooperation agreements 2001, 19).

Thus, the theory of harm in Article 101(1) relates to consumers' detriment.

The European appraisal implies that a comprehensive competition test has to be performed in Article 101(1) if certain evidence points in this direction. According to this rule, the anti-competitive effects of a certain practice are weighted in the light of its economic and legal context.[469] The ultimate consequences for competition are assessed under that paragraph and not under Article 101(3).

4.4.6 Economic Analysis in Article 101(3)

Article 101(3) tempers the prohibition of anti-competitive agreements and concerted practices by acknowledging that not all agreements restricting competition in the sense of Article 101(1) are bad for society and consumers. Article 101(3) recognises that some agreements may produce benefits that fully compensate for their negative effects on competition. These benefits can consist of lower costs, new products and services or products and services of a better quality. Assessments of this nature are not an exact science. Article 101(3) acknowledges that, and exempts those agreements of the prohibition of Article 101(1).

Where the criteria laid down in Article 101(3) are fulfilled, the prohibition in Article 101(1) may be declared to be inapplicable to agreements, decisions or concerted practices, or categories thereof. The application of Article 101(3) is commonly referred to as an *'exemption'* though this word does not appear in the Treaty itself.

Article 101(3) provides that:

> *The provisions of paragraph 1 may, however, be declared inapplicable in the case of:*
>
> - *any agreement or category of agreements between undertakings;*
> - *any decision or category of decisions by associations of undertakings;*
> - *any concerted practice or category of concerted practices;*
>   *wich contributes to improving the production or distribution of goods or to promoting technical or economic progress, while allowing consumers a fair share of the resulting benefit, and which does not:*
>   *(a) impose on the undertakings concerned restrictions which are not indispensable to the attainment of these objectives;*
>   *(b) afford such undertakings the possibility of eliminating competition in respect of a substantial part of the products in question.*

This provision means that agreements may benefit from an exemption when the pro-competitive effects of the agreements or practices outweigh the anti-competitive effects of an agreement or practice. The evaluation of pro- and anti-competitive effects must be based on both existing and future competitive conditions.

The Commission may exempt a class of similar restrictive agreements whose pro-competitive benefits are considered to outweigh their anti-competitive detriments under a so-called *'block exemption'* regulation. Such regulations automatically exempt

---

469. (Manzini 2002, 399).

agreements of the relevant type from the application of Article 101(1) if they do not exceed the limits set forth in the regulation.

To satisfy Article 101(3), an agreement must satisfy four cumulative conditions:

- It must contribute to improving the production or distribution of goods or contribute to promoting technical or economic progress.
- Consumers must receive a fair share of the resulting benefits.
- The restrictions must be indispensable to the attainment of these objectives.
- The agreement must not afford the parties the possibility of eliminating competition in respect of a substantial part of the products in question.

All four criteria need to apply in order to qualify for an exemption. In the following the four criteria are discussed.

The 2004 guidelines[470] set out the Commission's interpretation of the conditions for exception contained in Article 101(3) and provide guidance on how it will apply Article 101 in individual cases.

4.4.6.1 First Condition of Article 101(3)

According to the first condition of Article 101(3), the restrictive agreement must contribute to improving the production or distribution of goods or to promoting technical or economic progress. This provision defines types of efficiency gains that can be taken into account. In addition, the further tests of the second, third and fourth conditions of Article 101(3) have to be positive as well. While assessing efficiency gains the nature, the likelihood and magnitude and the date of the claimed efficiency are of great importance.

In general, efficiencies result from an integration of economic activities whereby assets are combined. It is essential that the efficiencies could not have been achieved alone. The Commission's guidelines on Article 101(3) distinguish between cost efficiencies and efficiencies of a qualitative nature which create value in the form of new or improved products. Figure 4.10 shows different types of efficiencies that can be generated by vertical or horizontal agreements.

Figure 4.10   Type of Efficiencies

Cost efficiencies	Qualitative efficiencies	Other effects
☐ Development of new production technologies ☐ Synergies ☐ Economies of scale ☐ Economies of scope ☐ Planning of production, stock optimisation	☐ R&D-Agreements ☐ Licence Agreements ☐ Agreements providing for joint production ☐ Distribution Agreements	☐ Stimulation of investment incentives by vertical agreements due to elimination of free-rider & hold-up-problems

---

470. (Commission Guidelines on Art. 81(3) 2004, 97–118).

Only objective benefits can be taken into account.[471] A subjective view of the parties has to be dismissed.[472]

Therefore, independent expertise is required which substantiates the following issues:

- Nature of the claimed efficiencies.
- Link between the agreement and the efficiencies.
- Likelihood and magnitude of each claimed efficiency.
- How and when each claimed efficiency would be achieved.
- Any cost of achieving the claimed efficiencies.[473]

In order to assess the efficiencies, there must be a causal link between the product/distribution conditions and the claimed efficiencies.[474] The efficiencies have to be caused by the economic activity that forms the object of the agreement. In addition, cost savings that arise from the exercise of market power are not taken into account. The monetary value of the claimed efficiencies must be as accurately as possible calculated including the methods by which the efficiencies have been or will be achieved. Only the net efficiencies are considered. Costs that are incurred in obtaining the efficiencies must be deducted. Efficiencies may be substantiated by the following types of evidence[475]:

- a company's internal plans and cost studies, as well as public statements;
- engineering and financial evaluations;
- industry studies from third party consultants;
- economics and engineering literature;
- testimony from industry, accounting and economic experts;
- information regarding past merger experience in the industry; and
- information on firm performance from the stock market.

In order to obtain a systematic understanding on efficiencies, it is important to provide a typology of the various kinds of efficiencies. The first typology is based on the concept of the production function and mainly used in the literature on productivity measurement: (1) Rationalisation, (2) Economies of scale, (3) Technological progress, (4) Purchasing economies and (5) Slack. A second distinction often made is between: (a) Real cost savings and (b) Redistributive (or pecuniary) cost savings. This distinction is important since typically only real cost savings are considered in a merger

---

471. See e.g., (CFI, Mg, Antena 3 de Televisión, SA, Gestevisión Telecinco, SA and SIC, SA v. Commission, Joined cases T-185/00, T-216/00, T-299/00 and T-300/00 2002, 86); (CFI, Matra Hachette SA v. Commission, Case T-17/93 1994, 85); and (ECJ, Vereniging ter Bevordering van het Vlaamse Boekwezen, VBVB, and Vereniging ter Bevordering van de Belangen des Boekhandels, VBBB, v. Commission, Joined cases 43/82 and 63/82 1984, 61).
472. See (CFI, CMA CGM and others v. Commission, Case T-213/00 2003, 226).
473. (Guidelines on the Art. 81(3) of the Treaty 2004, 51).
474. In an OFT paper, the relationship between the efficiency arguments for vertical restraints across different product/distribution conditions is discussed extensively. See in: (Waterson & Dobson 1996, 55).
475. (ICN Merger Guidelines Project 2004).

efficiency defence. Redistributive gains are cost savings that the firms may achieve for example in the form of lower taxes. However purchasing economies may be redistributive. Real cost savings are those savings that correspond to some savings of productive resources in the economy. Rationalisation, economies of scale, technological progress, and slack reduction are all real cost savings. Also some purchasing economies are real cost savings. A third distinction that is often made is between: (1) Fixed costs and (2) Variable costs. This distinction is important since savings in variable costs may almost immediately benefit the consumers. Savings in fixed costs normally come in the form of economies of scale, technological progress, and purchasing economies. Savings in variable costs may come in all five forms. A fourth distinction that is useful is between: (a) Firm level efficiencies and (b) Industry level efficiencies. An example of efficiencies at the level of the industry is cost savings due to a reallocation of production.[476]

The same agreement may give rise to several kinds of efficiencies, which even may overlap. It is essential that the efficiencies could not have been achieved alone. The Commission's guidelines on Article 101(3) discuss in particular cost efficiencies and efficiencies that create value in the form of new or improved products.

4.4.6.1.1 Cost Efficiencies

Cost efficiencies[477] can originate from a number of different sources. One very important source of cost savings is the development of new production technologies and methods.[478] Another very important source of efficiency is synergies resulting from an integration of existing assets.[479] Cost efficiencies may also result from economies of scale, i.e., declining cost per unit of output as output increases. Learning economies constitute a related type of efficiency.[480] Economies of scope are another source of cost efficiency, which occur when firms achieve cost savings by producing different products on the basis of the same input.[481] Efficiencies in the form of cost reductions can also follow from agreements that allow for better planning of production, reducing the need to hold expensive inventory and allowing for better capacity utilisation.

---

476. (Röller, Stennek & Verboven 2000, 13).
477. The following examples are illustrated in more detail in the Commission's guidelines on Art. 81(3).
478. For instance, the introduction of the assembly line led to a very substantial reduction in the cost of producing motor vehicles.
479. The combination of two existing technologies that have complementary strengths may reduce production costs or lead to the production of a higher quality product. Similarly, if one undertaking has optimised one part of the value chain and another undertaking has optimised another part of the value chain, the combination of their operations may lead to lower costs.
480. As experience is gained in using a particular production process or in performing particular tasks, productivity may increase because the process is made to run more efficiently or because the task is performed more quickly.
481. Such efficiencies may arise from the fact that it is possible to use the same components and the same facilities and personnel to produce a variety of products.

4.4.6.1.2 Qualitative Efficiencies

In the analysis of technological progress a distinction is often made between process and product innovations. A process innovation reduces the cost of producing an existing product; a product innovation increases the value (quality) of an existing product. Technical and technological progress in the form of new or improved goods and services may stem from research and development agreements, licence agreements, and agreements providing for joint production of new or improved goods or services. Improvements in product quality and service levels constitute yet another example of efficiencies forming part of this category.

4.4.6.2 Second Condition of Article 101(3)

According to the second condition of Article 101(3) consumers must receive a fair share of the efficiencies generated by the restrictive agreement. Consumers within the meaning of Article 101(3) are the customers of the parties to the agreement and subsequent purchasers. The concept of fair share implies that the pass-on of benefits must at least compensate consumers for any actual or likely negative impact. Within EC competition policy one goal is to maximise 'consumer' welfare. Therefore the distribution of the gains and pass-on issues are very important.[482]

If the agreement has both substantial anti-competitive effects and substantial pro-competitive effects a careful analysis is required. The following two sections describe in more detail the analytical framework for assessing consumer pass-on of efficiency gains.

In general, cost efficiencies may in some circumstances lead to increased output and lower prices for the affected consumers. If due to cost efficiencies the undertakings in question can increase profits by expanding output, consumer pass-on may occur. In the assessment, the following factors are taken into account:[483]

- Characteristics and structure of the market.
- Nature and magnitude of the efficiency gains.
- Elasticity of demand.
- Magnitude of the restriction of competition.

The degree of competition remaining on the market and the nature of this competition influences the likelihood of pass-on. In the assessment it is important to know if cost savings are passed on to consumers in the form of a lower price. From an empirical perspective, *pass-on studies* appear in various applications.

---

482. (Yao & Dahdouh 1993, 41–43) A provocative article argues that a pass-on requirement should be rejected for an entirely different reason. See (Yde & Vita 1996) (a prediction of economic theory that 'the more competitive the relevant market, the less likely it is that merger-specific efficiencies will be reflected in the post-merger market price.')
483. (Guidelines on the Art. 81(3) of the Treaty 2004, 96).

There is some scepticism about the pass-on proviso. In practice, cost efficiencies that lead to reductions in variable or marginal costs are more cognisable to competition authorities than reductions in fixed costs because they are more likely to result in lower consumer prices and to be achieved in the short-term. In other words, efficiencies are thought to be more clearly identifiable where they impact upon variable costs (and thus marginal cost), since such cost savings tend to stimulate competition and are more likely to be passed directly on to consumers in the form of lower prices (because of their importance in short run price setting behaviour). Critics remark that it would assume that efficiencies can be neatly segregated into 'variable' cost savings that presumably will be passed on and 'fixed' cost savings that presumably will not. These fixed cost/variable cost allocations superimposed on the already equivocal calculations add a further layer of imprecision to an already impressive exercise.[484] Further, determination of what costs might be 'variable' in any given instance is highly problematic and can be a matter of the analysis timeframe adopted. Reductions in fixed costs can eventually become variable in the long run and therefore can play an important role in longer-term price formation.

The degree of competition remaining on the market and the nature of this competition influences the likelihood of pass-on. If undertakings compete mainly on price and are not subject to significant capacity constraints, pass-on may occur relatively quickly. If competition is mainly on capacity and capacity adaptations occur with a certain time lag, pass-on will be slower. Pass-on is also likely to be slower when the market structure is conducive to tacit collusion. The nature of the efficiency gains also plays an important role. According to economic theory, undertakings maximise their profits by selling units of output until marginal revenue equals marginal cost. Marginal revenue is the change in total revenue resulting from selling an additional unit of output and marginal cost is the change in total cost resulting from producing that additional unit of output. It follows from this principle that as a general rule output and pricing decisions of a profit-maximising undertaking are not determined by its fixed costs (i.e., costs that do not vary with the rate of production) but by its variable costs (i.e., costs that vary with the rate of production). After fixed costs are incurred and capacity is set, pricing and output decisions are determined by variable cost and demand conditions. It follows that undertakings may have a direct incentive to pass-on to consumers in the form of higher output and lower prices efficiencies that reduce marginal costs, whereas they have no such incentive with regard to efficiencies that reduce fixed costs.[485]

The actual pass-on rate depends on the extent to which consumers respond to changes in price, i.e., the elasticity of demand. The greater the increase in demand caused by a decrease in price, the greater the pass-on rate. It must also be taken into account that efficiency gains often do not affect the whole cost structure of the undertakings concerned and the impact on the price to consumers is reduced. The general empirical finding from literature is that pass-on is indeed incomplete. The examples cited above suggest that pass-on roughly varies between 30% and 70%. That

---

484. (Leary 2002).
485. (Guidelines on the Art. 81(3) of the Treaty 2004, 98).

is if cost is reduced by 10%, price is reduced by 3–7%.[486] However, the net effect of the agreement must at least be neutral. In this context it is not necessary that consumers receive a share of each and every efficiency gain. It suffices that sufficient benefits are passed on. In some cases a certain period of time may be required before the efficiencies materialise. Pass-on to the consumer occurs with a certain time lag.[487]

Finally, and very importantly, it is necessary to balance the two opposing forces resulting from the restriction of competition and the cost efficiencies.

In addition, the second condition of Article 101(3) incorporates a *'sliding scale'* as defined in an OECD paper.[488] Under the sliding scale, the more that competition is restricted, the higher the efficiency claims and the pass-on to consumers must be in order to grant an exemption. This sliding scale approach implies that if the restrictive effects of an agreement are relatively limited and the efficiencies are substantial it is likely that a fair share of the cost savings will be passed on to consumers. If, on the other hand, the restrictive effects of the agreement are substantial and the cost savings are relatively insignificant, it is very unlikely that the second condition of Article 101(3) will be fulfilled.[489]

Consumer pass-on can also take the form of new and improved products, creating sufficient value for consumers to compensate for the anti-competitive effects of the agreement, including a price increase. Any such assessment necessarily requires value judgment. The availability of new and improved products constitutes an important source of consumer welfare. As long as the increase in value stemming from such improvements exceeds any harm from an increase in price caused by the restrictive agreement, consumers are better off than without the agreement and the consumer pass-on requirement of Article 101(3) is normally fulfilled.

4.4.6.3 *Third Condition of Article 101(3)*

In the context of the third condition of Article 101(3) the decisive factor is whether or not the restrictive agreement and individual restrictions make it possible to perform the activity in question more efficiently than would have been the case in the absence of the agreement or the restriction concerned.[490] This condition implies a two-fold test:

- First, the restrictive agreement as such must be necessary in order to achieve the efficiencies.
- Secondly, the individual restrictions of competition that flow from the agreement must also be necessary for the attainment of the efficiencies.

---

486. (Röller, Stennek & Verboven 2000, 53).
487. In order to allow for an appropriate comparison of a present loss to consumers with a future gain to consumers, the value of future gains must be discounted applying an appropriate discount rate.
488. (OECD Roundtable on Competition Policy and Efficiency Claims in Horizontal Agreements 1996, 53).
489. (Guidelines on the Art. 81(3) of the Treaty 2004, 90).
490. The question is not whether in the absence of the restriction the agreement would not have been concluded, but whether more efficiencies are produced with the agreement or restriction than in the absence of the agreement or restriction.

The first test contained in the third condition of Article 101(3) requires that the efficiencies be specific to the agreement in question in the sense that there are no other practicable and less restrictive means of achieving the efficiencies. In making this latter assessment the market conditions and business realities facing the parties to the agreement have to be taken into account. Undertakings invoking the benefit of Article 101(3) must explain and demonstrate why seemingly realistic and less restrictive alternatives to the agreement would be significantly less efficient.[491]

In particular, the examination is relevant whether the parties could have achieved the efficiencies without the restrictive agreement, either on their own or by means of another less restrictive type of agreement and, if so, when they would be able to obtain the efficiencies.[492] In this assessment, the minimum efficient scale[493] on the market concerned works as a benchmark. The larger the minimum efficient scale compared to the current size of either of the parties to the agreement, the more likely it is that the efficiencies will be deemed to be specific to the agreement. Where the agreements produce substantial synergies through the combination of complementary assets and capabilities, the very nature of the efficiencies give rise to a presumption that the agreement is necessary to attain them.[494]

Once it is found that the agreement in question is necessary in order to produce the efficiencies, the indispensability of each restriction of competition flowing from the agreement must be assessed. A restriction is indispensable if its absence would eliminate or significantly reduce the efficiencies that follow from the agreement or make it significantly less likely that they will materialise. In this context it must be assessed whether individual restrictions are reasonably necessary in order to produce the efficiencies.

The assessment of indispensability is made within the actual context in which the agreement operates and must in particular take account of the structure of the market, the economic risks related to the agreement, and the incentives facing the parties.[495]

In some cases a restriction may be indispensable only for a certain period of time, in which case the exception of Article 101(3) only applies during that period.

4.4.6.4 Fourth Condition of Article 101(3)

According to the fourth condition of Article 101(3), the agreement must not afford the undertakings concerned the possibility of eliminating competition in respect of a substantial part of the products concerned. This concept is an autonomous Community

---

491. (Guidelines on the Art. 81(3) of the Treaty 2004, 75).
492. For instance, where the claimed efficiencies take the form of cost reductions resulting from economies of scale or scope the undertakings concerned must substantiate why the same efficiencies would not be likely to be attained through internal growth and price competition.
493. The minimum efficient scale is the level of output required to minimise average cost and exhaust economies of scale.
494. (Guidelines on the Art. 81(3) of the Treaty 2004, 76).
495. (Guidelines on the Art. 81(3) of the Treaty 2004, 80).

Chapter 4: Competition Practice

law concept specific to Article 101(3). Article 101(3) requires that it is interpreted as precluding any application of this provision to restrictive agreements that concluded by a dominant undertaking constitute an abuse of a dominant position. The existence of an elimination of competition within the meaning of the last condition of Article 101(3) depends on the degree of competition existing prior to the agreement and on the impact of the restrictive agreement on competition, i.e., the reduction in competition that the agreement brings about. The greater the reduction of competition caused by the agreement the greater the likelihood that competition in respect of a substantial part of the products concerned risks being eliminated. The application of the last condition of Article 101(3) requires an analysis of the various sources of competition in the market, the level of competitive constraint that they impose on the parties to the agreement and the impact of the agreement on this competitive constraint. In the assessment of the impact of the agreement on competition it is also relevant to examine its influence on the various parameters of competition. Both actual and potential competition must be considered.[496]

The scale of remaining sources of *actual competition* is not purely on the basis of market share. More extensive qualitative and quantitative analysis is required. Therefore, the capacity of actual competitors to compete and their incentive to do so must be examined. Also, past competitive interaction may also provide an indication. If an agreement is concluded with a competitor that in the past has been a maverick, such an agreement may change the competitive incentives and capabilities of the competitor and thereby remove an important source of competition in the market. In cases involving differentiated products, the impact of the agreement may depend on the competitive relationship between the products sold by the parties to the agreement. When undertakings offer differentiated products the competitive constraint that individual products impose on each other differs according to the degree of substitutability between them. It must therefore be considered what is the degree of substitutability between the products offered by the parties. The more the products of the parties to the agreement are close substitutes the greater the likely restrictive effect of the agreement.[497]

While sources of actual competition are usually the most important, as they are most easily verified, sources of *potential competition* must also be taken into account. The assessment of potential competition requires an analysis of barriers to entry facing undertakings that are not already competing within the relevant market. Any assertions by the parties that there are low barriers to market entry must be supported by information identifying the sources of potential competition and the parties must also substantiate why these sources constitute a real competitive pressure on the parties.[498] In the assessment of entry barriers and the real possibility for new entry, it is relevant to examine, *inter alia*, the following:[499]

---

496. (Guidelines on the Art. 81(3) of the Treaty 2004, 107–108).
497. (Guidelines on the Art. 81(3) of the Treaty 2004, 109–113).
498. (Guidelines on the Art. 81(3) of the Treaty 2004, 114).
499. (Guidelines on the Art. 81(3) of the Treaty 2004, 115).

- The regulatory framework with a view to determining its impact on new entry.
- The cost of entry including sunk costs: Sunk costs are those that cannot be recovered if the entrant subsequently exits the market. The higher the sunk costs the higher the commercial risk for potential entrants.
- The minimum efficient scale within the industry, i.e., the rate of output where average costs are minimised. If the minimum efficient scale is large compared to the size of the market, efficient entry is likely to be more costly and risky.
- The competitive strengths of potential entrants. Effective entry is particularly likely where potential entrants have access to at least as cost efficient technologies as the incumbents or other competitive advantages that allow them to compete effectively. When potential entrants are on the same or an inferior technological trajectory compared to the incumbents and possess no other significant competitive advantage entry is more risky and less effective.
- The position of buyers and their ability to bring onto the market new sources of competition. It is irrelevant that certain strong buyers may be able to extract more favourable conditions from the parties to the agreement than their weaker competitors. The presence of strong buyers can only serve to counter a prima facie finding of elimination of competition if it is likely that the buyers in question will pave the way for effective new entry.
- The likely response of incumbents to attempted new entry. Incumbents may for example through past conduct have acquired a reputation of aggressive behaviour, thereby having an impact on future entry.
- The economic outlook for the industry may be an indicator of its longer-term attractiveness. Industries that are stagnating or in decline are less attractive candidates for entry than industries characterised by growth.
- Past entry on a significant scale or the absence thereof.

4.4.7 EU Competition Rules for Distribution

In 2010 the Commission adopted a Regulation[500] block exempting vertical agreements between manufacturers and distributors for the sale of products and services. The Regulation and the accompanying Guidelines will be valid until 2022. The principles from the previous guidelines remain namely that companies are free to decide how their products are distributed, provided their agreements do not contain price-fixing or other hardcore restrictions, and *both* manufacturer and distributor do not have more than a 30% market share. Approved distributors are free to sell on the Internet without limitation on quantities, customers' location and restrictions on prices. The 2010 rules address in particular aspects of the Internet as a force for online sales and for cross-border commerce.[501] Once authorised, distributors must be free to sell on their websites as they do in their traditional shops and physical points of sale. For selective

---

500. (Regulation (EU) 330/2010 on the application of Art. 101 (3) 2010).
501. (Commission Press Release IP/10/445 2010).

distribution, this means that manufacturers cannot limit the quantities sold over the Internet or charge higher prices for products to be sold online. Terminating transactions or re-routing consumers after they have entered their credit card details showing a foreign address are not accepted either. Manufacturers can still choose distributors on the basis of quality standards for the presentation of the products regardless of whether they operate off- or online. They may decide to sell only to dealers that have one or more 'brick and mortar' shops, so that consumers can physically see and try or test their products. However, in this regard, the Commission will be particularly attentive to concentrated markets to which price discounters either online only or traditional may not have access.

A channel of distribution is the structure of intra-company organisation units and extra-company agents and dealers, wholesale and retail, through which a commodity, product, or service is marketed. Distribution channel strategy is a challenging component of marketing products and services. With larger multinational companies, operating via country subsidiaries, distribution channel strategy is an integral part of the total marketing programme and must either fit or be fitted to product design, price and communications aspects of the total marketing programme.

In many cases, manufacturers are unable to sell their products abroad at all, unless a distributor handles them. It may be both costly and risky for the manufacturers to market their products themselves. On the other hand, a distributor might be unwilling to take on a manufacturer's products unless the distributor is protected from competition either from the manufacturer or from other distributors. In particular, the distributor intends to protect his investments from so-called 'free riders'. Free riders tend to enter a market, after a distributor has successfully developed it. Since free riders spend less money, they may undercut the prices and offer cheaper products of the same brand obtained from other sources.

Vertical restraints are broadly defined as provisions contained in agreements between a supplier of goods and services and an acquirer of those goods and services. The assumption is that the output of the supplier and the output of the acquirer are complementary. Vertical restraints typically restrict the supplier from supplying the same or similar goods or services to (certain) other potential acquirers and/or restrict the acquirer from acquiring such goods and services from (certain) other suppliers and/or from entering into supply agreements with (certain) potential acquirers. Similarly, terms that impose minimum, fixed or maximum resale prices constitute vertical restraints, as do conditions that the acquirer shall resell a minimum or fixed quantity of the acquired goods or shall provide specific services in connection with their resale.

Vertical agreements are therefore those that arise in a channel of distribution between firms at different levels of trade or industry i.e., between a manufacturer and wholesaler, between a supplier and customer or between a licensor of technology and his licensee. Examples of vertical restraints include non-linear pricing, quantity forcing, full-line forcing, RPM, territorial restrictions, exclusive dealing, partial exclusive dealing, tie-in sales, refusal to deal, etc. Vertical agreements often contain:

- Dealing restrictions such as exclusive territories, selective distribution or exclusive purchasing under which one firm undertakes not to deal with competitors, or certain competitors, of the other.
- Non-linear pricing like fixed per unit price.
- Price restrictions such as RPM and recommendations of resale prices.[502]

Vertical agreements are mostly the result of complex business negotiations. Agreements can therefore not be pushed into strait-jacket schemes, since they differ from one another as much as business relationships do. Hence for competition law purposes, classifications take place in the form of 'components' of vertical restraints. In practice, many vertical agreements make use of more than one of these components. To give an example, exclusive distribution usually limits the number of buyers the supplier can sell to and at the same time limits the area where the buyers can be active. The first component may lead to foreclosure of other buyers while the second component may lead to price discrimination. Before the assessment of these components is discussed in more detail, an overview of the most important vertical agreements is given.

4.4.7.1   Types of Vertical Restraints

4.4.7.1.1   Exclusive Distribution Group

Some producers deliberately limit the number of intermediaries handling their goods.[503] Under the heading of exclusive distribution come those agreements or components that have as their main element that the manufacturer is selling only to one or a limited number of buyers. In this agreement, a supplier appoints a distributor to sell the contract goods within a defined geographical[504] area and agrees not to appoint any other distributor in that area. At the same time, the distributor is usually limited in its active selling outside its territory. Either the number of buyers for a particular territory or a group of customers or the kind of buyers can be restricted.

The 'exclusive distribution group', as referred to in the Commission's guidelines, comprises exclusive distribution and exclusive customer allocation. It also comprises exclusive supply and quantity forcing on the supplier, where an obligation or incentive scheme agreed between the supplier and the buyer makes the former sell on a particular market only or mainly to one buyer.

Exclusive distribution is found to some extent in the distribution of appliances or women's apparel brands. By granting exclusive distribution, the manufacturer hopes for more aggressive and knowledgeable selling and more control over intermediaries'

---

502. (Hughes, Foss und Ross 2001, 424).
503. The analysis relates to both goods and services, although certain restraints are mainly used in the distribution of goods. This is why throughout this text the term good(s) means both good(s) and service(s) unless otherwise stated.
504. The relevant geographical territory in which the exclusive distributor operates must be clearly defined.

Chapter 4: Competition Practice

policies on prices, promotion, credit and various services. Exclusive distribution tends to enhance the product's image and allow higher mark-ups.

Exclusive distribution is also an instrument for developing markets and organising cooperation between manufacturers and traders, especially small and medium-sized enterprises. This is sometimes the only way for small or medium size undertakings to compete in the market since it may be difficult to find a non-exclusive dealer prepared to make the investment necessary to promote a new and/or foreign product. The costs of promotion, maintaining stocks and advertising, etc. may result in a loss during an initial period of months or years. A dealer might not be prepared to make such an investment, unless he is protected for a specific period of time from free riders (the manufacturer himself or other distributors) distributing the same brand that would benefit from his advertising.

It is broadly understood that exclusive distribution leads in principle to efficiencies where investments by distributors are required to protect or build up the brand image. This applies in particular to new products, complex products and products the qualities of which are difficult to assess. In addition, a combination of exclusive distribution and a non-compete obligation may help the distributor to focus on the particular brand. If such a combination does not lead to foreclosure, it is exempted for the whole duration of the agreement.

Exclusive distribution at the retail level is more likely to lead to anti-competitive effects than exclusive distribution at the wholesale level. This anti-competitive effect is more likely when retail territories are large and the choice of final consumers between high-price/high-service and low-price/low-service distributors is limited. On the other hand, at the wholesale level, appreciable anti-competitive effects are unlikely when the manufacturer is not dominant itself and the exclusive wholesaler is not restricted at all in its sales to retailers.

Exclusive customer allocation normally leads to efficiencies where the distributors are required to make investments in specific equipment, skills or know-how to adapt to the requirements of their customers. The depreciation period of these specific investments indicates the justified duration of an exclusive customer allocation system. In general, the case is strongest for new or complex products and for products requiring adaptation to the needs of the individual customer. Efficiencies are more likely for intermediate products, i.e., when the products are sold to different types of professional buyers. Allocation of final consumers is unlikely to lead to efficiencies and is therefore unlikely to be exempted.

A combination of several restrictions like the combination of exclusive distribution or exclusive customer allocation with exclusive purchasing enhances the competition risks of market partitioning and price discrimination. Exclusive distribution and exclusive customer allocation makes it more difficult for customers to take advantage of possible price differences for a certain brand. The combination with exclusive purchasing hinders the distributors from taking advantage of price differences. Requiring the exclusive distributor to buy its supplies of a particular brand directly from the manufacturer eliminates the possibility for the distributor to buy the goods cheaper from other exclusive distributors. This combination is therefore unlikely to be exempted unless there are clear and substantial efficiencies leading to lower prices for all final consumers under Article 101(3).

The Commission elaborated in its guidelines on a few aspects in order to facilitate the self-assessment of the companies. What is evident from these examples is that the whole market situation has to be assessed before any conclusion can be drawn. A simple guidance might be that the stronger the position of the supplier on the relevant market, the more problematic is the loss of intra-brand competition. Exclusive customer allocation is unlikely to be exempted above the 30% market share threshold, unless it leads to clear and substantial efficiencies. Efficiencies are calculated according to the Commission's guidelines on Article 101(3), which are discussed at a later stage.

4.4.7.1.2 Single Branding Group

Under the heading of single branding come those agreements and components which have as their main element that the buyer is induced to concentrate its orders for a particular type of product with one supplier. This component can be found amongst others in 'non-compete' and 'quantity-forcing' on the buyer. The same component can be found in tying, where the obligation or incentive scheme relates to a product that the buyer is required to purchase as a condition of purchasing another distinct product.[505]

There are a few negative effects on competition: (1) since other suppliers in that market cannot sell to the particular buyers, foreclosure on the market might be likely. (2) Collusion by several suppliers is a potential competition risk since market shares are inflexible. (3) As far as the distribution of final goods is concerned, the particular retailers will only sell one brand with the effect that inter-brand competition in their shops is eliminated (no in-store competition). (4) In the case of tying, the buyer may pay a higher price for the tied product than it would otherwise do. All these effects may lead to a reduction in inter-brand competition. This reduction in inter-brand competition on the other hand may be mitigated by strong initial competition between suppliers to obtain the single branding contracts.

4.4.7.1.3 Resale Price Maintenance Group

Under the heading of RPM come those agreements and components that have as their main element that the buyer is obliged or induced to resell not below a certain price, at a certain price or not above a certain price. This group comprises minimum, fixed, maximum and recommended resale prices. Maximum and recommended resale prices, although in theory unlikely to have negative effects, may work as fixed RPM. As RPM relates to the resale price it is mainly relevant for the distribution of final goods. There are two main effects of minimum and fixed RPM on competition: (1) the distributors can no longer compete on price for that brand, leading to a total elimination of

---

505. The first product is referred to as the 'tied' product and the second is referred to as the 'tying' product.

intra-brand price competition, and (2) there is increased transparency on price and responsibility for price changes, making horizontal collusion between manufacturers easier, at least in concentrated markets. The reduction in intra-brand competition may, as it leads to less downward pressure on the price for the particular good, have as an indirect effect a reduced level of inter-brand competition.

4.4.7.1.4 Market Partitioning Group

Under the heading of market partitioning come those agreements and components that have as their main element that the buyer is restricted in where it either sources or resells a particular good. This group comprises territorial sales restrictions, where a reseller agrees to refrain from actively selling the contract goods outside of the defined area; customer sales restrictions; after-market sales restrictions; prohibitions of resale; tying and exclusive purchasing. Exclusive purchasing are those agreements and components in which a distributor agrees to purchase certain goods for resale exclusively from a particular supplier.[506] The difference between exclusive dealing agreements and exclusive purchasing agreements is that the supplier does not undertake to grant the distributor exclusive territorial rights, i.e., the supplier is free to appoint competing distributors within the defined area, or indeed to compete directly with the distributor.

The main effect on competition is a reduction of intra-brand competition that may help the supplier or the buyer (in case of after-market sales restrictions) to partition the market and thus hinders market integration. This may facilitate price discrimination. Tying is slightly the odd one out. Its main effect is that the buyers may pay a higher price for the tied good than they would otherwise do but it may also lead to foreclosure of other suppliers and reduced inter-brand competition in the market of the tied good.

4.4.7.1.5 Combinations of Vertical Restraints

Combinations of different vertical restraints are likely and might increase the negative effects. Another argument is that certain combinations of vertical restraints are better for competition than their use in isolation from each other.

For example, a combination of one of the restraints of the single branding group with one of the exclusive distribution group combines a reduction of inter-brand competition with a reduction of intra-brand competition. In the case of final goods, a market is created with local brand monopolists without in-store competition. To the foreclosure at manufacturer level foreclosure at the retail level is added. It may not only be difficult for a manufacturer to sell a new brand as stores are tied, but also that new

---

506. Cases on exclusive purchasing agreements: (Decision IV/29.021 on BP Kemi-DDSF 1979, 26, 33–37, 57–71, 93–97); (ECJ, SA Brasserie de Haecht v. Consorts Wilkin-Janssen, Case 23-67 1967); (European Commission, Eleventh Report on Competition Policy 1982, Soda Ash. paras 73–76).

entrants may have difficulties obtaining some of the leading brands. This results in a situation where it may be both difficult to find outlets and unprofitable to set up new outlets.[507]

Another example is the combination of one of the restraints of the exclusive distribution group with one of the RPM group. The first contributes to a reduction of intra-brand competition whereas intra-brand price competition is eliminated by the second. This quickly leads to a total elimination of intra-brand competition. This market result may sustain collusion.

There are three combinations that are particularly negative from a market integration perspective: (1) territorial sales restriction combined with selective distribution at the same level of distribution, (2) exclusive distribution combined with exclusive purchasing, and (3) selective distribution combined with exclusive purchasing. These combinations help to make a distribution system tougher.

4.4.7.2 *Economics of Vertical Restraints*

4.4.7.2.1 Beneficial Effects of Vertical Restraints

Vertical restraints can be employed to reduce transaction costs or to achieve other efficiencies between firms at different levels of the production and distribution chain.[508] Vertical restraints, like exclusive distribution, can also help to solve the potential problem of under-investment.[509]

Another benefit that derives from vertical restraints relates to the so-called 'double marginalization'. The intuition behind double marginalisation is that if both producers and distributors add mark-ups over their costs, the resulting 'double' mark-up leads to excessive prices. This is of particular concern if both, the manufacturer and the retailer, have market power since they each will set its price above marginal cost.[510] They both add their margin that exceeds the one that would exist under competition. This may result in a final price that even exceeds the monopoly price an integrated company would charge. In this, arguably rather hypothetical case, quantity forcing on the buyer or maximum RPM could help the manufacturer bring the price down to a joint profit-maximising level.[511] The externality stems from the fact that each partner, when setting his price (the wholesale price for the producer and the retail price for the distributor), does not consider the effect of this price on the other partner's

---

507. (Peeperkorn 1998).
508. Rey from IDEI, Toulouse performed quite an extensive economic discussion on these aspects in various papers and speeches such as (Rey, The economics of vertical restraints, Speech at Cargese 2004).
509. Hold-up problems may also cause under-investment, e.g., when a component manufacturer does not commit the necessary client-specific investments in equipment. A possible solution may be an obligation not to purchase the component from third parties ('single branding') for a period of time.
510. (Lever & Neubauer 2000, 10).
511. (Peeperkorn 1998).

Chapter 4: Competition Practice

profit. For instance, the distributor, when setting the retail price, does not take into account that an increase in his price, which decreases the final demand, also decreases the producer's profit.

Another aspect is that there might be too many retailers from the point of view of the manufacturer. Individual retailers take into account only their private costs and the revenues they generate (some of which may be taken from other retailers). Therefore, it is possible that total retail costs may be increased to a greater extent than is justified by the increase in total sales generated by having an additional retailer. In order to have economies of scale exploited and thereby see a lower retail price for its product, a manufacturer may want to concentrate the resale of its products on a limited number of distributors.

Other justifications for vertical restraints are that they relate to a solution for the free rider problem.[512] Distributors might be unwilling to invest in the marketing of new products or services unless the manufacturer imposes a territorial restraint that ensures that late-entering distributors will not 'free ride' on the earlier distributors' initial efforts and investments to establish the manufacturer's position in the marketplace. This is particularly true where distributors provide pre-purchase services.[513] Each distributor's investment in such activities generates positive externalities on the rest boosting their sales regardless of whether they have contributed to these activities. The distributor who makes efforts may not be able to appropriate all the benefits the effort creates and may therefore be inclined to invest sub-optimally. In the absence of vertical restraints, it is likely that distributors may attempt to free ride on these investments by trying to get the benefits from the investment made by the rest. In order to benefit, the product needs to be relatively new or technically complex as the customer otherwise may very well know what he wants from past purchases. In addition, the product must be of a reasonably high value as it is otherwise not attractive for a customer to go to one shop for information and to another one to buy.[514] The results of free riding are too little service and innovation.

Free riding can also occur between manufacturers where one invests in promotion in the shops for its brand, thereby also attracting customers for its competitors. Non-compete type restraints can help to overcome this. On the other hand, free riding between manufacturers is also limited by rather strict conditions. It can be the case that a manufacturer who invests in promotion of his own product is also increasing demand for his competitors' products. Similarly, free riding might appear when a retailer has a strong reputation for selling only high quality products allowing other retailers to free ride on the investment made by the 'certifying' store by stocking the same goods.

A special form of free riding is the certification free rider argument. The hypothesis is that certain retailers sell new and complex products. Gradually its reputation becomes established and demand grows enough for it to be sold through low-price chains. If the manufacturer cannot initially limit its sales to the premium

---

512. See for example the work done by (Boyd 1996).
513. Free riding between retailers can only occur on pre-purchase services and not on after-sales services.
514. (Peeperkorn 1998).

327

stores, it runs the risk of being de-listed at those stores and the product introduction may fail. It may be necessary to provide temporary protection against price discounters to help the introduction of the new and complex product. However, a period of protection, which is too long, may only delay the product moving into the mature, price competitive stages of its life cycle, to the disadvantage of consumers. This means, at best, that there may be a reason to allow for a limited duration a restriction of the exclusive distribution or RPM.

Another issue that provides benefits is the so-called 'hold-up' problem. The risk of hold-up might arise when a firm needs to make an important long-term investment involving substantial sunk costs and that is particular to one purchaser or supplier. In such a case, after the investments have been made, the bargaining position of the firm is weakened. The fear is that free riding on investments is a possibility. However, there are a number of conditions that have to be met: Firstly, the investment must be sunk and specific to deal with only that other party. Secondly, it must be a long-term investment, which is not recouped in the short run. And thirdly, the investment must be asymmetric; i.e., one invests more than the other. Only when these conditions are met is there a reason to have a vertical restraint for a limited duration, of the non-compete type when the investment is made by the supplier and of the exclusive distribution or exclusive supply type when the investment is made by the buyer.

Vertical restraints can also increase sales and create brand image by imposing certain standards of quality on the distributors. In such cases exclusive or selective distribution can be justified when introducing a new product into the market for a limited period of time. There is a large measure of substitutability between the different vertical restraints. This means that the same inefficiency problem can be solved by different vertical restraints.[515] To conclude, the beneficial effects are quite comprehensive.

4.4.7.2.2 Anti-Competitive Effects of Vertical Restraints

Nevertheless, vertical restraints can also lead to anti-competitive effects. Negative anti-competitive effects, which may result from vertical restraints, are: foreclosure by raising barriers to entry, a reduction of inter-brand competition (including facilitation of collusion, both explicit and tacit), a reduction of intra-brand competition, and the creation of obstacles to market integration.[516] These negative effects are likely to emerge, if the undertakings hold a certain degree of market power. The main reason is that the profits of the vertical structure resulting from an efficiency-enhancing vertical restraint are more likely to benefit consumers in the form of reduced prices or better quality, if strong competition from other suppliers of goods exists. If, however, the vertical structure holds a sufficient degree of market power, it will tend to absorb those efficiency gains in the form of extra profits.

---

515. (Korah & O'Sullivan 2002); The authors discuss in their book the pro-intrabrand-restriction concepts as well as the rationales that express concern.
516. (Hughes, Foss und Ross 2001, 427).

Regarding market integration, vertical restraints are viewed ambivalently. They either may restrict competition in a harmful way or may introduce competition by the opening up of new markets.

By imposing restrictions to competition, vertical agreements having the purpose or effect of protecting Member State markets, clearly contravene the Community's goal of market integration. They directly or indirectly impair the free flow of goods between Member States and help to maintain different price levels. On the other hand, parallel imports may give rise to free rides from one exporting dealer on the promotional or servicing efforts of one local dealer. However, the free rider is considered by some to be a 'hero' because his sales foster the free movement of the brand within the Internal Market and thus contribute to market integration. Restraints which limit the distributors' room for manoeuvre have been subject to close scrutiny in the past. Because of the market integration objective, the relationship between manufacturers and distributors as well as other vertical relationships in the distribution chain were of particular concern. Since market integration proceeded quite well, this concern is of less importance today. So, vertical agreements can be beneficial to competition since they enable a producer to be present in a market for less than it would cost him to set up a subsidiary. At the same time, however, agreements of this kind can prove an extremely effective tool for establishing price differentials within a particular territory or for deterring new competitors from entering the market. Exclusive agreements backed by measures aimed at restricting imports can protect a distributor's territory, enabling him to keep his prices high.

In addition, when most or all of the manufacturers or suppliers apply exclusive distribution this may facilitate collusion, both at the suppliers and distributors level. Likewise, as the Court of Justice pointed out in its preliminary ruling judgment in the *Delimitis*[517] case, a series of exclusive distribution agreements between a producer and a large number of distributors can shield a market from new entrants, although each of the agreements may be admissible when looked at in isolation. In such cases, the positive effect on competition of vertical agreements is easily offset by their detrimental effect of hindering the emergence of new competitors.

The possible competition risks of exclusive territories are therefore that fewer distributors will offer this good, and market partitioning. Another competition risk is that certain buyers within that market can no longer buy from this particular supplier, i.e., it leads to foreclosure of certain buyers.[518] In the case of wide exclusive territories or customer allocation, the result may be total elimination of intra-brand competition. The basic idea is as follows: Suppose that two manufacturers supply two substitute goods. There is a positive externality between the manufacturers' choices of prices. If they delegate price decisions to retailers who compete in Bertrand fashion, the same externality between wholesale prices is still present. Any mechanism that allows the manufacturers or retailers to raise retail prices should benefit the manufacturers. One such mechanism is for the manufacturers to assign exclusive territories to their retailers. This arrangement eliminates intra-brand competition. And each retailer

---

517. (ECJ, Stergios Delimitis v. Henninger Bräu AG, Case C-234/89 1991).
518. See (Rey, The economics of vertical restraints, Speech at Cargese 2004).

enjoys some monopolistic power over a fraction of the final demand and tends to charge a price higher than by an incumbent firm offering exclusive dealing contracts.[519] *Rey/Stiglitz*[520] considers a situation in which oligopolistic manufacturers' and dealers' incentives to compete might be reduced by exclusive territories. With exclusive territories a cut in wholesale prices will only be translated in a partial cut in consumer prices and if one manufacturer's dealer cuts price following a reduction in wholesale prices then other dealers might react by reducing their prices as well. Both effects discourage manufacturers from reducing wholesale prices by reducing the increase in sales that can be expected to be generated. Thus exclusive territories make sales less sensitive to changes in wholesale prices.

When the exclusive distribution type of agreement is used rather selectively, that means that not many stores can carry the product, it also leads to less in-store competition and reduced inter-brand competition. If the exclusive distributorship leads to the empowerment of a distributor with buying power – if for instance at the retail level, he becomes the exclusive distributor for the whole or a substantial part of the market – foreclosure of other distributors may cause serious anti-competitive effects too. On the other hand, exclusive distribution agreements allow manufactures to enter new geographical markets thanks to the experience of exclusive importers already established in those markets and to facilitate the promotion of sales of their products while at the same time rationalising distribution.

It often goes with exclusive dealing that the manufacturer requires these dealers not to carry competing lines. Therefore, another negative effect is to prevent entry by potential efficient competitors. One possible strategy might be to sign-up available distributors into exclusive dealing arrangements, thereby forcing potential new suppliers to set up their own distribution systems. Such exclusive arrangements would raise the entry cost of potential rivals if there are large economies of scope or scale in distribution or retail entry is difficult and costly, e.g., if there is a limited supply of retailers, at least of comparable quality, or a scarcity of comparably good retail locations.[521]

Because they directly affect the nature of downstream intra-brand competition between distributors and thus, indirectly, the behaviour of the upstream manufacturer, vertical restraints alter the behaviour of the vertical structure and thus influence the strategic interaction with rival vertical structures. In short, altering intra-brand competition modifies inter-brand competition as well.[522] Whereas intra-brand competition

---

519. (Tan 2001).
520. (Rey & Stiglitz 1988).
521. (Rey 2003).
522. Several papers have shown for example that vertical restraints such as exclusive territories, which reduce intra-brand competition within a given distribution network, also reduce inter-brand competition between rival manufacturers, by reducing their incentives to undercut each other. Suppose for example that competing manufacturers distribute their products through distinct retail networks. If they maintain strong intra-brand competition within their retail networks, then the retail price of each product will closely reflect the evolution of the wholesale price for that product; as a result, the situation resembles one of direct, face-to-face competition between the manufacturers. If instead manufacturers reduce intra-brand competition by for example., assigning exclusive territories to their distributors, these distributors will

comes from other suppliers of the product derived from the same manufacturer,[523] inter-brand competition comes from products made by rival manufacturers'.[524]

Intra-brand competition is concerned with the product or service provided by an undertaking, but distributed only with certain 'strings attached', for instance RPM, tying agreements, or territorial protection. Vertical restraints, such as between a manufacturer and his dealer, may increase efficiency and competition between the brands of different manufacturers by enabling a supplier to give incentives to his dealers to supply services that may benefit the brand as a whole. The 'incentive' is created by offering the dealer some degree of protection against intra-brand competition. However, the presence of vigorous inter-brand competition may ensure that the 'protected' dealer is forced to provide services desired by consumers as effectively as possible. Inter-brand competition usually means talking about the fair play of market forces. Different enterprises compete on a certain market with different goods or services, which in the view of the consumer are interchangeable to satisfy needs, but still have different parameters of price, quality, and contract terms attached to them. Inter-brand competition would mean that the consumer has several options for obtaining the goods or services he needs: the consumer may be interested in price and therefore prefer cheap outlets not tied to manufacturers, or may insist on quality and after-sales services and therefore prefer vertical distribution systems which select and restrict the choice of outlets, or the consumer may want to buy a complex product including the prestige and exclusivity value of a certain distribution system, like in perfumes. Inter-brand competition would still be operating in these circumstances provided that the consumer has a free choice of outlets. It will only be restricted if consumers are forced to satisfy their needs on a market without having alternative distribution systems to choose from.

Except by producing better value for money, a manufacturer is seldom able to save his dealers from inter-brand competition, if such competition exists. To do so, the manufacturer would have to enter into a horizontal agreement with his competitors and this would clearly be contrary to the competition laws of most countries and, in particular, to Article 101. In some markets, there may be little effective inter-brand competition. The manufacturer may be the only firm providing a product for which there are no close substitutes and which is shielded by barriers to entry. Thus effective inter-brand competition between manufacturers provides them with strong incentives to adopt efficient distribution arrangements, or their products would be less competitive than their rivals. However, where inter-brand competition is limited, the pressure on firms to be competitive might be reduced.

---

have more freedom for setting their prices: and typically the retail price for one product will then (at least partially) respond to an increase in a rival manufacturers' wholesale prices, thereby encouraging them to raise indeed their prices. Thus, reducing intra-brand competition leads to an indirect mode of competition between manufacturers, which perceive less elastic demands upstream and are more inclined to maintain high prices.
523. For example, competition between all the dealers selling IBM computers.
524. An example of this would be competition between a dealer selling IBM computers and another selling, say, HP and a third selling Apple computers and so on. There may also be non-branded substitutes, but the phrase 'inter-brand competition' is often used to embrace them.

The type of vertical restraint does not itself determine whether it will increase or decrease economic efficiency. A provision may have either beneficial or detrimental effects, depending on the context. For example, RPM may promote economic efficiency and increase consumer surplus when, by placing a ceiling on retail prices, it eliminates double retail mark-ups. RPM that puts a floor under retail prices may also promote economic efficiency when its primary effect is to prevent free riding that undermines the supply of retail services or the development of reputations and uniform quality standards that are valuable to consumers. On the other hand, if the primary effect of RPM is to facilitate collusion among franchisors, economic efficiency will be reduced. Exclusive territories also may increase economic efficiency if they reduce free rider distortions; unfortunately, they have the potential to reduce not only intra-brand competition but also market competition and thus allow increased exercise of market power.[525]

Vertical restraints might increase price transparency and thereby facilitate explicit collusive behaviour or tacit oligopolistic coordination. Courts often argue that vertical restraints can help manufacturers to sustain a cartel. However, it is only recently that this argument has been captured in a formal analysis. *Jullien/Rey* demonstrated that by ensuring more uniform prices, RPM facilitates tacit collusion since price cuts are easier to detect.[526]

Vertical restraints that are in the manufacturer's interest are not always socially desirable. According to *Comanor*[527], the desirable quality of dealers' services for manufacturers might differ substantially from the interests of society. *Comanor* argues that the profitability of increasing the level of dealer services depends solely on the preferences of marginal consumers (consumers just willing to pay for the product at its prevailing price) if the marginal consumer's valuation of these services exceeds their cost, they will increase their purchases of the product, and the vertical restraint increasing the level of such services will be profitable. However, society's gains or losses from changes in the quality of a dealer's services depend on the preferences of all consumers' not only marginal consumers. If marginal consumers place a higher (lower) valuation on dealer services than infra marginal consumers (who are willing to pay significantly more than the prevailing price), then the level of dealer services chosen by manufacturers will be too high (low).[528]

4.4.7.2.3 Different Schools of Thought

In general, in economic theory two main schools of thought can be distinguished when dealing with vertical restraints:

---

525. (OECD, Brenner and Rey 1994, 57).
526. The argument is that, in the absence of RPM, while retail prices are partially driven by wholesale prices, they also respond to local shocks in retail costs or demand conditions. Therefore, short of checking the entire distribution of retail prices, it may be difficult to detect changes in wholesale prices. Instead, through RPM manufacturers can maintain uniform prices, and any deviation from a collusive agreement will be detected at once.
527. (Comanor 1985).
528. (Neven, Papandropoulos & Seabright 1998, 32).

- *The Chicago School:* The Chicago School[529] uses neoclassical insights to argue in general that only a limited number of cases concern anti-trust laws. Chicago School researchers assert that anti-trust law should mainly address horizontal arrangements and practices. For vertical arrangements, the Chicago School argues that the occurrence of allegedly anti-competitive practices spells no efficiency loss and may in fact even be pro-competitive.[530] Therefore, the Chicago School denies the anti-competitive character of vertical restraints and maintains that vertical restraints should be treated as completely lawful agreements.

  According to this wisdom, vertical restraints are agreements between producers of 'complementary' goods or services rather than competing suppliers of substitutes. Suppliers of such goods or services (complementary) have no interest in raising the price of a complementary product because by definition it will decrease the demand for its own product. So if manufacturers accept a vertical restraint, which limits retail competition, there must be – according to economic theory – some offsetting efficiency justifications. This reasoning can also be related to the well-known discussion on inter-brand versus intra-brand competition. From a Chicago-type perspective, a well-functioning inter-brand competition among producers can substitute intra-brand competition among retailers.

- *The European School:* Despite the tremendous impact of the Chicago School on the Commission, many European (as well as Post-Chicago US) scholars, practitioners of anti-trust and the Court of Justice of the EU have strong reservations about Chicago School applications to vertical restraints.

  The European approach does not support the view, as argued by the Chicago School, that all vertical restraints should be legal. Based on a detailed investigation of the relevant issues in a case, vertical restraints might have a negative impact on competition. Based also on the structure of Article 101 itself, a vertical restraint might restrict competition under Article 101(1) and any efficiency considerations can be evoked under Article 101(3) only. Thus, in the European School approach vertical agreements may contain certain restrictions to competition which, in the absence of significant market power by the companies involved, may improve production and distribution of the goods and services concerned. However, such agreements can also have negative effects on the market, in particular by partitioning markets or by foreclosing markets.[531]

---

529. See also Chapter one.
530. For example, Chicago School scholars have argued that resale price maintenance is likely to be pro-competitive unless it serves to facilitate a horizontal cartel. Otherwise, a rational manufacturer would only engage in this practice to induce retailers to provide consumers valuable but costly services that they would not otherwise provide. As a result of the impact of the Chicago School, the courts rarely consider non-price restraints illegal and the enforcement agencies in the US almost never challenge vertical restraints, even when price-related.
531. (Abbamonte und Rabassa 2001, 214).

To conclude, modern European economics supposes that vertical restraints can be but are not automatically efficiency-enhancing. They can help to eliminate some form of vertical externality in the manufacturer-retailer relationship as well as horizontal externality such as free riding problems among retailers.[532] However, the European school of thought does not follow the per se doctrine of the Chicago School that all vertical restraints are pro-competitive. According to the European school of thought, some of the vertical restraints can be anti-competitive since they may serve to eliminate competition either at the manufacturer level or at the retail level thereby reducing consumers' choices and welfare. Which of these effects dominates and which vertical restraints will be adopted in a particular situation depend critically on the informational environment (e.g., on what can be observed and enforced by the manufacturers) and on the vertical and horizontal market structures.[533]

It is not the Commission but the Court of Justice that guarantees that the European economic approach is applied.

The Commission instead uses as an underlying theoretical basis a patchwork-approach to vertical restraints influenced, among others by neoclassical, efficiency-oriented reasoning – stemming from Chicago School learning (e.g., Posner, 1976) –, transaction costs theories and incomplete contracts economics[534] (e.g., Williamson, 1979) as well as game-theoretic industrial organisation theory (e.g., Tirole, 1988).[535] In addition, the 'new' Harvard approach on market power is employed.[536] These influences altogether have led to a considerable liberalisation in the interpretation of the rules for exempting vertical agreements. However, the relaxed approach towards vertical agreements applied in the US is, even for the Commission from the methodology perspective, too removed. On the whole, it can be concluded that the Commission is basing its analysis and criteria on the recent neoclassical economic reasoning on vertical restraints.[537]

4.4.7.2.4 EU Policy Conclusions on Vertical Restraints

Vertical restraints have both pro and anti-competitive features. Chicago School learning disregards the possible adverse effects that vertical restraints can have on third parties whereas modern European economics qualify them as relevant in the assessment of vertical agreements. In fact, the same vertical restraint can have very different effects depending on the context.

---

532. (Tan 2001, 3).
533. (Tan 2001).
534. See also (Grossman & Hart 1986).
535. (Tirole 1988).
536. U.A. (Vezzoso 2004).
537. See, for example, (Rey & Caballero-Sanz 1996), (OECD, Brenner und Rey 1994), (Waterson & Dobson 1996) and (Motta 2004, 302–410).

However, a few general rules can be identified. For most vertical restraints competition concerns can only arise if there is insufficient inter-brand competition, i.e., if there exists a certain degree of market power[538] at the level of the supplier or the buyer or both. On the other hand, where there are many firms competing in an unconcentrated[539] market, it can be assumed that non-hardcore vertical restraints will not have appreciable negative effects.

As a general rule, exclusive agreements are generally worse for competition than non-exclusive agreements. Exclusive agreements make one party fulfil all or practically all its requirements from another party.[540]

Another general rule is that restraints agreed for intermediate goods are in general less harmful than restraints affecting the distribution of final goods. Intermediate goods and services are sold to undertakings for use as an input to produce other goods or services and are generally not recognisable in the final goods or services. At an intermediate level both the supplier and the buyer are usually professional and knowledgeable. The undertakings buying intermediate goods or services normally have specialist departments or advisers who monitor developments in the supply market. Because they affect sizeable transactions, search costs are in general not prohibitive. A loss of intra-brand competition is therefore less important at the intermediate level. This makes a possible loss of intra-brand competition less important because it stimulates specialisation, which leads to comparative advantages. Final goods are, directly or indirectly, sold to final consumers who often rely more on brand and image. As distributors (retailers, wholesalers) have to respond to the demand of final consumers, competition may suffer more when distributors are foreclosed from selling one or a number of brands than when buyers of intermediate products are prevented from buying competing products from certain sources of supply.

Vertical restraints agreed for non-branded goods and services are in general less harmful than restraints affecting the distribution of branded goods and services. Branding tends to increase product differentiation and reduce substitutability of the product, leading to a reduced elasticity of demand and an increased possibility to raise prices. The distinction between branded and non-branded goods or services will often coincide with the distinction between intermediate goods and services and final goods and services.

Vertical restraints from a limited distribution group, in the absence of sufficient inter-brand competition, may significantly restrict the choices available to consumers. They are particularly harmful when more efficient distributors or distributors with a different distribution format are foreclosed. This can reduce innovation in distribution and denies consumers the particular service or price-service combination of these distributors.

---

538. Conceptually, market power is the power to raise price above the competitive level and, at least in the short-term, to obtain supranormal profits.
539. A market is – according to the Commission – deemed unconcentrated when the HHI index, i.e., the sum of the squares of the individual market shares of all companies in the relevant market, is below 1,000.
540. For example, a non-compete obligation means that the buyer purchases only one brand, while quantity forcing may leave the buyer scope to purchase competing goods.

The more the vertical restraint is linked to the transfer of know-how, the more reason there may be to expect efficiencies to arise and the more a vertical restraint may be necessary to protect the know-how transferred or the investment costs incurred.

The more the vertical restraint is linked to investments, which are relationship-specific, the more justification there is for certain vertical restraints. The justified duration will depend on the time necessary to depreciate the investment.

In the case of a new product, or where an existing product is sold for the first time on a different geographic market, it may be difficult for the company to define the market or its market share may be very high. However, this should not be considered a major problem, as vertical restraints linked to opening up new product or geographic markets in general do not restrict competition. This rule holds, irrespective of the market share of the company, for two years after first putting the product on the market. It applies to all non-hardcore vertical restraints and, in the case of a new geographic market, to restrictions on active and passive sales imposed on the direct buyers of the supplier located in other markets to intermediaries in the new market. In the case of genuine testing of a new product in a limited territory or with a limited customer group, the distributors appointed to sell the new product on the test market can be restricted in their active selling outside the test market for a maximum period of one year without being caught by Article 101(1).

Another general rule is that the possible negative effects of vertical restraints are reinforced when not just one supplier with its buyers practices a certain vertical restraint but when also other suppliers and their buyers organise their trade in a similar way. These so-called 'cumulative effects' can be a problem in a number of sectors. Restrictions of resale and after-market sales restrictions in the form of market partitioning seem the worst as they allow market partitioning without clear possible efficiencies. Tying is in general considered a somewhat less serious restriction. It concerns the possible extension of market power from one market into another.

Vertical restraints that reduce inter-brand competition are generally more harmful than vertical restraints that reduce intra-brand competition. For instance, non-compete obligations are likely to have more net negative effects than exclusive distribution. The former, by possibly foreclosing the market to other brands, may prevent those brands from reaching the market. The latter, while limiting intra-brand competition, does not prevent goods from reaching the final consumer.

In general, a combination of vertical restraints aggravates their negative effects. However, certain combinations of vertical restraints are better for competition than their use in isolation from each other. For instance, in an exclusive distribution system, the distributor may be tempted to increase the price of the products as intra-brand competition has been reduced. The use of quantity forcing or the setting of a maximum resale price may limit such price increases.

A central conclusion is that market structure is important. For most vertical restraints, competition concerns can only arise if there is insufficient inter-brand competition, i.e., if there is some degree of market power at the level of the supplier or the buyer or at both levels. On the one hand, the fiercer inter-brand competition is, the more likely it is that vertical restraints have no negative effect or at least a net positive effect. On the other hand, if there is insufficient inter-brand competition, the protection

Chapter 4: Competition Practice

of inter- and intra-brand competition becomes important.[541] This means that the same vertical restraint can have different effects depending on the market structure and on the market power of the company applying the vertical restraint. The conclusion – based on modern economic insights – is that in the absence of significant market power at the manufacturer and/or retailer level, it is unlikely that vertical restraints will be socially undesirable. It is important and necessary to strike a balance between pro and anti-competitive effects.

For the purpose of assessing whether an agreement or its individual parts may restrict inter-brand competition and/or intra-brand competition consideration needs to be made of how and to what extent the agreement affects or is likely to affect competition on the market. The Commission guidelines on the application of Article 101(3) describes in paragraph 18 two questions that might provide a useful framework for making this assessment. The first question relates to the impact of the agreement on inter-brand competition while the second question relates to the impact of the agreement on intra-brand competition. Since restraints may be capable of affecting both inter-brand competition and intra-brand competition at the same time, a restraint has to be assessed in light of both questions before it can be concluded whether competition is restricted within the meaning of Article 101(1):

- Does the agreement restrict actual or potential competition that would have existed without the agreement? If the answer is a positive one, the agreement might be caught by Article 101(1). In making this assessment it is necessary to take into account competition between the parties and competition from third parties. For instance, where two undertakings established in different Member States agreed not to sell products in each other's home markets, (potential) competition that existed prior to the agreement is restricted. Similarly, where a supplier imposes obligations on his distributors not to sell competing products and these obligations foreclose third party access to the market, actual or potential competition, which would have existed in the absence of the agreement, is restricted. By evaluating whether the parties to an agreement are actual or potential competitors the economic and legal context must be taken into account. For instance, if due to the financial risks involved and the technical capabilities of the parties, it is unlikely that each party would be able to carry out its own activities covered by the agreement, the parties are deemed to be non-competitors in respect of that activity. It is for the parties to bring forward evidence to that effect.
- Does the agreement restrict actual or potential competition that would have existed in the absence of the contractual restraint(s)? If so, the agreement may be caught by Article 101(1). For example, where a supplier restricts its distributors from competing with each other, (potential) competition that could have existed between the distributors without the restraints is restricted. Such restrictions include RPM and territorial or customer sales restrictions between distributors. However, certain restraints are under certain

---

541. (Commission Guidelines on Vertical Restraints 2000, 6).

circumstances not caught by Article 101(1) when the restraint is objectively necessary for the existence of an agreement of that type or that nature. The question is whether given the nature of the agreement and the characteristics of the market a less restrictive agreement would not have been concluded by undertakings in a similar setting. For instance, territorial restraints in an agreement between a supplier and a distributor may for a certain period of time fall outside Article 101(1), if the restraints are objectively necessary in order for the distributor to penetrate a new market. Similarly, a prohibition imposed on all distributors not to sell to certain categories of end users may not be restrictive of competition if such a restraint is objectively necessary for reasons of safety or health related to the dangerous nature of the product in question. Claims that in the absence of a restraint the supplier would have resorted to vertical integration are not sufficient. Decisions on whether or not to vertically integrate depend on a broad range of complex economic factors, a number of which are internal to the undertaking concerned.

The importance of individual factors will vary from case to case and depend on all other factors. It is therefore not possible to provide strict rules on the importance of the individual factors.

The BER and the accompanying Guidelines discussed below are welcomed as they reflect the economic thinking on this subject.

By illustrating this theoretical background it becomes clear that competition analysis of vertical restraints under Article 101 is mostly centred on the demonstration of efficiencies and on the ascertainment of possible indicators of market power, such as the market position of the supplier and of competitors, and the presence of entry barriers. Accordingly, at the heart of the BER on vertical agreements the presumption holds that in the absence of market power, the pro-competitive (efficiency) gains of vertical restraints are superior to any possible anti-competitive effects. The approach chosen by means of the BER is a 'safe harbour' for all suppliers whose market share does not exceed a certain threshold – 30% for vertical restraints. Below this market share, vertical agreements are – with the exception of agreements with 'hardcore restrictions' – always exempted. By applying this cap, the Commission recognises that vertical agreements are in principle pro-competitive unless significant horizontal market imperfections exist. The purpose of a market share cap is to act as a filter for the cases potentially more likely to raise competition concerns. Only a small number of vertical restraints, such as RPM, certain forms of market partitioning by territory or by customer, and restrictions of active or passive sales to end users by members of a selective distribution network are nearly always seen as having anti-competitive effects ('hardcore restrictions') and benefit therefore not from the group exemption.

4.4.7.2.5 Block Exemption Regulation 330/2010

Where a vertical agreement is concluded between companies that have limited market power (reflected in a market share not exceeding 30%), and providing that it contains no hardcore restrictions of competition, the Commission's and the NCAs' experience with enforcement shows that the agreement will usually have no anti-competitive effects or, if it does, that the positive effects will outweigh any negative ones. Based on this positive presumption the Commission's BER 330/2010[542] exempts them from the prohibition principle set out in Article 101(1).

In contrast, for vertical agreements concluded by companies whose market share exceeds 30%, there is no such exemption, but there is also no presumption that the agreement is illegal: it is necessary to assess the agreement's negative and positive effects on the market. The Commission's Guidelines on vertical restraints that accompany the Regulation assist in making this assessment.[543]

The Regulation does not cover agreements containing 'hardcore restrictions', such as restraints on the buyer's ability to determine its sale price ('RPM') or certain types of resale restrictions, which may create barriers to the internal market.

Under the Regulation manufacturers can, however, implement certain types of distribution system such as exclusive distribution or selective distribution:

- Thus, the Regulation allows manufacturers to protect an exclusive distributor from active sales by other distributors, in order to encourage that distributor to invest in the exclusively allocated territory or customer group. But within an exclusive distribution system, the manufacturer cannot restrict its distributor from responding to customer demand and selling its products throughout the internal market (passive sales): any such restriction would be hardcore restriction.
- In selective distribution, the Regulation also allows manufacturers to choose their distributors on the basis of specified criteria and to prohibit sales to unauthorised distributors. But distributors can actively sell to other authorised distributors throughout the internal market and to any end consumer. Any other restriction of their freedom regarding where and to whom they may sell would be a hardcore restriction.

The same rules apply to online sales. Since the Internet allows distributors to reach different customers and different territories, restrictions of the use of the Internet by distributors generally are considered as hardcore restrictions. Similarly, any obligation that dissuades distributors from using the Internet, such as a limit on the proportion of overall sales which a distributor can make over the Internet, or the requirement that a distributor pays a higher purchase price for units sold online ('dual pricing'), is also considered as a hardcore restriction. However, as in the offline world, suppliers can set up an exclusive or a selective distribution network, which allow them to restrict active sales into exclusively allocated territories or customer groups, and to require quality standards for the use of an Internet site to sell their products. Where there are hardcore restrictions, the agreement cannot benefit from the block

---

542. (European Commission, Regulation (EU) 330/2010 on the application of Art. 101 (3) 2010) This Regulation came into force on 1 Jun. 2010.
543. (Commission Guidelines on Vertical Restraints 2010, 1).

exemption, and it is unlikely they will meet the conditions set out in Article 101(3) which would make them compliant with the competition rules.[544]

In the 2010 BER, the Commission also introduced a buyer's market share threshold. Just like suppliers, buyers can use their market power to put in place vertical restraints to the ultimate detriment of consumers. The introduction of a buyer's market share threshold is particularly beneficial to small and medium-sized enterprises, because they are the most likely (as competitors of the powerful buyer or as a supplier unable to countervail the market power of the buyer) to be harmed by buyer-led vertical restraints.

Restrictions suppliers can impose on the distribution of their products on the internet are limited. Suppliers should normally be free to decide on the number and type of distributors they want to have in their distribution systems. They may for example only want to sell to chain stores that provide for a uniform sales environment, or only to shops in exclusive areas which provide a particular quality of service. More generally, suppliers may only want to sell to distributors that have one or more physical points of presence ('brick and mortar' presence) where the suppliers' goods can be touched, smelled, tried, etc.

However, once a supplier has allowed a distributor into its distribution system, it cannot prevent that distributor from having a website and selling products online. The 2010 Guidelines provide examples of restrictions of online sales that amount to hardcore restrictions of competition, whose object is to segment markets to the detriment of consumers and the internal market. Such restrictions could include an obligation imposed on a distributor to automatically re-route customers to the website of another distributor, or to terminate a sales transaction if the credit card data shows an address outside the area to which a given distributor has been assigned.

However, certain vertical restraints on online sales can be justified because they eventually benefit consumers. For instance, a supplier may impose a requirement, as for offline sales, that, in a selective distribution system, a distributor must not sell online through a website that does not meet the agreed quality standards, or to unauthorised distributors. In the case of exclusive distribution, the supplier may require the distributor not to actively target online customer groups or customers in areas exclusively reserved for another distributor of the supplier. The exclusive distributor must, however, remain free to sell to customers that contact it on their own initiative, i.e., to do 'passive sales'.

When a majority of the main suppliers in a market have selective distribution systems, the loss of competition at the distribution level can be significant, and it is possible that certain types of distributors could be excluded from the market, as well as there being an increased risk of collusion between these main suppliers. Exclusion (or foreclosure) of potentially more efficient distributors is a risk with selective distribution systems, because these systems allow suppliers to restrict sales by their authorised dealers to non-authorised dealers, thus preventing non-authorised dealers from obtaining supplies.

---

544. (Commission Memo/138 2010).

Pressure by different distribution formats such as price discounters or cheaper online-only distributors is good for competition. Foreclosure of such distribution formats could result either from the cumulative application of selective distribution in a market (the main suppliers all having selective distribution systems) or from the actions of a single supplier with a market share exceeding 30%. In either situation, the lack of competitive pressure from price discounters or cheaper online-only distributors would reduce the possibilities for consumers to take advantage of the specific benefits offered by these alternative formats – such as lower prices, more transparency and wider access. In such instances, the Commission may find that there are unjustified restrictions of competition, and may act or withdraw the benefit of the BER.[545]

4.4.7.2.6 EU Guidelines on Vertical Restraints

In order to assist undertakings in carrying out the new economic based approach under the BER the Commission approved a set of guidelines on vertical restraints.

The guidelines explain in particular which vertical agreements generally do not distort competition and therefore fall outside Article 101(1). This concerns, in particular, agreements between SME's, true agency agreements and agreements where neither the supplier nor the buyer holds a significant degree of market power.

Additionally, the guidelines elaborate on which vertical agreements benefit from the 'safe harbour' created by the BER. This is achieved by describing the conditions for the application of the regulation. Moreover, circumstances are described which may require that the benefit of the BER has to be withdrawn by the Commission or by Member State authorities. Withdrawal may be necessary when access to the relevant market is considerably restricted by the cumulative effect of parallel networks of similar vertical agreements applied by competing suppliers or buyers. Withdrawal may also be required when, in the context of exclusive supply or exclusive distribution, the buyer has significant market power on the downstream market where it resells the goods or provides the services.

The guidelines discuss a number of market definition and market share calculation issues that may arise when companies apply the 30% market share threshold. Since the enforcement policy of the Commission in cases above the 30% market share threshold is not covered by the BER, a general framework of analysis is provided by the guidelines and applied to the most important specific vertical restraints, such as single branding, exclusive distribution and selective distribution.

The guidelines reflect the more economic based approach. The ultimate aim behind the guidelines is to identify agreements, which cause no competition problems at all and therefore qualify for exemption under Article 101(3). Where a competition problem is identified, the guidelines discuss whether there are suitable solutions for the treatment of the identified competition problem.

With the assistance of the guidelines companies are considered to be able to make their own assessment of vertical agreements. It is important to note that the standards

---

545. (Commission Memo/138 2010).

as described in the guidelines have to be applied on a case-by-case basis. Each case must be evaluated in the light of its own facts.

Section V discusses Market Definition and Market Share Calculation Issues. The guidelines explicitly make reference to the Commission's Notice on the Definition of the Relevant Market for the purposes of Community competition law.[546] The methodology on market definition is discussed in sections 87–92. In addition to the well-established methodology of market definition, the guidelines discuss some special aspects related to vertical restraints.

The guidelines continue in section VI (paragraphs 96–229) with the enforcement policy of the Commission in individual cases. Section VI represents a comprehensive guidance through the *European School of thought*.

In the section on the framework of the analysis (paragraphs 96–127) the negative and positive effects of vertical restraints (paragraphs 100–109) are discussed first. Paragraphs 110–127 elaborate on the general rules for the evaluation of vertical restraints. Although it has to be kept in mind that every assessment takes place on a case-by-case basis, the guidelines apply some basic rules:

- The first recommendation is that competition concerns can only arise if there is insufficient inter-brand competition. The guidelines indicate that vertical restraints, which reduce inter-brand competition, are generally more harmful than vertical restraints that reduce intra-brand competition.
- Additionally, exclusive dealing arrangements are generally viewed as worse for competition than non-exclusive arrangements. On the other hand, the guidelines indicate that vertical restraints agreed for non-branded goods and services are in general less harmful than restraints affecting the distribution of branded goods and services. The combination of vertical restraints is viewed as aggravating their negative effects. However, certain combinations of vertical restraints are better for competition than their use in isolation. This fact requires a case-by-case analysis.
- The issue of cumulative effects is elaborated in a very detailed way. The guidelines state that possible negative effects of vertical restraints are reinforced when several suppliers and their buyers organise their trade in a similar way. These so-called cumulative effects may be a problem in a number of sectors.
- Besides the more the vertical restraint is linked to the transfer of know-how, the more reasons there may be to expect efficiencies to arise and the more a vertical restraint may be necessary to protect the know-how transferred or the investment costs incurred.
- The more the vertical restraint is linked to investments, which is relationship-specific, the more justification there is for certain vertical restraints. The guidelines also state that the justified duration will depend on the time necessary to depreciate the investment.

---

546. (Commission Notice on the definition of relevant market 1997).

Chapter 4: Competition Practice

- The guidelines consider that in the case of a new product, or where an existing product is sold for the first time on a different geographic market, it may be difficult for the company to define the market, or its market share may be very high. However, this should not be considered a major problem, as vertical restraints linked to opening up new product or geographic markets in general do not restrict competition.

For an assessment under Article 101(1), the Commission's competition test, according to the *European School of thought*, analyses the following factors:

- Market position of the parties.
- Market position of competitors.
- Market position of buyers of the contract products.
- Entry barriers.
- Maturity of the market.
- Level of trade.
- Nature of the product.
- Other factors.

Paragraphs 111-121 explain the factors in more detail.

The guidelines continue with an analysis of specific vertical restraints on single branding (paragraphs 129-150), exclusive distribution (paragraphs 151-167), exclusive customer allocation (paragraphs 168-172), selective distribution (paragraphs 174-188), franchising (paragraphs 189-191), exclusive supply (paragraphs 192-202), upfront access payments (paragraphs 203-208), category management agreements (paragraphs 209-213), tying (paragraphs 214-222) and resale price restrictions (paragraphs 223-229).

4.4.8 EU Competition Rules for Cooperation

4.4.8.1 Block Exemption Regulations

The Commission adopted in 2010 block exemptions for research and development (R&D) agreements[547] and specialisation agreements.[548]

A cooperation is defined as horizontal in nature if an agreement or concerted practice is entered into between companies operating at the same level(s) in the market. In most instances, horizontal cooperation amounts to cooperation between competitors (as opposed to *vertical* agreements which are between companies at different levels in the supply chain). Horizontal cooperation is about cooperating on research and development, production, purchasing, commercialisation, standardisation, or exchange of information. These agreements can be pro-competitive and lead to substantial economic benefits, allowing companies to respond to increasing

---

547. (European Commission, Regulation 1217/2010 on the application of Art. 101(3), 2010).
548. (European Commission, Regulation 1218/2010 on the application of Art. 101(3), 2010).

competitive pressures and a changing market place driven by globalisation. However, where the parties have market power, horizontal cooperation can also lead to serious competition problems.

If parties to cooperation agree, for example, to fix prices or output, to share markets, or if the cooperation enables the parties to maintain, gain or increase market power, competition problems may arise. On the other hand, horizontal cooperation can lead to substantial economic benefits. Companies need to respond to increasing competitive pressure. Globalisation, the speed of technological progress and the generally more dynamic nature of markets require new modes of cooperation. Cooperation can be a means to share risk, save costs, pool know-how and launch innovation faster. A more economic approach means that an assessment of horizontal cooperation needs to take place. The basic aim of the more economic approach is to allow collaboration between competitors where it contributes to economic welfare without creating a risk for competition. In particular, for small and medium-sized enterprises, cooperation is an important means of adapting to the changing marketplace. Consumers may share these gains, provided that effective competition is maintained in the market. Thus, the more economic approach embodied in the two Regulations acknowledges efficiencies, which can be achieved by competitor collaboration. Moreover, the self-assessment by companies is facilitated. The guidelines cover research and development (R&D), production, purchasing, commercialisation, standardisation and environmental agreements and acknowledge that economic analyses are required to assess restrictions by effect.

Certain categories of agreements concluded between companies that have limited market power (reflected in a market share not exceeding 25% in the case of joint R&D agreements between competitors or not exceeding 20% in the case of specialisation or joint production agreements) *and* that respect certain conditions set out in the Commission's BERs, can be presumed to have no anti-competitive effects or, if they do, the positive effects will outweigh any negative ones. Based on this positive presumption, agreements falling under a BER are exempted from the prohibition of restrictive agreements under Article 101(1) and (2). With a 25% market share threshold, R&D agreements are the most favourably treated category of horizontal agreements as such agreements can lead to substantial efficiencies because they stimulate innovation. For R&D, specialisation or joint production agreements concluded by companies whose market shares exceed the *above*-mentioned thresholds, there is no such automatic exemption, but there is also no presumption that the agreement is illegal: it is necessary to assess the agreement's negative and positive effects on the market. The Commission's Horizontal Guidelines that accompany the R&D and Specialisation BERs assist in making this assessment.[549]

The safe harbour market thresholds for horizontal agreements are lower than the 30% threshold for vertical agreements between non-competitors. This is simply because agreements between competitors have a higher potential to harm competition than agreements between non-competitors.

---

549. (Commission memo 2010).

The two Regulations exempt from the competition rules certain R&D, specialisation and production agreements that are unlikely to raise competition concerns. The Commission has extended the scope of the R&D BER now covering R&D activities carried out jointly but also so-called 'paid-for research' agreements where one party finances the R&D activities carried out by the other party. In addition, the new Regulation gives parties more scope to jointly exploit the R&D results.

The 'Horizontal Guidelines'[550] provide a framework for the analysis of the most common forms of horizontal cooperation. While the two BERs exempt certain research and development (R&D) agreements and specialisation as well as joint production agreements, the scope of the Horizontal Guidelines is much wider. The Horizontal Guidelines describe the framework for the analysis of the most common forms of horizontal cooperation such as agreements in the areas of R&D, production, purchasing, commercialisation, standardisation, standard terms, and information exchange.

The Guidelines promote a standard-setting system that is open and transparent and thereby increases the transparency of licensing costs for IPR used in standards. The Commission included a 'safe harbour' and provides guidance on standardisation agreements that do not fulfil the safe harbour criteria, to allow companies to assess whether they are in line with EU competition law. Standard-setting organisations may wish to provide for their members to unilaterally disclose, prior to setting a standard, the maximum rate that they would charge for their IPR if those were to be included in a standard. Such a system could enable a standard-setting organisation and the industry to take an informed choice on quality and price when selecting which technology should be included in a standard. The revised rules clarify that such a system would normally not infringe EU competition rules.[551]

Information exchange can be pro-competitive, for example, when it enables companies to gather market data that allow them to become more efficient and better serve customers. However, there are also situations where the exchange of market information can be harmful for competition, for instance when companies use sensitive information to align their prices. The Guidelines give clear and comprehensive guidance on how to assess the compatibility of information exchanges with EU competition law.[552]

4.4.8.2. *EU Guidelines on Horizontal Cooperation Agreements*

The guidelines on horizontal cooperation agreements complement the BER. They describe the general approach, which should be followed when assessing horizontal cooperation agreements.

Point 5 of the guidelines explains the main purpose of these guidelines. They provide an analytical framework for the most common types of horizontal cooperation agreements dealing with research and development agreements, production agreements including subcontracting and specialisation agreements, purchasing

---

550. (Commission Corrigendum to Guidelines on the applicability of Art. 101 2011, 20).
551. (Commissions Press Release 2010).
552. (Commissions Press Release 2010).

agreements, commercialisation agreements, standardisation agreements including standard contracts, and information exchange. Economic criteria such as the market power of the parties and other factors relating to the market structure form a key element of the assessment of the market impact likely to be caused by a horizontal cooperation agreement and, therefore, for the assessment under Article 101. This explanation illustrates quite clearly that the Commission focuses in its assessment on the economic meaning of the agreement. This means that even agreements that at first sight contain anti-competitive elements, may provide significant pro-competitive elements, which may outweigh the negatives ones. This approach concentrates on the effect of the agreements in the relevant markets.

The framework can be summarised as follows: a horizontal cooperation agreement is only able to restrict competition if it is likely to reduce competition in the market to such an extent that negative market effects on prices, output, innovation or the variety or quality of goods and services can be expected. To cause a restriction of competition the parties normally need appropriate tools to coordinate their behaviour and a degree of market power. Consequently, cooperation has to be assessed in its economic context taking into account both the nature of the agreement and the parties' combined market power, which determine – together with other structural factors – the capability of the cooperation to reduce overall competition to such a significant extent. These two criteria normally have to be assessed together.

The nature of the agreement is determined by the area and objective of the agreement, the competitive relationship between the parties and the degree of coordination of activities. The issues that have to be analysed in this context, are about the possible effects on prices and output. In the assessment of market power the following factors have to be considered: the parties' market shares, the concentration, the position of competitors, the stability of market shares, entry barriers and the countervailing power of suppliers.

The guidelines reiterate in paragraph 20 that an assessment under Article 101 consists of two steps. (1) The first step, under Article 101(1), is to assess whether an agreement between undertakings, which is capable of affecting trade between Member States, has an anti-competitive object or actual or potential restrictive effects on competition. (2) The second step, under Article 101(3), which only becomes relevant when an agreement is found to be restrictive of competition within the meaning of Article 101(1), is to determine the pro-competitive benefits produced by that agreement and to assess whether those pro-competitive effects outweigh the restrictive effects on competition. The balancing of restrictive and pro-competitive effects is conducted exclusively within the framework laid down by Article 101(3). If the pro-competitive effects do not outweigh a restriction of competition, Article 101(2) stipulates that the agreement shall be automatically void.

The guidance on standardisation purpose should ensure that the process of selecting industry standards is competitive and that, once the standard is adopted, access is given on 'fair, reasonable and non-discriminatory' (FRAND) terms to interested users. The criteria under which the Commission will not take issue with a standard-setting agreement ('safe harbour') are the following: (i) that the procedure for adopting the standard is unrestricted with participation open to all relevant competitors on the market; (ii) transparency to ensure that stakeholders are able to inform themselves of upcoming, ongoing and finalised work and for standards involving IPR, and (iii) a balanced IPR policy with good faith disclosure of those IPRs which are essential for the implementation of a standard, and a requirement for all IPR holders that wish to have their technology included in the standard to provide an irrevocable commitment to license their IPR on fair, reasonable, and non-discriminatory terms (FRAND).[553]

Information exchange can be pro-competitive when it enables companies to gather general market data that allow them to become more efficient and better serve customers. However, there are also situations where the exchange of market information can be harmful for competition, for instance when companies use sensitive information to coordinate their behaviour. The new chapter on information exchanges in the Horizontal Guidelines is the first Commission document to give clear and comprehensive guidance on how to assess the compatibility of information exchanges within EU competition law and will therefore play a significant practical role for businesses and their legal advisors. In particular, the chapter on information exchange sets out that the exchange between competitors of individualised information regarding intended future prices or quantities is to be considered as having as its object the restriction of competition. Such exchanges are the most likely to lead to negative effects for consumers because they allow competitors to increase prices without incurring the risk of losing market shares or triggering a price war during the period of adjustment to new prices. This type of information exchange is also the most likely to be taking place for anti-competitive reasons. The subsequent part of the chapter provides guidance for the assessment of the restrictive effects and efficiencies of such information exchanges that do not aim at restricting competition (e.g., for statistical or benchmarking purposes), i.e., the vast majority of information exchanges. To this end, the chapter describes various factors relevant for the assessment and their interplay. Finally, the chapter contains a number of practical examples which will help businesses and their legal advisors to assess typical information exchange scenarios.[554]

4.5 EUROPEAN ECONOMIC APPROACH IN ARTICLE 102

This section discusses the role of economic analysis in Article 102 cases. Economics comes into play at several stages: market definitions, the economic assessment related to the finding of dominance and, last but not least, the economic effects of the behaviour of dominant undertakings. In particular exclusionary practices like abusive rebates are of relevance in Article 102 cases. This is elaborated on in the following.

---

553. (Commission memo 2010).
554. (Commission memo 2010).

4.5.1 Market Definitions in Article 102

Market definition is of particular significance in Article 102 procedures. Effective competition can only be assessed by reference to the market thus defined.[555]

In *SPO v. Others v. Commission*,[556] the Court of First Instance confirmed the necessity of market definition under Article 102:

> For the purposes of Article 86 (new Article 102), the proper definition of the relevant market is a necessary precondition for any judgement as to allegedly anti-competitive behaviour[557]... since, before an abuse of a dominant position is ascertained, it is necessary to establish the existence of a dominant position in a given market, which presupposes that such a market has already been defined.

Thus, in assessing whether an undertaking holds a dominant position, the definition of the relevant market is of fundamental importance. Market definition is not a mechanical or abstract process but requires an analysis of all available evidence on market structure, market behaviour and an overall understanding of the mechanics of a given sector. The Commission published its methodology with respect to market definition in the Commission's Notice on the Definition of the Relevant Market for the Purposes of Community Competition Law.[558] The detailed methodology of market definition is discussed in section 4.2.

In any case, the part of the common market on which the undertaking is supposed to have a dominant position must be *substantial*.[559] This is discussed in section 4.5.1.4. The use of the term 'relevant market' implies the description of the products and services that make up the market and the assessment of the geographical scope of that market.[560] This means that in order to determine whether the position of a company is dominant, it must be viewed in relation to the *relevant product market* and the *relevant geographical market*.[561] Depending on the case, the time factor may be considered as well.

A prospective analysis of market conditions which is applied in merger proceedings may in some cases lead to a market definition different from that resulting from a market analysis based on past behaviour.

---

555. (ECJ, FFAD v. Københavns Kommune, Case C-209/98 2000, 57) and (ECJ, GT-Link A/S v. DSB, Case C-242/95 1997, 36).
556. (CFI, Vereniging van Samenwerkende Prijsregelende Organisaties in de Bouwnijverheid and others v. Commission, Case T-29/92 1995, 73 and 74).
557. (CFI, SIV and Others v. Commission, Joined cases T-68/89, T-77/89 and T-78/89 1992, 159).
558. (Commission Notice on the definition of relevant market 1997).
559. (ECJ, Coöperatieve Vereniging 'Suiker Unie' UA and others v. Commission, Joined cases 40-48, 50, 54 to 56, 111, 113 and 114-73 1975, 1977 and 1991).
560. (ECJ, France and Others v. Commission, Joined Cases C-68/94 and C-30/95 1998, 221).
561. (ECJ, United Brands Company and United Brands Continentaal BV v. Commission, Case 27/76 1978).

Chapter 4: Competition Practice

4.5.1.1 *Product Market Definitions*

The Court of Justice has repeatedly required the Commission to define the relevant product market and to give reasons for its definition. In *Continental Can* the Court stated that:

> *the definition of the relevant market is of essential significance, for the possibility of competition can only be judged in relation to those characteristics of the products ... which ... are particularly apt to supply an inelastic need, and only to a limited extent interchangeable with other products.*[562]

The Commission had found in this case[563] that the firm in question was dominant in markets defined as 'light containers for canned meat products', 'light containers for sea food' and 'metal closures for the food packaging industry.' Most of its analysis was focused on the inclusion of glass and plastic containers in these markets. Because of the different physical characteristics of packaging materials and in the machines used for the packaging, the market was confined to metal containers. The failure of the Commission to explain how these three markets differed from one another, and therefore from the broader light metals container market, was critical. The Court recognised that a limited interchangeability with other products was insufficient to place them in the same market. The Court found inconsistencies in the Commission's analysis of glass and plastic containers. Instead, the Court in examining the market for metal cans and containers pointed to the existence of other sources of competition, such as containers made of glass or plastic, and the fact that food packers could manufacture their own containers. The Court thus came to the conclusion that Continental Can was not in a dominant position, as the metal container market was not distinguishable from the market for other food containers. At the very outset, the Court stressed supply-side substitutability in this case.

The emphasis shifted to *demand-side substitutability* in *United Brand*,[564] where the question for the Court was whether the market for bananas was a separate market, or whether it was part of the overall market for fruit. The Court considered that for a market to be separate, it must be sufficiently distinguishable from other markets. It must be possible to single out special factors, which make that market separate, so that it is only to a limited extent, if at all, interchangeable with other markets, and only exposed to imperceptible competition. The Court upheld the Commission's determination that the relevant market was bananas rather than all fresh fruit. Despite findings that at various times of the year sales of other fruits then in season exerted price pressure on bananas and reduces their volume of sales, the Court concluded that there was no long-term (apparently meaning year-long) cross-elasticity between bananas and other fruits; a result the Court explained in terms of physical characteristics such as taste, softness, and ease of handling, and the availability over the entire year at this

---

562. (ECJ, Europemballage Corporation and Continental Can Company Inc. v. Commission, Case 6/72 1973).
563. (Decision IV/26.811 on Continental Can Company 1971).
564. (ECJ, United Brands Company and United Brands Continentaal BV v. Commission, Case 27/76 1978).

time to a particular group whose need for bananas was constant namely 'the young, the old and the sick.' The decision has been criticised by a number of commentators for its reliance on the needs of a particular sub-group of purchasers without evidence of the volume of their purchases.[565] To conclude, the Court found that bananas were only to a limited extent interchangeable with other fruit, (there was a low cross-elasticity of demand), and that the market for bananas was quite distinct from the market for other fruit.[566]

A study of the objective characteristics of the products involved is not enough as demonstrated in the *Michelin*[567] case. In this case, where the issues were more complex than in other early cases, it was necessary to distinguish a new original equipment tyre from a new replacement tyre. Both products were seen as part of a different relevant market. The Commission found that Michelin held a dominant position in a market defined as new replacement tires for heavy vehicles, a market which did not include the same tires when sold to vehicle manufacturers (OEM's), auto or light van tires, and retreads. The Court upheld the Commission's market definition.

The Court held in *Michelin*, that it must be noted that the determination of the relevant product market is useful in assessing whether the undertaking concerned is in a position to prevent effective competition from being maintained and behave to an appreciable extent independently of its competitors and customers and consumers. For this purpose, therefore, an examination limited to the objective characteristics of the relevant products only cannot be sufficient: the competitive conditions and the structure of supply and demand on the market must also be taken into consideration. However, competitive conditions in the supply of the former are likely to be subject to materially different factors from those pertaining to the latter, judged from the point of view of users, distributors, consumers and suppliers. In other words, even goods, which, based on their objective characteristics could be considered as being reasonably interchangeable, may be used by different categories of customers, who are part of a different competitive environment. Under these circumstances, it may be appropriate to treat the different categories of customers as belonging to separate markets.[568] Thus the Court relied in *Michelin* upon a whole range of factors. The Court declined, however, to break the heavy tire market into further categories based on types and dimensions, finding that these differences were not relevant to the demands of distributors who carried a full-line, even though those differences might be relevant for consumers.

In the *Deutsche Post AG (DPAG)*[569] decision, the Commission distinguished the customer segment B-to-B from the C-to-X and the B-to-C segment. By reason of their characteristics, costs and uses, the Commission considered that mail-order parcel services form one relevant product market. Mail-order parcels are not processed through the postal counter system but are collected by DPAG directly at the customers'

---

565. (Korah 1994, 72).
566. (ECJ, United Brands Company and United Brands Continentaal BV v. Commission, Case 27/76 1978, 22).
567. (ECJ, NV Nederlandsche Banden Industrie Michelin v. Commission, Case 322/81 1983).
568. (Van Bael & Bellis 1987, 50).
569. (Decision COMP/35.141 on Deutsche Post AG 2001, 26–30).

premises. Furthermore, DPAG offers special prices to mail-order customers, who do not use the postal counter system for their parcel and catalogue deliveries. This distinguishes mail-order parcel services from over-the-counter parcels, which are processed against payment of a standard tariff through the postal counters. A mail-order firm expects German-wide delivery of parcels up to 31.5 kilograms and catalogues over 1 kilogram (heavy Infopost) or over 50 grams (Infopost) to a large number of private addressees scattered throughout the country. As a rule mail-order parcels weigh on average up to 2 kilograms; the maximum weight is 31.5 kilograms. Mail-order parcels are almost always in the category of so-called 'non-bulky' parcels. These are parcels that are 'machine-handle able', i.e., they can be stacked and lend themselves during sorting to being processed on a conveyor belt. Although they share the infrastructure at the sorting and transport stages, final delivery to private addressees makes much greater use of vehicles and postal delivery staff than do B-to-B services. In the case of mail-order services the dispersed addressee structure produces a very low 'stop factor' (i.e., number of parcels delivered per delivery vehicle stop), one parcel per stop being the rule. In the case of parcel services between business customers, i.e., B-to-B services, the stop factor is much higher, as here several parcels are normally delivered whenever the delivery vehicle stops. In addition, mail-order parcel services are characterised by a different price structure. That is why the Commission took account of the different customer segments in its decision.

In *Hoffmann-La Roche*, a case on exclusionary practices, thirteen categories of vitamins were characterised as separate markets based on bionutritive functions. With respect to these functions, vitamins were in a market separate from such things as food, which obviously perform the same functions. As the Court stated:

> the concept of the relevant market in fact implies that there can be effective competition between the products which form part of it and this presupposes that there is a sufficient degree of interchangeability between all the products forming part of the same market insofar as a specific use of such products is concerned.[570]

The general approach of the Commission and the Court has been to focus upon interchangeability: the extent to which the goods or services under scrutiny are interchangeable with other products.[571] There is no precise test for determining what a sufficient degree of interchangeability between products is. This issue can be answered, in principle, by looking at both the demand and supply-sides of the market.

The most striking Court of Justice opinion in a preliminary ruling is *Ahmed Saeed*.[572] It is also one of its most cryptic. At issue, was the validity of airline tariffs jointly proposed by airlines and approved by the German government. German law prohibited the sale of tickets below these approved fares. After two travel agents sold discounted tickets on a flight from Germany to international destinations, a suit was brought in German courts, which in turn referred several questions to the Court of

---

570. (ECJ, Hoffmann-La Roche & Co. AG v. Commission, Case 85/76 1979).
571. (ECJ, United Brands Company and United Brands Continentaal BV v. Commission, Case 27/76 1978).
572. (ECJ, Ahmed Saeed Flugreisen and Silver Line Reisebüro GmbH v. Zentrale zur Bekämpfung unlauteren Wettbewerbs e.V., Case 66/86 1989).

Justice. No discussion of the relevant market appears in its analysis under Article 101. Instead, with respect to Article 102, the Court of Justice had to deal with the question of whether scheduled flights could be deemed to constitute a separate market or whether alternative transport possibilities, such as charter flights, air and road transport, or scheduled flights on other routes capable of serving as substitutes, could be taken into consideration. In line with its established case law, the Court ruled that due regard had to be given to the possibilities of substitution. Although for some routes no effective competition was likely to occur, for other routes, in particular for intra-Community routes, the possibility existed that other transport undertakings on the same route or on a substitute route could offer effective competition.[573] The Court then simply concluded that:

> *The test to be employed is whether the scheduled flight on a particular route can be distinguished from the possible alternatives by virtue of specific characteristics as a result of which it is not interchangeable with those alternatives and is affected only to an insignificant degree by competition from them.*[574]

The Court placed great emphasis on the defendant firm's recognition of a narrow product market.

Ahmed Saeed has had an influence far beyond air transport markets. In *French-West African Shipowner's Committees*,[575] the Commission found in its decision that cargo sharing and other agreements of a ship owner's committee violated both Articles 101 and 102. Market definition was formally discussed only in the Article 102 analysis. Initially the Commission defined the market as regular liner cargo service, a market excluding air transport and chartered tramp vessels for reasons similar to Ahmed Saeed's exclusion of surface transport and air charter service. More specifically, the market was defined as regular liner cargo service between France and eleven African states, with little explanation beyond the statement that the logic of *Ahmed Saeed* has to be applied to sea routes.

The Commission once again in its decision *Sea Containers* extended this chain of logic.[576] Sea Containers desired to operate a vehicle and passenger ferry service on a route between Holyhead in Wales and Dublin and Dun Laoghaire in Ireland. Access was denied to the port of Holyhead by Sealink, which owned the port facilities and operated as the port authority. It also operated a ferry service on the route, Sea Containers sought to enter. The Commission found that while there were three ferry corridors between Great Britain and Ireland, the corridors were not substitutes. The northern and southern corridors brought passengers a considerable distance from Dublin, and were not therefore, according to the Commission, interchangeable in the eyes of consumers. It was then an easy step to conclude that the market was port services for the central corridor. The only British port on the corridor was Holyhead, and Sealink therefore held a dominant position.

---

573. (ECJ, Ahmed Saeed Flugreisen and Silver Line Reisebüro GmbH v. Zentrale zur Bekämpfung unlauteren Wettbewerbs e.V., Case 66/86 1989, 39–41).
574. *Ibid.*, para. 40.
575. (Decision IV/32.450 on French-West African shipowners' committees 1992).
576. (Decision IV/34.689 on Sea Containers v. Stena Sealink – Interim measures 1993).

Tetra Pak II,[577] a rejected appeal against a Court of First Instance judgment, concerns another important case. Tetra Pak, a company of Swedish origin established in Switzerland is the largest supplier for the packaging of liquid foods (chiefly milk and fruit juices) in cartons. In some of the markets in this sector, the market for machinery and the market for cartons for aseptic packaging of 'long life' liquids, the group holds a virtual monopoly (approximately 95% of the market). The Commission defined as the relevant product markets four markets:[578] (1) machines for aseptic packaging of ultra-high temperature treated liquid foods (primarily milk); (2) cartons for the same; (3) machines for packaging liquid foods in cartons in a non-aseptic manner; (4) cartons for the same. The Court of Justice agreed with the Commission's findings on the lack of sufficient substitutability between aseptic and non-aseptic systems, noting, as the Commission stressed, that small increases in machinery prices would not affect consumers' decision to shift between aseptic and non-aseptic milk. In the end, the critical factors were those relied upon by the Commission, namely differences in physical characteristics, consumer preferences based on taste and shelf-life, and the costs inherent in shifting from one system to another.

Much of the analysis in *Tetra-Pak II* reflects a conventional assessment of physical and technological characteristics and consumer needs and preferences. Nevertheless, according to *Kauper*[579], several things stand out. First, the Commission's explicit reference to the time frame to be used in assessing markets is noteworthy, even though it has used short time periods implicitly for some time. Second, the reliance on consumer demand as the critical element in concluding that small (increases) in machinery prices would not cause a shift in this intermediate market to other machinery types. Third, the Commission and the Court of Justice did consider supply-side substitutability, although factually both concluded rather easily that it was not relevant. And finally, the Commission and Court of Justice declined, although the machinery for aseptic packaging was basically the same for all types of liquids packages, to segregate the market further based on liquid type. In short, it rejected end user market definitions, at least in part, because there was no evidence of price discrimination among the proposed user categories.

Hugin/Liptons[580] was the most explicit example of limitation of the market to a firm's own product. In *Hilti AG v. Commission*[581], the Court of Justice returned to a single brand market. The Court of Justice dismissed the appeal brought by Hilti against the judgment of the Court of First Instance.[582] Hilti manufactured powder-actuated fastening (PAF) guns, power tools which drive nails with the use an exploding cartridge which is inserted into the gun along with the nails to be driven. Hilti produced not only the guns themselves, but also the cartridge strips and nails which were compatible with its guns. Acting on complaints by competing manufacturers of

---
577. (ECJ, Tetra Pak International SA v. Commission, Case C.333/94 P 1996).
578. *Ibid.*, point 92.
579. (Kauper 1996 1708).
580. (ECJ, Hugin Kassaregister AB and Hugin Cash Registers Ltd v. Commission, Case 22/78 1979).
581. (ECJ, Hilti AG v. Commission, Case C-53/92 P 1994).
582. (CFI, Hilti AG v. Commission, Case T-30/89 1991).

Hilti-compatible nails, the Commission[583] found that Hilti had violated Article 102 by refusing to provide cartridge strips without nails, and by taking a number of other steps to assure that cartridge purchasers were required to use cartridges only with Hilti nails. In essence, Hilti tied the sales of cartridges and nails together. The Commission defined three separate markets: (1) nail guns; (2) Hilti compatible cartridge strips; and (3) Hilti-compatible nails. Hilti was found to be dominant in each.

In its judgment, the Court of First Instance rejected Hilti's application for annulment of the Commission decision finding that Hilti had abused its dominant position within the meaning of Article 102 vis-à-vis independent producers of nails for Hilti nail guns. The Court of First Instance agreed that PAF guns, Hilti-compatible cartridges, and nails were three separate markets, not one integrated product. Other producers produce Hilti-compatible cartridges and nails, a fact that alone was deemed to be 'sound evidence' of separate markets. The Court of First Instance stated that Hilti's view that the nail guns, nails and cartridges all constituted one market:

> *is in practice tantamount to permitting producers of nail guns to exclude the use of consumables other than their own branded products in their tools. However, in the absence of general and binding standards or rules, any independent producer is quite free, as far as Community competition law is concerned, to manufacture consumables intended for the use in equipment manufactured by others, unless in doing so it infringes a patent or some other industrial or intellectual property right.*[584]

After pointing out that products form part of the same market only if they are sufficiently interchangeable with each other, the Court of Justice held that, contrary to what the applicant claimed, the Court of First Instance had duly considered whether or not PAF systems were interchangeable with other fastening systems. These grounds are questionable. Because the Court of First Instance and the Commission found that for a number of applications the PAF system was favoured, and for a number it was not, it is difficult to determine the actual degree of substitutability that may have existed. That each of several fastening systems held a significant part of overall fastening sales over a period of time may suggest that each system was technically superior in particular systems, but does not negate price responsiveness among them in the event of a significant price increase. Hilti argued also that there was a significant degree of supply substitutability between power drill and PAF gun manufacturers, between PAF nails and other nails and screws, and between cartridge strip manufacturers. The Court of Justice did not resolve any issue of supply-side substitutability.

Hilti is just one case concerning the issue of *secondary product markets*. Several complaints which the Commission received concern the alleged abuse of a dominant position in secondary product markets such as spare parts, consumables or maintenance services. These products are used in conjunction with a primary product and have to be technically compatible with it (e.g., software or hardware peripheral equipment for a computer). Thus, for these secondary products there may be no or few substitutes other than parts or services supplied by the primary product supplier. This

---

583. (Decision IV/30.787 and 31.488 on Eurofix-Bauco v. Hilti 1987).
584. (CFI, Hilti AG v. Commission, Case T-30/89 1991, 68).

prompts the question whether a non-dominant manufacturer of primary products can be dominant with respect to a rather small secondary product market, i.e., secondary products compatible with a certain type of that manufacturer's primary products.

The question raises many complex issues. Producers of primary equipment argue that there cannot be dominance in secondary products if there is lack of dominance in the primary product market because potential buyers would simply stop buying the primary products if the prices for parts or services were raised. This theory implies a timely reaction on the primary product market due to consumers' ability to calculate the overall lifetime costs of the primary product including all spare parts, consumables, upgrades, services, etc. It furthermore implies that price discrimination is not possible between potentially new customers and 'old' captive customers or that switching costs for the latter are low. On the other hand, complainants who produce consumables or maintenance services assume dominance in the secondary product market if market shares are high in this market, i.e., this approach focuses only on the secondary products without analysing possible effects emanating from the primary product market.

4.5.1.2 Geographic Market Definitions

The *relevant geographic market* is defined by the area in which the dominant firm may be able to engage in abuses, which hinder effective competition. The definition of the relevant geographic market therefore depends on the location of the company, which is the object of investigation, and on the nature of the practices, which are being investigated. In his opinion in *Michelin*,[585] the Advocate General *VerLoren Themaat* stressed that the relevant geographic market cannot be defined in the abstract.

The *Alsatel*[586] preliminary ruling judgment provides a welcomed clarification on the issue of market definition where products are available under different forms or through different means, each of which involves different substitution possibilities. Telecommunication equipment could be either purchased or leased by the user from Alsatel. Taking into consideration the fact that many users choose to rent their equipment and that competition in respect of rental and maintenance of equipment is limited to the local market – where Alsatel was dominant – the Commission suggested considering the *local market* as being the relevant geographic market for the purpose of assessing Alsatel's market position. The Court of Justice refused to follow this approach. Considering that users are free, if they wish to do so, to purchase their equipment rather than renting it and that it was not alleged that Alsatel had a dominant position on the entire French market, the Court of Justice rejected the Commission's narrow market definition.[587] The relevant market covered the sale and renting-out of telephone installations because the customer could choose between those alternatives.

---

585. (ECJ, NV Nederlandsche Banden Industrie Michelin v. Commission, Case 322/81 1983, 3534–3535).
586. (ECJ, Alsatel v. SA Novasam, Case 247/86 1988).
587. *Ibid.*, paras 16–18.

In the Italian *Flat glass*[588] case, the Commission found in its decision that flat glass became significantly less competitive as the distance from the production facility increased. In the Commission's view, transportation costs were significant in limiting the geographic market for flat glass to the Member State Italy. The Commission concluded that the Italian market was the relevant geographic market because it supplied at least four-fifths of the domestic consumption. In *Joint Cases Societa Italiano Vetro (SIV) Spa & ORS v. Commission (Flat Glass)*[589], the Court of First Instance suggested that it is not enough to allege simply that high transport costs mean that the geographic market should be limited to the Member States or a portion of the Member State in which production facilities are located. Rather, the analysis of the relevant geographic market should examine whether, in reality, transport costs are significant. Moreover, the relevant geographic market should be categorised by homogeneous competitive conditions. For this purpose, the objective conditions of competition applying to the product in question must be the same for all traders, or in other words, the area must be sufficiently homogeneous.[590]

In *United Brands*,[591] the Court of Justice upheld the Commission's exclusion of France, Italy and the UK from the market because defendant banana supplier (UBC) faced different objective conditions of competition in those three Member States as compared with the remainder. This arose primarily from the governmental system of import preferences in France and the UK, and quota restrictions in Italy; the remaining six Member States were held to constitute the relevant market despite varying tariffs. Similarly the Commission limited the geographical market in another case to the UK because of natural and trade barriers.

In the Commission decision *Napier Brown/British Sugar*,[592] for example, the cost of freight was a significant factor in defining the market. The Commission noted that the English Channel provided a natural barrier allowing British sugar producers to charge a premium price for sugar compared with Continental prices.

In *Hilti*,[593] the Court of First Instance upheld the Commission's determination that the relevant geographic market was the entire Community, on the grounds that parallel trade in Hilti products between Member States was likely due to low transport costs and large price differences.

In *Michelin*,[594] the Netherlands was considered to be the relevant geographic market. The reasons invoked were that Michelin's activities were concentrated on the Dutch market, and that, in practice, Dutch tyre dealers obtained their supplies only from suppliers operating in the Netherlands. Another argument was that Michelin's

---

588. (Decision IV/31.906 on Flat glass 1988).
589. (CFI, SIV and Others v. Commission, Joined cases T-68/89, T-77/89 and T-78/89 1992).
590. (ECJ, United Brands Company and United Brands Continentaal BV v. Commission, Case 27/76 1978).
591. *Ibid.*, para. 38.
592. (Decision IV/30.178 on Napier Brown – British Sugar 1988).
593. (CFI, Hilti AG v. Commission, Case T-30/89 1991).
594. (ECJ, NV Nederlandsche Banden Industrie Michelin v. Commission, Case 322/81 1983).

competitors were organised in the same way. The decision in Michelin contains no analysis of transport costs or cross-elasticity of supply factors. The Commission has been severely criticised for its failure to do so and also because of its almost single-minded reliance on the use of national marketing organisations.

In *Alsatel*,[595] the Commission tried to have the Court of Justice declare the Alsace region to be the relevant market. The Court of Justice refused to follow the Commission's suggestion, since under examination the company was authorised to operate on the entire French territory.

In *Tetra Pak II*,[596] the Commission had defined the markets for milk packaging machinery as EU-wide because such machines were sold in each Member State and transport costs were low. Before the Court of First Instance, Tetra Pak argued that the markets were national because distribution was organised through national subsidiaries, patterns of consumption varied between states and so did prices. Nevertheless, the Court agreed with the Commission on the scope of the geographic market. Price differences resulted from artificial partitioning of markets by Tetra Pak and others and were therefore not indicative of different conditions of competition. Finally, due to Tetra Pak's group-wide strategy of partitioning markets, weight was given to the use of national subsidiaries.

Some indications can be given as to how the Commission is dealing with relevant market definitions, although in most decisions there is little or no analysis of the relevant geographic market. In some cases, the outer limits of the relevant geographic market are set by government measures such as import restrictions or statutory monopolies. In other cases the decisive factors are the characteristics of the product, especially its transport costs,[597] technical requirements such as the range of television networks,[598] consumer tastes and preferences,[599] and more generally the realistic economic alternatives available to buyers and sellers.[600]

Reference must also be made to the geographic scope of the abusive conduct. The abusive conduct may constitute a general, community-wide strategy, as in the *Hoffmann-La Roche* case involving the sale of vitamins throughout the Community; it may also be directed only at distributors in a single Member State, as in the *Michelin* case explained above; or it may be directed at distributors in part of a Member State as in the *Sugar* case in which one of the abuses was limited to the southern part of Germany. In such cases, a single Member State or part of a Member State may be the relevant geographic market.

---

595. (ECJ, Alsatel v. SA Novasam, Case 247/86 1988).
596. (Commission Decisions (92/163/EEC) on Tetra Pak II Case IV/31043 1991).
597. For empty cans the Commission claimed in Continental Can that the geographic limits were between 150 and 300 kilometres for transporting large cans and between 500 and 1000 kilometres for smaller cans.
598. (ECJ, CBEM v. CLT and IPB, Case 311/84 1985).
599. (ECJ, Coöperatieve Vereniging 'Suiker Unie' UA and others v. Commission, Joined cases 40-48, 50, 54 to 56, 111, 113 and 114-73 1975).
600. (ECJ, Hoffmann-La Roche & Co. AG v. Commission, Case 85/76 1979).

4.5.1.3 *The Time Factor*

'*Dominance is economic power over a period of time, and not transient power*',[601] therefore the time period has to be considered carefully for assessing the relevant market (and at a later stage for assessing dominance) in cases of, for example, a temporary dominant position during emergencies. An oil shortage temporarily increases the customer's dependence on its traditional supplier. Due to special circumstances, the normal competitive process comes to an end. In such a case, each supplier finds himself in a dominant position.[602] Under normal conditions, however, the market must be considered over a longer period. Seasonal variations in demand were not accepted by the Court of Justice in the *United Brands* case as sufficient to consider bananas as belonging temporarily to a larger fresh fruit market. Such temporary changes in market shares are nevertheless relevant considerations when evaluating the existence of a dominant position.

In *Tetra Pak II*,[603] one of the aspects covered was the time factor. Tetra Pak argued that the market should include a variety of other forms of packaging, such as glass and plastic bottles. The Commission concluded that such packaging competes at best in the long-term, given their different physical characteristics, user needs and the differences in the machinery used in the packaging process. But '*in the short, and probably even the medium term*' the elasticity of substitution in response to prices 'is almost zero,' for two reasons.[604] First, packaging is but a very small part of the price of the packaged product, so even a 10% price increase would have little impact on the price of the packaged product. Given consumer preferences, the packager or producer will not shift to another form of packaging only in response to consumer acceptability. There can, in the Commission's words, be '*no elasticity of intermediate demand if there is no elasticity of final demand*'.[605] Second, changeover by producer or packagers to different equipment and packages is both costly and time-consuming, and may require alteration in storage, handling, and distribution systems. For perhaps the first time, the Commission explained in *Tetra Pak II* why markets must be defined based on short time periods. Over a long-term, consumer habits evolve, technology changes and market boundaries shift. A short time period corresponds more to the period in which a company exercises its market power and upon which therefore analysis must focus.

In this context, it is interesting to note that the time factor is not considered explicitly in the Commission's Notice on the Definition of the Relevant Market for the Purposes of Community Competition Law.[606]

---

601. (Baden-Fuller 1979, 424).
602. (Van Bael & Bellis 1987, 58).
603. (Commission Decisions (92/163/EEC) on Tetra Pak II Case IV/31043 1991).
604. *Ibid.*, para. 93.
605. *Ibid.*, para. 97.
606. (Commission Notice on the definition of relevant market 1997).

Chapter 4: Competition Practice

4.5.1.4 Substantial Part of the Common Market

Article 102 requires that an undertaking must be dominant within the common market or a substantial part of it, therefore making the geographical area an important factor. This language has been interpreted to include the entire common market, Member States, regional areas of a Member State and even a port. In *Suiker Unie S.A. v. Commission*[607], a case on market sharing, the Court of Justice stated that:

> For the purpose of determining whether a specific territory is large enough to amount to a 'substantial part of the common market' within the meaning of Article 86 (new Article 102) of the Treaty the pattern and volume of the production and consumption of the said products as well as the habits and economic opportunities of vendors and purchasers must be considered.[608]

On these grounds Holland on its own, Belgium and Luxembourg taken together and the Southern part of Germany were considered in *Suiker Unie* to be substantial parts. Similarly, the Commission held in its decision *Magill TV Guide/ITP, BBC and RTE*[609] that Ireland and Northern Ireland are a substantial part of the common market.

The territory of one Member State has on several occasions been deemed to be sufficiently large to be a substantial part. In most Article 102 cases, the relevant market has comprised the territory of at least one Member State, thus quasi-automatically satisfying the substantiality requirement. *Suiker Unie* (as described above) and *Hugin* moreover indicate that even a part of a Member State may qualify as a substantial part of the common market. In *Hugin*, it was the City of London. Similarly, in *Bodson v. Pompes Funebresdes*[610] the Court of Justice held in reply to a request for a preliminary ruling, that Article 102 might be applicable to activities carried out in only a part of the territory of a Member State, while leaving it to the national court to decide if there was in fact a dominant position in a substantial part of the Common market.

A problem could arise when considering whether essential facilities comprise a substantial part of the common market. Clearly, a facility such as a port can hardly in itself be a substantial part of the common market in a purely geographic sense. Consequently, the Court of Justice focused in *Merci Convenzionali Porto di Genova SpA v. Siderurgica Gabrielli SpA*,[611] also a preliminary ruling, on the importance of the port for a substantial part of the Community (namely Italy). It referred to the volume of traffic through the port, and its importance in relation to maritime export and export operations as a whole in that Member State. In *Port of Rodby*,[612] the Commission merely referred to the high percentage of sea traffic between Denmark and Germany handled by Rodby, its volume and value, and then stated: 'The port of Rodby thus constitutes a

---

607. (ECJ, Coöperatieve Vereniging 'Suiker Unie' UA and others v. Commission, Joined cases 40-48, 50, 54 to 56, 111, 113 and 114-73 1975, 371).
608. *Ibid.*, para. 371.
609. (Decision IV/31.851 on Magill TV Guide/ITP, BBC and RTE 1988).
610. (ECJ, Corinne Bodson v. SA Pompes funèbres des régions libérées, Case 30/87 1988).
611. (ECJ, Merci Convenzionali Porto di Genova SpA v. Siderurgica Gabrielli SpA, Case C-179/90 1991).
612. (Decision 94/119/EC concerning a refusal to grant access to the facilities of the port of Rødby 1993).

substantial part of the common market'.[613] Presumably the Commission is saying that, as in *Porto di Genova*, the importance of the port to the Member States concerned, which are themselves a substantial part of the common market, lends the port a similar standing.

4.5.2 Economic Analysis in Article 102

The first step in applying Article 102 is to define the relevant degree of economic power, *dominance*.[614] The Treaty gives no definition of dominance. It is thus left to the national courts or the Commission subject to the control of the Court of Justice of the EU to determine whether or not a dominant position exists by reference to the relevant market factors. However, the Commission, the Court of Justice of the EU as well as national courts need advice on which yardsticks should be used in order to define whether an undertaking has by law the necessary degree of market power. Economic analysis plays a critical part in this context. It is evident, that competition law has to employ economic concepts to judge which market structures and practices are harmful and which are beneficial for an economy.[615]

The existing case law provides some useful insights into the economic concept of dominance. In practice, there are four steps that have to be taken to establish whether a firm holds a dominant position:

- Definition of the relevant product and geographic market in which conditions of competition and the market power of the (supposed) dominant firm have to be assessed.
- Indication that the undertaking has a persistently high share of current activity in that market.
- Confirmation that there is no real likelihood of actual or potential rivals eroding the position of the dominant firm.
- Evidence that the dominant position exists in the common market or a substantial part thereof.

Although those four steps are analysed separately each step overlaps the others.

Thus, dominance exists in relation to a relevant market. Market definition therefore becomes a central part in any case as discussed in the previous sections. Indeed, the inquiry into dominance is divided from the economic perspective into two parts – first the definition of the relevant market, and then the investigation of dominance within 'that' market. Once dominance has been established, there is then the question of whether an abuse has occurred.

---

613. *Ibid.*, para. 8.
614. The attempt to define dominance can be traced back to the year 1621, when Leonardo Lessius in his work 'Gerechtigkeit, Recht und andere Kardinaltugenden' defined dominance as the ability of one or a few offerers to sell a specific kind of good for a certain price, which is freely chosen and independent from competitors as well as buyers in: (Albach 1978, 538).
615. (Bork 1978, 7).

The framework of an economic analysis contains, besides the size of market shares, the market structure, the firms structure and other competitive conditions on the relevant market. Except in the most obvious of cases, such as *Suiker Unie*[616], where one of the suppliers had a massive share of a commodity product on the market, the proof of significant market share is seldom a substitute for a full economic analysis of the issue of dominance.[617] Firstly, even if market share figures are reliable, maintenance of a significant market share tells one little about the competitive process unless one understands the reason for, and the pressures determining the output and price decisions made by the firms in the market. Secondly, even if the market has been defined correctly, market share figures do not show relative efficiencies and do not necessarily demonstrate that similar market shares can be sustained in the future. Thirdly, the decisions that any firm makes may be influenced by potential competitors who have not yet entered the market but who would do so if a profitable opportunity were to arise. By definition, market shares cannot measure this potential competition, even though the threat that it presents may be a powerful influence restraining the independence of an allegedly dominant firm. Fourthly, market power on the part of the customers of the undertaking may limit its ability to act independently of their wishes. Therefore, *'market shares are limited in their power of indication'* in dominance cases.[618] The case law indicates that concrete economic circumstances have to be analysed.[619]

Moreover, as the Court of Justice has emphasised, a finding of a dominant position does not preclude some competition in the market. It only enables the undertaking that enjoys such a position, if not to determine, at least to have an appreciable effect on the conditions under which that competition will develop, and in any case to act in disregard of any such competitive constraint so long as such conduct does not operate to its detriment.[620]

In an *ex post* analysis under Article 102 we are faced with a number of different examples of market behaviour each indicative of market power within the meaning of Article 102. Although market shares might be a prime surrogate for market power, other criteria have to be applied – depending on the specific circumstances of the case – to measure market power. These criteria include:

- overall size of the undertaking;
- technological advantages or superiority;
- absence of countervailing buying power;
- easy or privileged access to capital markets or financial resources;
- product and services diversification (e.g., bundled products or services);
- economies of scale;
- economies of scope;

---

616. (ECJ, Coöperatieve Vereniging 'Suiker Unie' UA and others v. Commission, Joined cases 40-48, 50, 54 to 56, 111, 113 and 114-73 1975).
617. (Bellamy and Child 1993, 605).
618. (Langen and Bunte 1994, 22).
619. Schröter in: (Von der Groeben, Thiesing and Ehlermann 1993, 542).
620. (ECJ, Hoffmann-La Roche & Co. AG v. Commission, Case 85/76 1979, 39).

- vertical integration;
- a highly developed sales network;
- absence of potential competition.

A dominant position can derive from a combination of the above-mentioned criteria, which taken separately may not necessarily be determinative.

4.5.2.1 *Market shares*

A valuable consideration in determining dominance is market share. 'The existence of a dominant position may derive from several factors, which separately, are not necessarily determinative but among these factors a highly important one is the existence of very large market shares.'[621] Though rarely sufficient alone to prove the existence of a dominant position, a large market share is indicative for its assessment. 'A trader can only be in a dominant position on the market for a product if he has succeeded in winning a large part of this market'.[622] Market shares above 80% are considerably high and are usually enough to conclude a dominant position.[623] Nevertheless a case-by-case analysis is required, since it is not possible to point to a specific market share of the market above which a firm is conclusively dominant, and below which it is not.[624] In its 2009 guidance paper,[625] the Commission takes into account that a finding of dominance requires a careful assessment of market conditions, without giving too much weight to market shares. The Commission points out that the market shares of the various players are just the starting point for the analysis of the market position of the allegedly dominant undertaking. They consider very high market shares as likely to indicate a dominant position, but emphasise that any indication based on market shares depends on the facts of each individual case.

An important argument in this context is the relationship between the market shares of the competitors and the mobility of the demand, in particular price elasticity, which follows a set pattern. The transition decision of the consumers depends on several factors. Those factors are the substitution ratio[626] of the products, the price level of the competitive products, the access to them, market transparency and the utilisation of the products by the consumers as well as, the readiness and possibility of the competitors to satisfy the demand. The consumer is not considering market shares as a decisive factor in his decision to switch over to other producers, nor is a competitor's market shares an indication of his future readiness to supply. Dominance is not indicated by market share, but is indicated by the change of market shares when

---

621. (ECJ, Hoffmann-La Roche & Co. AG v. Commission, Case 85/76 1979).
622. (ECJ, United Brands Company and United Brands Continentaal BV v. Commission, Case 27/76 1978).
623. (ECJ, Coöperatieve Vereniging 'Suiker Unie' UA and others v. Commission, Joined cases 40-48, 50, 54 to 56, 111, 113 and 114-73 1975).
624. (Faull and Nikpay 1999, 125).
625. (European Commission, Guidance on the Commission's enforcement priorities in applying Art. 82 of the EC Treaty to abusive exclusionary conduct by dominant undertakings 2009).
626. The substitution rate indicates whether products are easily replaced by similar products or not.

Chapter 4: Competition Practice

the dominant firm's supply deteriorates. This implies the necessity – after the identification of the market shares and the substitute products – to confirm the mobility of the demand.[627]

In Continental Can[628], the Court of Justice laid down the test of market dominance as the ability of competitors to constitute an adequate counterweight. In United Brands[629], where it was held that a market share of 45% of the banana market constituted market dominance, the fact that the largest competitor had a market share of only 9% was an important consideration. Other factors in this case were the high barriers against new entrants to the market, such as penetration costs, access to sources of supply, and the need for large investment. In Hoffmann-La Roche, the Court of Justice again stressed the importance of market shares and gave the reason why an undertaking with a very large market share is in a position of strength:

> Furthermore although the importance of the market shares may vary from one market to another the view may legitimately be taken that very large shares are in themselves, and save in exceptional circumstances, evidence of a dominant position. An undertaking which has a very large market share and holds it for some time, by means of the volume of production and the scale of the supply which it stands for - without those having much smaller market shares being able to meet rapidly the demand from those who would like to break away from the undertaking which has the largest market share - is by virtue of that share in a position of strength which makes it an unavoidable trading partner and which, already because of this secures for it, at the very least during relatively long periods, that freedom of action which is the special feature of a dominant position.
>
> ... The existence of a dominant position may derive from several factors which taken separately are not necessarily determinative but among these factors a highly important one is the existence of very large market shares.[630]

Whilst the Commission had placed in this case weight on the pure size of the company and the volume of turnover that it provided, the Court of Justice did not accept that size and turnover alone could indicate dominance. The Court of Justice also placed far less reliance than the Commission on the range of products produced by Roche as well as the fact that it had retained market shares over a continuous period of time, pointing out that this could be explained by a large number of other factors, including simply its ability to compete effectively in a normal manner. In that case Hoffmann-La Roche held very high market shares in a number of markets.

The Court of Justice indicated in *Hoffmann-La Roche,* that market shares over a three-year period ranging between 75% and 87% are held to be so large that they are in themselves evidence of a dominant position,[631] and market shares between 84% and 90% over a similar period so large that they prove the existence of a dominant position.

---

627. Koch in: (Grabitz 1984, Art. 82 para. 30).
628. (ECJ, Europemballage Corporation and Continental Can Company Inc. v. Commission, Case 6/72 1973).
629. (ECJ, United Brands Company and United Brands Continentaal BV v. Commission, Case 27/76 1978).
630. (ECJ, Hoffmann-La Roche & Co. AG v. Commission, Case 85/76 1979, 41).
631. *Ibid.*, para. 56, Market shares relate to the market for Vitamin B Group.

In *Hilti*,[632] the Court of First Instance held a 70–80% share as an indication for a dominant position. In *AKZO*,[633] a stable market share of 50% over at least three years was held to be proof of a dominant position. The Court added *'furthermore, AKZO has not adduced any evidence to show that it share decreased during subsequent years'*.[634] With reference to the *Hoffmann-La Roche* case, the Court stated additionally that if there is a market share of 50%, such as found in the AKZO case, this could be evidence for the existence of a dominant position. What is important to note in this context is the fact that only a case-by-case analysis might prove the existence of a dominant position. It is wrong to conclude at first sight that a company with high market share holds a dominant position per se. The Court of First Instance concluded in *Irish Sugar*[635] that a dominant position may derive from several factors which, taken separately, are not necessarily decisive. Amongst these factors, extremely large market shares are in themselves, save in exceptional circumstances, evidence of the existence of a dominant position. This means that besides the requirement of a case-by-case analysis, exceptional high market shares are only a point of departure for further market structure analysis. This is particularly true in the assessment of dominance in network-based industries like telecommunications.

In *Hoffmann-La Roche* market shares ranging between 63% and 66% over a three-year period, in the market for the vitamin C group, were held to be *'evidence of the existence of a dominant position'* and *'the gap between Roche's share (64.8%) and those of its next largest competitors (14.8% and 6.3%) was such as to confirm the conclusion which the Commission reached.'*[636] In *Michelin*, the Court of Justice held that a market share of 57% to 65% on the market in new replacement tyres for heavy vehicles (compared with the market shares of Michelin main competitors of between 4% and 8%) *'constitutes a valid indication of Michelin NV's preponderant strength in relation to its competitors.'*[637]

In *United Brands*, the Court of Justice found a market share of between 40% and nearly 45% 'does not ... permit the conclusion that UBC automatically controls the market. It must be determined having regard to the strength and number of competitors.'[638] A case-by-case analysis is required:

- In current case law, a dominant position is assumed if the market shares of the undertaking in question are about or above 60% and are in fact more than the cumulated shares of the following two smaller undertakings or if the distance between the leading undertaking and the second important one is in the range of 50% points. The same may be appropriate in the case that the

---

632. (CFI, Hilti AG v. Commission, Case T-30/89 1991).
633. (ECJ, AKZO Chemie BV and AKZO Chemie UK Ltd v. Commission, Case 53/85 1986).
634. *Ibid.*, para. 59.
635. (CFI, Irish Sugar plc v. Commission, Case T-228/97 1999).
636. (ECJ, Hoffmann-La Roche & Co. AG v. Commission, Case 85/76 1979, 63).
637. (ECJ, NV Nederlandsche Banden Industrie Michelin v. Commission, Case 322/81 1983).
638. (ECJ, United Brands Company and United Brands Continentaal BV v. Commission, Case 27/76 1978).

Chapter 4: Competition Practice

  distance between the leading undertaking with a market share between 45%
  and 60% and the second important one is very high.[639]
- Percentages above 40% are regarded as relevant and significant in an assessment of dominance, depending upon (i) changes in the absolute level of time, (ii) the level relative to that of the nearest competitors and (iii) the presence of other factors tending to entrench that leading position or, conversely, to threaten it. For example in *AKZO*,[640] emphasis was placed on AKZO's belief in its position as a world leader in the peroxide market, on its highly developed marketing organisation, and on its superior technological knowledge.
- Percentages varying between 30% and 40% seem to fall below the level at which dominance is indicated. Further evidence would be required of substantial disparities in market share, significant impediments to entry and so on before dominance could be established. In the light of the foregoing, it appears that a market share of below 30% in a correctly defined market would not be evidence of a dominant position save in exceptional cases.
- On the other side of the spectrum, some market shares conclusively show that an undertaking is not in a dominant position. For example in *Demo Studio Schmidt*,[641] a case on selective distribution, it was held that an undertaking with a market share of 1% cannot be considered to be dominant. However, the lower a company's market share, the more additional factors have been relied upon by the Commission and Court of Justice of the EU to support a finding of dominance. Such additional factors have included a number of structural elements, amounting to barriers of entry, as well as certain performance factors.

In its guidance paper on Article 102, the Commission clarified its view on market shares: It is very likely that very high markets shares, which have been held for some time, indicate a dominant position. This would be the case where an undertaking holds 50% or more of the market, provided that rivals hold a much smaller share of the market. In the case of lower market shares, dominance is more likely to be found in the market share range of 40%-50% than below 40%, although undertakings with market shares below 40% could be considered to be in a dominant position. However, undertakings with market shares of no more than 25% are not likely to enjoy a (single) dominant position on the market concerned.

In its Notice on the Definition of the Relevant Market[642], the Commission provides an indication of how it views the calculation of market shares. It is evident that the definition of the relevant market in both its product and geographic dimensions allows identifying the suppliers and customers and consumers active in that market. On that basis, a total market size and market shares for each supplier can be calculated

---

639. Schröter in: (Von der Groeben, Thiesing and Ehlermann 1993, 536).
640. (ECJ, AKZO Chemie BV and AKZO Chemie UK Ltd v. Commission, Case 53/85 1986).
641. (ECJ, Oswald Schmidt, trading as Demo-Studio Schmidt v. Commission, Case 210/81 1983, 21).
642. (Commission Notice on the definition of relevant market 1997).

on the basis of their sales of the relevant products on the relevant area. The Commission states that in practice the total market size and market shares are often available from other sources, for example, companies' estimates, studies commissioned to industry consultants or trade associations. In most cases, these studies refer to business markets and not to anti-trust markets as defined according to the Commission's Notice. In the case that these anti-trust data are not available or available estimates are not reliable, the Commission may ask each supplier in the relevant market to provide its own sales in order to calculate both total market size and market shares. The Commission's past decisions have shown, in practice, that often part of the required evidence is sufficient to reach a conclusion. The question is whether these Commission decisions really reflect the appropriate anti-trust market size and the market shares of the companies.

Competition economics uses market shares for other objectives too. For example, the correlation between market share and profit is much more central than the correlation between concentration and profits. *'Market share is the primary element while concentration and entry barriers are secondary'*.[643] In particular, Shepherd points out that as a rule of thumb 10% of added market share adds about 2% to the profit rate, whereas the concentration ratio by itself shows a weaker correlation with the profit rate.[644]

The *Chicago School* on the other hand does not deny a positive correlation between concentration and profits, but it views the relationship as spurious. According to the *Chicago School*, different levels of efficiency lead to weaker competitors being driven out and thereby to concentration (efficiency causes concentration). Therefore, *Demsetz* comes to the conclusion that the positive correlation between concentration and profits is only valid for firms with large market share (core of the oligopoly), but not for the fringe of small firms in a partial oligopoly.[645]

Higher than normal profits may be an indication of a lack of competitive constraints on an undertaking. The way in which a firm acts in a market may in itself be indicative of substantial market power, for instance, where an undertaking increases its price while benefiting from falling costs. However, an undertaking's economic strength cannot be measured by its profitability at any specific point in time; even short run losses are not incompatible with a dominant position.[646]

To conclude, market shares provide useful first indications of the market structure and of the competitive importance of various undertakings active on the market. If the undertaking concerned has a high market share compared to other players on the market, it is an indication of dominance, provided that this market share has been held for some time. If market shares have fluctuated significantly over time, it is an indication of effective competition. However, this is only true where fluctuations are caused by rivalry between undertakings on the market.

---

643. (W. Shepherd 1981, 66).
644. (W. Shepherd 1981, 129).
645. (Demsetz 1973, 7).
646. See (ECJ, United Brands Company and United Brands Continentaal BV v. Commission, Case 27/76 1978, 126) and (ECJ, NV Nederlandsche Banden Industrie Michelin v. Commission, Case 322/81 1983, 59).

Historic market shares may be used if market shares have been volatile, for instance when the market is characterised by large, lumpy orders. Changes in historic market shares may also provide useful information about the competitive process and the likely future importance of the various competitors, for instance, by indicating whether firms have been gaining or losing market shares. In any event, the Commission interprets market shares in the light of likely market conditions, for instance, whether the market is highly dynamic in character and whether the market structure is unstable due to innovation or growth.

What is remarkable in the 2009 Commission's guidance paper is that the importance of market shares are said to be qualified by an analysis of the degree of product differentiation. Furthermore the Commission points out correctly that it is unlikely that a company with high market shares will have the possibility of sustaining supra-competitive prices in the long run if barriers to expansion and entry are low. In order to determine whether or not there are barriers to expansion and entry in a market they propose a full analysis of the conditions of competition prevailing on the relevant market.

4.5.2.2 Barriers of Entry

So far, the case law analysis has shown that the Commission and the Court of Justice of the EU are too often prepared to infer dominance from the mere existence of large market shares, often on very narrowly defined markets. In this context the analysis of market power comes into play. Any analysis of market power must assess the possible competitive forces described as supply substitutability just as it must assess potential competition to the allegedly dominant firm in general. The notion of supply substitutability as a principle of market definition has already been discussed and it is probably more illuminating to consider this with other potential competition. That is why the discussion around entry barriers becomes so important. In addition to calculating market shares the Commission will, when assessing dominance, consider whether technical resources, overall strength, economies of scale, IPR or other attributes possessed by the dominant firm may give raise to *entry barriers*, a compendious phrase used to describe the difficulties new undertakings face in entering the market. The existence of entry barriers is seen as an important indicator in assessing market dominance. In particular, modern industrial organisation theories have stressed the need for a comprehensive analysis of entry barriers.[647]

Considerable market power over a period of time presupposes the absence of substitutes at lower prices to which the customers could turn and the existence of entry barriers preventing new competition from materialising, even when supply is profitable. This assumes no sharp distinction between monopoly and competition: market power is a matter of degree. The absence of new competition does not demonstrate market power.[648] This means that a finding of dominance depends on an assessment of

---

647. (Baden-Fuller 1979, 428).
648. (Korah 1981, 396).

ease of market entry. In fact, the absence of barriers to entry deters, in principle, independent anti-competitive behaviour by an undertaking with a significant market share. Dominance presupposes barriers to entry. Its proof requires an analysis of all the factors influencing the firm.

Entry barriers bear the potential to interfere seriously with new competitors or even to exclude them. This is apparent in cases of legal monopolies[649], invincible administrative barriers[650] or the economic impossibility for competitive offers.[651] In all these three cases, the lack of potential competition is clear evidence – in the opinion of the Court of Justice – that market dominance can be assumed. Firms, which are not able from the very beginning to produce and sell their products and services at cost-covering prices, are not viewed as potential competitors at all. This is especially the case if the production costs of those potential newcomers' competitors are higher than the costs of producers that are already at the market place.[652] Real (natural) entry barriers are legal impediments to market entry like patents or government licenses and the necessity, resulting from economies of scale, of a minimum efficient scale in relation to the market.

The discussion around entry barriers is a very controversial one, especially related to the *European School* that follows the *Harvard School* tradition and again, the *Chicago School*. Some economists emphasise the workability of competition as a control mechanism and start from the assumption that high entry barriers lessen the coordination, information and allocation function of competition. Those representatives view advertising, minimum capital requirements or vertical integration as a barrier to entry. The original concept can be traced back to *Joe S. Bain* who inquired into the question of potential competition in the case of oligopolistically structured markets.

Entry barriers are defined by *Bain*[653] as '... *the advantages of established sellers in an industry over potential entrants, these advantages being reflected in the extent to which established sellers ... raise their prices above a competitive level without attracting new firms to enter the industry.*' Bain grouped entry barriers under three headings: (1) absolute cost advantages, (2) product differentiation, and (3) economies of scale. Bain stated that for easy entry three conditions must in general be simultaneously fulfilled.

Bain extricated three different sources responsible for the observation that in some industries excess profits do not necessarily lead to market entry by potential competitors, thereby eroding excess profits. These sources were termed entry barriers and, originally, encompassed three conditions:[654]

---

649. (ECJ, General Motors Continental NV v. Commission, Case 26-75 1975).
650. (Decision IV/30.178 on Napier Brown – British Sugar 1988).
651. (ECJ, Hugin Kassaregister AB and Hugin Cash Registers Ltd v. Commission, Case 22/78 1979); in the same sense GEMA I.
652. (Abbott 1955), Schröter in: (Von der Groeben, Thiesing and Ehlermann 1993, 540).
653. (Bain 1956, 3).
654. (Bain 1986, 27).

- Newcomers have to be able to attain unit average costs comparable to those of their competitors because the competitors would otherwise experience absolute cost advantages that can serve as a shield of protection against potential competitors.
- Newcomers have to offer equivalent products on the basis of comparable price/quantity relationships. In the case of product heterogeneity or the inability of potential competitors, incumbents have product differentiation advantages.
- Size advantages are neither negligible for nor attainable by potential competitors, if advantages due to economies of scale are said to exist.

If at least one of these conditions is not fulfilled, easy entry for potential competitors into a market is not possible. Hence, the height of entry barriers is perceived to depend on the extent of absolute cost advantages, product differentiation advantages, and economies of scale. Entry into a market presupposes that the natural and artificial entry barriers, as well as the existing profit opportunities in a relevant market are well-known and that there are enough competitors possessing a spirit of competition to allow these chances for profit to be exploited by entering the market. If there is too little information on profit opportunities and/or little spirit of competition, there will be no market entry even in the case of low-entry barriers. Besides that, the product life cycle plays an important role in deciding whether to enter a market or not. Therefore, in particular economists of the *Harvard School* take the view that entry barriers resist the erosion of powerful positions as time goes on.[655]

At any stage in the relevant progression of entry (1) established firms have no absolute cost advantages over potential entrant firms; (2) established firms have no product differentiation advantages over potential entrant firms; and (3) economics of large-scale firms are negligible, in the sense that the output of a firm of optimal (lowest-cost) scale is an insignificant fraction of total industry output.[656] Although this classification remains useful, barriers need to be considered in a more dynamic context.

Stigler[657] gave a similar but slightly different definition namely 'a cost of producing which must be borne by a firm which seeks to enter an industry but is not borne by firms within the industry'. *Baumol*[658] argued that entry barriers can be effective only if expenditures required to overcome them are sunk costs; that is they would not be recovered on subsequent exit from the market. *Salop*[659] emphasised the time taken for new entry and the response of incumbent firms, which may be able to operate discriminatory practices to prevent entry on a limited scale (e.g., in one market segment), while entry on a large-scale would be uneconomic because of its effect on market price. Linked with this last point is the principle that entry will be easier into a

---
655. (W. Shepherd 1981, 71).
656. *Ibid.*, 13.
657. (Stigler 1968).
658. (Baumol 1982).
659. (Salop 1982).

market with expanding demand – a principle recognised in the Commission's decisions on a number of mergers in the computer industry.

This line of thought is again in complete contradiction with that of the *Chicago School*, where the discussion on entry barriers is reduced to a question of efficiency. The *Chicago School* views advertising, minimum capital requirements or vertical integration not as entry barriers but as competitive behaviour or the outcome of economic efficiency. Legal entry barriers, such as patents, are quite properly ignored as beyond the reach of anti-trust policy.[660]

Where Harvard economists had argued that higher barriers enabled incumbents to increase prices progressively further above marginal costs, and where therefore prima facie to be condemned, the Chicagoans are concerned with examining the nature of the barrier, tolerating those that are the result of efficiency considerations. *Bork* argued that:

> the question for antitrust is whether there exist artificial entry barriers. These must be barriers which are not forms of superior efficiency and which yet prevent the forces of the market ... from operating to erode market positions not based on efficiency.[661]

Discussions on the contestability approach on entry barriers are gaining ground in EU competition law. The contestability approach as outlined in section 3.3.3.3, with the assumption of zero sunk costs and ultra-free entry, reflects rather extreme assumptions and cannot be applied except in extreme cases. The contestability discussion shifts away from entry conditions to a non-existing post-entry struggle, which means that external conditions are assumed to dominate internal conditions.[662] The current discussion is about whether the assumptions the theory of contestable markets relies on, can be applied without adaptations.

In its 2009 guidance paper,[663] when identifying possible barriers of entry, the Commission considers that it is important to focus on whether rivals can reasonably replicate circumstances that give advantage to the allegedly dominant undertaking. The following factors are regarded as possible origins of barriers to expansion and entry:

- legal barriers;
- capacity constraints;
- economies of scale and scope;
- absolute cost advantages;
- privileged access to supply;
- a highly developed distribution and sales network;
- the established position of the incumbent firms on the market;
- other strategic barriers to expansion and entry, e.g., network effects.

---

660. (Posner 1979, 947).
661. (Bork 1978, 311).
662. (W. G. Shepherd 1984, 575).
663. (Guidance on the Commission's enforcement priorities in applying Art. 82 of the EC Treaty to abusive exclusionary conduct by dominant undertakings 2009).

Chapter 4: Competition Practice

The 2009 guidance paper also addresses the power of buyers to counteract supra-competitive prices by suppliers. They point out that certain strong buyers can pave the way for effective new entry or lead existing suppliers in the market to significantly expand their output so as to defeat the price increase.

Dominance can be related to one undertaking as single dominance or two or more undertakings as collective dominance.

4.5.2.3 Assessing Single Dominance

According to established case law, the almost classical definition of dominance is:

> *a position of economic strength enjoyed by an undertaking which enables it to prevent effective competition being maintained on the relevant market by affording it the power to behave to an appreciable extent independently of its competitors, its customers and ultimately of the consumers.*[664]

The notion of independence, which is the special feature of dominance, is related to the level of competitive constraint facing the undertaking(s) in question. For dominance to exist the undertaking(s) concerned must not be subject to effective competitive constraints. In other words, it must have *substantial market power*. Market power is defined as the power to influence market prices, output, innovation, the variety or quality of goods and services, or other parameters of competition on the market for a significant period of time.

The Court of Justice examined the concept of market dominance in a preliminary ruling in *Sirena v. Eda*,[665] where the Court defined dominance as the ability or power to prevent effective competition in an important part of the market, considering the position of producers or distributors of similar products.

In *Michelin*,[666] the Court of Justice clarified further the definition of dominant position:

> *It exists when an undertaking enjoys a position of economic strength which enables it to hinder the maintenance of effective competition on the relevant market by allowing it to behave to an appreciable extent independently of its competitors and customers and ultimately of consumers.*

In *United Brands*,[667] a reference case on excessive pricing, the Court of Justice held that dominance did not require the elimination of all competition. The fact that there had been *'a lively competitive struggle'* did not, therefore, negate dominance, especially in circumstances where the competition did not succeed in increasing their market share and the competition was limited in time and space.

---

664. (ECJ, United Brands Company and United Brands Continentaal BV v. Commission, Case 27/76 1978, 65), and (ECJ, Hoffmann-La Roche & Co. AG v. Commission, Case 85/76 1979, 38).
665. (ECJ, Sirena S.r.l. v. Eda S.r.l. and others, Case 40-70 1971).
666. (ECJ, NV Nederlandsche Banden Industrie Michelin v. Commission, Case 322/81 1983).
667. (ECJ, United Brands Company and United Brands Continentaal BV v. Commission, Case 27/76 1978).

In the Commission decision on *Continental Can*,[668] which involved a consideration of whether European subsidiaries of an American company would be in a dominant position before a proposed merger in the metal container market, the Commission again gave a similar definition and its opinion that '*undertakings are in a dominant position when they have the power to behave independently, which put them in a position to act without taking into account their competitors, purchasers, or suppliers*'. The Commission focused on the discretionary power of the undertaking to set its prices and to make other market decisions without being tightly constrained by competitive pressures. The Commission noted that such discretion presupposes entry barriers, meaning that other firms will not be able to enter the market if monopoly profits are being earned, and that few firms have surmounted these barriers.[669] Since *United Brands*, the Court of Justice has used a standard definition for dominance. The Court of Justice stated that:

> *Undertakings are in a dominant position when they have the power to behave independently without taking into account to any substantial extent, their competitors, purchasers and suppliers... . It is not necessary for the undertaking to have total dominance such as would deprive all other market participants of their commercial freedom, as long as it is strong enough in general terms to devise its own strategy as it wishes.*[670]

In *Gottrup-Klim v. Dansk Landbrugs Grovvareselska*,[671] a reference for a preliminary ruling, the Court of Justice confirmed again the well-established case law:

> *The concept of dominant position is defined in settled case law as a position of economic strength enjoyed by an undertaking which enables it to prevent effective competition being maintained on the relevant market by giving it the power to behave to an appreciable extent independently of its competitors, customers and ultimately of its consumers. In general the existence of a dominant position derives from a combination of several factors which, taken separately, are not necessarily decisive.*[672]

This definition of dominance consists of three elements, two of which are closely linked: (a) there must be a position of economic strength on a market which (b) enables the undertaking(s) in question to prevent effective competition being maintained on that market by (c) affording it the power to behave independently to an appreciable extent. The second and third elements concern the link between the position of economic strength held by the undertaking concerned and the competitive process, i.e., the way in which the undertaking and other players act and interact on the market.

---

668. (ECJ, Europemballage Corporation and Continental Can Company Inc. v. Commission, Case 6/72 1973).
669. (Korah 1981, 120).
670. (ECJ, United Brands Company and United Brands Continentaal BV v. Commission, Case 27/76 1978).
671. (ECJ, Gøttrup-Klim e.a. Grovvareforeninger v. Dansk Landbrugs Grovvareselskab AmbA, Case C-250/92 1994).
672. *Ibid.*, para. 47.

4.5.2.4 *Assessing Collective Dominance*

The application of collective dominance to oligopolies under Article 102 follows from the potential anti-competitive risks of such a market structure. Moreover, collective dominance, like single firm dominance, has to be analysed according to the effects it has on the market.

For collective dominance to exist under Article 102, two or more undertakings must from an economic point of view present themselves or act together on a particular market as a collective entity. It is not necessary that the undertakings concerned adopt identical conduct on the market in every respect. What matters is that they are able to adopt a common policy on the market and act to a considerable extent independently of their competitors, their customers, and also of consumers.

In order to establish the existence of such a collective entity on the market, it is necessary to examine the factors that give rise to a connection between the undertakings concerned. Such factors may flow from the nature and terms of an agreement between the undertakings in question or from the way in which it is implemented, provided that the agreement leads the undertakings in question to present them or act together as a collective entity. This may, for instance, be the case if undertakings have concluded cooperation agreements that lead them to coordinate their conduct on the market. It may also be the case if ownership interests and other links in law lead the undertakings concerned to coordinate behaviour.

Undertakings in oligopolistic markets may sometimes be able to raise prices substantially above the competitive level without having recourse to any explicit agreement or concerted practice. Coordination is more likely to emerge in markets where it is relatively simple to reach a common understanding on the terms of coordination. The simpler and more stable the economic environment, the easier it is for undertakings to reach a common understanding. Indeed, they may be able to coordinate their behaviour on the market by observing and reacting to each other's behaviour. In other words, they may be able to adopt a common strategy that allows them to present themselves or act together as a collective entity.

Coordination may take various forms. In some markets, the most likely coordination may involve directly coordinating prices in order to keep them above the competitive level. In other markets, coordination may aim at limiting production or the amount of new capacity brought to the market. Firms may also coordinate by dividing the market, for instance by geographic area or other customer characteristics, or by allocating contracts in bidding markets. In its 2009 guidance paper the Commission states that the ability to arrive at and sustain such coordination depends on a number of factors, the presence of which must be carefully examined in each case:

- Each undertaking must be able to monitor whether or not the other undertakings are adhering to the common policy. It is not sufficient for each undertaking to be aware that interdependent market conduct is profitable for all of them, because each undertaking will be tempted to increase its share of the market by deviating from the common strategy. There must, therefore, be

sufficient market transparency for all undertakings concerned to be aware, sufficiently precisely and quickly, of the market conduct of the others.
- The implementation of the common policy must be sustainable over time, which presupposes the existence of sufficient deterrent mechanisms, which are sufficiently severe to convince all the undertakings concerned that it is in their best interest to adhere to the common policy.
- It must be established that competitive constraints do not jeopardise the implementation of the common strategy. As in the case of single dominance, the market position and strength of rivals that do not form part of the collective entity, the market position and strength of buyers and the potential for new entry as indicated by the height of entry barriers must be analysed.

Thus, under Article 102, a dominant position can be held by several undertakings.

The Court of Justice has frequently held that the concept presupposes the economic independence of the entities concerned.[673] A finding that two or more undertakings held a collective dominant position must proceed upon an economic assessment of the position of the relevant market of the undertakings concerned, prior to any examination of the question whether those undertakings have abused their position in the market. Therefore, for the purpose of Article 102 it is necessary to consider whether the undertakings concerned together constitute a collective entity vis-à-vis their competitors, their trading partners and consumers on a particular market.

In *Flat Glass*, the Court of First Instance suggested the following concept of 'collective dominance':

There is nothing, in principle, to prevent two or more independent economic entities from being, on a specific market, united by such economic links that, by virtue of that fact, together they hold a dominant position vis à vis the other operators on the same market.[674]

This definition was supplemented by the Court of Justice in the *Almelo*[675] case, where it stated, *'in order for such a collective dominant position to exist, the undertakings must be linked in such a way that they adopt the same conduct on the market.'* The Court of Justice followed in subsequent judgments this concept. In *Compagnie Maritime Belge Transports SA and others v. Commission*, the Court of Justice offered the following definition on 'collective dominant position':[676]

It follows that the expression 'one or more undertaking' in Article 86 of the Treaty (new Article 102) implies that a dominant position may be held by two or more

---

673. (ECJ, Béguelin Import Co. v. S.A.G.L. Import Export, Case 22-71 1971).
674. (CFI, SIV and Others v. Commission, Joined cases T-68/89, T-77/89 and T-78/89 1992, 358) The Court of First Instance considered that the Commission had not proved the existence of a collective dominant position and therefore, partially, annulled its decision.
675. (ECJ, Municipality of Almelo and others v. NV Energiebedrijf Ijsselmij, Case C-393/92 1994).
676. (ECJ, Compagnie Maritime Belge Transports SA and Others v. Commission, Joined Cases C-395/96 P and C-396/96 P 2000).

economic entities legally independent of each other, provided that from an economic point of view they present themselves or act together on a particular market as a collective entity.[677]

The crucial element required is to demonstrate the existence of links between the undertakings in question. Evidence of collective dominance can be examined by investigating economic links or factors, which give rise to a connection between the undertakings concerned.[678]

In *Flat Glass*, examples of economic links are given. The Court of First Instance mentioned agreements or licences which give undertakings a technological lead over others, or agreements between members of liner conferences.[679] Collective dominant positions could also exist when the undertakings in question are not linked by contractual relationships, but where there is a structural link that leads them to behave as a single undertaking. In addition, it has to be determined whether the economic links and factors allow the undertakings to act together independently of their competitors, their customers and their consumers.

The issue whether collective dominance could also apply in the absence of any kind of links among the undertakings present in such a market, was raised at length by the Court of First Instance in *Gencor*. Parties argued that the Commission had failed to prove the existence of 'links' between the members of the duopoly within the meaning of the existing case law. The Court rejected the application by stating, *inter alia*, there was no legal precedent suggesting that the notion of economic links was restricted to the notion of structural links between the undertakings concerned. The Court extended the concept of collective dominance to members of a tight oligopoly even if there were no contractual or structural links between them. The Court explained the need for this extension as follows:

> *there is no reason whatsoever in legal or economic terms to exclude from the notion of economic links the relationship of interdependence existing between the parties to a tight oligopoly within which, in a market with the appropriate characteristics, in particular in terms of market concentration, transparency and product homogeneity, those parties are in a position to anticipate one another's behaviour and are therefore strongly encouraged to align their conduct on the market, in particular in such a way as to maximize their joint profits by restricting production with a view to increasing prices. In such a context, each trader is aware that highly competitive action on its part designed to increase its market share (for example a price cut) would provoke identical action by the others, so that it would derive no benefit from its initiative. All the traders would thus be affected by the reduction in price levels.*[680]

---

677. *Ibid.*, para. 36.
678. (ECJ, France and Others v. Commission, Joined Cases C-68/94 and C-30/95 1998).
679. (CFI, SIV and Others v. Commission, Joined cases T-68/89, T-77/89 and T-78/89 1992, 358).
680. (CFI, Gencor Ltd v. Commission, Case T-102/96 1999, 276) The case concerned the legality of a decision adopted by the Commission under the Merger Regulation prohibiting the notified transaction on the grounds that it would lead to the creation of a duopoly market conducive to a situation of oligopolistic dominance.

Market conditions are described by the Court as such that 'from market structures of an oligopolistic kind where each undertaking may become aware of common interests and, in particular, cause prices to increase without having to enter into an agreement or resort to a concerted practice'.[681]

The ruling of the Court of First Instance in Gencor and of the Court of Justice in Compagnie Maritime Belge established that a finding of collective dominance may be based on the existence of economic links and also on other factors which could give rise to a connection between the undertakings concerned.[682] In particular, it is necessary to ascertain whether economic links exist between the undertakings concerned. The existence of a collective dominant position may therefore flow from the nature and terms of an agreement, from the way in which it is implemented and, consequently, from the economic links or factors which give rise to a connection between undertakings, which result from it. The existence of an agreement or of other links in law is not indispensable to a finding of a collective dominant position. As the Court of Justice stated in Compagnie Maritime Belge, 'a finding of a collective dominant position may also be based on other connecting factors and would depend on an economic assessment and, in particular, on an assessment of the structure of the market in question'.[683]

Structural links, therefore, do not need to be proved in order to determine collective dominance. In Gencor, the Commission relied on other factors like market concentration, similarity of cost structures of the undertakings holding the collective dominant positions, market transparency, product homogeneity, moderate growth in demand, price inelastic demand, mature production technology, high entry barriers, and lack of negotiation power of purchasers.[684] In order to show that two or more undertakings hold a joint oligopolistic position, it is also necessary to prove that (a) there is no effective competition among the undertakings in question; and (b) the said undertakings adopt a uniform conduct or common policy in the relevant market. Only when these issues are answered in the affirmative, is it appropriate to consider whether the collective entity actually holds a dominant position. It follows from the Gencor and Compagnie Maritime Belge judgments that a market structure analysis has to be performed in order to enable a finding of an oligopolistic or highly concentrated market whose structure alone may be conducive to coordinated effects on the relevant market.

---

681. Ibid., para. 277.
682. See (CFI, SIV and Others v. Commission, Joined cases T-68/89, T-77/89 and T-78/89 1992, 358); (ECJ, Municipality of Almelo and others v. NV Energibedrijf Ijsselmij, Case C-393/92 1994, 43), (ECJ, Centro Servizi Spediporto Srl v. Spedizioni Marittima del Golfo Srl., Case C-96/94 1995, 33); (ECJ, DIP SpA v. Comune di Bassano del Grappa, LIDL Italia Srl v. Comune di Chioggia and Lingral Srl v. Comune di Chiogga, Joined cases C-140/94, C-141/94 and C-142/94 1995, 62); (ECJ, Sodemare SA, Anni Azzurri Holding SpA and Anni Azzurri Rezzato Srl v. Regione Lombardia, Case C-70/95 1997, 46); and (ECJ, France and Others v. Commission, Joined Cases C-68/94 and C-30/95 1998, 221).
683. (ECJ, Compagnie Maritime Belge Transports SA and Others v. Commission, Joined Cases C-395/96 P and C-396/96 P 2000, 45).
684. (CFI, Gencor Ltd v. Commission, Case T-102/96 1999, 159).

Chapter 4: Competition Practice

To ascertain collective dominance, the Court of Justice of the EU requires a detailed examination of whether the firms in the oligopoly have the power for collusive behaviour and to a significant extent have the possibility to act independently of competitors, customers and final consumers. The Court of Justice for example did not assume in 'Kali + Salz' that the collective market shares of 60% of Kali + Salz and SCPA was a reliable indication for collective dominance. The Court instead favoured an approach of a 'close examination in particular of the circumstances which, in each individual case, are relevant for assessing the effects of the concentration on competition in the reference market.'[685]

The Court refused to accept the Commission's argument that after a merger there would be a dominant duopoly on the market for potash, on the basis that the resulting duopoly was insufficiently close knit. Furthermore, the Court noted that there were other competitors, which would provide an effective competitive counterweight to the duopoly. Hence, the oligopoly was insufficiently tight to allow the two undertakings the ability to act on the market as a collective unit. The Court stated that it is:

> apparent that the Commission *has* not on any view established to the necessary legal standard that the concentration would give rise to a collective dominant position on the part of Kali + Salz/MdK and SCPA liable to impede significantly effective competition in the relevant market.[686]

Finally, the Court annulled the Commission's decision since the Commission had not adequately established that an oligopolistic dominant position would be created or strengthened.[687]

The Commission's finding that there was a collective dominant position was based on four main sets of criteria: (i) the stability of the market shares of the members of the oligopoly, (ii) the increase in the parties' market share as a result of the transaction, (iii) the nature of the products and the structural features of the market (homogeneous product, barriers to entry, mature market, limited cross-border trading between France and Germany); and above all (iv) the existence of structural links between Kali + Salz and SCPA. The Court of Justice rejected some of these arguments on the grounds that they were not conclusive in themselves (*'those facts cannot be regarded as lending decisive support to the Commission's conclusion'*).[688] The Court favoured a sectoral or case-by-case approach for the assessment of the risks of oligopolistic collusion. In particular, in performing its economic analysis the Commission should not simply rely on a checklist of descriptive factors that indicate the theoretical risk of oligopolistic dominance or on the fact that market shares exceed a certain threshold. Rather, those factors have to be analysed in the dynamic context of the relevant economic facts of each specific case. Application of this standard led the

---

685. (ECJ, France and Others v. Commission, Joined Cases C-68/94 and C-30/95 1998, 222).
686. *Ibid.*, para. 249.
687. After resumption of the case the Commission had approved the merger under Art. 6(1)b. The Commission denied a dominant duopoly between the two merging undertakings. Their combined market share on the relevant EU market for Kali was about 46% and the former structural interconnections had been resolved. (Decision IV/M.308 on Kali + Salz/MDK/Treuhand 1998).
688. See also (Ysewyn and Caffarra 1998, 470).

Court to annul in this case the Commission's findings concerning oligopolistic dominance given the presence of three factors: (i) the asymmetries between the allegedly jointly dominant companies; (ii) the absence of close structural links between them and (iii) the ability of third parties to exercise competitive constraint on the alleged duopolists.[689] Moreover, the Court's dismissal of the structural links aspect of the Commission's case ties in exactly with the economic theory of coordinated effects.[690]

4.5.2.5 Commission's Rules on Article 102

The 2009 Guidance Paper[691] of the Commission contributed to the process of introducing a more economics based approach in EU competition law enforcement. The effects-based approach advocated by the Commission discerns competition on the merits, which has beneficial effects for consumers and should therefore be promoted, from competition that is liable to lead to anti-competitive foreclosure, i.e., foreclosure that is likely to harm consumers.[692]

The main principles of the effects-based approach to Article 102 as defined by the Commission are the following:

- fair and undistorted competition is the best way to make markets work better for the benefit of EU business and consumers. Healthy competition, including by dominant undertakings, should be encouraged;
- the focus of the Commission's enforcement policy should be on protecting consumers, on protecting the process of competition and not on protecting individual competitors;
- the Commission does not need to establish that the dominant undertaking's conduct actually harmed competition, only that there is convincing evidence that harm is likely;
- since the focus of the Commission's enforcement policy is on conduct that harms the competitive process rather than individual competitors, for pricing conduct the Commission examines whether the conduct is likely to prevent competitors that are as efficient as the dominant undertaking from expanding on or entering the market and that can be expected to be most relevant to consumer welfare.

The first step in the Commission's analysis is to investigate whether a firm holds substantial market power over a significant period of time, allowing it to behave to an appreciable extent independently of its competitors and customers. The investigation continues by checking whether or not there are sufficient constraints on the firm's conduct by existing competitors and their output, by expansion or entry of rivals and/or by countervailing buying power.

---

689. (Venit 1998 1112).
690. (Lofaro and Ridyard 2000, 549).
691. (Guidance on the Commission's enforcement priorities in applying Art. 82 of the EC Treaty to abusive exclusionary conduct by dominant undertakings 2009).
692. (Commissions Memo 2008).

Chapter 4: Competition Practice

A soft safe harbour was created by the Guidance Paper by stating that dominance is not likely if the market share of the firm is below 40%.

Two forms of an abuse of a dominant position can be distinguished: exclusionary abuses (behaviours by a dominant firm likely to have a foreclosure effect on the market) and exploitative abuses (behaviours where companies take advantage of their market power, e.g., by charging excessive prices). The Guidance Paper just explains theories of harm on the basis of a sound economic assessment for the types of abusive exclusionary behaviour like exclusive dealing, tying and bundling, predatory practices and refusal to supply. These are discussed in the subsequent sections.

The Guidance Paper acknowledges that most of the types of conduct covered by Article 102 can have both anti-competitive and pro-competitive effects and therefore cannot always be legal or illegal. The challenge for the Commission is therefore to identify the core economic concern, and then to create transparent and workable proxies as rules for when such conduct is indeed illegal.

Some of the issues dealt with in the guidance paper are not new. However, they are discussed at length and in the context of the reform. What is new is the consequent focus on an 'effects-based' approach. In other words, what really counts are the measurable effects on the market. Such an approach requires sound economic analysis. The Guidance Paper not only provides instructions on how competition authorities should assess an abuse of a dominant position: the paper also gives guidance on defences companies can bring forward against allegations of an abuse or in which way competitors can plead their case in front of the competition authorities. In particular, the latter group is favoured by the effects-based approach. Hypothetical test procedures can be carried out even when first-hand information about the cost structures of the dominant company is missing.

4.5.2.6 More Economics Based Approach

An economics based approach focusing on consumer welfare requires a careful examination of how competition functions in each particular market. The centre of the economic appraisal is the analysis of the economic effects of certain behaviours. Thus, the standard for assessing whether a given practice is detrimental to competition or whether it is a legitimate tool of competition is derived, in such an approach, from the effects of the practice on consumers. If we think of competition as a regime in which the different suppliers vie to sell their products to participants on the other side of the market, then the benefits reaped by the other side of the market will themselves provide a measure of how well competition works. For final products markets, this observation leads directly to a consumer welfare standard. For primary- or intermediate-products markets, a consumer welfare standard is obtained by adding the observation that the vertical organisation of industry itself is a subject of competition, the ultimate beneficiaries of which are the final consumers. In either case, competition forces the supply-side of the economy to be responsive to consumers' needs with respect to price, quality, variety, etc.; business strategies that respond to these needs and raise consumer welfare are likely to be legitimate competitive strategies.[693]

In this review on Article 102, the Commission took account of established case law such as the judgment of the Court of Justice in *Hoffmann-La Roche*.[694] This case is a good starting point from which to define abuses that exclude. The Court emphasised that the behaviour under review has to have a certain effect on the market. Second, the Court values the protection of equal opportunities for residual competition, so that remaining competitors are able to improve in efficiency and thereby increase competition to the dominant company. This means two things: (1) the conduct of the dominant firm must have the potential to influence the position of residual competition on the market and therefore be likely to negatively impact prices, quantities or innovation in the market. This actually is a 'foreclosure effect'. (2) Such a market distorting foreclosure effect must be established. This may depend on factors such as the market coverage of the conduct or, for example, the selective nature of the conduct if it targets strategic customers that may be important for new entrants or residual competitors. These factors need to be analysed to check whether there is a credible 'theory of foreclosure' that fits the facts of the case.

What was really new for the Commission was the extensive focus on such an effects-based approach in Article 102. In the past, in the Commission's practice the discussion and management of Article 102 cases were often organised by categories of conduct, such as predatory pricing, discrimination, fidelity rebates or tying. Such a form-based approach was problematic since in many instances alternative practices can serve the same purpose. For example, predatory pricing can take the form of selective rebates, targeted at the rival's prospective customers. Alternatively, the predator can engage in explicit discrimination and charge more attractive prices or, more generally, offer better conditions to these customers. Other instruments in the predator's toolbox include implicit discrimination (e.g., in the form of fidelity or quantitative rebates that are formally available to all, but in fact tailored to the specific needs of the targeted customers) and mixed bundling or tying, when these customers are particularly interested in the bundle in question. To take another example, a firm that controls a key input may distort competition in a downstream market by refusing to deal with independent downstream firms; alternatively, it can engage in exclusive dealing arrangements or engage in explicit or implicit price discrimination such as mentioned above. The more consistent approach embodied in the guidance paper starts out from the effects of anti-competitive conduct, such as the exclusion of competitors in the same market or in a horizontally or vertically related market one and considers the competitive harm that is inflicted on consumers. Adopting such an effects-based approach ensures that these various practices are treated consistently when they are adopted for the same purpose.[695]

---

693. (Gual, et al. 2005).
694. (ECJ, Hoffmann-La Roche & Co. AG v. Commission, Case 85/76 1979).
695. (Gual, et al. 2005).

4.5.2.6.1 Economics of Exclusionary Conduct

Article 102 prohibits exclusionary conduct which produces actual or likely anti-competitive effects in the market and which can harm consumers in a direct or indirect way. Exclusionary abuses may be both price-based and non-price-based. Examples of non-price based abuses are contractual tying, 'naked' refusals to supply, and single branding obligations. The question is whether such exclusion may be characterised as anti-competitive, in other words impacting not only competitors, but also competition in the market. Similar exclusionary effects may be achieved through pricing. High stand-alone prices in comparison to a low bundled price for two products may 'tie' these two products together as effectively as contractual tying. Asking a very high-price for a product or combining a high upstream price with a low downstream price may amount to a 'constructive' refusal to supply. High rebates given on condition of single branding may have the same effect as contractual non-compete obligations. Predatory pricing is another means to exclude competitors. Certain forms of pricing conduct may have different exclusionary effects depending on how efficient the rivals are.

Harm to intermediate buyers is generally presumed to create harm to final consumers as well. Therefore, the central concern of Article 102 is to inhibit business practices that foreclose competitors and create harm to final consumers in terms of rising prices or declining quality. Thereby not only short-term harm, but also medium and long-term harm arising from foreclosure, is taken into account. Foreclosure means that actual or potential competitors are completely or partially denied profitable access to a market. Possible effects of foreclosure can be (1) that rivals are disadvantaged; (2) rivals compete less aggressively or (3) may even encourage rivals to leave the market or (4) inhibit market entry of newcomers. The assumption is that disadvantages that occur to rivals may potentially harm in the long run consumers as well.

The disadvantages for rivals are manifold: the dominant company can reduce demand for the rivals' products or directly raise rivals' costs. In the first case, foreclosure occurs because the dominant company is able to improve its market position by using exclusionary practices such as predatory pricing or unfair rebate systems. In the latter case, the dominant company is vertically integrated or disposes of a strong position on the relevant market as well as on the upstream market. The dominant company is then able to raise prices of input factors and thereby worsen the market position of the rivals on the relevant market. The issue is to differentiate between business conducts that are part of the normal functioning of markets and those that are part of an abusive strategy of the dominant company.

However, inefficient competitors should not be protected by competition policy from aggressive price-based actions of a dominant firm. Competition on its merits takes place when an efficient competitor that does not have the benefits of a dominant position, is able to compete against the pricing conduct of the dominant company. One possible approach to pricing abuses is that only the exclusion of 'equally efficient' competitors is abusive. The benchmark for 'as efficient' is normally the costs of the dominant company, except where it is not possible to determine such costs, or when the dominant company, for instance in a newly liberalised market, has some 'first-mover advantages' that later entrants cannot be expected to match.

The guidance paper suggests drawing the line by using the 'as-efficient-competitor-test' (the AEC test): The question that has to be answered is whether a competitor which is as efficient as the dominant company can compete against business practices used by the dominant company. The 'as efficient competitor' is a hypothetical competitor having the same costs as the dominant company. Foreclosure of an 'as efficient competitor' can only result if the dominant company prices below its own costs. The 'as-efficient-competitor-test' is thus a cost-benchmark test. To apply the test it is crucial to choose the appropriate cost benchmarks since the results of the assessment may vary depending on the costs under scrutiny: marginal costs (MCs), average variable costs (AVCs), average avoidable costs (AACs), long run incremental costs (LAICs) or ATCs. Other effects need to be considered as well including the existence of economies of scale and scope, learning curve effects or first mover advantages which may favour declining costs. The exact application of the 'as-efficient-competitor-test' as well as the chosen cost benchmarks vary on a case-by-case basis. In the following, the analysis of a rebate system is illustrated first as an example before continuing with the description of the test as illustrated in the guidance paper.

4.5.2.6.2   As-Efficient-Competitor Test

The 'as efficient' competitor test provides dominant firms with at least some degree of certainty as to the type of behaviour that might be considered lawful. Since the test is based on the costs and prices of the dominant firm, it is in principle possible for companies to assess whether their commercial behaviour is likely to comply with competition law. The principles described in the guidance paper for assessing alleged price-based exclusionary conduct are based on the premise that in general only conduct which would exclude a hypothetical 'as efficient' competitor is abusive. The 'as efficient' competitor is a hypothetical competitor having the same costs as the dominant company. Foreclosure of an AEC can in general only result if the dominant company prices below its own costs. In order to apply the hypothetical 'as efficient' competitor test the following are often mentioned as possible cost benchmarks[696]: MC, AVC, AAC, LAIC and ATC.

In the case of multi-product companies it may be difficult to calculate ATC because of certain common costs, which are fixed costs that are necessary for the production of more than one product and where it is difficult to allocate these costs to the different products. Where it is necessary to apply a cost benchmark based on ATC,

---

696. Marginal cost is the cost of producing the last unit of output. Average variable cost is the average of the costs that vary directly with the output of the company. Average avoidable cost is the average of the costs that could have been avoided if the company had not produced a discrete amount of (extra) output, in this case usually the amount allegedly subject to abusive conduct. Long run average incremental cost is the average of all the (variable and fixed) costs that a company incurs to produce a particular product. Average total cost is the average of all the variable and fixed costs.

the Commission will allocate common costs in proportion to the turnover achieved by the different products unless other cost allocation methods are for good reasons standard in the sector in question or in case the abuse biases the allocation based on turnover. Whereas ATC takes account of all variable and fixed costs, LAIC only takes account of the product-specific variable and fixed costs. The LAIC will thus usually fall below ATC because it does not take into account (non-attributable) common costs. The LAIC will usually be above AAC because LAIC takes into account all product-specific fixed costs, including product-specific fixed costs made before the period of abusive pricing, whereas AAC only takes product-specific fixed costs into account that are made in order to foreclose. The AAC will be higher than AVC to the extent that the company does make product-specific fixed costs behave abusively, otherwise AAC and AVC are the same by taking into account the variable costs only.

Finally, marginal cost, MC, because it concerns the additional cost made to produce one extra unit of output and does not concern an average, can be lower or higher than all the other cost benchmarks, depending on the actual output and capacity constraints of the company in question.

Thus for price-based alleged abuses, principles are provided in the guidance paper to evaluate whether a competitor, which is as efficient as the dominant company, can compete against the price schedule or rebate system of the dominant company. The question asked is whether the dominant company itself would be able to survive the exclusionary conduct in the event that it would be the target.

If examination of a dominant company's price schedule or rebate system according to these principles leads to the conclusion that an AEC can compete with the dominant company, the Commission will normally reach the conclusion that the dominant company's price schedule or rebate system is not abusive (*safe harbour*). If, however, an efficient competitor cannot compete with the dominant company, the Commission will consider the conduct to have the capability to foreclose competitors and therefore examine the likely market impact of the price schedule or rebate system.

To apply the 'as efficient' competitor test reliable information on the pricing conduct and costs of the dominant company is required. A number of remarks need to be made in this context. Firstly, it may be necessary to look at revenues and costs of the dominant company in a wider context. It may not be sufficient to only assess whether the price or revenue covers the costs for the product in question, but it may be necessary to look at incremental revenues where the dominant company's conduct negatively affects its revenues in other markets or of other products. Similarly, in the case of two-sided markets it may be necessary to look at revenues and costs of both products at the same time. Secondly, where reliable information on the dominant company's costs is not available it may be necessary to apply the 'as efficient' competitor test using cost data of apparently efficient competitors. Thirdly, where no reliable information on cost data is available but where the Commission has nonetheless been able to build on other arguments a credible case of abuse, the dominant company may show that it is not pricing below the appropriate cost benchmark. Fourthly, it may sometimes be necessary in the consumers' interest to also protect competitors that are not (yet) as efficient as the dominant company. Here too the assessment does not (only) compare cost and price of the dominant company but will apply the 'as efficient' competitor test in its specific market context, for instance taking account of economies of scale and scope, learning curve effects or first mover advantages that later entrants cannot be expected to match even if they were able to achieve the same production volumes as the dominant company.

Example: 'As-Efficient-Competitor-Test' for Rebate Systems

Issue: What is the economic effect of a fidelity rebate system? Do customers buy additional output from the dominant company by diverting purchases from other suppliers to the dominant company?

The analysis has to assess the likelihood and the extent of the economic incentive: What is the threshold level the customer applies? What is the economic effect once the threshold level is reached or passed? Is it possible that a hypothetical efficient undertaking is able to keep up with the price level of the dominant company and to set its own prices at the same threshold? Which other factors have an impact on the threshold?

Within the analysis, the following concerns have to be addressed:

- *'Suction' effect*: A suction effect emerges from the fact that exceeding the threshold will not only reduce the price for all purchases above the threshold, but also for all previous purchases. Prices for the last units which were bought before the threshold was exceeded are significantly lower and possibly even negative because the transaction triggers the rebate for all the purchases below the threshold as well. The extent of the suction effect depends on the relative size of the threshold and the applied rebates. This suction effect has to be assessed empirically.
- *Supply of commercially viable amounts*: As the majority of the competitors normally are not able to compete for the entire demand, the question is, whether the rebate system hinders them from supplying commercially viable amounts to individual customers. To answer this issue a market simulation has to be performed.
- *Price analysis*: What is the effective price level for the purchase of a commercially viable share with respect to the rebates offered by the dominant company?
- *Cost analysis*: What are the ATCs of the dominant company or of a hypothetical efficient competitor?
- *Price/cost analyses*: Is the effective price for a commercially viable share of a competitor below the ATCs of an efficient competitor?
- *Price/cost comparison*: Is the effective price below the ATCs of an efficient competitor, so that it is impossible to compete with the dominant undertaking for this part of the demand?

4.5.2.6.3 Possible Defences

Another widely debated issue is whether it is desirable and indeed possible for there to be an 'efficiency defence' under Article 102. Article 102 does not expressly foresee the possibility of 'exempting' abusive behaviour under Article 102 because of efficiencies. The same type of conduct can have efficiency-enhancing as well as foreclosure effects. This is reflected in the analytical framework.[697] This means that exclusionary conduct may escape the prohibition of Article 102 where the dominant undertaking can provide an objective justification for its behaviour or it can demonstrate that its conduct produces efficiencies which outweigh the negative effect on competition. The burden of proof for such an objective justification or efficiency defence will be on the dominant company. In general, there are two types of possible objective justifications:

(1) *Objective necessity defence*: The first type of objective justification is where the dominant company is able to show that the otherwise abusive conduct is actually necessary conduct on the basis of objective factors external to the parties involved and in particular external to the dominant company.
(2) *Meeting competition defence*: The second type of objective justification is where the dominant company is able to show that the otherwise abusive conduct is actually a loss minimising reaction to competition from others.
In relation to the *efficiency defence*, the dominant company must be able to show that the efficiencies brought about by the conduct concerned outweigh the likely negative effects on competition resulting from the conduct and moreover the likely harm to consumers that the conduct might otherwise have. For the efficiency defence, the dominant company must demonstrate that the following conditions are fulfilled:
   - that efficiencies are realised or likely to be realised as a result of the conduct concerned;
   - that the conduct concerned is indispensable to realise these efficiencies;
   - that the efficiencies benefit consumers;
   - that competition in respect of a substantial part of the products concerned is not eliminated.

Where all four conditions are fulfilled the net effect of such conduct is to promote the very essence of the competitive process, namely to win customers by offering better products or better prices than those offered by rivals.

Example: Efficiency Defence in Case of a Rebate System

When assessing the indispensability of the rebate system and when applying the efficiency defence, the following questions have to be addressed:

   – Can cost advantages be obtained and passed on to the customers?

---

697. (Kroes 2005).

- Can downstream customers be motivated to purchase welfare optimising amounts and can double marginalisation be avoided?
- Can incentives be introduced for the dominant company to make certain relationship-specific investments in order to improve the supply the downstream market?

In the guidance paper, the Commission provides a detailed description of how to assess those cases under Article 102. These guidelines offer direction if companies have to defend themselves against the allegations of an abuse of a dominant position, either by a NCA or the Commission or companies which are strongly disadvantaged by exclusionary abuses from a dominant company. In each case, the application of the 'more-economics-based-approach' means that market facts need to be presented based on sound economics and grounded on empirical evidence. The empirically collected market evidence needs to be linked to established economic theory and serves competition authorities as a foundation in their decision-making process.

With this approach, the Commission is in line with the critical remarks from the Court of Justice of the EU which complained that the economic analysis carried out in many cases by the Commission was inadequate. By implementing an efficiency defence, the Commission reflects the basic insight from economic theory that many business practices can both harm and promote competition and respectively consumer welfare. However, the realisation and practical implementation of this approach requires broad experiences and substantiated empirical analyses.

4.5.2.6.4 Predatory Pricing

For the purposes of Article 102 predatory pricing can be defined as the practice where a dominant company lowers its price and thereby deliberately incurs losses or foregoes profits in the short run so as to enable it to eliminate or discipline one or more rivals or to prevent entry by one or more potential rivals thereby hindering the maintenance or the degree of competition still existing in the market or the growth of that competition.

Pricing is not predatory just because a lower price means incurring losses or foregoing profits in the short run. An investment in temporarily lower prices may for instance be required to enter a market or to make more customers familiar with the product.

The predatory nature of charging lower prices to all or certain customers means the predator is making a sacrifice by deliberately incurring short run losses with the intention of eliminating or disciplining rivals or preventing their market entry. The company will make this sacrifice when it considers that it is likely to be able to recoup the losses or lost profits at a later stage after its actions have had the foreclosure effect. The exclusion should thus allow the predator to return to, maintain or obtain high prices afterwards. Although consumers may have benefited from the lower predatory prices in the short-term, in the longer-term they will be worse off due to weakened competition resulting in higher prices, reduced quality and less choice.

Chapter 4: Competition Practice

Under most market conditions, a dominant company is unlikely to have to price below ATC and make a loss. Its market share, the importance of its product on the market, the entry barriers, competitive constraints being absent or weak and its resulting power over the price usually enable the dominant company to price well above ATC and thus to avoid making losses. If therefore a dominant company reacts to entry or to competition from a smaller company in the market by lowering its price and making a loss, in general or on certain specific sales, there may be good reasons for the Commission to look into such behaviour.

Another important issue is to decide on the relevant time period over which to measure the costs. This is important because what is a fixed cost in the short run may become a variable cost in the longer run. In the long run all factors of production become variable as the production process, the plant and machines will be replaced. What are fixed and variable costs can only be determined in the actual situation of the case.

In general, the appropriate cost benchmark is the one that most accurately justifies the presumption that pricing below that benchmark can be expected to be predatory. The relevant question in that context is whether the dominant company, by charging a lower price for all or a particular part of its output over the relevant time period, incurred or incurs losses that could have been *avoided* by not producing that (particular part of its) output. If such avoidable losses are incurred, the pricing can be presumed to be predatory. At the same time the benchmark must be practical enough to be implemented.

The AAC benchmark is the appropriate and practical answer to the question about avoidable losses. Often the AAC benchmark will be the same as the AVC benchmark as in many cases only variable costs can be avoided. However, if the dominant company, for instance, had to expand capacity in order to be able to be predatory, then also the fixed or sunk investments made for this extra capacity will have to be taken into account and will filter into the AAC benchmark. In the latter case AAC will, for good reasons, exceed AVC.

If the price charged by the dominant company is below AAC this means that the dominant company incurred a loss that it could have avoided. It is, at least in the short run, not minimising its losses. This is sufficient to presume that the dominant company made this sacrifice in order to exclude the targeted competitor. This is however a rebuttable presumption; there may be exceptional circumstances under which a price below AAC is justified.

Where in general a dominant company may have no reason to price below AAC as it does not maximise profits in the short-term, it may have further reasons to price above AAC but below ATC. For instance, where there is a serious fall in demand the short run profit-maximising price may temporarily fall below ATC. Pricing below ATC will not entail losses by the mere production of that (particular part of it's) output. While the sales do not cover total costs, they still allow coverage of all variable costs and a part of the fixed costs.

In certain sectors the decisional practice of the Commission has deviated from the cost benchmark based on AAC and has chosen to use LAIC as the benchmark. In these cases the LAIC benchmark is used as the benchmark below which predation is presumed. Pricing above LAIC but below ATC in these sectors is assessed as pricing above AAC but below ATC in all other sectors. Thus pricing below LAIC is predatory in cases concerning sectors which recently have been liberalised or which are undergoing liberalisation, such as the telecom sector.

Price cuts where the resulting price remains above ATC are in general not considered to be predatory because such pricing can usually only exclude less efficient competitors.

In a case where a presumption of predatory pricing is established, the dominant company may rebut that finding by justifying its pricing behaviour even if the price is below the relevant cost benchmark.

A first justification could be that although the price is below the relevant cost benchmark and although there is a likely exclusionary effect, the dominant company is actually minimising its losses in the short run. This could for instance be the case where there is an issue of re-start up costs or strong learning effects. An efficiency defence can in general not be applied to predatory pricing.

4.5.2.6.5 Rebate Systems

To be consistent with the overall modernisation process, the economic effects of rebate systems need to be analysed more thoroughly in the future. The competition concern is to prevent exclusionary conduct of a dominant firm. Within the guidance paper, a basic distinction for rebates is drawn between unconditional and conditional rebates. Unconditional rebates, while granted to certain customers and not to others, are granted for every purchase of these particular customers, independently of their purchasing behaviour. On the other hand, conditional rebates are granted to customers to reward a (certain) purchasing behaviour of these customers.

The main possible negative effect of rebate systems is market foreclosure of actual and potential competitors. Thus, the purpose of Article 102 is to ensure that competitors are able to expand in or enter the market and compete therein on the merits, without facing competition conditions that are distorted or impaired by the dominant firm. Foreclosure effects are more likely if rebates are granted unconditionally and selectively. In particular, the Commission considers the occurrence of foreclosure as likely, if the dominant company applies a conditional rebate system where the rebates are granted on all purchases in a particular period once a certain threshold is exceeded, and:

- there is no indication that this threshold is set so low that for a good part of the dominant company's buyers it cannot hinder them from switching to and purchase substantial additional amounts from other suppliers without losing the rebate; and
- the required share exceeds the commercially viable amount per customer; and
- the dominant company applies the rebate system to a good part of its buyers and this system therefore affects at least a substantial part of market demand; and

Chapter 4: Competition Practice

- there are no clear indications of a lack of foreclosure effect such as aggressive and significant entry and/or expansion by competitors and/or switching of customers.

4.5.2.6.5.1   Relevance of Rebates

For manufacturers, rebate systems are an important tool to boost sales by providing incentives to buyers. Buyers benefit from rebates by lower prices. On the other hand, unbalanced rebate systems may damage the positioning of a product. However, because of the importance of rebate systems for sales figures, the giving up of rebates is not an economically feasible strategy: the abandonment of a rebate system can ultimately lead to a weakening of the market position. Ceasing to use rebates would also be problematic for consumer welfare reasons. The fact that rebates can be welfare-enhancing is an argument in favour of price cuts by means of rebates. In this context, it is crucial that the rebates are given without discrimination and are not harmful to competition. The burden of proof is on the dominant company. An economic analysis can generate legal certainty by exploiting at the same time the positive effects of rebates.

Rebates may come in the form of pure volume discounts: the firm then offers a rebate if the quantity bought by a customer exceeds a given threshold. In this case, the rebate may apply to the incremental quantities (only those above the threshold) or to all the units bought by the customer as soon as the threshold is reached. In the former case, the rebate scheme induces a progressive discount. By contrast, when it applies to the total quantities bought by the customer, it amounts to switching to a new price scheme as soon as the threshold is achieved. Rebates can also be offered to a customer whose growth in the volume of purchases lies above a given threshold.

Rebates on a particular product can also take the form of a more advantageous offer to customers who buy another product together with the initial one. Rebates then involve mixed bundling. Finally, fidelity rebates may be offered: for instance, rebates can be conditional on the client buying all its quantities, or at least a given percentage of them, from the firm.

4.5.2.6.5.2   Anti-competitive Effects of Rebates

Rebates can exclude actual or potential competitors from the market on which the firm is dominant. This is the case, for instance, for selective rebates offered to those of the customers of the firm that would switch to a new entrant were the rebate not offered, or if the rebate is conditional on the percentage of quantities bought by the customer from the firm. In most of these cases, rebates may be associated with predatory pricing on some of the units sold. Moreover, like predatory prices, rebates induce short run sacrifices and may have exclusionary effects either by inducing exit or by discouraging entry.

They can also involve horizontal foreclosure: this is for instance the case if the rebate is offered to a customer that buys the product from the dominant firm in an adjacent market together with the product on the main market. This is an example where rebates also tie together the products on two different markets.

Finally, rebates can induce vertical foreclosure. This is the case for instance when a producer offers rebates to its retailers in order to discourage them from selling competitors' products. They may then be associated with an exclusivity clause. Competitors are therefore unable to obtain access to a distribution network to sell their products. Of course, this mechanism may appear in any vertically related market, where one of the stages plays the role of an essential facility. In these 'essential facility cases', rebates may eliminate downstream or upstream competition in order to better exploit upstream or downstream market power.

To establish a market distorting foreclosure effect, it is in general necessary not only to consider the nature or form of the conduct, but also its incidence, that is the extent to which the dominant company is applying it in the market, including the market coverage of the conduct or the selective foreclosure of customers to newcomers or residual competitors. Other market characteristics including the existence of network effects and economies of scale and scope may also be relevant in establishing a foreclosure effect. In addition, the degree of dominance will be a relevant factor.

4.5.2.6.5.3 Pro-competitive Effects and Efficiency Considerations of Rebates

Efficiencies may be a cause or a consequence of rebates. A general way of assessing the dominance of pro-competitive effects over anti-competitive ones is to check whether total output has increased or not. Pro-competitive effects of rebates may for example appear in the following circumstances.

Since rebates allow high and low demand elasticity consumers to be treated differently, elastic demand segments tend then to generate lower margins. Consumers with a high elasticity of demand thus benefit from the practice, although consumers with a low elasticity may suffer from it; the overall effect on consumer welfare is thus *a priori* ambiguous. But in the spirit of Ramsey pricing, rebates may also allow for the recovery of fixed costs, and thus encourage R&D investments that involve such large fixed costs. As a result, rebates are more likely to have a pro-competitive effect when high fixed costs are involved.

Rebates that are targeted at those consumers who are more likely to switch to competitors imply a more intense competition for these consumers; they clearly benefit from this situation. The other consumers may indirectly benefit from an increased pressure on the price they face.

Moreover, prohibiting selective rebates as a reaction against competitive pressure may constitute excessive interventionism in the competitive strategies of firms on the part of competition authorities.

In a vertical relationship in particular, rebates that take the form of non-linear pricing may be used as an incentive mechanism to induce the efficient behaviour of retailers. For example, rebates can be used to increase retail margins on additional

Chapter 4: Competition Practice

volumes, so as to encourage retailers to promote the product. While a uniform reduction in the wholesale price might have the same impact on retailers' incentives, it would be more costly for the supplier. Hence, rebates allow suppliers to provide incentives at a lower cost, thereby encouraging suppliers to provide more incentives and thus to compete more intensively. More generally, rebate schemes can enhance efficiency by solving adverse selection or moral hazard problems.

Rebates may also generate efficiency gains for the dominant firm, for instance, economies of scale for this firm, or economies of transaction costs for the customers (the buyer concentrates its purchase on a single seller). These elements lead to a general intuition: rebates that take the form of pure quantity rebates are more likely to be motivated by efficiency considerations than fidelity rebates. In particular, the mere form of the rebate may not constitute a clear indicator; for instance, efficiency considerations might require personalised rebate schemes, tailored to the size of the retailer, which could take the simple form of market share fidelity rebates.

4.5.2.6.5.4 Possible Solutions: A Performance-Based Rebate System

Firms with high market shares need to pay close attention to the legal compliance of their rebate systems. The key to a successful rebate system which complies with Article 102 lies in the economic justification of the rebates: firms granting rebates need to receive a 'service' in return for their rebates. In addition, by applying economically rational strategies, producers are well advised to exploit the potential of influencing retailers' behaviour by means of a proper rebate system. The sacrifice of simple quantity rebates bears many promising opportunities: a performance-based rebate system facilitates the successful realisation of strategic goals, for example on brand policies by conditioning rebates such as on improved product presentations or on an increase in promotional activities.

In such a system, unconditional rebates do not occur. In line with the 'more economics based approach' or 'effects-based' approach, the impact of the rebate system on competition is the decisive criterion. It should be noted that the respective economic effects of rebate systems need to be assessed individually and may diverge case-by-case.

4.5.2.6.6 *Tying and Bundling*

Tying consists of making the purchase of one good (the tying good) conditional upon the purchase of another one (the tied good), whereas bundling refers to the sale of two products together. Bundling may be pure (the goods are available only together) or mixed (they are also available separately). Therefore, when tying is at work, the tied product may be bought alone, whereas when pure bundling is at work this is impossible.

The problem is to identify cases where tying is anti-competitive, that is, profitable for the firm that implements the practice, while inducing exclusion and hurting consumers. These cases are relatively scarce.

4.5.2.6.6.1   Anti-competitive Effects of Tying and Bundling

Bundling may serve an exclusionary purpose on the tied market. Since the consumer buys both good A and also good B from the dominant firm, either necessarily (if there is pure bundling) or because it is advantageous for him (in the case of mixed bundling), a competitor on market B cannot profitably sell its product, even if this was a better quality product or produced at a lower cost. Bundling may be used in order to protect the dominant firm's home market.

4.5.2.6.6.2   Pro-competitive Effects of Tying and Bundling

The analysis of the overall effect on consumers has to take into account the fact that the strategies of the dominant firm linking the two markets may also be the result, not of an attempt to exclude competitors, but rather of an attempt to improve the efficiency and quality of the products supplied in the market. Depending on the nature of competition, the cost structure on the tied market, the magnitude of costs savings associated with bundling, and the existence of strategic reasons, bundling can have both exclusionary effects and pro-competitive effects. The Commission's guidance paper provides some guidance about how the Commission intends to assess tying and bundling. Still, practical implementation to real-world cases remains a challenge.

4.5.2.7   *Economic Analysis in Cases on Rebates*

The Court of Justice of the EU has had several opportunities to rule on economic analysis in Article 102 cases in recent years. While *Michelin* was at the beginning of this saga, the 2014 *Intel* judgment by the General Court is the current climax of this epic. From the economic perspective it is interesting to note that these cases cause so much trouble. If the 'as-if competition principle' of the European School (see section 1.2) is applied coherently by companies (and their advisers), there would be fewer problems. 'As if competition' means that a dominant company competes in the market like any other competitor with no market power, namely just competing on the merits (Leistungswettbewerb). But in the Chicago School thinking so much weight is placed on efficiencies as *the tool* to escape Article 102, which as we see in the following case law in front of the Court of the EU, is so toothless.

4.5.2.7.1   *Michelin II*

In its *Michelin II* judgment[698] in 2003, the Court of First Instance upheld the Commission's decision,[699] which found that Michelin was dominant in the French markets for new replacement tyres as well as retreaded tyres for heavy vehicles and that it breached

---

698. (CFI, Manufacture française des pneumatiques Michelin v. Commission, Case T-203/01 2003).
699. (Michelin 2001).

Article 102 by setting up a system of bonuses, rebates and tying agreements that could potentially induce loyalty and exclude its competitors.

In many respects, this case is exemplary of the strict formalistic approach followed in abuse of dominance cases by the Commission and the Court of Justice of the EU, which severely limit the possibility of dominant firms resorting to certain business practices, such as exclusive dealing, rebates, and tying. As a matter of fact, *Michelin II* is even stricter than previous decisions and judgments because for the first time it is found that a dominant firm cannot even resort to pure (non-individualised) quantity discounts,[700] a practice until then accepted by the Courts.

The Commission concluded in its decision that Michelin adopted a complex system of rebates and discounts to maintain dominance, thus leading to the finding of Michelin's infringement of Article 102 and the imposition of a fine. Quantity discounts were criticised by the Commission because the purchase of some additional units might determine that a buyer reaches a higher quantity threshold and thus is entitled to a larger rebate on all units (additional and previously bought). The Commission was also critical that the discounts did not reflect economies of scale. Finally, according to the Commission, this system would have market partitioning effects, because rebates were applied only to purchases from Michelin France, thereby making parallel imports difficult, as tyres bought outside France do not qualify for the thresholds established by the rebate schemes. It is in this section devoted to parallel imports, that the Commission goes the closest to formulating a theory of foreclosure in the decision:

> thanks to its market shares, Michelin was able to absorb the cost of these rebates, while its competitors were unable to do likewise and therefore had to either accept a lower level of profitability or give up the idea of increasing their sales volume.[701]

The service bonus scheme showed, according to the Commission, similar abusive features as quantity discounts. In particular, it was unfair, because: a) it is subjective (Michelin has a wide margin of discretion in assigning 'points' to buyers); b) it asks dealers to provide market information, which would not be in their interest and for which they would have no return (e.g., in the form of market studies); c) subjectivity is inevitably a source of discrimination (i.e., that a dominant firm may not discriminate among customers, discrimination being abusive).

The Commission found the progress bonus, (as well as the 'achieved target bonus' which replaced it in 1997) as particularly abusive because it was loyalty-inducing, by pushing dealers to buy more than previous years (or meet the target), thus denying sales to rivals; The practice was unfair, because: a) it was discriminatory (two dealers who buy the same quantity but have different bases get different rebates); and b) it 'created insecurity' for the dealers (they do not know if they will get the bonus). Individual agreements were equally abusive, because they give extra incentives to large dealers, and put pressure on them to buy only from Michelin, so that they can reach the highest rebates.

---

700. Unless it can show that such discounts can be justified by per-transaction savings, see below for a discussion.
701. (Michelin 2001, 241).

The decision was appealed by Michelin. The Court of First Instance upheld the decision and accepted all the Commission's arguments.

The main element of novelty in the judgment is the fact that for the first time the Court of First Instance rejected the use of pure quantity discounts. According to the Court, they *induce loyalty* because the rebates were calculated on the overall turnover, and are abusive because they are not justified by cost savings:

> *a rebate system in which the rate of the discount increases according to the volume purchased will not infringe Article 82 EC unless the criteria and rules for granting the rebate reveal that the system is not based on an economically justified countervailing advantage but tends, following the example of loyalty and target rebate, to prevent customers from obtaining their supplies from competitors (...)*[702]
> *A quantity rebate system has no loyalty-inducing effect if discounts are granted on invoice according to the size of the order. If a discount is granted for purchases made during a reference period, the loyalty-inducing effect is less significant where the additional discount applies only to the quantities exceeding a certain threshold than where the discount applies to total turnover achieved during the reference period.*[703]

It is also interesting that the Court in *Michelin II* requested the defendant company to prove that linear quantitative rebate schemes are cost justified. It thereby reversed the current case law, which traditionally puts the burden of proof in this respect on the authority. However, the Court of First Instance condemned Michelin's quantitative rebates for having failed to demonstrate that the rebates reflected economies of scale.[704] In paragraph 258 of the judgment, the Court *'notes that, in the contested decision, the Commission did not examine the specific effects of the abusive practices. Nor can it be required to do so'*. According to the Court of First Instance in paragraph 241, *'for the purposes of applying Article 82 EC (now Article102), establishing the anticompetitive object and the anticompetitive effect are one and the same thing'*.

4.5.2.7.2 British Airways

British Airways is another Article 102 case on rebates. In 2007, the Court of Justice dismissed British Airways' (BA) appeal[705] against the judgment of the Court of First Instance,[706] which, in turn, had upheld the Commission's decision finding that BA's loyalty-inducing targeted scheme for travel agents infringed Article 102(b), and (c).[707]

---

702. (CFI, Manufacture française des pneumatiques Michelin v. Commission, Case T-203/01 2003, 59).
703. (CFI, Manufacture française des pneumatiques Michelin v. Commission, Case T-203/01 2003, 85).
704. (CFI, Manufacture française des pneumatiques Michelin v. Commission, Case T-203/01 2003, 98 and 108): 'Far from establishing that the quantity rebates were based on actual cost savings (...), the applicant merely states generally that the quantity rebates were justified by economies of scale in the areas of production costs and distribution'.
705. (ECJ, British Airways plc v. Commission, Case C-95/04 P 2007).
706. (CFI, British Airways plc v. Commission, Cast T-219/99 2003).
707. (Commission Decision 2000/74/EC relating to a proceeding under Art. 82 (IV/D-2/34.780 – Virgin/British Airways) 2000).

Chapter 4: Competition Practice

Whereas the judgment of the Court of Justice solved the legal proceedings in this case, the debate on competition concerns, with respect to discounts and rebates applied by dominant firms were still ongoing.

By following a complaint lodged by Virgin Atlantic Airways about agreements between British Airways and travel agents relating to commissions and other financial incentives for the sale of BA tickets the Commission initiated a proceeding in relation to BA's marketing agreements with UK travel agents. BA's bonus schemes provided travel agents with a basic commission, a separate additional performance bonus calculated with reference to the increase in sales compared to individualised volume targets, payable on all BA tickets sold. In 1997, BA adopted a third type of incentive scheme. Here the agent's performance was measured by comparing its sales in a given month with those of the same month in the previous year. In its decision the Commission condemned the incentive schemes established by BA as an abuse of its dominant position on the UK market for travel agencies.[708]

BA appealed this decision to the Court of First Instance in 2003. The Court of First Instance rejected all pleas and upheld the Commission's decision.

In particular, regarding whether there was an abuse of a dominant position, the Court of First Instance maintained that the Commission was correct to define the relevant market as air ticket distribution services in the UK,[709] and that BA held a dominant position in this market.[710] Consequently BA had applied dissimilar conditions to equivalent transactions given that different agents would receive different levels of commission for exactly the same level of revenue.[711] In addition, the Court confirmed that the loyalty enhancing scheme limited the access of BA's competitors.[712] The Court of First Instance also stated that there was no economic justification to the exclusionary practice.[713]

In 2007, the Court of Justice confirmed that in considering whether a system of discounts or bonuses constitutes an abuse, it first has to be determined whether those discounts or bonuses can produce an exclusionary effect. The relevant questions, according to the Court, are whether the discounts or bonuses are capable, (1) of making market entry very difficult or impossible for competitors of the dominant undertaking and, (2) of making it more difficult or impossible for its customers to choose between various sources of supply or commercial partners. If this first condition is fulfilled, consideration must then be given to whether there is an *objective economic justification* for the discounts or bonuses granted. Applying this approach to the facts of the case, the Court of Justice held that the Court of First Instance was right to examine whether BA's bonus schemes had a loyalty enhancing effect capable of producing an

---

708. (Commission Decision 2000/74/EC relating to a proceeding under Art. 82 (IV/D-2/34.780 – Virgin/British Airways) 2000).
709. As to the definition of the relevant product and geographic market see (CFI, British Airways plc v. Commission, Cast T-219/99 2003, 94–100 and 110–116).
710. (CFI, British Airways plc v. Commission, Cast T-219/99 2003, 189–197).
711. *Ibid.*, paras 233–40.
712. *Ibid.*, paras 270–278.
713. *Ibid.*, paras 279–293.

exclusionary effect and was without objective economic justification.[714] In particular, the Court observed in respect of the 'exclusionary effect' condition that the Court of First Instance had correctly considered the following three features:

(1) The schemes were based on individual targets, dependent on the growth in turnover of individual agents over a particular period.
(2) The schemes were retroactive: they rewarded the entire turnover achieved from BA sales, not just the incremental turnover (i.e., the part above the performance threshold). As a result, even small changes in sales could have a disproportionate effect and this provided a strong incentive not to switch.
(3) Other airlines would have to offer disproportionately higher rebates to outbid BA's rebates. Given the structure of the market and BA's position, other competitors were not able to do so.[715]

4.5.2.7.3 Tomra

The *Tomra* case is another Article 102 rebate case. The Commission decision in Tomra was on appeal at the General Court[716] and the Court of Justice.[717] Both Courts dismissed the appeal.

In 2006, the Commission found that Tomra abused its dominant position on the market for the supply of machines, usually installed in retail outlets, for the collection of used drink containers in return for a deposit, in Austria, Germany, the Netherlands, Norway and Sweden. Tomra was found to be a dominant supplier of reverse vending machines (used by supermarkets to collect empty beverage containers from, and return deposits to, consumers) by enjoying market shares of 80% or more in various national markets.

Tomra engaged in a number of exclusionary pricing practices aimed at denying rival suppliers access to the market. The Commission concluded that Tomra's practices, consisting of loyalty-inducing discounts restricted or at least delayed the market entry of other manufacturers.

The major competition concern was that the abuses were a series of rollback rebates. Just as it had done in previous cases the Commission ruled that the incentive properties of these discount schemes excluded competition. However, in contrast to the more formalistic approach that has been used in previous cases, in *Tomra* the Commission stated that it backed up its conclusion with an economic analysis of the effects of the rollback rebate scheme.

---

714. (ECJ, British Airways plc v. Commission, Case C-95/04 P 2007, 69–90).
715. *Ibid.*, paras 72–76.
716. (ECJ, Tomra and Others v. Commission, Case T-155/06 2010).
717. (ECJ, Tomra Systems ASA and Others v. Commission, Case C-549/10 P 2012).

Chapter 4: Competition Practice

4.5.2.7.3.1 Dominance and Economic Effects

The Court of Justice reconfirmed that abuse of a dominant position prohibited by Article 102 is an *objective concept* relating to the conduct of a dominant undertaking which, on a market where the degree of competition is already weakened precisely because of the presence of the undertaking concerned, through recourse to methods different from those governing normal competition in products or services on the basis of the transactions of commercial operators, has the effect of hindering the maintenance of the degree of competition still existing in the market or the growth of that competition.[718] This point was in particular stressed in section 1.2 as an essential feature of the European School.

On the issue of dominant position, the Court of Justice stated again in *Tomra* in 2012 that such a dominant position relates to a position of economic strength enjoyed by an undertaking which enables it to prevent effective competition being maintained on the relevant market by affording it the power to behave to an appreciable extent independently of its competitors and its customers. None the less, the degree of market strength is, as a general rule, significant *in relation to the extent of the effects of the conduct* of the undertaking concerned rather than in relation to the question of whether the abuse as such exists. This means that the Court of Justice reconfirmed the effects-based approach.

The Court continued by stating that the foreclosure by a dominant undertaking of a substantial part of the market cannot be justified by showing that the contestable part of the market is still sufficient to accommodate a limited number of competitors. (1) The customers on the foreclosed part of the market should have the opportunity to benefit from whatever degree of competition is possible on the market and competitors should be able to *compete on the merits* for the entire market and not just for a part of it. (2) It is not the role of the dominant undertaking to dictate how many viable competitors will be allowed to compete for the remaining contestable portion of demand.[719]

In line with previous case law, the Court stated that for the purposes of proving an abuse of a dominant position within the meaning of Article 102, it is sufficient to show that the abusive conduct of the undertaking in a dominant position *tends* to restrict competition or that the conduct is *capable of having that effect*. Accordingly, where there is a system of retroactive rebates which establishes a loyalty mechanism whereby a supplier drives out its competitors by means of the suction to itself of the contestable part of demand, it is *unnecessary to undertake an analysis of the actual effects* of the rebates on competition given that, for the purposes of establishing an infringement of Article 102, it is sufficient to demonstrate that the conduct at issue is capable of having an effect on competition.[720]

---

718. *Ibid.*, paras 17–21; See also (ECJ, Tomra Systems ASA and Others v. Commission, Case C-549/10 P 2012).
719. *Ibid.*, paras 38, 39, 42, 43, 46.
720. *Ibid.*, paras 68, 79,; See also (ECJ, Tomra Systems ASA and Others v. Commission, Case C-549/10 P 2012).

4.5.2.7.3.2   Rebates

The Court stated that a rebate scheme is anti-competitive where, in the first place, the incentive to obtain supplies exclusively or almost exclusively from certain undertakings is particularly strong when thresholds are combined with a system whereby the achievement of the bonus threshold or, as the case may be, a more advantageous threshold benefited all the purchases made by the customer during the reference period and not exclusively the purchasing volume exceeding the threshold concerned. Secondly, the combination of a rebate scheme individual to each customer and thresholds established on the basis of the customer's estimated requirements and/or past purchasing volumes therefore represents a strong incentive for buying all or almost all the equipment needed from that undertaking and artificially raises the costs of switching to a different supplier, even for a small number of units. Thirdly, the retroactive rebates often apply to some of the largest customers of that undertaking with the aim of ensuring their loyalty. Lastly, their conduct is not objectively justified or it does not generate significant efficiency gains which outweigh the anti-competitive effects on consumers. Further, the exclusionary mechanism represented by retroactive rebates does not require the dominant undertaking to sacrifice profits, since the cost of the rebate is spread across a large number of units. If retroactive rebates are given, the average price obtained by the dominant undertaking may well be far above costs and ensure a high average profit margin. However, retroactive rebate schemes ensure that, from the point of view of the customer, the effective price for the last units is very low because of the suction effect.[721]

4.5.2.7.4   Intel

In 2014, the General Court[722] dismissed the action of Intel against a Commission decision[723]. Intel appealed against this judgment at the Court of Justice.

In 2009, the Commission found that Intel, a company holding a market share of roughly 70% or more, had engaged in illegal anti-competitive practices to exclude competitors from the market for computer chips called x86 central processing units ('CPUs'). The fine imposed was EUR 1.06 billion.

According to the Commission, the abuse was characterised by several measures. Intel granted rebates to four major computer manufacturers (Dell, Lenovo, HP and NEC) on the condition that they purchased from Intel all or almost all of their x86 CPUs. Intel's anti-competitive conduct resulted in a reduction of consumer choice and in lower incentives to innovate.[724]

---

721. *Ibid.*, paras 73, 75, 78; See also (ECJ, Tomra Systems ASA and Others v. Commission, Case C-549/10 P 2012).
722. (ECJ, Intel Corp. v. Commission, Case T-286/09 2014).
723. *Ibid.*
724. (ECJ Press Release 2014).

The General Court found that the rebates granted to Dell, HP, NEC and Lenovo are exclusivity rebates. Such rebates are, when applied by an undertaking in a dominant position, incompatible with the objective of undistorted competition within the common market.

In competition matters, an undertaking which is in a dominant position on a market and ties purchasers – even if it does so at their request – by an obligation or promise on their part to obtain all or most of their requirements exclusively from that undertaking abuses its dominant position within the meaning of Article 102, whether the obligation in question is stipulated without further qualification or whether it is undertaken in consideration of the grant of a rebate. The same applies where that undertaking, without tying the purchasers by a formal obligation, applies, either under the terms of agreements concluded with these purchasers or unilaterally, a system of loyalty rebates, that is to say, discounts conditional on the customer's obtaining – whether the quantity of its purchases is large or small – all or most of its requirements from the undertaking in a dominant position.

4.5.2.7.4.1 Rebates

According to the General Court, exclusivity rebates are not based – save in exceptional circumstances – on an economic transaction which justifies such a financial advantage, but are designed to remove or restrict the purchaser's freedom to choose his sources of supply and to deny other producers access to the market. That type of rebate constitutes an abuse of a dominant position if there is no objective justification for granting it. Exclusivity rebates granted by an undertaking in a dominant position are, *by their very nature*, capable of restricting competition and foreclosing competitors from the market. It is thus – according to the General Court – not necessary to show that they are capable of restricting competition on a case-by-case basis in the light of the facts of the individual case.

As to whether the grant of a rebate by an undertaking in a dominant position can be characterised as abusive, the Court specified that a distinction should be drawn between three categories of rebates:[725]

(1) Quantity rebate systems ('quantity rebates') linked solely to the volume of purchases made from an undertaking occupying a dominant position are generally considered not to have the foreclosure effect prohibited by Article 102. If increasing the quantity supplied results in lower costs for the supplier, the latter is entitled to pass-on that reduction to the customer in the form of a more favourable tariff. Quantity rebates are therefore deemed to reflect gains in efficiency and economies of scale made by the undertaking in a dominant position.

(2) There are rebates which are conditional on the customer obtaining all or most of its requirements from a dominant company. These are 'fidelity rebates

---

725. (ECJ, Intel Corp. v. Commission, Case T-286/09 2014, paras 72–78).

within the meaning of *Hoffmann-La Roche*', otherwise known as 'exclusivity rebates'. That expression is not limited to rebates linked to an exclusive supply condition, but includes rebates which are conditional on the customer obtaining *most of its requirements* from the dominant company. Such exclusivity rebates, when applied by an undertaking in a dominant position, are incompatible with the objective of undistorted competition within the common market, because they are not based – save in exceptional circumstances – on an economic transaction which justifies this burden or benefit but are designed to remove or restrict the purchaser's freedom to choose his sources of supply and to deny other producers access to the market. Such rebates are designed, through the grant of a financial advantage, to prevent customers from obtaining their supplies from competing producers.

(3) There are other rebate systems where the grant of a financial incentive is not directly linked to a condition of exclusive or quasi-exclusive supply from the undertaking in a dominant position, but where the mechanism for granting the rebate may also have a *fidelity-building effect*. That category of rebates includes *inter alia* rebate systems depending on the attainment of individual sales objectives which do not constitute exclusivity rebates, since those systems do not contain any obligation to obtain all or a given proportion of supplies from the dominant undertaking. In examining whether the application of such a rebate constitutes an abuse of dominant position, it is necessary to consider all the circumstances, particularly the criteria and rules governing the grant of the rebate, and to investigate whether, in providing an advantage not based on any economic service justifying it, that rebate tends to remove or restrict the buyer's freedom to choose his sources of supply, to bar competitors from access to the market, or to strengthen the dominant position by distorting competition.

Thus the general rule is that in competition matters, the question whether an exclusivity rebate can be categorised as abusive does not depend on an analysis of the circumstances of the case aimed at establishing a potential foreclosure effect. The case law shows that it is only in the case of rebates falling within the *third category that it is necessary to assess all the circumstances*, and not in the case of exclusivity rebates falling within the second category. The existence of such an incentive does not depend on whether the rebate is actually reduced or annulled if the requirement of exclusivity on which it is conditional is not satisfied. It is sufficient, in that regard, that the dominant undertaking gives the impression to the customer that that would be the case. What counts are the circumstances which the customer could expect when making its orders – on the basis of what it was told by the dominant undertaking – and not the actual reaction of that undertaking to the customer's decision to change supplier.[726] That approach can be justified by the fact that exclusivity rebates granted

---

726. (ECJ, Intel Corp. v. Commission, Case T-286/09 2014, see paras 80, 84–86, 88, 91–93, 103, 104, 116, 117, 132, 527).

by an undertaking in a dominant position are *by their very nature* capable of restricting competition. The capability of tying customers to the undertaking in a dominant position is inherent in exclusivity rebates.

A foreclosure effect is produced not only where competitors' access to the market is made impossible but also where it is made more difficult. The grant of exclusivity rebates by an undertaking in a dominant position makes it more difficult for a competitor to supply its own goods to customers of that dominant undertaking. If a customer of the undertaking in a dominant position obtains supplies from a competitor by failing to comply with the exclusivity or quasi-exclusivity condition, it risks losing not only the rebates for the units that it switched to that competitor, but the entire exclusivity rebate.[727]

In *Intel*, the General Court states that, in order to submit an attractive offer, it is not sufficient for a competitor to offer Intel's customer attractive conditions for the units that that competitor can itself supply to the customer. It must also offer that customer compensation for the potential loss of the exclusivity rebate for having switched supplier. In order to submit an attractive offer, the competitor must therefore apportion solely to the share which it is able to offer the customer the rebate granted by Intel in respect of all or almost all of the customer's requirements (including the requirements which Intel alone – as an unavoidable supplier – is able to satisfy).

Moreover, it is inherent in a strong dominant position, for a substantial part of the demand, there are no proper substitutes for the product supplied by the dominant undertaking. The supplier in a dominant position is thus, to a large extent, an unavoidable trading partner. It follows from the position of unavoidable trading partner that customers will in any event obtain part of their requirements from the undertaking in a dominant position ('the non-contestable share'). The competitor of an undertaking in a dominant position is not therefore in a position to compete for the full supply of a customer, but only for the portion of the demand exceeding the non-contestable share ('the contestable share'). The contestable share is thus the portion of a customer's requirements which can realistically be switched to a competitor of the undertaking in a dominant position in any given period.[728]

Given that exclusivity rebates granted by an undertaking in a dominant position are, by their very nature, capable of restricting competition, the Commission was not required, contrary to what Intel claims, to make an assessment of the circumstances of the case in order to show that the rebates actually or potentially had the effect of foreclosing competitors from the market.

In order to submit an attractive offer, it is not therefore sufficient for the competitor of an undertaking in a dominant position to offer attractive conditions for the units that that competitor can itself supply to the customer; it must also offer that customer compensation for the loss of the exclusivity rebate. In order to submit an attractive offer, the competitor must therefore apportion the rebate that the undertaking in a dominant position grants in respect of all or almost all of the customer's

---

727. (ECJ, Intel Corp. v. Commission, Case T-286/09 2014, see paras 80, 84–86, 88, 91–93, 103, 104, 116, 117, 132, 527).
728. (ECJ Press Release 2014).

requirements, including the non-contestable share, to the contestable share alone. Thus, the grant of an exclusivity rebate by an unavoidable trading partner makes it structurally more difficult for a competitor to submit an offer at an attractive price and thus gain access to the market. The grant of exclusivity rebates enables the undertaking in a dominant position to use its economic power on the non-contestable share of the demand of the customer as leverage to also secure the contestable share, thus making access to the market more difficult for a competitor.[729]

When such a trading instrument exists, it is unnecessary to undertake an analysis of the actual effects of the rebates on competition or to prove a causal link between the practices complained of and actual effects on the market.

Finally, the possible small part of the market impacted by the exclusivity rebates granted by an undertaking in a dominant position is not capable of excluding their illegality, since an 'appreciable effect' criterion or a *de minimis* threshold is not taken into account for the purposes of applying Article 82 EC. Furthermore, the customers on the foreclosed part of the market should have the opportunity to benefit from whatever degree of competition is possible on the market and competitors should be able to compete on the merits for the entire market and not just for a part of. A dominant undertaking may not therefore justify the grant of exclusivity rebates to certain customers by the fact that competitors remain free to supply other customers. Similarly, an undertaking in a dominant position may not justify the grant of a rebate subject to a quasi-exclusive purchase condition by a customer in a certain segment of a market by the fact that that customer remains free to obtain supplies from competitors in other segments.[730]

4.5.2.7.4.2 As-Efficient-Competitor Test

The economic analysis concerning the 'as-efficient-competitor test' or 'the AEC test' carried out in the contested decision takes as a starting point the circumstance that an as-efficient competitor, which seeks to obtain the contestable share of the orders hitherto satisfied by a dominant undertaking which is an unavoidable trading partner, must compensate the customer for the exclusivity rebate that it would lose if it purchased a smaller portion than that stipulated by the exclusivity or quasi-exclusivity condition. The AEC test is designed to determine whether the competitor which is as efficient as the undertaking in a dominant position and faces the same costs as the latter, can still cover its costs in that case. Even if an assessment of the circumstances of the case were necessary to demonstrate the potential anti-competitive effects of the exclusivity rebates, it would still not be necessary to demonstrate those effects by means of an AEC test. An AEC test only makes it possible to verify the hypothesis that access to the market has been made impossible and not to rule out the possibility that

---

729. (ECJ Press Release 2014).
730. (ECJ, Intel Corp. v. Commission, Case T-286/09 2014) see paras 80, 84–86, 88, 91–93, 103, 104, 116, 117, 132, 527.

Chapter 4: Competition Practice

it has been made more difficult. It is true that a negative result means that it is economically impossible for an as-efficient competitor to secure the contestable share of a customer's demand. In order to offer a customer compensation for the loss of the exclusivity rebate, that competitor would be forced to sell its products at a price which would not allow it even to cover its costs. However, a positive result only means that an as-efficient competitor is able to cover its costs. That does not however mean that there is no foreclosure effect. The mechanism of the exclusivity rebates is still capable of making access to the market more difficult for competitors of the undertaking in a dominant position, even if that access is not economically impossible.[731]

The General Court found in that context, that it is not necessary to examine, by means of the 'as efficient competitor test', whether the Commission correctly assessed the ability of the rebates to foreclose a competitor as efficient as Intel. More precisely, such a test establishes at what price a competitor as efficient as the undertaking in a dominant position would have had to offer its products in order to compensate a customer for the loss of the rebate granted by the undertaking in a dominant position. Since the exclusivity rebates granted by an undertaking in a dominant position are, by their very nature, capable of restricting competition, the Commission was not required to show, in its analysis of the circumstances of the case, that the rebates granted by Intel were capable of foreclosing AMD from the market. Moreover, even if the competitor were still able to cover its costs in spite of the rebates granted, that would not mean that the foreclosure effect did not exist. The mechanism of the exclusivity rebates is such as to make access to the market more difficult for competitors of the undertaking in a dominant position, even if that access is not economically impossible.

4.5.2.7.5 Post Denmark II

Post Denmark II[732] is a rebates case about a request for a preliminary ruling.

4.5.2.7.5.1 Rebates

Post Danmark implemented a rebate scheme in respect of direct advertising mail. The rebate scale was standardised since all customers were entitled to receive the same rebate on the basis of their aggregate purchases over an annual reference period. The rebates were conditional too. Post Danmark offered a 6–16% discount to all its customers, on the basis of the overall volume of direct advertising mail that they would send over a reference period of one year. At the end of the year, Post Danmark adjusted the discounts where the quantities presented were not the same as those that had been estimated initially. The rebates were also retroactive. Where the threshold of mailings initially set was exceeded, the rebate rate applied to all mailings presented during the year and not only to mailings exceeding the estimated threshold initially set.

---

731. (ECJ, Intel Corp. v. Commission, Case T-286/09 2014) see paras 141, 146, 150.
732. (ECJ, Post Danmark A/S v. Konkurrenceradet, Case C-23/14 2015).

The Court of Justice recalled the established case law by distinguishing between two categories of rebates: (1) Purely quantity-based rebates. These are linked solely to the volume purchased and correspond to the cost savings the supplier gains. These standardised purely volume-based incremental rebates are compatible with EU competition law. (2) The second category relates to exclusive rebates. These encourage customers to place all of their orders with a single supplier.

The Court of Justice found that Post Danmark's rebate did not fall within one of these categories. It was not a harmless quantity rebate since it was granted on the basis of the aggregate orders placed over a year rather than individual orders and, on the other hand, it was not an exclusive rebate either because it did not oblige or incentivise customers to deal exclusively with Post Danmark.

4.5.2.7.5.2   Abuses by Object and by Effect

The ruling confirms that the object/effect divide exists in the context of Article 102. As the law stands, some practices are *prima facie* prohibited as abusive irrespective of the context and effects they produce (this category includes exclusive dealing and loyalty rebates). Other practices are only prohibited insofar as they have exclusionary effects (such as 'margin squeeze' practices and standardised rebate schemes).

The Court noted that the fact that the rebates under scrutiny are standardised and thus non-discriminatory does not prevent it from having an abusive exclusionary effect. The Court of Justice clarified that only dominant companies whose conduct is likely to have an anti-competitive effect on the market fall within the scope of Article 102. In that regard, the assessment of whether a rebate scheme is capable of restricting competition must be carried out in the light of all relevant circumstances, including the rules and criteria governing the grant of the rebates, the number of customers concerned and the characteristics of the market on which the dominant undertaking operates. Such an assessment seeks to determine whether the conduct of the dominant undertaking produces an actual or likely exclusionary effect, to the detriment of competition and, thereby, of consumers' interests.[733]

The Court then ruled that, in order to assess whether a rebate is exclusionary, regard must be had to the criteria and rules governing the granting of the rebates. The Court found that a rebate will be all the more exclusionary if it is: retroactive (based on a relatively long reference period – even a period of less than a year could still be too long); conditional upon the customer meeting the projected volumes for the year, i.e., the customer would have to reimburse the supplier if it failed to meet its target and applicable to the entire market, that is to say, the part of the market under Post Danmark's legal monopoly and the part of the market open to competition, i.e., the so-called 'contestable' part of the market. However, the Court also stated that once the exclusionary effect is established, the undertaking may demonstrate that this effect is counterbalanced by efficiency gains.

---

733. *Ibid.*, paras 67–69.

4.5.2.7.5.3 As-Efficient-Competitor Test

With respect to the 'as efficient competitor test' the Court stated that there is no obligation to apply this test. It is not possible to infer from Article 102 or the case law of the Court that there is a legal obligation requiring a finding to the effect that a rebate scheme operated by a dominant undertaking is abusive has to be based always on the AEC test.[734] The AEC test is just one tool amongst others for the purposes of assessing whether there is an abuse of a dominant position in the context of a rebate scheme.[735]

However in *Post Denmark II*, the 'as efficient competitor test' is of no relevance because the market is characterised by the holding by the dominant undertaking of a very large market share and by structural advantages conferred, *inter alia*, by that undertaking's statutory monopoly. Thus, the structure of the market makes the emergence of an as-efficient competitor practically impossible.[736]

Consequently, the 'as-efficient-competitor test' does not constitute a necessary condition for finding to the effect that a rebate scheme is abusive under Article 102.

4.5.2.8 Economic Analysis in Other Article 102 Cases

4.5.2.8.1 Tetra Pak II

In *Tetra Pak II*,[737] the Court of Justice rejected an appeal against a Court of First Instance judgment. Prior to *Tetra Pak II*, a dominant undertaking could be held to abuse its dominant position in cases where (1) the abusive conduct took place and produced effects *on the dominant market* (this is the most frequent case[738]), or (2) the abusive conduct took place on the dominant market but produced an effect on another, associated market (this is typically the case where the dominant undertaking exploits its dominant position in order to monopolise an associated market on which the dominant product or service is an indispensable input[739]), or (3) the abusive conduct took place on a non-dominated market but produced effects on the associated, dominated market (this is the case where the dominant undertaking adopts a restrictive conduct on a non-dominated market with a view to reinforcing its dominant position on the dominated market). In *Tetra Pak II*, the Court of Justice ruled that Article 102 prohibits exclusionary practices (4) which are implemented and produce effects in a market in which the undertaking concerned does *not* hold a dominant position, on the mere grounds that this market has associated links with another, distinct market dominated by this undertaking. It is possible that, in view of the links between the dominated market (the market for aseptic packaging) and the non-dominated market (the market for non-aseptic packaging), the elimination of competitors from the

---

734. Ibid., para. 57.
735. Ibid., para. 61.
736. Ibid., para. 59.
737. (ECJ, Tetra Pak International SA v. Commission, Case C.333/94 P 1996).
738. see (ECJ, Hoffmann-La Roche & Co. AG v. Commission, Case 85/76 1979).
739. see (ECJ, Istituto Chemioterapico Italiano S.p.A. and Commercial Solvents Corporation v. Commission, Joined cases 6 and 7-73 1974).

non-dominated market could *reinforce* Tetra Pak's position on the dominant market. However, *Tetra Pak II* did not enquire whether this was indeed the case.[740]

Tetra Pak, a company of Swedish origin established in Switzerland, is the largest supplier for the packaging of liquid foods (chiefly milk and fruit juices) in cartons. In some of the markets in this sector, the market for machinery and the market for cartons for aseptic packaging of 'long life' liquids, the group holds a virtual monopoly (approximately 95% of the market). The Commission concluded[741] that Tetra Pak had committed a number of varied infringements of Article 102 in these markets and the related markets for non-aseptic packaging of 'fresh liquids'. Infringements involved:

- marketing policy aimed at segregating national markets within the EC;
- customer contracts policy, aimed at artificially excluding potential competition by unduly binding users to the group through a series of exclusivity clauses, notably those stipulating that only Tetra Pak cartons could be used on Tetra Pak machines, inspection clauses and loyalty discounts;
- pricing policy: general application of discriminatory pricing with regard to users and ad hoc predatory pricing aimed at eliminating competitors;
- various practices aimed at eliminating competitors (where necessary by buying the companies or their machinery) and/or removing their technology from certain markets.

The Commission defined as the relevant product markets four markets:[742]

- machines for aseptic packaging of ultra-high temperature treated liquid foods (primarily milk);
- cartons for the same;
- machines for packaging liquid foods in cartons in a non-aseptic manner;
- cartons for the same.

While it concluded that market shares in both aseptic and non-aseptic markets were sufficiently high to find dominance in each, it concluded that such an approach ignored links between them. Milk and fruit juice are packaged in both ways, often by the same producers. In these circumstances, it was appropriate to find that conduct affecting the non-aseptic markets constituted an abuse of its aseptic market position. The Commission found that Tetra Pak has abused its position in these markets through the use of restrictive sales conditions, tying arrangements and discriminatory pricing.

4.5.2.8.1.1 Market Definition and Dominance

In the judgment of the Court of First Instance, the arguments in *Tetra Pak II*[743] grew yet more complex. It was argued that the Commission should have approached the market

---

740. (Art and Van Liedekerke 1997, 931).
741. (Commission Decisions (92/163/EEC) on Tetra Pak II Case IV/31043 1991).
742. *Ibid.*, point 92.
743. (CFI, Tetra Pak International SA v. Commission, Case T-83/91 1994).

Chapter 4: Competition Practice

definition by looking separately at packaging for a different liquid food group, i.e., milk, orange juice, etc. The Court of First Instance found that this approach was unwarranted, noting that whatever the product, aseptic and non-aseptic systems each fulfilled the same need, involved the same packager/producers in many cases, and, within each type of system, prices were uniform, regardless of liquid. Moreover, given the dominance of milk in each category, packaging of milk alone could provide a reasonable basis for assessing dominance.

The Court of Justice then agreed with the Commission's findings on lack of sufficient substitutability between aseptic and non-aseptic systems, noting, as the Commission stressed, that small increases in machinery prices would not affect consumers' decision to shift between aseptic and non-aseptic milk. Tetra-Pak's claim that it was the packager/producer's view that was critical and that they would switch even in response to a very small increase was flatly rejected. In the end, the critical factors were those relied upon by the Commission, namely differences in physical characteristics, consumer preferences based on taste and shelf-life, and the costs inherent in shifting from one system to another.

The Court of Justice also rejected supply substitutability arguments, finding that manufacturers of non-aseptic machinery in cartons would not be able, at least because of a lack of technological knowledge, to modify their machinery to make it useable for aseptic packaging. The same analysis was used in upholding the Commission's findings that aseptic packaging in containers of glass and plastic was not substitutable with aseptic packaging in cartons.

4.5.2.8.1.2   Predatory Pricing

The assessment of the practices under the Article 102 investigation in *Tetra Pak II* raised some concerns. The sales prices applied by Tetra Pak on the sale of the non-dominant product were found to be *predatory* under the test set forth in *AKZO*,[744] that is the comparison between the sales price and certain cost thresholds. Predation is economically rational only if the predator has a reasonable possibility of raising prices after the elimination of a competitor to a level permitting recoupment of the losses incurred as a result of sales below cost. Tetra Pak argued that the possibility of recouping losses is a constituting element of predatory pricing. The Court of Justice disagreed and ruled that '*it must be possible to penalise predatory pricing whenever there is a risk that competition will be eliminated.*'[745] Another critical point is that the Court did not consider the economic circumstances under which the dominant undertaking operates by stating that prices below AVCs are deemed to be 'always' predatory. '*There is no conceivable economic purpose other than elimination of a competitor.*'[746] However, prices below AVCs may be economically justified for instance upon the launch of a product or in case of perishable or old-fashioned goods. In supporting a mechanical application of the accounting formulae referred to in *AKZO*

---

744. (ECJ, AKZO Chemie BV v. Commission, Case C-62/86 1991).
745. (ECJ, Tetra Pak International SA v. Commission, Case C.333/94 P 1996, 44).
746. *Ibid.*, para. 41.

without regard to the relevant economic circumstances, *Tetra Pak II* makes it difficult to distinguish fair from unfair competition.

4.5.2.8.2 AstraZeneca

In 2012, the Court of Justice[747] dismissed the appeal of the AstraZeneca group against a General Court judgment.[748] The Anglo-Swedish group AstraZeneca (AZ) abused its dominant position by preventing the marketing of generic products replicating Losec.

In 2005, the Commission fined AZ EUR 60 million for misusing a patent system and procedures for marketing pharmaceuticals in order to block or delay market entry for generic competitors to its ulcer drug Losec. From 1993 to 2000, AstraZeneca infringed the competition rules by blocking or delaying market access for generic versions of Losec and preventing parallel imports of Losec. AstraZeneca did this by (1) giving misleading information to several national patent offices in the EEA resulting in AstraZeneca gaining extended patent protection for Losec through so-called supplementary protection certificates (SPCs) and by (2) misusing rules and procedures applied by the national medicines agencies which issue market authorisations for medicines by selectively deregistering the market authorisations for Losec capsules in Denmark, Norway and Sweden with the intent of blocking or delaying entry by generic firms and parallel traders.

4.5.2.8.2.1 Exclusionary Abuse

AZs abuse was exclusionary in nature in that it aimed to exclude (or at least delay) generic competition in the markets concerned. AZ's behaviour resulted in SPCs in three countries (Finland, Germany and Norway) as well as extended SPC protection in the Benelux countries and Austria (see recitals (760)–(762)). This, by itself, was capable of having at least a potential effect on the competitive structure and thereby on trade between at least two EEA Contracting Parties. It should also be noted that AZ's Norwegian SPC was only revoked after the expiry of the substance patent. Although AZ's German SPC was revoked before the expiry of the substance patent, AZ was still able to bring patent infringement proceedings against generic firms even after the expiry of the substance patent (see recital (231)). As a result, by preventing – actually or potentially – market entry for competitors operating in several EEA Contracting Parties (such as the complainant in this case and other generic producers of omeprazole based products such as ratiopharm), the economic activities, in which such undertakings are engaging, are affected. As regards the second abuse, through its tablet/capsule switch and the capsule deregistration in Denmark, Norway and Sweden, AZ intended to delay market entry of generic omeprazole. The Commission found that this second infringement produced effects on the market as well. The decision

---

747. (ECJ, AstraZeneca AB and AstraZeneca plc v. Commission, Case C-457/10 P 2012).
748. (ECJ, AstraZeneca AB & AstraZeneca plc v. Commission, Case T-321/05 2010).

Chapter 4: Competition Practice

confirmed the Commission's strict approach to sanctioning restrictions on parallel imports and on market access for generic products. AZ appealed against this decision.

In 2010, the General Court rejected most of the arguments put forward by AZ. However, it annulled in part the Commission's decision so far as concerns the finding of the second abuse. The General Court held that, although the Commission had proved that the deregistration of the marketing authorisations for Losec capsules in Denmark, Sweden and Norway were such as to delay the entry to the market of generic medicinal products in those three countries and, furthermore, to prevent parallel imports of Losec in Sweden, the Commission had not proved that that latter effect had been produced in Denmark and in Norway. The General Court therefore reduced the amount of the fine imposed jointly and severally on AstraZeneca AB and AstraZeneca plc to EUR 40.25 million and fixed the fine imposed on AstraZeneca AB at EUR 12.25 million.[749]

The Court of Justice rejected the appeal. As regards, in particular, the first abuse of a dominant position concerning SPCs, the Court observes that EU law prohibits a dominant undertaking from eliminating a competitor and thereby strengthening its position by using methods other than those which come within the scope of competition on the merits. The Court of Justice explained that in its judgment the concept of 'abuse' is an objective concept referring to the conduct of a dominant undertaking which is such as to influence the structure of a market where the degree of competition is already weakened precisely because of the presence of the undertaking concerned, and which, through recourse to methods different from those governing normal competition in products or services on the basis of the transactions of commercial operators, has the effect of hindering the maintenance of the degree of competition still existing in the market or the growth of that competition. It follows that Article 102 prohibits a dominant undertaking from eliminating a competitor and thereby strengthening its position by using methods other than those which come within the scope of competition on the merits. Thus the Court of Justice confirmed the European concept of 'as if competition' and 'competition on the merits' as defined section 1.2.

4.5.2.8.2.2 Competition on the Merits

The consistent and linear conduct of a pharmaceutical undertaking, characterised by the notification to the patent offices of highly misleading representations and by a manifest lack of transparency falls outside the scope of competition on the merits. A dominant company has the specific responsibility not to prejudice, by its conduct, effective and undistorted competition within the EU.[750] The Court reconfirmed that, although the importance of the market shares may vary from one market to another, the possession, over a long period, of a very large market share constitutes in itself,

---

749. (ECJ Press Release 2012).
750. Ibid., paras 74, 75, 93, 98.

save in exceptional circumstances, proof of the existence of a dominant position[751] and that market shares of more than 50% constitute very large market shares.[752],[753]

Although the practice of an undertaking in a dominant position cannot be characterised as abusive in the absence of any anti-competitive effect on the market, it is not, however, necessary for such an effect to be concrete, since it is sufficient to demonstrate that there is a potential anti-competitive effect.[754] The preparation by a pharmaceutical undertaking, even in a dominant position, of a strategy whose object it is to minimise the erosion of its sales and to enable it to deal with competition from generic products is legitimate and is part of the normal competitive process, provided that the conduct envisaged does not depart from practices coming within the scope of competition on the merits, which is such as to benefit consumers. An undertaking which holds a dominant position has a special responsibility in that latter regard and it cannot therefore use regulatory procedures in such a way as to prevent or make more difficult the entry of competitors on the market, in the absence of grounds relating to the defence of the legitimate interests of an undertaking engaged in competition on the merits or in the absence of objective justification.

The deregistration, without objective justification and after the expiry of the exclusive right to make use of the results of the pharmacological and toxicological tests and clinical trials granted by EU law, of marketing authorisations with the aim of hindering the introduction of generic products and parallel imports does not come within the scope of competition on the merits.[755]

So far as concerns the second abuse of a dominant position, the Court has held that the deregistration of the marketing authorisations, without objective justification and after the expiry of the exclusive right granted by EU law, with the aim of hindering the introduction of generic products and parallel imports, also does not come within the scope of competition on the merits.

4.5.2.8.3 Microsoft

An exciting Article 102 case was the *Microsoft* saga. In 2007, the Grand Chamber of the Court of First Instance upheld the fines and vast majority of rulings against Microsoft.[756]

The case originated with a December 1998 complaint from Sun Microsystems alleging that Microsoft was refusing to supply it with interoperability information necessary to interoperate with Microsoft's dominant PC operating system. In February 2000, following information obtained from the market, the Commission broadened the scope of its investigation to examine Microsoft's conduct with regard to its Windows

---

751. (ECJ, Hoffmann-La Roche & Co. AG v. Commission, Case 85/76 1979, para. 41).
752. (ECJ, AKZO Chemie BV v. Commission, Case C-62/86 1991, para. 60).
753. *Ibid.*, para. 176.
754. *Ibid.*, paras 106, 112.
755. *Ibid.*, paras 129, 130, 134.
756. (CFI, Microsoft Corp. v. Commission, Case T-201/04 2007).

Media Player product. Following an extensive analysis of the evidence on the file, the Commission concluded its investigation in March 2004 by way of a decision.[757] The Commission found that Microsoft had abused its dominant position in the PC operating system market by:

- refusing to supply competitors in the work group server operating system market interface information necessary for their products to interoperate with Windows, and hence to compete viably in the market;
- harming competition through the tying of its separate Windows Media Player product with its Windows PC operating system.

In its decision, the Commission found that Microsoft engaged in these two separate types of conduct. The Commission's competition concern with respect to bundling of Microsoft's Windows Media Player with Windows was that it allowed Microsoft to foreclose the media player market.

In assessing this concern the Commission applied four steps:

- First, the undertaking concerned must have a dominant position on the market for the tying product.
- Second, the tying product and the tied product must be two separate products.
- Third, consumers must not have a choice of obtaining the tying product without the tied product.
- Fourth, the practice must foreclose competition.

The Court of First Instance delivered its judgment in 2007, upholding the findings of abuse in the Commission's decision.

4.5.2.8.3.1 Market Definition

With respect to separate product markets, the Court confirmed that 'in the absence of independent demand for the allegedly tied product, there can be no question of separate products and no abusive tying'. Thus, the Court seems to set a minimum hurdle such that there must be independent demand for media players. Referring to *Hilti*, the Court argued that the fact that there is no demand for a Windows operating system without a media player does not mean that they are two separate products:

> To take Hilti, for example, it may be assumed that there was no demand for a nail gun magazine without nails, since a magazine without nails is useless. However, that did not prevent the Court of Justice of the European Union from concluding that those two products belonged to separate markets.[758]

---

757. On 23 Mar. 2004 the Commission imposed a fine of more than EUR 497 million on Microsoft.
758. (ECJ, Hilti AG v. Commission, Case C-53/92 P 1994, 921).

4.5.2.8.3.2 Dominance

With respect to the finding of dominance, the Court found that Microsoft's dominant position is characterised by market shares that have remained very high, at least since 1996 (above 90% in recent years), and by the presence of very high barriers to entry. These barriers to entry are in particular linked to the presence of indirect network effects. Indeed, the popularity of a PC operating system among users derives from its popularity among vendors of PC applications, which in turn choose to focus their development efforts towards the PC operating system that is most popular among users. This creates a self-reinforcing dynamic that protects Windows as the *de facto* standard for PC operating systems (an applications barrier to entry).

4.5.2.8.3.3 Bundling

The Court found that the existence of pure bundling de facto implies coercion:

> it cannot be disputed that, in consequence of the impugned conduct, consumers are unable to acquire the Windows client PC operating system without simultaneously acquiring Windows Media Player, which means... that the condition that the conclusion of contracts is made subject to acceptance of supplementary obligations must be considered to be ratified.[759]

This implies that whenever there are separate products, and pure bundling, there will always be coercion and no further evidence is required.

The Court restated well-known principles. Those factors are: first, the undertaking concerned must have a dominant position on the market for the tying product; second, the tying product and the tied product must be two separate products; third, consumers must not have a choice of obtaining the tying product without the tied product; and, fourth, the practice must foreclose competition.

Recent economic theories of exclusionary bundling investigate the circumstances in which mixed bundling acts as a form of predation, and can therefore exclude competitors of unbundled products. The predation-like test proposed by the Commission investigates whether the supply of the additional product in a bundle is profitable for the dominant firm. The cost-based test suggested by the Commission to assess the exclusionary effect of mixed bundling relies on a comparison of the incremental price of the product (B) added to the bundle with the LAICs of including that product in the bundle. The cost measure includes all the costs associated with producing B, assuming that A is already produced (where A is the product for which the dominant firm holds significant market power). This test is consistent with the Ortho Diagnostics Systems Inc v. Abbott Laboratories (1996) test developed in the US.[760] However, this test has been criticised for potentially condemning bundling void of exclusionary motives (or effects), and alternatives have been proposed – mainly to couple the cost test with other types of evidence (e.g., the size of the market being potentially

---

759. (CFI, Microsoft Corp. v. Commission, Case T-201/04 2007, para. 961).
760. (Papandropoulos 2006).

foreclosed). In fact, if the incremental price of the additional product is above its incremental cost of production, there should be a presumption that no exclusionary effect is likely. However, the Commission seems to take the opposite view: it may exceptionally be concluded that, although the price exceeds the LAICs, the mixed bundling nonetheless is considered exclusionary.

4.5.2.8.3.4 Competition on Equal Footing

With regards to interoperability, the Court considered that the Commission had been right to conclude that the work group server operating systems of Microsoft's competitors must be able to interoperate with Windows domain architecture on an *equal footing* with Windows operating systems to be able to compete in the market.

On the bundling of Windows Media Player to the Windows operating system, the Court endorsed the Commission's conclusion that there was abusive tying and that it would lead to a weakening of competition.

4.5.2.8.3.5 Consumer Benefits

By this ruling the Court confirmed that Microsoft cannot regulate the market by imposing its products and services on people. The Court has also confirmed that Microsoft can no longer prevent the market from functioning properly and that computer users are therefore entitled to benefit from choice, more innovative products and more competitive prices. In confirming the interoperability part of the Commission's decision, the Court acknowledges the importance of interoperability for consumer choice and innovation in high-tech industries. If competitors are unable to make their products 'talk to' or work properly with a dominant company's products, they are prevented from bringing new innovative products onto the market, and customers are locked into the products of the existing provider. Consumers want interoperable products, and companies that want to meet consumers' demands should be able to provide them.

4.5.2.8.3.6 Refusal to Supply

As regards the refusal to supply the interoperability information, the Court ruled that, although undertakings are usually free to choose their business partners, in certain circumstances a refusal to supply on the part of a dominant undertaking may constitute an abuse of a dominant position. It found that the Commission did not make an error in considering that the relevant conditions were indeed satisfied.

Arguments to the effect that the refusal is objectively justified because the technology concerned is covered by IPR were rejected and the Court noted that such justification would render ineffective the basic competition principles established in the case law which is referred to above. Microsoft failed to show that if it were required to disclose the interoperability information that would have a significant negative effect on its incentives to innovate.

The Microsoft saga continued: The Commission concluded in 2007 that up until 21 October 2007 Microsoft had not complied with its obligation pursuant to the decision to give access to the interoperability information on reasonable and non-discriminatory terms. Therefore, on 27 February 2008, the Commission adopted a decision pursuant to Article 24(2) of Regulation 1/2003 ('the second Article 24(2) Decision') imposing on Microsoft a penalty payment of EUR 899 million for non-compliance with its obligations.

4.6 EUROPEAN ECONOMIC APPROACH IN MERGERS

This section discusses the role of economic analysis in merger proceedings. In particular the European School of thought is clarified. Merger control is one of the areas in which the intellectual fights between Chicago School thinking and the European approach are the most striking. Whereas in Chicago School thinking a large company producing efficiencies might be coherent with competition law objectives, the European School of thought requires a more holistic assessment.

The EU Merger Regulation

On 21 December 1989, under pressure from industry, the Council adopted Regulation (EEC) 4064/89,[761] requiring the pre-notification to the Commission of concentrations within its scope – those above the thresholds – and providing for possible prohibition by the Commission. The Merger Control Regulation (the ECR) was amended by the Council Regulation (EC) 1310/97 of 30 June 1997.[762]

2002 marked a significant milestone: The Commission faced an important challenge when the General Court overruled three Commission decisions (Case M-1524, *Airtours v. First Choice*, Case M-2283, *Schneider v. Legrand* and Case M-2416, *Tetra Laval v. Sidel*), arguing that the Commission had misevaluated the competitive intensity in relevant industries. Following these remarkable decisions, the EMR was reformed in early 2004 and the new Council Regulation (EC) 139/2004 on the control of concentrations between undertakings (the ECMR) came into force on 1 May 2004.

A merger may significantly impede effective competition in a market, for example, by removing important competitive constraints on one or more sellers, who consequently may increase market power. The most direct effect of the merger will be the loss of competition between the merging firms. Another aspect covered occurs when merging firms are close competitors. Products may be differentiated within a relevant market such that some products are closer substitutes than others. The higher the degree of substitutability between the merging firms' products, the more likely it is that the merging firms will raise prices significantly.

---

761. (Regulation 4064/89 on setting forth control of concentrations between undertakings 1989).
762. (Regulation 1310/97 amending Regulation No. 4064/89 on the control of concentrations between undertakings 1997).

Article 2(2) and (3) ECMR implements these guiding principles by stating that:

2. A concentration which would not significantly impede effective competition in the common market or in a substantial part of it, in particular as a result of the creation or strengthening of a dominant position, shall be declared compatible with the common market.
3. A concentration which would significantly impede effective competition, in the common market or in a substantial part of it, in particular as a result of the creation or strengthening of a dominant position, shall be declared incompatible with the common market.

Thus, the novelty in the ECMR is the notion of 'significant impediment to effective competition' SIEC-Test in Article 2(2) and (3) requiring an extension beyond the concept of dominance.[763]

The SIEC-Test

In the past, a merger was blocked if it created a dominant position, and therefore would likely result in higher prices, less choice and innovation. This concept has been interpreted by the Commission and the Court of Justice of the EU along the years as applying also to situations of 'joint dominance' or duopolies[764] as well as to situations of 'collective dominance' or oligopolies.[765] However in the past, the dominance test did not apply in the case of a 'non-collusive oligopoly,' a scenario which typically involves (i) the merger of the second and third largest players in the market, (ii) where the two are the closest substitutes, and (iii) the merged entity would obtain market power and be able to raise prices unilaterally, i.e., what is known in the US as a unilateral competitive effect. Unilateral effects are changes to the economic equilibrium caused by an increase in concentration that materially changes the optimal behaviour of the merging firms. In differentiated product industries, unilateral effects are of higher importance than coordinated effects.

The importance of the SIEC-test is further highlighted indirectly in the ECMR's fifth recital where it is suggested that the ultimate objective of the ECMR is to prevent those mergers that lead to a significant impediment of effective competition:

Whereas it must be ensured that the process of reorganisation does not result in lasting damage to competition. Whereas community law must therefore include provisions governing those concentrations which may significantly impede effective competition in the common market or a substantial part of it.

The SIEC-test by stating that a merger must be blocked if it would 'significantly impede effective competition' now covers anti-competitive effects in oligopolistic markets where the merged company would not be strictly dominant in the usual sense

---

763. In the past, a merger was blocked if it created a dominant position, and therefore would likely result in higher prices, less choice and innovation. This concept has been interpreted by the Commission and the Court of Justice of the European Union along the years as applying also to situations of 'joint dominance' or duopolies (*Kali und Salz/MdK* and *Gencor/Lonrho*) as well as to situations of 'collective dominance' or oligopolies (*Airtours/First Choice*).
764. (Decision IV/M.308 on Kali und Salz v. MdK v. Treuhand 1993, para. 62); (Decision IV/M.619 on Gencor v. Lonrho 1996, paras 205–206).
765. (Decision IV/M.1524 on Airtours v. First Choice 1999, para. 97).

of the word (i.e., much bigger than the rest). The central question is whether sufficient competition remains after the merger to provide consumers with sufficient choice. Thus in principle, the SIEC-test embodies correctly the European concept as defined in section 1.2. The SIEC-test does not make reference to a consumer welfare standard at all as known in the Chicago School thinking.

The SIEC-test recognises the economic fact that there are at least two ways in which competition may be threatened, other than by single dominant firms. These two ways are conceptually distinct. The first is when a number of firms engage in what economists refer to as tacit collusion, as a result of which their behaviour may approximate that of a single dominant firm.[766] The second is when market concentration is high enough for non-competitive outcomes to result from the individual profit-maximising responses of firms to market conditions even when none of these firms would be considered individually dominant. Situations of the second kind are now captured by the SIEC-test.

The analyses in the SIEC-test are analyses of market outcomes or effects. Thus, another interpretation of the SIEC-test is that this is an 'effects based approach'.

An immediate implication of this economic approach is that the effect of the merger on the merging firms does not tell the whole story. Non-merging rivals will react to the merger and raise their prices, resulting in a new equilibrium. In other words, when firms compete on price, the final equilibrium effect will exceed the direct effect on the merging parties. In the end, there are two effects: the initial effect on the merging parties and the final equilibrium effect when the full set of reactions and counter reactions has occurred.

It is the equilibrium effect that affects consumers and that captures the effect of the merger on competition. A merger test – such as the dominance test – that focuses almost exclusively on the market power of the merged firm does not fully capture the full equilibrium effect. It is important to realise that these equilibrium effects do not arise from any collusion between firms, or from any trade-off of future or current profits. It is simply a change in the competitive equilibrium because of the transaction.[767]

On the other hand, a merger may lead to welfare gains for consumers in the form of lower prices or increased innovation. This can happen for at least two reasons. First, the merged entity may attain efficiencies such as marginal cost reductions, which give an incentive to lower prices. If these efficiencies are passed on, this may fully offset the opposite incentive to raise prices resulting from increased market power. Thus, it is possible for prices in the market to fall and total output to rise post-merger. Second, a merger between suppliers may create a dominant position, which enhances countervailing seller power *vis-à-vis* a dominant buyer. This may lead to increased input and output sales and lower output prices.

---

766. Tacit collusion is dealt in a number of judgments under the notion of collective dominance corresponding to the 'coordinated effects' studied in the US.
767. (Röller and De la Mano 2006, 18–19).

Chapter 4: Competition Practice

Role of Efficiencies

In order to determine the impact of a concentration on competition in the common market, the ECMR states that it is appropriate to take account of any substantiated and likely efficiencies put forward by the undertakings concerned. The assumption is that efficiencies brought about by the concentration may counteract the effects on competition. As a consequence, the concentration would not significantly impede effective competition in the common market or in a substantial part of it, in particular as a result of the creation or strengthening of a dominant position. The idea is that competition secures for the consumer the desired goods at the lowest price with the sacrifice of the fewest resources.

In this sense, competition is a mechanism for promoting economic efficiency. A merger can entail economic efficiency gains by reducing costs. Efficiency claims are accepted when the efficiencies are generated by the merger. These efficiencies need to be of direct benefit to consumers, as well as being substantial, timely, and verifiable. Case law analysis so far shows that the Commission is not really applying this 'efficiency defense' in merger cases thereby confirming that the application of economic analysis in merger proceedings is guided by other, more holistic objectives.

In this context it is important to note that the Commission needs to place its merger appraisal within the general framework of the achievement of the fundamental objectives referred to in section 1.2. Recitale (23) of the Merger Regulation states that:

> it is necessary to establish whether or not concentrations with a Community dimension are compatible with the common market in terms of the need to maintain and develop effective competition in the common market. In so doing, the Commission must place its appraisal within the general framework of the achievement of the fundamental objectives referred to in Article 2 of the Treaty establishing the European Community and Article 2 of the Treaty on European Union.

Based on the changes after the entry into force of the Treaty of Lisbon on 1 December 2009 as elaborated in section 1.3, the old numbering of Article 2 in the TEEC was replaced in substance by Article 3 TEU.[768] Article 3 TEU includes the provision that the Union shall work for a highly competitive social market economy. With respect to economic analysis in EU competition law, this requirement asks for a type of economic analysis that is becoming known as 'European School of thought' (see section 1.2).

This means that in EU merger proceedings the economics applied need to relate to the European approach as stated in the Treaty of Lisbon and developed by the Court of Justice of the EU.

4.6.1 Role of Economic Analysis in EU Merger Control

As elaborated on in Chapter One, the European ideology with respect to competition economics differs significantly from Chicago School thinking. However, Chicago

---

768. (European Commission, Annex – Tables of Equivalences referred to in Art. 5 of the Treaty of Lisbon 2007).

School thinking is sometimes applied by European economists to issues in EU competition law and interestingly to a lesser extent in US anti-trust law.

Contradicting Schools of Thought

In principle, merger control is the natural breeding ground for the fertilisation of sophisticated economic analysis. In 1990, the most influential event that marked the beginning of the new era in European competition economics was the entry into force of the Merger Control Regulation 4064/89 (MCR). The ability of the Commission to pass judgment on the biggest mergers occurring in Europe, in fact in the world, catapulted the Commission into a position of power and importance that no competition agency in Europe had ever enjoyed.[769]

In getting ready to apply the MCR, the Commission relied on experts from the US. In those times, the consumer welfare model of the Chicago School entered the arena in Europe. According to this Chicago School approach, the sole purpose of competition law is to ensure that consumer (or total) welfare is not jeopardised by actions of undertakings. Government actions are not of any concern in the Chicago School.

Subsequent to the enactment of the MCR, a process of Americanisation began. Some European scholars gradually adopted their own understanding of the term 'competition' towards a version of the consumer welfare approach developed by the Chicago School. Chicago's claim is that economic analysis is governed by basic price theory. This claim – the so-called 'sole value' thesis – has two remarkable consequences. (1) Other concerns, such as fairness, or the plight of small businesses, or the balancing of power, are irrelevant. (2) The sole value to be pursued by price-theoretic anti-trust must be a specific kind of economic value, namely, efficiency, in both allocative and productive terms. Thus, the focus of the Chicago School is on efficiency – or, as it is often said, consumer welfare. If efficiency is to be the sole yardstick, then another central thesis of the Chicago School is that competitive harm consists of adverse price and output effects. A third Chicago cornerstone is faith in freedom of entry.[770]

By replacing the idea that anti-trust is for competition with the idea that anti-trust is for efficiency, the Chicago School has created the 'efficiency paradox'.[771] Thus Chicago style is to place excessive trust in the efficiency produced by dominant firm strategies and vertical relationships, as well as in the possibility of free entry. This approach ends up protecting monopoly or oligopoly and suppressing innovative challenges, eventually stifling that very efficiency it was supposed to enhance. The paradox is more serious in high-tech industries and intellectual property markets, where the natural drift toward single firm dominance, caused by the joint action of patents, copyrights and network effects, is furthered by Chicago complacency towards monopoly power.[772]

---

769. (Weitbrecht 2008, 84).
770. (Giocoli 2012, 5).
771. (Fox 2008, 77).
772. (Giocoli 2012, 6).

Chicago views are heavily critised by some economists.[773] Some on them have never accepted this static, non-strategic approach to competition.[774] In sharp contradiction to the European competition model as identified in section 1.2, the logic of the Chicago School is to protect consumers' freedom in order to guarantee consumers' welfare. This means the production of a variety of products at reasonable prices. The Chicago 'pro-consumer' label is often traced to Robert H. Bork and his book 'The Antitrust Paradox'[775], as discussed in section 1.4.2.

Although the positions associated with the Chicago School never overturned mainstream anti-trust in the US, they retained significant influence on competition law in Europe. Some European scholars believe that modern EU competition policy needs to be inspired by the neoliberal ideas of the Chicago School which place great confidence in free markets.[776] Since the introduction of the SIEC-test as the new test in EU merger control, some scholars even think that EU merger analysis ought to apply modern industrial organisation theory, based on the Chicago consumer welfare standard.[777]

The argument in many scientific papers[778] is that the majority of economists generally support the application of an overall social welfare standard in merger control.[779] A further assumption is that the aim of the Commission is to increase consumer welfare.[780] Even members of the EU CET at DG Competition use Chicago School arguments: long ago it was established that under certain assumptions a monopolist cannot increase its profits by leveraging its monopoly power into another market. *'Against this background, it is clear that one needs to establish which of the (restrictive) assumptions of the one–monopoly profit theorem are violated before even considering the possibility of harm'.*[781] The Chief Economist Motta for example confirms that economic welfare is the objective EU competition authorities and courts should pursue.[782] He identifies economic welfare as a branch of economics that focuses on the optimal allocation of resources and goods and how this affects social welfare. In accordance with *Bork's* reading, he agrees that in each given industry, welfare is specified by total surplus: That is the sum of consumer surplus and producer surplus.[783] To conclude, there is a strong view that in merger policy anti-trust enforcers should focus on consumer welfare.[784]

---

773. (Giocoli 2007, 13).
774. (Martin 2007).
775. (Bork 1978, 7, 15, 50, 51).
776. (Geradin and Girgenson 2011, 353).
777. (Maier-Rigaud and Parplies 2009, 565).
778. See (Motta 2004, Ch. 1.3) for a discussion and (Anderson and Coate 2005, 947–972) for an overview of papers addressing the two merger policy standards.
779. (Bergman, et al. 2010, 4).
780. (Szilágyi 2011, 4).
781. (De Coninck 2010, 931); See, e.g., (Hart and Tirole 1990, 205–286); (Choi and Yi 2000, 717–743); (Chen 2001, 667–685); and (Nocke and White 2005).
782. (Motta 2004, 30).
783. *Ibid.*, 18.
784. (Coate 2005, 189–240).

European School of Thought

In contrast, as discussed in section 1.5, the European approach as expressed in EU competition law and developed by the Court of Justice of the EU is a constitutional market order that it is defined by its institutional framework and, as such, subject to (explicit or implicit) *constitutional choice*. It assumes that the working properties of market processes depend on the nature of the legal-institutional frameworks within which they take place.[785] A second element of the European approach is the willingness to place humanistic and social values on a par with economic efficiency.[786] The European rules of the game do not favour the powerful and wealthy but income redistribution instead.[787] The European approach is a normative ideology with specific claims about how society should be organised around conceptions of liberty and humanistic values.[788] As *Reinhard Behlke* wrote in 1961, '...*liberalism is not to be viewed as a direction in economics or economic policy, but as a humanistically based intellectual orientation*'.[789]

The concept of 'social market economy', now in Article 3 TEU, was coined by *Müller-Armack* in the 1950s to emphasise the egalitarian and humanistic bent of this new form of liberalism.[790] In 1952, *Eucken* claimed that '*social security and social justice are the greatest concerns of our time*'.[791] These claims are still valid today.

The concept of a 'social market economy' first appeared in scholarly writings on political economy in the period between the two World Wars. The instability of the interwar years, plagued by inflation and depression that bred radical ideologies and unleashed devastation on Europe, convinced many intellectuals and politicians that capitalism was untenable.

These thinkers agreed with earlier conceptions of liberalism in considering a competitive economic system to be necessary for a prosperous, free and equitable society. They were convinced that such a society could develop only where the market was embedded in a constitutional framework. This framework was necessary to protect the process of competition from distortion, as a means of preventing degeneration of the competitive process. The main issue of relevance with respect to economic analysis in EU competition law is the assurance that the benefits of the market need to be equitably distributed throughout society and that governmental intervention in the economy is minimised (see Chapter One).

European history has demonstrated that competition has tended to collapse, because enterprises preferred private (i.e., contractual) regulation of business activities rather than competition and because enterprises were frequently able to acquire such

---

785. (Vanberg 2004, 5).
786. (Boas and Gans-Morse 2009, 146).
787. (D. J. Gerber 1994, 38).
788. (Hanslowe 1960, 96).
789. (D. J. Gerber 1994, 36).
790. (Boarman 1964, 21); (D. J. Gerber 1994, 60).
791. (D. J. Gerber 1994, 37).

high levels of economic power that they could eliminate competition. Competition law is viewed as a means of preventing this degeneration of the competitive process. Competition law should enforce competition by creating and maintaining the conditions under which it can flourish.[792]

Thus, this School of liberalism emphasises the need for the state to ensure that the free market produces results close to its theoretical potential. The state must create a proper legal environment for the economy and maintain a healthy level of competition through measures that adhere to market principles. The concern is that, if the state does not take active measures to foster competition, firms with monopoly (or oligopoly) power will emerge. These companies will not only subvert the advantages offered by the market economy, but also possibly undermine good government.

A liberal market economy, the German scholar *Eucken* argued, cannot survive for long in a totalitarian state, nor can a democratic state under the rule of law survive if economic power is highly concentrated. He showed that the specific way in which an economic process develops is dependent upon the specific kind of economic system that prevails.[793] In this respect, competition and competition law is not viewed as automatism, but as a task of governmental economic policy. Monetary and other policies designed to foster competition would have little effect, if firms could act in concert in setting prices or determining output or if firms with economic power could use that power to foreclose opportunities for competition. Thus, one of the key concepts is the idea of an economic constitutional order.[794] Defining the 'rules of the game' of a competitive market society is the underlying mission.

The model or concept of a 'social market economy', takes a central position in the economic order. Article 3 TEU states:

> *The Union shall establish an internal market. It shall work for the sustainable development of Europe based on balanced economic growth and price stability, a highly competitive social market economy, aiming at full employment and social progress, and a high level of protection and improvement of the quality of the environment.*

Europeans consider such a social market mechanism as the most efficient way to meet the demand from consumers for goods and services.

The Court of Justice of the EU has repeatedly made reference in its judgments on competition issues to Articles 2 and 3 TEU as the basic principles underlying the Treaty's rules of competition. It is not only a pragmatic approach that EU competition law should be guided by the objectives of the TEU, but also a historically grown conclusion. The Court of Justice of the EU has repeatedly stated that the competition rules are designed to maintain effective competition, which means that in each market there must be sufficient competition to ensure the observance of the basic requirements and the attainment of the objectives of the TEU. The maintenance of effective

---

792. (D. Gerber 1995, 44).
793. (Eucken 1939, 24–37).
794. (Giocoli 2007, 3).

competition is viewed by the Court of Justice of the EU as so essential *'that without it numerous provisions of the Treaty would be pointless'*.[795] Thus, the economic concept embodied in the TEU and TFEU is a normative one: it is given.

In this regard, firstly, the EU is motivated, in coherence with the US, by concerns for consumers' interest, and secondly, but now in contrast to the US, by concerns for efficient businesses. The logic is that in the EU joint ventures, mergers, and other collaborations may be necessary to enhance technological development and thereby allowing European firms to compete effectively in global markets. This is in clear contradiction to the US which adheres to the logic that effectiveness is a natural result of market forces.

The important message is that in applying EU competition rules economists like lawyers are forced to respect that the underlying assumptions in EU competition law, the case law of the Court of Justice of the EU as well as the legal language required to address economic issues. Every economic analysis needs to correspond to the legal subject matter.

Where economists do not comprehend this point, the result is miscommunication and weak performances by economists in competition cases. Lawyers and judges are confused by those economists who do not accept that European competition economics is just a branch of economic science within a stable legal framework. The following chapter discusses this special branch of economic thinking with respect to EU merger control proceedings.

4.6.2 Guidance by the Court of Justice of the EU

Before we discuss the guidance of the Court of Justice of the EU in merger control cases, first we will elaborate on the different roles assigned to the Commission and the judicial review.

Role of the Commission

The single-sided interpretation of EU competition law with respect to a Chicago School thinking approach on the consumer welfare standard raises serious concerns. However, there is no evidence that the Commission adheres to the consumer welfare paradigm. Currently the Commission touches on this argument in only a few cases.

However, the Commission's competition policy could change towards a US based approach over time. This worry highlights another discussion: the Commission's powerful role in combining investigative, prosecutorial and decision-making powers. Those multiple roles of the Commission are controversial.[796] The risk of such a concentration of powers is thought to be compensated by procedural guarantees during the administrative proceedings and by the possibility of judicial review.[797] However,

---

795. *Ibid.*
796. (Bronckers and Vallery 2011, 537–539).
797. (Schweitzer 2009, 7.

Chapter 4: Competition Practice

undertakings and practitioners in EU competition law proceedings often feel that they are treated unfairly and that procedural rights are violated.[798] This argument holds for both – infringements as well as merger cases. With respect to judicial review, it seems that the Court of Justice of the EU views its mandate mainly as one of objective legality control: The European judiciary review restricts itself to some sort of 'light' review.

In principle the Commission's position as to questions of law, but also with respect to findings of facts, as well as the legal assessment of those facts, is open to the General Court's scrutiny. In the light of an alleged conflict between effectiveness of competition law enforcement and the full protection of individual rights, the General Court has opted for the first.[799]

Despite the admittedly numerous changes that have occurred both with respect to the Commission's role and the role of the Court of Justice of the EU, there is still a demand for more changes. In particular, the 'more economics based approach' calls for a 'more judicial approach'.[800] Such an increase in the judicial review would be even more important should the Commission decide to turn to the US Chicago School thinking, putting the consumer welfare standard at the forefront of its EU competition policy.

Role of the Courts

With respect to merger cases, the judiciary's review of past decisions already document that the Court of Justice of the EU has a strong tendency to intervene. By making reference to the basic objectives of the Treaty of Lisbon, the Courts are not reluctant to provide guidance to the Commission about how to apply, for example, the substantive test in merger control proceedings.

On the other side, the Court of Justice has held that the basic provisions of the ECMR, in particular Article 2, confer on the Commission a certain discretion, especially with respect to assessments of an economic nature. Consequently, any review by the Court of Justice of the EU of the exercise of that discretion, must take account of the margin of discretion implicit in the provisions of an economic nature that form part of the rules on concentrations.[801]

Whilst the Court of Justice of the EU recognizes that the Commission has a margin of discretion with regard to economic matters, that does not mean that the Court must refrain from reviewing the Commission's interpretation of information of an economic nature. Not only must the Court establish, in particular, whether the evidence relied on is factually accurate, reliable and consistent but also whether that

---

798. (Editorial comments: Towards a more judicial approach? EU antitrust fines under the scrutiny of fundamental rights 2011, 1406).
799. (Schweitzer 2009, 25).
800. (Editorial comments: Towards a more judicial approach? EU antitrust fines under the scrutiny of fundamental rights 2011, 1405).
801. See (ECJ, France and Others v. Commission, Joined Cases C-68/94 and C-30/95 1998, paras 223 and 224) and (CFI, Tetra Laval BV v. Commission, Case T-5/02 2002, para. 119).

evidence contains all the information which must be taken into account in order to assess a complex situation and whether it is capable of substantiating the conclusions drawn from it.[802]

According to settled case law, where institutions like the Commission have a power of appraisal, respect for the rights guaranteed by the legal order of the EU in administrative procedures is of even more fundamental importance. Those guarantees include, in particular, the duty of the Commission to examine carefully and impartially all the relevant aspects of the individual case, the right of the person concerned to make his views known and also his right to have an adequately reasoned decision.[803]

Emergence of an Economic Approach Defined by the Courts

Courts are actually applying these principles in a pro-active way. When the Court of Justice of the EU had the impression that economic analyses on the Commission were flawed, they passed tough judgments produced by the Commission: The Courts took the lead. Based on this jurisprudence, in fact a coherent economic methodology developed as a supplement to the legal rules and a A School of thought for proper economic analysis emerged. More than fifteen years of ongoing reform in EU competition law with respect to economics has shaped a comprehensive body of economic thinking. This body of economic thinking or European School is an independent School of thought – in particular independent from the insights of the Chicago School. In the following sections, some merger case reviews by the Courts are highlighted to illustrate that the European competition concept is interpreted by the Courts as it stands.

Whereas the majority of merger cases are only discussed on the Commission level, a few merger cases have been reviewed by the Court of Justice of the EU. In particular, these judgments shape European competition economics. With reference to the discussion of the Commission's powerful role combining investigative, prosecutorial and decision-making powers, the guidance from the merger cases reviewed by the Courts should get more attention.

4.6.2.1 GE/Honeywell

The Court of First Instance approved the contentious prohibition decision of the merger between General Electric (GE) and Honeywell.[804] However, several arguments contained in the Commission's decision were rejected by the Court. In the contested decision, the Commission applied some economic models and concepts in theory and explained certain conclusions on the basis of these models. The Court found that the Commission did not succeed in applying the economic theory correctly to market realities. The Court of First Instance claimed that the likely effects on the market were not properly evaluated.

---

802. See (ECJ, Commission v. Tetra Laval BV, Case C-12/03 P 2005, para. 31) and (ECJ, Bertelsmann AG and Sony Corporation of America v. Impala, Case C-413/06 P 2008, para. 69).
803. (ECJ, Hauptzollamt München-Mitte v. Technische Universität München, Case C-269/90 1991, para. 14) and (CFI, NVV and Others v. Commission, Case T-151/05 2009, para. 163).
804. (CFI, General Electric Company v. Commission, Case T-210/01 2005).

Chapter 4: Competition Practice

4.6.2.1.1 Theory of Harm/Competition Concerns

Among other issues, the Commission was worried that the merged firm could bundle jet engines with avionics and non-avionics products and offer those packages for very attractive prices that would lead to foreclosure of competitors. This rationale was based on the 'Cournot-effect-theory', which means that the profit-maximising price for two complementary products is lower if these are offered by one instead of two firms.[805]

4.6.2.1.2 The Judgment

This reasoning was partly flawed since the jet engines were produced jointly by GE and SNECMA. SNECMA had no stake in the manufacturing of the avionics and non-avionics products. Price reductions that lead to higher sales for avionics and non-avionics would not benefit SNECMA. Therefore, GE would need to compensate SNECMA for the price reductions or rather bear the full costs of the discounts. Such an action would reduce the profitability of this strategy for GE considerably. Therefore, the real likelihood of such a strategy was debatable.

Another major issue in this case is that the Commission did not examine demand side reactions to such product offers. The Court of First Instance argued that the Commission assumed a competitive threat through bundled offers without examining if the reaction of the demand side would lead in fact to such a foreclosure effect. This error was aggravated by the fact that the Commission stated several times during the investigation that an empirical survey would be necessary to substantiate such a theory. Such an empirical survey of the demand side reactions was never carried out in this case and the Court of First Instance therefore criticised this inaccuracy:

> In the absence of a detailed economic analysis applying the Cournot effect theory to the particular circumstances of the present case, it cannot be concluded from the Commission's brief mention of that theory in the contested decision that the merged entity would have been likely to engage in mixed bundling after merger.[806]

Thus, according to the Court a mere discussion of economic models does not suffice. The Court made clear that the application of these models to reality must go along with appropriate empirical studies. Convincing conclusions can only be drawn, if the applicability of theories to a specific case is given: *'The Commission could produce convincing evidence ... by relying on the Cournot effect only if it demonstrated its applicability to this specific case.'*[807]

---

805. The reason for this is that a price reduction for one good increases the demand for both goods since they are complementary. However, increase in demand for the second good is not taken into account, if the goods are produced by separate firms.
806. (CFI, General Electric Company v. Commission, Case T-210/01 2005, para. 462).
807. (CFI, General Electric Company v. Commission, Case T-210/01 2005, para. 462).

4.6.2.2 Schneider/Legrand

Schneider Electric SA (Schneider) and Legrand SA (Legrand) are two large French industrial groups. Schneider notified its proposed acquisition of Legrand to the Commission. The Commission prohibited the merger.[808] The markets that caused most concern were the markets for electrical switchboards, where the merged parties had combined market shares of 40%–70% in a number of countries, and the market for wiring accessories, with combined market shares in certain countries up to 90%. Although the Commission found that France was likely to be the country with the most severe competition issues, concerns were also raised in Denmark, Spain, Greece, Italy, Portugal and the UK.

4.6.2.2.1 Theory of Harm/Competition Concerns

The Commission claimed that the relevant markets were national because of differing standards and prices. Despite defining national markets, the Commission looked at the merged group's position across the EU as a whole and argued that the merged entity's range of products and wide geographic presence buttressed dominance in any single national market.

Another area of debate in this case was how to treat the sales of components used within vertically integrated channels. Three major competitors to Schneider and Legrand have vertically integrated retail arms that sell direct to end users. Schneider and Legrand do not. Thus for example, all Schneider and Legrand's circuit breakers are sold in wholesale markets. On the other hand, some circuit breakers manufactured by a competitor bypass this wholesale market, as they are directly installed by the retail arm at the end customer's location. The Commission argued that vertically integrated channel sales to end users are not 'sold' in the wholesale market where Schneider and Legrand operate, and therefore would not constrain the 'market power' of the merged entity.

The role of distributors was also important in this case. Essentially, the Commission argued that the merged entity would have an 'unassailable' position *vis-à-vis* distributors who would then favour the merged entity's products over those of other competitors. Regardless of the size or number of distributors in a market, these distributors would have no power or interest in resisting price increases by the merged entity despite vast differences in the structure of distribution across the seven countries in question. In some countries, such as Spain and Italy, hundreds of distributors exist and the top ten have a small fraction of sales. In other countries, such as France or Portugal, distribution is much more concentrated.

---

808. (Decision M-2283 on Schneider v. Legrand 2001, para. 99).

Chapter 4: Competition Practice

4.6.2.2.2 The Judgment

In its judgment, the Court of First Instance accepted in principle the Commission's analysis as to whether the operation leads to the creation or strengthening of a dominant position in the relevant national product markets, and that the Commission could take into consideration transnational effects,[809] i.e., effects resulting from the presence of the combined entity across Europe. On the facts however, the Court found that the Commission merely added the positions held by the merging parties on the various national product markets without really reviewing these positions in detail and had extrapolated certain characteristics from certain national product markets (in particular the French market). According to the Court, the Commission failed to demonstrate the relevance of these elements in its analysis of the competitive situation in the different national product markets under investigation. The Court found that the Commission was wrong to draw inferences from Schneider's position at an EU level for the various national markets.

The Court held that the Commission's analysis was insufficiently clear and lacked country-specific analysis on the detailed workings of individual countries' distribution networks. The Commission did not provide detailed country specific data; instead it relied on sweeping across-country statements. The Court called this type of analysis 'abstract and detached'. Hence, in future the Commission will be required to provide detailed country-by-country analyses. Thus, the generalisations and the specific local examples relied upon by the Commission were not supported by the facts. On the basis of very detailed and critical analysis of the contested parts of the Commission's reasoning, the Court stated that it was not convinced by the Commissions case. The Court concluded that in future, *a detailed case-by-case and market-by-market analysis* by the Commission is required to determine whether the terms 'portfolio' or 'captive' make sense in the particular circumstances of each product and geographic market.

4.6.2.3 Tetra Laval/Sidel

The case originated from the Commission's prohibition in 2001 of the merger between Tetra Laval, which, according to the Commission, had a dominant position in carton drinks packaging, and Sidel, a market leader in the production of machines used for making PET plastic bottles.[810]

4.6.2.3.1 Theory of Harm/Competition Concerns

The Commission concluded that the merger would have resulted in anti-competitive 'conglomerate effects'. In particular, although Tetra Laval and Sidel did not previously have a competitive relationship, either as direct competitors or through a vertical relationship, the Commission believed that the combination of the parties' businesses

---

809. (CFI, Schneider Electric SA v. Commission, Case T-310/01 2002, para. 171).
810. (Decision M-2416 on Tetra Lava v. Sidel 2001, para. 452).

in potentially converging areas would encourage Tetra Laval to leverage its existing market power to persuade its customers to choose Sidel's PET bottling machines in future.[811]

The Commission's *leveraging theory* was the most significant aspect of the decision. The Commission's approach was as follows: currently packagers of juice, milk and other 'sensitive' products primarily use carton. With advances in technology, they will increasingly be adding PET to their product offerings. Thus, the Commission assumed that in the future a substantial customer overlap might be possible. The supposition is that Tetra Laval will offer juice and milk packagers a good deal on future carton purchases if they agree to buy SBM machines from Sidel. The claim was that this would shift demand from rival SBM producers. Under the Commission's theory, the payoff to Tetra/Sidel post-merger would be reduced competition in the supply of SBM machines to the sensitive segment. By marginalising rivals, Tetra would be able to enjoy higher prices in this sector in the long run:

> *Leveraging is possible not only when the products in question are complements in the economic sense of the term, but also when they are commercial complements, that is to say, when the products are used by the same group of customers. This is so when, for example, as in the present case, the products in question are related and belong to closely neighbouring markets.*[812]

For its concern to have much plausibility the Commission needed to find that sales of SBM machines to packagers in the sensitive segment constituted a distinct market, separate from sales to other end uses such as carbonated soft drinks and water. Tetra Laval contended that even if it could discriminate by end use on the demand side (which it denied) it still could not exploit any market power even with 100% of the sensitive segment. This is because on the supply-side little, if any, extra investment or technology was needed to serve the sensitive segment. Any rival serving carbonated soft drink and water users (which are and will remain the major uses of PET) could equally well serve the sensitive segment.[813] Hence, any attempt to marginalise or foreclose competitors by shifting demand in the sensitive segments could not be profitable.

4.6.2.3.2 The Judgment

The Court did not accept that the Commission had demonstrated significant or growing competition between carton and PET. As a result, it rejected the potential competition argument.

The Court held also that the factual evidence was against the Commission's approach in the decision, which on this point had contained no relevant evidence.

---

811. (CFI, Tetra Laval BV v. Commission, Case T-5/02 2002, para. 336).
812. (CFI, Tetra Laval BV v. Commission, Case T-5/02 2002, para. 169).
813. Demand conditions and the degree of competition in the market for SBM machines were also relevant factors for the assessment of leveraging.

Chapter 4: Competition Practice

Special investments are needed, if at all, only in filling machines (in which Sidel is not a major player) not in SBM machines, which are generic across segments and interoperate with all filling equipment.

The Court's approach confirms that leverage theories can have a role to play in merger cases. The economics of leveraging focuses on the motivation that a firm has to extend its monopoly power in one market to an adjacent market. In principle it could accomplish this in several ways such as bundling products together through price discounts or through technological ties. But the fact that a firm has an ability to leverage does not mean it will have the incentive to do so.

The Tetra Laval/Sidel judgment recognises that most conglomerate mergers are neutral or pro-competitive and requires the Commission to produce convincing proof of anti-competitive effects before it can block a merger.[814]

4.6.2.4 Impala

The Court of Justice of the EU has qualified economic analyses performed by the Commission in merger proceedings several times as 'flawed'. However, the ruling of the Court of First Instance in the *Impala* judgment[815] is remarkable in this respect.

The interesting issue is that the Court annulled for the first time a merger approval and ruled in favour of Impala, an independent music label that had brought this case to the Court. The issue at hand was the question of whether the merger between Sony and BMG would lead to the creation of a collective dominant position on the market for recorded music.[816]

The Court in its judgment criticised as insufficient the line of argument and claimed that the Commission needed to apply detailed econometric analyses to support its conclusions.[817]

This judgment is of particular interest because the Court itself developed the required economic standard of proof to assess a collective dominant position. Other judgments discussed the collective dominance concept in theory. In the Impala judgment, the Court clarified which economic tools are mandatory to assess the effects. This means that in fact the Court itself specified the actual implementation of the 'more economics based approach' thereby providing legal certainty as required by many lawyers. The requirement of the Court is that:

> a delicate prognosis as regards the probable development of the market and of the conditions of competition on the basis of a prospective analysis, which entails complex economic assessments ...supported by a concrete analysis of the situation existing at the time of adoption of the decision.

The Court stated – consistent with game theory findings – that collusion is only possible if it is based on sufficient transparency, a deterrent mechanism, and low

---

814. (Decision M-2416 on Tetra Lava v. Sidel 2001, para. 327).
815. (CFI, Impala v. Commission, Case T-464/04 2006, para. 76).
816. (Decision COMP/M.3333 on SONY/BMG 2004, paras 60–154).
817. (CFI, Impala v. Commission, Case T-464/04 2006, para. 327).

potential competition. However, the Court made clear that the Commission failed again in applying economic theory correctly to a real-world case. According to the Court, it is not sufficient to describe the appropriate economic theory and assume that the prerequisites in a certain case are fulfilled. What is necessary is to investigate thoroughly if the preconditions are fully met. According to the Court, it is the task of the Commission to apply theories to market realities and perform complex economic assessments.[818]

4.6.2.5 Ryanair

In 2006, the Irish government privatised the flag-carrying airline Aer Lingus retaining 25.35% of the share capital. Ryanair, an Irish low cost carrier acquired 19.16% of Aer Lingus's issued share capital on the open market during this privatisation. On 5 October 2006 Ryanair launched a public bid for the company. During the course of the public bid, Ryanair increased its shareholding to 25.17%.

The Commission's decision is based on a detailed economic analysis of the merger. Whereas in the past the Commission was criticised for poor reasoning and for a failure to adopt modern sophisticated analytical tools, in this case the Commission has undertaken a detailed analysis. It appears that the decision is based largely on quantitative rather than qualitative analysis.[819]

4.6.2.5.1 Theory of Harm/Competition Concerns

The Commission considered that the implementation of the concentration would significantly impede effective competition, in particular as a result of the creation of a dominant position on thirty-five routes to and from Dublin, Shannon and Cork, and second, of the creation or strengthening of a dominant position on fifteen routes to and from Dublin and Cork. The effect would, the Commission felt, have been to reduce choice for consumers, leaving them exposed to a high risk of price increases.[820] The results of the Commission's fixed-effects regressions on Aer Lingus prices indicate consistently that Ryanair exerts a competitive constraint on Aer Lingus' prices.[821] The Commission opposed the transaction on the following grounds: very high market shares on a large number of routes, elimination of competition between the closest competitors on Irish routes, high barriers to entry to the affected markets and competitors were not likely to replace the loss of competition.[822]

---

818. (CFI, Impala v. Commission, Case T-464/04 2006, para. 250).
819. (P. Massey 2008, 13).
820. (Koch 2010, 41).
821. (De la Mano, Pesaresi and Stehman 2007, 78).
822. (Gadas, et al. 2007, 69-70).

4.6.2.5.2 The Judgment

The Commission's econometric analysis was contested by the parties. The price regression analysis was carried out in order to enable the Commission to test and assess the econometric observations submitted by Ryanair and Aer Lingus, and to evaluate what the likely impact of each of them on the other's fares might be.

The Court agreed with the Commission that the analysis confirmed and complemented the conclusions derived from the qualitative evidence, namely that Ryanair and Aer Lingus are close competitors. It stated that those results were also in line with the opinion of the majority of the people surveyed during the customer survey, from which it is apparent that the parties to the concentration are 'closest competitors' where other airlines operate on the route. Consequently, the Commission did not exceed the limits of the discretion in relation to economic matters that it enjoys under the case law.

The Court confirmed as well that efficiencies are relevant to the competitive assessment when they are a direct consequence of the notified concentration and cannot be achieved to a similar extent by less anti-competitive alternatives.

As regards consumer benefit, the Court stated that the relevant benchmark in assessing efficiency claims is that consumers will not be worse off as a result of the merger. For that purpose, efficiencies should be substantial and timely, and should, in principle, benefit consumers in those relevant markets where it is otherwise likely that competition concerns would occur. The incentive on the part of the merged entity to pass efficiency gains on to consumers is often related to the existence of competitive pressure from the remaining firms in the market and from potential entry. The greater the possible negative effects on competition, the more the Commission has to be sure that the claimed efficiencies are substantial, likely to be realised, and to be passed on, to a sufficient degree, to the consumer. As regards that point, the Commission's Guidelines state that it is highly unlikely that a merger leading to a market position approaching that of a monopoly, or leading to a similar level of market power, can be declared compatible with the common market on the grounds that efficiency gains would be sufficient to counteract its potential anti-competitive effects.

Ryanair did not dispute the assessment that any efficiencies are unlikely to be passed on to consumers in view of the very high market shares of the merged entity on most overlap routes. Therefore, even if Ryanair's claim that all cost savings are used to lower fares further in order to drive higher volumes were to be established, Ryanair's actual priority is still probably that of maximising profit. *'On markets where all competition is eliminated as a result of the merger, it is likely to be much more profitable not to pass on to consumers the claimed reduction in Aer Lingus's fixed costs.'*[823]

The Court of First Instance followed regarding the efficiency arguments the Commissions' guidelines. The Court of First Instance stated that those dominant positions that are monopolistic, quasi monopolistic or very significant are sufficient, in themselves, to validate the finding that the implementation of the merger should be

---

823. (ECJ, Ryanair v. Commission, Case T-342/07 2010, para. 441).

declared incompatible with the common market. If a merged undertaking does not have a dominant position, efficiency gains may outweigh the harm to competition on the condition that the benefits reach the consumers.[824]

4.6.3 EU Merger Guidelines

Based on the case law discussed in the previous section and some academic work commissioned by DG Competition, the Commission published two guidelines on merger assessments. These guidelines address selected economic topics in (1) horizontal and (2) non-horizontal mergers.

4.6.3.1 *Horizontal Merger Guidelines*

4.6.3.1.1 *Purpose of the Guidelines*

The Commission published in due course the ECMR guidelines on the appraisal of mergers between competing firms. These guidelines are known as the Horizontal Guidelines.[825] The guidelines comprehensively set out for the first time the analytical approach the Commission takes when assessing the competitive impact of mergers between competing firms.

The Commission states that there are two main ways in which horizontal mergers may significantly impede effective competition by creating or strengthening a dominant position:

- by eliminating important competitive constraints on one or more firms, which consequently would have increased market power, without resorting to coordinated behaviour (*non-coordinated or unilateral effects*);
- by changing the nature of competition in such a way that firms that previously were not coordinating their behaviour, are now significantly more likely to coordinate and raise prices or otherwise harm effective competition. A merger may also make coordination easier, more stable or more effective for firms that were coordinating their behaviour prior to the merger (*coordinated effects*).

The guidelines make clear that mergers and acquisitions will be challenged by the Commission only if they enhance the market power of companies in a manner which is likely to have adverse consequences for consumers, notably in the form of higher prices, poorer quality products, or reduced choice. The guidelines complement the wording of Article 2 of the ECMR with respect to the substantive test that underpins merger reviews, the SIEC-test. They explain in particular that mergers may result in harm to competition either because the concentration eliminates a competitor from the

---

824. (Szilágyi 2011, 9).
825. (Commission Guidelines on horizontal mergers 2004).

Chapter 4: Competition Practice

market, thereby removing an important competitive constraint, or because it makes coordination between the remaining firms more likely.[826]

The guidelines also provide clear indications as to when it will be unlikely for the Commission to intervene. Intervention will be unlikely when the merger does not result in market concentration levels exceeding certain specified levels, as measured by the firms' 'market share' or by the so-called 'HHI Index'. The HHI or Herfindahl-Hirschman Index is a recognised measure of market concentration. The HHI is obtained by summing the squares of the market shares of all the companies in the market, including the merging parties. It is unlikely that the Commission will identify horizontal competition concerns in a market with a post-merger HHI below 1.000 or with a post-merger HHI between 1.000 and 2.000 and a delta below 250, or a merger with a post-merger HHI above 2.000 and a delta below 150, except where special circumstances are present.

The guidelines also discuss, among other issues, how the Commission will apply the notion of dominance in oligopolistic markets. They also deal with particular factors that could mitigate an initial finding of likely harm to competition – factors such as buyer power, ease of market entry, the fact that the merger may be the only alternative to the demise of the firm being acquired, and efficiencies. Those factors will be discussed in the following sections.

4.6.3.1.2 Market Entry

Market entry is an aspect that needs a careful and thorough assessment. The parties to a transaction are already required in Form CO to submit answers to questions. For example, whether there has been any significant entry into any affected markets over the previous five years and if the answer is positive, information on these entrants, estimating their current market shares. Another question that needs to be addressed in Form CO is whether there are undertakings (including those at present operating only in extra-Community or extra EEA-markets) that are likely to enter the market. If the answer is 'yes,' an explanation as to why and information on these potential entrants needs to be provided. Furthermore, the undertakings are asked for an estimation of the time within which an entry is likely to occur.[827] There are various factors influencing market entry. They need to be provided in Chapter 8 of Form CO. The undertakings have to take into consideration the following where appropriate:

- the total costs of entry (R&D, establishing distribution systems, promotion, advertising, servicing etc.) on a scale equivalent to a significant viable competitor, indicating the market share of such a competitor;
- any legal or regulatory entry barriers, such as government authorisation or standard setting in any form;

---

826. (Commission adopts merger control guidelines 2003).
827. Sections 8.7. and 8.9. of Form CO.

- any restrictions created by the existence of patents, know-how and other IPR in these markets and any restrictions by licensing such rights;
- the extent to which each of the parties to the concentration are licensees or licensors of patents, know-how and other rights in the relevant markets;
- the importance of economies of scale for the production of products in the affected markets;
- access to sources of supply, such as the availability of raw materials.

The analysis of entry barriers is widely accepted as crucial for the understanding of competitive forces, and forms a convenient link between considerations of market structure and day-to-day competitive conduct. Following the contributions of *Baumol* and others[828] in developing the theory of contestable markets it could be argued that market shares are irrelevant and that entry conditions alone determine the degree of competition. Nevertheless, in any reasonable analysis market shares are relevant to the assessment of competition, but provide only a partial guide to market power. The easier it is to enter a market, the less concerns there should be for concentrations, which create high market shares.

The horizontal guidelines address market entry in a comprehensive way. When entering a market is sufficiently easy, a merger is unlikely to pose any significant anti-competitive risk. For entry to be considered a sufficient competitive constraint on the merging parties, it must be shown that entry is likely, timely and sufficient to deter or defeat any potential anti-competitive effects of the merger.[829]

4.6.3.1.2.1   Likelihood of Entry

The Commission examines whether entry is likely or whether potential entry is likely to constrain the behaviour of incumbents post-merger. For entry to be likely, it must be sufficiently profitable taking into account of the price effects of injecting additional output into the market and the potential responses of the incumbents. Entry is thus less likely if it would only be economically viable on a large-scale, thereby resulting in significantly depressed price levels. Additionally, entry is likely to be more difficult if the incumbents are able to protect their market shares by offering long-term contracts or giving targeted pre-emptive price reductions to those customers that the entrant is trying to acquire. Furthermore, high risk and costs of failed entry may make entry less likely. The costs of failed entry will be higher; the higher the level of sunk cost is associated with entry.

Potential entrants may encounter barriers to entry that determine entry risks and costs and thus have an impact on the profitability of entry. Barriers to entry are specific features of the market, which give incumbent firms advantages over potential competitors. When entry barriers are low, the merging parties are more likely to be constrained by entry. Conversely, when entry barriers are high, price increases by the

---

828. (Baumol, Panzar and Willig 1982).
829. (Commission Guidelines on horizontal mergers 2004, paras 68–75).

merging firms would not be significantly constrained by entry. Historical examples of entry and exit in the industry may provide useful information about the size of entry barriers.

Barriers to entry can take various forms:

- Legal advantages encompass situations where regulatory barriers limit the number of market participants by, for example, restricting the number of licences. They also cover tariff and non-tariff trade barriers.
- The incumbents may also enjoy technical advantages, such as preferential access to essential facilities, natural resources, innovation and R&D, or IPR, which make it difficult for any firm to compete successfully. For instance, in certain industries, it might be difficult to obtain essential input materials, or patents might protect products or processes.

Other factors such as economies of scale and scope, distribution and sales networks, access to important technologies, may also constitute barriers to entry. Furthermore, barriers to entry may also exist because of the established position of the incumbent firms on the market or it may be difficult to enter a particular industry because experience or reputation is necessary to compete effectively, both of which may be difficult to obtain as an entrant. Factors such as consumer loyalty to a particular brand, the closeness of relationships between suppliers and customers, the importance of promotion or advertising, or other advantages relating to reputation will be taken into account in this context. Barriers to entry also encompass situations where the incumbents have already committed to building large excess capacity, or where the costs faced by customers in switching to a new supplier may inhibit entry.

The expected evolution of the market should be taken into account when assessing whether or not entry would be profitable. Entry is more likely to be profitable in a market that is expected to experience high growth in the future than in a market that is mature or expected to decline. Scale economies or network effects may make entry unprofitable unless the entrant can obtain a sufficiently large market share.

Entry is particularly likely if suppliers in other markets already possess production facilities that could be used to enter the market in question, thus reducing the sunk costs of entry. The smaller the difference in profitability between entry and non-entry prior to the merger, the more likely such a reallocation of production facilities will be.

4.6.3.1.2.2 Timeliness

The Commission examines whether entry would be sufficiently swift and sustained to deter or defeat the exercise of market power. What constitutes an appropriate time period depends on the characteristics and dynamics of the market, as well as on the specific capabilities of potential entrants. However, entry is normally only considered timely if it occurs within two years.

4.6.3.1.2.3 Sufficiency

Entry must be of sufficient scope and magnitude to deter or defeat the anti-competitive effects of the merger. Small-scale entry, for instance into some market 'niche', may not be considered sufficient. Corporate reorganisations in the form of mergers may be in line with the requirements of dynamic competition and are capable of increasing the competitiveness of industry, thereby improving the conditions of growth and raising the standard of living in the Community. It is possible that efficiencies brought about by a merger counteract the effects on competition and in particular the potential harm to consumers that it might otherwise have. In order to assess whether a merger would significantly impede effective competition, through the creation or the strengthening of a dominant position, within the meaning of Article 2(2) and (3) of the Merger Regulation, the Commission performs an overall competitive appraisal of the merger. In making this appraisal, the Commission takes into account the factors mentioned in Article 2(1), including the development of technical and economic progress provided that it is to the consumers' advantage and does not form an obstacle to competition. The Commission considers any substantiated efficiency claim in the overall assessment of the merger. It may decide that, as a consequence of the efficiencies that the merger brings about, there are no grounds for declaring the merger incompatible with the common market pursuant to Article 2(3) of the Merger Regulation. This will be the case when the Commission is in a position to conclude on the basis of sufficient evidence that the efficiencies generated by the merger are likely to enhance the ability and incentive of the merged entity to act pro-competitively for the benefit of consumers, thereby counteracting the adverse effects on competition that the merger might otherwise have caused.

4.6.3.1.3 Efficiency

For the Commission to take account of efficiency claims in its assessment of the merger and be in a position to reach the conclusion that as a consequence of efficiencies there are no grounds for declaring the merger to be incompatible with the common market, the efficiencies have to benefit consumers, be merger-specific and be verifiable. These conditions are cumulative.

4.6.3.1.3.1 Benefit to Consumers

The relevant benchmark in assessing efficiency claims is that consumers will not be worse off as a result of the merger. For that purpose, efficiencies should be substantial and timely, and should, in principle, benefit consumers in those relevant markets where it is otherwise likely that competition concerns would occur.

Mergers may bring about various types of efficiency gains that can lead to lower prices or other benefits to consumers. For example, cost savings in production or distribution may give the merged entity the ability and incentive to charge lower prices following the merger. In line with the need to ascertain whether efficiencies will lead to a net benefit to consumers, cost efficiencies that lead to reductions in variable or marginal costs are more likely to be relevant to the assessment of efficiencies than reductions in fixed costs; the former are, in principle, more likely to result in lower prices for consumers. Cost reductions, which merely result from anti-competitive reductions in output, cannot be considered as efficiencies benefiting consumers.

Consumers may also benefit from new or improved products or services, for instance resulting from efficiency gains in the sphere of R&D and innovation. A joint venture company set up in order to develop a new product may bring about the type of efficiencies that the Commission can take into account.

In the context of coordinated effects, efficiencies may increase the merged entity's incentive to increase production and reduce prices, and thereby reduce its incentive to coordinate its market behaviour with other firms in the market. Efficiencies may therefore lead to a lower risk of coordinated effects in the relevant market.

In general, the later the efficiencies are expected to materialise in the future, the less weight the Commission can assign to them. This implies that, in order to be considered as a counteracting factor, the efficiencies must be timely. The incentive on the part of the merged entity to pass efficiency gains on to consumers is often related to the existence of competitive pressure from the remaining firms in the market and from potential entry. The greater the possible negative effects on competition, the more the Commission has to make sure that the claimed efficiencies are substantial, likely to be realised, and to be passed on to a sufficient degree, to the consumer. It is highly unlikely that a merger leading to a market position approaching that of a monopoly, or leading to a similar level of market power, can be declared compatible with the common market on the grounds that efficiency gains would be sufficient to counteract its potential anti-competitive effects.

4.6.3.1.3.2 Merger Specificity

Efficiencies are relevant to the competitive assessment when they are a direct consequence of the notified merger and cannot be achieved to a similar extent by less anti-competitive alternatives. In these circumstances, the efficiencies are deemed to be caused by the merger and thus are merger-specific. It is for the merging parties to provide in due time all the relevant information necessary to demonstrate that there are no less anti-competitive, realistic and attainable alternatives of a non-concentrative nature (e.g., a licensing agreement, or a cooperative joint venture) or of a concentrative nature (e.g., a concentrative joint venture, or a differently structured merger) than the notified merger which preserve the claimed efficiencies. The Commission only considers alternatives that are reasonably practical in the business situation faced by the merging parties having regard to established business practices in the industry concerned.

4.6.3.1.3.3 Verifiability

Efficiencies have to be verifiable such that the Commission can be reasonably certain that the efficiencies are likely to materialise, and be substantial enough to counteract a merger's potential harm to consumers. The more precise and convincing the efficiency claims are, the better the Commission can evaluate the claims. Where reasonably possible, efficiencies and the resulting benefit to consumers should therefore be quantified. When the necessary data are not available to allow for a precise quantitative analysis, it must be possible to foresee a clearly identifiable positive impact on consumers, not a marginal one. In general, the longer the start of the efficiencies is projected into the future, the less probable the Commission may be able to assign the efficiencies to the merger.

Most of the information that allows the Commission to assess whether the merger will bring about the sort of efficiencies that would enable it to clear a merger is solely in the possession of the merging parties. It is, therefore, the incumbent's task to provide in due time all the relevant information necessary to demonstrate that the claimed efficiencies are merger-specific and likely to be realised. Furthermore the notifying parties must demonstrate to what extent the efficiencies are likely to counteract any adverse effects on competition that might otherwise result from the merger, and therefore benefit consumers.

Evidence relevant to the assessment of efficiency claims includes internal documents that were used by management to decide on the merger, statements from the management to the owners and financial markets about the expected efficiencies, historical examples of efficiencies and consumer benefit, and pre-merger external experts' studies on the type and size of efficiency gains, and on the extent to which consumers are likely to benefit.

4.6.3.2 Non-Horizontal Merger Guidelines

The Commission adopted Guidelines for the assessment of mergers between companies that are in a so-called vertical or conglomerate relationship (also known as 'non-horizontal mergers'). The Guidelines intend to provide guidance to companies as to how the Commission will analyse the impact of such mergers on competition. During the preparation of the guidelines Professor Church performed an extensive literature review on the impact of vertical and conglomerate mergers on competition, the so-called Church-Report.[830]

4.6.3.2.1 Purpose of the Guidelines

The non-horizontal Merger Guidelines complement the existing Guidelines on horizontal mergers, which deal with mergers of companies who compete on the same markets. Non-horizontal mergers are aimed at broadening a company's activities either

---

830. (Church 2004).

by merging with a company at another level of the supply chain (vertical merger) or with a company active in a related market (conglomerate merger). Horizontal mergers – i.e., those between competitors on a particular market – can lead to a loss of direct competition between the merging firms. By contrast, vertical and conglomerate mergers do not immediately change the number of competitors active in any given market. As a result, the main potential source of anti-competitive effects in horizontal mergers is absent from vertical and conglomerate mergers. They are thus generally less likely to create competition concerns than horizontal mergers. In addition, vertical and conglomerate mergers may also improve a company's efficiency by better coordinating their different production stages.

While horizontal mergers may eliminate competition between the merging parties by increasing the scope of collusion or give rise to a SIEC, vertical mergers are less likely to produce negative economic effects. In fact, vertical mergers might even have some positive impacts on consumer welfare. In particular, it is generally accepted in economic theory that vertical mergers might eliminate the double marginalisation problem and opportunistic behaviour. Other positive results might be lower transaction costs, increasing efficiencies in input choices and other static and dynamic efficiencies.

The Guidelines by providing examples, based on established economic principles, of where vertical and conglomerate mergers may significantly impede effective competition in the markets concerned, represent the state-of-the art of the established economic literature in the field. For instance, they outline the circumstances under which a vertical merger could be likely to result in competing companies being denied access to an important supplier or facing increased prices for their inputs and thus ultimately lead to higher prices for consumers. The Guidelines also indicate levels of market share and concentration below which the Commission is unlikely to identify competition concerns (so-called 'safe harbours'). Competition concerns are less likely with non-horizontal mergers, when the post-merger market share of the new entity in each of the markets concerned is below 30%. In the following some important statements in the guidelines are reviewed.

The Commission explicitly emphasises in its guidelines the consideration of *efficiencies*. This progress is in line with economic literature and is widely accepted in the field of competition economics. Vertical mergers can give rise to considerable efficiencies and may enhance consumer welfare (e.g., because of the elimination of double marginalisation or a decrease in transaction costs). Efficiencies could outweigh the anti-competitive effects of non-horizontal mergers.

As with horizontal mergers there are two main ways in which non-horizontal mergers may significantly impede effective competition: non-coordinated effects and coordinated effects:

- *Non-coordinated effects* may arise when non-horizontal mergers give rise to foreclosure: the merger may grant the merging firms the ability to foreclose rival firms' access to supplies or markets. Two modes of foreclosure can be distinguished: 'input foreclosure' and 'customer foreclosure'. 'Input foreclosure' may arise, for example, if a paper producer with market power merges

with a printing plant and – after the merger – rival printing plants can purchase paper only on poor conditions, at higher prices or not at all. The 'new' rivals would need to purchase the paper somewhere at higher prices and would not be able to sell their products (e.g., books) at competitive prices. This would in turn allow the merged entity to raise their prices to the detriment of the customers.
- *Coordinated effects* arise where the merger alters the nature of competition in such a way that firms that were not coordinating their behaviour before the merger might change their view: coordination might be more likely, prices might increase or effective competition might be harmed in another way. Both conglomerate and vertical mergers can facilitate anti-competitive concerted practices. Thus, depending on the market circumstances coordination is easier to achieve when the number of market participants is reduced (e.g., due to the foreclosure of competitors).

4.6.3.2.2 Analysis of Tying and Bundling

4.6.3.2.2.1 Economic Theory on Tying and Bundling

Economic theory on tying and bundling has evolved over the years. Historically, liberal scholars like *Bork* and *Posner* have claimed that tying and bundling could hardly have any anti-competitive effects at all: tying and bundling is typically beneficial or associated with price discrimination.[831] This hypothesis is based on the so-called 'single profit theorem'. According to this theorem, there is only one monopoly profit. Therefore, a monopolist cannot increase his profits by leveraging his monopoly power into a competitive downstream market. In general, the problem with the single profit theorem is that the model is not robust if assumptions are changed. For example, if fixed costs are introduced bundling may be a profit-maximising strategy for the monopolist.[832] According to *Nalebuff*, monopoly leveraging might also be profitable, if the assumption that goods are consumed in fixed proportions is relaxed. On the other hand criticism of the single profit theorem applied to complements holds that – when consumers have homogenous preferences – a monopoly supplier of one complement can extract all of the monopoly profit through the price of his product. Plus he does not need to monopolise competitively supplied complements by tying or bundling. Thus, relaxing the assumptions changes the single profit result and may provide in some cases an incentive for vertical or conglomerate integration based on market power. Today, economic theory offers a more thorough picture of possible incentives and effects of tying and bundling. It is well understood that tying and bundling can serve many purposes, both pro-competitive and anti-competitive. There are possible efficiency-enhancing effects of bundling including cost saving, improvement of quality, and reduction of pricing inefficiencies. Also, bundling and tying is often used as a price

---

831. (Bork 1978); (Posner 1976).
832. (Whinston 1990).

discrimination device. The creation of entry barriers, foreclosure effects or the exclusion of competitors can be possible anti-competitive effects of bundling.

4.6.3.2.2.2 Models as Practical Guidance?

The application of theoretical models is difficult. Either the welfare effects are ambiguous, or the results are halted – like 'the single profit theorem' – because of specific assumptions. Some of the theories are not robust at all. For example, a critical issue is the mode of competition applied in the respective model. *Carbajo* et al. show that in the case of Bertrand competition tying can serve as a means to differentiate products and reduce competition between rival firms leading to higher prices and higher profits.[833] Introducing Cournot competition into the same framework leads to a totally different result: the monopolist sets the prices of his products more aggressively. This results in lower prices, lower profits for the competitor and a mitigated result for the monopolist's profits. Since there is no general rule about which mode of competition describes markets adequately, limited practical conclusions can be drawn from the different theoretical models. Another critical issue is that most of the theoretical models assume a monopolistic market structure in at least one of the markets. In theory, tying or bundling a monopoly product reduces the demand for the competitor's single product. It may force the competitor to enter the market on two stages or it may create other competitive disadvantages. As pure monopolies hardly ever exist in reality, the practical relevance of these discussions is uncertain. Another discussion is that anti-competitive effects are created by the unequal competition between a firm that produces a bundle and a single product firm. However, in an oligopolistic market there is the possibility that non-integrated competitors cooperate and sell competing bundles too. According to *Nalebuff*, competition in bundles may have strong pro-competitive effects as it might lead to lower prices and increased consumer welfare.[834] However, in the following a list of criteria is presented to assess tying and bundling.

4.6.3.2.2.3 List of Assessment Criteria

(1) *Market position in the tying market*
If the tying market is competitive, the product tie cannot force consumers to buy the tied good as they can easily switch to competing products that are offered without a tie. Therefore, a necessary but not sufficient condition for competitive harm is market power in the tying market. The higher the market power the easier is it for the tying firm to impose the tie on its customers.

(2) *Market position in the tied market*
Monopoly leveraging can arise, even if the market position in the tied market is a very weak one since a tying-strategy can lever market power on this 'weaker' market. However, tying two products also bears the risk for the tying

---

833. (Carbajo, de Meza and Seidmann 1990).
834. (Nalebuff 2000).

firm of losing those customers who don't find the tied product very attractive and want to avoid it. This risk is higher if a firm ties an unattractive product with low market share. Monopoly power can be leveraged more easily on a market if the tied good already enjoys high popularity and remarkable market shares.

(3) *Entry barriers*
An assessment should be considered if bundling and tying force new competitors to enter several markets at the same time and thus raise market entry barriers and lower potential competition.

(4) *Complementarity of the products*
Another factor that has to be taken into account when assessing the potential harm of bundling is the complementarity of the products included. Only if consumers usually consume the tied or bundled goods together, can a bundle or tie have a significant anti-competitive effect.

(5) *Feasibility of counterstrategies*
In a merger analysis, the European Commission should always assess the feasibility of counterstrategies. Competitors might form competing bundles leading to lower consumer prices. Also, strong buyer power can prevent leveraging or foreclosure effects. Special attention should be paid to the effect of bundling on prices and the market share of competitors.

(6) *Variety bundles*
This kind of bundle provides consumers with a greater variety of products with no or only a small increase in price, e.g., software bundles, bundled pay-TV offers or combined tickets for skiing areas, theme parks, museums etc. Generally, these bundles have pro-competitive effects as they create a wider product variety at almost no extra cost thereby enhancing consumer welfare. Anti-competitive effects can only arise, if the attractiveness of this bundle is so outstanding that the other market participants are not able to form competing bundles and are consequently foreclosed. However, the analysis of potential anti-competitive effects has to be a thorough one as false convictions can prevent the potential positive effects.

(7) *Efficiency effects*
The guidelines take into account possible efficiency-enhancing effects of an alleged bundling. Cost reductions, quality improvements or efficient pricing might offset suspected anti-competitive effects.

(8) *Allow commitment of the companies*
If the Commission fears that tying or bundling might harm competition, companies post-merger should be given the possibility to commit themselves not to bundle or tie. If the market is transparent, the Commission can easily supervise such commitments enabling firms to realise merger-specific efficiencies and to reduce at the same time possible anti-competitive effects.

4.6.3.2.3 Analysis of Input and Customer Foreclosure

Under exceptional circumstances, vertical mergers may give rise to two types of foreclosure concerns. One necessary (but not sufficient) condition for foreclosure to occur is that the merging parties have considerable market power in one market stage. If the merging firm has market power on the upstream level input foreclosure might arise. Input foreclosure may create the incentive for the combined entity to foreclose its competitors on the downstream market. This might occur if the merged firm can raise rival's costs by increasing their input prices whereas the downstream entity of the firm still has access to the input at marginal costs, thus, gaining a competitive advantage. Input foreclosure also arises, if the merged firm stops supplying rivals of its downstream entity, denying completely the access to the input. Alternatively, downstream or customer foreclosure occurs where the downstream firm exclusively purchases inputs from the upstream divisions of the combined firms post-merger.

However, customer foreclosure is generally seen as less harmful than input foreclosure. Due to vertical integration, unintegrated upstream firms may have a smaller addressable market, which could make it difficult for them to cover their fixed costs. But the unintegrated firms' pricing is not likely to change and the integrated firms' prices might even be lower due to efficiencies. Only if the unintegrated rivals exit the market, might the merged firm be able to raise prices above competitive levels. But these effects result in the long-term only and are subject to speculation.

Moreover, rivals have enough time to discover alternative ways to reach the customers. On the other hand, input foreclosure leads to immediate price effects. The unintegrated firms face higher input costs and, thus, have to raise their prices. If the supply of an input is denied, unintegrated firms must find alternative sources that are probably more expensive. If they cannot find a substitute for the input they might even exit the market, which increases the market power of the remaining firms and probably leads to further price increases. Therefore, input foreclosure is likely to be more harmful than customer foreclosure.

The Commission developed a three-step-approach to analyse non-coordinated effects of non-horizontal mergers. In assessing the likelihood of anti-competitive 'input foreclosure' the Commission will examine three questions:

- First, whether the merged entity would have, post-merger, the ability to substantially foreclose access to inputs?
- Second, whether it would have the incentive to do so?
- Third, whether a foreclosure strategy would have a significant detrimental effect on competition?

In the first step, the ability of the merged entity to foreclose the market by considering all different modes of foreclosure like raising prices, restricting supplies or a subtler mode like degrading the quality of inputs supplied is analysed. In the second step, whether the merged entity has an incentive to foreclose access to inputs is assessed. This incentive depends on the degree to which foreclosure would be profitable. In addition, since the adoption of a specific course of conduct by the merged entity is an essential element in the assessment of foreclosure, the factors liable to reduce, or even eliminate, those incentives, are examined including the possibility that the conduct is unlawful under Article 102. In the third step, the effects on competition are analysed and anti-competitive and pro-competitive effects are balanced. Anti-competitive 'input foreclosure' for example, may occur when a vertical merger allows the merging parties to increase the costs of downstream rivals thereby leading to an upward pressure on their sales prices. The higher the proportion of the rivals who would be foreclosed on the downstream market, the more likely the merger can be expected to result in a significant price increase in the downstream market and thus significantly impede competition. Subsequently, efficiencies are considered. Efficiencies may outweigh anti-competitive effects, if the efficiencies generated by the merger are likely to enhance the ability and incentive of the merged entity to act pro-competitively for the benefit of consumers.

As a first step, an assessment of the market conditions and the identification of the market position of the firms involved is required. With respect to 'input foreclosure', the ability to foreclose depends on whether an important input of the downstream product is concerned, whether the input concerned represents a significant cost factor relative to the price of the downstream product and if there are alternatives sources for the input. The purchase alternatives are worse if the merged entity has a strong market position on the upstream market. Thus, for 'input foreclosure' to be a concern, the vertical merger must involve a company that has market power in the upstream market. This assessment requires an in-depth market structure analysis that contains, among other things, the following elements:

- definition of the relevant product and geographic markets.
- calculation of the market shares of the firms concerned.
- upstream and downstream markets.
- development of market shares over time.
- analysis of actual competitors.
- assessment of product characteristics and value chains.

If a sufficient number of downstream competitors would remain whose costs are not raised due to the merger because they are themselves vertically integrated or they are capable of switching to alternative inputs, competition from those firms may constitute a sufficient competitive constraint on the merged entity. Moreover, the assessments of potential competitors and of market entry barriers play an important role. Sufficient market entrants in the upstream market could, for example, render a foreclosure strategy ineffective because the downstream rivals can switch their supplier. Therefore, an analysis is required to investigate whether legal, structural or strategic entry barriers exist and which modes of market entry are likely.

Chapter 4: Competition Practice

4.6.3.2.3.1 Cost-Benefit-Analysis

By means of cost-benefit-analysis, profitability and thus the incentive for foreclosure strategies can be examined. The likelihood of foreclosure can be identified. In the following example, this method is described: if a vertically integrated paper producer forecloses the market against other printing plants on the downstream markets by refusing supply, the costs of such a strategy would be the lost upstream margin on wholesale sales. The benefits would in turn arise from the weakened downstream competition from rivals, who are no longer able to sell at competitive prices. Thus, the paper producer's own integrated printing plant could increase sales and profits. Essentially, the merged entity faces a trade-off between the profit lost in the upstream market due to a reduction of input sales to (actual or potential) rivals and the profit gain from expanding sales downstream or, as the case may be, being able to raise price in that market. The trade-off is likely to depend on the level of profits the merged entity obtains upstream and downstream. The lower the margins upstream, the smaller the loss from restricting input sales. Similarly, the higher the downstream margins, the higher the profit gains from increasing market share downstream at the expense of foreclosed rivals. With economic cost-benefit-analysis the concrete costs and benefits of a foreclosure strategy can be calculated. If costs exceed the benefits the implementation of a foreclosure strategy is not rational from an economics point of view. Thus it is possible to prove empirically, that a foreclosure strategy following non-horizontal mergers is a) likely or b) irrational and unlikely.

4.6.3.2.3.2 Game Theory

The appearance of market coordination can be analysed with the support of game theory: game theory and its requirements (agreement, monitoring, and punishment) suit the analysis of coordinated effects. After *Airtours/First Choice*[835], the Court of First Instance confirmed the application of game theory again and discussed the requirements of economic analysis in Sony/BMG. Game theory can answer the question about which market outcome is likely in an oligopoly by assessing three essential conditions: first, if the coordinating firms can monitor to a sufficient degree whether the terms of coordination are being adhered to; second, if there is a credible deterrent mechanism; third, the reactions of outsiders. Besides an analytical evaluation of the facts, econometric merger modelling is required to forecast the behaviour post-merger. Special merger simulation models that are adjusted to the game theory questions are suitable.
    The following aspects need to be evaluated:

- Ability of the upstream *firm to raise the input price to downstream rivals*
  The degree of market power in the upstream market is essential. If the upstream market is still sufficiently competitive and if downstream firms are able to easily substitute to alternative inputs, the likelihood that the upstream

---

835. (Decision COMP/M.1524 on Airtours/First Choice 1999).

firm is able to raise the input prices to downstream competitors is small. Thus, it should be evaluated if there are a sufficient number of upstream firms that have an incentive to continue to sell their products to independent downstream firms. If downstream firms already buy from various upstream suppliers switching costs might be comparatively low. If there is only a low degree of market power on the upstream market, it is not likely that the upstream firm will be able to raise the input prices and thus input foreclosure is not likely to occur.

- *Likelihood that an increase in the input price leads to an increase in the price charged to end consumers*
Without an increase in the output price by the downstream firms, the incentive to raise the input price in order to raise a rival's cost vanishes. Thus, to harm competition an increase in the input price charged by the integrated or merged firm to downstream customers must result in an increase in the price charged by downstream firms to their customers, as the higher profit downstream constitutes the benefit to a vertically integrated firm that engages in a strategy of input foreclosure. Thus, if the likelihood that an increase in the input price results in a price increase to the end-consumer is low, input foreclosure is not likely to occur either.

- *Increase in downstream profits must exceed the costs of the input foreclosure*
While implementing input foreclosure, costs in the form of a loss in upstream profits arise. These costs, which can be traced back to the decision of the integrated firm to forego sales for its product to downstream rivals have to be considered as well. Input foreclosure thus is only rational if the higher downstream profits are greater than the lower upstream profits. Thus, input foreclosure will not arise if the costs in the form of lower upstream profits are high.

- *Counterstrategies*
Counterstrategies refer to the possibility that downstream rivals countermerge an upstream rival to ensure competition. Thus for input foreclosure to be likely, counterstrategies must be impossible to adopt on the relevant market. If counterstrategies are feasible, input foreclosure is not likely to arise.

- *Potential Benefits*
Possible efficiency-enhancing effects must be taken into account as well. For example, the elimination of double marginalisation constitutes a possible efficiency of a vertical merger. More efficiencies could result because of reduced costs and increased productivity. It has to be taken into account, that the conditions that lead to efficiencies, at the same time, create the possibility for foreclosure. The positive competitive effects in terms of efficiencies can countervail the negative effects. Thus, a careful balancing act is required while analysing the effects of vertical mergers.

Chapter 4: Competition Practice

4.6.3.2.3.3 Assessment of Customer Foreclosure

Customer foreclosure is less likely to be harmful than input foreclosure. The following shows the criteria which need to be assessed:

- *Exercise of market power*
  The ability to exercise market power is essential in this respect. Due to the fact that anti-competitive customer foreclosure is only credible if both the upstream and downstream markets are conducive to the exercise of market power, in particular, the ability of the merged firm to control the access to the end users needs to be assessed. Thus, a careful analysis of the distribution channels and the ways products are sold into the downstream market is required. If there is no evidence of market power on the downstream level, customer foreclosure is not very likely to arise.
- *Switching Costs*
  The assessment should consider the switching costs faced by customers. Whether customers are locked in depends on a variety of factors, such as terms and duration of supply contracts and the possibility of renegotiation. In the case of low switching costs the likelihood of customer foreclosure is also low.
- *Benefits of vertical mergers*
  The merger analysis must consider potential efficiency gains. As has already been pointed out, the potential harm caused by customer foreclosure is less severe than that caused by input foreclosure. Therefore, it is far less likely that the potential competitive harm outweighs the benefits a vertical merger might generate. The positive competitive effects in terms of efficiencies can countervail the negative effects. Thus, a careful evaluation is required while analysing the effects of vertical mergers.

4.6.3.2.4 *Actual and Potential Competition*

The Commission takes account of potential, as well as actual competition, regardless of whether undertakings belong to the Community or not. Potential competition, though invisible and not measurable in terms of market share, reduces market power. An example of potential competition could be a firm operating in the same product line but operating in another geographic market than the incumbent or a customer who may be in a position to start supplying the market in question. Similarly, a producer of related or complementary products may be able to switch manufacturing capacity to producing the relevant product. Potential competition may therefore be removed by a merger with the potential competitor. The evaluation of such a merger will depend on the actual competitor's market position and on the potential competitor's proximity to the relevant market in terms of both geographic and product offerings. The greater the ability of the potential competitor to become an actual competitor within a relatively short period of time, the greater is the potential of the merger to reduce competition.

Another significant issue that has arisen in assessing the likely competitive impact of a proposed transaction is the determination of whether sufficient potential competition exists in a market to constrain the merged entity's exercise of market power. In such cases, the Commission examines whether market entry is probable, whether it would be competitively meaningful and effective, and whether it could take place within a time frame short enough to deter the parties from exploiting their market power.

In two cases in particular, the ability of potential competitors to thwart the exercise of market power was considered to be an important factor in granting clearance. In *SNECMA/TI*,[836] involving a world market for landing gear, the continuing emergence of potential competition arising from licensees and subcontractor-manufacturers was taken into account to clear the operation. In *Mannesmann/Vallourec/Ilva*,[837] the Commission found that sufficient potential competition existed in the relevant market (for seamless stainless steel tubes) to prevent anti-competitive price increases or other illegal parallel behaviour by the duopolists in the market. It determined that Japanese producers, who were already present in the market, could increase their imports if a price rise made such business attractive. It further found that East European producers, who have modern production facilities, would be in a position to obtain rapidly appropriate certification to supply Western European customers and to serve as an additional constraining factor against anti-competitive behaviour.

In *Ryanair/Aer Lingus III*[838], potential competition was an important parameter of competition amongst Ryanair and Aer Lingus due to the bases of both companies being at Irish airports and as evidenced of past entry events. In its analysis, the Commission considered the extent to which the disappearance of one carrier's very close, if not closest, competitor might eliminate potential competition that would have constrained Ryanair and Aer Lingus in the absence of the Transaction. In its decision, the Commission considered that as a consequence of the dynamic pattern of entry in competition with each other and the very limited impact of entry by other carriers on the Parties, Ryanair and Aer Lingus exert a potential competitive constraint on each other. The Commission therefore concluded that the Transaction was likely to significantly impede effective competition, in particular as a result of the creation or strengthening of a dominant position, by eliminating the most credible potential entrant on five routes on which Aer Lingus or Ryanair respectively exert a significant constraining influence and on which there is not a sufficient number of other potential competitor that could maintain sufficient competitive pressure on the merged entity post-Transaction.

---

836. (Decision IV/M.368 on SNECMA/TI 1994).
837. (Decision IV/M.315 on Mannesmann/Vallourec/Ilva 1994).
838. (Decision COMP/M.6663 on Ryanair/Aer Lingus III 2013).

Chapter 4: Competition Practice

In *Deutsche Börse/NYSE Euronext*[839] the Commission found that potential competition could have a significant constraining effect on an incumbent exchange, in particular when the other competitor already has a large margin pool of closely correlated derivatives contracts.

Conversely, the lack of adequate potential competition thereby preventing anti-competitive effects in the market place has been an important factor in the assessment of whether an operation would have created or strengthened a dominant position. In *P&G*,[840] the Commission determined that there were no potential competitors capable of restraining Procter & Gamble's dominance in the German sanitary pads markets under consideration within a two to three-year time frame. After conducting an exhaustive search for potential competitors, it concluded that Japanese producers were not likely to enter the market within two to three years, due to a lack of marketing experience and distribution networks in Europe. Moreover, existing suppliers in Europe were either already present in the German market, albeit on a very small (and declining) basis, or had previously tried and failed to enter the German market and were deemed unlikely to attempt entry again. Finally, major consumer products companies (such as Unilever, Nestle, and Philip Morris), who were considered as the next most likely candidates in the light of their expertise in marketing consumer products (and, in some cases, had already been in the feminine protection market approximately twenty years before) were not likely to enter within the next few years.

In another case, the party was able to overcome the Commission's competitive concerns by offering divestitures and commitments to license industrial and IPR. In *Kimberly-Clark/Scott Paper*,[841] after a five-month investigation, the Commission cleared the merger of two American paper companies, Kimberly-Clark and Scott. The Commission was concerned about high levels of concentration in three product markets: toilet tissue, kitchen towels, and facial hankies in the UK and Ireland. In each of the product markets, the parties had 40–60% of the relevant market. The Commission's competitive concerns were alleviated by the parties' commitment to divest a major UK production facility and to license for a ten-year period the use of Kimberly-Clark's *Kleenex* brand for the sale of toilet paper in the UK and Ireland. Furthermore, Scott must sell certain brands of napkins. The surviving Kimberly-Clark will become the number one tissue paper producer at both the world and European levels. However, the European market is not highly concentrated and Kimberly-Clark will have less than 20% of the relevant market after the merger. Thus, it is guaranteed that sufficient potential competition exists.

In *MSG Media Service*,[842] a concentration consisting of three German enterprises, namely Bertelsmann AG, Taurus, part of the Kirch group, and Deutsche Bundespost a developing future market was of particular interest, As was the issue of future potential competition.

---

839. (Decision COMP/M.6166 on Deutsche Börse / NYSE Euronext 2012).
840. (Decision IV/M.430 on Procter & Gamble/VP Schickedanz (II). 1994).
841. (Decision IV/M.623 on Kimberly-Clark/Scott 1996).
842. (Decision IV/M.469 on MSG Media Service 1994).

The German companies planned to set up a joint venture, MSG Media Service, to operate on the market in technical and administrative services for digital pay-TV operators. The Commission analysed the effects of the proposed merger on the three product markets, in the knowledge that, in each case, the relevant geographic market is Germany.

The first market is that for administrative and technical services for pay-TV operators and other suppliers of audio-visual services, a market that is likely to expand rapidly with the introduction of digital technology. These services consist principally in the provision of decoders, the development of a system of access control and subscriber management. On this new market, MSG would have had a lasting dominant position liable to restrict or prevent access by competitors owing to the strength of Deutsche Telekom in the field of cable networks and the exceptional film and programming resources of Bertelsmann and Kirch. Another interesting perspective can be derived from the second defined product market. The market was defined as the market for pay-TV, the supply of which is set to grow rapidly thanks to digitalisation. Bertelsmann and Kirch already have sufficient resources to give them a very strong position on this market. If MSG had had a lasting dominant position in the area of services provided to pay-TV suppliers, these enterprises could have been able to control and influence the access of their competitors to consumers and hence to hold a dominant position on the market for pay-TV.

The Commission assessed the creation of a dominant position in a developing, future market. The Commission made clear that in general a single provider in a potential future market, is not considered to be creating a dominant position. However, in this particular case, it can be expected that the single market supplier position is not a temporary one. The competitive advantage of being the first provider could be used to block the market entrance for future competitors.

This analysis was supported by the fact that the joint venture would eliminate potential competition between the two undertakings that are considered to be the most likely competitors on this market. Another reason to block the concentration was found in the fact that the third market to be defined was that for cabled network for the transmission of television, where Deutsche Telekom held a virtual monopoly. Because of the size of the German cable network (14 million subscribers), other forms of transmission do not and will not constitute an adequate alternative. MSG would have allowed Telekom to strengthen its dominant position on this market and this was a sensitive issue particularly in view of liberalisation after 1998.

Therefore, the Commission took the view that the proposed merger was liable to create or strengthen lasting dominant positions on three product markets and should therefore be considered incompatible with the common market and the proper operation of the EEA Agreement.

On the other hand, the existence of potential competition from firms not involved in the merger will be a factor in favour of allowing the merger to proceed. For example, a firm that appears at first glance to hold a dominant position in a geographic market that consists of only one Member State may in fact not be dominant if producers of the

Chapter 4: Competition Practice

same or similar products in nearby Member States could quickly commence sales operations in the alleged dominant firm's market. These potential competitors might so reduce the alleged firm's ability to abuse its local market position as to make its acquisition of a smaller rival unlikely to strengthen its largely illusory dominant position.

4.6.4 Collective Dominance

This section discusses an economic topic of particular relevance in merger proceedings: collective dominance is sometimes referred to as coordinated effects. First, the developments in the Commission's practice and the jurisprudence are discussed before elaborating on the Commission's guidelines.

4.6.4.1 Developments in the Case Law

The Commission applies the test as laid down in Article 2(3) of the ECMR in cases where the result of the concentration would be the creation of collective dominance.

In examining collective dominance and its effects, the Commission is conscious of the peculiarities of each sector and sticks to an analysis carried out without preconceptions and on a case-by-case basis. The Court of Justice of the EU has confirmed the Commission's approach. The ruling of the Court of Justice in *Compagnie Maritime Belge*[843] and the ruling of the Court of First Instance in *Gencor*[844] established that a finding of collective dominance was based on the existence of economic links or other factors which could give rise to a connection between the undertakings concerned.[845]

In assessing collective dominance, it is necessary to ascertain whether economic links exist between the undertakings concerned which enable them to act independently of their competitors, customers and consumers. As the Court stated in *Compagnie Maritime Belge*, '*a finding of a collective dominant position may also be based on other connecting factors and would depend on an economic assessment and, in particular, on an assessment of the structure of the market in question*'.[846]

The issue was raised at length by the Court of First Instance in *Gencor* too. Parties argued that the Commission had failed to prove the existence of 'links' between the

---

843. (ECJ, Compagnie Maritime Belge Transports SA and Others v. Commission, Joined Cases C-395/96 P and C-396/96 P 2000).
844. (CFI, Gencor Ltd v. Commission, Case T-102/96 1999).
845. (CFI, SIV and Others v. Commission, Joined cases T-68/89, T-77/89 and T-78/89 1992, 358); (ECJ, Municipality of Almelo and others v. NV Energibedrijf Ijsselmij, Case C-393/92 1994, 43); (ECJ, Centro Servizi Spediporto Srl v. Spedizioni Marittima del Golfo Srl., Case C-96/94 1995, 33); (ECJ, DIP SpA v. Comune di Bassano del Grappa, LIDL Italia Srl v. Comune di Chioggia and Lingral Srl v. Comune di Chiogga, Joined cases C-140/94, C-141/94 and C-142/94 1995, 62); (ECJ, Sodemare SA, Anni Azzurri Holding SpA and Anni Azzurri Rezzato Srl v. Regione Lombardia, Case C-70/95 1997, 46); and (ECJ, France and Others v. Commission, Joined Cases C-68/94 and C-30/95 1998, 221).
846. (ECJ, Compagnie Maritime Belge Transports SA and Others v. Commission, Joined Cases C-395/96 P and C-396/96 P 2000, 45).

members of the duopoly within the meaning of the existing case law. The Court rejected the application by stating, *inter alia*, there was no legal precedent suggesting that the notion of economic links was restricted to the notion of structural links between the undertakings concerned. Thus, the Court extended the concept of collective dominance to members of a tight oligopoly even if there were no contractual or structural links between them. The Court explained the need for this extension as follows:

> *there is no reason whatsoever in legal or economic terms to exclude from the notion of economic links the relationship of interdependence existing between the parties to a tight oligopoly within which, in a market with the appropriate characteristics, in particular in terms of market concentration, transparency and product homogeneity, those parties are in a position to anticipate one another's behaviour and are therefore strongly encouraged to align their conduct on the market, in particular in such a way as to maximize their joint profits by restricting production with a view to increasing prices. In such a context, each trader is aware that highly competitive action on its part designed to increase its market share (for example a price cut) would provoke identical action by the others, so that it would derive no benefit from its initiative. All the traders would thus be affected by the reduction in price levels.*[847]

Structural links, therefore, do not need to be proved in order to determine collective dominance. In *Gencor*, the Commission relied on other factors like market concentration, similarity of cost structures of the undertakings holding the collective dominant positions, market transparency, product homogeneity, moderate growth in demand, price inelastic demand, mature production technology, high entry barriers, and lack of negotiation power of purchasers.[848] It follows from the *Gencor* and *Compagnie Maritime Belge* judgments that a market structure analysis has to be performed in order to enable a finding of an oligopolistic or highly concentrated market whose structure alone may be conducive to coordinated effects on the relevant market. In the early days, the so-called checklist provided some guidance.

4.6.4.1.1 The 'Checklist'

The Commission has applied the concept of collective dominance in relation to oligopolistic markets in a number of decisions adopted under the ECMR. The Commission has relied upon a certain number of criteria, which are summarised below. It has to be clearly stated that the application of a so-called 'checklist' is not appropriate. An evaluation of collective dominance has to be done on a case-by-case basis only. In individual cases the Commission focused on the following factors:

---

[847]. (CFI, Gencor Ltd v. Commission, Case T-102/96 1999, 276) The case concerned the legality of a decision adopted by the Commission under the Merger Regulation prohibiting the notified transaction on the grounds that it would lead to the creation of a duopoly market conducive to a situation of oligopolistic dominance.

[848]. (CFI, Gencor Ltd v. Commission, Case T-102/96 1999, 159).

Chapter 4: Competition Practice

- few market players;[849]
- a mature market;
- stagnant or moderate growth on the demand side;[850]
- low elasticity of demand;
- homogeneous product;
- similar cost structures;[851]
- similar market shares;[852]
- transparent market conditions;[853]
- lack of technical innovation, mature technology;
- absence of excess capacity;[854]
- high barriers to entry;[855]
- lack of countervailing buying power;[856]
- lack of potential competition;[857]
- various kinds of informal or other links between the undertakings concerned;[858]

---

849. As the Commission noted in (Decision IV/M.1016 on Price Waterhouse/Coopers & Lybrand 1998), 'collective dominance involving more than three or four suppliers is too complex and unstable to persist over time', cit., at paras 103 and 113. In that decision the Commission dismissed the possibility that the so-called Big Six accounting firms be considered collectively dominant. However, such an assessment will depend on each market's particular characteristics and indeed markets with more than three players may under certain circumstances be considered as being conducive to oligopolistic dominance.
850. (Decision IV/M.1225 on Enso/Stora 1998, para. 67).
851. Ibid., para. 67.
852. See in particular, France and Others v. Commission, at para. 226. Large imbalances of market share between the undertakings concerned may render the existence or creation of a collective dominant position highly unlikely, (Decision IV/M.1517 on Rhodia/Donau Chemie/Albright & Wilson 1999, 73). See also, (Decision IV/M.1527 on OTTO Versand/Freemans 1999, 31), and (Decision COMP/M.1882 on Pirelli/BICC 2000, 83). However, imbalances in market share among the members of an oligopoly have not been an obstacle to a finding of collective dominance in a number of cases; (Decision IV/M.1313 on Danish Crown/Vestjyske Slagterier 1999).
853. See also (Decision IV/M.942 on VEBA/Degussa 1997, 44) (market conditions were not found to be transparent). In (Decision IV/M.1225 on Enso/Stora 1998) the Commission also took into consideration the absence of market transparency regarding such key parameters as supplies and prices together with the existence of secret discounts, para. 68. See also, (Decision COMP/M.1882 on Pirelli/BICC 2000) 'the results of the market investigation indicate that price transparency for LV/MV products is rather low due to the absence of meaningful list prices and varying customer-defined specifications. Collusive strategies are thus further complicated', para. 91.
854. A finding of collective dominance may be negated if it can be established that there exist overcapacities distributed among the undertakings concerned 'in a way that would allow for breaking up of parallel anticompetitive behaviour', see in particular, (Decision IV/M.1517 on Rhodia/Donau Chemie/Albright & Wilson 1999, 71).
855. See for example, (Decision IV/M.1225 on Enso/Stora 1998, 75-77).
856. See (Decision IV/M.1313 on Danish Crown/Vestjyske Slagterier 1999, 171-174).
857. Ibid., para. 174.
858. In (Decision IV/M.1016 on Price Waterhouse/Coopers & Lybrand 1998) the Commission also took into account the fact that the undertakings concerned (accounting firms) were represented in various industry organisations and institutions responsible for matters of self-regulation and that their representatives met on a regular basis to discuss issues crucial to their profession.

- retaliatory mechanisms; and
- lack or reduced scope for price competition.[859]

The above is not an exhaustive list, nor are the criteria cumulative. Rather, the list is intended to illustrate the sort of evidence that could be used to support assertions concerning the existence of collective (oligopolistic) dominance. Indeed, the existence of structural links among the undertakings concerned is not a prerequisite for finding a collective dominant position. It is however clear that where such links exist, they can be relied upon to explain, together with any of the other above-mentioned criteria, why in a given oligopolistic market coordinated effects are likely to arise.

4.6.4.1.2 Development of the Collective Dominance Doctrine

In earlier years, the Commission dealt with the potential collusive effects of mergers in narrow oligopolies, drawing on the notion of a dominant position 'by one or more undertakings'.

In *Nestlé/Perrier*[860], the Commission explained in detail its opinion namely that Article 2 of the ECMR can also be applicable in oligopolistic market situations. This case presented a duopoly situation in the French market for bottled mineral water. Nestlé's acquisition of Perrier would reduce from three to two the number of significant players in the market, and would leave Nestlé and BSN each with market shares of about 44%. The Commission came to the conclusion that Nestlé and BSN would act together as a single firm, and therefore applied the dominance test against the jointly dominant firms. Nestle was obliged to sell a sufficient number of brands to an independent third party to re-create a third party in the market.

Kali + Salz[861] is another case where the Commission assessed collective dominance. With respect to the relevant geographic market (European Community without Germany) the Commission came to the conclusion that the proposed concentration would create a situation of oligopolistic dominance on the part of the merged entity and the French state owned producer SCPA. Four main reasons justified this conclusion: (1) Kali + Salz and SCPA together would account for about 60% of the market defined; (2) the market is a mature market characterised by a homogenous product and a lack of technical innovation. Moreover, the market is very transparent, and information on prices is generally available. (3) Both companies were members of an old export agreement dating from 1973. (4) The existence of exceptionally close links between the two companies extending over a long period of time. For these reasons, the Commission required before approval of the merger that Kali + Salz had to eliminate its links with SCPA.

In March 1998, the Court of Justice delivered its judgment in this case. The Court annulled the Commission's decisions and argued that the Commission's conclusion was over-reliant on the mere existence of structural links and had not established how

---

859. (Decision IV/M.1313 on Danish Crown/Vestjyske Slagterier 1999, 176).
860. (Decision IV/M.190 on Nestlé/Perrier 1992).
861. (Decision IV/M.308 on Kali und Salz v. MdK v. Treuhand 1993).

Chapter 4: Competition Practice

or why those links would in reality act to facilitate coordination of the two firms competitive behaviour. In the Court proceedings the Advocate General denied the application of collective dominance under the ECMR by arguing with the actual wording of Article 2(3) and with the evolution of the ECMR itself. However, he did not deny the application of the ECMR for such market situations. Finally, the Court of Justice approved its application in the case law.

In *Kali + Salz*,[862] the Court annulled the Commission's decision since the Commission had not adequately established that an oligopolistic dominant position would be created or strengthened.[863] The Commission's finding that there was a collective dominant position was based on four main sets of criteria: (i) the stability of the market shares of the members of the oligopoly, (ii) the increase in the parties' market share as a result of the transaction, (iii) the nature of the products and the structural features of the market (homogeneous product, barriers to entry, mature market, limited cross-border trading between France and Germany); and above all (iv) the existence of structural links between Kali + Salz and SCPA. The Court of Justice rejected some of these arguments on the grounds that they were not conclusive in themselves (*'those facts cannot be regarded as lending decisive support to the Commission's conclusion'*).[864] The Court favoured instead a sectoral or case-by-case approach for the assessment of the risks of oligopolistic collusion. In particular, in performing its economic analysis the Commission should not simply rely on a checklist of descriptive factors that indicate the theoretical risk of oligopolistic dominance or on the fact that market shares exceed a certain threshold. Rather, those factors have to be analysed in the dynamic context of the relevant economic facts of each specific case. Application of this standard led the Court to annul in this case the Commission's findings concerning oligopolistic dominance given the presence of three factors: (i) the asymmetries between the allegedly jointly dominant companies; (ii) the absence of close structural links between them and (iii) the ability of third parties to exercise competitive constraint on the alleged duopolists.[865] Moreover, the Court's dismissal of the structural links aspect of the Commission's case ties in exactly with the economic theory of coordinated effects.[866]

Thus to ascertain collective dominance the Court of Justice of the EU wants to have a detailed examination of whether the firms in the oligopoly have the power for collusive behaviour and to a significant extent have the possibility to act independently of competitors, customers and final consumers. The Court favours an approach of a

---

862. (Decision IV/M.308 on Kali und Salz v. MdK v. Treuhand 1993).
863. After resumption of the case the Commission had approved the merger under Art. 6(1)b. The Commission denied a dominant duopoly between the two merging undertakings. Their combined market shares on the relevant EU market for Kali was about 46% and the former structural interconnections had been resolved. (Decision IV/M.308 on Kali + Salz/MDK/Treuhand 1998).
864. See also (Ysewyn and Caffarra 1998, 470).
865. (Venit 1998, 1112).
866. (Lofaro and Ridyard 2000, 549).

455

'*close examination in particular of the circumstances which, in each individual case, are relevant for assessing the effects of the concentration on competition in the reference market.*'[867]

The first occasion that the Commission prohibited a merger on the grounds of collective dominance between more than two firms was that of *Airtours/First Choice*.[868] In April 1999, *Airtours*, international travel group, launched a hostile bid for First Choice, which was its effective vertically integrated and emerging rival in the UK. Following the Commission's examination of the case, the merger of those two companies would have left only three major travel groups in the UK, who would have held 70% of the UK short hauls foreign package holiday market. The Commission found that the full integration of the operators both upstream in the charter airline and downstream into distribution via the chains of travel agencies which they owned, would tend to align cost structures and increase transparency of the market. This in consequence would reduce the likelihood of strong price competition between them. Another key factor for the Commission was the relative inflexibility of supply, which would create an incentive for the larger integrated tour operators to keep the market 'tight' and not to expand capacity in order to compete aggressively with each other for market shares. The Commission additionally concluded that the remainder of the UK tour operating market was highly fragmented and was unable to obtain inputs and distribution at prices available to the integrated groups. Therefore, they would not be able to exercise effective competition against the oligopoly of *Airtours, Thomson Travel* and *Thomas Cook*. The Commission on these grounds declared the proposed operation incompatible with the Common Market and did not accept the remedies offered by the parties. The decision represents a significant development in E.C. merger control since the adoption of the Regulation itself. Companies will now need to consider their acquisition strategies under this background and anticipate where the Commission might have concerns about emerging oligopolies, which will include reviewing existing relationships with competitors in order to see whether these could be seen to support an oligopoly finding.

Only a few months later there was another acquisition in the travel sector, which was investigated by the Commission. This was the acquisition of the UK travel company *Thomson Travel Group Plc*[869] by the German *Preussag AG*. Preussag is a conglomerate with interests in the travel sector through its ownership of German travel company *TUI*. As already stated in *Airtours/First Choice* the Commission concluded that the UK market of short-haul package holidays is characterised by a significant degree of vertical integration. The main domestic operators are active in tour operating, travel agencies and charter airline services. The Commission cleared this merger in Phase I.

In the landmark judgment in 2002, the Court of First Instance in *Airtours v. Commission* annulled for the first time a prohibition decision under the ECMR. The Court of First Instance clarified the standard for finding collective dominance by

---

867. (ECJ, France and Others v. Commission, Joined Cases C-68/94 and C-30/95 1998, 222).
868. (Decision IV/M.1524 on Airtours v. First Choice 1999).
869. (Decision COMP/M.2002 on Preussag/Thomson 2000).

rejecting a routine application of a 'checklist' approach (analyzing the market characteristics conducive to coordination) but setting out three cumulative conditions, reflecting a more dynamic approach and looking at the sustainability mechanism of tacit collusion: First, the market must be transparent enough to allow for the monitoring of other firms' market conduct. Second, coordination must be sustainable, which means that the participants must be deterred from defection by fear of retaliation. Third, the benefits of coordination must not be jeopardised by the actions of current or future competitors or customers. The Court of First Instance also made clear that these conditions require a 'prospective analysis' of the specific circumstances.

The *Airtours* judgment, already discussed in section 4.5.2.4, influenced the adoption of the Horizontal Merger Guidelines, in which the Commission opted for a more economic approach. The Guidelines indicate that to assess the likelihood of coordinated effects it is first necessary to identify a plausible mechanism for coordination. The mechanical application of the checklist discussed above was put aside. That paved the way for the most important first steps from collective dominance toward the concept of coordinated effects.

The *Danish Crown/Vestjyske Slagterier*[870] case concerned the creation of a duopolistically dominant position of the parties together with another large Danish cooperative slaughterhouse. Danish Crown/Vestjyske Slagterier and Steff-Houlberg would have accounted for about 70% of the market for fresh pork meat sold through supermarkets. In addition to this fact, the Commission took into account several other elements. Due to the weekly pig price quotation, competitive actions would be very transparent; secondly there would be a number of structural and other similarities between the parties and the number two competitor, Steff-Houlberg, in terms of similar cost structures, technology and sales channels; in addition, there would be links between Steff-Houlberg and the parties. The Commission found that due to the market structure neither of the two duopolists would have had any incentive to compete with each other on the Danish market. The parties committed themselves to abolish the pig price quotation, in order to make the market less transparent. Since, due to this move, sourcing of pigs could be done at different prices, cost structures could become different. Additionally, the parties committed themselves to dissolve important structural links between them and Steff-Houlberg. The Commission's concerns also existed over the creation of a dominant position on the Danish market for the purchasing of live pigs for slaughtering and the sale of abattoir by-products.[871] To remove these concerns the parties committed themselves to dissolve all structural and operational links between themselves and Steff-Houlberg.

In the withdrawn operation of *EMI* and *Time Warner*[872] the Commission investigated whether such a concentration would lead to a collective dominance situation between four major players, *EMI/Time Warner*, *Universal*, *Sony* and *Bertelsmann*, holding together around 80% of the recorded music market at the EEA and worldwide

---

870. (Decision IV/M.1313 on Danish Crown/Vestjyske Slagterier 1999).
871. Parts of animals, which cannot be used for human consumption.
872. (Decision COMP/M.1852 on Time Warner/EMI 2000).

level. The market characteristics were the nature of the product[873], the high degree of market transparency, and of multi-market contacts, the existence of structural links, as well as the symmetry in the characteristics of the majors. These factors could have favoured tacit coordination. The Commission thus considered that the majors would have credible means to retaliate and discipline each other. This would take place in particular through their compilation joint ventures because such joint ventures would generate highly attractive returns. Finally, for a variety of reasons it was considered that the tacitly coordinated equilibrium would not easily be contested.

Veba/Viag[874] was a case, which the Commission considered in parallel with the German *Bundeskartellamt* investigation of *RWE/VEW*.[875] The new entities would have presided over a considerable market position in the German market for electricity delivered from the interconnected grid. The Commission examined a number of factors such as the total homogeneity of the product, the market transparency, similar cost structures, a number of jointly operated large power stations and numerous interrelationships between *Veba* and *Viag* and *RWE*. Both operations, the *Veba/Viag* and the *RWE/VEW* merger, were cleared due to several commitments given by the parties. Those undertakings mainly concerned holdings in *VEAG* in the eastern part of Germany. The undertakings also provided for improvements to the basic rules governing transmission through the network operated by the two interconnecting entities.

A series of mergers in the aluminium sector stimulated the Commission to examine the coordinated effects in these markets and investigate issues of collusion. In *Alcan/Pechiney*[876] the Commission's assessments were essentially based on the idea that the merging parties could use an existing structural link, which in this case was a joint venture, with a competitor as a retaliation mechanism to dissuade this competitor from engaging in a price war. The three-way merger between *Alcan, Pechiney* and *Alusuisse* would have brought together companies involved in all aspects of the aluminium industry and would have created the largest aluminium producer worldwide. Due to *Alcan's* market share, exchange offers between the two others meant one merger could have been performed without the other and therefore the Commission was able to investigate in-depth the two cases separately and on their own merits. The *Alcan/Pechiney* operation did not go through and was abandoned by the parties in view of a prohibition decision considered by the Commission. On the other hand, the Commission approved the *Alcan/Alusuisse*[877] operation due to divestment undertakings.

In examining the mergers *AirLiquide/BOC*[878] and *Linde/AGA*,[879] the Commission was faced with two cases of global consolidation in the industrial gases industry. In

---

873. While it would be too simplistic to say, that every record is unique, the Commission argued that from an economic point rather a high degree of standardisation does exist in pricing, distribution and format of the product, which would make the tacit coordination easier.
874. (Decision COMP/M.1673 on VEBA/VIAG 2000).
875. (BKartA Decision B8 – 40000 – U – 309/99 on RWE/VEW 2000).
876. (Commission Decision M 1715 withdrawn 14 Mar. 2000 on Alcan/Pechiney 2000).
877. (Decision COMP/M.1663 on Alcan/Alusuisse 2000).
878. (Decision COMP/M.1630 on Air Liquide/BOC 2000).
879. (Decision COMP/M.1641 on Linde/AGA 2000).

AirLiquide/BOC, the Commission identified distinct product markets in this sector based on the type of gas and method of distribution. The Commission took account of the inter-relation between these markets, implying for instance, that a strong position on the tonnage market will often confer competitive advantages on the bulk market and vice versa. The geographic market for cylinder and for bulk gases was found to be national in scope due to different prices, market structures and distribution systems in different Member States. On this basis, the operation would in the eyes of the Commission have strengthened the dominant position in certain bulk and cylinder markets of *AirLiquide* in France and of *BOC* in the UK and Ireland. Nevertheless, the *AirLiquide/BOC* transaction was cleared by the Commission. Finally, the parties following unsuccessful negotiations with the Federal Trade Commission in the US abandoned the operation.

When the Court of First Instance in its *Impala* judgment, discussed in section 4.6.2.4, annulled the Commission's *Sony/BMG* decision, this development was surprising for some observers. The core of the judgment is the detailed review of the Commission's assessment of the strengthening of an existing collective dominant position by the major record companies. On 10 July 2008, the Court of First Instance judgment was overturned by the Court of Justice. In the context of this judgment the Court of Justice fully endorsed the economic model of tacit coordination, elaborating on its most important aspects. The judgment highlights several elements that the Commission should examine in detail and analyse consistently.

The Court recognises that by its very nature and in contrast to cartel agreements, tacit coordination can rarely be proved by relying on hard evidence. Price-fixing or market sharing agreements in violation of Article 101 can generally be proved by way of hard evidence. In contrast, tacit coordination, is likely to emerge if competitors can easily arrive at a common perception as to how the coordination should work. Tacit coordination can thus only be inferred indirectly from observing and adequately interpreting the actual conduct of market players in light of existing market conditions, which affect their ability and incentives tacitly to coordinate their actions.

Reaching an agreement, however, is not sufficient. The agreement should be sustainable over time. The Court also refers to the need for the identification of a sufficient degree of sustainability. Monitoring to a sufficient degree, a credible deterrence mechanism, and a limited reaction by outsiders are the required elements. The coordinating undertakings must be able to monitor to a sufficient degree whether the terms of the coordination are being adhered to. Furthermore, discipline requires that there be some form of credible deterrent mechanism that can come into play if deviation is detected. The reactions of outsiders, such as current or future competitors, and also, the reactions of customers, should not be such as to jeopardise the results expected from the coordination.

The Court requires the Commission to link these aspects to the effects that the merger brings about. Thus, the Commission should further show, on the basis of a prospective analysis, the extent to which:

> the alteration in the [relevant market] structure that the transaction would entail, significantly impedes effective competition by making coordination easier, more

stable or more effective for the three firms concerned either by making the coordination more robust or by permitting firms to coordinate on even higher prices.[880]

In the following, the Commission's guidelines on collective dominance are discussed.

4.6.4.2 Assessment of Coordinated Effects in the Merger Guidelines

Traditional economic theory distinguishes between two main cases when studying the effects of mergers on social welfare. Firstly, the case where the merger might allow a firm to unilaterally exercise market power and profitably raise prices without losing customers. In the US, this is discussed as the unilateral effects of a merger. The other case arises when a merger might favour collusion in the affected industry. Here, the merging firm would not be able to unilaterally increase prices above a certain threshold, but the merger could introduce new industry conditions that enhance the scope for tacit collusion. Prices could then increase as firms are more likely to obtain supranormal profits where 'normal' profits correspond to the equilibrium situation (perfect competition). This issue falls under the category of collective dominance (also called joint dominance or oligopolistic dominance) or coordinated effects in the wording of the US Merger Guidelines. Today the Commission uses the wording of coordinating effects instead of collective dominance in its new horizontal merger guidelines.[881]

In some markets the structure may be such that firms would consider it possible, economically rational, and hence preferable, to adopt on a sustainable basis a course of action on the market aimed at selling at higher prices. A merger in a concentrated market may significantly impede effective competition, through the creation or the strengthening of a collective dominant position, because it increases the likelihood that firms are able to coordinate their behaviour in this way and raise prices, even without entering into an agreement or resorting to a concerted practice within the meaning of Article 101.

Coordination may take various forms. In some markets, the most likely coordination may involve keeping prices above the competitive level. In other markets, coordination may aim at limiting production or the amount of new capacity brought to the market. Firms may also coordinate by dividing the market, for instance by geographic area or other customer characteristics, or by allocating contracts in bidding markets.

Coordination is more likely to emerge in markets where it is relatively simple to reach a common understanding on the terms of coordination. In addition, three conditions are necessary for coordination to be sustainable. First, the coordinating firms must be able to monitor to a sufficient degree whether the terms of coordination are being adhered to. Second, discipline requires that there is some form of credible

---
880. (CFI, Airtours plc v. Commission, Case T-342/99 2002, para. 61).
881. (Commission Guidelines on horizontal mergers 2004, para. 39).

Chapter 4: Competition Practice

deterrent mechanism that can be activated if deviation is detected. Third, the reactions of outsiders, such as current and future competitors not participating in the coordination, as well as customers, should not be able to jeopardise the results expected from the coordination.

4.6.4.2.1 Reaching Terms of Coordination

Coordination is more likely to emerge if competitors can easily arrive at a common perception as to how the coordination should work. Coordinating firms should have similar views regarding which actions would be considered to be in accordance with the aligned behaviour and which actions would not. Generally, the less complex and the more stable the economic environment, the easier it is for the firms to reach a common understanding on the terms of coordination. For instance, it is easier to coordinate among a few players than among many. It is also easier to coordinate on a price for a single, homogeneous product, than on hundreds of prices in a market with many differentiated products. Similarly, it is easier to coordinate on a price when demand and supply conditions are relatively stable than when they are continuously changing. In this context volatile demand, substantial internal growth by some firms in the market or frequent entry by new firms may indicate that the current situation is not sufficiently stable to make coordination likely. In markets where innovation is important, coordination may be more difficult since innovations, particularly significant ones, may allow one firm to gain a comparative advantage over its rivals. Firms may find it easier to reach a common understanding on the terms of coordination if they are relatively symmetric, especially in terms of cost structures, market shares, capacity levels and levels of vertical integration. Structural links such as cross-shareholding or participation in joint ventures may also help in aligning incentives among the coordinating firms.

4.6.4.2.2 Monitoring Deviations

Coordinating firms are often tempted to increase their share of the market by deviating from the terms of coordination, for instance by lowering prices, offering secret discounts, increasing product quality or capacity or trying to attract new customers. Only the credible threat of timely and sufficient retaliation keeps firms from deviating. Markets therefore need to be sufficiently transparent to allow the coordinating firms to monitor to a sufficient degree the behaviour of other firms, and thus know when to retaliate. In some markets where the general conditions seem to make monitoring difficult, firms may nevertheless engage in practices which have the effect of easing the monitoring task, even when these practices are not necessarily intended for such purposes. These practices, such as meeting the competition or most-favoured customer clauses, voluntary publication of information, announcements, or exchange of information through trade associations, may increase transparency or help competitors interpret the choices made. Cross-directorships, participation in joint ventures and similar arrangements may also make monitoring easier.

4.6.4.2.3 Deterrent Mechanisms

Coordination is not sustainable unless the consequences of deviation are sufficiently severe to convince coordinating firms that it is in their best interest to adhere to the terms of coordination. It is thus the *threat of future retaliation* that keeps the coordination sustainable. However, the threat is only credible if, where deviation by one of the firms is detected, there is sufficient certainty that some deterrent mechanism will be activated. Retaliation that manifests itself after some significant time lag, or is not certain to be activated, is less likely to be sufficient to offset the benefits from deviating. The speed with which deterrent mechanisms can be implemented is related to the issue of transparency. If firms are only able to observe their competitors' actions after a substantial delay, then retaliation will be similarly delayed and this may influence whether it is sufficient to deter deviation. The credibility of the deterrence mechanism depends on whether the other coordinating firms have an incentive to retaliate. Some deterrent mechanisms, such as punishing the deviator by temporarily engaging in a price war or increasing output significantly, may entail a short-term economic loss for the firms carrying out the retaliation. This does not necessarily remove the incentive to retaliate since the short-term loss may be smaller than the long-term benefit of retaliating resulting from the return to the regime of coordination.

For coordination to be successful, the actions of non-coordinating firms and potential competitors, as well as customers, should not be able to jeopardise the outcome expected from coordination. Special consideration is given to the possible impact of market entry and the countervailing buyer power of customers.

4.6.5 Merger Simulation Models

This section discusses an economic tool which is becoming an essential element in critical merger proceeding: merger simulation models.

Traditionally, merger control in Europe has focused mainly on market share analysis: competition authorities have been concerned predominantly with the market share of the merged entity and with the level of concentration within the industry.[882] However, in differentiated product markets, market shares may provide a poor approximation of the extent to which a merger may give rise to unilateral effects. This is because market shares fail to accurately measure the closeness of substitution between the merging parties' products which is central to predicting the competitive effects.[883] Thus, merger simulation is one of a number of alternative approaches that may be used to evaluate unilateral effects in differentiated product industries instead of or to reciprocate market shares and concentration measures. Merger simulation takes into account the price response by non-merging firms, and second it predicts individual product as well as market-wide price changes.[884]

---

882. (Walker 2005, 474).
883. (Durand 2012, 1).
884. *Ibid.*

Chapter 4: Competition Practice

The need for more sophisticated quantitative analysis in merger control is also motivated by theoretical arguments. Both the current US and European merger guidelines stipulate that the anti-competitive effects of a merger should be assessed by quantifying the trade-off between efficiency gains and the increase in market power due to unilateral effects. In this context, there is a need for empirical techniques that can explicitly compare efficiency gains with the price increase that would be induced by the increase in market power, without any efficiencies. The merger guidelines thus call for an investigation process, which involves the comparison between the observed pre-merger situation and the hypothetical post-merger situation.[885]

Merger simulation models (MSM) are able to predict post-merger prices based on information about a set of pre-merger market conditions and certain assumptions about the behaviour of the firms in the relevant market.[886] MSM have been around since the mid-1990s. In a number of merger cases involving fast-moving consumer goods, the Commission relied on merger simulation to assess unilateral effects. Nevertheless, merger simulation is still a very young and innovative instrument of anti-trust and, therefore, its 'technical' potential is far from being comprehensively exploited and teething problems in its practical use in the anti-trust environment prevail.[887]

Merger simulation follows three distinct steps:[888]

- The first step specifies and estimates a demand system.
- The second step makes an assumption about the equilibrium behaviour, typically a multi-product Bertrand-Nash equilibrium to compute the products current profit margins and their implied marginal costs.
- The third step usually assumes that marginal costs are constant, and predicts how prices will change after the merger, accounting for increased market power, cost efficiencies and perhaps remedies.

These three steps are discussed below.

4.6.5.1 *The Specification Stage*

4.6.5.1.1 *Model Selection*

The first assumption we make when building a MSM is about the form of competition that best describes the behaviour of firms operating in the relevant market.

In the model of perfect competition firms charge their price at marginal costs. The conditions required to classify a market as perfectly competitive is a mixture of several different notions. Perfect information about the market and price distribution should be available. Besides product homogeneity, the size of agents does not matter either:

---

885. (J. Foncel 2009, 1).
886. (Epstein and Rubinfeld 2001).
887. (Budzinski and Ruhmer 2008).
888. (J. Foncel 2009, 3).

market participants can sell as much of the good as they wish at the equilibrium price but nothing at a higher price. The equilibrium or competitive price at marginal costs is reached when supply and demand are in equilibrium. Since equilibria happens before and after a merger, such models are inappropriate in estimating the unilateral effects of a merger.

Oligopoly models, in contrast, are more appropriate when applying game theory. Modern game-theoretic oligopoly theory is predominantly built upon three standard models: Cournot competition (quantity competition), Bertrand competition (price competition), and auction theory.

Whereas in traditional economic analysis, a company takes as given its cost structure and the demand curve that it is facing, game theory suggests that most companies are smarter than this and realise that competitors will respond to whatever strategy they choose. Thus, modern game theory strives to formalise the theory and mathematics of decision-making in a strategic environment by incorporating awareness of the consequences of strategic decisions. The consequences can be a response, such as matching a competitor's prices, or responses from consumers, such as lower future demand in response to quality issues with the company's product.

Oligopoly games have only a few players which is generally taken to be somewhere between three and ten. Thus, economic games tend to have a manageable number of players, although sometimes games are constructed with a few players and then the remaining part of the industry is represented as a competitive fringe which means that those firms act as if in perfect competition and do not practice strategic behaviour.

Repeated games occur when the same players repeat the same game, either a set number of times (called rounds) or an infinite number of times. A game in which the sum of all payoffs is constant is called a constant game; a non-constant game is one where the sum of payoffs varies depending on strategies chosen.

The Nash equilibrium is a solution concept of a non-cooperative game involving two or more players, in which each player is assumed to know the equilibrium strategies of the other players, and no player has anything to gain by changing only their own strategy. If each player has chosen a strategy and no player can benefit by changing strategies while the other players keep their's unchanged, then the current set of strategy choices and the corresponding payoffs constitute a Nash equilibrium.

Modern oligopoly theory is predominantly built upon three standard models: (1) Cournot competition, (2) Bertrand competition, and (3) auction theory:

(1) Cournot competition applies to markets with homogenous goods i.e., perfect substitutes, where firms compete in quantities. MSMs are rarely applied to Cournot competition because it is somehow counterintuitive to estimate unilateral effects caused by price changes when quantities (not prices) are the strategic parameters.

(2) Bertrand competition is the common framework adopted to evaluate horizontal mergers in differentiated product industries. In this model, firms compete on prices. More specifically, a firm sets its optimal price as a function of

marginal cost, own-price elasticity, and the prices of its competitors. The Bertrand paradox describes a situation in which two players (firms) reach a state of Nash equilibrium where both firms charge a price equal to marginal cost. Bertrand's result is paradoxical because if the number of firms goes from one to two, the price decreases from the monopoly price to the competitive price and stays at the same level as the number of firms increases further. The outcome would be the same as under perfect competition.

For merger simulation purposes, the Bertrand model is useful. A horizontal merger between two firms will give a strong incentive to the merged entity to raise its price due to the internalisation of the competition between the merging parties. A MSM based on a Bertrand model is able to illustrate these price movements.

(3) In some markets, products are traded at auctions. The assessment of unilateral effects arising as a result of a merger between two bidding firms can be performed through MSM using auction theory. Auction theory studies the efficiency of a given auction design, optimal and equilibrium bidding strategies, and revenue comparison.

In addition, simulation models require assumptions about supply or, more specifically, about how total cost responds to marginal changes in post-merger output. Most simulation analyses assume that marginal costs do not vary with output.[889] Finally, the relevant product and geographic markets as well as market size must be defined. However, such a delineation is in fact not strictly necessary *a priori*. Merger simulation can abstract from market definition because the estimation of substitution patterns provides all the relevant information without one having to start by delineating markets.[890]

In general, Cournot models are appropriate if products are rather homogenous whereas Bertrand models are adequate for markets with heterogeneous products. In some markets, products are traded in a way similar to auctions (e.g., markets for business software, services for the public sector like forest timber services or hospitals, etc.). If mergers occur on these kinds of markets, auction models represent the first choice for simulating the competitive effects.[891]

4.6.5.1.2 Auction Models

Merger simulation with an auction model is much like that in a Cournot or Bertrand market. However, instead of specifying functional forms for demand and cost, valuation or cost distributions for competing bidders are specified.

In some markets products are traded in an auction-like manner. Next to suppliers that actually auction their products, these markets approximate the following characteristics: products are mostly sold on a low-frequency basis and customers specify their

---

889. (Epstein and Rubinfeld 2001, 887).
890. (J. Foncel 2009, 4).
891. (Budzinski and Ruhmer 2008, 8–11).

needs by calling for tenders. Then suppliers propose offerings leading to a multiple-round selection procedure and finally to a transaction.

Typical auction-like markets are markets for business software, user-specific technical equipment and services for the public sector. If mergers occur on such auction-like markets, auction models represent the first choice to simulate the competitive effects.

Auction models vary depending on the detailed specifications of the bidding process. Game-theoretic models of auctions and strategic bidding generally fall into either of the following two categories:

- In a private value model, each participant (bidder) assumes that each of the competing bidders obtains a random *private value* from a probability distribution.
  The standard textbook example associated with this model is the selling of a painting; buyers' valuations for the painting may differ but are assumed to be independent.
- Common value auctions pertain to situations in which the object for sale is worth the same to everyone, but bidders have different private information about its true value.

A well-known example where the common value set up applies is the auctioning of oil drilling rights, which, to a first approximation, are worth the same to all competing bidders. In a common value model, each participant assumes that any other participant obtains a random signal from a probability distribution common to all bidders.

Based on these distinctions, two types of auction models are used for merger simulation: the first-price and second-price auction models.

4.6.5.1.1.1   First-Price Auctions

In this type of auction all bidders simultaneously submit sealed bids so that no bidder knows the bid of any other participant. The highest bidder pays the price they submitted.

First-price auction models are used for the simulation of merger effects in markets of asymmetric first-price, sealed-bid, and private value auctions. The lowest price each bidder is able to bid corresponds to its costs. Using this model, the merger effects are calibrated using pre-merger information on market shares and the range of density function of costs.

4.6.5.1.1.2   Second-Price Auctions

This is identical to the sealed first-price auction except that the winning bidder pays the second-highest bid rather than his or her own.

Chapter 4: Competition Practice

The second-price auction is built on a set of assumptions; first of all, valuations of bidders are comprised of two independent components: the idiosyncratic component and the common component. The winning probabilities of each bidder (corresponding to the expected market share), the prices (corresponding to the second-highest value) and the merger effects can be calculated using simplifying properties of the idiosyncratic components.

By using differences between losing bids, one can estimate distribution parameters. This is possible when employing a two-step, limited-information maximum-likelihood (LIML) estimator. For that estimation, data on bidder identities and bidder shares, bidder characteristics (also losing bidders' characteristics) and values of bids (again, including losing bids) across the sample of auction, have to be available. The estimation consists of three steps.

- First of all, firm or bidder specific characteristics are used to estimate the logit probability of winning, and simultaneously, the expected values of the winning bids. Here, shares are used as proxies for the probabilities of winning:

   - Secondly, the fitted probabilities are used to construct the difference between the second and third highest bids.
   - And thirdly, the merger price effect is calculated using estimated distribution parameters and the enhanced winning probability of the merger firm. The new winning probability equals the sum of the shares of each merging partner, as the merged firm will win each auction that either of the original firms would have won. The price effect of the merger mainly depends on the variance of the idiosyncratic component in two ways; a great variance indicates the increase of the amount and variance of the price effect.

4.6.5.2 The Estimation Stage

Next, the model is confronted with observed data in order to confirm that interactions in the market take place as the model suggests. This stage consists in fitting the model to the data by means of a specific procedure.

One-way is to use econometric techniques to achieve the best statistical approximation of the model to the data. The disadvantage of this method is that it requires a comprehensive set of information including prices, quantities and the objective attributes of most products sold on the market. For example, estimating a demand system for ten products would involve simultaneous estimation of at least 100 demand parameters. Assuming that useful data can be found and afforded, adequately estimating such a system would require many hours of labour by econometricians working with specialised computer software. Even then, there is no guarantee that the resulting econometric estimates would be economically reasonable or statistically significant, or that they would represent a fair approximation to the true parameter values.[892]

---

892. (Dalkir and Kalkan 2003, 8).

An alternative is to run calibrated simulation models which are used when data are scarce or when analysts face time limitations in the investigation process. They are deceptively easy to use and it takes little time to run these models once the codes are in place.[893]

Demand elasticities are important for merger simulation models. After a merger, the merged entity has reason to increase prices, as the merger lessens the price elasticity of demand for its products. The lost sales may be regained through the merged entity. The extent to which the elasticity falls depends largely on the closeness of substitution between the merging parties' products and the substitutability to goods of non-merged firms.

Thus, the first step in any merger simulation model is choosing a functional form of demand that matches consumer behaviour and choice. There exist four families of demand system used to estimate own- and cross-price elasticities: linear and log-linear demand, logit and nested logit demand systems, Almost Ideal Demand System (AIDS) and Proportionality Calibrated AIDS (PCAIDS).

4.6.5.2.1 *Linear and Log-Linear Demand System*

A linear demand curve is the graphical representation of the relationship between the price of a good and the quantities of that good consumer are willing to purchase. The first law of demand states that as price increases, less quantity is demanded. This is why the demand curve slopes down to the right.

Slope and elasticity are different concepts. Slope measures the steepness or flatness of a line in terms of the measurement units for price and quantity. Elasticity measures the relative response of quantity to changes in price. In other words, how much will a change in price affect the quantity demanded or supplied. The price elasticity of demand is different at each point on a demand curve with constant slope. In addition, price elasticity of demand is almost always negative because price and quantity move in opposite directions on the demand curve.

An alternative approach to a linear demand model is to consider a linear relationship among log-transformed variables. This is called a *log-log model*. The dependent variable as well as all explanatory variables are transformed to logarithms. Since the relationship among the log variables is linear some researchers call this a log-linear model. The parameters of the log-log model have an interpretation as elasticities. So the log-log model assumes a constant elasticity over all values of the data set. This assumption of constant elasticities is consequently criticised. As a result, linear and log-linear models are scarcely used.

Mathematically, these simplest models of demand can be expressed as follows:

Linear: $q_i = a_i + b_{ii}p_i + \sum_j b_{ij}p_j$

Log-linear: $ln(q_i) = a_i + b_{ii}ln(p_i) + \sum_j b_{ij}ln(p_j)$

---

893. (Durand 2012, 6).

Where q_i and p_i refer to quantity and price of product i respectively, p_j is the price of competing brand j, α_i is the constant term, and b_{ii} and b_{ij} are the own- and cross-price coefficients of the equations respectively.

The own- and cross-price elasticities in the linear demand system are calculated by taking the first-order derivative of the quantity with respect to the price, and multiplying it by the ratio of the price over quantity:

Own-price elasticity (linear): $\quad \varepsilon_{ii} = \dfrac{\partial q_i}{\partial p_i}\dfrac{p_i}{q_i} = b_{ii}\dfrac{p_i}{q_i}$

Cross-price elasticity (linear): $\quad \varepsilon_{ij} = \dfrac{\partial q_i}{\partial p_j}\dfrac{p_j}{q_i} = b_{ij}\dfrac{p_j}{q_i}$

We can see that one property of the linear demand system is that it allows elasticities to increase linearly with the price level.

On the other hand, the log-linear demand system has the property of constant own- and cross-price elasticities. In fact, these are equal to the own- and cross-price coefficients in the log-linear demand equation. More specifically:

Own-price elasticity (log-linear): $\quad \varepsilon_{ii} = \dfrac{\partial q_i}{\partial p_i}\dfrac{p_i}{q_i} = b_{ii}$

Cross-price elasticity (log-linear): $\quad \varepsilon_{ij} = \dfrac{\partial q_i}{\partial p_j}\dfrac{p_j}{q_i} = b_{ij}$

This assumption, however, receives considerable criticism. Indeed, it seems unrealistic that while a merger changes prices and market shares in a significant way, it does not change demand elasticities at all. Instead, own and cross-price elasticities are expected to change with the level of prices. As a result, log-linear models are scarcely used.

4.6.5.2.2 Logit and Nested Logit Demand Systems

A more popular form used in merger simulation models are (nested) logit demand models. This type of model is part of the discrete choice demand models family. Discrete choice models explain and predict choices between two or more discrete alternatives. Techniques such as regression or conjoint analyses are used for empirical analysis of discrete choice.

Discrete choice models are based on utility theory. Consumers choose to buy a unit of the product that maximises their personal utility function. The assumption is that the consumer utility function depends on observable product characteristics, including price, and unobservable product characteristics as well as individual-specific coefficients.

In contrast, a nested logit model relaxes the IIA property (independence of irrelevant alternatives) of the simple logit model, and allows consumers to have correlated preferences for products that belong to the same sub-group or group.

4.6.5.2.2.1 Logit Demand System

Mathematically, the logit demand takes the following form:

$$ln(s_i) - ln(s_0) = \beta^T x_i - \alpha p_i + \xi_i$$

Where s_i refers to brand i's market share, s_0 is the market share of the outside good[894], x_i is a vector of observed characteristics of brand i, p_i is that brand's price, and ξ_i is an unobserved product characteristic.[895]

The popularity of this equation is due to its simplicity and the fact that it can be easily estimated by instrumental variables techniques. Its drawback is that it is highly restrictive. To illustrate, let ε_{ii} and ε_{ij} denote the own- and cross-price elasticities of demand.[896] With the logit demand equation, those elasticities are calibrated in the following way:

Own-price elasticity: $\varepsilon_{ii} = \alpha p_i (s_i - 1)$

Cross-price elasticity: $\varepsilon_{ij} = \alpha p_j s_j$

Where p_i and p_j are the prices of goods i and j respectively and s_i and s_j are the respective market shares.

These two equations entail the principle of proportionality i.e., the fact that switching between individual brands is proportional to brand market share.[897] This is captured by the presence of s_i and s_j in both equations. So for instance, the own-price elasticity equation assumes that the larger the market share of the good is, the more inelastic will be the demand for that good which implies that it becomes harder for consumers to switch to other substitutes.

Clearly, the substitution patterns that are implied by these equations are unappealing. For example, all elasticities increase linearly with price and with market share. While this is an improvement over the linear and log-linear demand systems which assume constant price elasticities, it is still not perfectly realistic. Furthermore, since s_i is i's share of the total market, which includes the outside good, estimated elasticities are very sensitive to the choice of the outside good.

---

894. The concept of outside good is equivalent to market potential. More specifically, the size of the outside good refers to the number of consumers who considered the product but did not purchase it. Nevo (2001) estimates the size of the outside good as the share of the total population in the relevant market that is considering to buy the product but do not buy it because they consider the price to be too high. (Nevo 2000, 513–548).
895. (Slade 2006, 4).
896. The own-price elasticity of demand for good i (ε_{ii}) shows the percentage change in demand in response to a 1% increase in the price of that good. The higher the own-price elasticity is, the more substitutable that good will be. Furthermore, the cross-price elasticity of demand for good i with respect to the price of good j (ε_{ij}) shows the percentage change in the demand for good i in response to a 1% increase in the price of good j. The higher the cross-price elasticity is, the higher the degree of substitutability across goods will be.
897. This is also referred to as the Independence of Irrelevant Alternatives (IIA) assumption which implies that a consumer's switch to other products in reaction to a price increase for one product is proportional to the relative shares of these products. (Budzinski and Ruhmer 2008, 20).

4.6.5.2.2.2 Nested Logit Demand System

The nested logit (NL) is distinguished from the ordinary logit by the fact that the n brands or products are partitioned into G groups, referred to as 'nests' and indexed by g = 1,..., G, and the outside good is placed in group 0. Each nest contains different products which share common characteristics. For instance, the car market can be partitioned into the following nests: sports cars and non-sport cars, urban cars and rural cars, etc.

Mathematically, the NL estimating equation is expressed as follows:

$$ln(s_i) - ln(s_0) = \beta^T x_i - \alpha p_i + \sigma ln(\bar{s}_{i/g}) + \xi_i$$

Where $\bar{s}_{i/g}$ is brand i's market share of the group g to which it belongs and σ is the within-group correlation of tastes (it takes a value between 0 and 1). More specifically, the higher the value of σ is, the larger the degree of substitutability between two products belonging to the same group will be.

The NL model calibrates the own- and cross-price elasticities in the following way:

Own-price elasticity: $\varepsilon_{ii} = \alpha p_i [(s_i - 1)/(1 - \sigma) + \sigma/(1 - \sigma)\bar{s}_{i/g}]$

Cross-price elasticity: $\varepsilon_{ij} = \begin{cases} \alpha p_j [s_j + \sigma/(1 - \sigma)\bar{s}_{j/g}] & \text{when } j \neq i \text{ and } j \in g \\ \alpha p_j s_j & \text{when } j \neq i \text{ and } j \notin g \end{cases}$

The first equation for the cross-price elasticity corresponds to the within-group cross-price elasticity whereas the second one refers to the across-groups cross-price elasticity.

The attractive property of the NL model is that it relaxes the proportionality assumption by allowing for different degrees of substitutability across products with different characteristics i.e., belonging to different nests. In particular, the result of the nesting structure is that substitution across groups is smaller than within. This is captured by the equations for cross-price elasticities which indicate that within-group cross-price elasticity is always larger than across-group cross-price elasticity for any positive value of σ. However, within the nests, the proportionality assumption continues to hold. Hence, a certain restriction of the substitution possibilities still exists.[898]

4.6.5.2.3 Almost Ideal Demand System

One of the most popular models for empirical demand analysis is the so-called AIDS model. AIDS is a widely accepted and intuitively reasonable model in economics that allows a flexible representation of own-price and cross-price elasticities. It is also a user-friendly system, which makes it well-suited for merger analyses.

AIDS is based on the recognition that the 'average' consumer behaves in a way so as to maximise utilities subject to budget constraints. The analysis is primarily based on

---

898. (Budzinski and Ruhmer 2008, 21).

the assumption of a specific class of preferences that can be aggregated to represent the demand decisions of this particular 'average' consumer. These preferences lie on the cost function (expenditure function) of the consumer which attributes certain expenditures at given relative prices to respective consumer utilities.

A distinct feature of the AIDS model is that price and expenditure elasticities are not expected to be constant but instead vary with total expenditure. Accordingly, the richer consumers become, the less luxury goods exist on the market. As opposed to other estimation methods, an increase in total expenditure does not lead to a rise but to a fall of the expenditure elasticities. This relationship is close to reality: the share of food expenditure is, for instance, not likely to rise with total expenditure. This property of the AIDS model is directly derived from the assumption of stable preferences.

A major advantage of AIDS models lies in the fact that the demand functions derived from the utility functions are subject to numerous restrictions that can be empirically falsified. These restrictions are:

- The adding-up-restriction, where the expenditure elasticities weighted against their respective budget shares sum to one.
- The homogeneity restriction, where the expenditure-, price-, and cross-price elasticities sum to zero.
- The symmetry requirement, where the compensated cross-price elasticities weighted against budget shares are identical.
- The negativity restriction, where the compensated demand functions show a downward trend.

In addition, this system is indirect non-additive; this implies that consumption of one product can influence the marginal utility of another product.

From an econometric point of view, the AIDS model holds the major advantage, relative to other demand systems, that the model can be almost completely written in terms of linear equations. Based on expenditure shares and the estimated coefficients, price and expenditure elasticities can be easily calculated. Where a general price index depicting a linear homogenous function of the prices is used, estimating an AIDS demand function by using the OLS method is possible.

The major problem with AIDS is a practical one. AIDS typically requires econometric estimation of a large number of parameters, and it is not unusual for the estimated cross-price elasticities to have low precision and algebraic signs that are inconsistent with economic theory.

A simple example with three independent firms, each owning a single brand, helps to explain the logic of AIDS. The AIDS model specifies that the share of each brand depends on the prices of all brands. More formally, the share of the ith brand, s_i, as a percent of total market revenues is a function of the natural logarithms of the prices, p_i, of all of the brands in the relevant market:

$$s_1 = \alpha_1 + \beta_{11} ln(p_1) + \beta_{12} ln(p_2) + \beta_{13} ln(p_3)$$

$$s_2 = \alpha_2 + \beta_{21} ln(p_1) + \beta_{22} ln(p_2) + \beta_{23} ln(p_3)$$

$$s_3 = \alpha_3 + \beta_{31}ln(p_1) + \beta_{32}ln(p_2) + \beta_{33}ln(p_3)$$

The coefficients β_{ij} (for i,j = 1,2,3) must be determined to use this system to simulate the effects of a merger. The three 'own-coefficients' β_{11}, β_{22}, and β_{33} specify the effect of each brand's own-price on its share. The six other β_{ij}'s specify the effects of the prices of other brands on each brand's share.

When we use this AIDS model to simulate a merger, we wish to predict changes in the share of each brand resulting from the transaction. These changes (obtained formally by differentiating each equation totally) are given by the following:

$$ds_1 = \beta_{11}(dp_1/p_1) + \beta_{12}(dp_2/p_2) + \beta_{13}(dp_3/p_3)$$

$$ds_2 = \beta_{21}(dp_1/p_1) + \beta_{22}(dp_2/p_2) + \beta_{23}(dp_3/p_3)$$

$$ds_3 = \beta_{31}(dp_1/p_1) + \beta_{32}(dp_2/p_2) + \beta_{33}(dp_3/p_3)$$

The simple 3-brand example also allows us to illustrate the difficulty in estimating elasticities. In the example, a model with 3 brands has 9 β parameters: 3 own coefficients and 6 cross-effect coefficients, which correspond to 3 own elasticities and 6 cross-elasticities. To estimate the parameters of a demand model with many brands, it is necessary either to have a large data set, or to impose assumptions that reduce the number of independent parameters to be estimated.

4.6.5.2.4 Proportionally Calibrated AIDS

Calibrated-demand simulation models offer an alternative to models that rely on econometric estimation of demand. Because they reduce the number of required demand parameters, these models are especially valuable when there are data limitations or estimation problems, or when a rapid and less costly analysis is required. Budzinski and Ruhmer (2008) offer PCAIDS as a calibrated-demand model that provides analytical flexibility while retaining many of the desirable properties of AIDS. PCAIDS-models are especially valuable when data are limited or estimation problems exist, or when a rapid and less costly analysis is required. A PCAIDS model requires information on:

– market shares;
– the industry price elasticity[899;] and
– the price elasticity for one brand in the market.[900]

The logic of PCAIDS is simple. The share lost as a result of a price increase is allocated to the other firms in the relevant market in proportion to their respective shares.

---

899. The industry price elasticity shows the percentage change in sales in response to a 1% increase in price when all firms belonging to that industry simultaneously increase their price.
900. The own-price elasticity of a particular good gives the percentage change in the good's sales volume in response to a 1% increase in its price.

PCAIDS requires neither scanner data nor data on pre-merger prices. It requires information only on market shares, the industry price elasticity, and the price elasticity for one brand in the market. The logic of PCAIDS is simple. The share lost as a result of a price increase is allocated to the other firms in the relevant market in proportion to their respective shares. This is exactly the same proportionality assumption used in the logit demand system. In effect, the market shares define probabilities of making incremental sales for each of the competitors.

The PCAIDS model makes use of the proportionality property to extend the AIDS model. In light of the previous example, this property can be illustrated as follows. With proportionality, sales are diverted to brands 2 and 3 in proportion to the market shares of the two brands. For example, if brand 2 has a share of 40% and brand 3 a share of 20%, an increase in the price of brand 1 will increase the share of brand 2 by twice as much as it increases the share of brand 3. Formally, the proportionality assumption implies that the cross-effects associated with p can be expressed in terms of β_{11} and the observed shares; β_{21} is equal to:

$$-s_2/(s_2 + s_3)\beta_{11}$$

and β_{31} equals:

$$-s_3/(s_2 + s_3)\beta_{11}$$

The same relationships between own- and cross-effects hold for other prices; for example, β_{12} equals:

$$-s_1/(s_1 + s_3)\beta_{22}$$

The proportionality assumption reduces the number of unknown β's from 9 to 3. We only need to know the 3 own-effect coefficients (and market shares) to calculate the remaining 6 cross-effect coefficients. More generally, the proportionality assumption posits a direct relationship between all cross-effects associated with a particular price change and the corresponding own-effect.

The PCAIDS model can be calibrated with only two independent pieces of information (in addition to market shares): the elasticity of demand for a single brand and the elasticity for the industry as a whole. For example, only the industry elasticity and the own-price elasticity for brand 1 are needed as inputs in the calculation of the own-effect coefficient for brand 1, β_{11}:

$$\beta_{11} = s_1(\varepsilon_{11} + 1 - s_1(\varepsilon + 1))$$

In this equation, ε_{11} is the own-price elasticity for brand 1 and ε is the industry elasticity. All remaining unknown own-effect coefficients can be determined as simple multiples of β_{11}, as the following equation illustrates:

$$\beta_{ii} = \frac{s_i}{1-s_i}\frac{1-s_i}{s_i}\beta_{11}$$

Elasticities can be calculated directly from the values for the β parameters, the market shares (s^-_i), and the industry elasticity (ε), as follows.

Own-price elasticity for the ith brand:

$$\varepsilon_{ii} = -1 + \frac{b_i}{s_i} + s_i(\varepsilon + 1)$$

Cross-price elasticity of the ith brand with respect to the price of the jth brand:

$$\varepsilon_{ij} = \frac{b_{ij}}{s_i} + s_j(\varepsilon + 1)$$

The PCAIDS model faces the same pitfall as the logit and AIDS models: it relies on the proportionality assumption. However, as with nested logit demand systems, PCAIDS can be extended to include a nested structure. More specifically, products that are closer substitutes for each other than proportionality suggests may be placed together in 'nests.'

In the previous example, brand 2's market share of 30% and brand 3's share of 50% implied that 37.5% (30/80) of the share lost by brand 1 when its price increased would be diverted to brand 2 and 62.5% (50/80) would be diverted to brand 3. This effect can be characterised using an odds ratio. Here, the odds ratio between brand 2 and brand 3 is 0.6 (0.375/0.625). That is, under proportionality, brand 2 is only 60% as likely to be chosen by consumers leaving brand 1 as brand 3. Now suppose instead that brand 2 is relatively 'farther' from brand 1 in the sense that that fewer consumers would choose brand 2 in response to an increase in p_1 than would be predicted by proportionality. For example, brand 2 may only be 'half as desirable' a substitute as brand 3 and the appropriate odds ratio is really only 0.3. It is straightforward to calculate in this case that the share diversion to brand 2 becomes 23.1% and the diversion to brand 3 increases to 76.9% (an odds ratio of 0.3 = 0.231/0.769). As expected, fewer consumers leaving brand 1 would choose brand 2.

PCAIDS is generalised to cover such situations by constructing separate 'nests' of brands. Diversion among brands within each nest is characterised by proportionality. Share diverted to a brand in a different nest deviates from proportionality in the following sense: the odds ratio is equal to the odds ratio under proportionality, multiplied by an appropriate scaling factor ranging from 0 to 1. The result is that brands within a nest are closer substitutes than brands outside the nest. PCAIDS with nests allows a more flexible pattern of cross-elasticities, as the model is no longer fully constrained by the proportionality assumption.[901]

4.6.5.3 *The Simulation Stage*

Whereas the estimation stage involves the calculation of parameter values for a demand system that characterises the behaviour of purchasers of the relevant products before the merger, the calibration of the model involves 'fitting' the estimated demand

---

901. (Epstein and Rubinfeld 2001).

parameters to pre-merger market shares and profit margins. In particular, the model is used to carry out counterfactual thought experiments like the simulation of the prevailing prices in the post-merger world, under different assumptions about the magnitude and nature of efficiencies. At the simulation stage, estimated demand parameters and profit margins are used to predict the likely price increase resulting from exercise of incremental market power by the merging products. When solving for the model's equilibrium, all producers are assumed to maximise their short-term profits after, as well as before, the merger.

Since own- and cross-price elasticities have already been estimated, the last step to estimate unilateral effects is to simulate the post-merger equilibrium price derived from the First-Order Conditions (FOCs) of the merged entity's profit-maximisation problem. The post-merger equilibrium price is calculated as the price that maximises profits for the merged entity whereby the profit function of the merged entity is derived from the pre-merger demand and cost structure specifications.

Under short-term profit maximising behaviour, demand parameters and observed market shares imply a profit margin for each product. This profit margin is the gross margin also known as the Lerner Index (L) defined as follows:

$$L = \frac{1}{\varepsilon_{ii}} = \frac{P_i - MC_i}{P_i}$$

Where ε_{ii} is the own-price elasticity of demand for product i, p_i is the profit-maximising price of product i, and MC_i is the corresponding marginal cost. It can be shown that this expression derives from the profit-maximisation problem faced by a firm and satisfies the equality of marginal cost with marginal revenue.

Pre-merger margins are calculated from the pre-merger FOCs for profit-maximisation i.e., the Lerner Index as illustrated above, by using the pre-merger own-price elasticities obtained in the estimation stage. The post-merger FOCs are then obtained by solving the profit-maximisation problem faced by the merging firm and the non-merging firms. Finally, the post-merger equilibrium price is derived by finding the vector of prices that solves the system of post-merger FOCs for each firm in the market.[902]

Another issue that deserves particular attention is the assumption concerning the efficiency gains resulting from a merger. The advantage of MSM is that it incorporates efficiencies, as the model usually takes the extent to which the claimed efficiencies are likely to reduce incremental costs post-merger into account. Efficiency gains or synergies may occur from the fact that marginal costs of the merging firms both decrease as a result of the merger. The existence of these merger efficiencies may mitigate the effects of an increase in post-merger prices by increasing overall welfare through economies of scale. The consideration of merger efficiencies is an integral part in any MSM.

---

902. (Palmer 2010, 12).

Chapter 4: Competition Practice

4.6.6 Commission's Use of Merger Simulation Models

Since the entering into force of Regulation 139/2004, the Commission has employed simulation analysis in a number of cases.[903] In the following we discuss some of them in accordance with the merger simulation model applied.

4.6.6.1 *Linear Demand Model*

The Commission used a linear demand model in the *Honeywell/Novar*[904] case.

4.6.6.1.1 The Case

In that case from 2004, Honeywell announced its binding intention to acquire all of the outstanding shares of Novar. Honeywell is an advanced technology manufacturing company and Novar is an international group based in the UK focusing on Intelligent Building Systems (IBS), Indalex Aluminum Solutions (IAS) and Security Printing Services (SPS). Both companies overlap in relation to commercial building security systems (fire and intrusion alarms), and commercial building control systems.

One of the relevant markets was the fire alarm system market. In two other markets the Commission saw limited overlaps: the first one being the market of intrusion and other security systems and the second one being the market of building control systems.

4.6.6.1.2 Merger Simulation Model

The Commission calibrated a simulation model based on a linear pricing contract assumption between non-integrated upstream and downstream firms. As a result, it found that the quantities available on the market would be reduced by a significant amount. Prices would increase in turn.[905]

The Commission cleared the transaction.

4.6.6.2 *Nested Logit Models*

Cases in which the Commission has run merger simulations based on nested logit demand models include *Scania/Volvo*,[906] *Lagardère/Natexis/VU*,[907] and *Unilever/Sara*

---

903. (Decision M.3867 on Vattenfall/Elsam and E2 Assets 2005); (Decision 2007/353 on DONG/Elsam/Energi E2 (M.3868) 2006); (Decision COMP/M.3916 on T-Mobile Austria/tele.ring 2006); (Decision M.5224 on EDF/British Energy 2008); (Decision M.5467 on RWE/Essent 2009); (Decision M.5549 on EDF/Segebel 2009); (Decision COMP/M.5644 on Kraft Foods/Cadbury 2010); (Decision COMP/M.5658 on Unilever/Sara Lee 2010).
904. (Decision COMP/M.3686 on Honeywell/Novar 2005).
905. (J. Foncel 2009, 6).
906. (Decision M.1672 on Volvo/Scania 2000).
907. (Decision COMP/M.2978 on Lagardère/Natexis/VUP 2004).

477

Lee[908]. Furthermore, in *Kraft Foods/Cadbury*[909], results of a nested logit demand model for chocolate were presented to the Commission by the different parties.

All mergers, except *Scania/Volvo*, were cleared conditional upon remedies by the Commission. The following subsections cover each individual case.

4.6.6.2.1 Scania/Volvo

The merger between Scania and Volvo, which the Commission blocked in March 2000 is probably the first case of a fully-fledged merger simulation exercise. This case showed that sometimes economists disagree significantly over the merits and value of a particular model and that the findings of merger simulation exercises can therefore be highly controversial.[910]

4.6.6.2.1.1 The Case

The main concerns in the merger between Volvo and Scania related to the truck market. The truck market can be segmented into three categories: light duty trucks, medium duty trucks and heavy duty trucks (further divided into rigid trucks and tractor trucks). The Commission decided to focus its analysis on the heavy truck segment only and to restrict the investigation to Sweden, Norway, Finland, Ireland and Denmark because the merger would not have created any dominant position in the remaining Member States.

In the five countries mentioned, the joint market share of Scania and Volvo would have been in the 49%–91% range. The Commission defined the relevant geographic markets as the national markets of these five countries.

4.6.6.2.1.2 Merger Simulation Model

The econometric analysis performed simulated the consequences of the merger. The model chosen by Ivaldi and Verboven was the nested logit model, as discussed above. Such a model has the advantage of allowing some flexibility into the analysis by dividing products into nests. In the Volvo/Scania case, the two nests corresponded to rigid and tractor trucks. Products belonging to the same nest are closer substitutes than products belonging to another nest. Within the same nest, the proportionality assumption of the simple logit and PCAIDS model applies. Therefore, the nested logit model is not a fully flexible model as it somewhat restricts the cross-price elasticties, although in many cases it is considered a reasonably good approximation.

The main results of the merger simulation exercise were computed assuming that Volvo and Scania were under common ownership and that the merger would not have induced any change in the degree of collusion in the industry.

---

908. (Decision COMP/M.5658 on Unilever/Sara Lee 2010).
909. (Decision COMP/M.5644 on Kraft Foods/Cadbury 2010).
910. (Conti 2006, 8).

Although DG Competition commissioned the merger simulation exercise from Professors Ivaldi and Verboven, the decision was ultimately based on a conventional market share analysis. The Commission justified its decision with the argument that the large market shares of the merging parties, coupled with a large difference between the market share of the merged entity and that of the closest competitor (in the range of 36%–85%), strong brand loyalty, little customer bargaining power and high entry costs.

4.6.6.2.2 Lagardère/Natexis/VUP

4.6.6.2.2.1   The Case[911]

In 2003, the French group Lagardère acquired part of the publishing business of Editis (formerly known as Vivendi Universal Publishing or VUP), through its subsidiary Hachette Livre. Editis is the biggest publisher, marketer and distributor of French books, while Hachette is second in the market.[912]

4.6.6.2.2.2   Merger Simulation Model

The Commission used a nested logit model to estimate the demand for literature. Consumers' demand decisions are assumed to be hierarchical in that first, the type of book (humour, thriller, etc.), and then, on the second level, a specific book is chosen.[913]

Data on prices and volumes concerning the 5,000 bestsellers in pocket-format in 2002 and 1,500 bestsellers in large-format were provided by IPSOS. The sample covered a big share of the market in 2002. These books accounted for over 96% of pocket-format sales and 44% of large format sales. The econometric study was based on a Bertrand competition model in which consumer preferences were represented by a nested logit model.

The resulting simulated price increase was 4.84%. Differentiating between hardcover and paperback books there were an increase of 5.51% for paperback and 1.59% for hardcover ones so that the average price increase was based on the increase in paperback books.

The merging parties were critical that the model did not differentiate sufficiently between hardcover and paperback books. Their final point was that the Commission hadn't taken into account how publishing and book price determination work in reality. Nonetheless the Commission judged all the criticism unfounded and so the study was used.

The merger was cleared subject to conditions.

---

911. (Decision COMP/M.2978 on Lagardère/Natexis/VUP 2004).
912. (Foncel, Ivaldi and Rabassa 2007, 2).
913. (Budzinski and Ruhmer 2008, 38).

4.6.6.2.3   Unilever/Sara Lee

4.6.6.2.3.1   The Case

The *Unilever/Sara Lee* case[914] concerned the sale of branded deodorants in some Member States.

4.6.6.2.3.2   Merger Simulation Model

The Commission itself developed a nested logit demand model. To simulate the demand function, a one-level and a two-level nested logit model was applied. The nests were male and non-male deodorants brands, the sub-nests skin friendly or not. A standard Bertrand-Nash market equilibrium was used.

The Commission used different data sources for the model. First of all, they used retail scanner data (data that is gathered by the cashier's scanner device) produced by Nielsen from April 2006 to March 2009. These detailed store and transaction level data are generally available. The Commission used country level datasets for four countries: Belgium, the Netherlands, Spain, and the UK.

Secondly, the Commission used data on the individual product level also covering the years 2006 to 2009 on a weekly basis. For each product, the following variables were observed: the total value and volume of sales, the number of units sold and also some product characteristics (size, gender proposition, format). For the estimations, the data were aggregated to a quarterly level. In addition, Unilever provided its classification of the scanner data along with further dimensions of product differentiation.

Thirdly, Unilever and Sara Lee, submitted their own (separate) internal transaction data. This data tracked the companies' sales to their customers, mostly retailers. The data covered 2007–2009 on a monthly basis on a detailed product level (brand, sub-brand, gender, format, size). The observed variables included the value of sales, volume of sales, gross profits, and gross profit margins.

The Commission carried out a simulation for eight markets (male and non-male deodorants in the four countries), finding estimated price increases between 1% and 6%. Competition concerns were ultimately raised for five of these markets, all with estimated price increases of 2% or higher. The largest overall predicted price increases were those for Belgium around 4–5%. The figures for the Dutch market were somewhat lower (3.8%) followed by the UK and Spanish estimates (2–2.5%).

The methodology employed gave the Commission the opportunity to look at compensating efficiency gains that would offset anti-competitive effects, in particular a substantial decrease in the post-merger marginal costs. The nested logit model used

---

914. (Decision COMP/M.5658 on Unilever/Sara Lee 2010).

generally relied on simplifying assumptions, a crucial feature being that the switching between individual brands is proportional to brand market share.

The decision is also noteworthy for the importance awarded by the Commission to statistical reliability and robustness checks. The latter were particularly necessary in view of the inherent limitations of the econometric evidence presented in this case.

The Commission cleared the transaction.

4.6.6.2.4 Kraft Foods/Cadbury

4.6.6.2.4.1 The Case

On 9 November 2009, Kraft Foods announced a hostile bid for Cadbury plc. The companies overlapped primarily in the supply of chocolate confectionary. Chocolate confectionary can broadly be grouped into three categories: count lines, tablets and pralines. Kraft and Cadbury produced chocolates in all three segments but their main overlap was in the tablets segment.[915]

4.6.6.2.4.2 Merger Simulation Model

First, the parties' economic advisers estimated a nested logit demand system[916] for confectionary chocolate in the UK and Ireland econometrically. Secondly, a merger simulation was carried out to predict the impact of the transaction. The effect of the transaction was then simulated with a Bertrand model of competition (ignoring product repositioning and entry). It was estimated that the proposed operation would lead to an overall weighted average price increase of 1% in the UK (even less in Ireland) in the absence of efficiencies.[917]

In the nested logit model each nest corresponded to a relevant market (the three nests were tablets, pralines and count lines). In this type of model, substitution is proportional to market shares within each nest, whilst the fact that Kraft sells continental chocolate and Cadbury supplies British Heritage plays absolutely no role, even though it was one of the main reasons for clearing the transaction. Thus in fact the added value to a simple analysis of market shares was limited.[918]

The Commission cleared the takeover.[919]

---

915. (Andreu, Edwards and Requejo 2010).
916. The nested logit demand system is a particular functional form of demand from which own- and cross-price elasticities are derived. It is based on discrete choice modelling and allocates each product into a particular product category or 'nest' (in this case, countlines, tablets or pralines) to allow for some correlation of consumer tastes across products (see (S. Berry 1994)).
917. (Decision COMP/M.5644 on Kraft Foods/Cadbury 2010, paras 64–65).
918. (Durand 2012, 8).
919. (Slaughter and May 2010).

4.6.6.2.5   Tomtom/Tele Atlas

4.6.6.2.5.1   The Case

The merger between TomTom and Tele Atlas was a case of backward integration, where a downstream manufacturer (TomTom) acquired one of its input providers (Tele Atlas). The Commission calculated in this case the value of sales TomTom would be able to capture downstream post-merger. To estimate the downstream elasticities, the Commission used a nested logit model.

4.6.6.2.5.2   Merger Simulation Model

The model used retail data covering monthly sales and volumes of the product for the last three years. On the basis of the estimated own-price and (inter and intra-nest) cross-price elasticity parameters for each product, it was calculated that a price increase of 1% by all TomTom's competitors (except Garmin) would lead to an increase in the number of PNDs sold by TomTom in the range of 0.3–0.5%.

The result of the Commission's model was that the sales captured by the merged entity downstream by raising its rivals' costs would not be sufficient to compensate for the lost sales upstream if it engaged in input foreclosure.

The Commission cleared the transaction.

4.6.6.3   Use of Auction Models

There were at least four cases in which the Commission or one of the concerned parties used auction models: *Sydkraft/Graninge, Oracle/PeopleSoft, Vattenfall/Elsam and E2 assets* and *Thales/Finmeccanica/Alcatel Alenia Space/Telespazio*.

4.6.6.3.1   Sydkraft/Graninge

4.6.6.3.1.1   The Case

On 29 September 2003, the Commission received a notification of a proposed concentration by which Sydkraft AB belonging to the German E.ON Group, would acquire sole control of the whole of the undertaking Graninge AB, by purchasing shares.[920] The two energy companies are active in Sweden and Finland. At the time, it came forth that the local grid operator in western Denmark, Eltra, was in possession of a model of the Nordic power market.[921]

---

920. (Decision M.3268 on Sydkraft/Graninge 2003, para. 1).
921. (Hofer 2012, 56).

Chapter 4: Competition Practice

4.6.6.3.1.2   Merger Simulation Model

MARS is a model developed by the grid operator for Western Denmark, Elkraft, which is now part of Energinet.dk. The model seeks to emulate the market conditions under which each electricity producer is operating on Nord Pool; based on these conditions the model tries to predict what their optimal bidding strategy for each hour of a hypothetical year would be.

In addition to being based on sophisticated game-theoretic principles, the simulation model also took an array of industry-specific features into account. These – among others – included the different technologies for producing electricity, the varying fuel prices and resulting marginal cost fluctuations, the substantial variation of demand over time, and the possibility of transmission constraints in the Nordic power grids.[922]

After having compared the outcome with and without the merger by using MARS, it was concluded that: *'It appears from market power simulations with MARS that the merger between Sydkraft and Graninge does not result in higher average prices in Sweden'*. The simulations indicated that Sydkraft prior to the merger is not sufficiently large to have the incentive to withhold capacity, in order to generate a price increase. This absence of market power is not significantly altered by the acquisition of Graninge.[923]

The Commission cleared the transaction.

4.6.6.3.2   Oracle/Peoplesoft

Merger simulation has also been used in *Oracle/PeopleSoft*. This was the first case in which the Commission's use of econometric methods was particularly decisive for the outcome of the case. It was also the first merger in which the merger simulation model was realised by an in-house economist of the Commission.[924]

4.6.6.3.2.1   The Case

Oracle and PeopleSoft were two of many companies active in the part of the software industry that is called Enterprise Application Software (EAS).[925] In 2003, Oracle made a public bid to purchase PeopleSoft. The Commission was concerned that the merger would lead to a reduction in the number of viable contenders in a bidding contest from three to two, which could lead to significant harm to customers due to a combination of reduced choice and increased prices.

---

922. (Hofer 2012, 56).
923. (Decision M.3268 on Sydkraft/Graninge 2003, para. 37).
924. (Budzinski and Ruhmer 2009, 41).
925. (Bengtsson 2005).

4.6.6.3.2.2   Merger Simulation Model

The in-house experts designed a 'sealed-bid auction model where the vendors know the identity of their competitors but cannot observe the monetary value customers assign to the different competing products'.

The vendors choose their bids based on a calculation of the expected profits depending on price and the probability to win the auction while not having information on their competitors. The costs were ignored in the Commission's model because most of the costs occur before the auction starts and the distribution is very cheap.

The relevant markets were Human Resources (HR) and Financial Management Systems (FMS). The Commission also used two scenarios for efficiency gains: the first one was rather pessimistic by keeping product quality constant, while the second one let product quality increase. Additionally, the model calibrated quality levels and different levels of uncertainty about product quality which led to a wide spread among the results of consumer surplus and price.[926]

The Commission used data submitted by Oracle itself. Oracle submitted data for 728 bids between 2001 and 2003 with an average licence value of EUR 708,851. This data contains a number of bids for niche products and best-of breed solutions not falling into the product market and having a much lower licence value (e.g., 235 bids with licence values between EUR 2,000 and EUR 100,000). As Oracle was not able to specify the modules contained in these bids, the Commission could not verify whether or not they fell within the markets for high-function FMS and HR solutions.

The results of the merger model were that in the HR market, the price increase varied from 6.8% to 25.5% whereas in the FMS price changes from 13.9% to 30% with a 10% quality improvement were observed. The loss of customer surplus was about 37.8% in the pessimistic and 15.5% in the optimistic scenario for the HR market and 17.9% to 25.2% loss of customer surplus in the FMS market. However, the modelling also showed that the outcome of the sealed-bid auction model were unreliable and that false market definitions were used, which is why the Commission had to abandon the model.[927]

The following excerpt of the Commission's decision is of particular interest for the evidential value of the simulation method in general:

> *As a general matter Oracle submits that the use of simulation models is controversial due to the unavoidable need to make simplifying assumptions. (...) The Commission agrees that the use of simulation models depends critically on the ability of the model to adequately capture the fundamental mechanisms that drive the behaviour of the different market participants and that, in principle, the assessment as to whether that is the case in any particular case may be a subject of debate. (...) The Commission therefore maintains as a general point that this kind of simulation model can be a useful tool in assisting the Commission in making the economic assessment of the likely impact of a merger.*

The Commission cleared the transaction.

---

926. (Bengtsson 2005).
927. *Ibid.*

Chapter 4: Competition Practice

4.6.6.3.3 Vattenfall/Elsam and E2 Assets

4.6.6.3.3.1 The Case

On 18 October 2005, the Commission received the notification of a proposed concentration in which Vattenfall AB (Sweden) would acquire control of parts of the companies ElsamA/S (Denmark) and Energi E2 (Denmark), through a swap agreement with DONG A/S (Denmark).

4.6.6.3.3.2 Merger Simulation Model

Based on its market simulation model of the Nordic electricity market (MARS), Energinet.dk has performed a number of simulations for the Commission, in order to assess the potential effects of the merger on prices in Denmark and the rest of the Nord Pool area.

MARS is a model developed seeking to emulate the market conditions under which each electricity producer is operating on Nord Pool. Based on these conditions the model tries to predict what their optimal bidding strategy for each hour of a hypothetical year would be.

The strategies of the producers are calculated on the basis of a number of exogenous factors that describe the hypothetical year, including electricity prices in the Kontek area, the prices of production inputs, as well as the amount of rain and thus the water levels in the reservoirs. Based on this information, as well as information about the transmission capacity between the different price areas and the production facilities available for each producer, the model predicts the bid that each bidder will submit to Nord Pool. On the basis of the bids and assumed consumption patterns, as well as transmission capacity, the model then calculates the resulting prices in each price area for each hour of the year.

It was predicted by MARS that the transfer of assets to Vattenfall would lead to a small fall in average prices in Denmark of less than 1% while the effect in other price areas would be *de minimis*.[928]

The Commission cleared the transaction.

4.6.6.3.4 Thales/Finmeccanica/Alcatel Alenia Space/Telespazio

4.6.6.3.4.1 The Case

Thales S.A. and Finmeccanica intended to acquire joint control of the undertakings Alcatel Alenia Space SAS (ASS) and Telespazio Holding srl by purchasing shares in two existing joint ventures to which additional assets are contributed.[929]

---

928. (Decision M.3867 on Vattenfall/Elsam and E2 Assets 2005).
929. (Decision COMP/M.4403 on Thales/Finmeccanica/Alcatel Alenia Space & Telespazio 2007).

4.6.6.3.4.2   Merger Simulation Model

In this case, the Commission considered a vertical simulation model, which was submitted by the parties and which analysed the pricing strategies of upstream and downstream firms.[930] The model assesses the new entity's economic incentive to foreclose its rival prime contractors with a view to increasing AAS's chances of winning satellite contracts. Therefore the study used two economic models: a relatively simple vertical arithmetic analysis and a more sophisticated bidding model.[931]

The conclusions of the study were that the new entity would have a strong economic incentive to foreclose its rival prime contractors and that, under certain assumptions, these foreclosure practices would result in very significant price increases.

The objective of the first model (vertical arithmetic analysis) was to compare the margins. The model in fact evaluated the critical diversion ratio. The critical diversion ratio is necessary to make the foreclosure profitable and it obtained a result of about 6.5%, which is quite low. The Commission made its own calculation using the margins and price data obtained during its market investigation and obtained results of between 27% and 40% depending on the data.

The second model was much more sophisticated and sought to model the bidding process. While the model was relatively complex to reflect the bidding process and market players' strategies, it applied extreme assumptions in order to simplify the calculation. Under these very unlikely conditions, the model showed that the new equilibrium would be significantly different from the current market conditions and that prices would increase. AAS would acquire a 53% market share of the commercial satellite market (compared to 10–20% pre-merger). This strategy would be profitable for the new entity.

The Commission reviewed the economic study and reached the conclusion that the proposed models failed to reflect the competitive dynamics and the various segments of the industry appropriately and that the models' assumptions and conclusions were not supported by the market investigation.

In 2007, the transaction was cleared, among other reasons because the Commission did not find foreclosure to be a concern.

4.7   STATE AID PROVISIONS

State aid consists of *'an advantage in any form whatsoever conferred on a selective basis to undertakings by national public authorities'*.[932] A company which receives government support gains an advantage over its competitors. Therefore, the Treaty of Lisbon generally prohibits State aid unless it is justified by reasons of general economic

---

930. (J. Foncel 2009, 6).
931. (Decision COMP/M.4403 on Thales/Finmeccanica/Alcatel Alenia Space & Telespazio 2007, para. 411).
932. (Commission on State Aid control 2013).

development. To ensure that this prohibition is respected and that exemptions are applied equally across the EU, the European Commission is in charge of ensuring that State aid complies with EU rules.

Historical Development

The existence of state aid control in Europe dates back to the creation of the European Coal and Steel Community (ECSC) by the Treaty of Paris which set out a strict ban on State Aid in its Article 4(c). In fact, the latter declared incompatible with the common market for coal and steel *'subsidies or aids granted by States, or special charges imposed by States, in any form whatsoever'*.[933]

2005 was a turning point in European state aid control. Indeed, in response to the growing need to rethink the balance between the various objectives of state intervention, the European Commission adopted the State Aid Action Plan (SAAP) which launched a comprehensive reform of state aid policy that covered a five-year period (2005–2009). The aim of that reform was to encourage Member States to help achieve the objectives of the Lisbon Strategy. In particular, the SAAP was the initial step towards the implementation of a more economics, effect-based approach in state aid and state aid control, also called the 'refined economic approach'.[934] Such an approach should be based on a detailed economic analysis of the balancing between the positive and negative effects of aid (the so-called Balancing Test). Both at national and European level, the political mandate has since then been for *'less and better targeted state aid'*.[935]

The latest developments in state aid control were initiated on 8 May 2012, in the light of Europe 2020, Europe's growth strategy for this decade, when the Commission set out an ambitious State aid reform programme in the Communication on State aid modernisation (SAM). In a changing world, the Commission is targeting its policies at making Europe a smart, sustainable and inclusive economy. Those three mutually reinforcing objectives should help the EU and the Member States deliver high levels of employment, productivity and social cohesion.[936] The modernisation has three main, closely linked objectives:

- Foster growth in a strengthened, dynamic and competitive internal market.
- Focus enforcement on cases with the biggest impact on the internal market.
- Streamlined rules and faster decisions.

Under the SAM, the Commission has revised and consolidated State aid guidelines and regulations specific to the exemption of some types of aid from State aid rules. This shall reinforce the principle of less and better targeted state aid.

---

933. (European Coal and Steel Community 1951).
934. (Friederiszick, Röller and Verouden 2007).
935. (Commission Discussion Paper on the application of Art. 82 of the Treaty to exclusionary abuses 2005).
936. (Commission Communication on EU State Aid Modernisation 2012).

In the following sections, the economic principles are reviewed underlying the role of state aid control, the economic rationale behind the granting of state aid, and the refined economic approach adopted by the Commission in its assessment of state aid.

4.7.1 Economics in the EU State Aid Rules

The point of departure of EU State aid policy is laid down in Article 107(1) TFEU. This article provides that State aid is, in principle, incompatible with the common market. Under Article 108, the Commission is given the task of controlling State aid. This article also requires Member States to inform the Commission in advance of any plan to grant State aid ('notification requirement').

The definition of state aid is embedded in Article 107(1) as follows:

> *Save as otherwise provided in the Treaties, any aid granted by a Member State or through State resources in any form whatsoever which distorts or threatens to distort competition by favouring certain undertakings or the production of certain goods shall, in so far as it affects trade between Member States, be incompatible with the internal market.*[937]

According to this provision, there are four criteria to be met in order for a measure to qualify as state aid.

First, state aid needs to be a *transfer of government funds*. In other words, it should constitute an intervention by the State or through State resources, which can take a variety of forms (e.g., grants, interest and tax reliefs, guarantees, government holdings of all or part of a company, or providing goods and services on preferential terms, etc.). Furthermore, the aid does not necessarily need to be granted by the State itself. It may also be granted by a private or public intermediate body appointed by the State.

Second, this state measure should confer an *economic advantage* upon the recipient, which it would not obtain under 'normal' market conditions. This therefore excludes the cases in which the state, for example, awards a contract to a supplier after a tender, as long as the services of the supplier are compensated reasonably and not excessively by the state. Economic analysis establishes the extent to which an aid measure confers an economic advantage to the recipient of the aid. In many cases, it is easy to determine the size of the economic advantage, i.e., for direct subsidies granted to firms. In many other situations, however, it is much more difficult, in particular where governments invest in companies or provide loans or guarantees.[938]

---

937. (Consolidated version of the Treaty on the Functioning of the European Union, Art. 107 2008).
938. Prominent examples include the assessment of whether a government acts like a 'private investor' in providing (financial) support to a selected undertaking or a group of undertakings, as well as the exemption rule under Art. 86 EC Treaty for the provision of services of general economic interest, the so-called 'net additional cost test'. For the private investor test see (CFI, Westdeutsche Landesbank Girozentrale v. Commission, Joined Cases T-228/99 and T-233/99 2003) and for the so-called 'private creditor test' see (CFI, Lenzing AG v. Commission, Case T-36/99 2004). The net additional cost test is discussed in Commission, 'Proposal on a

Third, the state transfer must be conducted *selectively*, thus benefiting some companies more than others. This criterion excludes fundamental or general measures of the state, which generally benefit all companies within the measure. The selective character thus distinguishes State aid measures from general economic support measures. Most nationwide fiscal measures would be regarded as general measures as they apply across the board to all firms in all sectors of activity in a Member State. The distinction is, however, not always clear-cut. For example, a measure that is open to all sectors may be selective if there is an element of discretion by the awarding authorities. On the other hand, the fact that certain companies might benefit more than others from a measure does not necessarily mean that the measure is selective. The interpretation of the concept of selectivity has evolved over the years following various Commission decisions and Court rulings.[939]

Fourth, the *competition and trade* between two or more Member States must be affected by the award of state funds. This criterion is sufficiently met if it can be demonstrated that the beneficiary is situated on a market where companies from other Member States are also active. This criterion constitutes what can be called an economic assessment of the effects of an aid on the economic reality of competition and trade between Member States.[940] Prior to the application of the refined economic approach, distortions of competition and effects on trade were assumed to be already present when the measure was selective, that is when the market position of the aid beneficiary vis-à-vis its competitors was improved by the aid.[941]

According to Article 107(1), aid measures that satisfy all the criteria outlined above are, in principle, incompatible with the common market.

Article 107(2) and 107(3) specify in addition a number of cases in which State aid could be considered acceptable (the so-called 'exemptions'). The existence of these exemptions justifies the vetting of planned State aid measures by the Commission, as foreseen in Article 108. This Article provides that Member States must notify the Commission of any plan to grant State aid before putting such a plan into effect. It also gives the Commission the single power to decide whether the proposed aid measure qualifies for exemption or whether the '*State concerned shall abolish or alter such aid*'. Exemptions only become relevant when the State measure is found to be a State aid in accordance with Article 107(1). The intention of Article 107(3) is to determine the pro-competitive benefits produced by that State aid and to assess whether these pro-competitive effects outweigh the anti-competitive effects.

Community Framework for State Aid in the Form of Public Service Compensation', 2004. The Commission applied this approach in its RAI decision. See (Decision 2004/339 on RAI SpA 2003).
939. See (Kociubinski 2012).
940. (Schmauch 2012, 121).
941. (Friederiszick, Röller and Verouden 2006, 627).

4.7.2 Balancing Test in Article 107(3)

The balancing test in Article 107(3) weighs the positive effects of, for example, risk capital measures or aid to research and innovation against potential crowding-out or other negative effects on competition and trade.[942] The economic argument is that State aid may correct market failures and thereby restore competition again. In this analysis, several types of market failures are relevant which are discussed in more detail below.[943]

The three steps balancing test operates upon the approval of a State aid measure. The first two steps address the positive effects of State aid whereas the third addresses the negative effects thereby resulting in a balancing of the positive and negative effects. The following issues need to be addressed from an economic perspective:

The aid needs to address a well-defined market failure or a well-defined objective of common interest (e.g., growth, employment, cohesion, environment).

The aid must be well targeted. The question is whether the aid is well-designed to deliver the objective of common interest i.e., does the proposed aid address the market failure or other objective? In this context an assessment is made as to whether State aid is the appropriate policy instrument, whether there is an incentive effect, i.e., does the aid change the behaviour of firms; and whether the aid measure is proportional, i.e., could the same change in behaviour be obtained with less aid.[944]

Another aspect is that the distortions to competition and trade resulting from the State aid measure must be limited enough so that, on balance, it can be declared compatible.

Thus, the first step of the balancing test focuses on the objective. Objectives of common interest can be divided between those targeting efficiency (increasing wealth in the economy) and those targeting equity (better division of the wealth between stakeholders, notably to reflect social and regional cohesion). As a result, an appropriate starting point in any assessment of State aid is to ask whether there is a market failure or an equity objective. This transparency *vis-à-vis* the objective of the aid measure is needed in order to assess the effectiveness or necessity of the aid. Moreover, transparency between efficiency and equity is essential in order to assess possible trade-offs between the two objectives.

However, it is not sufficient for State aid to target a market failure. Before resorting to State aid, which is in general only the 'second best' option to achieve an optimal allocation of resources, it should be verified whether other less distortive measures could remedy the market failure. An assessment will be made as to whether there are other, better placed instruments, which are either more effective or less costly

---

942. (Fingleton, Ruane and Ryan 1999, 77). For example in the case of environmental protection the possible instruments would include taxation, regulation, tradable emission licences and also State aid.
943. See also (Meiklejohn 1999, 25).
944. (Friederiszick, Röller and Verouden 2006, 648).

in reaching the objective chosen.[945] According to European case law, the amount and the intensity of State aid must be limited to the necessary minimum.[946] Therefore, also examined is whether any alternative instrument exists, which is considerably milder while still having the same effect as the chosen one.[947]

A State measure needs to involve a change in behaviour of the firms in order to be justified. This change in behaviour is assessed by means of the *incentive effect*. In order to identify the incentive effect of the State measure, reference values are used.[948] The Commission applies the following assessment (e.g., with respect to risk capital). The first question to be asked is exactly which changes should be produced by the State funding. By means of a counterfactual analysis important findings are gained: The incentive impact is expressed as the difference between two scenarios comparing a situation with and without the State measure. Furthermore, a continuous evaluation guarantees the observation of the incentive effect. The implementation of pilot projects and the definition of benchmarks ensure documentation. These references serve as indicators of the incentive effect.[949] From the economic perspective it is important that the incentive effect generates benefits for the consumers as a result of the State measure. Without an incentive effect, a firm's behaviour is not affected and consumers are not affected either, since the aid is simply transferred from the taxpayer to the firm. The consumer standard plays a crucial role in this context. If there is no incentive effect, there cannot be any benefit to consumers, hence the necessity of the incentive effect. In this sense, the consumer standard (as operationalised by the incentive effect) is a safeguard against windfall profits to firms.[950] If the result of this analysis is that the desired incentives cannot be achieved with a lower intensity and the impacts involved, the conclusion can be drawn that no milder instrument solves the market failure, therefore the chosen measure is necessary. Thus by analysing the incentive effect and proportionality, State aid is tested as to whether it is an appropriate policy instrument and whether it is designed in such a way that it effectively solves the market failure. In assessing this *appropriateness*, a determination is made as to whether the aid measure is suitable to solve the observed problem.[951]

The balancing of the positive and negative effects of the State aid is the next step. Whether generated positive effects outweigh the negative effects caused by the distortion of competition is analysed.

---

945. See also (ECJ, Commission v. Germany, Case C-209/00 2001, 9, 31, 34, 38, 40, 42, 45, 46, 48, 50, 54).
946. (CFI, Schmitz-Gotha Fahrzeugwerke GmbH v. Commission, Case T-17/03 2006, 4).
947. (CFI, Deutsche Bahn AG v. Commission, Case T-351/02 2006, 86).
948. The Commission developed for example reference values in the Community framework for State aid for research and development and innovation. See (Community framework for state aid for research and development and innovation 2006).
949. For indicators of the incentive effect for risk capital see (Community guidelines on State aid to promote risk capital investments in small and medium-sized enterprises 2006, 12).
950. (Friederiszick, Röller and Verouden 2006, 650).
951. For example, (Community framework for state aid for research and development and innovation 2006, 8).

To conclude, the balancing test is the measurement of positive effects in relationship to possible negative effects.[952] If the positive effects dominate the negative effects, an exemption under Article 107(3) is likely.[953]

Market Failures

The assessment of market failures is another area where economic analysis is important. There are a number of market failures that prevent the market from functioning.

Externalities are the most frequently discussed type of market imperfection in the context of State aid policy.[954] An externality exists whenever one individual's actions affect the well-being of another individual, whether for the better or for the worse, in ways that need not be paid for according to the existing definition of property rights in the society. Externalities of either the 'positive' or the 'negative' sort create a problem for the effective functioning of the market to maximise the total utility of the society. The 'external' portions of the costs and benefits of producing a good will not be factored into its supply and demand functions because rational profit-maximising buyers and sellers do not take into account costs and benefits they do not have to bear. Hence a portion of the costs or benefits will not be reflected in determining the market equilibrium prices and quantities of the good involved.[955] Accordingly, aggregate supply and demand for goods that entail positive externalities is too small. On the contrary, goods that entail negative externalities may encounter demand above the socially optimal level.[956]

The term *public good* is used to describe goods that are characterised by non-rivalry and non-excludability.[957] Public goods cannot practically be withheld from one individual consumer without withholding them from all ('non-excludability') and for which the marginal cost of an additional person consuming them, once they have been produced, is zero ('non rivalrous consumption'). Consequently, private production of the good is unprofitable, and the good may not be provided at all by the free market.[958] National defence is an example of a public good.

A market failure can also arise through differently distributed information. Information asymmetry models assume that at least one party to a transaction has relevant information whereas the others do not. *Information asymmetry* occurs when one party to a transaction has more or better information than the other party. If the buyers are less informed than the suppliers of a good, this might be exploited by suppliers providing products with reduced quality and thus at lower costs, which is not realised by buyers due to their information deficit. The consequence is a so-called adverse selection: worse products drive out qualitatively better products.[959]

---

952. Heidhues, Nitsche in: (Bartosch, et al. 2006, 23–24, 33).
953. (CFI, Schmitz-Gotha Fahrzeugwerke GmbH v. Commission, Case T-17/03 2006, 3, 34, 41, 43); (CFI, Technische Glaswerke Ilmenau Gmbh v. Commission, Case T-198/01 2004, 170 and 174).
954. (Meiklejohn 1999, 28).
955. (P. M. Johnson n.d.).
956. (Fritsch, Wein and Ewers 1996, 81).
957. (Samuelson 1954).
958. (Musgrave, Musgrave and Kullmer 1990, 55–56).
959. (Akerlof 1970).

Chapter 4: Competition Practice

Markets may also not function efficiently when there is a *coordination problem* between market actors. This aspect plays a key role in standards setting. Another aspect is *market power*. Notably, market power leads to prices that are too high from society's point of view, thereby not achieving efficiency.[960]

The aims of State intervention and implementation of State aid are to correct market failures because it would be more efficient and welfare-enhancing than market solutions. In the case of an identified market failure the government can calculate the net benefit caused by the intervention. Its objective is to grant aid where that net benefit is positive: the benefits outweigh the costs. Because of these economic considerations a thorough economic analysis is necessary to disclose the real intention and the justification for a State measure.

The economic objective of state aid in correcting a market failure can be explained by the use of the graph below. In this chart, it is assumed that there exists a private domestic supply and demand curves for health services. These are expressed as S_0 and D_0 respectively. Consequently, with a world price of P^*, equilibrium quantities of health services provided and consumed domestically are Q_0 and Q_d.

Now suppose that there is a positive externality in the provision of health services. This is highly relevant to the case of health services as private treatment for contagious diseases provides a considerable benefit to others, for which they do not pay. Consequently, the initial supply curve is not representative of the benefits of the provision of health services. In fact, the social costs of providing each unit of the service would be lower than what is portrayed by the supply curve S_0 which only displays the private cost. If the externalities are taken into account, the new supply curve would be S_1, which indicates a lower unit cost of health service provision.

Figure 4.11 Economic Effect of Health Services

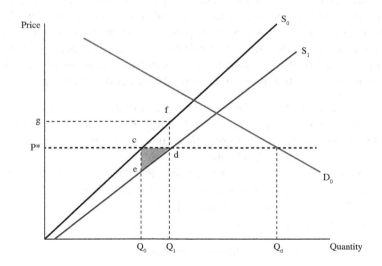

---

960. (Friederiszick, Röller and Verouden 2006, 634).

If the world price and the demand curve are assumed to reflect the true social costs, then the domestic provision of health care services at Q_0 would be less than the socially optimum level of provision Q_1. The cost to society of this under provision would be the area *cde*. To see this, assume a total subsidy of the amount *dfgP** is granted, which expands the amount of health service to Q_1. The total cost of the imports being replaced as a result of the subsidy is Q_0Q_1dc, but the total cost to society from providing the incremental service would be Q_0Q_1de. The difference is the area *cde*.

Therefore, if a positive externality in the provision of health care services exists, a production subsidy could be used to increase welfare.

The third area for the use of the refined economic approach is the *justification of the conditions for compatibility*. In so doing, a distinction is made between a lighter and a more detailed assessment, depending on the risks of distortion of competition and trade. There are a limited number of cases a detailed assessment is required.

4.7.3 State Aid Modernisation

4.7.3.1 *EU Guidelines*

In 2012, the Commission adopted a Communication on SAM, setting out the objectives of an ambitious reform package for state aid control. In the broader context of the EU's agenda to foster growth, state aid policy should focus on facilitating well-designed aid targeted at market failures and objectives of common European interest. The Commission also aims at focusing its enforcement on cases with the biggest impact on the internal market, streamlining rules and taking faster decisions. Thus, one of the main objectives of the SAM is to revise, streamline and consolidate State aid guidelines to make them consistent with common principles to assess the compatibility of aid with the internal market. As a result, the Commission modernised a set of horizontal rules which set out the Commission's position on particular categories of aid. The SAM consists of the revision, introduction, or strengthening of the following:

- State aid guidelines on: Rescue and restructuring aid, Regional Aid, Research & Development & Innovation, Agriculture, Environmental and Energy aid, Promotion of important projects of common European interest, Risk Finance, Broadband, Aviation Guidelines.
- Regulations of: General Block Exemption Regulation (GBER), Enabling Regulation, *De minimis* Regulation, and Procedural Regulation.
- Clarification of the notion of state aid.
- Evaluation of aid schemes.

These are reviewed in the following subsections.

4.7.3.1.1   Rescue and Restructuring Aid

The first category of aid concerns state aid for rescuing and restructuring non-financial undertakings in difficulty. Rescue and restructuring ('R&R') aid is among the most distortive types of State aid. By preventing exit, it impedes a key mechanism of productivity growth, namely the displacement of inefficient firms by more efficient and innovative competitors. R&R aid can also set off wasteful subsidy races that undermine the internal market.[961]

The guidelines introduce a new concept of temporary restructuring support to simplify the provision of aid while also reducing distortions to competition. More specifically, it allows liquidity support to be made available to SMEs in difficulty for a period which is longer than the six-month period for which liquidity assistance in the form of rescue aid can currently be granted (the two options are either twelve or eighteen months).

The guidelines also contain new filters designed to verify that aid is truly in the public interest. First, it must be shown that the aid pursues an objective of common interest, in the sense that saving the undertaking would prevent social hardship or address market failures. The guidelines set out a non-exhaustive list of situations in which aid would be justified under this provision; a separate provision for SMEs applies a less strict standard and identifies situations that are more relevant to the position of SMEs. Aid will also only be in the public interest if it can make a difference to the situation that would prevail without aid. The draft guidelines therefore require Member States to present a comparison with a credible alternative scenario not involving State aid. For reasons of simplification, this requirement does not apply to rescue aid or temporary restructuring support.

The Commission also developed the concept of 'burden sharing' for undertakings benefiting from restructuring aid: undertakings should make a contribution to the restructuring costs from their own resources. The guidelines make clear that the type of contribution must match the nature of the undertaking's difficulties. Specifically, equity shortages should be dealt with by capital-enhancing measures, while liquidity problems require contribution in a form that raises cash for the business.

Other changes include a clarification of the definition of 'undertaking in difficulty', an increase in the minimum level of remuneration for rescue aid, more detailed provisions on the required content of a restructuring plan, and the introduction of measures to limit distortions of competition.

4.7.3.1.2   Regional Aid

A major reform affecting regional aid is the extension of the GBER to include three types of regional aid which will no longer be subject to notification to the Commission:

---

961. (Commission Note on State aid for rescuing and restructuring non-financial undertakings in difficulty 2013).

- Ad hoc aid (individual aid granted outside a scheme) below the notification threshold.
- Aid for newly created small enterprises.
- Certain types of operating aid for outermost regions and sparsely populated areas.

On the other hand, the measures that are assessed by the new guidelines on regional aid are:

- Regional investment aid schemes targeted at specific sectors of economic activity.
- Individual aid (including ad hoc aid) above the notification threshold: between EUR 15 million and EUR 37.5 million depending on the region.
- Investment aid potentially linked to a closure of a similar or same activity in the EEA.
- Certain regional operating aid schemes, namely: (i) aid to reduce certain specific difficulties faced by SMEs in 'a' areas, (ii) aid to compensate for certain additional costs (other than transport costs) in the outermost regions, (iii) aid to prevent or reduce depopulation in areas with a very low population density.[962]

In line with the refined economic approach, which requires an assessment of whether the positive impact of an aid measure outweighs its potential negative effects on trade and competition, the Commission developed a series of criteria which need to be met in order for the measure to be considered compatible with the internal market. These criteria are the following:

- Contribution to a well-defined objective of common interest.
- Absence of market delivery of the equity objective.
- Appropriateness of the aid measure.
- Incentive effect of the aid.
- Aid limited to the minimum.
- Avoidance of undue negative effects.
- Transparent aid award.

In cases where these criteria are all met, the Commission will conduct a balancing test of the positive effects of the measure in terms of its contribution to the development of the area against the potential distortions of competition it could cause.

4.7.3.1.3 State Aid for Research and Development and Innovation (R&D&I)

In light of the revision of conditions under which Member States can grant state aid for research, development and innovation activities (R&D&I), the new framework allows

---

962. (Commission note on the DG Competition regional aid guidelines 2014–2020 2013).

more effective R&D&I aid, fewer distortions of competition and less red tape.[963] The framework[964] identifies five categories of R&D&I activities for which state aid may, under specific conditions, be compatible with Article 107(3)(b) and 107(3)(c):

- Aid for R&D projects where the aided part of the research project falls within the categories of fundamental research and applied research, of which the latter can be divided into industrial research and experimental development.
- Aid for feasibility studies related to R&D projects.
- Aid for the construction and upgrade of research infrastructures.
- Aid for innovation activities.
- Aid for innovation clusters.

The framework highlights the necessity for any R&D&I aid to be subject to the balancing test in order to be declared as compatible with the internal market. More specifically, the measure must contribute to a well-defined objective of common interest, it must be a necessary intervention, it should be appropriate, it should induce an incentive effect, it should be proportionate, it should avoid undue negative effects on competition and trade, and it should be transparent.

4.7.3.1.4 State Aid in Agriculture, Forestry and Rural Areas

The revision of the rules on state aid in the agriculture and forestry sectors and in rural areas aims at modernising state aid and adapting it to the new Common Agricultural Policy agreed in December 2013.[965] The new rules widen the scope of the Agricultural Block Exemption Regulation ('ABER', i.e., the set of rules defining the categories of State aid that can be granted by Member States without prior notification to the Commission) to include new categories of aid. They make it, for example, possible to grant aid to the forestry sector through funding from the Rural Development Fund.[966]

4.7.3.1.5 Environmental and Energy Aid

The rules for state aid in the energy and environmental fields have been revised too.[967] The Commission exempts certain categories of aid from prior scrutiny under the state aid rules by including them in the GBER. These include for instance, public support to clean up or remediate contaminated sites, aid to promote district heating and public loans to improve the energy efficiency in buildings. Exempted measures may cover up to 40% of the public expenditure in the energy and environmental field.

---

963. (Commission Press Release 2013).
964. (DG Competition Paper on a draft Framework for state aid for research and development and innovation 2013).
965. (European Commission 2013).
966. (Commission Press Release 2014).
967. (Commission Press Release 2013).

4.7.3.1.6 State Aid to Promote Important Projects of Common European Interest

Important projects of common European interest (IPCEIs) may make an important contribution to boosting economic growth, job creation and competitiveness. They make it possible to bring together knowledge, expertise, financial resources and economic players throughout Europe, so as to overcome very important market or systemic failures and address societal challenges. IPCEIs may range from cross-border transport projects to energy infrastructure projects, to research infrastructure or pan-European investments linked to the development of key enabling technologies.

The guidance provided by the Commission on state aid granted to IPCEIs introduces more flexibility with respect to the form of public support by Member States (repayable advance, loans, guarantees, grants), as well as the possibility to cover up to 100% of the funding gap on the basis of a large set of eligible costs. In order to reduce red tape and to facilitate the assessment of the financing of IPCEIs by the Member States, the Commission introduces the possibility to submit a joint notification to the Commission by the participating Member States.[968]

4.7.3.1.7 Risk Finance

The Commission has also adopted guidelines setting out the conditions under which Member States can grant aid to facilitate access to finance by European SMEs and companies with a medium capitalisation (the so-called midcaps). Certain SMEs and midcaps, in particular innovative and growth-oriented SMEs in their early development stages, have difficulties to get funding, independently of the quality of their business potential. State aid can help address this funding gap, not by replacing existing funding channels but by attracting fresh money into new ventures through well-designed financial instruments and fiscal measures.

The guidelines have radically enlarged scope, now including (i) SMEs (ii) small midcaps, and (iii) innovative midcaps and set out compatibility criteria for amounts above EUR 15 million per company, since the next GBER will exempt aid below this threshold from prior Commission scrutiny.

The revision also includes a wider range of financial instruments admissible – including equity, quasi-equity, loans and guarantees – to better reflect market practices. The financial intermediaries and investment funds involved will therefore be able to offer companies the amount and form of financing that is appropriate to their development stage and to the sector in which they operate.

A third major revision is the mandatory participation of private investors tailored to the development stage and riskiness of the company: Such participation alongside public investors ensures that aid measures serve to attract rather than replace private funding.[969]

---

968. (Commission Press Release 2014).
969. (Commission Press Release 2014).

4.7.3.1.8 Broadband

The Commission also revised the Guidelines to the application of state aid rules in the broadband sector. This became necessary as the Commission had limited experience in the assessment of very high speed broadband networks at the time of adoption of the former guidelines in 2009. The main changes in the new guidelines concern the alignment of the rules with the Digital Agenda for Europe (DAE) objectives, the fine tuning of the effective wholesale access obligation, the role of the National Regulatory Authority (NRA), increased transparency, and the clarifications, simplification and ease of administrative burden.

The guidelines highlight the steps of the balancing test to assess the compatibility of aid under Article 107(3). More specifically, in order to qualify as aid compatible with the internal market, the measure should comply with the following necessary conditions:

- Contribution to the achievement of objectives of common interest.
- Absence of market delivery due to market failures or important inequalities.
- Appropriateness of State aid as a policy instrument.
- Existence of incentive effect.
- Aid limited to the minimum necessary.
- Limited negative effects.
- Transparency.

If all necessary conditions are met, the Commission balances the positive effects of the aid measure in reaching an objective of common interest against the potential negative effects (third step of the balancing test).[970]

4.7.3.1.9 Aviation Guidelines

The Commission adopted guidelines on how Member States can support airports and airlines in line with EU state aid rules. The guidelines are aimed at ensuring good connections between regions and the mobility of European citizens, while minimising distortions of competition in the Single Market.[971]

4.7.3.2 EU Regulations

In addition to the refinement and consolidation of the various guidelines and frameworks described in the previous section, the Commission also revised the regulations declaring some categories of aid automatically compatible with the internal market.

---

970. (Commission Guidelines for the application of State aid rules in relation to the rapid deployment of broadband networks 2013).
971. (Commission Press Release 2014).

4.7.3.2.1   General Block Exemption Regulation

Since 1998, the Commission has put in place a regulation that allows it to declare specific categories of State aid compatible with the Treaty if they fulfil certain conditions, thus exempting them from the requirement of prior notification and Commission approval. As a result, Member States are able to grant aid that meets the conditions laid down in these regulations without the formal notification procedure and only have to submit information sheets on the implemented aid.[972] This is the co-called GBER.

The scope of the GBER is enlarged after the adoption of the Enabling Regulation, by means of higher thresholds and new exemptions. This adoption creates the legal basis for future block exemptions in the following new categories:

- Innovation.
- Culture and heritage conservation.
- Making good the damage caused by natural disasters.
- Making good the damage caused by certain adverse weather conditions in fisheries.
- Forestry.
- Promotion of food sector products not listed in Annex I of the TFEU.
- Conservation of marine and freshwater biological resources.
- Sports; social aid for transport for residents of remote regions.
- Certain broadband infrastructure.
- Infrastructure in support of the objectives of the Enabling Regulation and objectives of common interest.

Additionally, the Commission improved the transparency requirement of aid awarded under the GBER.[973] An example of the stricter requirement of transparency is the obligation by Member States to publish on a comprehensive State aid website information on each individual aid award in excess of EUR 200,000.

4.7.3.2.2   De Minimis Regulation

The *de minimis* rule sets a ceiling below which aid is deemed not to fall within the scope of Article 107(1) and is therefore exempt from the notification requirement laid down in Article 108(3). Under the *de minimis* rule, aid of no more than EUR 200,000 granted over a period of three years is not regarded as state aid within the meaning of Article 107(1). Furthermore, a specific ceiling of EUR 100,000 applies to road transport. Finally, under the SAM, the Commission introduced a ceiling of EUR 500,000 per

---

972. (Commission on Block Exemption Regulation 2013).
973. (Commission Memo/13/1175 2013).

company for services of general economic interest (SGEI).⁹⁷⁴ This higher ceiling is justified on the grounds that the support measures are at least in part compensating for the extra costs incurred for the provision of a public service.⁹⁷⁵

4.7.3.2.3 Procedural Regulation

In addition to the revision of the Enabling Regulation which provides the legal basis for the definition of categories of aid that can be exempted from notification, the Commission also revised the Procedural Regulation. The Procedural Regulation sets out the rules of procedure governing state aid investigations which are built around three main pillars:

- Member States may not grant state aid before the Commission has authorised it ('standstill obligation'), except if it is covered by a BER.
- The Commission is required to conduct a diligent and impartial examination of complaints and take a decision without undue delay.
- The Commission must keep under constant review all existing aid measures in Member States.

The new Procedural Regulation also introduces new market information tools (MIT). It allows the Commission to seek targeted information directly from concerned market players with effective means of enforcement when incomplete or incorrect data is submitted.⁹⁷⁶ Finally, the revised Procedural Regulation introduces a tool allowing the Commission to conduct sector inquiries.⁹⁷⁷

4.7.3.3 Notion of State Aid

Another point on the agenda of the SAM is the clarification of the notion of State aid. The Commission has compiled a guidance notice explaining and illustrating the various elements constitutive of state aid in the meaning of EU state aid control:⁹⁷⁸

- The presence of an economic activity (notion of 'undertaking').
- The imputability of the measure to the State.
- Financing through State resources.
- The presence of an economic advantage for the beneficiary.
- Selectivity.
- Effect on trade and competition.

---

974. (Commission Press Release 2012).
975. (Commission Press Release 2013).
976. *Ibid.*
977. *Ibid.*
978. (Commission Notice on the notion of State aid pursuant to Art. 107(1) TFEU 2014).

4.7.3.4 **Ex Post** *Evaluations*

Up to SAM, aid schemes were approved *ex ante* on the basis of pre-defined criteria on the assumption that their overall balance will remain positive, without a proper evaluation of their impact on the markets over time. SAM introduced the *ex post* evaluation of aid providing analysis on the effectiveness and efficiency of an aid measure and suggesting improvements and lessons to be learnt.[979] The need for *ex post* evaluation is particularly relevant for aid schemes which consisted of 55% of total aid amounts granted in 2011.[980] Evaluation is already a common practice is some subsidy schemes at both national and EU level. For instance, in the context of EU Structural Funds, projects are subject to systematic *ex ante* and *ex post* evaluation. More specifically, Member States are responsible for *ex ante* evaluation and the European Commission for the *ex post* evaluation.

In performing *ex post* evaluation, DG Competition intends to apply different methods depending on the availability of data and time constraint. Measuring the direct and indirect effects of a policy normally requires the use of different tools. The following econometric techniques are often used to perform such evaluations:[981]

- Linear regression.
- Matching techniques.
- Difference-in-Difference.
- Instrumental variables.
- Regression Discontinuity Design.

4.7.3.4.1 Linear Regression

Linear regression seeks to control for the influence of observed characteristics on the outcomes. It assumes a linear relationship between the outcome, for instance the investment in R&D, and other characteristics of the firm, for instance the sector, age, size etc., including the granting of the aid. It is possible to see linear regression as a linear approximation of more complicated relationships. Linear regressions can be seen as general purpose techniques and are used in many different evaluation contexts.

4.7.3.4.2 Matching Techniques

Matching techniques aim at pairing each beneficiary with another firm that 'looks' very similar but did not receive aid. The observables used for matching can be firm

---

979. (Issue Paper on Evaluation in the field of State aid 2013).
980. (Commission State aid scoreboard 2011, 2012).
981. (Commission Draft Methodological Guidance Paper on Evaluation in the field of State aid 2013).

characteristics or the estimated probability to receive aid (propensity score matching). Matching can be a useful way to control for observables in the context of a valid empirical strategy.

4.7.3.4.3 Difference-in-Difference

The general idea of this approach is to consider the difference in outcome between firms over time. Pre-existing differences would be attributed to other factors than the State aid. Only the change in these differences (the Difference-in-Difference) would be attributed to the aid. In other words, the method compares the difference in the performance between beneficiaries and control group before the aid as well as after the aid and then attributes the change in the difference to the aid. The method works if, over time, both the beneficiaries and the control group are affected by the other factors that also affect performance in the same way. It can then be concluded that the aid is the only relevant factor that explains the observed change in performance of beneficiaries relative to the control group.

4.7.3.4.4 Instrumental Variables

Using instrumental variables (IV) is a classical method to deal with endogeneity of explanatory variables. Since benefiting from aid can be seen as an endogenous explanatory variable of the performance of a firm in a linear regression context, it is natural to use instrumental variables to evaluate the effect of aid.

For the evaluation of State aid, an instrumental variable is a variable that can explain the fact of receiving the aid but has no direct impact on the other unobserved determinants of the outcome that has to be measured. Instrumental variables then allow focusing on the participation in the scheme without interference from the selection effects. For illustrative purposes, one can see the logics of instrumental variable as follows. In a first step, programme participation is regressed on all the exogenous variables, including the instrumental variables. In a second step, the participation variable (the variable indicating whether the aid was received) is replaced with the participation as predicted in the first step: this expected participation is not correlated with the unobserved element that also determines the outcome.

4.7.3.4.5 Regression Discontinuity Design

This method exploits the existence of a variable which has a discontinuous impact on the probability to be affected by a policy. In the context of State aid schemes, several types of discontinuities can be useful. The first one is geographical borders: the eligibility of schemes can be linked to precise administrative borders, like localities, NUTS regions, etc. The second one comes from conditions imposed on the firms to benefit from a scheme, in particular in terms of age and size.

As an example, we consider a situation in which some firms are formally excluded from the scheme even though they are very close to some firms who benefit from the scheme. Imagine for instance that projects presented by firms are rated by points (out of 100) and firms who get at least 70 points get aid while the others get no aid. A firm who scores 71 has a marginally better project than a firm who scores 69. However, the consequence of this marginal difference is dramatic: one gets some aid, while the second gets no aid at all. Comparing the outcomes for these two firms is thus very indicative of the causal effect of the aid.

Bibliography

2004/339/EC: Commission Decision of 15 October 2003 on the measures implemented by Italy for RAI SpA (European Commission 15 October 2003).

2007/353/EC: Commission Decision of 14 March 2006 declaring a concentration compatible with the common market and the functioning of the EEA Agreement (DONG/Elsam/Energi E2), Case COMP/M.3868 (European Commission 14 March 2006).

91/619/EEC: Commission Decision of 2 October 1991 declaring the incompatibility with the common market of a concentration (Case No. IV/M.053 - Aerospatiale-Alenia/de Havilland) - Council Regulation (EEC) No. 4064/89, Case No. IV/M.053 (European Commission 2 October 1991).

92/553/EEC: Commission Decision of 22 July 1992 relating to a proceeding under Council Regulation (EEC) No. 4064/89 (Case No. IV/M.190 - Nestlé/Perrier), Case No. IV/M.190 (European Commission 22 July 1992).

93/9/EEC: Commission Decision of 30 September 1992 declaring the compatibility of a concentration with the common market (Case No. IV/M214 - Du Pont/ICI), Case No. IV/M214 (European Commission 30 September 1992).

94/119/EC: Commission Decision of 21 December 1993 concerning a refusal to grant access to the facilities of the port of Rødby (Denmark) (European Commission 21 December 1993).

A. Ahlström Osakeyhtiö and others v. Commission of the European Communities, Joined cases C-89/85, C-104/85, C-114/85, C-116/85, C-117/85 and C-125/85 to C-129/85 (European Court of Justice (Fifth Chamber) 31 March 1993).

Aaker, D. A., Kumar, V. & Day, G. S. (2003). *Marketing Research.* Hillside: Wiley.

ABB/Daimler-Benz, Case No. IV/M.580 (European Commission 18 October 1995).

Abbamonte, G. B. & Rabassa, V. (2001). Foreclosure and vertical mergers – the Commission's review of vertical effects in the last wave of media and Internet mergers: AOL/Time Warner, Vivendi/Seagram, MCI Worldcom/Sprint. *European Competition Law Review*, S. 214–226.

Abbott, L. (1955). *Quality and Competition.* New York: Columbia UP.

Accor/Wagons-Lits, Case No. IV/M.126 (European Commission 28 April 1992).

Adams, W. (1976). Antitrust, Laissez-faire, and Economic Power. In F. Neumark, H. Dawar & H. Hölzler, *Wettbewerb, Konzentration und wirtschaftliche Macht* (11–17). Duncker & Humblot.

Aerospatiale-Alenia/de Havilland, Case No. IV/M.53 (European Commission 2 October 1991).
Agnew, J. H. (1985). *Competition Law*. London: Allen & Unwin.
Ahdar, R. (2002). Consumers, Redistribution of Income and the Purpose of Competition Law. *European Competition Law Review*, 23(7), 341–353.
Ahlborn, C. & Berg, C. (2003). Can State Aid Control Learn from Antitrust? The Need for a Greater Role for Competition Analysis under the State Aid Rules. In A. Biondi, P. Eeckhout & J. Flynn, *The Law of State Aid in the European Union* (41–66). Oxford University Press.
Ahmed Saeed Flugreisen and Silver Line Reisebüro GmbH v. Zentrale zur Bekämpfung unlauteren Wettbewerbs e.V., Case 66/86 (European Court of Justice 11 April 1989).
Air Liquide/BOC, Case No. COMP/M.1630 (European Commission 18 January 2000).
Airtours plc v. Commission of the European Communities., Case T-342/99 (Court of First Instance (Fifth Chamber, extended composition) 6 June 2002).
Airtours/First Choice, Case No. IV/M.1524 (European Commission 22 September 1999).
Akerlof, G. A. (August 1970). The Market for 'Lemons': Quality Uncertainty and the Market Mechanism. *The Quarterly Journal of Economics*, 488–500.
AKZO Chemie BV and AKZO Chemie UK Ltd v. Commision of the European Communities, Case 53/85 (European Court of Justice (Fifth Chamber) 24 June 1986).
AKZO Chemie BV v. Commission of the European Communities, Case C-62/86 (European Court of Justice (Fifth Chamber) 3 July 1991).
Albach, H. (1978). Zur Messung von Marktmacht und ihres Missbrauchs. *Wirtschaft und Wettbewerb*, 535–548.
Alcan/Alusuisse, Case No. COMP/M.1663 (European Commission 14 March 2000).
Alcan/Pechiney, withdrawn 14 March 2000, M 1715 (European Commission 14 March 2000).
Allenby, G. M., Arora, N. & Ginter, J. L. (1995). Incorporating Prior Knowledge into the Analysis of Conjoint Studies. *Journal of Marketing Research*, 152–162.
Allgemeine Elektrizitäts-Gesellschaft AEG-Telefunken AG v. Commission of the European Communities, Case 107/82 (European Court of Justice 25 October 1983).
Allianz Hungária Biztosító Zrt and Others v. Gazdasági Versenyhivatal, Case C-32/11 (ECJ 14 March 2013).
Allied Lyons/HWE-Pedro Domecq, Case No. IV/M.400 (European Commission 28 April 1994).
Almunia, J. (24 November 2011). *Competition – what's in it for consumers?* Poznan. Retrieved August 2015, from http://europa.eu/rapid/press-release_SPEECH-11-803_en.htm.
Alonso, J. B. (1994). Market Definition in the Community's Merger Control Policy. *European Competition Law Review*, 195–208.
Altmark Trans GmbH and Regierungspräsidium Magdeburg v. Nahverkehrsgesellschaft Altmark GmbH, and Oberbundesanwalt beim Bundesverwaltungsgericht, Case C-280/00 (European Court of Justice 24 July 2003).

Bibliography

Amelio, A. & Donath, D. (2009). Market definition in recent EC merger investigations: The role of empirical analysis. *Concurrences N°3-2009*, 1-6.

Amelio, A., De La Mano, M. & Godinho de Matos, M. (2008). Ineos/Kerling merger: an example of quantitative analysis in support of a clearance decision. *Competition Policy Newsletter*, 65-69.

Anderson, S. & Coate, S. (2005). Market provision of broadcasting: a welfare analysis. *The review of economic studies, 72*(4), 947-972.

Andreu, E., Edwards, K. & Requejo, A. (2010). Merger simulation as a screening device: simulating the effects of the Kraft/Cadbury transaction. *European Commission DG Competition*, 1-20.

Arjowiggins/M-real Zanders Reflex, COMP/M. 4513 (European Commission 4 June 2008).

Arsenal/DSP, COMP/M.5153 (European Commission 9 January 2009).

Art, J.-Y. & Van Liedekerke, D. (1997). Developments in EC Competition Law. *Common Market Law Review*, 895-956.

Associazione Italiana Tecnico Economica del Cemento and British Cement Association and Blue Circle Industries plc and Castle Cement Ltd and The Rugby Group plc and Titan Cement Company SA v. Commission of the European Communities, Joined cases T-447/93, T-448/93 and T-449/93 (Court of First Instance 6 July 1995).

Associazione Italiana Tecnico Economica del Cemento v. Commission of the European Communities, Case T-447/93 (Court of First Instance 28 November 1996).

AstraZeneca AB & AstraZeneca plc v. European Commission, Case T-321/05 (General Court (Sixth Chamber, Extended Composition) 1 July 2010).

AstraZeneca AB and AstraZeneca plc v. European Commission, Case C-457/10 P (European Court of Justice 6 December 2012).

Auerbach, P. (1988). *Competition: The Economics of Industrial Change*. Oxford: Basil Blackwell.

Baden-Fuller, C. (1979). Article 86 EEC: Economic Analysis of the Existence of a Dominant Position. *European Law Review*, 423-441.

Bain, J. S. (1956). *Barriers to New Competition*. Harvard University Press.

Bain, J. S. (1968). *Industrial Organization*. New York: John Wiley & Sons Inc.

Bain, J. S. (1986). Structure Versus Conduct as Indicators of Market Performance. *Antitrust Law and Economics Review*.

Bajari, P. & Ye, L. (2003). Deciding Between Competition and Collusion. *The Review of Economics and Statistics*, 971-989.

Baker, J. (1989). Recent Developments in Economics that Challenge Chicago School Views. *Antitrust Law Journal*.

Baldwin, W. L. (1987). *Market Power, Competition and Antitrust Policy*. Homewood, Illinois: Irwin Professional Publishing.

Bartosch, A., Braun, J.-D., Koenig, C. & Romes, M. (2006). *EC Competition and Telecommunications Law*. Kluwer.

Baumann, M. G. & Godek, P. E. (1995). Could and Would Understood: Critical Elasticities and the Merger Guidelines. *The Antitrust Bulletin: The Journal of American and Foreign Antitrust and Trade Regulation*, 885-899.

Baumbach, A. & Hefermehl, W. (1993). *Wettbewerbsrecht*. München: C.H. Beck.

Baumol, W. J. (1982). Contestable Markets: An Uprising in the Theory of Industry Structure. *The American Economic Review*, 1–15.

Baumol, W. J. (1988). *Contestable Markerts and the Theory of Industry Structure*. San Diego: Harcourt Brace Jovannich.

Baumol, W. J., Panzar, J. C. & Willig, R. D. (1982). *Contestable Markets and the Theory of Industry Structure*. New York: Harcourt Brace Jovanovich.

Bayer AG and Maschinenfabrik Hennecke GmbH v. Heinz Süllhöfer, Case 65/86 (European Court of Justice 27 September 1988).

Bayerische Motorenwerke AG v. ALD Auto-Leasing D GmbH, Case C-70/93 (European Court of Justice 24 October 1995).

Bayliss & El-Agraa. (1990). Competition and Industrial Policies with Emphasis on Competition Policy. In A. M. El-Agraa, *Economics of the European Community*. London: Allan.

BBI/Boosey & Hawkes, IV/32.279 (Commission Decision (87/500/EEC) 29 July 1987).

Begg, D. K., Fischer, S. & Dornbusch, R. (1997). *Economics*. Sydney and London: McGraw Hill.

Béguelin Import Co. v. S.A.G.L. Import Export, Case 22-71 (European Court of Justice 25 November 1971).

Bellamy, G. D. & Child, C. (1993). *Common Market Law of Competition*. London: Sweet & Maxwell.

Bengtsson, C. (2005). Simulating the Effect of Oracle's Takeover of PeopleSoft. In P. van Bergeijk & E. Kloosterhuis, *Modelling European Mergers Theory, Competition Policy and Case Studies* (133–149). Cheltenham: Elgar.

Bergman, M., Coate, M., Jakobsson, M. & Ulrick, S. (4 March 2010). Merger Control in the European Union and the United States: Just the Facts. *Working Paper*.

Berry S. (1994). Estimating discrete choice models of product differentiation. *RAND Journal of Economics, 25*, S. 242–263.

Bertelsmann AG and Sony Corporation of America v. Independent Music Publishers and Labels Association (Impala), Case C-413/06 P (European Court of Justice 10 July 2008).

Betrand, J. (1883). Théorie mathématique de la richesse sociale. *Journal des Savants, 67*, 499–508.

Blackstone/Acetex, Case No. COMP/M.3625 (European Commission 13 July 2005).

Blair, R. D. & Sokol, D. D. (2012). The Rule of Reason and the Goals of Antitrust: An Economic Approach. *Antitrust Law Journal, 78*(2), 471–504.

BMW/Rover, Case No. IV/M.416 (European Commission 14 March 1994).

Boarman, P. (1964). *Germany's economic dilemma: inflation and the balance of payments*. United States: Yale University Press.

Boas, C. & Gans-Morse, J. (2009). Neoliberalism: From new liberal philosophy to anti-liberal slogan. *Studies in Comparative International Development, 44*, 137–161.

Böhm, F. (1980). *Freiheit und Ordnung in der Marktwirtschaft*. (E.-J. Mestmäcker, Hrsg.) Bade-Baden: Nomos Verlag.

Böhm, F. (1982). The Non-State ('Natural') Laws Inherent in a Competitive Economy. In H. F. Wünsche, W. Stützel & D. Rutter, *Standard Texts on the Social Market Economy* (107-113). Stuttgart: Fischer.
Böhm, F. (1989). Private Law Society and the Market Economy. In A. Peacock & H. Willgerodt, *Germany's Social Market Economy: Origins and Evolution* (46-67). London: Macmillan.
Bork, R. (1966). Legislative Intent and the Policy of the Sherman Act. *The Journal of Law and Economics, 9*.
Bork, R. (1967). The Goals of Antitrust Policy. *American Economic Review*.
Bork, R. (1968). *Report of the White House Task Force on Antitrust Policy*. Chicago: University of Chicago.
Bork, R. (1978). *The Antitrust Paradox: A Policy at War with Itself*. New York: Basic Books.
Bos, P. V., Stuyck, J. & Wytinck, P. (1992). *Concentration Control in the European Economic Community*. London: Graham & Trotman.
Bowie, R. R. (15 June 1981). Réflexions sur Jean Monnet in Témoignages à la mémoire de Jean Monnet. *Transcript on file at the Fondation Jean Monnet pour l'Europe*. Lausanne.
Bowie, R. R. (15 March 1988). Oral History Project. (C. S. Kennedy, Interviewer) The Association for Diplomatic Studies and Training Foreign Affairs. Retrieved from http://www.adst.org/OH%20TOCs/Bowie,%20Robert%20R.toc.pdf.
Boyd, D. W. (1996). Vertical Restraints and the Retail Free Riding Problem: An Austrian Perspective. *The Review of Austrian Economics*, 119-134.
BP Kemi - DDSF, Case No. IV/29.021 (European Commission 5 September 1979).
BP/Petromed, Case No. IV/M.111 (European Commission 29 July 1991).
Brauerei A. Bilger Söhne GmbH v. Heinrich Jehle and Marta Jehle, Case 43-69 (European Court of Justice 18 March 1970).
Breeder's rights - maize seed, Case No. IV/28.824 (European Commission 21 September 1978).
Brighton West Pier, United Kingdom, Joined Cases N 560/01 and NN 17/02 (European Commission 4 October 2002).
British Airways plc v. Commission of the European Communities, Cast T-219/99 (Court of First Instance (First Chamber) 17 December 2003).
British Airways plc v. Commission of the European Communities, Case C-95/04 P (European Court of Justice (Third Chamber) 15 March 2007).
British Airways/American Airlines/Iberia (BA/AA/IB), Case COMP/39.596 (European Commission 14 July 2010).
British Leyland Public Limited Company v. Commission of the European Communities, Case 226/84 (ECJ (Fifth Chamber) 11 November 1986).
British Telecom/MCI, Case No. IV/M.353 (European Commission 13 September 1993).
British-American Tobacco Company Ltd and R. J. Reynolds Industries Inc. v. Commission of the European Communities, Joined cases 142 and 156/84 (European Court of Justice (Sixth Chamber) 17 November 1987).

Brodley, J. F. (November 1987). The Economic Goals of Antitrust: Efficiency, Consumer Welfare, and Technological Progress. *New York University Law Review, 62*, 1020–1053.
Bronckers, M. & Vallery, A. (2011). No longer Persumed Guilty: The Impact of Fundamental Rights on Certain Dogmas of EU Competition Law. *World Competition: Law and Economics Review, 34*(4), 535–570.
Brozen, J. (1977). The Concentration-Collussion Doctrine. *Antitrust Law Journal*, 826–856.
BSN/Euralim, Case No. IV/M.445 (European Commission 7 June 1994).
Budzinski, O. & Ruhmer, I. (29 May 2008). *Merger Simulation in Competition Policy: A Survey*. Retrieved 22 January 2014, from Social Science Research Network: http://papers.ssrn.com/sol3/papers.cfm?abstract_id = 1138682.
Budzinski, O. & Ruhmer, I. (January 2009). Merger Simulation in Competition Policy: A Survey. *Working Papers 82/09, University of Southern Denmark*.
Building and construction industry in the Netherlands, Cases IV/31.572 and 32.571 (European Commission 5 February 1992).
Bundeskartellamt. (2000). Auslegungsgrundsätze zu Prüfung von Marktbeherrschung in der deutschen Fusionskontrolle. BKartA Grundsatzabteilung E/G 4.
Bundeskartellamt. (October 2010). Principles of Interpretation. General Policy Division E/G 4.
Bundeskartellamt v. Volkswagen AG and VAG Leasing GmbH., Case C.266/93 (European Court of Justice 24 October 1995).
Bureau national interprofessionnel du cognac (BNIC) v. Guy Clair, C-123/83 (ECJ 30 January 1985).
Cambridge University Press. (2013). *Cambridge Dictionaries*. Cambridge.
Canenbley, C. (1993). Die Abgrenzung des Geographisch Relevanten Marktes in der EWG-Fusionskontrolle. In U. Everling, *Europarecht, Kartellrecht, Wirtschaftsrecht* (226–245). Baden-Baden: Nomos.
Carbajo, J., de Meza, D. & Seidmann, D. J. (1990). A Strategic Motivation for Commodity Bundling. *The Journal of Industrial Economics*, 283–298.
Cargill/Unilever, Case No. IV/M.26 (European Commission 20 December 1990).
Carlo Bagnasco and Others v. Banca Popolare di Novara soc. coop. arl. (BNP) (C-215/96) and Cassa di Risparmio di Genova e Imperia SpA (Carige) (C-216/96), Joined cases C-215/96 and C-216/96 (European Court of Justice (Sixth Chamber) 21 January 1999).
Carlsberg, Case No. IV/30.129 (European Commission 12 July 1984).
Carlton, D. & Bishop, W. (1994). Merger Policy and Market Definition under the EC Merger Regulation. In B. Hawk, *Annual Proceedings of the Fordham Corporate Law Institute*. The Netherlands: Kluwer.
Centro Servizi Spediporto Srl v. Spedizioni Marittima del Golfo Srl., Case C-96/94 (European Court of Justice 5 October 1995).
CGP/GEC Alsthom/KPR/Kone, Case No. IV/M.420 (European Commission 14 April 1994).
Chamberlin, E. (1933). *The Theory of Monopolistic Competition*. Cambridge: Harvard University Press.

Chen, Y. (2001). On Vertical Mergers and their Competitive Effects. *The RAND Journal of Economics, 32*(4), 667–685.
Child, G. D. & Bellamy, C. W. (1993). *Common Market Law of Competition* (Fourth Edition ed.). (V. Rose, Ed.) London: Sweet & Maxwell.
Choi, J. & Yi, S. (2000). Vertical Foreclosure with the Choice of Input Specifications. *The RAND Journal of Economics, 31*(4), 717–743.
Church, J. (2004). *The Impact of Vertical and Conglomerate Mergers on Competition.* Directorate B Merger Task Force (DG Competition, European Commission).
Ciba-Geigy/Sandoz, Case No. IV/M.737 (European Commission 17 July 1996).
Clapham, R. (1981). Das wettbewerbspolitische Konzept der Wettbewerbsfreiheit. In H. Cox, U. Jens & K. Markert, *Handbuch des Wettbewerbs: Wettbewerbstheorie, Wettbewerbspolitik, Wettbewerbsrecht.* München: Vahlen.
Clark, J. M. (June 1940). Toward a Concept of Workable Competition. *The Amreican Economic Review,* 241–256.
Clark, J. M. (May 1955). Competition: Static Models and Dynamic Aspects. *The American Economic Review,* 450–462.
Clark, J. M. (December 1962). Competition as a Dynamic Process. *Political Science Quarterly,* 632–634.
CMA CGM and others v. Commission of the European Communities, Case T-213/00 (Court of First Instance (Third Chamber) 19 March 2003).
Coate, M. (2005). Efficiencies in Merger Analysis: An Institutionalist View. *George Mason Supreme Court Economic Review, 13,* 189–240.
CODAN/HAFNIA, Case No. IV/M.344 (European Commission 3 August 1993).
Coditel SA, Compagnie générale pour la diffusion de la télévision, and others v. Ciné-Vog Films SA and others, Case 262/81 (European Court of Justice 6 October 1982).
Comanor, W. S. (1985). Vertical Price-Fixing, Vertical Market Restrictions, and the New Antitrust Policy. *Harvard Law Review,* 983–1002.
Commission Decision of 7 November 1990 declaring a concentration to be compatible with the common market (Case No. IV/M.0004 - RENAULT / VOLVO) according to Council Regulation (EEC) No. 4064/89, No. IV/M.0004 (European Commission 7 November 1990).
Commission Decision of 24 July 2000 providing for a compulsory beef labelling system in Denmark (notified under document number C(2000) 2157), (2000/490/EC) (European Commission 07 24, 2000).
Commission Decision of 25 February 1991 declaring a concentration to be compatible with the common market (Case No. IV/M.0017 - Aérospatiale / MBB) according to Council Regulation (EEC) No. 4064/89, No. IV/M.0017 (European Commission 25 February 1991).
Commission Decision of 4 May 1993 declaring the compatibility of a concentration (Case No. IV/M.291 - KNP/Bührmann-Tetterode and VRG) Council Regulation (EEC) No. 4064/89, Case No. IV/M.291 (European Commission 4 May 1993).
Commission of the European Communities v. Federal Republic of Germany, Case C-209/00 (European Court of Justice 20 September 2001).

Bibliography

Compagnie nationale Air France v. Commission of the European Communities, Case T-358/94 (Court of First Instance (Second Chamber, extended composition) 12 December 1996).

Compagnie Royale Asturienne des Mines SA and Rheinzink GmbH v. Commission of the European Communities, Joined cases 29/83 and 30/83 (European Court of Justice (Fourth Chamber) 28 March 1984).

Confederación Española de Transporte de Mercancías (CETM) v. Commission of the European Communities, Case T-55/99 (Court of First Instance 29 September 2000).

Consolidated version of the Treaty on the Functioning of the European Union, Article 107. (9 May 2008). *Official Journal of the European Union C115/47*, 47–199.

Consorzio italiano della componentistica di ricambio per autoveicoli and Maxicar v. Régie nationale des usines Renault, Case 53/87 (ECJ 5 October 1988).

Conti, M. (9 May 2006). EU Merger Analysis. *Competition Law Insight*.

Continental Can Company, Case No. IV/26.811 (European Commission 9 December 1971).

Continental Can v. Commission, 6/72 (ECJ 1973).

Cook, J. & Kerse, C. (1996). *EEC Merger Control - Regulation 4064/89*. London: Sweet & Maxwell.

Coöperatieve Vereniging 'Suiker Unie' UA and others v. Commission of the European Communities, Joined cases 40-48, 50, 54 to 56, 111, 113 and 114-73 (European Court of Justice 16 December 1975).

Corinne Bodson v. SA Pompes funèbres des régions libérées, Case 30/87 (European Court of Justice (Sixth Chamber) 4 May 1988).

Cornell University Law School. (1992). *NORTHERN PACIFIC RAILWAY COMPANY AND NORTHWESTERN IMPROVEMENT COMPANY, APPELLANTS, V. UNITED STATES OF AMERICA*. Retrieved 23 January 2014 from Legal Information Institute: http://www.law.cornell.edu/supremecourt/text/356/1.

Costa Crociere/Chargeurs/Accor, Case No. IV/M.334 (European Commission 19 July 1993).

Council of European Union. (9 September 2000). Interinstitutional File 2000/0243 (CNS) 11791/02 from the Competition Working party to the Permanent Representatives Committee. *Report of the Institutional File 2000/0243 (CNS) 11791/02*. Brussels: Council of European Union.

Council of European Union. (11 January 2001). Interinstitutional File 2000/0243 (CNS) 11848/00 RC 13- COM(2000) 582 Final. *Note from General Secreteriat of the Council to the Delegations 5158/01*. Brussels: Council of European Union.

Council of European Union. (27 June 2001). Interinstitutional File 2000/0243 (CNS), regarding 5158/01 RC 1. *Note from the General Secreteriat of the Council to the Delegations*. Brussels: Council of European Union. Retrieved 5 February 2015, from http://register.consilium.europa.eu/doc/srv?l=EN&f=ST%209999%202 001%20INIT.

Council of European Union. (20 November 2001). Progress Report from the presidency to the COREPER/Council (Industry/Energy) 13563/01, Interinstitutional file 2000/0243 (CNS). *Proposal for a Council Regulation on the implementation of the* rules on competition laid down in Articles 81 and 82 of the Treaty and amending Regulations (EEC) No 1017/68, (EEC) No 2988/74, (EEC) No 4056/86 and (EEC) No 3975/87. Brussels: Council of European Union.

Council of European Union. (11 October 2002). Interinstitutional File 2000/0243 (CNS). *Report from Competition Working Party to the Permanent Representatives Committee 12998/02*. Brussels: Council of European Union. Retrieved from http://data.consilium.europa.eu/doc/document/ST-12998-2002-INIT/en/pdf.

Council of European Union. (15 November 2002). Interinstitutional File 2000/0243(CNS) 14327/02. *Report from General Secreteriat of the Council to the Permanent Representatives Committee*. Brussels: Council of European Union. Retrieved from http://data.consilium.europa.eu/doc/document/ST-14327-2002-INIT/en/pdf.

Council of European Union. (21 November 2002). Interinstitutional File 2000/0243(CNS) 14471/02. *Report from Permanent Representatives Committee to the Council*. Brussels: Council of European Union.

Council of European Union. (28 October 2002). Note from General Secretariat of the Council to the Competition Working Party 13451/02, Interinstitutional file 2000/0243 (CNS). *Proposal for a Council Regulation on the implementation of the rules on competition laid down in Articles 81 and 82 of the Treaty and amending Regulations (EEC) No 1017/68, (EEC) No 2988/74, (EEC) No 4056/86 and (EEC) No 3975/87*. Council of European Union.

Council of European Union. (21 May 2002). Progress Report from the presidency to the permanent representatives Committee/Council 8383/02, Interinstitutional File 2000/0243 (CNS). *Proposal for a Council Regulation on the implementation of the rules on competition laid down in Articles 81 and 82 of the Treaty and amending Regulations (EEC) No 1017/68, (EEC) No 2988/74, (EEC) No 4056/86 and (EEC) No 3975/87*. Council of European Union.

Cournot, A. A. (1838). Recherches sur les Principes Mathematiques de la Theorie des Richesses. Paris: Hachette.

Cox, H. & Hübner, H. (1981). Einführung in die Wettbewerbstheorie und -politik. In H. Cox, U. Jens & K. Markert, *Handbuch des Wettbewerbs: Wettbewerbstheorie, Wettbewerbspolitk, Wettbewerbsrecht*. München: Vahlen.

Cox, H., Jens, U. & Markert, K. (1981). *Handbuch des Wettbewerbs: Wettbewerbstheorie, Wettbewerbspolitik, Wettbewerbsrecht*. München: Vahlen.

Crown Cork & Seal/CarnaudMetalbox, Case No. IV/M.603 (European Commission 14 November 1995).

Cseres, K. (2005). *Competition Law and Consumer Protection*. The Hague: Kluwer Law International.

Cseres, K. (March 2007). The Controversies of the Consumer Welfare Standard. *The Compeition Law Review, 3*(2), 121–173.

CVCE, I. E. (11 August 2015). *The origins of the Schuman Plan*. Retrieved from http://www.cvce.eu/collections/unit-content/-/unit/en/02bb76df-d066-4c08-a58a-d4686a3e68ff/53babf84-f8e0-4810-bb80-2ed15706efad.

Cyanamid/Shell, Case No. IV/M.354 (European Commission 1 October 1993).

Dalkir, S. & Kalkan, E. (2003). Application of the Proportionality-Calibrated AIDS Model to Predicting Potential Welfare Effects of Mergers Between Fertilizer Sellers as Part of the Turkish Privatization Program. *International Conference on Policy Modeling*, 1–19.

Danish Crown / Vestjyske Slagterier, IV/M.1313 (European Commission 3 September 1999).

DASA/Fokker, Case No. IV/M.237 (European Commission 10 May 1993).

De Coninck, R. (2010). Application of the nonhorizontal merger guidelines. *The Antitrust Bulletin*, 55(4), 929–951.

de Jong, H. W. (1985). *Dynamische Markttheorie*. Leiden: Stenfert Kroese.

de Jong, H. W. (1990a). On Market Theory. In B. Dankbaar, J. Groenewegen & H. (Schenk, *Perspectives in Industrial Organization*. The Netherlands: Springer.

de Jong, H. W. & Shepherd, W. G. (2007). *Pioneers of Industrial Organization*. Cheltenham: Edward Elgar Publishing.

De la Mano, M., Pesaresi, E. & Stehman, O. (2007). Econometric and Survey Evidence in the Competitive Assessment of the Ryanair-Aer Lingus Merger. *Competition Policy Newsletter*, 73–81.

Demsetz, H. (1973). *The Market Concentration Doctrine: An Examination of Evidence and a Discussion of Policy*. Washington D.C.: American Enterprise Institute for Public Policy Research.

Demsetz, H. (1976). Economics as a Guide to Antitrust Regulation. *The Journal of Law and Economics*.

DeSarbo, W. S., Ramaswamy, V. & Cohen, S. H. (1995). Market Segmentation with Choice-Based Conjoint Analysis. *Marketing Letters*, 137–147.

Deutsche Bahn AG v. Commission of the European Communities, Case T-351/02 (Court of First Instance (First Chamber, extended composition) 5 April 2006).

Deutsche Börse / NYSE Euronext, COMP/M.6166 (European Commission 1 February 2012).

Deutsche Post AG, Case COMP/35.141 (Commission Decision (2001/354/EC) 20 March 2001).

Devroe, W. (23 May 2013). The protection of non-economic interests in European competition law. Groningen: Europa Law Publishing.

Dijkstra, J. & Timmermans, H. (1997). Exploring the Possibilities of Conjoint Measurement as a Decision-Making Tool for Virtual Wayfinding Environments. Eindhoven, The Netherlands: Eindhoven University of Technology.

Dijkstra, J. & Timmermans, H. (1997). Exploring the possibilities of conjoint measurement as a deision-making tool for virtual wayfinding environments. In Y.-T. Liu (Ed.), *CAADRIA '97 [Proceedings Second Conference on Computer Aided Architectural Design Reseach in Asia]* (61–72). Taiwan: Hu's Publishers.

DIP SpA v. Comune di Bassano del Grappa, LIDL Italia Srl v. Comune di Chioggia and Lingral Srl v. Comune di Chiogga, Joined cases C-140/94, C-141/94 and C-142/94 (European Court of Justice 17 October 1995).

Directorate-General for Agriculture and Rural Development, JRC-IPTS. (December 2013). *Prospects for Agricultural Markets and Income in the EU 2013-2023*.

Retrieved 10 October 2014, from ec.europa.eu/agriculture: http://ec.europa.eu/agriculture/markets-and-prices/medium-term-outlook/2013/fullrep_en.pdf.

Dixit, A. & Skeath, S. (2004). *Games of Strategy 2nd edition*. New York and London.

Dobbs, I. M. (2007). Defining Markets for Ex Ante Regulation using the Hypothetical Monopoly Test. *International Journal of the Economics of Business*, 83–109.

Dole Food and Dole Fresh Fruit Europe v. Commission, C-286/13 P (European Court of Justice (Second Chamber) 19 March 2015).

Du Pont/ICI, Case No. IV/M214 (European Commission 30 September 1992).

Durand, B. (2012). Merger simulation is back: Should we worry about it? *Concurrences N° 2-2012*, 1–11.

Durand, B. & Pesaresi, E. (2007). Empirical estimation of a discrete choice model for filler calcium carbonates in the paper industry. *Competition Policy Newsletter*, S. 92–99.

Eastman Kodak Company v. Image Technical Services, Inc., 504 U.S. 451 (112 S. Ct. 2072 8 June 1992).

EDF/British Energy, Case COMP/M.5224 (European Commission 22 December 2008).

EDF/Segebel, Case COMP/M.5549 (European Commission 12 November 2009).

Editorial comments: Towards a more judicial approach? EU antitrust fines under the scrutiny of fundamental rights. (2011). *Common Market Law Review*, 48(5), 1405–1416.

EDP - Energias de Portugal SA v. Commission of the European Communities, Case T-87/05 (Court of First Instance (Second Chamber) 21 September 2005).

Edwards, C. D. (1949). *Maintaining Competition: Requisites for a Governmental Policy*. McGraw-Hill.

Eibl, S. & Schultze, J.-M. (2005). From Freiburg to Brussels and Back again: The Seventh Revision of Germany's Competition Law. *European Competition Law Review*, 26(9), 526–531.

Electrolux/AEG, Case No. IV/M.458 (European Commission 21 June 1994).

ELF/BC/Cepsa, Case No. IV/M.98 (European Commission 18 June 1991).

Elliot, M. (8 July 2001). *The Anatomy of the GE-Honeywell Disaster*. Retrieved 13 January 2014 from Time Business and Money: http://content.time.com/time/business/article/0,8599,166732,00.html.

Elzinga, K. G. & Hogarty, T. F. (1973). The Problem of Geographic Market Delineation in Antimerger Suits. *Antitrust Bulletin*, 45–83.

Emmerich, V. (1991). *Kartellrecht, 6th completely revised and comprehensively extended edition Wettbewerbsrecht*. München: C.H. Beck.

Endemol Entertainment Holding BV v. Commission of the European Communities, Case T-221/95 (Court of First Instance (Fourth Chamber, extended composition) 28 April 1999).

Enso/Stora, Case No. IV/M.1225 (European Commission 25 November 1998).

Entreprenørforeningens Affalds/Miljøsektion (FFAD) v. Københavns Kommune, Case C-209/98 (European Court of Justice 23 May 2000).

EPAC - Empresa para a Agroalimentação e Cereais, SA v. Commission of the European Communities, Case T-204/97 (Court of First Instance 13 June 2000).

Epstein, R. J. & Rubinfeld, D. I. (2001). Merger Simulation: A Simplified Approach with New Applications. *Antitrust Law Journal, 69*, 886.

Erhard, L. (14 October 1946). Freie Wirtschaft oder Planwirtschaft? *Die Neue Zeitung.*

Établissements Consten S.à.R.L. and Grundig-Verkaufs-GmbH v. Commission of the European Economic Community, Joined cases 56 and 58-64 (European Court of Justice 13 July 1966).

Eucken, W. (1938). Die Überwindung des Historismus. *Schmollers Jahrbuch für Gesetzgebung, Verwaltung und Volkswirtschaft im Deutschen Reiche*, S. 63–86.

Eucken, W. (1939). *Die Grundlage der Nationalökonomie.* Berlin: Fischer.

Eucken, W. (1959). *Die Grundsätze der Wirtschaftspolitik.* Hamburg: Rowohlt.

Eucken, W. (1990). *Grundsätze der Wirtschaftspolitik* (6 Ausg.). Tübingen: J.C.B. Mohr (Paul Siebeck).

Eucken, W. (1999). *Ordnungspolitik.* (W. Oswalt, Hrsg.) Münster: LIT.

Eurofix-Bauco v. Hilti, Case No. IV/30.787 and 31.488 (European Commission 22 December 1987).

Europe Meat and Food Exporters. (n.d.). *Europe and South-America frozen meat and poultry exporter.* Retrieved 23 January 2015, from http://www.exportforum.com/europe/frozen-meat-exporter.htm.

European Coal and Steel Community. (18 April 1951). *Treaty establishing the European Coal and Steel Community and Annexes I-III.* Retrieved from http://eur-lex.europa.eu/: http://eur-lex.europa.eu/LexUriServ/LexUriServ.do?uri=CELEX:11951K:EN:PDF.

European Commisison. (25 April 2012). State aid: Commission adopts de minimis Regulation for services of general economic interest (SGEI). *European Commission Press Release.*

European Commission. (14 December 2010). Competition: Commission adopts revised competition rules on horizontal co-operation agreements. *Memo/10/676.* Brussels.

European Commission. (1982). *Eleventh Report on Competition Policy.* Luxembourg: Office for Official Publications of the European Communities.

European Commission. (30 December 1989). Council Regulation (EEC) No. 4064/89 of 21 December 1989 on the control of concentrations between undertakings. *Official Journal L395*, 1–12.

European Commission. (16 February 1993). Commission Notice concerning the assessment of cooperative joint ventures pursuant to Article 85 of the EEC Treaty. *Official Journal C43/2*, 2–13.

European Commission. (9 December 1997). C 372 Commission Notice on the definition of relevant market for the purposes of Community competition law. *Official Journal of the European Communities.* European Commission.

European Commission. (30 June 1997). Council Regulation (EC) No. 1310/97 of 30 June 1997 amending Regulation (EEC) No. 4064/89 on the control of concentrations between undertakings. *OJ L180*, S. 1–6.

European Commission. (22 January 1997). Green Paper on Vertical Restraints in EC Competition Policy. *COM (96) 721 final.* Brussels.

European Commission. (28 April 1999). White Paper on Modernization of The Rules Implementing Articles 85 and 86 of the EC Treaty Commission Programme No. 99/027. *White Paper*. Brussels: European Commission. Retrieved 5 February 2015, from http://europa.eu/documents/comm/white_papers/pdf/com99_101_en.pdf.

European Commission. (4 February 2000). 2000/74/EC: Commission Decision of 14 July 1999 relating to a proceeding under Article 82 of the EC Treaty (IV/D-2/34.780 - Virgin/British Airways) (notified under document number C(1999) 1973). *Official Journal*, 1-24.

European Commission. (27 September 2000). Competition: Commission proposes regulation that extensively amends system for implementing Articles 81 and 82 of the Treaty. *IP/00/1064*. Brussels.

European Commission. (27 September 2000). Proposal for a Council Regulation on the implementation of the rules on competition laid down in Articles 81 and 82 of the Treaty and amending Regulations (EEC) No. 1017/68, (EEC) No. 2988/74, (EEC) No. 4056/86 and (EEC) No. 3975/87. *Procedure 2000/0243/CNS*. Brussels. Retrieved 5 February 2015, from http://eur-lex.europa.eu/procedure/EN/158821.

European Commission. (19 December 2000). Proposal for a Council Regulation on the implementation of the rules on competition laid down in Articles 81 and 82 of the Treaty and amending Regulations (EEC) No. 1017/68, (EEC) No. 2988/74, (EEC) No. 4056/86 and (EEC) No. 3975/87. *OJ C 365 E*, 284-296.

European Commission. (31 May 2001). Article 3- The Relationship between EC Law and National Law SEC(2001) 871. *Staff Working Document*. Brussels: European Commission.

European Commission. (6 January 2001). Commission Notice - Guidelines on the applicability of Article 81 of the EC Treaty to horizontal cooperation agreements. *Official Journal C 003*, 2-30.

European Commission. (29 May 2001). Opinion of the Economic and Social Committee on the 'Proposal for a Council Regulation on the implementation of the rules on competition laid down in Articles 81 and 82 of the Treaty and amending Regulations'. *OJ C 155*, 73-80.

European Commission. (16 December 2003). Commission adopts merger control guidelines. *IP/03/1744*. Brussels.

European Commission. (27 April 2004). Commission Notice — Guidelines on the effect on trade concept contained in Articles 81 and 82 of the Treaty (Text with EEA relevance). *Official Journal of the European Union C101*. Brussels. Retrieved 9 February 2015, from http://eur-lex.europa.eu/legal-content/EN/TXT/?uri = OJ:C:2004:101:TOC.

European Commission. (27 April 2004). Communication from the Commission Notice Guidelines on the application of Article 81(3) of the Treaty. *Official Journal of the European Union C 101/97*. Brussels: European Commission. Retrieved 24 February 2015, from http://eur-lex.europa.eu/LexUriServ/LexUriServ.do?uri = OJ:C:2004:101:0097:0118:EN:PDF.

European Commission. (5 February 2004). Guidelines on the assessment of horizontal mergers under the Council Regulation on the control of concentrations between

Bibliography

undertakings. *Official Journal of the European Union C31/5*. Brussels: European Commission. Retrieved 17 February 2015, from http://eur-lex.europa.eu/legal-content/EN/TXT/PDF/?uri = CELEX:52004XC0205(02)&from = EN.

European Commission. (5 February 2004). Guidelines on the assessment of horizontal mergers under the Council Regulation on the control of concentrations between undertakings. *OJ C31/03*, 5–18.

European Commission. (21 December 2005). Mergers: Commission clears acquisition of German slaughterhouse company Südfleisch by Dutch group Sovion. *Press Release*. Brussels.

European Commission. (2006). Community framework for state aid for research and development and innovation. *OJ C 323*, 1–26.

European Commission. (18 August 2006). Community guidelines on State aid to promote risk capital investments in small and medium-sized enterprises. *OJ C 194*, 2–21.

European Commission. (19 July 2006). Regulation (EC) No. 139/2004 on Merger Procedure. *Case No COMP/M.3796 - OMYA/HUBER PCC*.

European Commission. (17 December 2007). Annex - Tables of Equivalences reffered to in Article 5 of the Treary of Lisbon amending the Treaty on European Union and the Treaty establishing the European Community. *OJ C 306*, 202–229.

European Commission. (15 February 2007). Vademecum Community Rules on State Aid.

European Commission. (3 December 2008). Antitrust: Guidance on Commission enforcement priorities in applying Article 82 to exclusionary conduct by dominant firms – frequently asked questions. *Memo/08/761*. Brussels.

European Commission. (28 October 2009). A better functioning food supply chain in Europe COM (2009) 591. *Communication from the Commission*. Brussels: European Commission. Retrieved 5 February 2015, from http://ec.europa.eu/economy_finance/publications/publication16065_en.pdf.

European Commission. (24 February 2009). Communication from the Commission — Guidance on the Commission's enforcement priorities in applying Article 82 of the EC Treaty to abusive exclusionary conduct by dominant undertakings (Text with EEA relevance). *OJ-C- 45*. (E. Commission, Ed.) Brussels. Retrieved 26 February 2015, from http://eur-lex.europa.eu/legal-content/EN/ALL/?uri = CELEX:52009XC0224(01).

European Commission. (29 April 2009). Communication from The Commission to the European Parliament and the Council COM(2009) 206 Final. *Report on the functioning of Regulation 1/2003 SEC(2009)574*. Brussels: European Commission. Retrieved 5 February 2015, from http://www.ipex.eu/IPEXL-WEB/dossier/files/download/082dbcc530b1bf490130bbcc65f66893.do.

European Commission. (28 October 2009). Competition in the food supply chain SEC(2009) 1449 accompanying the document 'A better functioning food supply chain in Europe' COM (2009) 591. *Commission Staff Working Document*. Brussels: European Commission. Retrieved 5 February 2015, from http://ec.europa.eu/economy_finance/publications/publication16065_en.pdf.

European Commission. (11 November 2009). Summary of Commission Decision of 19 December 2007 relating to a proceeding under Article 81 of the EC Treaty and Article 53 of the EEA Agreement (Case COMP/34.579 — MasterCard, Case COMP/36.518 — EuroCommerce, Case COMP/38.580 — Commercial Cards). *OJ C 264*, S. 8–11.

European Commission. (20 April 2010). Antitrust: Commission adopts revised competition rules for distribution of goods and services. *Press Release IP/10/445*. Brussels.

European Commission. (20 April 2010). Antitrust: Commission adopts revised competition rules for vertical agreements: frequently asked questions. *Memo/138*. Brussels.

European Commission. (22 February 2010). Call for Tender for Study on the impact of national rules on unilateral conduct that diverge from Article 102 of the Treaty on the Functioning of the European Union. *Specifications to Invitation to tender COMP/2009/A4/021*. Brussels: European Commission. Retrieved 24 February 2015, from http://ec.europa.eu/competition/calls/2010_nationalrules/annex1.pdf.

European Commission. (18 December 2010). Commission Regulation (EU) No. 1217/2010 of 14 December 2010 on the application of Article 101(3) of the Treaty on the Functioning of the European Union to certain categories of research and development agreements. *OJ L 335*, 36–42.

European Commission. (18 December 2010). Commission Regulation (EU) No. 1218/2010 of 14 December 2010 on the application of Article 101(3) of the Treaty on the Functioning of the European Union to certain categories of specialisation agreements. *OJ L 335*, 43–47.

European Commission. (23 April 2010). Commission Regulation (EU) No. 330/2010 of 20 April 2010 on the application of Article 101(3) of the Treaty on the Functioning of the European Union to categories of vertical agreements and concerted practices. *OJ L 102*, 1–7.

European Commission. (14 December 2010). Competition: Commission adopts revised competition rules on horizontal co-operation agreements. *Press Release IP/10/1702*. Brussels.

European Commission. (2010). Guidelines on Vertical Restraints. *OJ C 130*, 1–46.

European Commission. (2 February 2011). Corrigendum to Communication from the Commission, Guidelines on the applicability of Article 101 of the Treaty on the Functioning of the European Union to horizontal co-operation agreements (OJ C 11, 14.1.2011). *OJ C 33*, 20.

European Commission. (2012). Communication from the Commission to the European Parliament, the Council, the European Economic and Social Committee and the Committee of the Regions: EU State Aid Modernisation (SAM). *European Commission*, 1–9.

European Commission. (2012). *State aid scoreboard 2011*. Retrieved from http://ec.europa.eu/: http://ec.europa.eu/competition/state_aid/scoreboard/index_en.html.

Bibliography

European Commission. (8 May 2012). State aid: Commission launches major initiative to modernise state aid control. *European Commission - Press Release.*

European Commission. (18 December 2013). *Block Exemption Regulation.* Retrieved from http://ec.europa.eu/: http://ec.europa.eu/competition/state_aid/legislation/block.html.

European Commission. (31 July 2013). COUNCIL REGULATION (EU) No. 734/2013 amending Regulation (EC) No. 659/1999 laying down detailed rules for the application of Article 93 of the EC Treaty. *Official Journal of the European Union L 204/15*, 15–22.

European Commission. (December 2013). Directorate General of Agriculture and Development Statistical and Economic Information Report. Retrieved 23 January 2015, from Directorate General of Agriculture and Development Statistical and Economic Information Report: http://ec.europa.eu/agriculture/statistics/agricultural/2013/pdf/full-report_en.pdf.

European Commission. (26 January 2013). EU Guidelines for the application of State aid rules in relation to the rapid deployment of broadband networks. *Official Journal of the European Union C 25/1*, 1–26.

European Commission. (December 2013). Overview of CAP Reform 2014–2020. *Agricultural Policy Perspectives Brief*, 1–10.

European Commission. (2013). *Prospects for Agricultural Markets and Income in the EU 2013-2023.* Brussels: European Commission.

European Commission. (18 December 2013). State Aid: Commission adopts revised exemption for small aid amounts (de minimis Regulation). *European Commission Press Release.*

European Commission. (18 December 2013). State aid: Commission consults on draft rules for state support in energy and environmental field. *European Commission Press Release.*

European Commission. (20 December 2013). State aid: Commission's competition service consults on draft rules on state aid for research, development and innovation. *European Commission Press Release.*

European Commission. (18 December 2013). State aid: Transparency and Evaluation in the draft General Block-Exemption Regulation. *European Commission Memo/13/1175.*

European Commission. (2014). Communication from the Commission — Notice on agreements of minor importance which do not appreciably restrict competition under Article 101(1) of the Treaty on the Functioning of the European Union (De Minimis Notice). *OJ C 291*, 1–4.

European Commission. (2 October 2014). Competition: Commission publishes results of retail food study. *Press Release.* Brussels: European Commission. Retrieved 5 February 2015, from http://europa.eu/rapid/press-release_IP-14-1080_en.htm.

European Commission. (2014). Enhancing competition enforcement by the Member States' competition authorities:institutional and procedural issues COM(2014) 453, SWD(2014) 230. *Commission Staff Working Document.* Brussels: European Commission. Retrieved 5 February 2015, from http://ec.europa.eu/competition/antitrust/legislation/swd_2014_231_en.pdf.

European Commission. (8 April 2014). European Commission Press Release. Retrieved 1 November 2014, from http://europa.eu/rapid/press-release_IP-14-389_en.htm.
European Commission. (2014). Ten Years of Antiturst Enforcement under Regulation 1/2003 SWD(2014) 230/2:Achievements and Future Perspectives COM(2014) 453. *Commission Staff Working Document*. Brussels: European Commission. Retrieved 5 February 2015, from http://ec.europa.eu/competition/antitrust/legislation/swd_2014_230_en.pdf.
European Commission. (2014). *The Economic Impact of Modern Retail on Choice on Innovation in the EU Food Sector*. Luxembourg: European Commission.
European Commission. (4 November 2015). Antitrust: Commission consults on boosting enforcement powers of national competition authorities. *Press release IP/15/5998*. Brussels.
European Commission. (2015). ECN Plus: Empowering the national competition authorities to be more effective enforcers - Consultation Strategy. Retrieved January 2016, from http://ec.europa.eu/competition/consultations/2015_effective_enforcers/strategy_en.pdf.
European Commission. (3 June 2015). Guidance on restrictions of competition 'by object' for the purpose of defining which agreements may benefit from the De Minimis Notice Accompanying the Commission De Minimis Notice. *Commission Staff Working Document*. Brussels.
European Commission. (n.d.). Article 81 of the EC Treaty (ex Article 85). Brussels.
European Commission DG Competition. (December 2005). DG Competition discussion paper on the application of Article 82 of the Treaty to exclusionary abuses. *Discussion paper*. Brussels: European Commission.
European Commission DG Competition. (November 2013). *Evaluation in the field of State aid, Draft Methodological Guidance Paper*. Retrieved from http://ec.europa.eu/: http://ec.europa.eu/competition/consultations/2013_state_aid_modernisation/draft_guidance_paper_en.pdf.
European Commission DG Competition. (12 April 2013). *Evaluation in the field of State aid, Issues Paper*. Retrieved from http://ec.europa.eu/: http://ec.europa.eu/competition/state_aid/modernisation/evaluation_issues_paper_en.pdf.
European Court. (19 February 2009). Opinion of Advocate General Kokott Case C-8/08 T-Mobile Netherlands BV and Others. *European Court Reports 2009 I-04529*. European Court. Retrieved 5 February 2015, from http://eur-lex.europa.eu/legal-content/EN/TXT/HTML/?uri=CELEX:62008CC0008&from=EN.
European Night Services Ltd (ENS), Eurostar (UK) Ltd, formerly European Passenger Services Ltd (EPS), Union internationale des chemins de fer (UIC), NV Nederlandse Spoorwegen (NS) and Société nationale des chemins de fer français (SNCF) v. Commission, Joined cases T-374/94, T-375/94, T-384/94 and T-388/94 (Court of First Instance (Second Chamber) 15 September 1998).
European Parliament. (21 June 2001). Draft Legislative Resolution A5-0229/2001. *Draft Legislative Resolution*. European Parliament. Retrieved 5 February 2015, from http://www.europarl.europa.eu/sides/getDoc.do?pubRef=-//EP//NONSGML+REPORT+A5-2001-0229+0+DOC+PDF+V0//EN.

Eurostat. (2013). *Pocketbooks: Agriculture, forestry and fishery statistics*. Brussels: Eurostat.
Eurostat. (1 November 2014). *Eurostat*. Retrieved 1 November 2014, from http://epp.eurostat.ec.europa.eu/statistics_explained/index.php/Pig_farming_sector_-_statistical_portrait_2014.
Ewans, L. (2006). Delivering the State aid reform. *Concurrences N° 4-2006*, 7–9.
Expedia Inc. v. Autorité de la concurrence and Others, C-226/11 (European Court of Justice (Second Chamber) 13 December 2012).
Faull, J. & Nikpay, A. (1999). *the EC Law of Competition*. Oxford: Oxford University Press.
Fikentscher, W. (1983). *Wirtschaftsrecht I*. München: Beck.
Fingleton, J., Ruane, F. & Ryan, V. (1999). Market Definition and State Aid Control. *European Reports and Studies*. DG Economic and Financial Affairs,.
Fishwick, F. & Denison, G. (1992). *The Geographical Dimension of Competition in the European Single Market*. Amt für Amt. Veröff. d. Europ.
Flat glass, Case No. IV/31.906 (European Commission 7 December 1988).
Foncel, J. (2009). Horizontal merger analysis and the use of simulation techniques. *Concurrences N° 2*, 1.
Foncel, J., Ivaldi, M. & Rabassa, V. (2007). The case for econometrics under the new European merger regulation: Hachette/Editis. *Université de Lille*, 2.
Ford of Europe Incorporated and Ford-Werke Aktiengesellschaft v. Commission of the European Communities, Joined cases 228 and 229/82 (ECJ 28 February 1984).
Ford/Volkswagen, IV/33.814 (European Commission 23 December 1992).
Fox, E. (2008). The Efficiency Paradox. In R. Pitofsky, *How the Chicago School Overshot the Mark: The Effect of Conservative Economic Analysis on U.S. Antitrust 77* (77–88). New York: Oxford University Press.
Fox, E. (2009). *The Efficiency Paradox*. Law & Economics Research Paper Series Working Paper No. 09-26, New York.
Fox, E. M. (1986). Monopolization and Dominance in the United States and the European Community: Efficiency, Opportunity, and Fairness. *Notre Dame Law Review*, 981–1017.
Frank, R. (1997). *Microeeconomis and Behavior* (3rd ed.). Boston: McGraw-Hill.
Franz Völk v. S.P.R.L. Ets J. Vervaecke, Case 5/69 (European Court of Justice 9 July 1969).
French Republic and Société commerciale des potasses et de l'azote (SCPA) and Entreprise minière et chimique (EMC) v. Commission of the European Communities, Joined cases C-68/94 and C-30/95 (European Court of Justice 31 March 1998).
French Republic v. Commission of the European Communities, Case C-482/99 (European Court of Justice 16 May 2002).
French-West African shipowners' committees, Case No. IV/32.450 (European Commission 1 April 1992).
Friederiszick, H. W., Röller, L.-H. & Verouden, V. (2006). *European State Aid Control: An Economic Framework*. DG Competition, European Commission.

Friederiszick, H. W., Röller, L.-H. & Verouden, V. (2007). European State Aid Control: an economic framework. *Paolo Buccirossi (Ed.) Advances in the Economics of Competition, MIT press*, 1-58.

Friesland Foods/Campina, Case COMP/M.5046 (European Commission 17 December 2008).

Fritsch, M., Wein, T. & Ewers, H.-J. (1996). *Marktversagen und Wirtschaftspolitik: Mikroökonomische Grundlagen staatlichen Handelns*. Verlag Vahlen.

Froeb, L. M. & Werden, G. J. (1991). Residual Demand Estimation for Market Delineation: Complications and Limitations. *Review of Indsutrial Organization*, 33-48.

Froeb, L. & Werden, G. (1992). The reverse Cellophane fallacy in market delineation. *Review of Industrial Organization*, 7, 241-247.

Fudenberg, D. & Tirole, J. (1991). *Game Theory*. Cambridge: The MIT Press.

Gadas, R., Koch, O., Parpilies, K. & Beuve-Méry, H. (2007). Ryanair/Aer Lingus: Even 'low cost' monopolies can harm consumers. *Competition Policy Newsletter*, 65-72.

Gasmi, F., Laffont, J.-J. & Sharkey, W. (2002). The natural monopoly test reconsidered: an engineering process-based approach to empirical analysis in telecommunications. *International Journal of Industrial Organization*, 435-459.

Gencor Ltd v. Commission of the European Communities, Case T-102/96 (Court of First Instance (Fifth chamber, extended composition) 25 March 1999).

Gencor/Lonrho, Case No. IV/M.619 (European Commission 24 April 1996).

General Court of the European Union. (6 December 2012). The Court dismisses the appeal of the AstraZeneca group, which abused its dominant position by preventing the marketing of generic products replicating Losec. *Press Release No 158/12*. Luxembourg.

General Court of the European Union. (12 June 2014). The General Court upholds the fine of €1.06 billion imposed on Intel for having abused its dominant position on the market for x86 central processing units between 2002 and 2007. *Press Release No 82/14*. Luxembourg.

General Electric Company v. Commission of the European Communities, Case T-210/01 (Court of First Instance (Second Chamber, extended composition) 14 December 2005).

General Motors Continental NV v. Commission of the European Communities, Case 26-75 (European Court of Justice 13 November 1975).

Gensch, D. H. & Recker, W. W. (1979). The Multinominal, Multiattribute Logit Choice Model. *Journal of Marketing Research*, 124-132.

Geradin, D. & Girgenson, I. (2011). Industrial policy and European merger control. In *Fordham law Institute* (353-382).

Gerber David J. (2013-2014). Searching for a modernised voice: Economics, Institutions, and Predictability in European Competition Law. *37 Fordham International Law Journal*, S. 1442-1449.

Gerber, D. (1995). Competition law and international trade: The European Union amd the neo-liberal factor. *Pacific Rim Law & Policy Journal*, 4(1), 37-57.

Gerber, D. (2001). *Law and Competition in Twentieth Century Europe Protecting Prometheus*. New York: Oxford University Press.

Gerber, D. J. (1994). Constitutionalizing the Economy: German Neo-Liberalism, Competition Law and the 'New' Europe. *The American Journal of Comparative Law*, 25–84.

Gerber, D. J. (1998). *Law and Competition in Twentieth Century Europe - Protecting Prometheus*. New York: Oxford University Press.

Germany Freizeitbad Dorsten, N 258/00 (European Commission 16 June 2001).

Giocoli, N. (30 May 2012). Old Lady charm: explaining the persistent appeal of Chicago antitrust. Pisa, Italy: University of Pisa.

Giovanni Anania, Maria Rosaria. (April 23–25 2007). *The Global Market for Olive Oil:Actors, Trends, Policies, Prospects and Research Needs*. Retrieved 5 December 2014, from The Global Market for Olive Oil:Actors, Trends, Policies, Prospects and Research Needs: http://ageconsearch.umn.edu/bitstream/6109/2/wp080 002.pdf.

GlaxoSmithKline Services Unlimited v. Commission of the European Communities, Case T-168/01 (Court of the First Instance (Fourth Chamber, extended composition) 27 September 2006).

Gormsen Liza Lovdahl. (December 2007). The conflict between economic freedom and consumer welfare in the modernisation of Article 82. *European Competition Journal*, 329–344.

Gormsen, L. (2006). Article 82 EC: Where are we coming from and where are we going to? *The Competition Law Review*.

Gøttrup-Klim e.a. Grovvareforeninger v. Dansk Landbrugs Grovvareselskab AmbA, Case C-250/92 (European Court of Justice (Fifth Chamber) 15 December 1994).

Grabitz, E. (1984). *Kommentar zum EWG-Vertrag*. München: Beck.

Green, P. E. & Srinivasan, V. (1990). Conjoint Analysis in Marketing: New Developments with Implications for Research and Practice. *Journal of Marketing*, 3–19.

Groeneveld, K., Maks, J. & Muysken, J. (1990). *Economic Policy and the Market Process - Austrian and Mainstream Economics*. Amsterdam: Elsevier Science Publishers BV.

Grossman, S. J. & Hart, O. D. (1986). The Costs and Benefits of Ownership: A Theory of Vertical and Lateral Intergration. *Journal of Political Economy*, 691–719.

Groupement des cartes bancaires (CB) v. European Commission, Case C-67 / 13 P (European Court of Justice (Third Chamber) 11 September 2014).

GT-Link A/S v. De Danske Statsbaner (DSB), Case C-242/95 (European Court of Justice (Sixth Chamber) 17 July 1997).

Gual, J., Hellwig, M., Perrot, A., Polo, M., Rey, P., Schmidt, K. & Stenbacka, R. (July 2005). An Economic Approach to Article 82: Report by the European Advisory Group on Competition Policy. Retrieved from http://ec.europa.eu/comm/competition/publications/studies/eagcp_july_21_05.pdf.

Gustafsson, A., Herrmann, A. & Huber, F. (2000). *Conjoint Measurement: Methods and Applications*. Berlin: Springer Verlag.

H.G. Oude Luttikhuis and others v. Verenigde Coöperatieve Melkindustrie Coberco BA., Case C-399/93 (European Court of Justice 12 December 1995).

Haberler, G. (1986). *Selected Essays of Gottfried Haberler*. Cambridge: The MIT Press.
Hancher, L., Ottervanger, T. & Slot, P. (1999). *E.C. State Aids*. London: Sweet & Maxwell.
Hanslowe, K. (1960). Neo-liberalism: An analysis and proposed application. *Journal of Public Law*, 9(1).
Harris, B. C. & Simons, J. J. (1989). Focusing Market Definition: How Much Substitution is Necessary? *Research in Law and Economics*, S. 207–226.
Harrisons & Crosfield/AKZO, Case No. IV/M.310 (European Commission 29 April 1993).
Hart, O. & Tirole, J. (1990). Vertical Integration and Market Foreclosure. *Brookings papers on economic activity, Microeconomics, 1990*, 205–286.
Hasselblad (GB) Limited v. Commission of the European Communities, Case 86/82 (ECJ 21 February 1984).
Hasselblad, IV/25.757 (Commission Decision (82/367/EEC) 2 December 1981).
Hauptzollamt München-Mitte v. Technische Universität München, Case C-269/90 (European Court of Justice 21 November 1991).
Havas Voyage/American Express, Case No. IV/M.564 (European Commission 6 April 1995).
Hawk, B. E. (1990). *United States Common Market and International Antitrust, Volume II*. Prentice Hall Law & Business.
Hawk, B. E. (1995). System Failure: Vertical Restraints and EC Competition Law. *35 Common Market Law Review*, 973–989.
Heidhues, P. & Nitsche, R. (2006). Comments on State Aid Reform: Some implications of an Effects-based Approach. *European State Aid Law Quarterly*.
Heintz van Landewyck SARL and others v. Commission of the European Communities, Joined cases 209-215 and 218/78 (ECJ 29 October 1980).
Heistermann, F. (1995). Praxis der EG-Kommission und des Bundeskartellamtes zur Fusionskontrolle. In *Schwerpunkte des Kartellrechts: Verwaltungs- u. Rechtsprechungspraxis Bundesrepublic Deutschland und EG*. (51–70). Köln: Heymann.
Henkel/Colgate, IV/26.917 (European Commission 23 December 1971).
Henkel/Nobel, Case No. IV/M.186 (European Commission 23 March 1992).
Heyer, K. (March 2006). Welfare Standards and Merger Analysis:Why not the Best? Retrieved from http://www.justice.gov/atr/welfare-standards-and-merger-analysis-why-not-best#N_4_.
Hilti AG v. Commission of the European Communities, Case T-30/89 (Court of First Instance (Second Chamber) 12 December 1991).
Hilti AG v. Commission of the European Communities, Case C-53/92 P (European Court of Justice 2 March 1994).
Hirsch, W. Z. (1988). Law and Economics: An Introductory Analysis 2nd edition. In T. Frazer & M. Waterson, *Competition Law and Policy* (7–10). London: Academic Press.
Hoffmann-La Roche & Co. AG v. Commission of the European Communities, Case 85/76 (European Court of Justice 13 February 1979).
Honeywell/Novar, Case No. COMP/M.3686 (European Commission 30 March 2005).

Hoppmann, E. (1966). Das Konzept der optimalen Wettbewerbsintensität. Rivalität oder Freiheit des Wettbewerbs: Zum Problem eines wettbewerbspolitisch adäquaten Ansatzes der Wettbewerbstheorie. In J. o. Statistics, *Jahrbuch für Nationalökonomie und Statistik*.

Hoppmann, E. (1977). *Marktmacht und Wettbewerb: Beurteilungskriterien und Lösungsmöglichkeiten*. Tübingen: JCB Mohr.

Horowitz, I. (1981). Market Definition in Antitrust Analysis: A Regression-Based Approach. *Southern Economic Journal*, 1–16.

Horspool, M. & Korah, V. (1992). Competition. *Antitrust Bulletin 37*, 337–385.

Hovenkamp, H. (1985). Antitrust Policy after Chicago. *Michigan Law Review*, 256–260.

Hovenkamp, H. (1994). *Federal Antitrust Policy: The Law of Competition and Its Practice*. St. Paul Minnesota: Place West.

Hovenkamp, H. (2001). Symposium: Post-Chicago Economics. *Antitrust Law journal*, 445–695.

Hovenkamp, H. (2010). The Harvard and Chicago Schools and the Dominant Firm.

Hughes, M., Foss, C. & Ross, K. (2001). The economic assessment of vertical restraints under UK and EC competition law. *European Competition Law Review*, S. 424–433.

Hugin Kassaregister AB and Hugin Cash Registers Ltd v. Commission of the European Communities, Case 22/78 (European Court of Justice 21 May 1979).

ICN, I. C. (April 2015). Online Vertical Restraints Special Project Report. *2015 International Competition Network Annual Meeting*. Sydney. Retrieved from http://www.icn2015.com.au/download/ICN2015-special-project-online-vertical-restraints.pdf.

IFTRA rules for producers of virgin aluminium, IV/27.000 (European Commission 15 July 1975).

Imperial Chemical Industries Ltd. v. Commission of the European Communities, Case 48-69 (ECJ 14 July 1972).

Independent Music Publishers and Labels Association (Impala, international association) v. Commission of the European Communities, Case T-464/04 (Court of First Instance (Third Chamber) 13 July 2006).

INEOS/Kerling, Case No. COMP/M.4734 (European Commission 30 January 2008).

Intel Corp. v. European Commission, Case T-286/09 (European Court of Justice 12 June 2014).

International Competition Network. (2004). Efficiencies. In *ICN Merger Guidelines Project*.

International Competition Network. (2008). *Report on Abuse of Superior Bargaining Position*. ICN Kyoto Annual Conference Report, Kyoto.

Irish Sugar plc v. Commission of the European Communities, Case T-228/97 (Court of First Instance (Third Chamber) 7 October 1999).

Istituto Chemioterapico Italiano S.p.A. and Commercial Solvents Corporation v. Commission of the European Communities, Joined cases 6 and 7-73 (European Court of Justice 6 March 1974).

Bibliography

Italian Republic (T-304/04) and Wam SpA (T-316/04) v. Commission of the European Communities, Joined cases T-304/04 and T-316/04 (Court of First Instance 6 September 2006).

Jacquemin, A. P. (1990). Introduction: Competition and Competition Policy in Market Economies. In A. P. Jacquemin, *Competition Policy in Europe and North America: Economic Issues and Institutions* (1-6). Chur: Harwood Academic Publishers.

Jenny, F. (1994). Competition and Efficiency. In (B. Hawk, *Annual Proceedings of the Fordham Corporate Law Institute*. The Netherlands: Kluwer.

Johnson, F. (1989). Market Definition under the Merger Guidelines. *Research in Law and Economics*, 235-246.

Johnson, P. M. (n.d.). *A Glossary of Political Economy Terms - Externality*. (Auburn University, Editor) Retrieved from http://www.auburn.edu/~johnspm/gloss/externality.

Jones, A. & Sufrin, B. (2008). *EC Competition Law. Texts, Cases and Materials*. Oxford: Oxford University Press.

Jones, A. & Sufrin, B. (2010). *EU Competition Law: Text, Cases & Materials*. United States of America: Oxford University Press.

Kali und Salz AG and Kali-Chemie AG v. Commission of the European Communities, Joined cases 19 and 20/74 (European Court of Justice 14 May 1975).

Kali + Salz/MdK/Treuhand, Case No. IV/M.308 (European Commission 14 December 1993).

Kantzenbach, E. & Kalfass, H. H. (1981). Das Konzept des funktionsfähigen Wettbewerbs. In H. Cox, U. Jens & K. Markert, *Handbuch des Wettbewerbs* (103-127). München.

Kantzenbach, E., Kottmann, E. & Krüger, R. (1996). *Kollektive Marktbeherrschung: Neue Industrieökonomik und Erfahrungen aus der Europäischen Fusionskontrolle*. Nomos.

Kattan, J. (1993). Market Power in the Presence of an Installed Base. *Antitrust Law Journal*.

Kauper, T. E. (1996). The Problem of Market Definition Under EC Competition Law. *Fordham International Law Journal*, 1682-1767.

Kerber, W. (2007). Should Competition Law Promote Efficiency? - Some Reflections of an Economist on the Normative Foundations of Competition law. In J. Drexl & L. a. Idot, *Economic Theory and Competition Law*. Cheltenham: Edward Elgar.

Kerber, W. & Vezzoso, S. (2004). *EU Competition Policy, Vertical Restraints, and Innovation: Analysis from an Evolutionary Perspective*. Marburg: Phillipps-Universität Marburg.

Kesko/Tuko, Case No. IV/M.784 (European Commission 20 November 1996).

Kimberly-Clark/Scott, Case No. IV/M.623 (European Commission 16 January 1996).

Kingdom of Belgium v. Commission of the European Communities, Case C-142/87 (European Court of Justice 21 March 1990).

Kingdom of Spain v. Commission of the European Communities., Joined cases C-278/92, C-279/92 and C-280/92 (European Court of Justice 14 September 1994).

Kingdom of the Netherlands and Leeuwarder Papierwarenfabriek BV v. Commission of the European Communities, Joined cases 296 and 318/82 (European Court of Justice 13 March 1985).

Kirch/Richemont/Telepiù, Case No. IV/M.410 (European Commission 2 August 1994).

Kirkwood, J. B. & Lande, R. H. (2009). *The Chicago School's Foundation is Flawed: Antitrust Protects Consumers, Not Efficiency*. Baltimore: University of Baltimore.

Kirzner, I. (1992). *The Meaning of Market Process: Essays in the Development of Modern Austrian Economics*. London: Routledge.

Kledingverkoopbedrijf de Geus en Uitdenbogerd v. Robert Bosch GmbH and Maatschappij tot voortzetting van de zaken der Firma Willem van Rijn, Case 13/61 (European Court of Justice 6 April 1962).

Klees, A. (2006). Breaking the Habits:The German Competition Law after the 7th Amendment to the Act against Restraints of Competition (GWB). *German Law Journal* 7(4), 400–420. German Law Journal. Retrieved 26 February 2015, from http://heinonline.org/HOL/LandingPage?handle = hein.journals/germlajo2006&div = 44&id = &page = .

Klein, N. M. & Bither, S. W. (14 September 1987). An Investigation of Utility-Directed Cut off Selection. *Journal of Consumer Research*.

Klemperer, P. (June 2005). *Nuffield College – University of Oxford*. Retrieved from http://www.nuff.ox.ac.uk/users/klemperer/biddingmarkets.pdf.

Knight, F. H. (2002). *Risk, Uncertainty, and Profit*. Boston: Mifflin 1921 Reprint Washington: Beard Books.

KNP/Bührmann-Tettorde/VRG-Group, Case No. IV/M.291 (European Commission 4 May 1993).

Koch, O. (2010). Yes we can prohibit - The Ryanair/Aer Lingus merger before the Court. *Competition Policy Newsletter*, 41–45.

Kociubinski, J. (2012). Selectivity Criterion in State Aid Control. *Wroclaw Review of Law, Administration and Economics, 2*(1), 1–15.

Konsortium ECR 900, IV/32.688 (European Commission 27 July 1990).

Korah, V. (1981). The Rise and Fall of Provisional Validity: The Need for a Rule of Reason in EEC Antitrust. *Northwestern Journal of International Law & Business*, 320–357.

Korah, V. (1990). *An Introductory Guide to EEC Competition Law and Practice*. Law Book Co. of Australasia.

Korah, V. (1994). *An Introductory Guide to EC Competition Law and Practice*. London: Sweet & Maxwell.

Korah, V. & O'Sullivan, D. (2002). *Distribution Agreements Under the EC Competition Rules*. Hart Publishing.

Kraft Foods/Cadbury, COMP/M.5644 (European Commission 6 January 2010).

Krattenmaker, T. & Salop, S. (1986). Anticompetitive Exclusion: Raising Rival's Cost to Achieve Power over Price. *Yale Law Review*, 209–293.

Krimphove, D. (1992). *Europäische Fusionskontrolle*. Köln: Heymanns.

Kroes, N. (23 September 2005). Preliminary Thoughts on Policy Review of Article 82. *Speech at Fordham Corporate Law Institute*. New York.

Kroes, N. (21 September 2006). The refined economic approach in state aid law: a policy perspective. *SPEECH/06/518*. Brussels.

L.C. Nungesser KG and Kurt Eisele v. Commission of the European Communities, Case 258/78 (European Court of Justice 8 June 1982).

La Redoute/Empire, Case No. IV/M.80 (European Commission 25 April 1991).

La Roche/Syntex, Case No. IV/M.457 (European Commission 20 June 1994).

Lagardère/Natexis/VUP, COMP/M.2978 (European Commission 7 January 2004).

Lagrange, M. (23 September 1980). Interview. *Transcript on file with the Fondation Jean Monnet Pour l'Europe.* Lausanne.

Lande, R. (1989). Chicago's False Foundation: Wealth Transfers (Not Just Efficiency) Should Guide Antitrust. *Antitrust Law Journal*, 631–644.

Lande, R. (1994). Beyond Chicago: Will Activist Antitrust Arise Again? *Antitrust Bulletin*.

Landes, W. & Posner, R. (1981). Market Power in Antitrust Cases. *Harvard Law Review*, 937–996.

Langnese Iglo GmbH v. Commission of the European Communities, Case T-7/93 (Court of First Instance (Second Chamber, extended composition) 8 June 1995).

Lao, M. (n.d.). Free Riding: An Overstated, and Unconvincing, Explanation for Resale Price Maintenance. 196–230.

LdPE, IV/31.866 (European Commission 21 December 1988).

Le Levant 001 and Others v. Commission of the European Communities, Case T-34/02 (Court of First Instance 22 February 2006).

Leagle. (2013). *OLYMPIA EQUIP. LEASING CO. v. WESTERN UNION TELEGRAPH CO.* Retrieved 23 January 2014 from http://www.leagle.com/decision/19861167797 F2d370_11096.xml/OLYMPIA%20EQUIP.%20LEASING%20CO.%20v.%20WE STERN%20UNION%20TELEGRAPH%20CO.

Leary, T. B. (2002). Efficiencies and Antitrust: A Story of Ongoing Evolution. *Prepared Remarks before ABA Section of Antitrust Law, 2002 Law Forum*. Washington, D.C., USA: Federal Trade Commission.

Leibenstein, H. (1966). Allocative Efficiency versus X-Efficiency. In: American Economic Review, 56, 392–415. In *Beyond Economic Man. A New Foundation or Microeconomics 2nd edition 1980* (S. 29–47). Cambridge: Harvard University Press.

Lenk, P. J., DeSarbo, W. S., Green, P. E. & Young, M. R. (1996). Hierarchical Bayes Conjoint Analysis: Recovery of Partworth Heterogeneity from Reduced Experimental Designs. *Marketing Science*, 173–191.

Lenzing AG v. Commission of the European Communities, Case T-36/99 (Court of First Instance (Fifth Chamber, extended composition) 21 October 2004).

Lever, J. & Neubauer, S. (2000). Vertical Restraints, Their Motivation and Justification. *European Competition Law Review*, 7–23.

Linde/AGA, Case No. COMP/M.1641 (European Commission 9 February 2000).

Lipps, W. (1975). *Kartellrecht; 2nd edition*. Bonn: Stollfuss.

Lipsey, R. & Lancaster, K. (1956). The General Theory of Second Best. *The Review of Economic Studies*, 11–32.

Lofaro, A. & Ridyard, D. (September 2000). The Economic Analysis of Joint Dominance under the EC Merger Regulation. *European Business Organization Law Review*, 539–559.

Loriot, G., Rouxel, F.-X. & Durand, B. (2004). GE/Instrumentarium: A Practical Example of the Use of Quantitative Analyses in Merger Control. *Competition Policy Newsletter*, 58–62.

Lowe, P. (1995). Recent Developments in EC Merger Control. In B. Hawk, *Annual Proceedings of the Fordham Corporate Law Institute*. The Netherlands: Kluwer.

Luce, R. & Raiffa, H. (1957). *Games and Decisions. Introduction and Critical Survey*. New York: Wiley.

Lutz, C. H., Kemp, R. G. & Dijkstra, S. G. (July 2010). Perceptions Regarding Strategic and Structural Entry Barriers. *Small Business Economics*, 19–33.

Magill TV Guide/ITP, BBC and RTE, Case No. IV/31.851 (European Commission 21 December 1988).

Magneti/Marelli/CEAc, Case No. IV/M.43 (European Commission 29 May 1991).

Maier-Rigaud, F. & Parplies, K. (2009). EU Merger Control Five Years After The Introduction Of The SIEC Test: What Explains the Drop in Enforcement Activity? *European Competition Law Review 11*, 565–579.

Mannesmann/Boge, Case No. IV/M.134 (European Commission 23 September 1991).

Mannesmann/Hoesch, Case No. IV/M.222 (European Commission 12 November 1992).

Mannesmann/Vallourec/Ilva, Case No. IV/M.315 (European Commission 31 January 1994).

Manufacture française des pneumatiques Michelin v. Commission of the European Communities, Case T-203/01 (Court of First Instance (Third Chamber) 30 September 2003).

Manzini, P. (2002). The European Rule of Reason: Crossing the Sea of Doubt. *European Competition Law Review*, 392–399.

Marenco, G. (2002). The Birth of Modern Competition Law in Europe. In C.-D. Ehlermann, A. von Bogdandy & P. C. Mavroidis (eds), *European Integration and International Co-ordination: Studies in Honour of Claus-Dieter Ehlermann* (279–304). Kluwer Law International.

Markham, J. W. (1950). An Alternative Approach to the Concept of Workable Competition. *The American Economic Review*, 349–361.

Mars/Langnese, Case IV/34.072 (European Commission 23 December 1992).

Mars/Schöller, Cases IV/31.533 and IV/34.072 (Commission 23 December 1992).

Marshall, A. (1890). *Principles of Economics*. London: MacMillan.

Martin, S. (1994). *Industrial Economics: Economic Analysis and Public Policy 2nd edition*. New York: MacMillan.

Martin, S. (2007). Remembrance of Things Past: Antitrust, Ideology, and the Development of Industrial Economics. In V. Ghosal & J. Stennek (eds), *The Political Economy of Antitrust* (25–57). Elsevier.

Martin, S. (2007). *The goals of antitrust and competition policy*. West Lafayette, Indiana.

Mason, E. S. (November 1937). Monopoly in Law and Economics. *The Yale Law Journal*, 34–49.
Mason, E. S. (March 1939). Price and Production Policies of Large-Scale Enterprise. *The American Economic Review*, 61–74.
Massey, P. (2000). Market Definition and Market Power in Competition Analysis - Some Practical Issues. *Economic and Social Review*, 309–328.
Massey, P. (2008). Commission's Economic Analysis Shoots Down Ryanair's Proposed Acquisition of Aer Lingus. *Compecon*.
MasterCard Inc. and Others v. European Commission, C-832/12 P (European Court of Justice 11 September 2014).
MasterCard Inc. and others v. European Commission, Case T-111/08 (European of Justice (Seventh Chamber) 24 May 2012).
Matra Hachette SA v. Commission of the European Communities, Case T-17/93 (Court of First Instance (Second Chamber) 15 July 1994).
Maurice, C. S., Phillips, O. R. & Ferguson, C. E. (1982). *Economic Analysis: Theory and Application*. R.D. Irwin.
Medeol SA/Elosua SA, Case No. IV/M.431 (European Commission 6 June 1994).
Meiklejohn, R. (1999). The economics of State aid, European Commission, DG Economic and Financial Affairs. *European Reports and Studies*, 25–31.
Mercedes-Benz/Kässbohrer, Case No. IV/M.477 (European Commission 14 February 1995).
Merci Convenzionali Porto di Genova SpA v. Siderurgica Gabrielli SpA, Case C-179/90 (European Court of Justice 10 December 1991).
Merkin, R. M. & Williams, K. (1984). *Competition Law: Antitrust Policy in the United Kingdom and the EEC*. London: Sweet & Maxwell.
Mestmäcker, E. (1980). *Freiheit und Ordnung in der Marktwirtschaft (Collected Articles)*. Nomos: Baden-Baden.
Mestmäcker, E. (1984). *Der verwaltete Wettbewerb*. Tübingen: Mohr.
Mestmäcker, E. J. (1994). Meinungsfreiheit und Medienwettbewerb. *Sandai Law Review*, 293–306.
Metro SB-Großmärkte GmbH & Co. KG v. Commission of the European Communities, Case 26-76 (European Court of Justice 25 October 1977).
Metro SB-Großmärkte GmbH & Co. KG v. Commission of the European Communities, Case 75/84 (European Court of Justice 22 October 1986).
Métropole télévision (M6), Suez-Lyonnaise des eaux, France Télécom and Télévision française 1 SA (TF1) v. Commission of the European Communities, Case T-112/99 (Court of First Instance (Third Chamber) 18 September 2001).
Métropole Télévision SA (M6) (T-185/00), Antena 3 de Televisión, SA (T-216/00), Gestevisión Telecinco, SA (T-299/00) and SIC - Sociedade Independente de Comunicação, SA (T-300/00) v. Commission of the European Communities, Joined cases T-185/00, T-216/00, T-299/00 and T-300/00 (Court of First Instance (Second Chamber, extended composition) 8 October 2002).
Michelin, Case No. COMP/E-2/36.041/PO (European Commission 20 June 2001).
Microsoft Corp. v. Commission of the European Communities, Case T-201/04 (Court of First Instance (Grand Chamber) 17 September 2007).

Miksch, L. (1947). *Wettbewerb als Aufgabe: Grundsätze einer Wettbewerbsordnung.* Godesberg: Verlag Helmut Küpper.
Miller International Schallplatten GmbH v. Commission of the European Communities, Case 19/77 (European Court of Justice 1 February 1978).
Mirowski, P. & Plehwe, D. (2009). *The Road from Mont Perlin - The Making of the Neoliberal Thought Collective.* Camnridge, Massachusetts: Harvard University Press.
Monti, M. (9 November 2000). *Competition in a Social Market economy.* Freiburg. Retrieved from http://ec.europa.eu/competition/speeches/text/sp2000_022_en.pdf.
Möschel, W. (1983). *Recht der Wettbewerbsbeschränkungen.* Köln: Heymanns.
Möschel, W. (1989). Competition Policy from an Ordo Point of View. In A. Peacock & H. Willgerodt (eds), *German Neo-Liberals and the Social Market Economy* (142-159). London: MacMillan.
Möschel, W. (2001). The Proper Scope of Government Viewed from an Ordoliberal Perspective: The Example of Competition Policy. *Journal of Institutional and Theortical Economics*, 3-13.
Motta, M. (2004). *Competition Policy, Theory and Practice.* Cambridge: Cambridge University Press.
MSG Media Service, Case No. IV/M.469 (European Commission 9 November 1994).
Müller-Armack, A. (1956). Soziale Marktwirtschaft. In *Handwörterbuch der Sozialwissenschaften.* Stuttgart and Tübingen.
Müller-Armack, A. (1989). The Meaning of the Social Market Economy. In A. Peacock & H. Willgerodt, *Germany's Social Market Economy: Origins and Evolution* (82-86). London: Macmillan.
Municipality of Almelo and others v. NV Energiebedrijf Ijsselmij, Case C-393/92 (European Court of Justice 27 April 1994).
Musgrave, R. A., Musgrave, P. B. & Kullmer, L. (1990). *Die öffentlichen Finanzen in Theorie und Praxis.* Stuttgart: UTB.
Nalebuff, B. J. (2000). Competing Against Bundles. *Yale School of Management Working Papers.*
Napier Brown - British Sugar, Case No. IV/30.178 (European Commission 18 July 1988).
Nazzini, R. (2006). Article 81 Between Time Present and Time Past: A Normative Critique of 'Restriction of Competition' in EU Law. *Common Market Law Review*, 43(2), 497-536.
Nederlandse Vakbond Varkenshouders (NVV), Marius Schep and Nederlandse Bond van Handelaren in Vee (NBHV) v. Commission of the European Communities, Case T-151/05 (Court of First Instance 7 May 2009).
Nestlé/Italgel, Case No. IV/M.362 (European Commission 15 September 1993).
Nestlé/Perrier, Case No. IV/M.190 (European Commission 22 July 1992).
Neven, D. & De la Mano, M. (2009). Economics at DG Competition, 2008-2009. *Industrial Organisation Review 35*, 317-347.
Neven, D. & De la Mano, M. (2010). Economics at DG Competition, 2009-2010. *Industrial Organisation Review, 37*, 309-333.

Neven, D., Papandropoulos, P. & Seabright, P. (1998). *Trawling for Minnows: Europea Competition Policy and Agreements between Firms*. London: Centre for Economic Policy Research.

Nevo, A. (2000). A Practitioner's Guide to Estimation of Random-Coefficients Logit Models of Demand. *Journal of Economics & Management Strategy, 9*(4), 513-548.

Newspaper Publishing, Case No. IV/M.423 (European Commission 14 March 1994).

Nicholls, A. J. (2000). *Freedom with Responsibility: The Social Market Economy in Germany, 1918-1963*. Clarendon Press.

Nocke, V. & White, L. (8 March 2005). Do Vertical Mergers Facilitate Upstream Collusion? *PIER Working Paper No. 05-013*.

Northern Pacific Railway Company and Northwestern improvement company v. United States of America, Case No. 356 U.S. 1, 4-5 (District Court 1958).

NV IAZ International Belgium and others v. Commission of the European Communities, Joined cases 96-102, 104, 105, 108 and 110/82 (ECJ 8 November 1983).

NV Nederlandsche Banden Industrie Michelin v. Commission of the European Communities, Case 322/81 (European Court of Justice 9 November 1983).

O2 (Germany) GmbH & Co. OHG v. Commission of the European Communities, Case T-328/03 (Court of the First Instance (Fourth Chamber) 2 May 2006).

O'Brien, D. P. & Wickelgren, A. L. (14 January 2003). A Critical Analysis of Critical Loss Analysis. *FTC Bureau of Economics Working Paper No. 254*. Federal Trade Commission.

OECD. (1993). *Glossary of Industrial Organisation Economics and Competition Law*. compiled by R. S. Khemani and D. M. Shapiro. Paris: Directorate for Financial, Fiscal and Enterprise Affairs.

OECD. (1996). *Policy Roundtables: Competition Policy and Efficiency Claims in Horizontal Agreements*. Paris.

OECD. (17 December 2009). Monopsony and Buyer Power DAF/COMP(2008)38. *Policy Roundtables*. OECD. Retrieved 5 February 2015, from http://www.oecd.org/daf/competition/44445750.pdf.

OECD. (2013, October). Competition Issues in the Food Chain Industry. OECD. Retrieved 5 February 2015, from http://www.oecd.org/daf/competition/competition-issues-in-food-chain.htm.

OECD, Brenner, S. & Rey, P. (1994). *Competition Policy and Vertical Restraints: Franchising Agreements*. Paris: OECD Secretary-General.

Office of Fair Traiding. (December 2004). Market definition - Understanding competition law. UK: Office of Fair Traiding.

Olympia Equipment Leasing Company, ALFCO v. Western Union Telegraph Company, Case No. 85-3150 (United States Court of Appeals, Seventh Circuit 18 July 1986).

OMYA/J.M. HUBER PCC, Case No. COMP/M.3796 (European Commission 19 July 2006).

Ordover, J. A. (1990). Economic Foundations of Competition Policy. In (A. Jacquemin, *Competition Policy in Europe and North America: Economic Issues and Institutions* (7-42). Chur: Harwood Academic Publishers.

Ordover, J. & Willig, R. (1985). Antitrust for High-Technology Industries: Assessing Research Joint Ventures and Mergers. *Journal of Law & Economics*, 311-333.

Orkla/Volvo, Case No. IV/M.582 (European Commission 20 September 1995).
Österreichische Postsparkasse AG, Bank für Arbeit und Wirtschaft AG v. Commission of the European Communities, Joined Cases T-213/01 and T-214/01 (Court of First Instance (Fifth Chamber) 7 June 2006).
Oswald Schmidt, trading as Demo-Studio Schmidt v. Commission of the European Communities, Case 210/81 (European Court of Justice 11 October 1983).
Ottervanger, T. (2010). Maatschappelijk verantwoord concurreren: Mededingingsrecht in een veranderende wereld. *Markt & Mededinging, 3*, 93-99.
OTTO Versand/Freemans, Case No. IV/M.1527 (European Commission 16 June 1999).
Otto/Grattan, Case No. IV/M.070 (European Commission 21 March 1991).
Overtveldt Johan Van. (2007). *The Chicago School: how the University of Chicago assembled the thinkers who revolutionised economics and business.* Chicago: Agate Publishing.
Owen, B. M. (1987). Defining Geographic Market under the 1984 Merger Guidelines: An Economic Perspective (Outline). *Practicing Law Institute, 27th Annual Advanced Antitrust Seminar.* PLI.
P & I Clubs, IGA and P & I Clubs, Pooling Agreement, Cases No. IV/D-1/30.373 and No. IV/D-1/37.143 (European Commission 12 April 1999).
Palmer, J. L. (2010). Merger Simulation with PCAIDS: A More Informative Screen? *University of California, Berkeley*, 1-36.
Papandropoulos, P. (2006). Article 82: Tying and bundling. *Competition Law Insight*, 3-5.
Peeperkorn, L. (1998). The Economics of Verticals. *Competition Policy Newsletter*, 10-17.
Peeters, J. (1989). The Rule of Reason revisited: Prohibition and Restraints of Competition in the Sherman Act and the EEC Treaty. *American Journal of Comparative Law*, 521-570.
Pheasant, J. & Weston, D. (1997). Vertical restraints, foreclosure and Article 85: developing and analytical framework. *European Competition Law Review*, 323-328.
Philips/Grundig, Case No. IV/M.382 (European Commission 3 December 1993).
Philips/Hoechst, Case No. IV/M.406 (European Commission 11 March 1994).
Phillips, A. (June 1976). A Critique of Empirical Studies of Relations Between Market Structure and Profitability. *The Journal of Industrial Economics*, 241-249.
Pilkington-Techint/SIV, Case No. IV/M.358 (European Commission 21 December 1993).
Pirelli/BICC, Case No. COMP/M.1882 (European Commission 19 July 2000).
Pitelis, C. N. (1991). *Market and Non-Market Hierarchies: Theories of Institutional Failure.* London: Blackwell.
Polypropylene, IV/31.149 (European Commission 23 April 1986).
Posner, R. (1977). *Economic Analysis of Law 2nd edition.* Boston: Little Brown.
Posner, R. (1979). The Chicago School of Antitrust Analysis. *University of Pennsylvania Law Review*, 925-942.
Posner, R. (1981). *The Economics of Justice.* Harvard: Harvard University Press.

Posner, R. A. (1976). *Antitrust Law - An Economic Perspective*. Chicago and London: The University of Chicago Press.
Posner, R. A. (1976). *Economic Analysis of Law*. Chicago and London: The University of Chicago Press.
Posner, R. A. (2001). *Antitrust Law* (2nd edition).
Post Danmark A/S v. Konkurrenceradet, C-23/14 (European Court of Justice 6 October 2015).
Preussag/Thomson, Case No. COMP/M.2002 (European Commission 26 July 2000).
Price Waterhouse/Coopers & Lybrand, Case No. IV/M.1016 (European Commission 20 May 1998).
Procordia/Erbamont, Case No. IV/M.323 (European Commission 29 April 1993).
Procter & Gamble/VP Schickedanz (II), Case No. IV/M.430 (European Commission 21 June 1994).
Promodes/BRMC, Case No. IV/M.242 (European Commission 13 July 1992).
Promodes/Dirsa, Case No. IV/M.27 (European Commission 17 December 1990).
Pronuptia de Paris GmbH v. Pronuptia de Paris Irmgard Schillgallis, Case 161/84 (European Court of Justice 28 January 1986).
Punj, G. N. & Staelin, R. (1978). The Choice Process for Graduate Business Schools. *Journal of Marketing Research*, 588–598.
PVC, IV/31.865 (Commission Decision (89/190/EEC) 21 December 1988).
Radio Telefis Eireann (RTE) and Independent Television Publications Ltd (ITP) v. Commission of the European Communities, Joined cases C-241/91 P and C-242/91 P (ECJ 6 April 1995).
Radio Telefis Eireann v. Commission of the European Communities, Case T-69/89 (Court of First Instance (Second Chamber) 10 July 1991).
Rao, V. R. (2008). Developments in Conjoint Analysis. *International Series in Operations Research & Management Science*, 23–53.
Rapoport, A. & Chemmah, A. (1965). *Prisoner's Dillema: A Study in Conflict and Cooperation*. Ann Arbor: University of Michigan Press.
Remia BV and others v. Commission of the European Communities, Case 42/84 (European Court of Justice (Fifth Chamber) 7 July 1985).
Renault/Volvo, Case No. IV/M.4 (European Commission 6 November 1990).
Rewe/Billa, Case No. IV/M.803 (European Commission 27 August 1996).
Rewe/Meinl, Case No. IV/M.1221 (European Commission 3 February 1999).
Rey, P. (2003). The economics of vertical restraints. In R. Arnott, *Economics for an Imperfect World: Essays in Honor of Joseph E. Stiglitz* (247–268). Massachusetts: MIT Press.
Rey, P. (2004). The economics of vertical restraints. *Speech at Cargese*.
Rey, P. & Caballero-Sanz, F. (1996). The Policy Implications of the Economic Analysis of Vertical Restraints. Brussels: European Commission, DG Economic and Financial Affairs.
Rey, P. & Stiglitz, J. E. (1988). Vertical Restraints and Producers' Competition. *European Economic Review*, 561–568.
Rhodia/Donau Chemie/Albright & Wilson, Case No. IV/M.1517 (European Commission 13 July 1999).

Rhône-Poulene/SNIA (II), Case No. IV/M.355 (European Commission 8 September 1993).
Riordan, M. & Salop, S. (1995). Evaluating Vertical Mergers: A Post-Chicago Approach. *Antitrust Law Journal, 63*(2), 513–546.
Ritter, L. K., Braun, W. D. & Rawlinson, F. (1993). *EEC Competition Law: A Practitioner's Guide.* Deventer: Kluwer.
Robinson, J. (1933). *The Economics of Imperfect Competition.* London: MacMillan.
Röller, L.-H. & De la Mano, M. (April 2006). The Impact of the New Substantive Test in European Merger Control. *European Competition Journal, 2*(1), 9–28.
Röller, L.-H., Stennek, J. & Verboven, F. (2000). Efficiency Gains from Mergers. *Working Paper No. 543.* Sweden: The Research Institute of Industrial Economics.
Röpke, W. (1934). *German Commercial Policy.* London: Longmans, Green.
Röpke, W. (1950). *The Social Crisis of Our Time.* Glasgow: William Hodge and Co. Ltd.
Röpke, W. (1960). *A Humane Economy: The Social Framework of the Free Market.* South Bend, Ind.: Gateway Editions.
Rosenbluth, G. (1955). Measures of Concentration. In N. B. Research, *Business Concentration and Price Policy* (57–99). Princeton: Princeton University Press.
Royall, S. (1995). Symposium: Post-Chicago Economics - Editor's Note. *Antitrust Journal*, 445–454.
RWE/Essent, Case COMP/M.5467 (European Commission 23 June 2009).
RWE/VEW, B8 - 40000 - U - 309/99 (Bundeskartellamt 30 July 2000).
Ryanair Holdings plc v. European Commission, Case T-342/07 (European Court of Justice 6 July 2010).
Ryanair/Aer Lingus III, COMP/M.6663 (European Commission 27 February 2013).
SA Brasserie de Haecht v. Consorts Wilkin-Janssen, Case 23-67 (European Court of Justice 12 December 1967).
SA Musique Diffusion française and others v. Commission of the European Communities, Joined cases 100-103/80 (ECJ 7 June 1983).
SABA, IV/847 (European Commission 15 December 1975).
Salop, S. C. (1982). Practices that Credibly Facilitate Oligopoly Coordination, Paper presented at IEA Symposium. Ottawa, Canada.
Samuelson, P. A. (1954). The Pure Theory of Public Expenditure. *Review of Economics and Statistics*, 387–389.
Sandoz prodotti farmaceutici SpA v. Commission of the European Communities, Case C-277/87 (European Court of Justice (Sixth chamber) 11 January 1990).
Sanitec/Sphinx, Case No. IV/M.1578 (European Commission 1 December 1999).
Sanofi/Sterling Drug, Case No. IV/M.72 (European Commission 10 June 1991).
SC Belasco and others v. Commission of the European Communities, Case 246/86 (European Court of Justice (Fifth Chamber) 11 July 1989).
Schaub, A. (1997). State aid in the ECSC steel sector. *EC Competition Policy Newsletter, 3*(2).
Scheffmann, D. T. & Spiller, P. T. (1987). Geographic Market Definition under the U.S. Department of Justice Merger Guidelines. *The Journal of Law and Economics*, 123–147.

Scherer, F. M. (1986). On the Current State of Knowledge in Industrial Organization. In H. W. De Jong & W. G. Shepherd, *Mainstreams in Industrial Organization* (5-22). Springer Netherlands.
Scherer, F. M. (1993). *Monopoly and Competition Policy - Volume I and II.* Edward Elgar.
Schmauch, M. (2012). *EU Law on State Aid to Airlines: Law, Economics and Policy.* Berlin: Lexxion Publisher.
Schmidt, I. (2012). *Wettbewerbspolitik und Kartellrecht: Eine Einführung* (9. Auflage). München.
Schmidt, I. L. & Rittaler, J. B. (1989). *A Critical Evaluation of the Chicago School of Antitrust Analysis.* Dordrecht: Kluwer.
Schmidt, I. & Haucap, J. (2012). *Wettbewerbspolitik und Kartellrecht: Eine interdisziplinäre Einführung.* München: Oldenbourg Wissenschaftsverlag GmbH.
Schmidtchen, D. (1978). *Wettbewerbspolitik als Aufgabe: Methodologisch (Competition Policy as Task: Methodological and System Theoretical Foundations for Reorientation).* Nomos: Baden-Baden.
Schmitz-Gotha Fahrzeugwerke GmbH v. Commission of the European Communities, Case T-17/03 (Court of First Instance (Fourth Chamber, extended composition) 6 April 2006).
Schneider Electric SA v. Commission of the European Communities, Case T-310/01 (Court of First Instance 22 October 2002).
Schneider v. Legrand, Case No. COMP/M.2283 (European Commission 10 October 2001).
Schöller Lebensmittel GmbH & Co. KG v. Commission of the European Communities, Case T-9/93 (Court of First Instance (Second Chamber, extended composition) 8 June 1995).
Schumpeter, J. A. (1942). *Capitalism, Socialism and Democracy.* London: George Allen & Unwin.
Schweitzer, H. (2007). The History, Interpretation and Underlying Principles of Section 2 Sherman Act and Article 82 EC. (1-42). Florence: European University Institute / Hart.
Schweitzer, H. (2009). The European Competition Law Enforcement System and the Evolution of Judicial Review. *European University Institute, Robert Schuhman Centre for Advanced Studies, EU Competition Law and Policy Workshop, European University Institute.* Florence.
Sea Containers v. Stena Sealink - Interim measures, Case No. IV/34.689 (European Commission 21 December 1993).
Shell/Monecatini, Case No. IV/M.269 (European Commission 8 June 1994).
Shepherd, W. (1981). *Public Policies Toward Business* (Eighth Edition ed.). R.D. Irwin.
Shepherd, W. G. (February 1972). The Elements of Market Structure. *The Review of Economics and Statistics*, 25-37.
Shepherd, W. G. (1984). 'Contestability' vs. Competition. *The American Economic Review*, 572-587.
Shepherd, W. G. (1985). *The Economics of Industrial Organization.* London: Prentice-Hall.

Shepherd, W. G. (1986). The Twilight of Antitrust. *Antitrust Law and Economics Review*, 21–27.

Shepherd, W. G. (1991). Some Aspects of Dynamic Analysis and Industrial Change. In P. de Wolf, *Competition in Europe: Essays in Honour of Henk W. de Jong* (9–31). Springer Netherlands.

Sirena S.r.l. v. Eda S.r.l. and others, Case 40-70 (European Court of Justice 18 February 1971).

Slade, M. E. (2006). Merger Simulations of Unilateral Effects: What Can We Learn from the UK Brewing Industry? *Journal of Economic Literature*, 1–29.

Slaughter and May. (2010). Commission conditionally clears Kraft Foods/Cadbury. *EU Competition & Regulatory*, 1–3.

Smith, A. (1776). *An Inquiry into the Nature and Causes of the Wealth of Nations*.

SNECMA/TI, Case No. IV/M.368 (European Commission 17 January 1994).

Società Italiana Vetro SpA, Fabbrica Pisana SpA and PPG Vernante Pennitalia SpA v. Commission of the European Communities, Joined cases T-68/89, T-77/89 and T-78/89 (Court of First Instance (First Chamber) 10 March 1992).

Société alsacienne et lorraine de télécommunications et d'électronique (Alsatel) v. SA Novasam, Case 247/86 (European Court of Justice (Sixth Chamber) 5 October 1988).

Société de Vente de Ciments et Bétons de l'Est SA v. Kerpen & Kerpen GmbH und Co. KG., Case 319/82 (ECJ (Fourth Chamber) 14 December 1983).

Société Technique Minière (STM) v. Maschinenbau Ulm GmbH (MBU), Case 56-65 (European Court of Justice 30 June 1966).

Sodemare SA, Anni Azzurri Holding SpA and Anni Azzurri Rezzato Srl v. Regione Lombardia, Case C-70/95 (European Court of Justice 17 June 1997).

Solvay-Laporte/Interox, Case No. IV/M.197 (European Commission 30 April 1992).

SONY/BMG, Case No. COMP/M.3333 (European Commission 19 July 2004).

SPAR/Dansk Supermarked, Case No. IV/M.179 (European Commission 3 February 1992).

Sraffa, P. (1926). The Laws of Returns under Competitive Conditions. *The Economic Journal*, 535–550.

Standard Oil Co. of New Jersey v. United States, 221 U.S. 1 (U.S. Supreme Court 15 May 1911).

Steetley/Tarmac, Case No. COMP/M.180 (European Commission 12 February 1992).

Stergios Delimitis v. Henninger Bräu AG, Case C-234/89 (European Court of Justice 28 February 1991).

Stigler, G. (1957). Perfect Competition, Historically Contemplated. In G. Stigler, *Essays in the History of Economics* (234–267). Chicago: The University of Chicago Press.

Stigler, G. (1968). *The Organization of Industry*. Chicago: University of Chicago Press.

Stigler, G. J. (1986). In K. R. Leube & T. G. Moore, *The Essence of Stigler*. Standford University: Hoover Institution Press.

Stigler, G. J. & Sherwin, R. A. (1985). The Extent of the Market. *Journal of Law and Economics*, 555–585.

Sullivan, L. (1995). Post-Chicago Economics: Economists, Lawyers, Judges, and Enforcement Officials in a Less Determinate Theoretical World. *Antitrust Law Journal*, 669–681.

Sydkraft/Graninge, Case COMP/M.3268 (European Commission 30 October 2003).

Szilágyi, P. (31 August 2011). How to Give a Meaningful Interpretation to the Efficiency Defence in European Competition Law? *CLRC Working Papers WP/2011/3*.

Talanx International/Meiji Yasuda Life Insurance Company/HDI Poland, COMP/M.6743 (European Commission 19 November 2012).

Tan, G. (2001). *The Economic Theory of Vertical Restraints*. Vancouver: University of British Columvia.

Technische Glaswerke Ilmenau Gmbh v. Commission of the European Communities, Case T-198/01 (Court of First Instance 8 July 2004).

Télémarketing (CBEM) v. SA Compagnie luxembourgeoise de télédiffusion (CLT) and Information publicité Benelux (IPB), Case 311/84 (European Court of Justice (Fifth Chamber) 3 October 1985).

Tetra Lava v. Sidel, Case No. COMP/M.2416 (European Commission 30 October 2001).

Tetra Laval BV v. Commission of the European Communities, Case T-5/02 (Court of First Instance (First Chamber) 25 October 2002).

Tetra Pak II, IV/31043 (Commission Decisions (92/163/EEC) 24 July 1991).

Tetra Pak International SA v. Commission of the European Communities, Case T-83/91 (Court of First Instance (Second Chamber) 6 October 1994).

Tetra Pak International SA v. Commission of the European Communities, Case C.333/94 P (European Court of Justice (Fifth Chamber) 14 November 1996).

Tetra Pak/Alfa-Laval, Case No. IV/M.68 (European Commission 19 July 1991).

Thales/Finmeccanica/Alcatel Alenia Space & Telespazio, COMP/M.4403 (European Commission 4 April 2007).

Thomson/Shorts, Case No. IV/M.318 (European Commission 14 April 1993).

Time Warner/EMI, Case No. COMP/M.1852 (European Commission 14 June 2000).

Tirole, J. (1988). *The Theory of Industrial Organization*. Cambridge: The MIT Press.

Tizzano, A. (10 October 2014). *IL RUOLO DEI CONSUMATORI NEL DIRITTO ANTITRUST ALLA LUCE DELLA GIURISPRUDENZA DELLA CORTE DI GIUSTIZIA*. European Competition Day, Rome.

T-Mobile Austria/tele.ring, Case No. COMP/M.3916 (European Commission 26 April 2006).

Tomra Systems ASA and Others v. European Commission, Case T-155/06 (General Court 9 September 2010).

Tomra Systems ASA and Others v. European Commission, Case C-549/10 P (European Court of Justice (Third Chamber) 19 April 2012).

Tractebel/Distrigaz II, Case No. IV/M.493 (European Commission 1 September 1994).

Tréfileurope Sales SARL v. Commission of the European Communities, Case T-141/89 (Court of First Instance (First Chamber) 6 April 1995).

U.S. Department of Justice. (14 June 1984). Non-Horizontal Merger Guidelines.

U.S. Department of Justice & Federal Trade Commission. (2 April 1992). Horizontal Merger Guidelines.

Bibliography

Uitermark, P. J. (1990). *Economische Mededinging en Algemeen Beland: een Onderzoek naar de Economisch-theoretische Fundering van de Mededingingspolitiek*. Groningen: Wolters-Noordhoff.

Unilever France/Ortiz Miko (II), Case No. IV/M.422 (European Commission 15 March 1994).

Unilever/Sara Lee, COMP/M.5658 (European Commission 17 November 2010).

Union Carbide/Enichem, Case No. IV/M.550 (European Commission 13 March 1995).

United Brands Company and United Brands Continentaal BV v. Commission of the European Communities, Case 27/76 (European Court of Justice 14 February 1978).

United States v. E. I. du Pont de Nemours & Co., 351 U.S. 377 (U.S. Supreme Court 11 June 1956).

University of Basel. (27 June and 1 July 2002). The Law and Economics of Mergers. *Presentation*. Retrieved from http://www.wwz.unibas.ch/wifor/zaeslin/courses2002/mergers%20overheads.ppt (Link does not work; access to document on Wayback Machine).

Van Bael & Bellis. (1987). *Competition Law of the European Community*. Oxfordshire: CCH Editions Limited.

Van Gerven, G. & Varona, E. N. (1994). The Wood Pulp Case and the Future of Concerted Practices. *Common Market Law Review*, 575–608.

van Miert, K. (10 November 1997). *Role of Competititon Policy in Modern Economics*. Danish Competition Council, Copenhagen.

Vanberg, V. (2004). The Freiburg School: Walter Eucken and Ordoliberalism. *Freiburg discussion papers on constitutional economics, No. 04/11*.

Vanberg, V. J. (2002). *The Constitution of markets - Essays in Political Economy*. Taylor & Francis.

Varta/Bosch, Case No. IV/M.12 (European Commission 31 July 1991).

Vattenfall/Elsam and E2 Assets, Case COMP/M.3867 (European Commission 22 December 2005).

VEBA/Degussa, Case No. IV/M.942 (European Commission 3 December 1997).

VEBA/VIAG, Case No. COMP/M.1673 (European Commission 13 June 2000).

Vedder, H. H. (2003). Legal and Economic Analysis of Competition and its Regulation. In H. H. Vedder, *Competition Law and Environmental Protection in Europe* (19-40). Groningen: European Law Publishing.

Venit, J. S. (1998). Two steps forward and no step back: Economic analysis and oligopolistic dominance after Kali & Salz. *Common Market Law Review*, 1101–1134.

Verband der Sachversicherer e.V. v. Commission of the European Communities, Case 45/85 (European Court of Justice 27 January 1987).

Vereeniging van Cementhandelaren, Case 8/72 (European Commission 17 October 1972).

Vereniging ter Bevordering van het Vlaamse Boekwezen, VBVB, and Vereniging ter Bevordering van de Belangen des Boekhandels, VBBB, v. Commission of the European Communities, Joined cases 43/82 and 63/82 (European Court of Justice 17 January 1984).

Vereniging van Samenwerkende Prijsregelende Organisaties in de Bouwnijverheid and others v. Commission of the European Communities, Case T-29/92 (Court of First Instance (First Chamber) 21 February 1995).

Vereniging van Samenwerkende Prijsregelende Organisaties in de Bouwnijverheid and Others v. Commission of the European Communities, Case C-137/95 P (European Court of Justice 25 March 1996).

Verouden, V. (2003). Vertical Agreements and Article 81(1) EC: The Evolving Role of Economic Analysis. *Antitrust Law Journal*, 525–575.

Verouden, V. (2008). Vertical Agreements: Motivation and Impact. *Issues in Competition Law and Policy (ABA Section of Antitrust Law)*, 3, 1813–1840.

Vestager, M. (15 June 2015). *The State of the Union: Antitrust in the EU in 2015-2016*. Paros. Retrieved from http://ec.europa.eu/commission/2014-2019/vestager/announcements/state-union-antitrust-eu-2015-2016_en.

Vezzoso, S. (6 December 2004). Evolutionary economics: an alternative approach to competition policy - the case of automobile distribution. Florence: University of Trento.

VIAG/Continental Can, Case No. IV/M.81 (European Commission 6 June 1991).

Vickers, J. & Hay, D. (1987). *The Economics of Market Dominance*. Oxford: Basil Blackwell.

Vienna Insurance Group/EBV, COMP/M.5075 (European Commission 17 June 2008).

Vitamins, IV/29.020 (Commission Decision (76/642/EEC) 9 June 1976).

Volvo/Scania, Case No. COMP/M.1672 (European Commission 14 March 2000).

von der Groeben, H. (1995). *Deutschland und Europa in einem unruhigen Jahrhundert*. Nomos.

von der Groeben, H. (2002). Europäische Integration aus historischer Erfahrung. *Discussion Paper*. (M. Gehler, Interviewer) Retrieved from http://www.zei.uni-bonn.de/dateien/discussion-paper/dp_c108_groeben.pdf.

Von der Groeben, H., Thiesing, J. & Ehlermann, C. D. (1993). *Kommentar zum EWG-Vertrag*. Baden-Baden: Nomos.

von Hayek, F. (1949). *Individualism and Economic Order*. Chicago: The University of Chicago Press.

von Hayek, F. (1960). *The Constitution of Liberty*. London: Routledge & Kegan Paul.

von Hayek, F. (1969). *Freiburger Studien*. Tübingen: Mohr.

von Hayek, F. (1978). Competition as a Discovery Procedure. In F. von Hayek, *New Studies in Philosophy, Politics, Economics and the History of Ideas*. Chicago: University of Chicago Press.

von Mises, L. (1949). *Human Action: A Treatise on Economics*. (B. B. Greaves, Hrsg.) Indianapolis: Liberty Fund 2007.

Walker, M. (2005). The Potential for Significant Inaccuracies in Merger Simulation Models. *Journal of Competition Law & Economics*, 473–496.

Walt Wilhelm and other v. Bundeskartellamt, Case 14/68 (European Court of Justice 13 February 1969).

Waterson, M. & Dobson, P. (1996). *Vertical Restraints and Competition Policy*. London: Office of Fair Trading.

Weitbrecht, A. (2008). From Freiburg to Chicago and Beyond - the First 50 Years of European Competition Law. *European Competition Law Review, 29*(2), 81–88.

Welded steel mesh, Case No. IV/31.553 (European Commission 2 August 1989).

Werden, G. J. (1992). Four Suggestions on Market Delineation. *Antitrust Bulletin*.

Werden, G. J. (1998). Demand Elasticities in Antitrust Analysis. *Antitrust Law Journal*, 363–414.

Werden, G. J. & Froeb, L. M. (1993). Correlation, Causality, and All that Jazz: The Inherent Shortcomings of Price Tests for Antitrust Market Delineation. *Review of Industrial Organization*, 329–353.

Werden, G. J., Froeb, L. M. & Scheffman, D. T. (2004). A Daubert Discipline for Merger Simulation. *Antitrust*, 89–95.

Westdeutsche Landesbank Girozentrale, Land Nordrhein-Westfalen, and Federal Republic of Germany v. Commission of the European Communities, Joined Cases T-228/99 and T-233/99 (Court of First Instance (Second Chamber, extended composition) 6 March 2003).

Whinston, M. D. (September 1990). Tying, Foreclosure and Exclusion. *American Economic Review*, 837–859.

Williamson, O. (1968). Economics as an Antitrust Defense: The Welfare Tradeoffs. *American Economic Review, 58*(18).

Wood pulp, IV/29.725q (European Commission 19 December 1984).

Yao, D. A. & Dahdouh, T. N. (1993). Information Problems in Merger Division Making and Their Impact on Development of an Efficiencies Defense. *Antitrust Law Journal*, 23–45.

Yde, P. L. & Vita, M. G. (1996). Merger Efficiencies: Reconsidering the 'Passing-On' Requirement. *Antitrust Law Journal*, 735–747.

Ysewyn, J. & Caffarra, C. (1998). Two's Company, Three's a Crowd: The Future of Collective Dominance After Kali & Salz Judgment. *European Competitive Law Review*, 468–471.

Zarembka, P. (1974). *Frontiers in Econometrics*. New York: Academic Press.

Index

A

ABB/Daimler Benz, 242
Absence of restraints, 139
Absolute territorial protection, 279, 283–286, 292, 293
Abuse of dominant position, 72, 78, 400
Accor/Wagons-Lits, 236
Aftermarkets, 222
Agreements
   network of, 276, 277, 301, 338, 341
   restrictive, 79, 249, 265, 267, 270, 279, 286, 299, 307, 311, 312, 315, 317–318, 338, 344, 346
Ahmed Saeed, 351, 352
AirLiquide/BOC, 458–459
Airtours/FirstChoice, 445, 456
AKZO, 76, 82, 237, 240, 364, 365, 407
Alcan/Alusuisse, 458
Alcan/Pechiney, 458
Allied Lyons/HWE-Pedro Domecq, 216, 234
Allocation of common costs, 382, 383
Allocation of resources
   efficient, 51, 89, 103, 105, 109
   optimal, 57, 130, 145, 159, 160, 419, 490
Alsatel, 355, 357
American Cyanamid/Shell, 237, 241
Ancillary restraints, 266, 267, 269, 293, 294
Anti-competitive
   conduct, 380, 398
   practices, 60, 171, 333, 398

Anti-competitive agreements, 14, 69, 147, 264, 307, 311
Anti-competitive behavior, 56, 175, 176, 348, 368, 448
Arrangements, restrictive, 270, 272
Article 3, 1, 5, 11, 14, 18–22, 57, 81, 162–167, 170, 173, 174, 417, 420, 421
Article 101, 3, 56, 162
Article 102, 4, 39–40, 56, 72–85, 89, 90, 162, 163, 166, 167, 170, 173, 174, 176, 177, 272, 288, 347–414, 444
Article 106, 56
Article 107, 56, 488–494, 497, 499, 500
Assessment of Market Power, 346
Assets, intangible, 208
Austrian school, 139–141, 159–160

B

Bailey, E.E., 120
Bain, J.S., 115, 116, 368
Barriers, regulatory, 59, 237
Barriers to entry, 96, 117, 119, 128, 231, 232, 235, 236, 239, 250, 253, 254, 319, 338, 343, 346, 366–370, 372, 374, 376, 387, 433–435, 441, 442, 444, 452
Barriers to expansion, 367, 370
Baumol, W.J., 118, 120, 121, 369, 434
Bayrische Motorenwerke AG, 291
BBC, 359
Beer, 208, 295–297
Bertelsmann AG, 449

543

Index

Bertrand model, 126, 158, 465, 481
Bidding studies, 258-262
Block exemption Regulation, 277, 311, 338-341, 343-345, 494, 497, 500
Block exemptions, 278, 297, 311, 320, 338-341, 343-345, 494, 500
BMW/Rover, 240
Bork, R.H., 419
Bosch/De Geus, 284
Bouwnijverheid, 306
BP Kemi, 65
Brand loyalty, 157, 192, 231, 234, 235, 242, 253, 256, 479
Brand names, 241, 296
Breweries, 294-296, 310
British Leyland, 78
British Telecom/MCI (BT/MCI), 236
BSN/EURALIM, 232, 234
Bundeskartellamt, 7, 269, 458
Bundling and tying, 440-442
Business secrets, 461

C

Camelia brand, 220
Capacity, 43, 62, 100, 105, 126, 127, 158, 185, 202, 203, 206, 225, 231, 237, 247, 255, 257, 272, 288, 314, 316, 319, 370, 373, 383, 387, 435, 447, 453, 456, 460, 461, 483, 485
Cargill/Unilever, 244
Car manufacturers, 217, 222
Cars, 78, 217, 218, 222, 240, 471
Cartel behaviour, 70, 101, 308, 332
Cartels, 14, 25, 34, 36, 47, 58, 60, 69, 70, 95, 100, 101, 105, 131, 144, 147, 171, 175, 179, 202, 204, 206, 231, 273, 281, 304-306, 308, 332, 459
Cartons, 83, 353, 406, 407, 427, 428
Cellophane fallacy, 192, 193
CGP/GEC ALSTHOM/KPR/Kone Corporation, 237
Chicago School, 6-10, 17, 22-32, 38, 40, 43, 46, 48-49, 51, 52, 89, 116, 117, 128-138, 140, 143, 149, 160, 333, 334, 366, 368, 370, 392, 414, 416-419, 422-424
Chicago trap, 26, 30, 32
Ciba-Geigy/Sandoz, 218
Clark, J.M., 102-107, 109
Clearance, negative, 448
Collective dominance, 371, 373-378, 415, 429, 451-462
Collusion, 25, 66, 110, 115, 125, 128, 131, 159, 250, 257, 263, 307, 308, 316, 324-326, 328, 329, 332, 340, 377, 416, 429, 439, 455, 457, 458, 460, 478
Commercial solvents, 81
Commission
    analysis of, 179, 221, 231, 241, 243, 265, 304, 349, 367, 411, 427, 430
    approach of, 7, 16, 89, 179, 180, 275, 451
    assessment of competition of, 434
    decisions of, 219
    guidelines, 169, 220, 272, 312, 314, 322, 324, 337, 339, 341, 347, 431, 432, 438, 439, 451, 457, 460, 499
    notice, 16, 169, 179, 181, 190, 210, 211, 227-229, 239, 310, 342, 348, 358, 365, 366, 501
Community-wide, 205, 230, 237, 240, 357
Compagnie Maritime Belge Transports SA, 374, 376, 451
Companies, parent, 300, 301
Competition
    allocation function of, 368
    application of EC, 297, 315, 414
    appreciable restriction of, 175, 275, 277, 294
    degree of, 19, 110, 186, 262, 289, 315, 316, 319, 386, 397, 402, 409, 434
    distortion of, 64, 68, 166, 177, 262, 271, 275, 277, 282, 284, 285, 310, 491, 494
    economic concept of, 92, 99
    effective intensity of, 105

544

geographic scope of, 181, 211, 229, 357
monopolistic, 14, 95, 100, 101, 103, 112, 133, 147, 156, 157
neo-classical concept of, 94, 138, 143
ordoliberal concept of, 35, 144, 145, 148
policy, 15, 17, 40, 55-90, 93, 103, 105, 120, 131, 138, 141, 143, 147, 148, 160, 164, 171, 172, 280, 290, 304, 315, 381, 419, 422, 423
process, 6, 23, 29, 36, 38, 88, 89, 103, 106-108, 160
restraints of, 112, 121, 134, 164, 325, 326
restrictions, 267
theory, 87-160, 297
undistorted, 72, 378, 399, 400, 409
Competitive
conditions, 72, 89, 177, 241, 242, 256, 257, 311, 350, 356, 361
constraints, 174, 180-182, 184, 200, 201, 206, 209, 246, 250, 252, 253, 319, 361, 366, 371, 374, 378, 387, 414, 430, 432-434, 444, 448, 455
forces, 51, 88, 181, 253, 275, 296, 367, 434
markets, 1-3, 32, 36, 38, 40, 66, 87, 88, 90, 92, 101, 108, 110, 112, 113, 123, 134, 145, 152, 249, 421
pressures, 45, 52, 176, 181, 225, 228, 230, 259-262, 319, 341, 344, 372, 390, 431, 437, 448
Competitors
foreign, 177, 255, 296, 299
market entry of, 255, 381, 408
Concentrated power, political fears of, 146, 421
Concentration
doctrine, 114, 115, 128, 131-133
ratios, 115, 116, 118, 129, 366
Concerted practices, 56, 64-68, 71, 162, 177, 262, 278, 294, 307-309, 311, 343, 373, 376, 440, 460

Conditions of competition, 66, 162, 181, 217, 227, 238, 244, 301, 302, 356, 357, 360, 367, 429
Conjoint analysis, 44, 194-199, 201
Consten, 59, 270, 280, 283-285, 292, 293
Consumables, 354, 355
Consumer
food, retail distribution of, 238
preferences, 3, 7, 9, 99, 172, 207, 211-213, 216, 221, 229, 231, 234, 353, 358, 407, 479
welfare, 1, 5, 7, 23-26, 28-32, 38, 48, 88, 89, 91, 92, 131-133, 149, 159, 172, 279, 285, 310, 315, 317, 378-380, 386, 389, 390, 416-419, 422, 423, 439, 441, 442
Consumption habits, 235
Containers, 349, 352, 372, 396, 407
Contestability, 101, 118-121, 370
Contestable Markets, 118-121, 370, 434
Contract, exclusive, 255
Copyright, 81, 82, 292, 418
Counterfactual analysis, 46, 47, 136, 265, 303, 491
Cournot, 96, 124-126, 156-158, 425, 441, 464, 465
Cross-elasticity, 205, 220, 349, 350, 357
Customer fidelity, 275, 296, 297
Customers
distinct group of, 214
typical, 195

D

Danish Crown/Vestjyske Slagterier, 457
Dansk Landbrugs Grovvareselskab AmbA, 266, 300, 372
DASA/Fokker, 237
Dealers
quantitative selection of, 287-288
Delimitis, 16, 68, 178, 265, 275, 295-297, 303, 329

Demand
  curve, 26, 27, 97, 99, 103, 149–151, 153–157, 193, 196, 464, 468, 493, 494
  elasticity, 52, 110, 150, 190, 390, 468, 469
  factors, 234
  side substitutability, 181, 189, 208, 209, 216, 218, 319
Demo-Studio Schmidt, 365
Demsetz, H., 117, 128, 133, 143, 366
Department of Justice Merger Guidelines, 189, 220
Deregulation, 120, 134, 160
Deutsche Telekom, 450
Dirlam, 106
Dirsa, 238, 243, 244
Distribution
  channels, 110, 217, 228, 232, 321, 447
  network, 222, 228, 338, 339, 390, 427, 449
Distribution agreements
  exclusive, 329, 330
  selective, 287
Distributors, 73, 79, 214, 218, 235, 251, 263, 277, 279, 280, 283–285, 287, 288, 295–297, 320–330, 335–341, 350, 357, 371, 426, 479
Diversion ratios, 188, 486
Dominance, 14, 58, 72–76, 79, 80, 86, 99–100, 113–114, 170, 172, 173, 192, 218–219, 242, 347, 355, 358, 360–368, 371–379, 390, 393, 397, 406–407, 412, 415, 416, 418, 426, 429, 433, 449, 451–462
Dominant position, 4, 13, 72–79, 81, 83–85, 90, 120–121, 166, 173, 176, 219, 220, 243, 319, 348–350, 352, 354, 355, 358–366, 371, 372, 374–377, 379, 381, 386, 395–397, 399–403, 405, 408–413, 415–417, 427, 429–432, 436, 448–452, 454, 455, 457, 459, 460, 478

Double marginalisation, 326, 386, 439, 446
Dynamic process, 94, 106, 107, 129, 142, 230, 249

E

Eastman Kodak Company, 135
Economic
  analysis, 6–10, 16, 22–24, 27, 28, 32–34, 44, 52, 61, 67, 76, 85, 86, 93, 96, 97, 100, 112, 116, 118, 130, 133, 136–138, 175, 183, 204, 262, 275, 277–320, 347, 360–414, 417–422, 424, 425, 430, 445, 455, 464, 487, 488, 492, 493
  assessment, 3, 7, 9, 64, 90, 91, 258, 278, 279, 285, 297, 299, 302, 309, 347, 374, 376, 379, 429, 430, 451, 484, 489
  concept, 18, 22, 26, 57, 92, 99, 360, 422
  concrete application of, 361
  Darwinism, 130
  efficiency, 25, 31, 32, 35, 39, 61, 88, 89, 97, 99, 131–133, 135, 137, 143, 160, 332, 370, 417, 420
  performance, 4, 19, 88, 102, 109, 114, 115, 133, 141, 146
  policy, 20, 37, 38, 60, 113, 144, 147, 420, 421
  power
    large aggregations of, 58
    society, core problem of, 87
  theory, 60, 90, 98, 101, 102, 122, 123, 134, 136, 140, 142, 148, 149, 205, 316, 332, 333, 378, 386, 412, 424, 430, 439–441, 455, 460, 472
  thinking, 10, 17, 22, 24, 33, 49, 93, 116, 130, 338, 422, 424
  values, 78, 418
ECS/Akzo, 76, 82, 237, 240, 364, 365, 407
ECSC Treaty, 55
EC-wide markets, 236, 237

Eda, 73, 78, 371
EEA
  agreement, 450
  level, 228
Effective competition, 59, 74, 75, 86, 89, 106–109, 177, 285, 344, 348, 350–352, 355, 366, 371, 372, 377, 397, 414, 415, 417, 421, 430, 432, 436, 439, 440, 448, 456, 459, 460
Effectiveness, 132, 208, 256, 302, 422, 423, 490, 502
Eisele, 291, 292
Elasticities, 47, 52, 103, 110, 133, 150, 152, 155, 180, 183, 184, 187, 188, 190–192, 194, 200, 201, 204, 205, 209, 212, 220, 221, 223, 231, 235, 237, 246, 247, 315, 316, 335, 349, 350, 357, 362, 390, 453, 465, 468–476, 482
Electrolux/AEG, 236, 238
Elzinga-Hogarty test, 204, 239
EMI/Time Warner, 457
Enichem, 219
Enso/Stora, 178, 358
Entrants
  potential, 118, 119, 254, 255, 320, 368, 369, 433–435, 448
Entrepreneurs
  strategic actions of, 108, 140, 141, 143
  superior abilities of, 131
Entry
  barriers, 96, 115, 117, 119, 128, 231, 232, 235, 236, 239, 250, 253, 254, 319, 338, 343, 346, 366–370, 372, 374, 376, 387, 433–435, 441, 442, 444, 452
  conditions, 235, 370, 434
Environment, 16, 35, 47, 50, 59, 88, 93, 97, 113, 122, 127, 129, 141, 145, 147, 236, 256, 257, 334, 340, 344, 350, 373, 421, 461, 463, 464, 490, 494, 497
Equilibrium
  models, 27, 47, 96, 102, 130, 140, 142, 464

Erhard Kantzenbach, 104–106
Essential facilities, 253, 359, 435
Eugen von *Böhm*-Bawerk, 139
European Commission (EC), 7, 9, 15, 16, 59–63, 70, 90, 93, 116, 120, 121, 148, 442, 487, 502
European Community. *See* European Commission (EC)
European school, 5, 6, 8–17, 22, 24, 29, 32–41, 44–47, 49–52, 58, 61, 91, 92, 144–149, 333, 334, 342, 343, 368, 392, 397, 414, 417, 420–422, 424
European Union (EU)
  administrative decisions
  Commission (*see* Commission)
  competition law, 1–10, 15, 17, 18, 23, 24, 27, 29, 32–34, 36–39, 53, 56–62, 64, 89–93, 116, 145, 148, 149, 166, 179, 181, 227, 279, 281, 299, 302, 309, 310, 345, 347, 370, 378, 404, 417, 418, 420–424
  competition policy, 55–91, 171, 172, 419, 423
  concept of competition, 94–96, 114, 131, 283
  Court of Justice, 7, 59, 162
  integration, 10, 11, 13, 59, 60, 62, 89, 92, 165, 230, 234
  integration objective results, 329
  market, 60, 219, 234, 236, 238, 240, 242, 449
  policy area, 32, 63
  policy goal
  rules of competition, 421
Excess capacity, 127, 202, 237, 255, 257, 435, 453
Excessive pricing, 78, 371
Exclusive license, 268, 292
Exclusive purchasing agreements, 177, 276, 294–298, 325
Exclusivity, 84, 174, 291, 294, 298, 331, 390, 399–403, 406
Exploitation, 170
Export bans, 283, 285

Exports, 134, 203, 231, 239, 240, 271, 281, 283–285, 287, 359, 424

F

Federal Trade Commission (FTC), 459
Fines, 175, 410
Firms
  group of, 181
  merging, 189, 203, 262, 414–416, 435, 439, 443, 460, 476
Foreclosure, refined understanding of, 137
Form CO, 212, 433
Fox, 144, 418
Franchise agreements, 267, 293
Free competition, 13, 20–22, 37, 38, 57, 58, 96, 112, 134, 141, 144, 147
Freiburg school, 10, 144–146, 148, 149
Fringe, competitive, 49, 202, 253, 261, 464
Fritz Machlup, 140
FTC. *See* Federal Trade Commission (FTC)

G

Gegengiftthese, 104
Gencor, 375, 376, 451, 452
General Motors, 78
Geographic
  area, 183, 189, 204, 213, 227, 230, 373, 460
  market, 13, 42, 77, 176, 180, 181, 185, 190, 200, 202–204, 206, 214, 224, 227–249, 259, 274, 336, 343, 355–357, 360, 427, 444, 447, 450, 454, 459, 465, 478
German competition law, 141, 148
German market, 179, 220–221, 241, 242, 449, 458
Glass, 235, 237, 243, 349, 356, 358, 374, 375, 407
Goals of competition law, 5

Goods
  distribution of, 3, 39, 71, 100, 304, 311, 312, 324, 333, 335, 342
  free movement of, 56
Grosfield/AKZO, 237
Grundig, 59, 270, 280, 283–285, 292, 293

H

Hafnia/Codan, 241
Harvard school, 8, 31, 34, 109, 112, 116, 128, 131, 132, 134, 159, 160, 368, 369
Hawk, 149
Hayek, 106, 140, 141
Henninger Bräu, 68, 265, 275, 295
Herfindahl-Hirschman Index (HHI), 135, 433
Hilti, 353–354, 356, 364, 411
HMT. *See* Hypothetical Monopolist Test (HMT)
Hoffmann-La Roche, 75, 76, 84, 351, 357, 363, 364, 380, 400
Hogarty, 203
Horizontal agreements, 45–47, 160, 263, 274, 281, 300–312, 331, 344
Horizontal mergers, 131, 189, 432–451, 457, 460, 464, 465
Horizontal restraints, 34
Hugin, 81, 353, 359
Hypothetical Monopolist Test (HMT), 187, 189–192, 194, 196, 198, 200, 201, 231
Hypothetical price, 192–194, 196, 198, 200–202, 204, 237

I

ICI, 215, 216
Importers, parallel, 67, 78, 282, 283, 285, 291, 292, 329, 393, 408–410
Incremental cost test, 90
Industrial organization, 7, 25, 109, 113–118, 121, 128, 129, 135–137, 334, 367, 419

Index

Inefficiency, managerial, 99
Integration, 10, 11, 13, 51, 59, 60, 62, 89, 92, 120, 137, 165, 182, 185, 230, 234, 240, 244, 253, 269, 278, 285, 312, 314, 325, 326, 328, 329, 338, 362, 368, 370, 440, 443, 456, 461, 482
Intellectual property rights (IPR), 60, 81, 82, 134, 253, 345, 347, 354, 367, 413, 418, 434, 435, 449
Interchangeability, 177, 181, 210, 220, 349, 351
Inter-State trade, 294
IPR. *See* Intellectual property rights (IPR)

J

Joint ventures, 219, 225, 267, 269, 273, 300, 301, 422, 437, 450, 458, 461, 485

K

Kali + Salz, 176, 377, 454, 455
Kesko/Tuko, 238
KNP/BT/VRG, 235
Kodak, 135

L

Legal assessment, 89, 93, 423
Legal certainty, 16, 130, 159, 389, 429
Leverage, 402, 428, 429, 442
Licenses, 79, 235, 268, 291, 292, 295, 321, 347, 368, 434, 448, 449
Licensing agreements, 437
LIFO ratio, 204
Linde/AGA, 458
Lisbon Treaty, 1, 5, 7, 9, 17-19, 22, 23, 33, 35, 39, 56-62, 68, 87, 89, 90
Local markets, 171, 202-204, 237-239, 244, 274, 355, 451
LOFI ratio, 203
Loyalty rebates, abusive nature of, 404

M

Magneti Marelli/CEAc, 242
Maintenance, resale price of, 25, 171, 263, 324-325
Mannesmann/Boge, 217, 222
Mannesmann/Hoesch, 241
Mannesmann/Vallourec/Ilva, 233, 234, 237, 239, 448
Manufacturing, 47-49, 81, 85, 97, 201, 209, 210, 214-217, 219, 220, 222, 231, 235, 238, 258, 269, 284, 285, 289, 290, 308, 320-327, 329-334, 337, 339, 349, 350, 353-355, 389, 392, 394, 396, 398, 407, 425, 426, 447, 448, 477, 482
Marginal costs, 42, 46, 97-99, 101, 112, 118, 125-127, 151-156, 158, 193, 194, 237, 250, 316, 326, 370, 382, 383, 416, 437, 443, 463-465, 476, 480, 483, 492
Market
    analysis, 16, 180, 240, 248-262, 265, 280, 294, 296, 348, 427
    artificial partitioning of, 357
    behaviour, 86, 130, 134, 139, 348, 361, 437
    common, 11-15, 19, 37, 61, 64-68, 72, 73, 81, 85, 177, 215, 262, 263, 270, 271, 282, 285, 292, 303, 348, 359-360, 399, 400, 415, 417, 431, 432, 436, 437, 450, 456, 487-489
    competitive, 1-3, 32, 36, 38, 40, 66, 87, 88, 90, 92, 101, 108, 110, 112, 113, 123, 134, 145, 152, 249, 421
    conditions, 18, 46, 58, 121, 122, 137, 171, 176, 249, 259, 298, 318, 348, 362, 367, 376, 387, 416, 444, 453, 459, 463, 483, 485, 486, 488
    conduct, 109, 115, 159, 160, 256, 373, 374, 457
    definition, 8, 16, 17, 175-249, 341, 342, 347-360, 367, 406-407, 411, 465, 484

distinct, 206, 208, 214, 216, 222, 405, 428
domestic, 59, 204, 206, 228, 237, 289
dominance, 72, 73, 76, 363, 367, 368, 371, 405
entry, 41, 43, 51, 60, 106, 118, 141, 153, 157, 249, 252-257, 319, 368, 369, 381, 386, 395, 396, 408, 433-434, 442, 444, 448, 450, 462
forces, 2, 6, 18, 38, 57, 59, 92, 110, 136, 154, 245, 331, 422
geographic, 13, 42, 77, 176, 180, 181, 185, 190, 200, 202-204, 206, 214, 224, 227-249, 259, 274, 336, 343, 355-357, 360, 427, 444, 447, 450, 454, 459, 465, 478
imperfections, 107, 113, 129, 136, 338, 492
integration, 11, 60, 92, 240, 278, 285, 325, 326, 328, 329
large, 75, 76, 114, 242, 249, 256, 257, 362-364, 366, 367, 405, 409, 410, 435, 479
power, 27-29, 31-32, 39-41, 49, 56, 74, 75, 77, 97, 108, 113-118, 125, 131, 133, 136, 146, 154, 160, 171, 172, 176, 180, 184, 185, 192, 202, 203, 227, 246, 249-251, 253-255, 257, 279, 313, 326, 328, 332-341, 344, 346, 358, 360, 361, 366, 367, 371, 378, 379, 390, 392, 412, 414-416, 426, 428, 431, 432, 434, 435, 437, 439-441, 443-448, 460, 463, 476, 482, 483, 493
secondary, 82, 354, 355
segments, 217, 221, 369
share threshold, 49, 274, 276, 277, 281, 324, 340, 341, 344
single, 12, 60, 71, 162, 179, 212, 214, 221, 237, 270, 271, 277, 289, 450, 499
structure, 1, 38, 88, 98, 100-102, 106, 109, 111, 113, 126, 128, 131, 134, 137, 139, 159, 160, 179, 250, 297, 298, 307, 308, 316, 334, 336, 337, 346, 348, 360, 361, 364, 366, 367, 373, 376, 434, 441, 444, 452, 457, 459
transparency, 104, 105, 147, 362, 374, 376, 452, 458
Marshall, 26, 27, 41, 96, 233
Mars/Langnese, 297, 298
Mars/Schöller, 297, 298
Mason, 109-112
MBB/Aérospatiale, 214, 215
MCI, 236
Medeol/Elosua, 217, 219
Mercedes-Benz/Kässbohrer, 242
Merger
  average productivity of, 187
  control, 41, 85-86, 160, 224, 232, 414, 417-423, 433, 456, 462, 463
  guidelines, 182, 189, 220, 432-451, 457, 460-463
  potential consequences of, 478
  Regulation, 15, 86, 414-415, 417, 436
Merger simulation, 445, 462-486
Metro, 267, 287-291, 302
Michelin, 43, 178, 350, 355-357, 364, 371, 392-394
Miert, Karel van, 16, 17, 179
Minor importance, agreements of, 276
Monopolies, 4, 13, 14, 51, 56, 58, 60, 95, 96, 98, 105, 108, 130, 131, 144, 147, 228, 357, 368, 441
Monopolist
  hypothetical, 184, 187-202, 223, 226, 231, 237, 246
More economics based approach, 5, 16, 179, 278, 378-392, 423, 429

N

National
  authorities, 162, 163, 167, 168, 180
  courts, 9, 63, 64, 162-164, 166-169, 175, 278, 279, 292, 297, 300, 359, 360
  markets, 13, 78, 224, 230, 232, 236, 238, 240, 242, 246, 271, 274, 284,

286, 295, 357, 396, 406, 426, 427, 478
Neal Report, 131
Neoclassicists, market equilibrium of, 130
Nestle, 208, 449, 454
Nestle/Italgel, 232, 234, 241
Nestle/Perrier, 208, 240, 454

O

Oligopolies, 14, 75, 101, 147, 373, 415, 454, 456
Oligopolistic
 dominance, 377, 378, 454, 455, 460
 markets, 118, 308, 373, 415, 433, 441, 452, 454
One-stop shop principle, 86
Ordoliberalism, 35–38, 144–146, 148
Ortiz Miko, 218
Otto/Grattan, 221
Otto Versand/Freemans, 453

P

Parallel agreements, cumulative, effect of possible, 67, 275
Parallel imports, 67, 78, 282, 283, 285, 291, 292, 329, 393, 408–410
Parties, third, 48, 77–79, 81–83, 139, 214, 219, 221, 222, 266, 267, 286, 288, 291, 292, 301, 302, 307, 313, 334, 337, 378, 454, 455
Patents, 141, 145, 250, 310, 354, 368, 370, 408, 409, 418, 434, 435
Perfect competition
 abstract criteria of, 97, 120
Philip Morris, 86, 309, 449
Philips/Grundig, 236
Philips/Hoechst, 236
P&I Clubs, 268
Pirelli/BICC, 453
Pompes Funèbresdes, 359
Pont/ICI, 215, 216, 220
Porto di Genova, 359, 360

Posner, 5, 89, 96, 99, 128, 133, 135, 143, 202, 209, 237, 334, 440
Post-Chicagoans, 136, 137
Potential competition, 76, 103, 105, 119, 155, 181, 183, 209, 211, 235, 240, 252–256, 265, 301, 303, 319, 324, 337, 361, 362, 367, 368, 406, 428, 430, 442, 447–451, 453
Predatory, 51, 77, 80–83, 90, 110, 115, 170, 379–381, 386–389, 406–408
Preferences, 2, 3, 7, 9, 27, 38, 42, 44, 129, 140, 158, 171, 172, 196, 198–200, 206, 207, 211–213, 216, 221, 226, 228, 229, 231, 232, 234, 240, 256, 332, 353, 356–358, 407, 440, 469, 472, 479
Preussag/Thomson, 456
Price
 concentration study, 185
 correlation, 183, 205–207, 225, 226, 233, 234, 244
 differences, 79, 183, 204, 207, 214, 219, 220, 228, 231, 232, 260–262, 323, 356, 357
 differentials, 60, 78, 329
 discrimination, 25, 77, 79, 80, 100, 110, 120, 131, 183, 212, 214, 221–223, 232–233, 257, 322, 323, 325, 353, 355, 380, 440
 elasticity, 183, 184, 187, 188, 191, 192, 200, 201, 205, 209, 220, 362, 465, 468–471, 473–476, 482
 favourable level of, 78
 levels, 42, 51, 78, 82, 115, 126, 192, 204, 205, 209, 212, 219, 228, 234, 243, 290, 329, 362, 375, 384, 434, 452, 469
 selling, 64, 73, 77, 237, 281
 theory, 25, 26, 41, 96, 98, 100–102, 109, 128, 130, 135, 149, 418
Pricing, 51, 66, 77–84, 90, 99, 110, 114, 115, 118, 119, 125, 126, 131, 145, 167, 170, 181, 191, 192, 195, 208, 209, 211, 213, 214, 224, 225, 228, 234, 246, 255, 259, 299, 308, 309,

Index

316, 321, 322, 339, 371, 378, 380, 381, 383, 386–390, 396, 406, 407, 440, 442, 443, 458, 477, 486
Product
  differentiation, 100, 101, 105, 108, 114, 115, 117, 125, 127, 157, 211, 226, 228, 229, 335, 367–369, 480
  market definition, 182, 190, 210, 214, 223, 227, 229, 349–355
  markets, 74, 176–179, 181, 183–185, 189, 190, 207–227, 229, 240, 244, 245, 274, 348–350, 352–355, 406, 411, 427, 449, 450, 459, 462, 484
Productive efficiency implications, 156
Profitability, 111, 115, 117, 118, 128, 133, 172, 186, 197, 200–201, 235, 246, 332, 366, 393, 425, 434, 435, 445
Promodes/BRMC, 238
Promodes/Dirsa, 238, 243, 244
Pronuptia, 266, 270, 292, 293
Proportionality, 254, 468, 470, 471, 474, 475, 478, 491
Public authorities, 286, 486
Public policy, 60, 102, 111, 112, 130, 132
Purchasers, 31, 74, 79, 84, 85, 216, 232, 308, 315, 328, 350, 354, 359, 372, 376, 399, 400, 452, 475

Q

Qualitative criteria, 288
Quantitative tests, 212, 229, 271
Quotas, 204, 228, 230, 235, 281

R

Radio Telefis Eireann (RTE), 75, 81
Raw materials, 81, 100, 200, 219, 230, 434
Rebates
  fidelity, 80, 84, 85, 90, 380, 384, 389, 391, 399
Reference markets, geographic, 234

Refusal to supply, 67, 79–82, 291, 379, 381, 413–414
Region, 11, 43, 181, 182, 184, 186, 203, 204, 228, 231, 233, 235, 238, 240, 241, 243–245, 274, 357, 359, 490, 494–496, 499, 500, 503
Regression analysis, 118, 431
Relationship, vertical, 282, 329, 390, 418, 427
Relative prices, 183, 190, 191, 198, 204, 205, 208, 210, 212, 213, 216, 228, 231, 232, 261, 472
Relevant geographic market, 42, 176, 181, 202–204, 206, 227–248, 274, 355–357, 450, 454, 478
Relevant product market, 74, 176, 179, 181, 185, 189, 190, 207–227, 229, 274, 348–350, 353, 406
Remedial imperfections theory, 104, 129
Renault/Volvo, 214, 215
Resale Price Maintenance (RPM), 25, 31, 48, 50, 171, 263, 279, 281, 321, 322, 324–326, 328, 331, 332, 337–339
Research & development agreements, 315, 345
Restraints, 4, 30, 35, 48, 49, 66, 94, 105, 108, 112, 133, 139, 141, 143, 251, 257, 266, 267, 269, 279, 293, 299, 307, 325, 326, 329, 335–339, 342
Restraints of competition, 14, 105, 116, 121, 134, 141, 164, 278
Restrictions, 16, 59, 89, 175
Retailers, 47–50, 172, 174, 178, 209, 211, 213, 221, 222, 238, 244, 248, 249, 254, 268, 275, 276, 287, 288, 290, 293, 297, 298, 323, 324, 326, 327, 329, 330, 334, 335, 337, 390, 391, 480
Rewe/Meinl, 239
Rhodia/Donau, 453
Rhone-Poulenc/SNIA, 232
Roche, 76, 84, 85, 363, 364
Roche/Syntex, 236
Royal Dutch Shell group, 219

552

Index

RPM. *See* Resale Price Maintenance (RPM)
RTE. *See* Radio Telefis Eireann (RTE)
Rules
    minimis, 500
    procedural, 168, 175
RWE/VEW, 458

S

SABA, 287–290
Sales
    outlets, 275, 276
    promotion, 287, 330
    total, 203, 258, 261, 274, 327
Sanitec/Sphinx, 243
Schmidtchen, D., 138
Schöller, 177, 178, 275, 276, 297, 298
Schumpeter, 107–109, 113
Selective distribution
    systems, 48, 268, 287, 289–291, 340, 341
Sellers, distant, 202, 237
Shell/Montecatini, 219
Shell petroleum NV, 219
Sherman Act, 131, 135
Shipments
    test, 202, 234
    trade flows/pattern of, 229, 230
Shock analysis, 212
Siderurgica Gabrielli SpA, 359
Significant market power, 172, 333, 337, 341, 412
Smith, A., 88, 94–98, 130, 138, 154
Social market economies, 1–3, 5, 6, 8–11, 14, 15, 18, 20–22, 24, 34, 37–39, 53, 57–58, 60–61, 87, 89, 92, 141, 144, 148, 417, 420, 421
Specialized goods, non-dominant supplier of, 290
SPO, 72, 176, 272, 306, 348
SSNIP Test, 189, 190, 246
State interventions, 35, 57, 94, 106, 116, 130, 131, 141, 147, 213, 487, 493
Stigler, 94, 95, 128–130, 205, 369

Structure-conduct-performance paradigm (SCP paradigm), 109–111, 128
Substitutability
    near-impossibility of direct assessment of, 233
Substitutes, 64, 66, 76, 98, 100, 103, 108, 156–157, 181–184, 186, 187, 189, 191–193, 204, 207, 208, 210–213, 216, 219, 221, 227, 252, 319, 329, 331, 333, 352, 354, 361, 363, 367, 401, 414, 415, 443, 445, 454, 470, 475, 478
Suiker Unie, 76, 359, 361
Supply-side substitutability, 182, 185, 208–210, 215, 224, 225, 349, 353, 354

T

Tacit collussion, 316, 332, 416, 457, 460
Tariffs, 53, 204, 228, 230, 232, 234–237, 255, 351, 356, 399, 435
Technique Minière, 68, 280–282, 292
Technological development, 186, 422
Territorial protection, 279, 283–286, 291–293, 331
Tetra Pak, 83, 219, 353, 357, 358, 405–408
TEU. *See* Treaty on European Union (TEU)
TFEU. *See* Treaty on the Functioning of the European Union (TFEU)
Total welfare, 5, 28–31, 41, 43, 61, 91, 418
Trade
    associations, 66, 115, 271, 308, 366, 461
    constituted unreasonable restraints of, 299
    flows, 202–204, 228–230, 242–244, 270
    restraints of, 112
    traditional, 178, 276

Index

Trade-offs, 27–29, 59, 195, 246, 284, 416, 445, 463, 490
Trading conditions, other unfair, 73, 77
Transport costs
  high, 232, 237, 238, 308, 356
Treaty on European Union (TEU), 5, 11, 14, 17–21, 56, 57, 161, 294, 417, 420–422, 504
Treaty on the Functioning of the European Union (TFEU), 3, 4, 12, 18–22, 24, 39–40, 56, 57, 62–64, 71–73, 85, 161, 170, 282, 422, 488, 500
Turnover, calculation of, 200
TV
  advertising market, 450
  broadcasting, 82, 234
  guides, 81, 82, 359
  programmes, 82
  stations, 81, 82
Tying and bundling, 25, 171, 379, 391–392, 440–442

U

UBC, 356, 364
Undertakings
  associations of, 64, 66, 71, 306, 311
  entry interests of, 410
  public, 56
Unfair prices, 77–79
Unilateral effects, 242, 415, 432, 460, 462–465, 476
Unilever, 218, 263, 449, 480, 496
Union Carbide/Enichem, 219
United Brands, 74, 76, 78, 81, 227, 349, 356, 358, 363, 364, 371, 372

US antitrust law, 8

V

Variable costs, 43, 82, 83, 102, 110, 151, 152, 187, 193, 194, 200, 223, 224, 314, 316, 382, 383, 387
Varta/Bosch, 217, 242
VEBA/VIAG, 458
Vereniging van Samenwerkende Prijsregelnde Organisaties, 306
Vertical
  agreements, 41, 47, 49, 131, 160, 253, 263, 279–281, 285, 295, 299, 312, 320–322, 329, 333, 334, 338, 339, 341, 343, 344
  arrangements, 333
  mergers, 106, 137, 138, 439, 440, 443, 444, 446, 447
Vertical restraints
  anti-competitive effects of, 328–332
VIAG/Continental, 243
Von Hayek, F.A., 140

W

Werden, G., 184, 185, 195
Wholesalers, 218, 268, 283, 286–288, 290, 321, 323, 335
Workable competition
  dynamic theory of, 104
  objective criteria of, 289
World market, 110, 136, 204, 219, 240, 244, 245, 448

X

X-inefficiency, 100

INTERNATIONAL COMPETITION LAW SERIES

1. Ignacio De Leon, *Latin American Competition Law and Policy: A Policy in Search of Identity*, 2001 (ISBN 90-411-1542-0).
2. Wim Dejonghe & Wouter Van de Voorde (eds), *M & A in Belgium*, 2001 (ISBN 90-411-1594-3).
3. Yang-Ching Chao, Gee San, Changfa Lo & Jiming Ho (eds), *International and Comparative Competition Law and Policies*, 2001 (ISBN 90-411-1643-5).
4. Martin Mendelsohn & Stephen Rose, *Guide to the EC Block Exemption for Vertical Agreements*, 2002 (ISBN 90-411-9813-X).
5. Clifford A. Jones & Mitsuo Matsushita (eds), *Competition Policy in the Global Trading System: Perspectives from the EU, Japan and the USA*, 2002 (ISBN 90-411-1758-X).
6. Christian Koenig, Andreas Bartosch, Jens-Daniel Braun & Marion Romes (eds), *EC Competition and Telecommunications Law*. Second Edition, 2009 (ISBN 978-90-411-2564-4).
7. Jürgen Basedow (ed.), *Limits and Control of Competition with a View to International Harmonization*, 2002 (ISBN 90-411-1967-1).
8. Maureen Brunt, Economic Essays on Australian and New Zealand Competition Law, 2003 (ISBN 90-411-1991-4).
9. Ky P. Ewing, Jr., *Competition Rules for the 21st Century: Principles from America's Experience*, Second Edition, 2006 (ISBN 90-411-2477-2).
10. Joseph Wilson, *Globalization and the Limits of National Merger Control Laws*, 2003 (ISBN 90-411-1996-5).
11. Peter Verloop & Valérie Landes (eds), *Merger Control in Europe: EU, Member States and Accession States,* Fourth Edition, 2003 (ISBN 90-411-2056-4).
12. Themistoklis K. Giannakopoulos, *Safeguarding Companies' Rights in Competition and Anti-dumping/Anti-subsidies Proceedings*, Second Edition, 2011 (ISBN 978-90-411-3404-2).
13. Marjorie Holmes & Lesley Davey (eds), *A Practical Guide to National Competition Rules across Europe,* Second Edition, 2007 (ISBN 978-90- 411-2607-8).
14. Sigrid Stroux, *US and EU Oligopoly Control*, 2004 (ISBN 90-411-2296-6).
15. Tzong-Leh Hwang and Chiyuan Chen (eds), *The Future Development of Competition Framework*, 2004 (ISBN 90-411-2305-9).

16. Phedon Nicolaides, Mihalis Kekelekis and Maria Kleis, *State Aid Policy in the European Community: Principles and Practice*, Second Edition, 2008 (ISBN 978-90-411-2754-9).
17. Doris Hildebrand, *Economic Analyses of Vertical Agreements: A Self- Assessment*, 2005 (ISBN 90-411-2328-8).
18. Frauke Henning-Bodewig, *Unfair Competition Law: European Union and Member States*, 2005 (ISBN 90-411-2329-6).
19. Duarte Brito & Margarida Catalão-Lopes, *Mergers and Acquisitions: The Industrial Organization Perspective*, 2006 (ISBN 90-411-2451-9).
20. Nikos Th. Nikolinakos, *EU Competition Law and Regulation in the Converging Telecommunications, Media and IT Sectors*, 2006 (ISBN 90-411- 2469-1).
21. Mihalis Kekelekis, *The EC Merger Control Regulation: Rights of Defence. A Critical Analysis of DG COMP Practice and Community Courts' Jurisprudence*, 2006 (ISBN 90-411-2553-1).
22. Mark R. Joelson, *An International Antitrust Primer: A Guide to the Operation of United States, European Union and Other Key Competition Laws in the Global Economy*, Third Edition, 2006 (ISBN 90-411-2468-3).
23. Themistoklis K. Giannakopoulos, *A Concise Guide to the EU Anti-dumping/ Anti-subsidies Procedures*, 2006 (ISBN 90-411-2464-0).
24. George Cumming, Brad Spitz & Ruth Janal, *Civil Procedure Used for Enforcement of EC Competition Law by the English, French and German Civil Courts*, 2007 (ISBN 978-90-411-2471-5).
25. Jürgen Basedow (ed.), *Private Enforcement of EC Competition Law*, 2007 (ISBN 978-90-411-2613-9).
26. Jung Wook Cho, *Innovation and Competition in the Digital Network Economy: A Legal and Economic Assessment on Multi-tying Practices and Network Effects*, 2007 (ISBN 978-90-411-2574-3).
27. Akira Inoue, *Japanese Antitrust Law Manual: Law, Cases and Interpretation of the Japanese Antimonopoly Act*, 2007 (ISBN 978-90-411-2627-6).
28. René Barents, *Directory of EC Case Law on Competition*, 2007 (ISBN 978-90-411-2656-6).
29. Paul F. Nemitz (ed.), *The Effective Application of EU State Aid Procedures: The Role of National Law and Practice*, 2007 (ISBN 978-90-411-2657-3).
30. Jurian Langer, *Tying and Bundling as a Leveraging Concern under EC Competition Law*, 2007 (ISBN 978-90-411-2575-0).
31. Abel M. Mateus & Teresa Moreira (eds), *Competition Law and Economics – Advances in Competition Policy and Antitrust Enforcement*, 2007 (ISBN 978-90-411-2632-0).
32. Alberto Santa Maria, *Competition and State Aid: An Analysis of the EC Practice*, 2007 (ISBN 978-90-411-2617-7).
33. Barry J. Rodger (ed.), *Article 234 and Competition Law: An Analysis*, 2007 (ISBN 978-90-411-2605-4).
34. Alla Pozdnakova, *Liner Shipping and EU Competition Law*, 2008 (ISBN 978-90-411-2717-4).

35. Milena Stoyanova, *Competition Problems in Liberalized Telecommunications: Regulatory Solutions to Promote Effective Competition*, 2008 (ISBN 978-90-411-2736-5).
36. *EC State Aid Law/Le Droit des Aides d'Etat dans la CE. Liber Amicorum Francisco Santaolalla Gadea*, 2008 (ISBN 978-90-411-2774-7).
37. René Barents, *Directory of EC Case Law on State Aids*, 2008 (ISBN 978-90-411-2732-7).
38. Ignacio De Leon, *An Institutional Assessment of Antitrust Policy: The Latin American Experience*, 2009 (ISBN 978-90-411-2478-4).
39. Doris Hildebrand, *The Role of Economic Analysis in EU Competition Law: The European School*, Fourth Edition, 2016 (ISBN 978-90-411-6245-8).
40. Eugène Buttigieg, *Competition Law: Safeguarding the Consumer Interest. A Comparative Analysis of US Antitrust Law and EC Competition Law*, 2009 (ISBN 978-90-411-3119-5).
41. Ioannis Lianos & Ioannis Kokkoris (eds), *The Reform of EC Competition Law: New Challenges*, 2010 (ISBN 978-90-411-2692-4).
42. George Cumming & Mirjam Freudenthal, *Civil Procedure in EU Competition Cases before the English and Dutch Courts*, 2010 (ISBN 978-90-411-3192-8).
43. A.E. Rodriguez & Ashok Menon, *The Limits of Competition Policy: The Shortcomings of Antitrust in Developing and Reforming Economies*, 2010 (ISBN 978-90-411-3177-5).
44. Mika Oinonen, *Does EU Merger Control Discriminate against Small Market Companies? Diagnosing the Argument with Conclusions*, 2010 (ISBN 978-90-411-3261-1).
45. Eirik Østerud, *Identifying Exclusionary Abuses by Dominant Undertakings under EU Competition Law: The Spectrum of Tests*, 2010 (ISBN 978-90-411-3271-0).
46. Marco Botta, *Merger Control Regimes in Emerging Economies: A Case Study on Brazil and Argentina*, 2011 (ISBN 978-90-411-3402-8).
47. Jürgen Basedow & Wolfgang Wurmnest (eds), *Structure and Effects in EU Competition Law: Studies on Exclusionary Conduct and State Aid*, 2011 (ISBN 978-90-411-3174-4).
48. George Cumming (ed.), *Merger Decisions and the Rules of Procedure of the European Community Courts*, 2012 (ISBN 978-90-411-3671-8).
49. Eduardo Molan Gaban & Juliana Oliveira Domingues (eds), *Antitrust Law in Brazil: Fighting Cartels*, 2012 (ISBN 978-90-411-3670-1).
50. Giandonato Caggiano, Gabriella Muscolo & Marina Tavassi (eds), *Competition Law and Intellectual Property: A European Perspective*, 2012 (ISBN 978-90-411-3447-9).
51. Ben Van Rompuy, *Economic Efficiency: The Sole Concern of Modern Antitrust Policy? Non-efficiency Considerations under Article 101 TFEU*, 2012 (ISBN 978-90-411-3870-5).
52. Liyang Hou, *Competition Law and Regulation of the EU Electronic Communications Sector: A Comparative Legal Approach*, 2012 (ISBN 978-90-411-4047-0).

53. Barry Rodger, *Landmark Cases in Competition Law: Around the World in Fourteen Stories*, 2012 (ISBN 978-90-411-3843-9).
54. Andreas Scordamaglia-Tousis, *EU Cartel Enforcement: Reconciling Effective Public Enforcement with Fundamental Rights*, 2013 (ISBN 978-90-411-4758-5).
55. Bernardo Cortese (ed.), *EU Competition Law: Between Public and Private Enforcement*, 2014 (ISBN 978-90-411-4677-9).
56. Barry Rodger (ed.), *Competition Law: Comparative Private Enforcement and Collective Redress across the EU*, 2014 (ISBN 978-90-411-4559-8).
57. Nada Ina Pauer, *The Single Economic Entity Doctrine and Corporate Group Responsibility in European Antitrust Law*, 2014 (ISBN 978-90-411-5262-6).
58. Urška Petrovčič, *Competition Law and Standard Essential Patents: A Transatlantic Perspective*, 2014 (ISBN 978-90-411-4960-2).
59. David Telyas, *The Interface between Competition Law, Patents and Technical Standards*, 2014 (ISBN 978-90-411-5418-7).
60. Katerina Maniadaki, *EU Competition Law, Regulation and the Internet: The Case of Net Neutrality*, 2014 (ISBN 978-90-411-4140-8).
61. Horacio Vedia Jerez, *Competition Law Enforcement and Compliance across the World: A Comparative Review*, 2015 (ISBN 978-90-411-5815-4).
62. Kadir Baş, *The Substantive Appraisal of Joint Ventures under the EU Merger Control Regime*, 2015 (ISBN 978-90-411-5816-1).
63. Alberto Santa Maria, *Competition and State Aid: An Analysis of the EU Practice*, Second Edition, 2015 (ISBN 978-90-411-5818-5).
64. Lúcio Tomé Feteira, *The Interplay between European and National Competition Law after Regulation 1/2003: "United (Should) We Stand?"*, 2016 (ISBN 978-90-411-5663-1).
65. Giovanni Pitruzzella & Gabriella Muscolo(eds), *Competition and Patent Law in the Pharmaceutical Sector: An International Perspective*, 2016 (ISBN 978-90-411-5927-4).